Implications of Social Media Use in Personal and Professional Settings

Vladlena Benson
Kingston Business School, Kingston University, UK

Stephanie Morgan
Kingston Business School, Kingston University, UK

A volume in the Advances in Social Networking
and Online Communities (ASNOC) Book Series

An Imprint of IGI Global

Managing Director:	Lindsay Johnston
Managing Editor:	Austin DeMarco
Director of Intellectual Property & Contracts:	Jan Travers
Acquisitions Editor:	Kayla Wolfe
Production Editor:	Christina Henning
Development Editor:	Hayley Kang
Typesetter:	Amanda Smith
Cover Design:	Jason Mull

Published in the United States of America by
    Information Science Reference (an imprint of IGI Global)
    701 E. Chocolate Avenue
    Hershey PA, USA 17033
    Tel: 717-533-8845
    Fax: 717-533-8661
    E-mail: cust@igi-global.com
    Web site: http://www.igi-global.com

        Library of Congress Cataloging-in-Publication Data

Implications of social media use in personal and professional settings / Vladlena Benson and Stephanie Morgan, editors.
    pages cm
 Includes bibliographical references and index.
 ISBN 978-1-4666-7401-1 (hardcover) -- ISBN 978-1-4666-7402-8 (ebook) -- ISBN 978-1-4666-7404-2 (print & perpetual access) 1. Online social networks. 2. Social media. 3. Education, Higher--Effect of technological innovations on. I. Benson, Vladlena, 1976- II. Morgan, Stephanie J.
 HM742.I47 2015
 302.30285--dc23
              2014040312

This book is published in the IGI Global book series Advances in Social Networking and Online Communities (ASNOC) (ISSN: 2328-1405; eISSN: 2328-1413)

Advances in Social Networking and Online Communities (ASNOC) Book Series

Hakikur Rahman
University of Minho, Portugal

ISSN: 2328-1405
EISSN: 2328-1413

Mission

The advancements of internet technologies and the creation of various social networks provide a new channel of knowledge development processes that's dependent on social networking and online communities. This emerging concept of social innovation is comprised of ideas and strategies designed to improve society.

The **Advances in Social Networking and Online Communities** book series serves as a forum for scholars and practitioners to present comprehensive research on the social, cultural, organizational, and human issues related to the use of virtual communities and social networking. This series will provide an analytical approach to the holistic and newly emerging concepts of online knowledge communities and social networks.

Coverage

- Information and Data Management
- Leveraging Knowledge Communication in Social Networks
- Meta-data Representation and Management (e.g., Semantic-Based Coordination Mechanisms, Use of Ontologies, etc.)
- Strategic Management and Business Process Analysis
- Communications and the Internet
- Flourishing Knowledge Creation Environments
- Communication and Agent Technology
- Business Process Modeling
- Community Practices
- Knowledge Management System Architectures, Infrastructure, and Middleware

IGI Global is currently accepting manuscripts for publication within this series. To submit a proposal for a volume in this series, please contact our Acquisition Editors at Acquisitions@igi-global.com or visit: http://www.igi-global.com/publish/.

Titles in this Series

For a list of additional titles in this series, please visit: www.igi-global.com

Handbook of Research on Interactive Information Quality in Expanding Social Network Communications
Francisco V. Cipolla-Ficarra (Latin Association of Human-Computer Interaction, Spain & International Association of Interactive Communication, Italy)
Information Science Reference • copyright 2015 • 435pp • H/C (ISBN: 9781466673779) • US $235.00 (our price)

Identity and Leadership in Virtual Communities Establishing Credibility and Influence
Dona J. Hickey (University of Richmond, USA) and Joe Essid (University of Richmond, USA)
Information Science Reference • copyright 2014 • 321pp • H/C (ISBN: 9781466651500) • US $205.00 (our price)

Harnessing the Power of Social Media and Web Analytics
Anteneh Ayanso (Brock University, Canada) and Kaveepan Lertwachara (California Polytechnic State University, USA)
Information Science Reference • copyright 2014 • 305pp • H/C (ISBN: 9781466651944) • US $215.00 (our price)

Educational, Psychological, and Behavioral Considerations in Niche Online Communities
Vivek Venkatesh (Concordia University, Canada) Jason Wallin (University of Alberta, Canada) Juan Carlos Castro (Concordia University, Canada) and Jason Edward Lewis (Concordia University, Canada)
Information Science Reference • copyright 2014 • 465pp • H/C (ISBN: 9781466652064) • US $225.00 (our price)

Gender and Social Computing Interactions, Differences and Relationships
Celia Romm Livermore (Wayne State University, USA)
Information Science Reference • copyright 2012 • 343pp • H/C (ISBN: 9781609607593) • US $195.00 (our price)

Virtual Worlds and Metaverse Platforms New Communication and Identity Paradigms
Nelson Zagalo (University of Minho, Portugal) Leonel Morgado (University of Trás-os-Montes e Alto Douro, Quinta de Prados, Portugal) and Ana Boa-Ventura (The University of Texas at Austin, USA)
Information Science Reference • copyright 2012 • 423pp • H/C (ISBN: 9781609608545) • US $195.00 (our price)

Youth Culture and Net Culture Online Social Practices
Elza Dunkels (Umeå University, Sweden) Gun-Marie Franberg (Umea University, Sweden) and Camilla Hallgren (Umea University, Sweden)
Information Science Reference • copyright 2011 • 472pp • H/C (ISBN: 9781609602093) • US $180.00 (our price)

Collaborative Search and Communities of Interest Trends in Knowledge Sharing and Assessment
Pascal Francq (Universite Libre de Bruxelles, Belgium)
Information Science Reference • copyright 2011 • 312pp • H/C (ISBN: 9781615208418) • US $180.00 (our price)

www.igi-global.com

701 E. Chocolate Ave., Hershey, PA 17033
Order online at www.igi-global.com or call 717-533-8845 x100
To place a standing order for titles released in this series, contact: cust@igi-global.com
Mon-Fri 8:00 am - 5:00 pm (est) or fax 24 hours a day 717-533-8661

Editorial Advisory Board

Table of Contents

Detailed Table of Contents

This chapter analyses privacy concerns of students and faculty resulting from the adoption of social media as teaching resources in higher education. In addition, the chapter focuses on privacy concerns that social media can cause to faculty when they are used for social networking. A trans-cultural study was carried out which involved three Spanish universities, a Colombian university, and an American university. A focus group was organized with PhD students to brainstorm the topic. Afterwards, 94 undergraduate students completed a survey and 18 lecturers participated in a written interview. Results indicate that social media are widely adopted in the university and are perceived as valuable resources for teaching. However, privacy concerns can easily emerge among students and faculty when these applications are used for this purpose. Concerns may appear when social media are used for social networking as well. The text also offers some guidelines to overcome them.

The use of Social Networking Sites (SNSs) has become an integral part of daily life, particularly for adolescents. The chapter examines the negative impact of social networking sites and how they may expose alcohol-related consumption and behavior to young adults, especially college students. In particular, the focus is on the use of two specific social networking sites, Facebook and Twitter, and their association with alcohol use. The review of existing literature reveals that the depiction of alcohol use on social networking sites has a deleterious effect on alcohol use through the creation of positive social norms toward use and abuse. Further, the chapter looks at the Theory of Differential Association to explain the use of SNS as a pivot to increased alcohol use by adolescents and young adults.

Chapter 3

Daniela Crisan, Tilburg University, The Netherlands

This chapter discusses personality traits of Facebook users, how personality traits and motivations explain Facebook use, and the potential beneficial and detrimental effects of Internet usage, in general, and online social networking sites usage, in particular, on social and psychological well-being. First, the author provides short definitions of concepts such as social media and Social Network Sites (SNS). Next, the author describes Nadkarni and Hofmann's (2012) two-factor model of motives associated with Facebook use, including the need to belong and the need for self-presentation. Afterwards, a literature review of the most cited studies on the association between Facebook use and personality traits, as conceptualized by the Big Five Model (Costa & McCrae, 1992), is provided, followed by research on the relationships between Facebook use and psychological dimensions, such as self-esteem, loneliness, narcissism, self-worth, and depression and suicide. Finally, conclusions are drawn and final remarks are made.

Chapter 4

Hemamali Tennakoon, Kingston University, UK

Information security and privacy are multi-faceted concepts, and earlier definitions of information security and privacy seem inadequate in the context of emerging technologies such as social media. Hence, this chapter presents an analysis of the concept of information security followed by a discussion of computer security, information security, network security, personal privacy, informational privacy, etc. Then the discussion narrows down to information security and privacy on Social Networking Sites (SNS) followed by an analysis of the consequences of information security and privacy breaches from individualistic and organizational perspectives. The lack of understanding of the complex nature of security and privacy issues are preventing businesses from gaining the full economic benefit, especially on SNS. Therefore, some solutions and recommendations are suggested towards the end of the chapter, including the need for a common legal framework. Finally, the chapter ends with suggestions for future research.

Chapter 5

Fritz Kohle, University of Edinburgh, UK
Sony Jalarajan Raj, MacEwan University, Canada

Despite the criticism in the mainstream press regarding the use and abuse of digital and social media, its use has been increasingly encouraged and supported in schools and universities. This chapter examines the social media behaviour of techy-savvy undergraduate students at NHTV, University of Applied Sciences, Breda, The Netherlands, from the perspective of an independent documentary producer and educator, to determine whether any correlation between the amount of time spent online and the use of cognitive functions exists. Media producers require an audience capable of critical thought, and teachers educate future audiences to acquire the necessary cognitive skills. Hence, the chapter analyses how the viewer's cognitive functions impaired by the use of social and digital media affects the reception of media products. This further leads to a more critical concern about the educators' response to the challenges provided by social and digital media.

Chapter 6

As the social technology matured in recent years, so did the threat landscape of the online medium. Fears about breaches of privacy and personal information security seem to dominate the list of concerns of social media users described in literature. Popular press continually reports cases of inadvertent and malicious information disclosure and breaches, cyberbullying, and stalking. Yet, social networking sites proliferated into all areas of human activity. The factor causing this phenomenon lies in the trusted nature of networks and the sense of trustworthiness of this easy-to-use technology. The formation of trust into social technology has attracted much attention, and this chapter offers an overview of the trust predictors in social settings. It continues with a retrospective into the threat landscape and the use of personalisation by social networking services to counter some of these threats. Further research directions are discussed.

Chapter 7

Education has evolved over time from face-to-face teaching to computer-supported learning, and now to even more sophisticated electronic tools. In particular, social technologies are being used to supplement the classroom experience and to ensure that students are becoming increasingly engaged in ways that appeal to them. No matter how educationally beneficial, however, new technology is affected by its users. To investigate this, lecturers at the Eynesbury Institute of Business and Technology (EIBT)—a Higher Education pathway provider—were surveyed to determine their perception and application of social technolog(ies) in their personal, but predominantly 'professional' lives. Utilising a qualitative and autoethnographic approach, one author provides an insight into their own attitude toward social technologies, coupled with responses to three open-ended questions. Thereafter, the same questions were posed to EIBT academic staff to understand their willingness or reluctance to use social technologies in their practice as part of their first-year pathway course(s).

This chapter analyses how autonomy, collaboration, and cooperation are built in a class designed to use digital technologies for a teacher development syllabus. For the purpose of this chapter, data was collected using an empirical-qualitative approach through active observation in participative action, using a questionnaire and Moodle e-portfolio that addressed learning in several virtual tools including

Facebook. The final analysis demonstrates that it is possible to understand the autonomous and collaborative teaching and learning process when online tools such as social networks are used, and it is also possible to determine students' participation through authorship. However, such acknowledgment requires that participants be prepared in terms of methodology, including teachers, and have the means to consider accepting new ways of teaching through the cooperation enabled by social networks and virtual learning environments.

Chapter 9

Effective social media usage has particular challenges for HE institutions. The many opportunities afforded by social media, increasingly demanded by students, have negative potential. Social technology requires substantial investment to do well, and in particular, it can be very hard to measure its performance. In this chapter, the authors focus on how aligning with strategic objectives can reduce the risk and enhance the effectiveness of social media use throughout the student lifecycle. They also consider the risks which social media investment entails in HE. Using a case study of a UK university, the authors identify common themes for social media adoption in educational settings. They offer practical recommendations and key areas to consider before launching or enhancing a social media strategy in the field of HE.

This chapter focuses on the extent of the usage of Short Message Services (SMS) in three universities in Southwest Nigeria, with 243 participants drawn from Covenant University, Bells University, and Lagos State University, who responded to a questionnaire on SMS. Data generated from the study confirmed the high usage of SMS among subjects in general and males in particular, within the age range of 31 to 40 years; a large number of subjects, especially those in administrative positions, were affected by the usage of SMS; most of the subjects are more tolerant when the messages are related to religion, are work-related, or are from family members. Subjects expressed concern when the contents of the SMS are related to adverts, when SMS are used when there are network problems, and the possible exploitation of recipients. Steps to minimize the disadvantages of the use of SMS are discussed.

Chapter 11

Social media is being increasingly utilised within society as an interactive communication platform. It has revolutionised the manner in which organisations communicate with their stakeholders, from the old way of simply designing messages and transmitting them across a desired medium, described as a static, one-way communication channel. Communications are the means by which organisations achieve their strategic goals through influencing their stakeholders. Social media allows stakeholders to connect to one another in relational, interactional networks. This means that stakeholders can now interact with organisations and each other and have a greater influence on the outcomes of communication strategies, which was impossible with traditional media. Organisations have less power dictating communications to stakeholders who in turn have more power in co-creating communication with each other. Social media is likely to have a major competitive impact on higher education institutions and these institutions should be accounting for these changes in their future strategy development. This chapter explores how social media is being utilized in organisations.

Chapter 12

Evangelia Marinakou, Royal University for Women, Bahrain
Charalampos Giousmpasoglou, Bahrain Polytechnic, Bahrain
Vasileios Paliktzoglou, University of Eastern Finland – Joensuu, Finland

Social networks have become very popular recently in the tourism sector. This chapter presents the use of social media and more specifically Trip Advisor in reference to reviews of cultural attractions and their potential influence on the development of cultural tourism in Bahrain. The findings propose that people use Trip Advisor to collect information about a destination and share experiences with other community members. They also suggest that cultural tourism has a potential to grow in the region; however, there should be more information available. The cultural attractions should be more organized, offer more information, and enhance the cultural experience. This chapter recommends that social networks and Trip Advisor should be used by the local tourism authorities for the development and promotion of cultural tourism in Bahrain. Finally, the attraction websites should be further enhanced and other social media could be used to communicate with visitors in Bahrain.

Chapter 13

Tuba Bircan, Bahçeşehir University, Turkey
Esra Çeviker-Gürakar, Okan University, Turkey

In this chapter, the authors quantitatively analyze the role of network membership in the performance of firms within the public procurement market in Turkey. They use a unique public procurement dataset of all high-value public procurement contracts—those with a contract value worth over TL 1,000,000—awarded between 2005 and 2010. The authors consider two types of networks: (1) Internet-based procurement-specific networks and (2) business networks established through business associations. Internet-based procurement-specific business networks provide their members with a wide range of procurement related services, access to critical resources, and timely information. Business associations help member firms establish a strong and unified presence, effectively protect their shared interests, and thus collectively influence governmental economic policies. The findings suggest that both types of network memberships are effective in winning public procurement contracts. There is also an overlap among network memberships, with 8.4% of contracts awarded to the firms that have membership in both networks.

This chapter reviews the current literature on the types of social media practices in college and university libraries, and suggests some new strategic agendas for utilizing these tools for teaching and learning about the research process, as well as other means to connect libraries to their users. Library educators continually hope to "meet students where they are" and use social media to "push" library content toward interested or potential university patrons. One new way to improve engagement and "pull" patrons toward an understanding of the usefulness of licensed resources and expert research help is through the channels of social media. By enhancing awareness of library resources at the point of need, and through existing social relationships between library users and their friends, libraries can encourage peer interaction around new research methods and tools as they emerge, while increasing the use of library materials (both online and within the library facility) in new and different ways.

Research in mobile learning (m-learning) about technology and software and mobile learning's application to educationally related undertakings and a long-term sustainability remain unclear. This chapter untwines the tangled information surrounding m-learning strategy through examining the drivers and perceptions for m-learning in the 21st century. The data will unearth the value of employing diverse modalities of m-learning. Administrators will gain knowledge to develop and implement mobile strategy. Faculty will enhance their familiarity on the diverse types of m-learning tools and the value of employing m-learning in the classroom. Administrators and faculty members will gather knowledge that guides efforts to diminish barriers in support of a successful m-learning implementation. In addition, administrators will garner developed knowledge to analyze, gather requirements, develop, and then implement a strategic m-learning plan for long-term sustainability. Academics and practitioners will gain insight into understanding the balance of a mobile strategy amid economic value and the required controls.

Foreword

Social media can be viewed as a multi-edged sword that works in unforeseeable ways and does not follow expected patterns. Although social media was intended as a technology to build and maintain connections (with friends, family, colleagues, etc.), it also contributes to social isolation and reduces face-to-face communication. On one hand, social media supports communal spirit and development of sound self-esteem; on the other hand, it can encourage addiction and foster narcissism. Social media presence is almost expected from any business; however, an organisation's reputation online can be damaged either momentarily or in the long term. Facebook is said to strengthen friendships; nonetheless, it can harm relationships and destroy careers. The paradoxical nature of social media continuously presents challenges in personal and professional settings.

Not only members of the generations X and Y but also users of all ages are challenged regarding how to competently navigate the social media landscape. This remains an underexplored domain. Extant literature continually reveals results of new psychological effects that social networking has on people, their relationships, and egos. Organisations, including higher education institutions, tend to launch social media channels without a complete understanding of the risks and legal implications involved.

While extant literature reports accounts of exciting developments in learning and teaching supported by social media, the area of privacy and information protection in this context has been understated in Higher Education. In the same manner, the adverse psychological impacts of social media exposure are not considered fully. However, awareness of the "dark side" of social media is growing.

Academics argue that social media is inherently different than other types of media. Online social networks are self-developing, dynamic, interconnected, and interactive entities that span beyond the control of an organisation, with a specific set of management principles and analysis metrics. The distinct nature of social media presents a challenge in applying known theories and principles from the traditional online media. Consequently, a new set of insights is required to explain the behaviour of actors in social media settings.

Through an in-depth discussion of a range of issues surrounding the impact of social media and technologies on individuals, firms, and HE organisations, this book creates a rich account of the dual side of social networking applications. It opens a long-awaited debate on further exploration of the unchartered social media territory and instigates new ideas for illumination of this challenging topic.

Ronald S. J. Tuninga
Kingston University, UK

Ronald S. J. Tuninga *is Pro Vice Chancellor and Dean of the Faculty of Business and Law at Kingston University and Dean at AVT Business School in Copenhagen, Denmark. AVT Business School cooperates for its Executive MBA is with faculty members from MIT, Harvard University, and the UC-Berkeley. He has been the Director of the PhD Program and Professor of International Management and Marketing at the Open University of The Netherlands, Visiting Professor at various international business schools such as Hult International Business School and King Abdul-Aziz University (Kingdom of Saudi Arabia), and is the former Director Dean and Professor of International Business and Marketing at the Maastricht School of Management. During his tenure at the Maastricht School of Management, he developed MBA programs in 24 countries across the world. He was the Associate Dean and Director MBA Programs and Professor of Marketing and International Business at Nyenrode Business University (The Netherlands). Professor Tuninga has lectured extensively both in North and South America, Europe, Asia, the Middle East, and Africa. His PhD is from Temple University (Philadelphia, USA). He completed his dissertation in Comparative Marketing in 1987. He also holds an MA in Economics, an MBA in International Business, and an MSc in Marketing. His research publications have appeared in such journals as the Journal of Macromarketing, Managerial and Decision Economics, The Irish Marketing Review, The Scandinavian International Business Review, The International Journal of Physical Distribution and Materials Management, Journal of Transnational Management, International Journal of Business and Globalization, South African Journal of Business and Management, Bedrijfskunde, and Proceedings of International Conferences. Prof. Tuninga has been involved in many international projects funded by the Dutch Government, World Bank, European Union, United Nations, and other international organizations. From 2007 until 2009, he was the President of the International Management Development Association. He was the Vice-Chair of the International Management Board (Board of Trustees) of the Association of MBAs (AMBA – UK) and currently is the Chair of the Faculty of Assessors of AMBA. He has been a member or chair of more than 40 assessment teams to business schools around the globe. He has been a consultant for companies such as for example Melitta North America and GE and a partner of the Holland Consulting Group.*

Preface

With the proliferation of smart devices, 4G, and other advancements in the information technology field, social media has become pervasive. Organisations, both in the public and private sector, see the impact of social technologies at the personal and professional levels. One of the greatest challenges of the moment is to create a balanced insight into the positive effects of social media as well as the negative implications created by this relatively new technology. This book attempts to present this view by balancing the vision of the effectiveness of social technologies with the adverse effects it may bring to its users. Being especially relevant in Higher Education settings, the dimensions of the social media adoption discussed in this book touch upon e-commerce, information security, business networks, libraries, the tourism sector, and raise issues linked to the psychological consequences and legal implications. The book is comprised of the following chapters:

Chapter 1, "Social Media in Higher Education: Examining Privacy Concerns among Faculty and Students," reports the results of a trans-cultural study that involved three Spanish universities, a Colombian university, and an American university. This chapter analyses the privacy concerns of students and faculty resulting from the adoption of a range of social media as teaching resources in higher education. Video-sharing sites and blogs are the most used resources for academic purposes. However, privacy concerns can easily emerge among students and faculty. Using videoconferencing to discuss work with lecturers and the obligation of including pictures in the social network profiles are the activities with the highest risk of raising privacy concerns among students when social media is implemented for classroom purposes. Faculty may also experience privacy concerns when they are requested to send pictures for publication online. In addition, the work focuses attention on the privacy concerns that social media can create for faculty when they are used for social networking.

Chapter 2, "Social Media and Alcohol Use: Adverse Impact of Facebook and Twitter on College Students," examines the negative impact of social networking use and how it may expose alcohol-related consumption and behaviour to young adults, college students in particular. The chapter uses the Theory of Differential Association to explain social networking as a pivot to increased alcohol use by adolescents and young adults. Alcohol marketing has expended to various SNSs. This new environment allows for an additional source of exposure to alcohol and supports the hypothesis of increased likelihood of alcohol consumption and abuse amongst young adults, especially college students. The review of existing literature reveals that the depiction of alcohol use on social networking sites has a deleterious effect on alcohol use through the creation of positive social norms toward use and abuse. Similar to Facebook, Twitter, although showing benefits for improved academic outcomes for students, is also a platform that exposes students to alcoholic brands and behaviours.

Chapter 3, "Face to Face(book): Users' Traits and Motivations and Effects of Facebook Use on Well-Being," assesses how personality traits and motivations explain Facebook use, and the potential beneficial and detrimental effects of social network usage on social and psychological well-being. The positive effects of social technologies on social well-being are well known and include communication, feeling of connectedness, number of ties in personal networks, and others. The authors of the chapter explore the adverse effects amplified through SNS: negative personality traits, reduced self-esteem, feelings of loneliness, depression, etc. These effects may represent a real concern for many individuals who use SNSs and parents of teenagers, who wish to ensure their children's well-being. Specifically, the chapter presents the results of analysis for users of Facebook and opens the discussion for ways to mitigate these negative effects.

Chapter 4, "Information Security and Privacy in Social Media: The Threat Landscape," opens with an analysis of the foundations of the concept of information security and narrows down to information security and privacy on social networking sites. For instance, SNS services have found successful application in many areas in recent years as a powerful marketing and promotional tool, as well as a platform for international trade. However, the issues of information security and privacy are preventing businesses from gaining the full economic benefit of such applications. The lack of understanding of the complex nature of security and privacy issues are at the core of the problem. The chapter suggests some solutions and highlights the need for a common legal framework guiding the usage of personal information and ensuring information security on social media.

Chapter 5, "Abuse of the Social Media Brain: Implications for Media Producers and Educators," highlights that social technology use has been increasingly encouraged and supported in schools and universities. Authors of the chapter argue that due to the proliferation of social media, information is no longer processed by users at a deeper level but absorbed superficially instead. Critics argue that using social and digital media in this way does not improve the development of cognitive skills, making it even more difficult for students to acquire new knowledge and retain it in the long term. The authors express concerns about the educators' response to the challenges provided by social and digital media and urge them to provide clear guidelines on the use of social media in the classroom

Chapter 6, "Social Networking: A Retrospective into the Trust Formation and Threats," presents a five-year reflection on the development of mechanisms for trust formation on social networks. The chapter draws on a literature review of privacy protection techniques suggested in academic debate over the past five years and draws conclusions on the technology development patterns on personalisation and information protection mechanisms used on current SNS.

Chapter 7, "Reflections on the Impact of Social Technologies on Lecturers in a Pathway Institution," was influenced in part by the recognition that although there are demonstrable benefits of integrating social tools in HE, there are some challenges that prevent their enthusiastic integration. For social technologies to expand and flourish in HE, it is necessary to gain insights into academics' conceptions and obtain an in-depth understanding into why they may or may not incorporate social technologies into their courses. The chapter reports results of an autoethnographic study of HE lecturers and their perceptions of social media and challenges presented by the fast changing educational technology landscape.

Chapter 8, "Facebook and Moodle as Classroom Extensions: Integrating Digital Technologies in the Curriculum," explores the ways in which autonomy, collaboration, and cooperation are built into the curriculum of a teacher development class designed to use digital technologies. The chapter reports the results of an empirical-qualitative approach through active observation of the uses of Moodle e-portfolio and social sites including Facebook. The authors argue that it is possible to gain an understanding of the autonomous and collaborative teaching and learning processes when online tools such as social networks are used. However, this requires that participants (including teachers) be prepared in terms of methodology and be accepting of new ways of teaching through the cooperation enabled by social networks and virtual learning environments.

Chapter 9, "Measuring the Social Impact: How Social Media Affects Higher Education Institutions," opens the discussion around social media adoption in HE contexts. Uptake is arguably driven by the end users—students—being increasingly demanding in their expectations of technology support provided by universities. The chapter discusses a new set of challenges to HE institutions regarding how to adopt social media effectively in a range of modes provided to students, alumni, external stakeholders, etc. The authors aim to close the gap in the literature on social media applications in higher education and present the academic view on the benefits and challenges that surface during the technology adoption.

Chapter 10, "The Prevalence, Effects, and Reactions to the Use of Short Message Services in University Settings in South West Nigeria," reports a study of messaging services and the implications of their use in the workplace. The study indicates that administrative staff at a Nigerian University is more likely to use messaging than academics. While the study acknowledges the positive role of messaging technology in professional settings, the authors report the negative effects including unsolicited messages, distraction, and inconvenience of messaging after work hours or in situations requiring undivided attention. The chapter draws attention to the fact that concern has been expressed on its effects in encouraging poor grammatical expressions and the possibility of distorting the message sent, especially when the abbreviations cannot be correctly decoded or interpreted by the recipient. They offer practical recommendations.

Chapter 11, "The Role of Social Media in Creating and Maintaining Social Networks Including its Impact on Enhancing Competitive Positioning within the Education Sector," draws readers' attention to the fact that social networks represent a disruptive medium that enhances the power of end customers and stakeholders to enter a dialogue regarding organisations and their offerings. The author argues that a different emergent strategy approach is required in planning social media strategies. The chapter utilises theoretical foundations from network theory and adopts the Service Dominant Logic to gain insights into the process of development and implementation of organisational social media strategies. It is recommended that managers in HE institutions think about how their organisation engages with and plans its future social media strategies as it can affect both social capital and competitive advantage.

Chapter 12, "The Impact of Social Media on Cultural Tourism," explores the role of social media in the tourism sector. This chapter opens a discussion on the use of social media for reviews of cultural attractions, and their potential influence on the development of cultural tourism in Bahrain. The authors emphasise that as people use TripAdvisor to collect information about tourist destinations and share experiences with other community members, cultural tourism has a potential to grow in the region. This chapter recommends that social networks and TripAdvisor should be used by the local tourism authorities for the development and promotion of cultural tourism in Bahrain. The chapter concludes with a discussion on how social media could be used to communicate with visitors in Bahrain – advice which is transferable elsewhere.

Chapter 13, "Business Networks and Public Procurement in Turkey," explores the role of network membership on the performance of firms in the public procurement market in Turkey. The authors use a unique public procurement data set of all high-value public procurement. The study considered professional Internet-based procurement-specific networks and business networks established through business associations. The authors conclude that despite the earlier blockade of Internet-based networks, such as

Twitter and Facebook, in Turkey, Internet-based procurement-specific business networks provide their members with a wide range of procurement-related services, access to critical resources, and timely information.

Chapter 14, "New Social Media Agendas for Teaching and Learning in Libraries," looks at today's students as creators of knowledge through social media that are profoundly changing the way they use and reuse knowledge. In supporting their learning at each higher level, librarians must stay well versed in new technologies and their applications in order to assist students in navigating a world full of content created by everyone and anyone. The authors emphasise that fundamental aspects of critical engagement, appreciation of the multiple "ways of knowing," engaging the world ethically, and recognising diverse points of view are necessary for lifelong learning and for informed citizenship. The chapter outlines the unique roles of libraries in assisting users over time to develop these skills and deploy them strategically over the course of their degrees and careers.

Chapter 15, "Educational Edifices Need a Mobile Strategy to Fully Engage in Learning Activities," provides an insight into the principles of developing a mobile learning strategy and policy for HE institutions. The authors explore the connections between social learning and mobile technology. The chapter offers strategic and pedagogical considerations to keep in mind when designing a mobile learning strategy in today's socially networked world.

Vladlena Benson
Kingston Business School, Kingston University, UK

Stephanie Morgan
Kingston Business School, Kingston University, UK

Chapter 1
Social Media in Higher Education:
Examining Privacy Concerns among Faculty and Students

Laura Aymerich-Franch
GRISS, Image, Sound, and Synthesis Research Group, Spain

ABSTRACT

This chapter analyses privacy concerns of students and faculty resulting from the adoption of social media as teaching resources in higher education. In addition, the chapter focuses on privacy concerns that social media can cause to faculty when they are used for social networking. A trans-cultural study was carried out which involved three Spanish universities, a Colombian university, and an American university. A focus group was organized with PhD students to brainstorm the topic. Afterwards, 94 undergraduate students completed a survey and 18 lecturers participated in a written interview. Results indicate that social media are widely adopted in the university and are perceived as valuable resources for teaching. However, privacy concerns can easily emerge among students and faculty when these applications are used for this purpose. Concerns may appear when social media are used for social networking as well. The text also offers some guidelines to overcome them.

INTRODUCTION

Why Do We Need Privacy?

Privacy is the claim of individuals to determine what information about themselves should be known to others, when such information is obtained and what uses are made of it (Westin, 1967, 2003). Privacy has also been defined as the selective control of access to the self (Altman, 1975).

Privacy is perceived as a basic human need and, its loss, as an extremely threatening experience (Trepte, 2011). Westin (1966) postulates four functions of privacy: personal autonomy, emotional release, self-evaluation, and limited and protected communication.

The arrival of new technologies has generated an important privacy debate at the academic, political, and social level. Westin (2003) notes the rise of the Internet in the mid-1990's and the arrival of

DOI: 10.4018/978-1-4666-7401-1.ch001

wireless communication devices (cell phones) as two major developments in technology that have generated privacy alarms and framed the privacy debates since their appearance in the nineties.

The Communication Privacy Management (CPM) theory (Petronio, 2002) is the most valuable privacy theory for understanding interpersonal computer-mediated communication (Margulis, 2011). According to Petronio and Caughlin (2006), privacy can be most effectively understood in terms of "a dialectical tension with disclosure" (p.37). The CPM theory envisages privacy boundaries to illustrate individual versus collective information ownership (Child & Petronio, 2011) and proposes a series of principles to understand the way people manage private information both personally and in conjunction with others (Child, Pearson, & Petronio, 2009). The first principle of the CPM theory states that people believe their private information belongs to them. The second one posits that people believe they also have the right to control the flow of that information. The third principle announces that people develop and use privacy rules to control the flow of private information based on criteria important to them. The fourth says that once an individual shares his or her private information, that information enters into collective ownership and a collective privacy boundary is formed. The discloser expects an acceptance of responsibility for the information within that collective owner-ship. The fifth principle explains that once the information becomes co-owned and collectively held, the parties negotiate privacy rules for third-party dissemination. Finally, the last one affirms that given that people do not consistently negotiate privacy rules for collective private information, there is a possibility of boundary turbulence, which occurs when co-owners fail to effectively control the flow of private information to third parties (Child, Pearson, & Petronio, 2009: 2080-1).

These principles provide an effective theoreti-cal framework for understanding the adoption of social media as teaching resources in the university context as well as the privacy management prac-tices that students and faculty apply in relation to this adoption. Social networks such as Facebook have been initially adopted in the private sphere of individuals as a new way of communication with friends and are perceived as belonging to the individual's private sphere, as opposed to the aca-demic and professional sphere (Aymerich-Franch & Fedele, 2014). In adopting these networks for educational purposes, privacy boundaries need to be redefined to fit the relationship *lecturer – student*, as opposed to the relationship *friend – friend*. At the same time, though, this new adoption cannot overlap the previous structure as both uses sometimes will coexist under the same medium and account. If, for instance, a student decides to use her personal Facebook account to join a group that a lecturer has created for class, she will need to adjust the privacy settings so her lecturer and classmates only have partial access to the information she has in the social network.

Despite the rules that individuals design to fit their privacy needs in this new context, break-downs or boundary turbulences may still occur (Child, Haridakis, & Petronio, 2012). When this happens, the individual needs to address the disrup-tion and recalibrate the satisfactory functioning of privacy rules (Child, Haridakis, & Petronio, 2012). This disturbance may occur for several reasons. In a hypothetical situation, if a professor accepted a Facebook invitation from a colleague and later found out that the colleague used the information she published on the social network to inform the head of department that she was taking days off without notifying it, the professor would probably experience privacy turbulence. As a result, she would probably readjust the access to private in-formation she grants to her work mates through the social network. Conversely, a professor might also have a general policy of never accepting students to social networks and later find out that, in the case of doctoral students, the relationship becomes more fruitful when they share more professional and personal experiences. In that case, she might decide to readjust her privacy practices to allow students follow her on Twitter or LinkedIn.

As seen in these examples, a tension between privacy and disclosure of personal information characterizes social media, not only in the adoption of these tools as teaching resources, but as an intrinsic characteristic. Frequently, disclosing information about the self becomes unavoidable in order to obtain the benefits from social media. In other words, "the more users disclose of themselves, the more they may enjoy the benefits these systems have to offer. At the same time, the more they disclose, the more they risk what they themselves consider breaches of their privacy" (Walther, 2011: 3).

Implementing Social Media in Higher Education: Uses and Consequences

Social media are "internet-based applications that build on the ideological and technological foundations of Web 2.0 and that allow the creation and exchange of user generated content" (Kaplan & Haenlein, 2010: 61). Social media include, among others, social networks, microblogging platforms, blogs, wikis, forums, video and photo sharing platforms, document sharing platforms, social bookmarks managers, instant messaging services, voice-over-IP services, live streaming video platforms, and virtual social worlds and games. Although the first social media could be dated earlier, the real boom of these applications as we know them today started at the end of the nineties, with the popularization of blogging sites such as Open Diary (1998) or Blogger (1999), and mainly evolved in the first decade of the two thousands, with the arrival of Wikipedia (2001), MySpace (2003), LinkedIn (2003), Skype (2003), Flickr (2004), Youtube (2005), Facebook (2004), or Twitter (2006), among others (Aymerich-Franch & Carrillo, 2014). At present, some social media reach astronomic numbers of users. For instance, in 2012, the social network Facebook achieved over one billion users (Facebook Newsroom,

2012), and Twitter, over five-hundred million users (Semiocast, 2012).

There is considerable value in social media as teaching resources and therefore these applications are also expanding into the educational arena. Although educational institutions usually have available their own virtual platforms such as the virtual campus or adopt open-source software e-learning platforms such as Moodle to carry out these functions, social media that were initially created for other purposes are also being implemented in the educational context. Faculty consider these applications valuable for teaching (Moran, Seaman, & Tinti-Kane, 2011). Therefore, educational institutions that apply these tools for communication purposes and faculty that use them to support classroom work are increasing (Alexander, 2006; Amstrong & Franklin, 2008; Anderson, 2007; Bennett, Bishop, Dalgarno, Waycott, & Kennedy, 2012; Conole & Alevizou, 2010; Kennedy et al., 2009). Examples of social media use in the classroom include uploading lectures in YouTube, writing blogs to complement class content, creating class groups in Facebook, using Twitter to notify course-related news, videoconferencing through Skype with students to discuss work, or asking students to build wikis as part of classroom work (Fernando, 2008; Jaya, 2008; Kirkpatrick, 2005; Ricardo & Chavarro, 2010; Toro-Araneda, 2010; Weisgerber, 2009). Overall, social media in higher education have mainly been implemented to develop the following roles or functions (Aymerich-Franch, 2011):

- **Communication Channels:** Voice-over-IP services and instant messaging services allow real time communication which can be used by faculty and students to communicate without the constraint of sharing the same physical space. These applications might be particularly useful in online education or to communicate during stays abroad. Also, faculty can use these platforms to offer lessons or conferences live.

- **Information Channels:** One of the most valuable characteristics of social media as information channels is its immediacy. In addition, smartphones facilitate permanent access to these applications. Microblogging platforms such as Twitter can be used as information channels to notify class cancelations and changes, or announce events relevant to the course.
- **Participation and Integration to Class Content:** Faculty can encourage student participation through the use of wikis or forums as part of class activities. In addition, social media are very relevant to some disciplines such as Communication or Information Sciences. Thus, these applications are being adopted as part of class content and integrated in the projects students carry out.
- **Content Support:** Faculty can use video-sharing platforms such as YouTube or blogs to offer or share useful materials to complement class content.

Regarding the process of adopting social media in the classroom, previous studies indicate that students perceive the use of social media for learning purposes in a positive manner (Kumar, 2009; Madge, Meek, Wellens, & Hooley, 2009; Mazer, Murphy, & Simonds, 2007; Roblyer et al., 2010). Also, students are much more likely than faculty to use social networks to support classroom work and are significantly more open to the possibility of using them for this purpose (Roblyer et al., 2010).

However, controversy surrounds the use of these sites, particularly in terms of privacy, safety, and revealing too much personal information (Cain, 2008). Concerning this, mediated communications contribute to blur the boundaries between the private and the public spheres (Meyrowitz, 1985). In particular, social media are likely to blur these boundaries by making information that belongs to the private sphere, public

(Aymerich-Franch & Fedele, 2014). Also, new privacy concerns may appear as a consequence of the new uses attributed to these applications in the educational context.

Thus, even if students generally accept using social media in the instructional arena, privacy concerns can easily emerge among them (Aymerich-Franch & Fedele, 2014). A major concern is the overlapping between their academic and private lives as a result of using the same social media in the classroom that they are already using in their private lives (Jones, Blackey, Fitzgibbon, & Chew, 2010). In addition, students believe that certain social media such as Facebook are not designed for education but for socializing (Hewitt & Forte, 2006; Jones et al. 2010; Kumar, 2009; Madge et al., 2009; Minocha, 2010; Philip & Nicholls, 2009; Roblyer et al., 2010). Also, they may experience privacy and identity management concerns when certain social networks are implemented for class purposes (Hewitt & Forte, 2006; Selwyn, 2009).

Similarly, teaching faculty see considerable value in social media as teaching resources. However, they also perceive privacy as an important barrier to their implementation for educational purposes (Moran, Seaman, & Tinti-Kane, 2011).

On the other hand, social media, and particularly social networks, might generate privacy conflicts to faculty in their working environments with students and colleagues, not only as a result of their implementation as teaching resources but as a result of their general expansion for social networking purposes. Some social networks such as Facebook are mainly used in the private sphere. Therefore, getting an invitation from a student or a colleague to connect on these online environments might generate conflict to faculty as the action might be perceived as an attempt of invasion of their private lives.

The current work deals with both aspects of the adoption of social media in the university context. First, it analyses students and faculty privacy concerns resulting from the implementation of social media as teaching resources in higher education. In addition, the work focuses attention to privacy concerns that social media *per se* can cause to faculty when they are used for social networking. The following research questions are explored:

1. What social media do students use, how often, and in what kind of activities do they get involved?
2. What social media are being implemented in the classroom in higher education?
3. What privacy concerns can the adoption of social media in the classroom generate to students?
4. Do faculty experience privacy conflicts as a result of adopting social media as teaching resources?
5. Do faculty experience privacy conflicts when social media are used for networking?

METHODOLOGY

A trans-cultural study was designed which involved faculty and student participants from three Spanish universities located in Catalonia and the Balearic Islands, a Colombian university on the Atlantic coast, and an American university in California. Quantitative and qualitative methods were combined to give response to the research questions.

In the first stage of the project, a focus group was organized to brainstorm the topic which involved the participation of five PhD students (three females and two males, aged 23 to 40) from the Communication and the Education departments at the American university. PhD students hold a position in between the student and the lecturer. They attend classes but, at the same time, they also usually get involved in teaching activities as teaching assistants at the university level. Thus, they can provide valuable information from multiple perspectives. The researcher posed the

questions and acted as a moderator. Participants were asked about

1. The use of social media as teaching resources in the university compared to the use of virtual environments specifically designed for educational purposes,
2. What makes some social media appropriate and some others not in the academic sphere,
3. Where are the boundaries between a responsible and non responsible use of social media by faculty, with special attention to avoiding privacy issues, and
4. Whether they could recall experiences that had raised privacy concerns either with their students, a professor, or an advisor, which involved social media.

The participants were given total freedom to discuss the questions for 30 minutes. Some relevant conclusions emerged after the discussion. Regarding a possible explanation to faculty adoption of social media in the classroom, PhD students believe that even if university online platforms offer more control and safety, faculty might decide to adopt social media because these media offer a wider range of possibilities. On the other hand, PhD students expressed their concerns regarding the adoption of social media at university as they believe the lines between public and private may easily blur if the same media are used for personal and academic purposes. Also, they consider that using the same social media for class purposes that are also used for personal purposes can distract towards personal things. In addition, PhD students assume that being professional as a lecturer involves maintaining a line of privacy between students' lives and their private lives and that some social media such as Facebook have the risk to put them in contact if they are implemented in the classroom. However, participants consider that privacy concerns do not affect all social media alike. Therefore, their implementation needs to be analyzed case by case: aspects such as the purpose of the implementation (e.g. communication *vs.* sharing content) or the degree of personal information that is shared through the medium need to be considered.

Based on the results of the focus groups and the results of a previous work on the same topic (Aymerich-Franch & Fedele, 2014), a survey was designed and distributed online among undergraduate students and a series of interviews were conducted among faculty.

The survey contained questions regarding

1. The use of the most relevant social media applications,
2. The participation in a series of activities through social media,
3. The use of social media during class for personal purposes,
4. Faculty use of social media in the classroom, and
5. Privacy concerns resulting from the use of social media in the educational context.

In particular, respondents answered

- How often they use email, Facebook, Google+, Twitter, chat rooms, online forums, Skype, Gtalk or Google Hangout, YouTube, Flickr, Instagram, Pinterest, Blogs, MySpace, LinkedIn, Tumblr, and Wikipedia, and rated their responses on a scale with seven categories (never, monthly, weekly, daily - once or twice, daily - 3-5 times, daily - 6-10 times, or daily - 10+ to permanently connected).
- How often they participate in the activities of emailing (reading / responding), reading and posting on Twitter, Facebook wall or in the shared spaces of other social networks, chatting from computer or smartphone, video or voice chatting using Skype, Google Hangout or similar video-conferencing services, editing their profile in social networks (LinkedIn, Facebook...),

watching videos in YouTube or in other social media (Tumblr, Pinterest...), photo sharing and editing (Flickr, Instagram, Pinterest...), reading blogs and forums, and writing blogs and participating in forums. They rated their responses on a 7-point scale ranging from 'never' to 'daily'.

- How often they use social media for personal purposes while they attend class and rated their responses on a 6-point scale ranging from 'very frequently' to 'never'.
- What social media their lecturers use for class purposes and how often (Facebook, Twitter, Wikis, Blogs, Podcasts, Online Video, and SlideShare) and rated their responses on a 6-point scale ranging from 'very frequently' to ''never'.
- Whether they would experience privacy concerns if their lecturers created a Facebook group for class which they were invited to join, posted class content on a social network and they had to sign up with their names and emails to get access, asked them to create a profile including their picture in a social network (such as Facebook) for class purposes, asked them to create a profile with no picture in a social network (such as Facebook) for class purposes, asked them to create a profile including their picture in a virtual space owned by the university which was used for class purposes only (e.g. virtual campus), asked them to create a profile with no picture in a virtual space owned by the university which was used for class purposes only, proposed them a meeting using video-voice conferencing (e.g. Skype) to discuss the results of their work instead of a face-to-face meeting in the office, proposed them a meeting using instant messaging service (e.g. Gtalk) to discuss the results of their work instead of a face-to-face meeting in the office, asked them to write a blog as part of a class activity, had a

blog with class content that they had to fol-low, uploaded lessons in YouTube for stu-dents to watch, asked them to participate in a discussion forum with their name, asked them to participate in a discussion forum anonymously, suggested them to follow a specific Twitter account the lecturer used to announce class-related news, sent them an invitation to connect in LinkedIn, and sent them an invitation to be friends on Facebook. Students rated their responses on a 5-point scale that ranged from 'ex-tremely unlikely' to 'extremely likely'.

- An open-ended question to describe their main privacy concerns regarding the use of social media as teaching resources.

The survey was filled out by 94 undergraduate students from the Communication faculties of the participant universities (56.4% respondents from the Spanish universities, 37.2% from the Colombian university, and 6.4% from the Ameri-can university). Participants were aged 17 to 29 (=19.8, SD=2.58). Females represented 60% of the sample. Responses were codified using the statistical software package SPSS.

In addition, a total of 18 written interviews with open-ended questions were conducted among teaching faculty from the Communication depart-ments at the participant Spanish and Colombian universities. Eleven females and seven males participated in the interviews, their ages ranged 30 to 60 (=41.9, SD=8.39). The interviewees answered questions regarding privacy concerns resulting from the use of social media in their profession. Both faculty-students and faculty-faculty relationships were explored. In particular, they answered whether

1. They have encountered situations in their jobs in which they had to offer more personal information than desired to institutions and organizations for distribution in social media,

2. They think that being professional as a lecturer implies making sure that lives of faculty and students do not converge,
3. They would accept students in their social networks and what factors would they evalu-ate in taking that decision,
4. They believe social media generate more privacy conflicts with students or with col-leagues according to their experience and what type of conflicts have they encountered, if any, and
5. They use social media as teaching resources and whether they have encountered privacy conflicts as a result of their implementation.

RESULTS

Social Media Use among Students

To explore what social media students use more often and in what kind of activities they get in-volved, students reported their frequency of use of a total of 17 applications. In addition, they reported how often they carry out a series of activities such as online chatting or updating their profiles in the social networks they belong.

Figure 1 shows frequency of social media use in a descending order (from the most frequently used to the least). Students in the sample are heavy users of social networks, in particular, Facebook. More than 90% of the students in the sample visit Facebook daily and 37% visit the site more than ten times per day or are permanently connected. This social network is the most visited social me-dia among students and it is even more used than email, which is the second medium in frequency of use. Email is used daily by 85% of the students and most daily users check the email five times per day or less. The video-sharing site YouTube is the third most visited social media among students. Of the total sample, 70% visits YouTube daily and 27% visits it weekly. Facebook, email, and

YouTube are used, more or less often, by nearly all students in the sample.

The microblogging service Twitter follows next as the fourth most used social media, with 60% of students being daily users of Twitter. However, 15% of the sample never uses Twitter. Instagram follows next. Of the sample, 56% of students use this online photo and video sharing social network daily and 25% do it more than 10 times a day or are permanently connected. However, 26% of the sample never uses this medium. Wikipedia is also a site frequently visited by students. Slightly over 38% of students use this collaboratively edited encyclopedia online. Almost 44% use it weekly and only 4.5% of students never use it. Blogs follow next, with 43% of the sample visiting them weekly. It follows Google+, visited weekly by 23% of the sample. However, 33% never uses it. Regarding chat rooms, almost 70% of the sample never uses it. Interestingly, though, 11% of students visit chat rooms more than 10 times per day or are permanently connected to them. Skype is next. This voice-over-IP service is used monthly by 40% of students. Regarding forums, almost 40% of the sample visits them weekly or monthly.

Other social media on the list are considerably less popular among students in the sample. In total (including daily, weekly, and monthly users), 30% of students use the microblogging platform Tumblr, 20.5% use the IM service Gtalk or the video-voice service Google Hangout, 17% use the photo-sharing website Pinterest, 18% use the professional social network LinkedIn, and 16% use the image and video hosting site Flickr. The social network MySpace is the least visited social media, with only 2% of students using it.

Figure 2 illustrates how often students participate in a series of activities involving social media. Chatting using the computer or the smartphone is the most frequent activity. More than 95% of students chat daily and over 72% engage in this activity more than 10 times per day or are permanently connected. Reading and posting on Twitter, Facebook wall or in the shared spaces of other

social networks is the second most popular activity. Over 80% of students carry out this activity daily and nearly 29% of them do it more than 10 times per day or are permanently connected. Watching videos in YouTube or in other social media such as Tumblr or Pinterest is the third most frequent activity, with 67% of students participating on it daily and 15% doing it more than 10 times per day or being permanently connected. Emailing comes next with over 70% of students emailing daily and 15% doing it more than 10 times per day or being permanently connected. Next, 41% practice photo sharing and editing daily using social media such as Flickr, Instagram, or Pinterest. However, 32% never get involved in these activities. Over 86% of students edit their profiles in their social networks at least once a month and over 17% do it daily. Regarding blogs, 84% of the students read blogs at least once a month and 70% write blogs at least once a month as well. Finally, 67% of the sample engages in video or voice chatting using Skype, Google Hangout or other videoconferencing services at least once a month.

Lastly, participants also reported their habits regarding social media use during class hours for personal purposes. Figure 3 shows frequency of social media use by students during class. Most part of students in the sample state that they use social media for personal purposes during class hours and almost 40% do it frequently or very frequently. Only a small number (less than 14%) never do it or do it very rarely.

Social Media as Teaching Resources

Student participants also reported what social media their professors use for class purposes and how often they use them. In addition, professors that participated in the interviews were also asked whether they use social media for teaching purposes and what social media they use. The results of the survey indicate that online video is the most frequently used by teaching faculty in their classes. According to students, nearly 69% of their faculty

Figure 1. Frequency of social media use among students

use this resource at least occasionally. Blogs are the second social media most widely adopted for class purposes. Over 52% of student's lecturers use blogs as a resource for teaching purposes at least occasionally. Twitter follows next. According to students in the sample, 36.5% of the lecturers use it at least occasionally. Almost 30% of teaching faculty use Wikipedia at least occasionally, nearly 26% use SlideShare at least occasionally, about 23% use podcasts at least occasionally, and 16% use Facebook at least occasionally. Figure

4 shows the results of the survey regarding how often lecturers use social media in the classroom.

Faculty that participated in the interviews also reported the use of social media for class purposes. These tools are used, with more or less frequency, by nearly all interviewees, with only one exception. Most lecturers are familiar with virtual campus and Moodle, online platforms intended for educational purposes. These tools are mainly used to share materials such as readings or the syllabus and to communicate with

Figure 2. Frequency of participation in social media activities among students

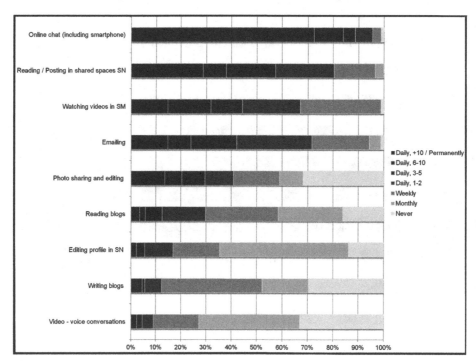

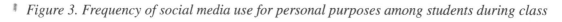

Figure 3. Frequency of social media use for personal purposes among students during class

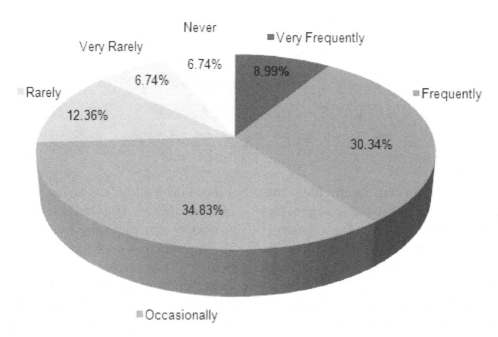

Figure 4. Frequency of faculty use of social media in the classroom

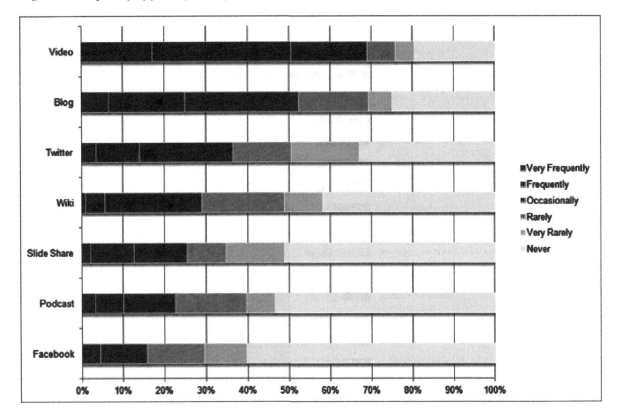

students. In addition, most lecturers also have experiences of using other social media in their classes. Lecturers are implementing social media as learning resources, as communication tools, and as part of class content. Several interviewees mentioned they have integrated social media as part of some subjects such as online Journalism. Regarding particular media, six of them specifically mentioned they have used or use YouTube. Lecturers use this platform to recommend or show videos to students as learning resources, upload and share videos of their own, or ask students to produce and upload videos as part of a class activity. Three interviewees mentioned they had created Facebook groups for class purposes and another one had asked students to create a Facebook and a Twitter account as part of a class activity. Three other lecturers also mentioned they use their Twitter accounts to recommend links or readings and

to communicate news. Four interviewees mentioned they have implemented Skype for online tutoring and meetings with students. Of them, one had done it with doctoral students only and two in exceptional circumstances in which either the lecturer or the student was abroad. Three lecturers also mentioned they had created blogs for their subjects or had asked students to create a blog as part of coursework. Finally, an interviewee also mentioned he had used the social library Pearltrees and the social bookmarking web service Delicious for class purposes.

Privacy Concerns among Students

Students reported their levels of privacy concerns regarding a series of implementations of social media in the educational context. Figure 5 illustrates the levels of privacy concerns in a

Figure 5. Students' probabilities of experiencing privacy concerns regarding social media implementation in the classroom (by activity)

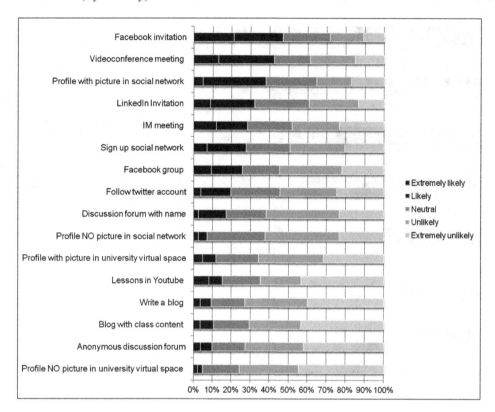

descending order that each activity might generate to students if their lecturers used social media for this purpose (from most likely to least likely to generate privacy concerns among students).

Nearly 47% of students claim that if one of their lecturers sent them an invitation to be friends on Facebook their chances of experiencing privacy concerns would be 'likely' or 'extremely likely'. This action is the most likely to generate privacy concerns to students. Although lower than an invitation to connect on Facebook, receiving an invitation from a lecturer to connect on LinkedIn might also generate distress as 32% of the students say they would 'likely' or 'extremely likely' experience privacy concerns if lecturers sent them an invitation to join in this professional network.

Proposing a meeting through video-conference to discuss work is the second most likely action to generate privacy concerns to students. Over

42% of students state that they would 'likely' or 'extremely likely' experience privacy concerns if a lecturer proposed them a Skype meeting instead of a face-to-face meeting. A meeting through instant messaging would also generate privacy concerns, but to a lesser extent. Of the sample, 28.3% states that using chat to discuss work instead of a face-to-face meeting in the office would 'likely' or 'extremely likely' cause them privacy concerns.

Asking students to create a profile with a picture in a social network such as Facebook for class purposes can easily generate them privacy concerns as well. Regarding this, 38% of students state that the probabilities of experiencing privacy concerns if their lecturers requested them to do that would be 'likely' or 'extremely likely'. Nonetheless, the same request but without including a picture drastically descends privacy concerns. Only 7% of the students consider that creating a profile with no picture would 'likely' or 'extremely likely' generate them privacy concerns. Creating a profile in the university virtual space significantly reduces students' privacy concerns as well. Nearly 12% would 'likely' or 'extremely likely' experience privacy concerns if they were requested to create a profile with their pictures in a virtual space owned by the university for class purposes, such as the virtual campus, and only 4.6% would 'likely' or 'extremely likely' experience privacy concerns if they were requested to do the same but without including their picture.

Posting class content on a social network in which students had to sign up with their names and emails to get access or creating a Facebook group for class in which students were invited to join are activities that might also generate uneasiness to more than a quarter part of the sample. The first one is 'likely' or 'extremely likely' to generate privacy concerns to 27.6% of students and the second one, to 25.6% of students.

Suggesting students to follow a specific Twitter account that the lecturer uses to announce class-related news would be 'likely' or 'extremely likely' to generate privacy concerns to 19.7% of students.

Regarding participation to discussion forums, privacy concerns would be 'likely' or 'extremely likely' to affect over 17% of students if lecturers asked them to participate using their names. Those concerns would descend to 10% if students could participate anonymously.

Uploading lessons in YouTube for students to watch would 'likely' or 'extremely likely' create privacy concerns to 15.3% of the sample.

Finally, having a blog with class content that students had to follow would 'likely' or 'extremely likely' generate concerns to 10.6% of students and asking students to write a blog as part of a class activity would 'likely' or 'extremely likely' raise privacy concerns to 9.4% of them.

Lastly, students reported their privacy concerns regarding the implementation of social media as teaching resources in higher education in an open-ended response. Students reported a wide range of answers, from those who stated that they "honestly don't have any" (male, 21) to those who would be "most concerned with the blurring of the line between professional or academic and personal" (female, 18).

Those students more in favor of implementing social media in higher education consider them "applications with interesting possibilities for learning" (male, 18) and "absolutely not a problem, but just the opposite, if these media are evolving, education needs to evolve with them, as quick as they do, and take advantage of them" (male, 22).

Other students also see the advantages of using social media in the classroom but "consider more appropriate using the tools that the university has developed for this purpose, such as the virtual campus" (male, 28).

Several students make a distinction between those social media that can cause privacy concerns and those that cannot as "privacy conflicts would depend on the medium. If we would have to use Facebook I would experience a lot of concerns because this is a space I just want to share with family and friends and I would not like to share it with my professors." On the other hand "if a professor started to follow me on Twitter I would need to change the type of comments I normally post because I would feel uncomfortable knowing that he could read what I write." Finally, "I don't see that other social media such as the virtual campus, blogs, forums, etc. would create me concerns unless I had to put photos there or some kind of information that I could consider very personal" (female, 18).

Some other students state that privacy concerns would appear if they were obliged to sign up to a social media they do not want to belong because "when you sign up to a social network you are already giving up your privacy and deciding that you want to exhibit your life to everyone" (female, 21). Thus, privacy conflicts would appear if someone "did not have a profile on a social network and they felt compelled to sign up in order to follow class content" (male, 18). Also, "professors should take into consideration that some of us don't like social networks, for instance, I don't like Facebook for personal reasons, and, in this case, would I be forced to sign up to follow class? I don't think I am willing to do that" (female, 24). This type of concerns might "bring conflicts in the classroom if some students refused to participate in some activities because they are against social networks, since it is a personal decision and professors should respect that" (male, 20).

One of the most important concerns expressed by students was that adopting social media for class purposes would "blurry the boundaries between the professional and the personal" (female, 18) as well as the "times and spaces for academy and for hobby" (male, 19). Many of them "don't want to mix the academic and social lives" (male, 19) as they "don't want people that are not friends to be connected in such an intimate setting" (female, 18). Also, they consider that "it would be strange and awkward to share things you only want to share with some people in a certain setting" (female, 18).

Some students consider that the adoption of social media in this setting might damage or modify the image that students have of their faculty. Concerning this, students believe that "if a professor adopted social media for class would change the relationship with the students and they would see him closer as a person but less professional" (female, 18). Students holding this view also believe that "some social media would be fine for educational purposes but some others which we consider more personal such as Facebook would modify our relationship with the professor, we would see him with different eyes as in the social networks we only have friends" (female, 18).

Finally, some other students expressed other type of concerns associated to social media such as "the need of being permanently connected and the contribution to an online addiction" (fermale, 18).

Privacy Concerns among Faculty

Teaching faculty that participated in the interviews presented a wide variety of opinions. Age or gender did not help to group the different points of view that emerged in the interviews.

The first question examined whether lecturers had encountered situations in their jobs in which they had to offer more personal information than desired to be published online. About half of the interviewees had encountered this situation. The principal request that creates uneasiness on these cases is the obligation to send a picture for its publication in online academic publications, the university website, or the website of the research group, among other sites. Also, a professor (female, 39) mentioned that "a situation that makes me feel particularly uncomfortable is when conference organizers upload pictures of the event where I appear to the website without previously requesting my permission. When this situation has happened I have not requested them to remove it but I did not like the fact that they did that without my consent."

Concerning the second question, an important number of interviewees agree that being professional as a lecturer implies that lives of faculty and students do not converge. This separation "is necessary to guarantee privacy to professors and students" (female, 33) as "students and professors develop different roles and relationships cannot be totally symmetric" (female, 47). However, "keeping this distance does not imply creating a hierarchy or exclude a relationship of proximity with students" (female, 33). On the other hand, about a quarter of them believe that a closer relationship can sometimes benefit students as "sharing some personal experiences can enrich our role as professional educators" (female, 60). Also, one of the interviewees stated that "it is very important to keep this distance with undergraduate students. However, it is not so important with graduate and doctoral students. With them, we can establish a closer relationship without losing professionalism" (female, 39). Finally, another professor mentioned that "I have a very good relationship with some of my former students. However, this friendship is now possible because while they were still my students we all strictly kept our roles" (male, 53).

The third question explored whether teaching faculty tend to accept students in their social networks and what factors they evaluate in taking the decision. Different positions emerged regarding that question. About a third of the interviewees do not have accounts in social networks or have never been invited to join their social networks by students. About another third have accounts on social networks and generally accept students: "I generally accept everyone that wants to connect with me on Twitter, Facebook, LinkedIn, Academia, etc. as I believe social networks have been created with the purpose of facilitating relationships, projects, and to create proximity" (male, 32). However, many of them do not use social networks (including Facebook) for personal purposes or do not publish information that can be considered private. Finally, about another third have accounts on social networks and accept students only in the networks that they use for professional purposes (mainly Twitter and LinkedIn) and refuse invitations to join social networks they use for personal purposes (mainly Facebook). An interviewee holding this position commented that: "as a general rule, I don't accept students on Facebook, in some cases I can accept former students. It is different with Twitter, I follow the students and former students that follow me, also because I use this medium as a professional tool, to inform about news and events that can be of their interest as well" (female, 31). Another interviewee with a similar perspective mentioned that: "whereas I would accept students on LinkedIn I would not do that on Facebook, as I use it for my close relationships, friends and family, and I

don't want to mix it with my academic life" (female, 33). An interviewee do not accept students to join any social network as a general rule and two of them generally accept invitations to join their social networks from doctoral students and refuse invitations from undergraduate students.

The fourth question evaluated whether social media generate more privacy conflicts to faculty in their relationship with students or with other faculty and what type of conflicts they may encounter. More than a third of interviewees stated that they do not use social media for personal purposes or do not publish aspects that consider private and therefore they had not encountered privacy concerns. In many cases, they decide not to use them "precisely, to avoid privacy conflicts" (female, 47). A professor mentioned that: "I have not encountered any problem, fundamentally, because I am not that foolish to put my private life online" (male, 39). Some of them said they are extremely careful when they set up the privacy settings of their social media accounts and that this is why they do not generally encounter privacy concerns. Among this group, one of the interviewees mentioned that "social media cannot be blamed of creating privacy conflicts. Users have the responsibility to learn how to manage privacy settings and control them in their social media accounts" (male, 32). Other lecturers also use social media for personal and professional purposes with no special precaution and have not encountered conflicts either. However, some lecturers have faced serious privacy conflicts. Facebook is the social media that has generated more conflicts among the interviewees. A professor (female, 44) explained that: "I was defamed on Facebook by some doctoral students that did not even know me in person." Another professor mentioned that: "in the past, I had a public profile in my social networks and experienced serious conflicts at work. Some colleagues commented on my behavior and misjudged my work schedule based on my status updates or the content I had in my accounts" (female, 31).

Social media have created privacy conflicts both with students and with colleagues. Some interviewees experience concern if they receive an invitation from a student to be friends on Facebook. They generally solve the conflict by not accepting the invitation. However, some interviewees consider accepting them if the relationship is good and "they are already alumni or last year students that won't be my students anymore" (female, 49). Privacy concerns that have to do with colleagues are experienced even in a more sensitive manner and are more difficult to handle than those that have to do with students. Receiving a Facebook invitation from a colleague can generate important concerns when the lecturer is not willing to add the person to his or her social network. Generally, the interviewees solve the conflict by accepting the invitation and modifying the privacy settings so the person only sees some information. Yet, they do it reluctantly as "I generally use Facebook for my relationships with close friends and family because I do not mind sharing my private life with them...I do not like having to add colleagues or my superiors to Facebook, unless we have a friendship in the real world." However, "sometimes I have to do this because refusing the invitation would be rude. When this happens, I modify the privacy settings so they can only see what I want them to see" (female, 33). A different solution an interviewee adopted to avoid dealing with privacy conflicts was "to have two different profiles and using a nickname for my personal profile that only friends know" as "it is very easy to encounter a situation in which you have to unwillingly add people from your work to your social networks if you don't take precautions, for instance, they can easily find your profile if it is associated to your email" and, if this happens, "you have no option but to add them" (female, 39). Despite the precautions, there are problems which cannot easily be solved such as "if you are tagged on a picture in Facebook by someone else you do not have control over who is going to see it" (female, 39).

Finally, faculty responded whether they use social media as teaching resources and whether they have encountered privacy conflicts as a result of their implementation. Social media use among teaching faculty has been reported in a previous section. As mentioned, an important number of interviewees use different social media as teaching resources. A few do not use them as they do not feel the need of doing so or consider that they "have the virtual campus for this purpose", as "social media are communication channels for students in their private life" (female, 49). Nearly a third of the interviewees have encountered privacy conflicts after implementing social media as teaching resources. A professor (female, 33) explained that in one of the institutions where she works she uses the official Moodle and has not found problems with that. However, in a different institution she created "a Facebook group for a specific subject with the intention to exchange practical information and help students to solve doubts." She opened "an account ad hoc for this purpose that did not contain personal information." The first problem she encountered was that "a couple of students didn't want to participate because they didn't have a Facebook account and were against having one." Second, "students were sending messages at all times, taking for granted that I would be available 24 hours to respond them immediately." In addition, "the tone and the format of the messages was completely inappropriate, it reminded more the type of interpersonal communication someone would have with their friends than a formal exchange of information between students and their professor." Another lecturer (female, 31) commented that "I use Twitter as a teaching resource for my students. Sometimes, I have to see aspects of their private lives that are not of my interest, which causes me conflict." Also, "as a result of important privacy conflicts I experienced in the past I made the decision to not publish some aspects of my private life in the social networks where I have students, former students, or colleagues." Some lecturers that use social media as part of class content take privacy of their students very seriously. A professor (female, 30) remarked that "in my classes I am constantly using social media as part of some subjects and I force my students to divide their personal profiles in social networks from the professional and academic projects we carry out." According to this professor, "if social media are used separately for personal or for professional purposes, with different accounts, there shouldn't be privacy conflicts." She also recommends her students to "use nicknames in their personal accounts so companies cannot find them in the results of the search engines. This way they will be able to protect better their digital identities." Another professor (female, 39) explained that "in one of the subjects students had to create an online media and created Twitter and Facebook accounts. Although I made sure they created the accounts using the profiles we created for the media and not their private ones, I encountered problems when some students used their Instagram and YouTube private accounts to upload videos and images. Even if students were not concerned, I forced them to redo the exercise creating new profiles."

FUTURE RESEARCH DIRECTIONS

This study examined privacy concerns of university students and faculty resulting from the adoption of social media as teaching resources. Also, it analyzed the concerns that faculty experience when social media are used for social networking in the academic context.

While the study uncovered several unique privacy conflicts occurring in the field of higher education, several other areas of research could enhance understanding of this research area. For instance, although this is a cross-cultural study, all results were explored as a whole. It would be interesting that other studies compared privacy concerns among different cultures and countries

or between males and females. Also, the study found a wide variety of responses among faculty regarding their opinions about social media and privacy concerns. However, it was not able to determine opinion tendencies among them. Larger samples might help identify potential tendencies.

On the other hand, the interviews and the survey were carried out with participants from Communication faculties. Social media are very relevant to this field and are also becoming part of class content and activities, which allowed the examination of many types of social media uses in the classroom. Future research could address how social media are implemented and received in other educational areas in which these applications are not as directly linked to the discipline as in Communication.

Finally, there are two important findings in the study which were not thoroughly reported in the results. One, the study found that an important number of students are permanently connected to some social media, specially, to social networks. This data might indicate that a substantial number of students suffer an addiction to these technologies. Also, there might be the possibility that using social media for educational purposes contributed to increase this addiction Two, the use of social media during class hours for personal purposes is a widely extended practice among students, which might affect attention during class. Researchers are strongly encouraged to examine these topics.

CONCLUSION

Social media are rapidly expanding into the educational arena. Although virtual environments specifically created for educational purposes exist with similar functionalities, professionals of education also want to take advantage of the possibilities that social media have to offer. In addition, the expansion of social media to many professional spheres requires the integration of social media as part of class content.

Both the survey and the interviews carried out in this study indicate that teaching faculty are broadly implementing social media for class purposes. According to the survey, video-sharing sites such as YouTube and blogs are the resources most frequently used for class purposes. On the other hand, the results of the interviews show that lecturers are mainly implementing social media in the classroom as learning resources, as communication tools, and as part of class content. Nearly all interviewees have implemented some kind of social media in the classroom. In addition, several lecturers have integrated social media as part of some subjects such as New Media or Online Journalism. The application most widely implemented by interviewees is YouTube, which is consistent with the results of the survey. Some of them have also created blogs with class content, created Facebook class groups or used it as part of class activities, used Twitter to inform of class related news or used it as part of class activities, and used Skype for meeting with students or giving conferences.

Also, this study found that students at university level are heavy users of social media. Facebook is the most widely used social media, with more than 90% of the sample visiting this site daily and 37% visiting it more than ten times per day or being permanently connected. Among the activities involving social media in which students participate, chatting is the most practiced, with 95% of the students chatting daily and over 72% doing it more than 10 times per day or being permanently connected. The other most practiced activity among students is reading and posting on Twitter, Facebook wall or in the shared spaces of other social networks, with over 80% doing it daily and nearly 29% doing it more than 10 times per day or being permanently connected.

A considerable number of social media are mainly used for personal purposes and are conceived as part of the private sphere (Aymerich-Franch & Fedele, 2014). Thus, the advent of social media in the academic sphere can easily raise privacy concerns to students and faculty. These concerns do not only appear when social media are implemented as teaching resources but also when students or faculty intend to use them for social networking in the academic sphere.

This study explored both types of concerns. Results suggest that using social media for social networking in the university context may easily generate privacy conflicts. Almost half of the students that participated in the survey think they would experience privacy concerns if they received a Facebook invitation from one of their lecturers and about a third would also experience concerns if they received an invitation to connect on LinkedIn, even if this is a professional social network. More varied opinions exist among faculty that participated in the interviews. About a third would generally accept students on Facebook, some professors would only accept graduate students, some others would only accept students to their professional social networks, and some of them do not use social networks. Lecturers who also use Facebook for personal purposes generally experience greater concerns when they get an invitation to connect on this social network from a colleague than from a student. This is explained because refusing an invitation from a student is perceived as the "correct thing" to do whereas refusing an invitation from a colleague is considered "rude." Given this general perception, faculty believes that rejecting a colleague might also negatively affect the relationship they have at work. Lecturers usually solve this issue accepting colleagues' invitations to join and modifying the privacy settings so that the colleague only has limited access to personal information.

On the other hand, using social media in the classroom may also create privacy conflicts. Consistent with the results of a previous work (Aymerich-Franch & Fedele, 2014), this study found that using social media for communication purposes between students and faculty may easily raise privacy concerns among students. More than 40% of the students in the sample believe that they would experience privacy concerns if a lecturer suggested them to discuss work through Skype or similar services and almost 30% of students believe they would experience concerns if a lecturer suggested them to discuss work using instant messaging services. Another activity which is likely to create concerns among students is the need to create a profile with a picture on a social network for class purposes. Interestingly, the concerns significantly decrease if the profile they are asked to create does not include a picture.

Even if it is to a minority of students, all implementations of social media may potentially generate some kind of concern. However, there are social media and activities more likely to create privacy concerns than others. According to the results of the study, the uses of social media that present lower risks of creating concerns to students are writing a blog as part of a class activity, following a lecturer's blog with class content, participating anonymously in a discussion forum, and creating a profile in the university virtual learning space with no picture.

Lecturers have also experienced some concerns as a result of implementing social media as teaching resources. Among them, it needs to be highlighted that using social networks such as Facebook might contribute to excessively blur the hierarchy existing between faculty and students. Some students alerted that students in general normally use Facebook for their personal purposes and, because of that, interacting with a lecturer through this network might invite them to address faculty in an excessive informal manner. Indeed, one of the professors that participated in the study had already encountered this situation.

Finally, some faculty that participated in the study also stated they had experienced privacy concerns for having to include a picture to online academic publications, the university website, or the website of their research group.

To conclude, the implementation of social media in the educational context is already a fact. Since social media commingle personal and pro-

fessional relationships, the risk of creating privacy turbulence is very high. Nonetheless, teaching faculty believe social media are interesting resources for the classroom. In addition, these applications are expanding into the professional sphere and need to be included as part of class content. Therefore, the adoption of social media in education needs to be accompanied of self-regulation and regulation from institutions. Faculty using social media in the classroom need to take privacy seriously and consider privacy issues beforehand to ensure a safe implementation. What is more, faculty need to develop an e-professionalism in relation to behaviors and communications that occur online (Cain, 2008). They need to decide what practices represent professionalism regarding behaviors and decisions that take place in the online sphere. These guidelines will also help faculty in developing better privacy protection strategies in their professional environments.

Most likely, both students and faculty will experience boundary turbulence as a result of implementing social media in the classroom. However, they will progressively learn how to adequate their uses in the educational context and will readjust privacy rules over time until privacy needs and expectations are met.

REFERENCES

Alexander, B. (2006). Web 2.0: A new wave of innovation for teaching and learning? *Educational Review*, *41*(2), 32–44.

Altman, I. (1975). *The environment and social behavior: Privacy, personal space, territory, crowding*. Monterey: Brooks/Cole.

Amstrong, J., & Franklin, T. (2008). *A review of current and developing international practice in the use of social networking (web 2.0) in higher education*. Franklin Consulting. Retrieved January 4, 2014, from http://arthurmckeown.typepad.com/files/web-2.0-in-higher-education.pdf

Anderson, P. (2007). What is web 2.0? Ideas, technologies and implications for education. *JISC Technology and Standards Watch*, 1-64.

Aymerich-Franch, L. (2011). *Aulas 2.0: The use of social media as learning tools*. Paper presented at Congreso Internacional de Comunicación y Educación: Estrategias de Alfabetización Mediática, Bellaterra, Spain.

Aymerich-Franch, L., & Carrillo, M. (2014). The adoption of social media in financial journalism. In B. Çoban (Ed.), *Sosyal medya d/evrimi*. Istanbul: Yayinlari.

Aymerich-Franch, L., & Fedele, M. (2014). Students' privacy concerns on the use of social media in higher education. In V. Benson & S. Morgan (Eds.), *Cutting-edge technologies and social media use in higher education*. Hershey, PA: IGI Global. doi:10.4018/978-1-4666-5174-6.ch002

Bennett, S., Bishop, A., Dalgarno, B., Waycott, J., & Kennedy, G. (2012). Implementing web 2.0 technologies in higher education: A collective case study. *Computers & Education*, *59*(2), 524–534. doi:10.1016/j.compedu.2011.12.022

Cain, J. (2008). Online social networking issues within academia and pharmacy education. *American Journal of Pharmaceutical Education*, *72*(1), 1–7. doi:10.5688/aj720110 PMID:18322572

Child, J. T., Haridakis, P., & Petronio, S. (2012). Blogging privacy rule orientations, privacy management, and content deletion practices: The variability of online privacy management activity at different stages of social media use. *Computers in Human Behavior*, *28*(5), 1859–1872. doi:10.1016/j.chb.2012.05.004

Child, J. T., Pearson, J. C., & Petronio, S. (2009). Blogging, communication, and privacy management: Development of the blogging privacy management measure. *Journal of the American Society for Information Science and Technology*, *60*(10), 2079–2094. doi:10.1002/asi.21122

Child, J. T., & Petronio, S. (2011). Unpacking the paradoxes of privacy in CMC relationships: The challenges of blogging and relational communication on the internet. In K. Wright & L. Webb (Eds.), *Computer-mediated communication in personal relationships* (pp. 21–40). New York: Peter Lang.

Conole, G., & Alevizou, P. (2010). *A literature review of the use of web 2.0 tools in higher education*. Higher Education Academy, The Open University, UK. Retrieved December 12, 2013, from http://www.heacademy.ac.uk/assets/documents/subjects/bioscience/event-report-2009-leicester-literature-review.pdf

Facebook Newsroom. (2012). One billion people on Facebook. *Facebook*. Retrieved September 20, 2013, from http://newsroom.fb.com/News/457/One-Billion-People-on-Facebook

Fernando, A. (2008). Baby steps in web 2.0 education. *Communication World*, *25*(3), 8–9.

Hewitt, A., & Forte, A. (2006). *Crossing boundaries: Identity management and student/faculty relationships on the Facebook*. Paper presented at the CSCW Conference, Canada.

Jaya, R. (2008). Advantages of learner-centered approach to learning English. *Language in India*, *8*(12), 40–45.

Jones, N., Blackey, H., Fitzgibbon, K., & Chew, E. (2010). Get out of MySpace! *Computers & Education, 54*(3), 776–782. doi:10.1016/j.compedu.2009.07.008

Kaplan, A. M., & Haenlein, M. (2010). Users of the world, unite! The challenges and opportunities of Social Media. *Business Horizons, 53*(1), 59–68. doi:10.1016/j.bushor.2009.09.003

Kennedy, G., et al. (2009). *Educating the net generation: A handbook of findings for practice and policy.* Australian Learning and Teaching Council. Retrieved December 12, 2013, from http://www.netgen.unimelb.edu.au/downloads/handbook/NetGenHandbookAll.pdf

Kirkpatrick, G. (2005). Online 'chat' facilities as pedagogic tool. *Active Learning in Higher Education, 6*(2), 145–159. doi:10.1177/1469787405054239

Kumar, S. (2009). Undergraduate perceptions of the usefulness of web 2.0 in higher education: Survey development. In: D. Remenyi (Ed.), *Proceedings of 8th European Conference on E-learning* (pp. 308-314). Academic Press.

Madge, C., Meek, J., Wellens, J., & Hooley, T. (2009). Facebook, social integration and informal learning at university: 'It is more for socialising and talking to friends about work than for actually doing work'. *Learning, Media and Technology, 34*(2), 141–155. doi:10.1080/17439880902923606

Margulis, S. (2011). Three theories of privacy: An overview. In S. Trepte & L. Reinecke (Eds.), *Privacy online: Perspectives on privacy and self-disclosure in the social web.* Berlin: Springer.

Mazer, J. P., Murphy, R. E., & Simonds, C. J. (2007). 'I'll see you on 'Facebook': The effects of computer-mediated teacher self-disclosure on student motivation, affective learning, and classroom climate. *Communication Education, 56*(1), 1–17. doi:10.1080/03634520601009710

Meyrowitz, J. (1985). *No sense of place.* Oxford, UK: Oxford University Press.

Minocha, S. (2009). A case study-based investigation of students' experiences with social software tools. *New Review of Hypermedia and Multimedia, 15*(3), 245–265. doi:10.1080/13614560903494320

Moran, M., Seaman, J., & Tinti-Kane, H. (2011). *Teaching, learning, and sharing: How today's higher education faculty use social media.* The Babson Survey Research Group, and Converseon.

Petronio, S. (2002). *Boundaries of privacy: Dialectics of disclosure.* State University of New York.

Petronio, S., & Caughlin, J. (2006). Communication privacy management theory: Understanding families. In D. Braithwaite & L. Baxter (Eds.), *Engaging theories in family communication: Multiple perspectives.* Thousand Oaks, CA: Sage. doi:10.4135/9781452204420.n3

Philip, R., & Nicholls, J. (2009). Group blogs: Documenting collaborative drama processes. *Australasian Journal of Educational Technology, 25*(5), 683–699.

Ricardo, C., & Chavarro, A. (2010). El uso de Facebook y Twitter en la educación. *Instituto de Estudios en Educación, 11*, 1–9.

Roblyer, M. D., McDaniel, M., Webb, M., Herman, J., & Witty, J. V. (2010). Findings on Facebook in higher education: A comparison of college faculty and student uses and perceptions of social networking sites. *The Internet and Higher Education, 13*(3), 134–140. doi:10.1016/j.iheduc.2010.03.002

Semiocast. (2012). Twitter reaches half a billion accounts. *Semiocast.* Retrieved September 20, 2013, from http://semiocast.com/en/publications/2012_07_30_Twitter_reaches_half_a_billion_accounts_140m_in_the_US

Toro-Araneda, G. (2010). Usos de Twitter en la educación superior. *Serie Bibliotecología y Gestión de Información*, *53*, 1–30.

Trepte, S. (2011). Preface. In S. Trepte & L. Reinecke (Eds.), *Privacy online: Perspectives on privacy and self-disclosure in the social web*. Berlin: Springer.

Walther, J. (2011). Introduction to privacy online. In S. Trepte & L. Reinecke (Eds.), *Privacy online: Perspectives on privacy and self-disclosure in the social web*. Berlin: Springer.

Weisgerber, C. (2009). Teaching PR 2.0 through the use of blogs and wikis. *Communication Teacher*, *23*(3), 105–109. doi:10.1080/17404620902974782

Westin, A. F. (1966). Science, privacy, and freedom: Issues and proposals for the 1970's: Part I--The current impact of surveillance on privacy. *Columbia Law Review*, *66*(6), 1003–1050. doi:10.2307/1120997

Westin, A. F. (1967). *Privacy and freedom*. New York: Atheneum.

Westin, A. F. (2003). Social and political dimensions of privacy. *The Journal of Social Issues*, *59*(2), 431–453. doi:10.1111/1540-4560.00072

ADDITIONAL READING

Barnes, S. B. (2006). A privacy paradox: Social networking in the United States. *First Monday*, *11*(9), 1–11. doi:10.5210/fm.v11i9.1394

Bovill, M., & Livingstone, S. (2001). Bedroom culture and the privatization of media use. In S. Livingstone & M. Bovill (Eds.), *Children and their changing media environment. A European comparative study*. Mahwah, New Jersey, London: Lawrence Erlbaum Associates Publishers.

Buckingham, D. (1998). Review essay: Children of the electronic age? Digital media and new generation rhetoric. *European Journal of Communication*, *14*(4), 557–565. doi:10.1177/0267323198013004007

Buckingham, D., & Sefton-Green, J. (1999). Children, young people and digital technology. *Convergence*, *5*, 5–7.

Chong, E. (2010). Using blogging to enhance the initiation of students into academic research. *Computers & Education*, *55*(2), 798–807. doi:10.1016/j.compedu.2010.03.012

Debatin, B., Lovejoy, J. P., Horn, A. K., & Hughes, B. N. (2009). Facebook and Online Privacy: Attitudes, Behaviors, and Unintended Consequences. *Journal of Computer-Mediated Communication*, *15*(1), 83–108. doi:10.1111/j.1083-6101.2009.01494.x

Drotner, K. (2000). Difference and diversity: Trends in young Danes' media use. *Media Culture & Society*, *22*(2), 149–166. doi:10.1177/016344300022002002

Dwyer, C., Hiltz, S. R., & Passerini, K. (2007). Trust and privacy concern within social networking sites: A comparison of Facebook and MySpace. *Proceedings of AMCIS 2007*, Keystone, CO.

Frau-Meigs, D. (2010). From Secrecy 1.0 to Privacy 2.0: Who Controls What? Critical Review Essay. *Revue Francaise d'Etudes Americaines*, *123*(1), 79–95.

Fuchs, C. (2010). StudiVZ: Social networking in the surveillance society. *Ethics and Information Technology*, *12*(2), 171–185. doi:10.1007/s10676-010-9220-z

Fuchs, C. (2012). *Internet and surveillance: the challenges of Web 2.0 and social media*. New York: Routledge.

Harwood, P. G., & Asal, V. (2007). *Educating the first digital generation*. Westport, Conn.: Praeger Publishers.

Hodge, M. J. (2006). The Fourth Amendment and privacy issues on the "new" Internet: Facebook. com and MySpace.com. *Southern Illinois University Law Journal. Southern Illinois University at Carbondale. School of Law*, *31*, 95–123.

Huang, W., Hood, D., & Yoo, S. (2012). Gender divide and acceptance of collaborative Web 2.0 applications for learning in higher education. *The Internet and Higher Education*, *16*, 57–65. doi:10.1016/j.iheduc.2012.02.001

Jones, N., Blackey, H., Fitzgibbon, K., & Chew, E. (2010). Get out of MySpace! *Computers & Education*, *54*(3), 776–782. doi:10.1016/j.compedu.2009.07.008

Joosten, T. (2012). *Social media for educators: strategies and best practices*. San Francisco: Jossey-Bass.

Jukes, I., McCain, T. D. E., & Crockett, L. (2010). Understanding the digital generation: teaching and learning in the new digital landscape. Kelowna, BC, Canada: 21st Century Fluency Project.

Kabilan, M. K., Ahmad, N., & Abidin, M. J. Z. (2010). Facebook: An online environment for learning of English in institutions of higher education? *The Internet and Higher Education*, *13*(4), 179–187. doi:10.1016/j.iheduc.2010.07.003

Karahasanovic, A., Brandtzaeg, P. B., Vanattenhoven, J., Lievens, B., Nielsen, K. T., & Pierson, J. (2009). Ensuring Trust, Privacy, and Etiquette in Web 2.0 Application. *Computer*, *42*(6), 42–49. doi:10.1109/MC.2009.186

Laermans, R. (2010). *Beyond privacy: new perspectives on the public and private domains*. Rotterdam, The Netherlands: NAi Publishers/SKOR.

Lewis, K., Kaufman, J., & Christakis, N. (2008). The Taste for Privacy: An Analysis of College Student Privacy Settings in an Online Social Network. *Journal of Computer-Mediated Communication*, *14*(1), 79–100. doi:10.1111/j.1083-6101.2008.01432.x

Livingstone, S. (2002). *Young people new media. Childhood and their changing media environment*. London: Sage.

Livingstone, S. (2008). Taking risky opportunities in youthful content creations: Teenagers' use of social networking sites for intimacy, privacy and self-expression. *New Media & Society*, *10*(3), 393–411. doi:10.1177/1461444808089415

Mitrano, T. (2006). A Wider World: Youth, Privacy, and Social Networking Technologies. *EDUCAUSE Review*, *41*(6), 16–29.

Neal, D. (2012). *Social media for academics: a practical guide*. Oxford, UK: Chandos Pub. doi:10.1533/9781780633190

Nissenbaum, H. (2011). *Why privacy online is different, and why it isn't*. Stanford, CA: Stanford Law School.

Öqvist, K. (2009). *Virtual shadows: your privacy in the information society*. Swindon, UK: BCS.

Palfrey, J., & Gasser, U. (2008). *Born digital: understanding the first generation of digital natives*. New York: Basic Books.

Rössler, B. (2005). *The value of privacy*. Oxford: Polity.

Samoriski, J. (2002). *Issues in cyberspace: communication, technology, law, and society on the Internet frontier*. Boston: Allyn and Bacon.

Selwyn, N. (2009). Faceworking: Exploring students' education-related use of Facebook. *Learning, Media and Technology, 34*(2), 157–174. doi:10.1080/17439880902923622

Seo, K. (2013). *Using social media effectively in the classroom: blogs, wikis, twitter, and more*. New York: Routledge.

Squicciarini, A. C., Shehab, M., & Wede, J. (2010). Privacy policies for shared content in social network sites. *The VLDB Journal - The International Journal on Very Large Data Bases, 19* (6), 777-796.

Strandburg, K., & Raicu, D. (2006). Privacy and technologies of identity: a cross-disciplinary conversation. New York: Springer Science+Business Media. doi:10.1007/0-387-28222-X

Trottier, D. (2012). *Social media as surveillance: rethinking visibility in a converging world*. Farnham: Ashgate.

Veletsianos, G., & Kimmons, R. (2012). Scholars and faculty members' lived experiences in online social networks. *The Internet and Higher Education, 16*, 43–50. doi:10.1016/j.iheduc.2012.01.004

Wankel, C., Marovich, M., Miller, K., & Stanaityte, J. (2011). *Educating educators with social media*. Bingley, UK: Emerald. doi:10.1108/S2044-9968(2011)1

Wankel, L. A., Wankel, C., Marovich, M., Miller, K., & Stanaityte, J. (2011). *Higher education administration with social media: including applications in student affairs, enrollment management, alumni relations, and career centers*. Bingley, UK: Emerald.

Zheleva, E., & Getoor, L. (2009). To join or not to join: The illusion of privacy in social networks with mixed public and private user profiles. In *Proc. WWW'09*, Madrid, Spain.

KEY TERMS AND DEFINITIONS

Disclosure: The act of revealing private information.

Microblogging: Web services that allow users to post short messages and follow other users' messages. Twitter is one of the most popular microblogging sites, which limits posts to 140 characters.

Privacy: The right of an individual to withhold information about the self or to isolate from the rest of the society.

Private Sphere: The domain in individuals' life that belongs to themselves in which personal and family relationships take part. It is the opposite or the complement of the public sphere.

Public Sphere: The social arena in society in which public interactions -including relations with the community, the government, etc.- take part. It is the opposite or the complement of the private sphere.

Social Bookmarking: Web services that allow their users store, classify and share bookmarks (i.e. links to a website). Delicious is one of the most popular social bookmarking sites.

Social Media: On-line communication applications that allow users to create and exchange contents in an accessible and simple way.

Social Network: Online platform intended to promote social relations. Connections are made based on real-life acquaintances or shared interests. Users build personal profiles and share information and communicate with other users on their personal network. Facebook is the most popular social network.

Virtual Campus: An online space from an educational institution, generally a college or a university, to support learning activities and administrative services. It is also a space of communication between students and lecturers. Access is restricted to students from the institution.

Chapter 2
Social Media and Alcohol Use:
Adverse Impact of Facebook and Twitter on College Students

Gulzar H. Shah
Jiann-Ping Hsu College of Public Health, USA

Moya L. Alfonso
Jiann-Ping Hsu College of Public Health, USA

Nina Jolani
National Association of County and City Health Officials (NACCHO), USA

ABSTRACT

The use of Social Networking Sites (SNSs) has become an integral part of daily life, particularly for adolescents. The chapter examines the negative impact of social networking sites and how they may expose alcohol-related consumption and behavior to young adults, especially college students. In particular, the focus is on the use of two specific social networking sites, Facebook and Twitter, and their association with alcohol use. The review of existing literature reveals that the depiction of alcohol use on social networking sites has a deleterious effect on alcohol use through the creation of positive social norms toward use and abuse. Further, the chapter looks at the Theory of Differential Association to explain the use of SNS as a pivot to increased alcohol use by adolescents and young adults.

INTRODUCTION

This chapter examines the use of SNSs by young adults, specifically college students, and further describes how these platforms might shape alcohol use amongst this age group, and in turn negatively impact social and academic aspects of their lives. Based on a systematic review of most recent studies conducted in the United States and elsewhere, the thrust is on synthesizing the manner in which SNSs facilitate underage drinking. The chapter offers comprehensive conceptual, theoretical, and empirical bases of association between use of SNSs and use of alcohol in adolescence and early adulthood. The chapter focuses on Edwin Sutherland's Theory of Differential Association (TDA) to explain the manner in which interaction and socialization with peers in virtual communities

DOI: 10.4018/978-1-4666-7401-1.ch002

facilitates formation of alcohol-identities and peer influence grouping. The TDA also explains why some adolescents are impacted by social media use negatively whereas others might experience socially desirable outcomes.

BACKGROUND

The alcohol culture in the United States has significantly increased in the past 25 years (Newport, 2010). Large amounts of alcohol consumption, or "binge" drinking, is connected to immediate fatalities and long-term health outcomes. While alcohol consumption varies between colleges (Lorant, Nicaise, Soto, & D'Hoore, 2013), on average four out five students drink alcohol, and about a half of college students who drink, consume four or more drinks in one sitting (Fact Sheets-Binge Drinking, 2012). The risk-taking behavior is developed through the positive outlook that is modeled from a direct or indirect encouragement of popular activities, alcohol consumption (Santor, Messervey, & Kusumakar, 2000). In addition, this deleterious culture is further amplified by print and media marketing. In one study, adolescents' exposure to alcohol marketing increased their likeliness of drinking, and further increased consumption level for those already drinking (Bruijn, Angus, Gordon, & Hastings, 2009). With the new digital age, alcohol marketing has expended to various SNSs. This new environment allows for an additional source of exposure to alcohol, and builds the hypothesis of increased likelihood of alcohol consumption and abuse amongst young adults, especially college students.

SOCIAL NETWORKING SITES AND ALCOHOL CONSUMPTION

In recent years, the use of SNSs has become inescapable. As of May 2013, 72 percent of Americans use SNSs, a 5 percent increase from 2012; and amongst young adults ages 18-29, SNS use is 89 percent (Duggan & Brenner, 2013). There are many methods of using these platforms: entertainment, information sharing, socializing, etc. College students use SNS to extensively communicate: given that it allows them to connect and efficiently interact with their peers and instructors. These academic needs may involve sharing information related to group projects, brainstorming on common assignments, and organizing meetings with study groups. Unfortunately, they also allow creation of virtual meeting space to display shared interests relating to drinking behavior (e.g. parties, sporting events, games, etc.). Whilst there are many social networking sites used by young adults; for the focus of this study Facebook and Twitter have been analyzed.

The first platform, Facebook, was developed in 2004 for users at participating colleges and universities across the United States. Its exclusivity grew its popularity to a larger audience of users across the globe. Facebook users develop profiles to connect with friends, relatives, and other networks. Facebook functionalities range from photo-sharing, story-telling format for information sharing, and private messaging. As of recent, 86 percent of those in the 18-29-age bracket are Facebook users (Duggan & Brenner, 2013). Students in this age bracket may use Facebook to create open and private Facebook groups to share updates with their fellow peers on various academic related or social related events. Regrettably, in addition to many positive functions that Facebook's platform can provide to college students, it can also allow students and other youth to interact and virtually connect for purposes other than academic.

A supportive evidence of increased drinking behavior, as a result of Facebook use by college students, is a study conducted collecting data on Facebook use by college students. In this study, the Alcohol Use Disorder Identification Test (AUDIT) scale was used as a screening tool to measure Facebook alcohol references. The study surveyed undergraduate students, ages 18-20 years, at two universities with public Facebook profiles. Researchers categorized the profiles into three categories: non-displayers, alcohol displayers, and intoxication/problem (I/PD) drinking displayers. The results of the study showed that those Facebook accounts whose profile owners displayed I/PD were more likely to face drinking problems on the AUDIT scale (Moreno, Christakis, Egan, Brockman, & Becker, 2012).

The second platform, Twitter, is an online micro-blogging platform that allows users to send 140-character messages, or tweets in real-time. Twitter has many functions for information sharing and encourages the use of hashtags (#), mentions (@), and retweets (RT) to its users. Hashtags are used to create conversations or information sharing around a specific topic. Popular and widely used hashtags often make the Twitter list of trending topics for users of a specific geographic location. The use of hashtags not only elevates the marketing of the user's tweet but also connects the user with other users of similar interest. The practice of mentions in tweets is to indicate a message to a specific user, which can include replying directly to that user (e.g., @johnsmith). The retweet function on Twitter is used to re-share what another user has tweeted.

According to recent data, about three out of ten (30%) young adults (18-29 year olds) use Twitter (Duggan & Brenner, 2013). Twitter is used for various academic purposes by college students and young-adults. Most evidently, in one study, Twitter was found to increase a number of positive academic outcomes, including: higher grades, positive engagement between instructor and student, and overall increased academic engagement (Junco, Heiberger, & Loken, 2011). However, similar to Facebook, whereas Twitter has its benefits for improved academic outcomes for students, it also is a platform that exposes students to alcoholic brands and behaviors. Researchers from the University of Western Sydney's School of Business studied the promotion of seven popular alcohol brands on Twitter over the course of six

months. They discovered that these companies' tweets reached to a broader secondary audience through the retweets of their followers; an audience that could be under the drinking age. Indeed, the study showed hashtags were also effective in popularizing drinking during social events such as concerts or sporting events (Burton, Dadich, & Soboleva, 2013). This study is one example of ways Twitter may stimulate a positive display for alcohol consumption and exposure for both college students and young adults.

CONNECTION BETWEEN SOCIAL MEDIA AND DRINKING: THE THEORETICAL EXPLANATIONS

Studies have used many explanations to reason why young adults get involved in socially undesirable behaviors. Tickle, Hull, Sargent, Dalton, & Heatherton (2006) used Ajzen and Fishbein's (1980) Theory of Reasoned Action to explain how social influences, such as portrayal of influential characters smoking cigarettes and smoking by family members, predict adolescent smoking. A classic theory of deviance, Edwin Sutherland's Theory of Differential Association (TDA) offers the best explanation for linkage between increased use of social media and socially undesirable behaviors such as smoking and drinking. Some criticisms of Sutherland's theory (Akers, 1988; Matsueda, 1988; Warr & Stafford, 1991) might suggest TDA is less relevant due to new realities created by social media. Social media, and virtual reality created with its help, play a decisive role in creating hyperreality (Baudrillard, 2012) for those living in the virtual reality. Consequently, young adults' responsibility to conform to mainstream societal norms weakens, because some youth are able to forget realities of the mainstream culture in favor of a simulation of reality created by sub-group norms, such as desirability of underage drinking, pre-marital sex, etc. Social media can facilitate seamless blending of reality and hyperrealist.

With increasing use of social media, parental control over adolescents is diminishing. Parents held much more control over adolescents in the absence of virtual meeting spaces. Who they met and were influenced by could be controlled by manipulating situations, so negative influence could be avoided. With social media facilitating togetherness and communications independent of physical presence, strict control is not possible. Even when parents and guardians are aware of associations causing negative influences, they are helpless in preventing networking. With virtual meeting places, parents can be deceived about the identities of others in the network. To complicate the matter, easily created fake identities can severely hamper efforts to prevent negative influences. Much like the real world, identity and impression management (Goffman, 1959) by hiding the undesirable characteristics and exaggerating more desirable characteristics also characterizes the cyber communities (Zweir, Araujo, Boukes, & Willemsen, 2011).

Theory-Based Explanations of Influence of Use of SNSs on Alcohol Use in Adolescence: Theory of Differential Association

Use of main propositions in Sutherland's theory helps understand the phenomenon in question relatively well. Sutherland would suggest that deviation from mainstream norms is a learned behavior. The primary learning about smoking and alcohol use often happens as youngsters learn these behaviors from their parents. Research on etiology of alcohol use shows that youth behavior is heavily shaped by parents' drinking habits; parents who are heavy alcohol consumers have children who are more likely to be involved in underage drinking (Armstrong, Ruttle, Burk, Costanzo, Strauman, & Essex, 2013). Perhaps more important is the influence of the secondary socialization of youth with their peers. Birds of feather flock together is true when it comes

to underage drinking. Having friends who were deviant in general also increased the odds of underage drinking among youth (Armstrong, et al., 2013). Adolescent peer group identification is often clearly captured in their names making it easy for distinguishing self from others. Sussman, Pokhrel, Ashmore, and Brown (2007), through an exhaustive review of 44 peer reviewed studies on adolescent peer group identification in offline environments (e.g., school) showed that discrete peer group identities can be categorized into five life style categories; deviant group of adolescents was one of those five categories. This group was categories separately in 37 of the deviants 44 studies. The deviant group reported caring least about school work, school-related extra-curricular activities and preparation for career. Their engagement into tobacco alcohol, drug use was much higher in deviant group (Sussman et al., 2007). Risky behaviors are not really inherited and adolescents with no one to teach them about these behaviors cannot really invent them. Social media and networking created through this becomes a major source of learning.

The premise of the Differential Association Theory that humans learn deviant behavior through interaction and communications with others is perhaps most relevant in explaining the linkage between social media and youth behaviors like smoking and drinking. Social media as communication landscape is ever more popular and is maturing fast, offering diverse functions to facilitate communication (Kietzmann, Hermkens, McCarthy, & Silvestre, 2011). The communication landscape of SNSs works much like regular communication in that it results in social bonding and adherence to the "virtual" norms (Garas, Garcia, Skowron, & Schweitzer, 2012). Consistent with Berger and Luckmann's theory of social construction of reality (Berger & Luckmann, 1966), norms evolve for social media users through frequent interactions and communications, gradually becoming routinized and leading to construction of their realities. Such communications facilitated by

SNS may also play a latent function of learning of otherwise deviant behaviors like drinking and smoking by the youth. Social context, particularly availability of other underage drinkers to participate in drinking has been shown by research to increase underage drinking (Reboussin, Song & Wolfson, 2012).

The premise of the TDA proposes that the core of the deviant behavior learning happens within intimate personal groups. Subrahmanyam, Reich, Waechter, and Espinoza (2008), found that the online social networks of communications, particularly MySpace and Facebook, are not just popular means for connecting with other "emerging adults," the core of online communication networks is made up of intimate friends and family. Through online social interactions, participants co-construct the spheres of their virtual existence, but due to major overlap with the circle of offline friends, psychological connections and social bonds are constructed through shared online and offline experiences. Online social networks are not only helpful in maintaining offline relationships; they are also used by some subgroups to find friends and romantic partners (DeHaan, Kuper, Magee, Bigelow, & Mustanski, 2013). Empirical evidence shows that online networking and instant messaging is done primarily with offline friends to converse about offline events being planned for the day or week. Social media, therefore, can be argued as a catalyst in promoting deviant behaviors through intimate circle of friends maintained by youth. Prior to the popularity of social media, tobacco industry and alcoholic beverages industry pushed the imagery of tobacco and alcoholic beverages through television and movies adds various other means (Arora, Mathur, Gupta, Nazar, Reddy, & Sargent, 2013). The imagery of smoking and alcohol use portrayed in movies can influence adolescents' attitudes, intentions, and behaviors towards initiating smoking and drinking as well as increased use. Positive imagery, such as drinking and smoking by credible lead characters holding prestigious social positions,

particularly those portrayed as heroes gives a sense of social desirability of these otherwise socially undesirable behaviors. Tickle et al. (2006) used the theory of reasoned action to conceptualize their research by using data from 150 schools from New Hampshire and Vermont to examine the impact of smoking imagery in movies on adolescent smoking behavior. Viewing smoking in movies was among the most important predictors of underage smoking intentions and behavior. The increasing regulations against targeting of minors and underage individuals in cigarette and alcohol advertisements may have protected youth from aggressive targeting by these industries. However, the increased use of social media over the past decade or so, have created an alternative source of alcohol and cigarette imagery displays. By Sutherland's theory, indirect influences such as mass media might not have much influence in promoting deviant behavior.

For acting out deviance, association with deviant friends alone is insufficient. One must also have skills required to perform the deviant acts. For instance, for cigarette smoking or alcohol consumption, children and youth not permitted to buy cigarettes and alcohol through legal means need to have skills to acquire them through other means. Thus, the learning of deviant behaviors means having skills of committing the deviant acts, as well as justification and rationalization for those acts. The etiology of alcohol use among underage college students is complex, but SNS communications can be private enough to organize underage smoking and drinking occasions, thus, the skills can be obtained through online circle of friends to perform offline acts of deviance. Factors that affect student drinking include: student expectations and social pressure (National Institute on Alcohol Abuse and Alcoholism (NIAAA), 2013), particularly during freshman year, social factors, such as, involvement in fraternities or sororities and peer behavior (Borsari & Carey, 2001; NIAAA, 2013; Testa, Kearns & Livingston, 2009), culture, e.g., race/ethnicity (Borsari &

Carey, 2001; Metlife Foundation, 2013), and biological and psychological factors (Schulte, Ramo, & Brown, 2009). Location might also play an important role in underage alcohol consumption, with youth in rural areas reporting more frequent use and problematic use (Atav & Spencer, 2002; Borders & Booth, 2007).

Sutherland's theory would suggest that the specific direction of the motives and drives for alcohol use is learned from definitions of proscriptive and prescriptive norms about alcohol use. One factor that consistently predicts underage alcohol consumption is social norms, more specifically the misperception that peers are using alcohol at high rates (when compared to self-reported use) (Litt & Stock, 2011; Perkins, Meilman, Leichliter, Cashin, & Presley, 1999). Young adults who consume alcohol might subscribe to subgroup norms with alcohol use, even binge drinking, as socially desirable behavior (Ridout, Campbell, & Ellis, 2012). Young adults also consistently misjudge the frequency of alcohol use by their peers, which leads to increased beliefs that underage alcohol use is a normative behavior and increased alcohol consumption (Litt & Stock, 2011; Perkins et al., 1999) SNSs such as Facebook provide a unique platform for the development and maintenance of alcohol use social norms among college students. Adolescents with self-reported alcohol displays reported greater willingness to use alcohol, more positive attitudes toward alcohol use, and lower vulnerability to the consequences of alcohol consumption (Litt & Stock, 2011). Through sharing of alcohol-related images, comments, and videos and supporting alcohol related-advertisements (Anderson, De, Angus, Gordon, Hastings, 2009), young adults create and maintain intoxigenic social identities as well as intoxigenic digital spaces that further contribute to the normalization of underage alcohol consumption (Griffiths & Casswell, 2010).

The principal of differential association, the central premise of Sutherland's theory, demonstrates how social media might be more crucial facilitator of underage drinking and smoking than any other factors. The primary assumption is that a person's capability to perform deviant acts without worrying about violation of values, mores, norms, and laws depends on availability of a subculture or a counter culture often found among teenagers that will reinforce the non-conformity to mainstream cultural norms, and values as not only something normal but desirable. Peer influences in digital space enable youth create a hyperreality (Baudrillard, 2012), that blurs the line between what is desirable by mainstream culture and what is considered desirable by the simulation of social desirability within the closed circles of youth. Young adults who consume alcohol might represent a counter-culture with alcohol use as socially desirable behavior. Young adults also consistently misjudge the frequency of alcohol use by their peers, which leads to increased beliefs that underage alcohol use is a normative behavior and increased alcohol consumption (Litt & Stock, 2011; Perkins et al., 1999). SNSs such as Facebook provide a unique platform for the development and maintenance of alcohol use social norms among college students.

The premise that differential association may vary in frequency, duration, priority, and intensity is equally applicable to association through SNSs. Studies have shown that the frequency and intensity of alcohol use displays differ across users. For instance, Fournier and Clarke (2011) found that profiles of Facebook users varied considerably for percent of alcohol-related content, ranging from 0% to 29%. Variation was also found in motives for use of SNSs (Yang & Brown, 2013).

Learning of deviant behavior through association with other deviants and non-deviants comprises processes involved in form of learning. Those adolescents who belong to online peer groups involved in activities more in line with broader cultural norms can lead to socially desirable outcomes. For instance, adolescents who also include their parents in their social networking not only have stronger bonding with parents, their use of SNSs leads to better behavioral outcomes, improved pro-social behavior, and reduced relational aggression (Coyne, Padilla-Walker, Day, Harper, & Stockdale, 2013). Also, social media specially designed for the young adults who are mentally impaired are known provide many positive functions for their leaning needs (Gowen, Deschaine, Gruttadara, & Markey, 2012). Social media is expected to actually help young adults to deal with their mental health problems through positive peer reinforcement (O'Dea & Campbell, 2011).

Social media can be also a deterrent to underage smoking and drinking. Just as social media can promote underage smoking and drinking, it can also be used as prevention. Social media can be used by those concerned with population health to post anti-smoking and anti-drinking messages. Twitter, Facebook, YouTube and other social media has increasingly been used by public health geneses to perform efficient monitoring using generated contents and educating fellow Tobacco control population education against to prevent smoking (Myslín, Zhu, Chapman, & Conway, 2013).Twitter offers large amounts of user centric information for public health professionals, reflecting perspective not available from surveys. Twitter data can be harvested with minimal effort on real–time basis (Myslín et al., 2013).

SOCIAL MEDIA, ALCOHOL USE, AND SOCIAL OUTCOMES

Research on college students suggests that references to and display of alcohol use (i.e., pictures of intoxication, alcohol brand images, comments regarding alcohol use) on SNSs are associated with self-reported alcohol use, perceptions of friends' alcohol use (Fournier & Clarke, 2011; Westgate, Neighbors, Heppner, Jahn & Lindgren, 2014), and increased risk for problematic drinking (Hoffman, Pinkleton, Austin & Reyes-Velázquez, 2014; Moreno et al., 2009; Westgate et al., 2014). Studies suggesting absence of relationship between alcohol use displays and alcohol use are rare, if

any. On the other hand, the impact of imagery of drinking on youth attitudes and behaviors towards these habits is documented globally. Such imagery often glorifies and, in turn, promotes tendencies to engage in smoking and drinking, even though mainstream social norms are increasingly proscriptive of both underage smoking and drinking (Davey & Zhao, 2012).

The transition from childhood into adolescence involves interactions that are beyond small groups. In this age group, larger peer groups are involved, and the peer pressure tends to overshadow the parental controls and guidance. Even before the predominance of digital space in our lives, peer group pressures tended to have profound impacts on adolescents' attitudes and behaviors. Membership of one or more peer influence group is desirable for a multitude of functions associated with it. Such membership helps adolescents with finding emotional/instrumental support, foster friendships and social interactions (Brown, Eicher & Petrie, 1986). Peer influences are different in pre-adolescence than in adolescence, in that in the former, peer groups are defined on the basis of common activity, whereas in adolescence, peer group influence is global and far reaching, affecting attitudes, behaviors and engagement in illicit acts (O'Brien & Bierman, 1988). Peer influences are documented by many recent studies, particularly showing that alcohol use during adolescence is significantly a function of peer pressure and use of alcohol by peer groups (Becker & Curry, 2013; Boyd-Ball, Veronneau, Dishion, & Kavanagh, 2013; Huang et al., 2013; Mundt, Mercken & Zakletskaia, 2012; Visser, Winter, Veenstra, Verhulst, & Reijneveld, 2013).

Social media can enable youth to share their drinking stories online and photos of alcohol-use during parties. McCreanor et al., (2012) found that SNSs can create conducive environments for encouraging underage drinking. Virtual norms are constructed through online interaction and social construction of shared understanding of prescriptive and prospective principles of online behaviors. However, research supports the premise that online behaviors and attitude are governed by same broader social norms prevalent in physical social world. This implies that in relationships built and maintained in virtual social environment, the group norms might be equally applicable in both social and virtual situations. By the same token, the youth norms formed through interactions at SNSs that govern drinking intentions, can lead to actual consumption of alcohol.

Alcohol use displays allow SNS users to explicitly declare their alcohol-identity, which is argued to be a crucial component of identity exploration for adolescents and young adults. Exaggerated alcohol identities, e.g. self-labeling "binge drinker", are also a means of persuading others with similar identities to reach out for planning and acting out these identities (Ridout et al., 2012). Persuasive alcohol advertisement has been found to not only influence initiation of underage drinking but also to increase the risk of regular alcohol use, resulting in alcohol-related problems later in adolescence (Grenard, Dent & Stacy, 2013; Moreno, Briner, Williams, Brockman, Walker & Christakis, D.A., 2010).

Studies suggest that substantial amounts of al-cohol-related content are found on SNSs (Fournier & Clarke, 2011). Alcohol-related content revealing alcohol identities significantly predicts underage alcohol consumption (Ridout et al., 2012). Empirical evidence supporting deleterious effects of adolescents' networking in virtual communities with deviant peers is mounting. A large scale study of 1,563 10th-grade students showed that online connection with friends who display pictures of partying or drinking significantly increased the risk of both smoking and alcohol use in adolescence. The impact of alcohol displays on underage drinking was compounded when adolescents had social media connections with other adolescents who were also involved in drinking. In other words, independent of the influence of alcohol displays, the risk for alcohol use grew in the virtual company of other alcohol users, implying that friendships

facilitated and maintained online had substantial peer influence (Huang et al., 2012). In one of the largest studies of young adults (*N*-3,448) in the United States, the quantity of alcohol content on social media websites was found to be a significantly predictor of alcohol and marijuana use (Stoddard, Bauermeister, Gorden-Messer, Johns, & Zimmerman, 2012).

Facebook users' modalities of and attitudes toward alcohol consumption, and perceived vulnerability is impacted significantly by the norms about alcohol use posted on Facebook profiles. Litt and Stock (2011) found that young adults who are frequently exposed to alcohol use displays were likely to internalize the subjective norm about desirability of alcohol consumption, which increased their risk of actual alcohol consumption compared to adolescents less frequently exposed to alcohol use displays on Facebook. Studies indicate that social media presents a digital space that can be used by young people to communicate messages created for marketing of alcohol, thus, presenting an intoxigenic social environment (i.e., an environment that promote alcohol use and abuse). The online networking can be used in other ways conducive to underage drinking, including to decide safe meeting places for drinking, communicate ways to consume alcohol, convey positive features of certain alcohol products, and to create a value system that is supportive of alcohol use. The communications can be accomplished through a variety of means, including digital photographs, short personal messaging, and online status titles (Griffiths & Casswell, 2010).

The prevalence of underage drinking is high enough to be considered a public health issue. Alcohol use among youth aged 12 to 20 years of age is common, with 10.4 million reporting that they drank alcohol beyond "just a few sips" in the past month (NIAAA, 2013). Roughly one-fifth of college students meet the criteria for alcohol abuse or dependence; however, seeking treatment is uncommon (i.e., 5%) (NIAAA, 2013). The rates are higher in some ethnic and age groups than others (Johnston, O'Malley, Bachman, Schulenberg, 2013; Nishimura, Hishinuma, & Goebert, 2013). Since initiation of drinking in very early age increases the span of alcohol use during their life course and increases the risk for subsequent abuse of prescription opioids (Fiellin, Tetrault, Becker, Fiellin, & Hoff, 2012), the initiation in early teens is even more disconcerting. Empirical evidence indicates the percentage of students in 8th grade who have experienced alcohol is alarmingly at 30 percent in the US, whereas in 10th and 12th graders it is 54 percent and 69 percent respectively. The current use of alcohol within past 30 days is also of note. In 2012, respectively 5 percent, 6 percent, and 24 percent of 8th, 10th, 12th graders reported such heavy drinking (Johnston et al., 2013).

Unfortunately, alcohol related harms (i.e., negative outcomes related to alcohol use) are prevalent as well. According to NIAAA (2013), 1,825 young adults die in the United States alone from unintentional injuries each year. Further, 97,000 young adults report alcohol-related sexual assault or date rape each year (NIAAA, 2013). The ill effects of drinking are major public health concern even among adult populations, but increasingly among youth (Maimon & Browning, 2012). Underage drinking can lead to memory disorders and risk of such disorders is increased for individuals with family history of alcoholism (Silveri, 2012). Studies have also shown elevated risks of morbidity and mortality due to alcohol consumption by American youth and young adults. The negative consequences of underage drinking range from academic problems to intentional and unintentional injuries, and raised risk of mortality. It is imperative to prevent or delay the initiation of drinking, both from individual and public health point of views (Jones & Waite, 2013).

The use of social media and mobile internet offers many advantages but also ill-effects including cyber-bullying (Tokunaga, 2010) and use of alcohol, drugs and tobacco. Peer pressure resulting

in alcohol use can lead to other undesirable social outcomes, particularly a decline in subjective well-being among young adults. (Kross et al., 2013) used several scales such as SWLS (Satisfaction with Life Questionnaire), Beck depression Inventory, the Rosenberg self-esteem scale and social provision scale to assess subjective well-being of adolescents, concluding that Facebook had negative impact on two aspects of subjective well-being:

1. How the participating adolescents felt moment-to-moment, and
2. Their level of satisfaction with life.

This study, therefore, concluded that rather than improving well-being, Facebook undermines it. In contrast, an earlier study presented slightly different findings. Kim and Lee (2011) studied 391 college students and found that for users with larger numbers of Facebook friends, use of Facebook led to improved subjective well-being. Kalpidou, Costin, and Marris (2011) had mixed results compared to the other two studies. Among first year college students, larger number of Facebook friends led to diminished academic adjustments, and lower self-esteem. Among students in their later years at college, this effect of Facebook on self-esteem and academic adjustment became positive, suggesting that younger adults are more vulnerable to negative consequences of Facebook.

Apparently conflicting evidence from the aforementioned studies may not be inexplicable. Since users' intensity of Facebook and other social media might differ, studies drilling down into details found that variation in how social media use impacts self-esteem might be attributable to intensity of both the use of social media and that of relationships (e.g., number of Facebook friends). To illustrate, a study of students at a large Northeastern university revealed that students with frequent visits of their Facebook scored better on Rosenberg Self-Esteemed Scale, indicating that they had higher objective self-esteem. This study also suggested that "selective self-presentation … leads to intensified relationship formation" which influences impression of self-esteem in a negative manner (Gonzalez & Hancock, 2011, p. 79). In addition, although Facebook and other social media are used for relationship forming, the impact of connecting with friends through SNSs is also not the same for all because of differences in self-esteem independent of on-line relationships. Adolescents with low self-esteem who participate in online networking tend to consider it safer for self-expression, but end up antagonizing online friends and losing online peer support (Forest, & Wood, 2012). The principle of relative depreciation equally governs the cyber communities and peer groups in that communicating with or just looking at people with impressive profile attributes (e.g., pictures) can lead to negative self-evaluations (Haferkamp & Kramer, 2011). Also, the peer group is not always homogenous. Instead, an individual might have membership of multiple peer groups. For instance, Dolcini and Adler (1994) found that in their study, students had four different peer groups in the offline social world – Elite popular Black, Elite Smart, Elite Floaters, and Elite Outsiders, and there was a substantial membership overlap. Alcohol use varied significantly by type of peer group af-filiation in this study.

Use of Facebook and other social media does not affect all youth in the same manner also due to variation in motives for use. Individu-als' motives for the use of certain social media are a product of their primary upbringing and socialization as well as secondary socializa-tion influences, including peer pressure. These motives, in turn, predict the type of activities for which the use occurs, the nature of social adjustments adults and adolescents make, and effectiveness in accomplishing level of positive social adaptation. Research shows that Facebook is used by late adolescents (college students) for two primary purposes:

1. Relationship formation, and
2. Relationship maintenance (Yang & Brown, 2013).

Motives for use can include finding out more about someone the user had recently met, knowing with whom the other users maintain friendship, checking out possibilities for po-tential future friendships, developing romantic relationship, and finding more interesting people than offline friends. Relationship maintenance encompassed motives such as staying connected with college friends, and other acquaintances, maintain social ties rather than attempting to find new friends (Yang & Brown, 2013).

The connection between social media and underage risky behaviors is crucial to assess and consider in public policy because the use of SNSs has grown dramatically over the past decade, with a 233% increase from 2010 to 2011 in Facebook usage among college students alone (Alacron-del-Amo, Lorenzo-Romero, & Gomez-Borja,2011; Corbett, 2011). Most (80%) college students use at least one SNS (Peluchette & Karl, 2008). Approximately half of those with SNS accounts log in to their site at least once per day (Peluchette & Karl, 2008), with roughly 34% spending more than an hour on their site (Espinoza & Juvonen, 2011) Young adults' use of SNSs provides an avenue for communicating with friends, with young adults reporting an average of 196 contacts ('friends') (Espinoza & Juvonen, 2011; Ross et al., 2009). Most smart phones have apps that allow 24/7 access to social media sites, updates, postings, etc. Many people don't logout, allowing alerts and messages to come straight to their phones at all times. Most young adult Facebook profiles are set to public (i.e., information is shared with the public – not just friends) (Lewis, Kaufman & Christakis, 2008), leaving open the possibility of negative outcomes related to public content.

CONCLUSION

SNSs play an important role in college students' lives, hence the development of Facebook for college students (Yang & Brown, 2013). Often, the literal moving away from parents and other family and friends, college students, particularly freshman, use SNSs to stay in touch with existing friends while connecting with new friends on campus (Yang & Brown, 2013). SNSs have come to play a vital role in adolescent peer group formation and dynamics. Adolescents of all ages use social networking to maintain connections with their peers and to make new connections to enhance their social networks (Yang & Brown, 2013). Social networking enables college students to maintain relationships, development new peer relationships, and manage social activities within their peer group (Lampe, Ellison, & Steinfield, 2006; Pempek, Yermolayeva, & Calvert, 2009; Subrahmanyam et al., 2008; Urista, Dong, & Day, 2009). Overall, SNSs serve an organizational function that allows college students to effectively manage their social networks (Yang & Brown, 2013). Females in particular use SNSs such as Facebook to manage friendships (Yang & Brown, 2013). However, SNSs might be even more important to adolescent males, who report greater sense of belonging as a result of SNS than do girls (Quinn & Oldmeadow, 2013).

Existing evidence on peer group formation supports the use of SNSs as a means to increasing interactions that extend beyond small groups, which results in increased opportunities for peer pressure. Peer pressure in virtual environments is evident through the posting of alcohol use displays (i.e., images including videos), endorsement of alcohol advertisements, and comments regarding

alcohol use and alcohol-related events. Identifying oneself as a 'drinker' is considered by many young adults to be a socially desirable component of identity in a social networking environment (Ridout et al., 2012). Being known as a 'drinker' might be particularly important to young adult males, as evidence suggests males were more likely than females to post self-promoting pictures or comments involving alcohol (Peluchette & Karl, 2008). Overall, alcohol use displays on SNSs play a key role in the expression of identity for many adolescents and young adults, particularly during the college years.

Alcohol related displays are common on SNSs (Fournier & Clarke, 2011) and predict underage alcohol consumption (Ridout et al., 2012). Alcohol use displays create an environment in which youth misperceive the frequency of alcohol use among their peers (i.e., social norms theory), which results in increased use and abuse (Litt & Stock, 2011). Thus, based on their role in alcohol use among youth and young adults, available evidence suggests that use of SNSs contributes to the public health problem of underage drinking. Prevalence studies suggest that alcohol use is common among 12 to 20 year olds, with approximately 10 million reporting that they consumed alcohol within the past month. Additional public health problems related to alcohol consumption, such as driving under the influence and related unintentional injuries, sexual assault, and alcohol abuse and addiction, are prevalent among youth and young adults. Thus, the relationship between social media and underage alcohol use is ripe for consideration in the public policy arena, especially given the tremendous increase in social networking site use in recent years.

Research supports relationships between high rates of underage drinking in the United States and prevalence of alcohol harms among college students. Unfortunately, the control of virtual environments by parents is quite limited. Policy changes and legal implications cannot promise the prevention of using SNSs as forms of display for alcohol abuse amongst college students and young adults. Several theories give the benefit of understanding the linkages between increased use of SNSs and negative behaviors. The strongest supporting theory in this study is TDA. The theory supports that deviant behavior occurs most often within intimate and personal networks (Sutherland, 1939). While SNSs also can be promising for prevention of poor health behaviors, further research and application is needed to guide its use for positive behavioral changes in alcohol attenuation.

Future Research Directions

Whereas existing evidence suggests a strong relationship between alcohol use displays on SNSs and positive attitudes toward underage alcohol use and related behaviors, little is known about the dynamics or mechanisms that underlie the relationships. For example, our review located no studies that extended the offline investigation of adolescent subcultures into the virtual world. Adolescent peer group formation has been studied extensively offline (Brown, Eicher, & Petrie, 1986; Dolcini & Adler, 1994; O'Brien, & Bierman, 1988; Sussman et al., 2007); however, studies on peer group formation in online environments are virtually nonexistent. SNSs naturally enhance adolescents' tendency to form social groups based on social similarities in social needs and behaviors. Our literature search found research on nature of peer group formation in offline interactions (Dolcini & Adler, 1994). Future research should use qualitative approach to explore the possible existence of adolescent subgroups in virtual environments and their perceived relationships with alcohol-related intentions and behaviors. Once possible subgroups are identified, segmentation (i.e., identification of unique subgroups) research using chi-squared interaction detection (CHAID) (Alfonso & Kaur, 2013) or cluster analysis techniques such as those used in the classification of social networking site uses in Alarcon-del-Amo et

al. (2011) can be used to verify the continuation of offline peer groups into online communities. Cluster analysis techniques would allow for the identification of unique subgroups of young adults who use social networking sites. For example, cluster analysis could be used to test whether the concept of 'deviant' subgroups identified offline persists in virtual environments.

Most studies have used quantitative approaches to looking at the influence of SNSs on alcohol use. Qualitative methods are useful in exploration and identification of the mechanisms behind relationships (Creswell, 2009), such as the relationship between SNS use and underage drinking. Qualitative studies that look at the nature of online interactions and alcohol use are needed. Qualitative research methods such as focus group discussions or in-depth interviews could be used to gather young adults' perceptions of the influence of SNSs on their behavior and perceived relationships between online behavior and future outcomes. Currently there is no firm explanation of how alcohol use displays affect behavior. Specifically, future research should use qualitative research methods to identify risk and protective factors at play in the virtual world that might be associated with underage alcohol use. Quantitative research could then be used to verify the risk and protective factors identified using qualitative research and identify levers of change to target in intervention research.

Perhaps most important to address is the lack of theoretical frameworks used so far in the literature. The use of theoretical constructs is vital in the explanation of human behavior. Theories such as the one discussed herein (i.e., Edwin Sutherland's Theory of Differential Association) could be used to identify key constructs to measure in the exploration of mechanisms that explain relationships between alcohol use displays on SNSs and alcohol-related behavior and to interpret the results of both qualitative and quantitative research studies in this area. For example, quantitative studies could test the theoretical premise that young adults learn alcohol use related behaviors and skills through interaction and communication with their peers through social networking use. In turn, qualitative research could be used to explore the principal of differential association in relation to alcohol-related displays on SNS and related behavior. More specifically, future research could explore values, mores, and norms expressed through SNS and their perceived relationships with alcohol-related beliefs, attitudes, and behavior.

Finally, there is a real need for intervention research in the area of social networking and alcohol-related related behavior. As stated earlier, social media can be also a deterrent to underage drinking. There is very little research in the area of using social media to combat underage drinking. Future research should address this dearth through the identification of levers of change to target with social media interventions. Theoretically driven, mixed method research (Creswell, 2009) could be used to identify strategies that could be effective in changing online behavior and social norms. For example, qualitative research could investigate strategies for using social media to change social norms among youth and young adults, while quantitative research could be used to identify the most significant predictors of social norms to address with interventions. Further, media literacy could be effective in alerting youth and young adults to the influence of alcohol related imagery and behaviors and the virtual world that may influence their behavior (Bergsma & Carney, 2008). Media literacy could be used to educate youth on the role of SNS use and their behaviors. Strategies similar to those used in anti-tobacco prevention campaigns could be used to inform youth of the influence, for example, of virtual alcohol advertisements on their behavior. The potential for differential response to interventions based on gender should be explored in future intervention research, as males report higher rates of alcohol use displays on their SNSs (Peluchette & Karl, 2008) and also report a greater sense of belonging from social networking activities (Quinn & Oldmeadow, 2013). In light of this, gender specific intervention strategies might be required. Future research should seek to confirm this possibility.

REFERENCES

Ajzen, I., & Fishbein, M. (1980). *Understanding attitudes and predicting social behavior*. Englewood Cliffs, NJ: Prentice-Hall.

Akers, R. L. (1996). Is differential association/social learning cultural deviance theory? *Criminology*, *34*(2), 229–247. doi:10.1111/j.1745-9125.1996.tb01204.x

Alarcón-del-Amo, M., Lorenzo-Romero, C., & Gómez-Borja, M. (2011). Classifying and profiling social networking site users: A latent segmentation approach. *Cyberpsychology, Behavior, and Social Networking*, *14*(9), 547–553. doi:10.1089/cyber.2010.0346 PMID:21288133

Alfonso, M., & Kaur, R. (2013). Self-injury among early adolescents: Identifying segments protected and at risk. *The Journal of School Health*, *82*(12), 537–547. doi:10.1111/j.1746-1561.2012.00734.x PMID:23151115

Anderson, P., De Bruijn, A., Angus, K., Gordon, R., & Hastings, G. (2009). Impact of alcohol advertising and media exposure on adolescent alcohol use: A systematic review of longitudinal studies. *Alcohol and Alcoholism (Oxford, Oxfordshire)*, *44*(3), 229–243. doi:10.1093/alcalc/agn115 PMID:19144976

Armstrong, J., Ruttle, P., Burk, L., Costanzo, P., Strauman, T., & Essex, M. (2013). Early risk factors for alcohol use across high school and its covariation with deviant friends. *Journal of Studies on Alcohol and Drugs*, *74*(5), 746–756. PMID:23948534

Arora, M., Mathur, N., Gupta, V., Nazar, G., Reddy, K., & Sargent, J. (2012). Tobacco use in Bollywood movies, tobacco promotional activities and their association with tobacco use among Indian adolescents. *Tobacco Control*, *21*(5), 482–487. doi:10.1136/tc.2011.043539 PMID:21730099

Atav, S., & Spencer, G. (2002). Health risk behavior among adolescents attending rural, suburban, and urban schools: A comparative study. *Family & Community Health*, *25*(2), 53–64. doi:10.1097/00003727-200207000-00007 PMID:12010115

Baudrillard, J. (1983). *The precession of simulacra* (2nd ed.). New York, NY: Durham & Kellner.

Becker, S., & Curry, J. (2014). Testing the effects of peer socialization versus selection on alcohol and marijuana use among treated adolescents. *Substance Use & Misuse*, *49*(3), 234–242. doi:10.3109/10826084.2013.824479 PMID:23965039

Berger, P., & Luckmann, T. (1966). *The social construction of reality: A treatise in the sociology of knowledge*. Garden City, NY: Anchor Books.

Bergsma, L., & Carney, M. (2008). Effectiveness of health-promoting media literacy education: A systematic review. *Health Education Research*, *23*(3), 522–542. doi:10.1093/her/cym084 PMID:18203680

Borders, T., & Booth, B. (2007). Rural, suburban, and urban variations in alcohol consumption in the United States: Findings from the National Epidemiologic Survey on Alcohol and Related Conditions. *The Journal of Rural Health*, *23*(4), 314–321. doi:10.1111/j.1748-0361.2007.00109.x PMID:17868238

Borsari, B., & Carey, K. (2001). Peer influences on college drinking: A review of the research. *Journal of Substance Abuse*, *13*(4), 391–424. doi:10.1016/S0899-3289(01)00098-0 PMID:11775073

Boyd-Ball, A., Véronneau, M., Dishion, T., & Kavanagh, K. (2013). Monitoring and peer influences as predictors of increases in alcohol use among American Indian youth. *Prevention Science*. PMID:23775578

Brown, B., Eicher, S., & Petrie, S. (1986). The importance of peer group ("crowd") affiliation in adolescence. *Journal of Adolescence*, *9*(1), 73–96. doi:10.1016/S0140-1971(86)80029-X PMID:3700780

Bruijn, A., Angus, K., Gordon, R., & Hastings, G. (2009). Impact of alcohol advertising and media exposure on adolescent alcohol use: A systematic review of longitudinal studies. *Alcohol and Alcoholism (Oxford, Oxfordshire)*, *44*(3), 229–243. doi:10.1093/alcalc/agn115 PMID:19144976

Burton, S., Dadich, A., & Soboleva, A. (2013). Competing voices: Marketing and counter-marketing alcohol on Twitter. *Journal of Nonprofit & Public Sector Marketing*, *25*(2), 186–209. doi:10.1080/10495142.2013.787836

Center for Disease Control and Prevention. (2012). *Fact sheets - Binge drinking*. Retrieved December 5, 2013 from http://www.cdc.gov/alcohol/factsheets/binge-drinking.htm

Corbett, P. (2011). *Facebook demographics and statistics including federal employees and gays in the military*. Retrieved on October 5, 2013 from http://istrategylabs.com/2011/01/2011-facebook-demographics-and-statistics-including-federal-employees-and-gays-in-the-military

Coyne, S., Padilla-Walker, L., Day, R., Harper, J., & Stockdale, L. (2013). A friend request from dear old dad: Associations between parent-child social networking and adolescent outcomes. *Cyberpsychology, Behavior, and Social Networking*, 2152–2723. PMID:23845157

Creswell, J. (2009). *Research design: Qualitative, quantitative, and mixed methods approaches* (3rd ed.). Thousand Oaks, CA: Sage Publications, Inc.

Davey, G., & Zhao, X. (2012). 'A real man smells of tobacco smoke'—Chinese youth's interpretation of smoking imagery in film. *Social Science & Medicine*, *74*(10), 1552–1559. doi:10.1016/j.socscimed.2012.01.024 PMID:22445156

DeHaan, S., Kuper, L., Magee, J., Bigelow, L., & Mustanski, B. (2013). The interplay between online and offline explorations of identity, relationships, and sex: A mixed-methods study with LGBT youth. *Journal of Sex Research*, *50*(5), 421–434. doi:10.1080/00224499.2012.661489 PMID:22489658

Dolcini, M., & Adler, N. (1994). Perceived competencies, peer group affiliation, and risk behavior among early adolescents. *Health Psychology*, *13*(6), 496–506. doi:10.1037/0278-6133.13.6.496 PMID:7889904

Duggan, M., & Brenner, J. (2013). *The demographics of social media users, 2012* (Vol. 14). Pew Research Center's Internet & American Life Project.

Espinoza, G., & Juvonen, J. (2011). The pervasiveness, connectedness, and intrusiveness of social network site use among young adolescents. *Cyberpsychology, Behavior, and Social Networking*, *14*(12), 705–709. doi:10.1089/cyber.2010.0492 PMID:21668346

Fiellin, L., Tetrault, J., Becker, W., Fiellin, D., & Hoff, R. (2012). Previous use of alcohol, cigarettes, and marijuana and subsequent abuse of prescription opioids in young adults. *The Journal of Adolescent Health*, *52*(2), 158–163. doi:10.1016/j.jadohealth.2012.06.010 PMID:23332479

Forest, A., & Wood, J. (2012). When social networking is not working individuals with low self-esteem recognize but do not reap the benefits of self-disclosure on Facebook. *Psychological Science*, *23*(3), 295–302. doi:10.1177/0956797611429709 PMID:22318997

Fournier, A., & Clarke, S. (2011). Do college students use facebook to communicate about alcohol? An analysis of student profile pages. *Cyberpsychology (Brno)*, *5*(2), 1–12.

Garas, A., Garcia, D., Skowron, M., & Schweitzer, F. (2012). Emotional persistence in online chatting communities. *Scientific Reports*, *2*(204), 402. PMID:22577512

Goffman, E. (1959). *The presentation of self in everyday life*. New York: Doubleday.

Gonzales, A. L., & Hancock, J. T. (2011). Mirror, mirror on my Facebook wall: Effects of exposure to Facebook on self-esteem. *Cyberpsychology, Behavior, and Social Networking*, *14*(1-2), 79–83. doi:10.1089/cyber.2009.0411 PMID:21329447

Gowen, K., Deschaine, M., Gruttadara, D., & Markey, D. (2012). Young adults with mental health conditions and social networking websites: Seeking tools to build community. *Psychiatric Rehabilitation Journal*, *35*(3), 245–250. doi:10.2975/35.3.2012.245.250 PMID:22246123

Grenard, J., Dent, C., & Stacy, A. (2013). Exposure to alcohol advertisements and teenage alcohol-related problems. *Paediatrics*, *131*(2), e369–e379. doi:10.1542/peds.2012-1480 PMID:23359585

Griffiths, R., & Casswell, S. (2010). Intoxigenic digital spaces? Youth, social networking sites and alcohol marketing. *Drug and Alcohol Review*, *29*(5), 525–530. doi:10.1111/j.1465-3362.2010.00178.x PMID:20887576

Haferkamp, N., & Krämer, N. (2011). Social comparison 2.0: Examining the effects of online profiles on social-networking sites. *Cyberpsychology, Behavior, and Social Networking, 14*(5), 309–314. doi:10.1089/cyber.2010.0120 PMID:21117976

Hoffman, E. W., Pinkleton, B. E., Austin, E. W., & Reyes-Velázquez, W. (2014). Exploring college students' use of general and alcohol-related social media and their associations to alcohol-related behaviors. *Journal of American College Health*. Retrieved from http://www.tandfonline.com/doi/abs/10.1080/07448481.2014.902837#.U3Tk0PldV8E

Huang, G., Unger, J., Soto, D., Fujimoto, K., Pentz, M., Jordan-Marsh, M., & Valente, T. (2013). Peer influences: The impact of online and offline friendship networks on adolescent smoking and alcohol use. *The Journal of Adolescent Health*, 1–7. PMID:24012065

Johnston, L. D., O'Malley, P. M., Bachman, J. G., & Schulenberg, J. E. (2012). *Monitoring the future, national survey results on drug use, 1975-2012, volume 1: Secondary school students*. Retrieved from http://www.monitoringthefuture.org//pubs/monographs/mtf-vol1_2012.pdf

Jones, S., & Waite, R. (2013). Underage drinking: An evolutionary concept analysis. *The Nursing Clinics of North America, 48*(3), 401–413. doi:10.1016/j.cnur.2013.05.004 PMID:23998767

Junco, R., Heiberger, G., & Loken, E. (2011). The effect of Twitter on college student engagement and grades. *Journal of Computer Assisted Learning, 27*(2), 119–132. doi:10.1111/j.1365-2729.2010.00387.x

Kalpidou, M., Costin, D., & Morris, J. (2011). The relationship between Facebook and the well-being of undergraduate college students. *Cyberpsychology, Behavior, and Social Networking, 14*(4), 183–189. doi:10.1089/cyber.2010.0061 PMID:21192765

Kietzmann, J., Hermkens, K., McCarthy, I., & Silvestre, B. (2011). Social media? Get serious! Understanding the functional building blocks of social media. *Business Horizons, 54*(3), 241–251. doi:10.1016/j.bushor.2011.01.005

Kim, J., & Lee, J. (2011). The Facebook paths to happiness: Effects of the number of Facebook friends and self-presentation on subjective well-being. *Cyberpsychology, Behavior, and Social Networking, 14*(6), 359–364. doi:10.1089/cyber.2010.0374 PMID:21117983

Kross, E., Verduyn, P., Demiralp, E., Park, J., Lee, D., & Lin, N. et al. (2013). Facebook use predicts declines in subjective well-being in young adults. *PLoS ONE, 8*(8), 1–6. doi:10.1371/journal.pone.0069841 PMID:23967061

Lampe, C., Ellison, N., & Steinfield, C. (2006). A Face(book) in the crowd: Social searching vs. social browsing. In *Proceedings of the 2006 20th Anniversary Conference on Computer Supported Cooperative Work* (pp. 167-170). New York, NY: ACM Press.

Lewis, K., Kaufman, J., & Christakis, N. (2008). The taste for privacy: An analysis of college student privacy settings in an online social network. *Journal of Computer-Mediated Communication, 14*(1), 79–100. doi:10.1111/j.1083-6101.2008.01432.x

Litt, D. M., & Stock, M. L. (2011). Adolescent alcohol-related risk cognitions: The roles of social norms and social networking sites. *Psychology of Addictive Behaviors, 25*(4), 708–713. doi:10.1037/a0024226 PMID:21644803

Lorant, V., Nicaise, P., Soto, V., & D'Hoore, W. (2013). Alcohol drinking among college students: College responsibility for personal troubles. *BMC Public Health, 13*(615), 1–6. PMID:23805939

Maimon, D., & Browning, C. (2012). Underage drinking, alcohol sales and collective efficacy: Informal control and opportunity in the study of alcohol use. *Social Science Research, 41*(4), 977–990. doi:10.1016/j.ssresearch.2012.01.009 PMID:23017864

Matsueda, R. (1988). The current state of differential association theory. *Crime and Delinquency, 34*(3), 277–306. doi:10.1177/0011128788034003005

McCreanor, T., Lyons, A., Griffin, C., Goodwin, I., Barnes, H., & Hutton, F. (2013). Youth drinking cultures, social networking and alcohol marketing: Implications for public health. *Critical Public Health, 23*(1), 110–120. doi:10.1080/09581596.2012.748883

Metlife Foundation. (2013). *Partnership attitude tracking study*. Retrieved from http://www.drug-free.org/tag/partnership-attitude-tracking-study

Moreno, M., Christakis, D., Egan, K., Brockman, L., & Becker, T. (2012). Associations between displayed alcohol references on Facebook and problem drinking among college students. *Archives of Pediatrics & Adolescent Medicine, 166*(2), 157–163. doi:10.1001/archpediatrics.2011.180 PMID:21969360

Moreno, M., Parks, M., Zimmerman, F., Brito, T., & Christakis, D. (2009). Display of health risk behaviors on MySpace by adolescents: Prevalence and associations. *Archives of Pediatrics & Adolescent Medicine, 163*(1), 27–34. doi:10.1001/archpediatrics.2008.528 PMID:19124700

Moreno, M. A., Briner, L. R., Williams, A., Brockman, L., Walker, L., & Christakis, D. A. (2010). A content analysis of displayed alcohol references on a social networking web site. *The Journal of Adolescent Health: Official Publication of the Society for Adolescent Medicine, 47*(2), 168–175. doi:10.1016/j.jadohealth.2010.01.001 PMID:20638009

Mundt, M., Mercken, L., & Zakletskaia, L. (2012). Peer selection and influence effects on adolescent alcohol use: A stochastic actor-based model. *BMC Pediatrics, 12*(115), 1–10. PMID:22867027

Myslín, M., Zhu, S., Chapman, W., & Conway, M. (2013). Using Twitter to examine smoking behavior and perceptions of emerging tobacco products. *Journal of Medical Internet Research, 15*(8), e174. doi:10.2196/jmir.2534 PMID:23989137

National Institute on Alcohol Abuse and Alcoholism (NIAAA). (2013). *College drinking*. Retrieved on October 5, 2013 from http://pubs.niaaa.nih.gov/publications/CollegeFactSheet/CollegeFactSheet.pdf

National Institute on Drug Abuse. (1998). National survey results on drug use from the monitoring the future study, 1975-1997 (Vol. 1). Rockville, MD: Author.

Newport, F. (2010, July 30). U.S. drinking rate edges up slightly to 25-year high. *Gallup Well-Being*. Retrieved December 5, 2013, from http://www.gallup.com/poll/141656/drinking-rate-edges-slightly-year-high.aspx

Nishimura, S., Hishinuma, E., & Goebert, D. (2013). Underage drinking among Asian American and Pacific Islander adolescents. *Journal of Ethnicity in Substance Abuse, 12*(3), 259–277. doi:10.1080/15332640.2013.805176 PMID:23967886

O'Brien, S., & Bierman, K. (1988). Conceptions and perceived influence of peer groups: Interviews with preadolescents and adolescents. *Child Development, 59*(5), 1360–1365. doi:10.2307/1130498 PMID:3168646

O'Dea, B., & Campbell, A. (2011). Healthy connections: Online social networks and their potential for peer support. *Studies in Health Technology and Informatics, 168*, 133–140. PMID:21893921

Peluchette, J., & Karl, K. (2008). Social networking profiles: An examination of student attitudes regarding use and appropriateness of content. *Cyberpsychology & Behavior, 11*(1), 95–97. doi:10.1089/cpb.2007.9927 PMID:18275320

Pempek, T., Yermolayeva, Y., & Calvert, S. (2009). College students' social networking experiences on Facebook. *Journal of Applied Developmental Psychology, 30*(3), 227–238. doi:10.1016/j.appdev.2008.12.010

Perkins, H., Meilman, P., Leichliter, J., Cashin, J., & Presley, C. (1999). Misperceptions of the norms for the frequency of alcohol and other drug use on college campuses. *Journal of American College Health, 47*(6), 253–258. doi:10.1080/07448489909595656 PMID:10368559

Pew Research Center's Internet & American Life Project. (2013). *72% of online adults are social networking site users* (Report). Retrieved December 5, 2013 from http://pewinternet.org/Reports/2013/social-networking-sites.aspx

Pew Research Center's Internet & American Life Project. (2013). *The demographics of social media users – 2012* (Report). Retrieved December 5, 2013 from http://pewinternet.org/~/media/Files/Reports/2013/PIP_SocialMediaUsers.pdf

Quinn, S., & Oldmeadow, J. (2013). Is the igeneration a 'we' generation? Social networking use among 9-to 13-year-olds and belonging. *The British Journal of Developmental Psychology, 31*(1), 136–142. doi:10.1111/bjdp.12007 PMID:23331112

Reboussin, B., Song, E., & Wolfson, M. (2012). Social influences on the clustering of underage risky drinking and its consequences in communities. *Journal of Studies on Alcohol and Drugs, 73*(6), 890–898. PMID:23036206

Ridout, B., Campbell, A., & Ellis, L. (2012). 'Off your face(book)': Alcohol in online social identity construction and its relation to problem drinking in university students. *Drug and Alcohol Review, 31*(1), 20–26. doi:10.1111/j.1465-3362.2010.00277.x PMID:21355935

Ross, C., Orr, E., Sisic, M., Arseneault, J., Simmering, M., & Orr, R. (2009). Personality and motivations associated with Facebook use. *Computers in Human Behavior, 25*(2), 578–586. doi:10.1016/j.chb.2008.12.024

Santor, D. A., Deanna Messervey, D., & Kusumakar, V. (2000). Measuring peer pressure, popularity, and conformity in adolescent boys and girls: Predicting school performance, sexual attitudes, and substance abuse. *Journal of Youth and Adolescence, 29*(2), 163–182. doi:10.1023/A:1005152515264

Schulte, M., Ramo, D., & Brown, S. (2009). Gender differences in factors influencing alcohol use and drinking progression among adolescents. *Clinical Psychology Review*, *29*(6), 535–547. doi:10.1016/j.cpr.2009.06.003 PMID:19592147

Silveri, M. (2012). Adolescent brain development and underage drinking in the United States: Identifying risks of alcohol use in college populations. *Harvard Review of Psychiatry*, *20*(4), 189–200. doi:10.3109/10673229.2012.714642 PMID:22894728

Stoddard, S., Bauermeister, J., Gordon-Messer, D., Johns, M., & Zimmerman, M. (2012). Permissive norms and young adults' alcohol and marijuana use: The role of online communities. *Journal of Studies on Alcohol and Drugs*, *73*(6), 968–975. PMID:23036215

Subrahmanyam, K., Reich, S., Waechter, N., & Espinoza, G. (2008). Online and offline social networks: Use of social networking sites by emerging adults. *Journal of Applied Developmental Psychology*, *29*(6), 420–433. doi:10.1016/j.appdev.2008.07.003

Sussman, S., Pokhrel, P., Ashmore, R., & Brown, B. (2007). Adolescent peer group identification and characteristics: A review of the literature. *Addictive Behaviors*, *32*(8), 1602–1627. doi:10.1016/j.addbeh.2006.11.018 PMID:17188815

Sutherland, E. (1939). *Principles of criminology* (3rd ed.). Philadelphia, PA: J.B. Lippincott.

Testa, M., Kearns-Bodkin, J., & Livingston, J. (2009). Effect of precollege drinking intentions on women's college drinking as mediated via peer social influences. *Journal of Studies on Alcohol and Drugs*, *70*(4), 575–582. PMID:19515298

Tickle, J. J., Hull, J. G., Sargent, J. D., Dalton, M. A., & Heatherton, T. F. (2006). A structural equation model of social influences and exposure to media smoking on adolescent smoking. *Basic and Applied Social Psychology*, *28*(2), 117–129. doi:10.1207/s15324834basp2802_2

Tokunaga, R. (2010). Following you home from school: A critical review and synthesis of research on cyber bullying victimization. *Computers in Human Behavior*, *26*(3), 277–287. doi:10.1016/j.chb.2009.11.014

Urista, M., Dong, Q., & Day, K. (2009). Explaining why young adults use MySpace and Facebook through uses and gratification theory. *Human Communication*, *12*(2), 215–229.

Visser, L., de Winter, A., Veenstra, R., Verhulst, F., & Reijneveld, S. (2013). Alcohol use and abuse in young adulthood: Do self-control and parents' perceptions of friends during adolescence modify peer influence? The TRAILS study. *Addictive Behaviors*, *38*(12), 2841–2846. doi:10.1016/j.addbeh.2013.08.013 PMID:24018228

Warr, M., & Stafford, M. (1991). The Influence of delinquent peers: What they think or what they do? *Criminology*, *29*(4), 851–866. doi:10.1111/j.1745-9125.1991.tb01090.x

Westgate, E. C., Neighbors, C., Heppner, H., Jahn, S., & Lindgren, K. P. (2014). I will take a shot for every' like' I get on this status": Posting alcohol-related Facebook content is linked to drinking outcomes. *Journal of Studies on Alcohol and Drugs*, *75*(3), 390–398. PMID:24766750

Yang, C., & Brown, B. (2013). Motives for using Facebook, patterns of Facebook activities, and late adolescents' social adjustment to college. *Journal of Youth and Adolescence*, *42*(3), 403–416. doi:10.1007/s10964-012-9836-x PMID:23076768

Zwier, S., Araujo, T., Boukes, M., & Willemsen, L. (2011). Boundaries to the articulation of possible selves through social networking sites: The case of Facebook profilers' social connectedness. *Cyberpsychology, Behavior, and Social Networking, 14*(10), 571–576. doi:10.1089/cyber.2010.0612 PMID:21476838

KEY TERMS AND DEFINITIONS

Deviation: Deviation or deviance refers to departure from acceptable standards for behaviors, beliefs, and values.

Norm: Formal or informal rules created by a society or a subgroup through ongoing interactions that are used for determining appropriateness of behaviors, attitudes, beliefs, and values.

Peer Group: A social group of individual that are homogenous with respect to one or more socio-demographic characteristics such as age, education, occupation, etc.

Social Media: Web-based applications or platforms such as Facebook, Twitter, LinkedIn, MySpace, and Instagram, that are easily accessible by user, to allow interactive creation and sharing of contents.

Social Networking Sites: Web-based services that enable users to create public profiles and share contents with other users whose connections/profiles are made available within the same Website.

Social Outcomes: Positive or negative consequences for or changes in statuses, roles, and accomplishments that are important within the norms of a group.

Chapter 3
Face to Face(book):
Users' Traits and Motivations and Effects of Facebook Use on Well-Being

Daniela Crisan
Tilburg University, The Netherlands

ABSTRACT

This chapter discusses personality traits of Facebook users, how personality traits and motivations explain Facebook use, and the potential beneficial and detrimental effects of Internet usage, in general, and online social networking sites usage, in particular, on social and psychological well-being. First, the author provides short definitions of concepts such as social media and Social Network Sites (SNS). Next, the author describes Nadkarni and Hofmann's (2012) two-factor model of motives associated with Facebook use, including the need to belong and the need for self-presentation. Afterwards, a literature review of the most cited studies on the association between Facebook use and personality traits, as conceptualized by the Big Five Model (Costa & McCrae, 1992), is provided, followed by research on the relationships between Facebook use and psychological dimensions, such as self-esteem, loneliness, narcissism, self-worth, and depression and suicide. Finally, conclusions are drawn and final remarks are made.

INTRODUCTION

From its humble beginning in 2004 to over 1 billion active users world-wide, Facebook has become a unique social phenomenon at the global level. Facebook's unique characteristics, the rapid growth of its use as a distribution medium and as a form of communication, the power and potential it has to change social behavior, and the impact it has on its users at a psychological level, are topics of constant debate amongst specialists.

Given the complexity of Facebook phenomenon and its rapid growth, we, as individuals who aim at understanding it, seem to always find ourselves a few steps behind it, regardless of the position we stand on or our expertise in the field.

The Facebook phenomenon needs to be approached scientifically, like any other phenomenon that influences human behavior. Scholars from a wide variety of disciplines (ranging from psychology, sociology and economics, to management, marketing and computer-mediated

DOI: 10.4018/978-1-4666-7401-1.ch003

communication) have recognized the impact of Facebook on human behavior (Wilson, Gosling, & Graham, 2012).

This chapter aims to discuss the findings of the past eight years' literature on personality characteristics of Facebook users, findings that might ease our understanding of the reasons why so many people are incorporating Facebook in their everyday activities.

BACKGROUND

Social Media, Web 2.0, User Generated Content

There seems to be confusion, even among scholars, regarding the definition of social media and the types of online services and applications that may be included in this category. The term "social media" is defined by Oxford Dictionaries as "websites and applications that enable users to create and share content or to participate in social networking" ("Social Media", n.d.). Often, related concepts such as Web 2.0, user generated content and social media are used as synonyms; although these three revolve around the same general idea, they are different concepts and should not be used interchangeably (Kaplan & Haenlein, 2010). For a better understanding of the concept of social media, and to eliminate confusion, a short discussion of how social media came into existence, and of the link between the aforementioned concepts, is necessary.

In 1980, Duke University graduate students Tom Truscott and Jim Ellis created Usenet, a world-wide chat room that allowed users to read and post public messages. However, as Kaplan and Haenlein (2010) argue, Social Media as we know it had appeared twenty years earlier, when Bruce and Susan Abelson had founded *Open Diary*, a rudimentary online social network that brought diary writers together in a community. The term "weblog" was used for the first time around the same period (1960's), and was truncated in "blog" a year later, when a blogger transformed the noun "weblog" into the sentence "we blog". The availability of high-speed Internet and the growing performance of web-based technologies had led to the growing popularity of the concept and to the invention of the online social networks such as MySpace (2003) and Facebook (2004).

As mentioned earlier, the concept of social media is related to - but not interchangeable with - the concepts of Web 2.0 and User Generated Content (*UGC*).

The term Web 2.0 was first used to describe a new way of using the World Wide Web, i.e., as a web platform where contents and applications are created and distributed both by webmasters (software creators) and end-users (regular internet surfers), in a collaborative and participative manner (Kaplan & Haenlein, 2010). Thus, Web 2.0 is not a new technology (although it is based on new technologies), but rather it represents a generic term for the new World Wide Web wave. Whereas before the Web 2.0 era the Internet had served only to feeding passive users with information posted by webmasters, after the Web 2.0 trend was introduced, the Internet became much more interactive. Now, the main purpose of the Internet is to generate and share new contents, reflecting the concept of participative web. Another feature of the Web 2.0, besides the participative culture, is that it facilitates users' access to a large number of applications (and not only data or information). Hence, Web 2.0 represents a stage for the evolution of social media (Kaplan & Haenlein, 2010).

Along with the apparition of Web 2.0 applications, the main paradigm regarding media-content creation and distribution has changed. In the old media (e.g., radio, television, etc.) the audience of the media-contents was very restricted in their capabilities of creating or modifying these contents, whereas the new media broadens consumers' range of possibilities (Jenkins, 2006).

There are several assumptions underlying the concept of participative culture and that of User

Generated Content. First, the meaning of the term user is often moved back and forth between two extremes: the user as a passive recipient (this view characterizes the old media) and the user as an active participant who is, ideally, a skilled individual regarding the abilities required by the new media. However, scholars have argued (see, for instance, Van Dijck, 2009) that viewing these two perspectives as totally opposed would be inaccurate, since the audience in the old media had actively engaged in the transformation of the media-contents that were transmitted. For example, within the past two decades, more and more viewers have been participating in programmes such as telecasted games, contests, talk-shows, etc. What the new media or the new digital era has brought is much more accessibility to media networks, which allow users to voice their opinions regarding transmitted contents, and make themselves heard (in the old media voicing opinions was only possible in studios). UGC sites have had the highest contribution in this direction, as they allow users to freely create and share media-contents (Organization for Economic Co-operation and Development, 2007). Moreover, we are far from saying that in the new technological era all users are active participants. For a better understanding of the meaning of participation in the context of mass-media, in general, and in the online environment, in particular, we need to acknowledge that there are several levels of participation (van Dijck, 2009). A relatively recent study (2006) conducted on American population by Forrester Research Inc., a private research corporation, categorizes users' behaviors in six categories on a participation ladder (van Dijck, 2009): active creators (13% of all UGC website users) - individuals who actively create and distribute media-content such as weblogs, videos, and photos; critics (19%) - individuals who evaluate media contents created and distributed by members of the previously mentioned category of users; collectors (15%) - individuals who bookmark URL's; joiners (19%) - individuals who register to social networking sites such

as MySpace or Facebook but do not create new contents, passive spectators (33%) - individuals who merely view other people's blogs and videos, and inactives (52%) - users who do not engage in any of the activities that are specific for these web sites. This categorization shows that "participation" is a relative term and does not equal "active contribution" to UGC sites.

A second assumption underlying the concept of participative culture in the context of the new media pertains to the fact that participation is highly related to the notions of citizens and active community members. But can we speak about communities and cultural citizenship on the Internet? José van Dijck (2009) argues that theoreticians who studied the new trend of participative culture have stressed users' high propensity to share with the online community their knowledge and cultural characteristics. The possibility to share media content has indeed become a default option of the UGC websites' interface, such as YouTube, MySpace, or Facebook. Although the notion of "community" has several meanings, in the context of web services that support UGC, it most likely denotes groups of individuals with common interests in terms of music, movies, books, etc. Hence, communities in the context of media platforms represent groups of individuals who have in common either their tastes for the same brands, or their preference for the same entertainment activities.

The third assumption underlying the concept of participative culture in the context of the new media pertains to the role of Web platforms' owners, designers and administrators, and the strategies they use to influence and control individuals and online communities. However, this aspect is beyond the scope of this chapter.

Social Networking Sites (SNS)

Danah M. Boyd and Nicole B. Ellison (2008) define online social network sites as "web-based services that allow individuals to: (1) construct a public or semi-public profile within a bounded system; (2) articulate a list of other users with whom they share a connection, and (3) view and traverse their list of connections and those made by others within the system." (p. 211). The first online social networking site that satisfies this definition was launched in 1997 and it was called SixDegrees. The website allowed users to create profiles, make a contact list and, starting with 1998, to view other users' - with which they were connected - contact lists. All these elements were present before 1997, scattered across websites, however, SixDegrees was the first website inspired enough to combine them on a single digital platform (boyd & Ellison, 2008).

The name and nature of connection types between users may vary across websites. However, immediately after a user registers to a website, he is asked to fill in some blanks with some personal information. Based on the information that the new user had introduced (descriptors for age, location, interests, and the *About me* section), the system generates the user's brand new profile page. Most websites encourage users to upload a profile picture. Also, most SNSs allow users to personalize and improve their profile pages by changing its aspect and / or adding multimedia content. The amount of information on a users' profile page that can be viewed by others also varies across SNS's. Facebook allows users to control the visibility of any information on their profile page, except for their profile name (however, users' profile name does not necessarily have to be the same as their real name) and cover photo (which is public since Facebook introduced Timeline in 2012). Nevertheless, security settings represent one of the most salient aspects that differentiates SNS's (boyd & Ellison, 2008).

After new users are finished setting up their personal profile page, they are encouraged to identify, within the same network, other users with whom they might a relationship. Public display of users' contact lists is a crucial component of SNS's (however, Facebook allows its users to make

their lists of friends private, if they wish to do so). Friends lists contain links to the profile pages of these people, allowing users to access them. Most often a user's friends list can be viewed by other users who are allowed to view the former's profile page; however, there are a few exceptions, one of which is Facebook, which allows users to control the visibility of their lists of friends. Possible actions on SNS's range from sending private messages to photo- and video-sharing and, lately, document transfers and video calls (Facebook).

Although SNS's are created so that they are widely accessible, many of them attract homogenous populations, thus it is not uncommon on these sites to come across several groups that are segregated by features such as nationality, age, education, or other socio-demographic and cultural variables which generally segment populations (Harghittai, 2008), even though this was not web-designers' intention.

Today, SNS's represent one of the most popular (and populated) websites on the Internet. In 2006, the Federal Bureau of Investigation had announced that they possessed a list comprising of at least 200 SNS's (Magid & Collier, 2007, as cited in Special & Li-Barber, 2012). In 2008, the number of SNS's had reached 850 (Swartz, 2008).

MAIN FOCUS OF THE CHAPTER

About Facebook

Facebook is a social network, as it enables users to initiate connections with others and to share photos, videos and other forms of media content (Kaplan & Haenlein, 2010; Lewis, Kaufman, Gonzales, Wimmer, & Cristakis, 2008).

Unlike other SNS's, Facebook was created to host student networks. It was invented by Mark Zuckerberg, a programming prodigy and Psychology student at Harvard University, and launched at the beginning of 2004 as a Harvard University intranet network (Cassidy, 2006). In order to register on the network, users had to own a harvard. edu email address. As the network extended to other colleges, users were asked to provide an email address associated to their institution; this conditional registration kept the network relatively closed, contributing to users' perception of the network as a private community.

In September 2005, Facebook opened its doors to high school students, welcoming them into the Facebook community. In time, the network was available to corporate professionals and, ultimately, to the entire world (boyd & Ellison, 2008).

In 2008, Facebook was the 6th most popular website in the world and number 1 in photo-sharing, with over 80 million active users in more than 55000 school and high-school networks. In 2009, Facebook registered more than 175 million active users. To put things in perspective, the number of active users on Facebook at that time was a little bit smaller than the population of Brazil (190 million) and twice the population of Germany (80 million) (Kaplan & Haenlein, 2010).

In 2011, Facebook registered over 500 million active users; in 2012, this number grew to 800 million, and, in 2013, the network reached over 1 billion active users worldwide (Social Media Marketing, Statistics, and Monitoring Tools, n.d.). According to the same reports, Europe is the second continent with the highest number of Facebook active users, following Asia, with more than 250 million users. Since February 2010, Facebook is available in more than 70 languages, reflecting the network's global expansion (Vasalou, Joinson, & Courvoisier, 2010).

In 2013, the *Forbes* website posted a short visualization of the evolution of Facebook since 2004, in term of redesigns and features: http://www.forbes.com/pictures/efjl45fhkg/the-evolution-of-facebook/.

Motivational Factors of Facebook Use

There are several studies that investigated possible motivational factors that drive Internet users to create and maintain profiles on SNS's (Burngarner, 2007; Joinson, 2008; Sheldon, 2008). The conclusion that can be drawn from these studies is that the major reasons for which individuals are creating and maintaining profiles on online SNS's are social in nature, the purpose being that of transferring offline social relations into the online environment, of disclosing information about the self to other members of the network, and of strengthening offline relationships through online self-disclosure and communication (Special & Li-Barber, 2012).

Distinguishing the main motives associated with creating and maintaining personal Facebook profiles is an important step towards understanding why has Facebook become, practically overnight, a genuine Internet phenomenon. Nevertheless, the extent to which Facebook manages to meet the social needs of its users is of equal importance. Most likely, users' satisfaction with the network comes from its ability to bring social payoffs to them (Special & Li-Barber, 2012).

Following an extensive literature review on the topic, Nadkarni and Hofmann (2012) advanced a two-factor explanatory model of Facebook use. According to the model, Facebook use is best explained on the basis of two motives: the need to belong and the need for self-presentation. The need to belong refers to the intrinsic desire for connections to others and for social approval. The need for self-presentation refers to impression management processes. The aforementioned needs or motives may co-exist or they may independently explain Facebook use (Nadkarni & Hofmann, 2012).

The Need to Belong

Many researchers, such as Baumeister & Leary, 1995; Baumeister & Tice, 1990; Stillman, Baumeister, Lambert et al., 2009; Zadro, Boland, & Richardson, 2006, have brought evidence that people in general are very dependent on the social support from others, with ostracization from social groups bearing negative effects on both mental and physical well-being (Nadkarni & Hofmann, 2012). Self-worth and self-esteem are intimately related to the need to belong. It can be asserted that self-esteem has a sociometric function by representing a measure of group inclusion.

Yu and her colleagues (Yu, Tian, Vogel, & Kwok, 2010) show that Facebook use has positive effects on the socialization of students within universities, and on learning outcomes. The increased efficacy of the learning process leads to an increase in students' self-esteem, satisfaction with student life, and academic performance. The authors argue that these findings indicate the presence of two socialization processes that transform users' engagement in Facebook activities in learning situations: first, Facebook use facilitates the formation of relationships and the acceptance from peers, and second, Facebook use features the aculturalization of students to the university. Thus, the first process facilitates students' cognitive functioning and skills attainment, whereas the second process increases students' satisfaction with life.

The Need for Self-Presentation

As an online environment, Facebook assumes the possibility that its users might display an idealized identity rather than a realistic one. To make reference to this phenomenon, the concept of idealized virtual-identity hypothesis has been advanced (Back, Stopfer, Vazire, Gaddis, Schmukle, Egloff, & Gosling, 2010). The authors tested this hypothesis by comparing self-evaluations and objective evaluations of Facebook users' profile pages on their personality traits. Observers made accurate evaluations of users' personality characteristics, showing that rather than expressing an idealized self-image, users present their true self within the online social network (Back et al., 2010).

Another study, that examines the relationship between the self-image that users want to promote and the extent to which they post inappropriate contents, shows that users post inappropriate content because they want to impress their peers through their self-image (Peluchette & Karl, 2010).

Mazer, Murphy, and Simonds show in a study conducted in 2007 that teachers' use of Facebook is perceived by students as a positive thing. The students who participated in the study were asked to look up a teacher that they did not know on Facebook and evaluate what would they think if they were to participate to a lecture held by that particular teacher. Results show that students find significantly more similarities between the teachers and themselves when the formers engage in self-disclosure on their Facebook profile page (e.g., they post pictures with themselves, messages between themselves and their families and friends, their opinions on certain topics, etc.). These perceived similarities have a positive effect on students' participation and emotional involvement (Mazer, Murphy, & Simonds, 2007). A follow-up of this study shows that the lecturer's self-disclosure has a positive effect on the extent to which the students perceive that lecturer as having credibility (Mazer, Murphy, & Simonds, 2009).

In addition to the studying of the effects of Facebook use on relationship formation, researchers examined its effects on the impression formation in the context of existing relationships. Thus, Weisbuch and his colleagues (2009) examined the impressions formed in the online environment and they were consistent with the impressions formed during face-to-face interactions. Their results show that individuals who receive positive evaluations during direct interactions, also receive positive evaluations through their personal Facebook profiles. Furthermore, the authors point out that social expressivity is what stands at the basis of both online and offline, face-to-face, impression formation. Thus, it seems that impressions that are formed based on someone's Facebook profile page provide rather valid information on the offline agreeableness of their owners (Weisbuch, Ivcevic, & Ambady, 2009).

Tong and her colleagues (2008) examined the relationship between users' number of Facebook friends and their levels of attractiveness and extraversion as perceived and rated by independent observers. Their results suggest a curvilinear relationship between the sociometric popularity and social attractivity, such that users with fewer contacts in their Facebook list (approximately 100) and those with higher numbers of contacts in their Facebook list (approximately 300) are perceived, on average, as being less socially attractive than users with average numbers of Facebook friends (Tong, Van Der Heide, Langwell, & Walther, 2008). Thus, an abundant number of Facebook friends creates the impression that these users are less socially attractive and desirable.

All these studies considered together suggest that Facebook users' profile pages are reflections of their public self, which seems to be shaped based on the need for self-presentation and the need to belong. This need or motive seems to direct users' specific behaviors, such as choosing a certain kind of profile picture or gathering a certain number of online contacts, which in turn reflect the self-image that the users wish to display (Nadkarni & Hofmann, 2012).

A study conducted by Daniela Crisan in 2013 on a Romanian sample population of 159 Facebook users aimed to identify the major factors that would explain Facebook use. According to the findings, Facebook use and commitment can be predicted directly from the number of contacts, the preference for Facebook applications that involve active participation, and the need for self-presentation. The need to belong has an indirect, positive effect, through users' preference for Facebook applications that involve active participation. Self-disclosure has an indirect, positive effect on the use of- and commitment to Facebook, through the need for self-presentation and the need to belong (which, in turn, operates through the preference for Facebook applications that involve active participation). The effect of self-disclosure on Facebook use and commitment is stronger when it runs through the need for self-presentation. Accordingly, a Facebook user who has many friends on their contact list, likes applications such as status, timeline, news feed, comments, like, messages, photos, chat and share, and has an intense need for self-presentation, can be predicted to have higher levels of commitment to Facebook (Crisan, 2013). Below the reader can find a table with the means and standard deviations

Table 1. Means and standard deviations of motivations of Facebook use across age groups

Age Category	Need to Belong			Need for Self-Presentation		
	Mean	N	Std. Deviation	Mean	N	Std. Deviation
18-24 years	11.867	98	4.996	8.949	98	4.070
25-34 years	11.268	41	4.006	8.756	41	4.646
35-44 years	11.059	17	4.437	7.176	17	2.404
45-54 years	12.333	3	3.215	6.667	3	1.528
Total	11.669	159	4.662	8.751	159	4.089

of the motivations for Facebook use across age groups, for the participants included in the study. There are no statistically significant differences between means.

Facebook Use and Psychological and Social Well-Being

Among scientific literature on social networks there is a growing body of studies focusing on Facebook in particular. These studies examine a wide variety of topics, ranging from social capital to information disclosure. Previous research has treated a small range of possible topics, using only a small portion of the data that could be extracted from Facebook. For example, Lampe, Ellison, and Steinfield (2006) and Ellison, Steinfield, and Lampe (2007) have used only data collected by means of questionnaires, ignoring the information posted by users on the site.

It is not surprising that social psychologists have focused on this particular field of human social behavior, advancing diverse and complex hypotheses and methodologies, and hoping to catch a glimpse of how human social interactions occur in the cyberspace. Early studies examining SNS's had focused predominantly on characteristics of these SNS's, their history, effects on the Internet (Boyd, 2007; Boyd & Ellison, 2008), and whether they bear upon face-to-face interactions or not (Sheldon, 2008). More recently, however, studies have shifted attention on the potentially beneficial social and psychological outcomes associated with creating and maintaining a profile on an online SNS.

The scientific literature abounds with controversies and debates regarding the effects of Internet use in general, and the use of online SNS in particular, on people's psychological and social well-being. Some of the first authors who tackled with this issue (the effects of Internet use on people's well-being) were Robert Kraut, Michael Patterson, Vicki Lundmark, Sara Kiesler, Tridas Mukopadhyay, and William Scherlis, from Carnegie Mellon University, Pittsburgh, who published their work in their classical study "Internet paradox: a social technology that reduces social involvement and psychological well-being?" (Kraut et al., 1998). The authors found that Internet use caused a decline in communication with family and an increase in loneliness and depression. This finding is called "the displacement hypothesis". However, a 3-year follow-up of 208 of these participants found that these negative effects had disappeared (Kraut et al., 2002). Instead, positive effects of Internet use on communication, social-involvement, and well-being were found, and these positive effects are consistent with the "rich get richer" paradigm: better outcomes of using the Internet are predicted for those individuals with higher levels of extraversion and less social support, but worse outcomes are predicted for individuals with lower levels of extraversion (or higher levels of introversion) and less social support.

Another relevant study, conducted by Valkenburg and Peter (2009), incorporates the displacement hypothesis in a model but predicts an overall indirect positive effect of online communication on adolescents' social connectedness and well-being. The authors called this model the "Internet-enhanced self-disclosure hypothesis".

In the following two paragraphs we will discuss these two papers in more detail, as we feel that they speak for the controversial relationship between Internet use, in general, and online social media, in particular, and well-being.

Kraut et al.'s (1998) study is a longitudinal study and a real-life experiment which aimed to investigate the causal relationship between Internet use, social involvement, and the psychological consequences of Internet use. Data were collected from a total of 169 persons in 72 households from Pittsburgh, Pennsylvania, in 1995 and 1996, in their first or second year of Internet use. The amount of Internet use was recorded automatically, with the help of specialized software, and measures of social involvement and well-being were collected twice by self-report scales. Individuals' demographic characteristics and indicators of their levels of social involvement and psychological well-being were collected in the pretest phase, before they were given unlimited access to the Internet, and also in the follow-up phase, after 12-24 months of unlimited Internet use. During the interval between the pretest phase and the follow-up phase, measures of Internet use were collected automatically, with specialized software. Sociodemographic variables were included as control variables; likewise, a measure of participants' extraversion was also included as a control variable, since this trait has an influence on communication patterns, on one's social networks, social support, feelings of loneliness, and it can also interact with measures of Internet use (as we will discuss in greater detail later in this chapter). The most important findings of this study are as follows: regarding social involvement: Internet use led to a decrease in communication with family; when controlling for extraversion and sociodemographic variables, more time spent on the Internet led to a decrease in the number of both local and distant social ties. There is a negative association between Internet use and social support, however, it is not statistically significant. Regarding psychological well-being: after controlling for personal characteristics and the initial levels of loneliness, individuals who spent more time on the Internet reported higher levels of feelings of loneliness; stress in general increased with Internet use. After controlling for other variables, the authors found that Internet use was significantly associated with a subsequent increase in depression. Paradoxically, the authors argue, the Internet, which is a technology meant to facilitate inter-personal communication, has nevertheless inevitable negative effects on communication.

Since Kraut et al.'s (1998) paper, there has been an accumulation of evidence that Internet usage does not decrease social interaction and well-being (e.g.: Ellison, Steinfield, & Lampe, 2011; Shapira, Barak, & Gal, 2007; Steinfield, Ellison, & Lampe,

2008). The second paper that is mentioned, by Valkenburg and Peter (2009), advances the idea of a shift from focusing on bad effects of Internet usage, to focusing on the positive effects that the Internet and online social media have on several aspects of life. The authors advance a hypothesis known as the "internet-enhanced self-disclosure hypothesis", which states that the positive effects of the Internet on social connectedness and well-being can be explained by enhanced online self-disclosure (Valkenburg & Peter, 2009). The authors define online self-disclosure as "online communication about personal topics that are typically not easily disclosed, such as one's feelings, worries, and vulnerabilities" (p. 2). There are three assumptions underlying this hypothesis:

1. Online communication stimulates online self-disclosure,
2. Internet-enhanced online self-disclosure enhances the quality of adolescents' relationships, and
3. Internet-enhanced self-disclosure indirectly promotes adolescents' well-being by enhancing the quality of their relationships.

Well-being is measured here with the five-item satisfaction-with-life scale developed by Diener (1985). Based on prior literature, the authors identified three moderating factors on the Internet effects:

1. **The Type of Internet Use:** Internet use only has positive effects when adolescents talk with their existing friends or when they use instant messaging (IM); technologies that are mainly use to communicate with strangers (e.g., chat rooms) or more solitary Internet use (e.g., surfing) might have adverse effects on connectedness and well-being;
2. **Users' Gender:** Boys seem to benefit more from communicating in the online environment with their friends than do girls;

3.   **Users' Level of Social Anxiety:** There are two hypotheses on the relationship between online communication and social anxiety: the social compensation hypothesis (which states that reduced audiovisual cues of the Internet may help socially anxious individuals overcome the inhibitions they usually experience in real-life interactions, thus driving them to turn to online conversations), and "the rich get richer" hypothesis (which assumes that especially socially competent individuals use the Internet for online communication; these individuals possess the necessary social skills, so they may consider the Internet as just another way to keep in touch with peers (Kraut et al., 2002)); most studies seem to support the "rich get richer" hypothesis rather than the social compensation hypothesis (Valkenburg & Peter, 2009).

Regarding the social networking site Facebook, in particular, its effects on people's psychological well-being are puzzling. Again, there is a strong debate among specialists and researchers whether Facebook use has more detrimental effects on people than it has beneficial effects, or vice-versa. There are concerns that using Facebook might have negative effects on individuals' well-being. Most recent studies, however, indicate that Facebook use is a good measure of students' social integration (Kalpidou, Costin, Morris, 2011), and that belonging to a social network is positively correlated with life satisfaction and positive emotions, under the right circumstances (Seder & Oishi, 2009). It appears that Facebook users perceive the time that they spend online more like an extension, rather than a substitution, of face-to-face interactions with their friends (Cheung, Chiu, Lee, 2011; Kujath, 2011). This is an illustration that Facebook, unlike most of the other online SNS's, enables its users to make visible their offline ties rather than form new ties with people they do not know from their offline social environment (boyd & Ellison, 2008). On average, users do not perceive

belongingness to an online social network to be more rewarding, socially speaking, than offline, face-to-face human interactions (Reich, 2010).

For a better understanding of the effects of Facebook use on individuals' social and psychological well-being, we need to examine the relationship between different measures of Facebook use (e.g., time spent on Facebook) and individuals' personality particularities and other psychological characteristics (e.g., feelings of loneliness, narcissism, etc.), and then we need to ask ourselves whether the use of Facebook has produced these characteristics or vice-versa. But first, we want to see to what extent people present their true selves on Facebook.

Online Identities: One's True Self on Facebook

Self-disclosure represents the act of sharing personal information with someone else. Self-presentation is disclosing factual information about one's self (Johnson, 1981). Self-disclosure and self-presentation are important processes in face-to-face interactions. Research shows that people tend to self-disclose to other people who have also self-disclosed. As stable relationships with others become more personal and intimate, people tend to make known their true selves [in Jungian theory, the self is defined as a coherent whole that unifies both the consciousness and the unconscious mind of a person, that is realized as the process of integrating one's personality, resulting in a certain predisposition of responding to the world in particular ways; hence, the self is the center of the total personality (Jung & Franz, 1978, p. 208)]. The average college student spends between 10-60 minutes a day on Facebook (Hew, 2011) and is constantly engaged in activities that involve self-disclosure and self-presentation (Hum, Chamberlin, Hambright, Portwood, Schat, & Bevan, 2011).

Past research had suggested that the online environment might alter individuals' identities, so that they are inclined to reveal more personal information online, compared to other forms of communication (Christofides, Muise, & Desmarais, 2009; Gibbs, Ellison, & Heino, 2006). A recent literature review shows that people reveal their true identities on sites such as Facebook (Hew, 2011), because they realize that false information could be exposed and confronted by their friends. Conversely, literature also shows that people tend to stretch the truth so that it would favor them (Gibbs, Ellison, & Heino, 2006). Hence, it remains unclear to what extent online self-disclosure reflects the reality, compared to the forms of communication *in persona*.

Shy individuals and those low on self-esteem admit that Facebook helps them to increase the number of their social ties, but it is unclear at the moment whether they actually benefit from these ties (Ellison, Steinfield, & Lampe, 2007; Forest & Wood, 2012; Orr, Sisic, Ross, Simmering, Arseneault, & Orr, 2009; Valkenburg, Petev & Schouten, 2006). Self-disclosure on Facebook may be done explicitly, by expressing thoughts and feelings in writing, or implicitly, through more subtle means (e.g., photos). Recent research shows that users tend to construct their identity implicitly, by posting photos and videos of themselves, rather than explicitly, through self-portretization (Zhao, Grasmuck, & Martin, 2008).

Scholars argue whether Facebook activity is more about impression management and expressing one's identity, compared to simple social interaction, as long as Facebook can be a public expression of the "ideal self" (Mehdizadeh, 2010). Several researchers believe that impression management is the most important reason for somebody to create a Facebook profile (Krämer & Winter, 2008). Undoubtedly, virtual impression management exists and can be effective; however, studies that tested the hypothesis that Facebook activity is foremost associated with impression management, have concluded that there are instances in which this kind of hypotheses are not confirmed. Back and colleagues (2010) have found

that Facebook users' self-portrayals are accurate reflections of their personalities, rather than ideal versions of them. Pempek, Yermolayeva, & Calvert (2009) asked 92 students to keep a one week journal of their Facebook activities, and, after analyzing them, they found that, in general, students mainly spend their time on Facebook interacting with others rather than expressing their identities. The fact that extraverts engage in more activities on Facebook than introverts (we will discuss this next in greater detail) brings additional evidence to the fact that Facebook use is mainly driven by the need for social interaction.

Personality Traits and Facebook Use

Many studies have focused on how psychological factors, such as personality traits, influence the use of online social networks (Amichai-Hamburger & Vinitzky, 2010; Ross, Orr, Arseneault, Simmering, & Orr, 2009; Ryan & Xenos, 2011). In general, researchers have used Costa and McCrae's (1992) personality model; according to this model, variability in human personality is best explained by five dimensions: neuroticism, extraversion, openness, agreeableness, and conscientiousness. Two such studies that are most cited in the literature are those of Ross et al. (2009), and Amichai-Hamburger and Vinitzky (2010).

Extraversion

Extraversion is a personality dimension "underlying a broad group of traits, including sociability, activity, and the tendency to experience positive emotions such as joy and pleasure" (Costa & McCrae, 1992, p. 5). Craig Ross and his colleagues had studied the association between personality traits, as conceptualized by the Big Five personality model, and Facebook activity, using a sample of 92 students, and they found that extraverts, as compared to introverts, engage in considerably more social activities, both online (on Facebook) and offline, outside the network, and use this online service to maintain and strengthen existing offline ties, not as an alternative to direct social activities and relations. Moreover, Mayer and Puller (2008) reported that only 0.4 percent of Facebook friendships that they had studied were exclusively online connections, and these findings are supported by other studies which show that to the utmost extent Facebook is used to preserve friendships that have already been built offline, rather than to initiate new ones (Skues, Williams, & Wise, 2012).

Amichai-Hamburger and Vinitzky (2010) partially replicated the study conducted by Ross et al., using a larger sample of 237 students; their findings indicate that individuals with low and high levels of extraversion differ on the number of Facebook friendships, with the latter category of individuals having significantly more friends than the former. Consistent with Ross et al., Amichai-Hamburger and Vinitzky conclude that extraverted individuals "transfer" their social connections from the real social environment to the virtual social environment, and this is why their online ties are more numerous compared to those of introverted individuals.

A study conducted by Wilson, Fornasier and White (2010) points out that extraverted individuals are prone to develop addictions towards Facebook, suggesting that the unlimited contact with their friends gratifies their need for stimulation and wide social networks (Nadkarni & Hofmann, 2012).

Neuroticism

Neuroticism represents "the individual's tendency to experience psychological distress" (Costa & McCrae, 1992, p. 5). This trait seems to have an impact on the ways people use Facebook but not on the number of their online friends or groups. Ross et al. (2009), for example, found that individuals with high levels of neuroticism are less inclined to reveal personal information, and they prefer the Wall (now Timeline) postings than photo-postings.

Neurotics' preference for Timeline postings may be explained by the fact that this provides them more control over the content of the postings; they can also control when they post and for how long the posted content remains visible to others. Contrary to Ross et al.'s findings, Amichai-Hamburger and Vinitzky (2010) argue that, on the contrary, individuals high in neuroticism tend to post more photos compared to individuals low in neuroticism. Moreover, individuals with high and low levels of emotional stability (the opposite of neuroticism) tend to disclose significantly more personal information than individuals with average levels of this characteristic.

Openness to Experience

The term refers to a broader constellation of traits. Individuals with high levels of openness "are imaginative and sensitive to art and beauty and have a rich and complex emotional life; they are intellectually curious, behaviorally flexible, and nondogmatic in their attitudes and values" (Costa & McCrae, 1992, p. 6). Studies show that individuals who are open to new experiences use significantly more applications provided by Facebook compared to individuals with lower levels of openness (Amichai-Hamburger & Vinitzky, 2010). It might be that individuals with high levels of openness to new experiences possess a broader range of interests and are more willing to pursue their interests, and Facebook allows them to do so.

Agreeableness

This dimension relates primarily to interpersonal behavior. Individuals high on agreeableness are trusting, sympathetic, and cooperative, whereas individuals low on agreeableness are cynical, callous, and antagonistic (Costa & McCrae, 1992). It is surprising that agreeableness doesn't seem to be related to the number of Facebook friends, according to Amichai-Hamburger & Vinitzky's (2010) study. However, Wilson et al. (2010) argue that individuals with low levels of agreeableness spend on average more time online, inasmuch as there are fewer requirements for agreeable behaviors in the online social environment.

Conscientiousness

Conscientiousness is a dimension that "contrasts scrupulous, well-organized, and diligent people with lax, disorganized, and lackadaisical individuals" (Costa & McCrae, 1992, p. 6). Of all studies that have examined the relationship between Big Five personality traits and Facebook use, only a very limited number found a statistically significant relationship between conscientiousness and different measures of Facebook use. One of these studies was conducted by Wilson, Fornasier and White (2010), and the authors found that as Facebook use increases, conscientiousness decreases, possibly due to the limited rules and policies enforced by the network on its users (Wilson et al., 2010).

Associations of Facebook Use with Other Psychological Constructs

On account of the findings regarding the association between personality traits (Big Five model) and Facebook use, there is a consensus among researchers on the fact that personality traits alone cannot efficiently predict users' online behavior; we need to take into consideration other psychological constructs as well (Amichai-Hamburger & Vinitzky, 2010). Most studied such constructs are self-esteem and self-worth (Ellison, Steinfield & Lampe, 2007; Kalpidou, Costin & Morris, 2011; Mehdizadeh, 2010), loneliness (Amichai-Hamburger & Ben-Artzi, 2003; Kraut, Patterson, Lundmark, Kiesler, Mukopadhyay, & Scherlis, 1998), *narcissism* (Buffardi & Campbell, 2008; Mehdizadeh, 2010), and depression.

Self-Esteem and Self-Worth

Self-esteem represents a person's overall cognitive and emotional evaluations of his/her self-worth, and is the strongest predictor of life satisfaction (in the United States), outweighing all demographic and objective measure, such as age, income, education, physical health, etc., and all other psychological variables (Diener. 1984). Regarding the association between self-esteem and the use of online social networks, findings are rather inconsistent. For instance, studies conducted by Ellison, Steinfield, and Lampe (2007) and Mehdizadeh (2010) argue that individuals low on self-esteem access the online social network *Facebook* more often and they spend more time on it; thus, Facebook has a compensatory function for these individuals, allowing them to construct their social capital [social capital is defined as "resources embedded in one's social networks, resources that can be accessed or mobilized through ties in the networks" and "then generate a return for the actor" (Lin, 2005, p. 61)]. Social ties and building relationship with others is related to measures of well-being, satisfaction with life, and self-esteem (Bargh, McKenna, & Fitzsimon, 2002). Gonzales and Hancock (2011) reported a positive effect of Facebook use on self-esteem: by selecting which information to post online, more specifically, by posting self-enhancing information, individuals low on self-esteem manage to improve their self-esteem. However, other studies found no statistically significant association between self-esteem and Facebook use variables (Kalpidou, Costin, & Morris, 2011).

Nevertheless, most of the studies on the relationship between Facebook use and self-esteem use a global measure of self-esteem, whereas behavior might be better and more reliably understood as a function of domain-based, rather than global self-esteem (Stefanone, Lackaff, & Rose, 2011).

Such domain-based aspects on which self-esteem is based are called contingencies of self-worth (Crocker & Wolfe, 2001). Crocker, Luhtanen, Cooper, & Bouvrette (2003) proposed a model with seven domains of contingencies: competencies, competition, approval from generalized others, family support, appearance, God's love, and virtue. A study conducted by Stefanone et al. (2011) on the relationship between Facebook use and these contingencies of self-worth, suggests that public-based contingencies (approval, appearance, and competition) explain online photo sharing, while private-based contingencies (family, virtue, and God's love) demonstrate a negative relationship with time spent online. The appearance contingency has the strongest relationship with the intensity of online photo-sharing, but no relationship with time spent managing profiles.

Loneliness

On the association between loneliness and Internet use, there is a debate regarding the direction of causality. Kraut and colleagues (1998) advance the idea of Internet paradox, according to which, paradoxical, high levels of Internet use are associated with intense loneliness. On one hand, intense Internet use may physically isolate the individual, who ends up feeling lonely (Kim, LaRose, & Peng, 2009). Conversely, individuals prone to loneliness seem to use the Internet more (Amichai-Hamburger & Ben-Artzi, 2003). This might happen because the Internet enables lonely people to find and interact with others via online social networks (Skues, Williams, & Wise, 2012). However, we may notice that these effects on loneliness are mostly found when the measure of Internet usage is the time spent online (see, for example, Stepanikova, Nie, & He, 2010).

Narcissism

Narcissism can be conceptualized as "one's capacity to maintain a relatively positive self-image through a variety of self-, affect-, and field regulatory processes, and it underlies individuals' needs for validation and affirmation as well as the motivation to overtly and covertly seek out self-enhancement experiences from the social environment" (Pincus et al., 2009, p. 365). Narcissism may be the only personality characteristic that might pinpoint the individuals who are tempted to use Facebook for self-eulogizing purposes, given that narcissism is positively associated with the frequency of Facebook activities, activities such as checking one's own profile, status update, and posting self-enhancing information and images (Mehdizadeh, 2010; Ong, Ang, Ho, Lim, Goh, Lee, & Chua, 2011). According to a study led by Buffardi & Campbell (2008), narcissism is positively related to levels of attractiveness and sexuality of posted images, and with posting self-enhancing ideas and personal information. The study showed that observers were able to estimate accurately the level of narcissism of several individuals based on their Facebook profile pages. It is likely that individuals with high levels of narcissism are more attracted by the fact that SNS's such as Facebook entail them a greater amount of control over the contents of their postings, thus giving them the possibility of selecting what personal information to reveal; hence, they might only share information that puts them in a favorable light (Skues et al., 2012).

Depression and Suicide

There is now extensive research on the relationship between media use and mood disorders, such as depression and dysthymia (a mild, but long-term form of depression) (e.g., Allam, 2010; Augner & Hacker, 2012; Chen & Tzeng, 2010; Cristakis, Moreno, Jelenchick, Myaing, & Zhou, 2011; Dong, Lu, Zhou, & Zhao, 2011; Huang, 2010; Kalpidou, Costin, & Morris, 2011; Lu et al., 2011; Morrison & Gore, 2010; Van der Aa et al., 2009). Some research indicates a statistically significant positive relationship between SNS activities and symptoms of depression, while other more recent studies indicate that there is no relationship, and in one condition a negative relationship, between Facebook use and depression. Moreover, Davila et al. (2012) suggest that the quality of social networking interactions, and not their quantity, is associated with depressive symptoms. Consistent with Davila et al. (2012), Datu, Valdez, & Datu (2012) show that there is no significant correlation between the number of hours a week Filipino adolescents spend on Facebook and depressive symptoms. However, a Croatian study conducted by Pantic et al. (2012) shows a positive association between time spent on Facebook and depression in high-school students. The act of unfriending is shown to be associated with strong negative emotional responses (Bevan, Pfyl, & Barclay, 2012).

Jelenchick, Eickhoff, & Moreno (2013) studied a sample of 190 older adolescents and they found no relationship between Facebook use and depression. Simoncic (2012) found that not only there is no positive correlation between Facebook use and depression, but for female users with high levels of neuroticism, the correlation is negative. These results are corroborated by other three studies, one on Dutch adolescents (Selfhout, Brantje, Delsing, ter Bogt, & Meeus, 2009), one on American adolescents (Ohannessian, 2009), and one on older Americans (Cotton, Ford, Ford, & Hale, 2012).

Rosen, Whaling, Rab, Carrier, & Cheever (2013) studied a large sample of 1143 adult Americans and tested hypotheses of correlations between use of specific technologies / media (including certain types of Facebook use) and clinical symptoms of several personality disorders and mood disorders (as defined by the *Diagnostic and Statistical Manual of Mental Disorders*, 4th edition). The study shows that the most predictors for these disorders involve mostly Facebook use. For example, more Facebook impression management (self-presentation techniques used by individuals to manipulate the impressions they make on others) predicts more signs of major depression. In contrast, having more friends on Facebook predicts less dysthymia.

The studies mentioned above fail to provide an understanding of the mechanisms behind the relationship between Facebook use and mental health outcomes. Following this line, Feinstein at al. (2013) propose a model of the effects of Facebook use on depressive symptoms. The model suggests that there is a significant indirect effect of Facebook negative social comparison (the tendency to negatively compare oneself with others while on Facebook) on increases in depressive symptoms through increases in rumination (the tendency to overly focus on bad feelings and experiences from the past). In other words, the relationship between Facebook social comparison and depressive symptoms is mediated by rumination. The model controls for general social comparison to test for specific effect of Facebook social comparison.

Suicide announcements on Facebook is a rather recent phenomenon that has even more recently made the focus of researchers and health care professionals (e.g.: Ahuja, Biesaga, Sudak, Draper, & Womble, 2014; Lehavot., Ben-Zeev, & Neville, 2012; Ruder, Hatch, Ampanozi, Thali, & Fischer, 2011). However, many cases of individuals across the world posting suicide notes on Facebook had been reported by the popular press. As a reaction to this problem, Facebook operators offer contact information for helplines and services to individuals who post suicidal notes and to individuals who want to help them by intervening (Facebook Help Center, 2014). Existing literature suggests that media reports of suicidal attempts may produce the so called Werther effect, named after Johann Wolfgang von Goethe's novel "Die Leiden des jungen Werther" ("The Sorrows of Young Werther"): the induction of copycat suicides (Pirkis, Blood, Beautrais, Burgess, & Skehan, 2006; Stack, 2003). Hence, suicidal notes on Facebook may encourage predisposed individuals to attempt suicide (Ruder et al., 2011). However, to the author's knowledge, this effect has not yet been tested. There also may be a positive effect of suicide announcements on Facebook. Because these announcements can be seen by other users immediately after they have been posted, it allows a prompt direct or indirect reaction and intervention of other concerned users, who might inform the health care professionals or emergency medical services (Ruder et al., 2011). Moreover, Facebook might confer a sense of community and belonging to vulnerable individuals, thus preventing them from committing suicide, at least until professional help is provided.

It is important to consider the limitations of these studies; more specifically, we need to acknowledge and consider the fact that they focus mainly on analyzing one or two psychological variables in relation with the use of SNS's, with no consideration for the joint effect of several such variables taken together. Only few of these studies have included psychological variables such as narcissism, loneliness or self-esteem together with the Big Five personality traits. One of these studies, conducted by Ryan and Xenos (2011), investigates the relationship between the Big five markers, shyness, narcissism and loneliness, on one hand, and patterns of Facebook use, on the other. This study, conducted on a sample of 1635 Australian Facebook users, shows that Facebook users register, on average, higher levels of extraversion and lower levels of conscientiousness, compared to non-users. Additionally, users score, on average, higher levels on narcissism compared to non-users. However, effect sizes are small.

In a study that examines the relationship between narcissism and Facebook use, Buffardi and Campbell (2008) correlate participants' scores on the Narcissistic Personality Inventory (NPI-16) with objective measures of Facebook use, such as number of Facebook friends and number of posts on participants' personal Facebook profile pages. The results indicate a positive association between narcissism and Facebook use, especially with respect to activities involving photos and

personal profile pages, which facilitate excessive self-enhancement (Buffardi & Campbell, 2008). Mehdizadeh (2010) reports similar results: he administered the NPI-16 and Rosenberg's self-esteem scale to a sample and, additionally, evaluated the contents of the "About me" section of their Facebook profile pages, the contents of their photos, the contents of the "Notes" section, and participants' status updates. Study's results suggests that, on average, individuals with high levels of narcissism and low levels of self-esteem spend more than an hour per day on Facebook and are more likely to post edited photos of themselves.

Similarly, Ong and his colleagues (2011) examined the relationship between narcissism, extraversion and adolescents' self-presentation on their personal Facebook profile pages. Results show that, when controlling for extraversion, narcissism is a significant predictor of Facebook activities involving user generated content (e.g., photos, frequency of status updates) (Ong et al, 2011).

Yet another limitation of most of these studies is that they are correlational in nature, thus the directionality of the relationships between measures of Facebook use and psychological outcomes is unclear. Facebook use measures seem to predict several psychological outcomes, but the mechanisms that account for these relationships, thus causal relationships, are yet to be researched.

Facebook Use and Sociodemographic Variables: Age and Gender

Despite the amount of research that has been done so far, we know surprisingly little about the influence of sociodemographic factors on Facebook use. We know that young people disclose more personal information than do older people (Christofides, Muise & Desmarais, 2009, 2012); analogous, individuals who are in search of an intimate relationship also disclose more personal information that those who are not actively looking for a new relationship (Nosko, Wood, & Molema, 2010). Facebook users' gender is nonetheless a promising and an under studied variable. Stefanone et al. (2011) have shown that women have more extensive online social networks than men, and Walker, Cohen & Sibbald (2008, as cited in McAndrew & Sun Jeong, 2012) have shown that women are more likely to post contents that might lead to rumors about themselves. The studies on gossip conducted by McAndrew & Milenkovic (2002), and by McAndrew, Bell and Garcia (2007) suggest that most people are more interested in rumors about other people of same gender and similar age, and women are particularly interested in this. The authors have concluded that this propensity is rooted in the phylogenetic need to keep up to date with information about potential competitors for one's status and partners, and, traditionally, our most important competitors are found in our own entourage and have the same age and gender as us.

Women engage in Facebook activities far more often than men, they spend more time online, have more friends and, like other studies have shown, they engage in more rumor searching and provoking behaviors; women are more interested than men in the relationship status of other people, and they are also more interested than men in what other women do. Also, compared to men, women spend more energy in transforming their profile pictures as tools for impression management and spend more time studying other people's photos. Though men also want to know the number of their friends' friends, they are not as interested in their academic and career achievements as are women. Perhaps the most intriguing finding on the relationship between gender and Facebook use is that men's relationship status is a significant predictor for their Facebook use, whereas for women it is not. Men involved in committed relationships spend less time viewing other women's profile pages and less time posting, viewing or commenting on pictures. Curiously, women's involvement

in committed relationship is irrelevant for their Facebook use (McAndrew & Sun Jeong, 2012). Why men act like this is very intriguing, insofar as replicas of several studies show that men are more interested in occasional sex compared to women, even if they are involved in a serious relationship. It is possible that men who are committed to a relationship have less spare time; however this doesn't explain why women don't show the same pattern. It is also possible that men, unlike women, only use Facebook to search for potential partners, but this argument needs additional support from future research.

Studies on the relationship between age and Facebook use yield consistent results. As people increase in age, they tend to use Facebook less, have fewer friends on their online contacts list, and engage in fewer activities, compared to their younger counterparts. When they do use Facebook, however, older people prefer to interact with others rather than inspect their own profile pages, and they are more likely than younger people to look at posted family pictures (McAndrew & Sun Jeong, 2012).

The need for an in-depth analysis of the simultaneous effects of psychological variables on the use of online social networks, such as Facebook, is made clear, more since online social behaviours have complex causes, being determined by the interactions between individual particularities and contextual factors (Skues, Williams, & Wise, 2012).

Thus far there is a vast body of research on the association between different measures of Facebook use and several psychological and social outcomes. These studies, however, are not as consistent in their findings as one would hope, thus Facebook (and other online SNS's) users are in need of a few recommendations on how to maintain and improve their well-being while using these social media services. In the following paragraphs, I will discuss some general recommendations for users, and I will also emphasize the importance of keeping an open and critical mind regarding the conclusions one might draw from these studies.

SOLUTIONS AND RECOMMENDATIONS

In the previous section, we have seen that there is a lot of debate among scholars and researchers whether the Internet, in general and online social networking websites, in particular, have more negative or more positive effects on our social well-being - communication, feelings of connectedness, number of ties in our personal networks, etc. - and on psychological well-being - personality traits, self-esteem, feelings of loneliness, depression etc.; the case of the online SNS Facebook was analyzed in depth. These effects may represent a real concern for many individuals who use SNS's, but also for parents of teenagers, who wish to ensure their children's well-being.

I would advise such individuals to keep in mind that any form of technology is not harmful in itself, but rather the ways it is used and users' attitudes towards it makes it beneficial or detrimental for well-being. As for SNS's in general, and Facebook, in particular, their purpose is to facilitate communication and make it more efficient, not to replace face-to-face social interactions. In order to preserve and improve their well-being while using SNS's, people need to be aware of the advantages and disadvantages these SNS's have, they need to be aware of their own limitations that could make them vulnerable to negative effects of SNS use (for example, lack of social skills, the tendency to engage in conversations with strangers rather than with friends, and the tendency to engage in more solitary forms of use, such as surfing), and ultimately, they ought to be mindful and to self-regulate their online behavior such that SNS's

preserve their initial purpose, that of facilitating communication, and do not become the main means for fulfilling social needs.

As for the research conducted thus far on the relationships between SNS use and well-being, it is important to keep in mind that there is a continuum of positive and negative effects, and we can never actually say that there is an absolute positive or negative effect of online social media on personal and/or professional well-being. Also, we need to be aware of several limitations that many of the studies we reviewed have: one limitation is that most of these studies are cross-sectional, comparing two or three groups of people on their average scores on particular outcomes, thus drawing conclusion from these cross-sectional studies to the individual level would be an ecological fallacy. A second limitation of many of these studies is that they use samples of students to test their hypotheses on, because this strategy is cost-effective: students are easy to find in large groups (in their classes, during lectures), they are easy to please in terms of compensation for their participation (in most of the cases, one or two extra credits should do the trick), and they probably all have Facebook accounts; however, students represent a particular population, thus generalizations of the findings on the general population should be made with caution. A third limitation of most of these studies is that they generally use cutoff points for their variables, transforming them into (ordinal) categorical variables (e.g.: low and high levels of extraversion); this procedure allows for group comparisons, however, it hides non-linear relationships. Finally, a fourth limitation is that most of the studies have a correlational design, being able to predict, at best, social and psychological outcomes from measures of Facebook use, but leaving the issue of causality unattended.

Consequently, I would advise the readers of this chapter and the audience of this volume to think critically about all the findings in the literature and to have high consideration for both positive and negative potential effects of online social media on its consumers.

FUTURE RESEARCH DIRECTIONS

Now, with the rapid changes in technology, and not only, trends are getting harder and harder to predict. As the Greek philosopher Heraclitus of Ephesus said: "Change is the only constant." Regarding the online SNS Facebook, it constantly changes and innovates in order to provide its users with the best possible experience. Researchers from various fields, such as psychology and social and behavioral sciences, make real efforts to advance articulated models that would explain and predict Facebook use and its effects on well-being in personal and professional settings. An interesting line of research pertains to suicide announcements on Facebook, a subject that is rather recent and under studied. The posting of *selfies* [photographic self-portraits, especially ones taken manually (not using a timer, tripod, etc.), with a small camera or mobile phone] on Facebook and other SNS's is another interesting and novel topic that may be researched.

Given the complexity of human online behavior, I would say that we are far from having a complete paradigm or set of models to explain and predict it. The field is in need of more longitudinal studies in order to be able to advance causal relationships. Thus, future research to support or contradict existing findings, or to propose new models, are always desirable.

CONCLUSION

Through this chapter, I tried to tackle one of the most controversial and debated topics of the modern world: online social media. The purpose of this chapter was to lay down in as concise and coherent manner as possible the main findings within the literature with regard to the relationship between online SNS's, as the most popular medium for long-distance communication, and social and psychological well-being. Since Facebook is by far the most popular SNS, I felt that it would adequately speak for the arguments made in this chapter.

Within the existing literature, there are thousands of studies that try to figure out what made Facebook the number one online social network site practically overnight, what are the relationships between different measures of Facebook use and individual differences such as personality traits, self-esteem, narcissism, gender, age, culture, etc., and what are the effects of Facebook use on social and psychological well-being.

Regarding the question of why Facebook has become such a success practically overnight, one of the possible explanations could be that its creator Mark Zuckerberg, a programming prodigy and Psychology student at Harvard University, understood that any product or service that satisfies the most fundamental needs of human beings determines them to return to that product or service over and over again. Hence, he designed Facebook such that it meets two of the most fundamental human needs: the need to belong and the need for self-presentation. All the motivational factors that are found in the literature that are said to explain Facebook usage (e.g.: communication, passing time, staying informed, and so on) can be conveyed under these two social-based needs. Research suggests that Facebook use is positively correlated with acceptance by peers and feelings of connectedness. It is also shown that, in general, people use Facebook to transfer their existing relationship from the offline environment to the online environment, rather than to meet new people. Hence, although features that enable the enhancement of self-image are broadly used, people in general present their public selves on Facebook.

As for the potential effects of Internet use in general, and Facebook use in particular, the issue is highly controversial, since there is a constant debate among literature whether or not there are more positive or rather more negative personal and social outcomes of online social media use. Two of the most well-known hypotheses of this kind are the "displacement hypothesis" and the "internet-enhanced self-disclosure hypothesis". The former predicts negative effects of Internet usage, such as decreased face-to-face communication and increased loneliness and depression. The latter hypothesis predicts rather beneficial outcomes of Internet use, such as increased satisfaction with life, indirectly through online self-disclosure. However, these effects are moderated by the type of use (instant messaging with friends rather than joining chat rooms with strangers, or more solitary forms of use, such as surfing), the gender of the user (boys benefit more than girls from Internet-enhanced self-disclosure), and users' levels of social anxiety (socially skilled individuals are the ones who benefit from online communication - the "rich get richer" paradigm). In the past few years, there has been an accumulation of evidence supporting the positive effects of social media use on social and psychological well-being.

The success of Facebook is an illustration of how powerful social needs are, driving individuals to engage in behaviors aimed to maintain and strengthen ties with others and, ultimately, to increase or maintain social capital.

REFERENCES

Ahuja, A. K., Biesaga, K., Sudak, D. M., Draper, J., & Womble, A. (2014). Suicide on Facebook. *Journal of Psychiatric Practice*, *20*(2), 141–146. doi:10.1097/01.pra.0000445249.38801.d1 PMID:24638049

Allam, M. F. (2010). Excessive internet use and depression: Cause-effect bias? *Psychopathology*, *43*(5), 334. doi:10.1159/000319403 PMID:20664310

Amichai-Hamburger, Y., & Ben-Artzi, E. (2003). Loneliness and internet use. *Computers in Human Behavior*, *19*(1), 71–80. doi:10.1016/S0747-5632(02)00014-6

Amichai-Hamburger, Y., & Vinitzky, G. (2010). Social network use and personality. *Computers in Human Behavior*, *26*(6), 1289–1295. doi:10.1016/j.chb.2010.03.018

Augner, C., & Hacker, G. W. (2012). Associations between problematic mobile phone use and psychological parameters in young adults. *International Journal of Public Health*, *57*(2), 4437–4441. doi:10.1007/s00038-011-0234-z PMID:21290162

Back, M. D., Stopfer, J. M., Vazire, S., Gaddis, S., Schmukle, S. C., Egloff, B., & Gosling, S. D. (2010). Facebook profiles reflect actual personality, not self-idealization. *Psychological Science*, *20*(10), 1–3. PMID:20424071

Bargh, J. A., McKenna, K. Y. A., & Fitzsimons, G. M. (2002). Can you see the real me? Activation and expression of the "true self" on the internet. *The Journal of Social Issues*, *58*(1), 33–48. doi:10.1111/1540-4560.00247

Bevan, J. L., Pfyl, J., & Barclay, B. (2012). Negative emotional and cognitive responses to being unfriended on Facebook: An exploratory study. *Computers in Human Behavior*, *28*(4), 1458–1464. doi:10.1016/j.chb.2012.03.008

boyd, d. (2007). Why youth (heart) social network sites: The role of networked publics in teenage social life. In D. Buckingham (Ed.), *McArthur Foundation series on digital learning - Youth, identity, and digital media*. McArthur Foundation.

boyd, d. m., & Ellison, N. B. (2008). Social network sites: Definition, history, and scholarship. *Journal of Computed-Mediated Communication, 13*, 210-230.

Buffardi, L. E., & Campbell, W. K. (2008). Narcissism and social networking web sites. *Personality and Social Psychology Bulletin, 34*(10), 1303–1314. doi:10.1177/0146167208320061 PMID:18599659

Burngarner, B. A. (2007). You have been poked: Exploring the uses and gratifications of Facebook among emerging adults. *First Monday, 12*(11).

Cassidy, J. (2006, May 15th). *Me media: How hanging out on the internet became big business.* Accessed on May 23rd, 2013, from The New Yorker Website: http://www.newyorker.com/archive/2006/05/15/060515fa_fact_cassidy

Chen, S.-Y., & Tzeng, J.-Y. (2010). College female and male heavy internet users' profiles of practices and their academic grades and psychosocial adjustment. *Cyberpsychology, Behavior, and Social Networking, 13*(3), 257–262. doi:10.1089/cyber.2009.0023 PMID:20557244

Cheung, C. M., Chiu, P.-Y., & Lee, M. K. (2011). Online social networks: Why do students use Facebook? *Computers in Human Behavior, 27*(4), 1337–1343. doi:10.1016/j.chb.2010.07.028

Christofides, E., Muise, A., & Desmarais, S. (2009). Information disclosure and control on Facebook: Are they two sides of the same coin or two different processes? *Cyberpsychology (Brno), 12*(3). PMID:19250020

Christofides, E., Muise, A., & Desmarais, S. (2012). Hey mom, what's on your facebook? Comparing Facebook disclosure and privacy in adolescents and adults. *Social Psychological & Personality Science, 3*(1), 48–54. doi:10.1177/1948550611408619

Costa, P. T., & McCrae, R. R. (1992). Normal personality assessment in clinical practice: The NEO personality inventory. *Psychological Assessment, 4*(1), 5–13. doi:10.1037/1040-3590.4.1.5

Cotton, S. R., Ford, G., Ford, S., & Hale, T. M. (2012). Internet use and depression among older adults. *Computers in Human Behavior, 28*(2), 496–499. doi:10.1016/j.chb.2011.10.021

Crisan, D. (2013). *To the Romanian Facebook user: May your life be as awesome as you describe it on your Facebook profile* [translated from Romanian]. Unpublished thesis.

Cristakis, D. A., Moreno, M. M., Jelenchick, L., Myaing, M. T., & Zhou, C. (2011). Problematic internet usage in US college students: A pilot study. *BMC Medicine, 9*(77). http://www.biomedcentral.com/content/pdf/1741-7015-9-77.pdf PMID:21696582

Crocker, J., Luhtanen, R. K., Cooper, M., & Bouvrette, A. (2003). Contingencies of self-worth in college students: Theory and measurement. *Journal of Personality and Social Psychology, 85*(5), 894–908. doi:10.1037/0022-3514.85.5.894 PMID:14599252

Crocker, J., & Wolfe, C. T. (2001). Contingencies of self-worth. *Psychological Review, 108*(3), 593–623. doi:10.1037/0033-295X.108.3.593 PMID:11488379

Datu, J. A., Valdez, J. P., & Datu, N. (2012). Does Facebooking make us sad? Hunting relationship between Facebook use and depression among Filipino adolescents. *International Journal of Research Studies in Educational Technology, 1*(2), 83–91. doi:10.5861/ijrset.2012.202

Davila, J., Hershenberg, R., Feinstein, B. A., Gorman, K., Bhatia, V., & Starr, L. R. (2012). Frequency and quality of social networking among young adults: Associations with depressive symptoms, rumination, and co-rumination. *Psychology of Popular Media Culture, 1*(2), 72–86. doi:10.1037/a0027512 PMID:24490122

Diener, E. (1984). Subjective well-being. *Psychological Bulletin, 95*(3), 542–575. doi:10.1037/0033-2909.95.3.542 PMID:6399758

Diener, E., Emmons, R. A., Larsen, R. J., & Griffin, S. (1985). The satisfaction with life scale. *Journal of Personality Assessment, 49*(1), 71–75. doi:10.1207/s15327752jpa4901_13 PMID:16367493

Dong, G., Lu, Q., Zhou, H., & Zhao, X. (2011). Precursor or sequela: Pathological disorders in people with internet addiction disorder. *PLoS ONE, 6*(2), 1–5. doi:10.1371/journal.pone.0014703

Ellison, N. B., Steinfield, C., & Lampe, C. (2007). The benefits of Facebook "friends": Social capital and college students' use of online social network sites. *Journal of Computer-Mediated Communication, 12*(4), 1143–1168. doi:10.1111/j.1083-6101.2007.00367.x

Ellison, N. B., Steinfield, C., & Lampe, C. (2011). Connections strategies: Social capital implications of Facebook-enabled communication practices. *New Media & Society, 13*(6), 873–892. doi:10.1177/1461444810385389

Facebook Help Center. (2014). Retrieved from https://www.facebook.com/help/384834971571333

Feinstein, B. A., Hershenberg, R., Bhatia, V., Latack, J. A., Meuwly, N., & Davila, J. (2013). Negative social comparison on Facebook and depressive symptoms: Rumination as a mechanism. *Psychology of Popular Media Culture, 2*(3), 161–170. doi:10.1037/a0033111

Forest, A. L., & Wood, J. V. (2012). When social networking is not working: Individuals with low self-esteem recognize but do not reap the benefits of self-disclosure on Facebook. *Psychological Science, 23*(3), 295–302. doi:10.1177/0956797611429709 PMID:22318997

Gibbs, J. L., Ellison, N. B., & Heino, R. D. (2006). Self-presentation in online personals: The role of anticipated future interaction, self-disclosure, and perceived success in internet dating. *Communication Research, 33*(2), 152–177. doi:10.1177/0093650205285368

Gonzales, A. L., & Hancock, J. T. (2011). Mirror, mirror on my Facebook wall: Effects of exposure to Facebook on self-esteem. *Cyberpsychology, Behavior, and Social Networking, 14*(1-2), 79–83. doi:10.1089/cyber.2009.0411 PMID:21329447

Harghittai, E. (2008). Whose space? Differences among users and non-users of social network sites. *Journal of Computer-Mediated Communication, 13*(1), 276–297. doi:10.1111/j.1083-6101.2007.00396.x

Hew, K. F. (2011). Students' and teachers' use of Facebook. *Computers in Human Behavior, 27*(2), 662–676. doi:10.1016/j.chb.2010.11.020

Huang, C. (2010). Internet use and psychological well-being: A meta-analysis. *Cyberpsychology, Behavior, and Social Networking, 13*(3), 241–249. doi:10.1089/cyber.2009.0217 PMID:20557242

Hum, N. J., Chamberlin, P. E., Hambright, B. L., Portwood, A. C., Schat, A. C., & Bevan, J. L. (2011). A picture is worth a thousand words: A content analysis of Facebook profile photographs. *Computers in Human Behavior, 27*(5), 1826–1833. doi:10.1016/j.chb.2011.04.003

Jelenchick, L. A., Eickhoff, J. C., & Moreno, M. A. (2013). ''Facebook depression?'' Social networking site use and depression in older adolescents. *The Journal of Adolescent Health, 52*(1), 128–130. doi:10.1016/j.jadohealth.2012.05.008 PMID:23260846

Jenkins, H. (2006). *Convergence culture: Where old and new media collide.* Cambridge, MA: MIT Press.

Johnson, J. A. (1981). The "self-disclosure" and "self-presentation" views of item response dynamics and personality scale validity. *Journal of Personality and Social Psychology, 40*(4), 761–769. doi:10.1037/0022-3514.40.4.761

Joinson, A. N. (2008). Looking at, looking up or keeping up with people? Motives and use of Facebook. In *Proceedings of CHI '06* (pp. 1027–1036). New York: ACM.

Jung, C. G., & Franz, M.-L. (1978). *Man and his symbols.* London: Pan Books.

Kalpidou, M., Costin, D., & Morris, J. (2011). The relationship between Facebook and the well-being of undergraduate college students. *Cyberpsychology, Behavior, and Social Networking, 14*(4), 183–189. doi:10.1089/cyber.2010.0061 PMID:21192765

Kaplan, A. M., & Haenlein, M. (2010). Users of the world, unite! The challenges and opportunities of social media. *Business Horizons, 53*(1), 59–68. doi:10.1016/j.bushor.2009.09.003

Kim, J., LaRose, R., & Peng, W. (2009). Loneliness as the cause and the effect of problematic internet use: The relationship between internet use and psychological well-being. *Cyberpsychology & Behavior, 12*(4), 451–455. doi:10.1089/cpb.2008.0327 PMID:19514821

Krämer, N. C., & Winter, S. (2008). Impression management 2.0: The relationship of self-esteem, extraversion, self-efficacy, and self-presentation within social networking sites. *Journal of Media Psychology, 20*(3), 106–116. doi:10.1027/1864-1105.20.3.106

Kraut, R., Kiesler, S., Boneva, B., Cummings, J., Helgeson, V., & Crawford, A. (2002). Internet paradox revisited. *The Journal of Social Issues, 58*(1), 49–74. doi:10.1111/1540-4560.00248

Kraut, R., Patterson, M., Lundmark, V., Kiesler, S., Mukopadhyay, T., & Scherlis, W. (1998). Internet paradox: A social technology that reduces social involvement and psychological well-being? *The American Psychologist, 53*(9), 1017–1031. doi:10.1037/0003-066X.53.9.1017 PMID:9841579

Kujath, C. L. (2011). Facebook and MySpace: Complement or substitute for face-to-face interaction? *Cyberpsychology, Behavior, and Social Networking, 14*(1-2), 75–78. doi:10.1089/cyber.2009.0311 PMID:21329446

Lampe, C., Ellison, N., & Steinfield, C. (2006). A Face(book) in the crowd: Social searching vs. social browsing. In *Proceedings of CSCW-2006.* ACM. doi:10.1145/1180875.1180901

Lehavot, K., Ben-Zeev, D., & Neville, L. E. (2012). Ethical considerations and social media: A case of suicidal postings on Facebook. *Journal of Dual Diagnosis*, *8*(4), 341–346. doi:10.1080/1550426 3.2012.718928

Lewis, K., Kaufman, J., Gonzales, M., Wimmer, A., & Cristakis, N. (2008). Taste, ties, and time: A new social network dataset using Facebook.com. *Social Networks*, *30*(4), 330–342. doi:10.1016/j.socnet.2008.07.002

Lin, N. (2005). A network theory of social capital. In D. Castiglione, J. Van Deth, & G. Wolleb (Eds.), *The handbook of social capital*. Oxford University Press.

Lu, X., Watanabe, J., Liu, Q., Uji, M., Shono, M., & Kitamura, T. (2011). Internet and mobile phone text-messaging dependency: Factor structure and correlation with dysphoric mood among Japanese adults. *Computers in Human Behavior*, *27*(5), 1702–1709. doi:10.1016/j.chb.2011.02.009

Mayer, A., & Puller, S. L. (2008). The old boy (and girl) network: Social network formation on university campuses. *Journal of Public Economics*, *92*(1-2), 329–347. doi:10.1016/j.jpubeco.2007.09.001

Mazer, J., Murphy, R., & Simonds, C. (2007). I'll see you on "Facebook": The effects of computer-mediated teacher self-disclosure on student motivation, affective learning, and classroom. *Communication Education*, *56*(1), 1–17. doi:10.1080/03634520601009710

Mazer, J. P., Murphy, R. E., & Simonds, C. J. (2009). The effects of teacher self-disclosure via Facebook on teacher credibility. *Learning, Media and Technology*, *34*(2), 175–183. doi:10.1080/17439880902923655

McAndrew, F. T., Bell, E. K., & Garcia, C. M. (2007). Who do we tell and whom do we tell on? Gossip as a strategy for status enhancement. *Journal of Applied Social Psychology*, *37*(7), 1562–1577. doi:10.1111/j.1559-1816.2007.00227.x

McAndrew, F. T., & Milenkovic, M. A. (2002). Of tabloids and family secrets: The evolutionary psychology of gossip. *Journal of Applied Social Psychology*, *32*(5), 1064–1082. doi:10.1111/j.1559-1816.2002.tb00256.x

McAndrew, F. T., & Sun Jeong, H. (2012). Who does what on Facebook? Age, sex, and relationship status as predictors of Facebook use. *Computers in Human Behavior*, *28*(6), 2350–2365. doi:10.1016/j.chb.2012.07.007

Mehdizadeh, S. (2010). Self-presentation 2.0: Narcissism and self-esteem on Facebook. *Cyberpsychology, Behavior, and Social Networking*, *13*(4), 357–364. doi:10.1089/cyber.2009.0257 PMID:20712493

Morrison, C., & Gore, H. (2010). The relationship between excessive internet use and depression: A questionnaire-based study of 1,319 young people and adults. *Psychopathology*, *43*(2), 121–126. doi:10.1159/000277001 PMID:20110764

Nadkarni, A., & Hofmann, S. G. (2012). Why do people use Facebook? *Personality and Individual Differences*, *52*(3), 243–249. doi:10.1016/j.paid.2011.11.007 PMID:22544987

Nosko, A., Wood, E., & Molema, S. (2010). All about me: Disclosure in online social networking profiles: The case of Facebook. *Computers in Human Behavior*, *26*(3), 406–418. doi:10.1016/j.chb.2009.11.012

Ohannessian, C. M. (2009). Media use and adolescent psychological adjustment: An examination of gender differences. *Journal of Child and Family Studies*, *18*(5), 582–593. doi:10.1007/s10826-009-9261-2 PMID:21359124

Ong, E. Y., Ang, R. P., Ho, J. C., Lim, J. C., Goh, D. H., Lee, S., & Chua, A. Y. (2011). Narcissism, extraversion and adolescents' self-presentation on Facebook. *Personality and Individual Differences*, *50*(2), 180–185. doi:10.1016/j.paid.2010.09.022

Organisation for Economic Cooperation and Development. (2007). *Participative web: User-created content*. OECD Committee for Information, Computer and Communications Policy Report, April. Retrieved from http://www.oecd.org/internet/ieconomy/38393115.pdf

Orr, E. S., Sisic, M., Ross, C., Simmering, M. G., Arseneault, J. M., & Orr, R. R. (2009). The influence of shinness on the use of Facebook in an undergraduate sample. *Cyberpsychology & Behavior*, *12*(3), 337–340. doi:10.1089/cpb.2008.0214 PMID:19250019

Pantic, I., Damjanovic, A., Todorovic, J., Topalovic, D., Bojovic-Jovic, D., & Ristic, S. et al. (2012). Association between online social networking and depression in high school students: Behavioral physiology viewpoint. *Psychiatria Danubina*, *24*(1), 90–93. PMID:22447092

Peluchette, J., & Karl, K. (2010). Examining students' intended image on Facebook: What were they thinking?! *Journal of Education for Business*, *85*(1), 30–37. doi:10.1080/08832320903217606

Pempek, T. A., Yermolayeva, Y., & Calvert, S. L. (2009). College students' social networking experiences on Facebook. *Journal of Applied Developmental Psychology*, *30*(3), 227–238. doi:10.1016/j.appdev.2008.12.010

Pincus, A. L., Ansell, E. B., Pimentel, C. A., Cain, N. M., Wright, A. C., & Levy, K. N. (2009). Initial construction and validation of the pathological narcissism inventory. *Psychological Assessment*, *21*(3), 365–379. doi:10.1037/a0016530 PMID:19719348

Pirkis, J., Blood, R. W., Beautrais, A., Burgess, P., & Skehan, J. (2006). Media guidelines on the reporting of suicide. *Crisis*, *27*(2), 82–87. doi:10.1027/0227-5910.27.2.82 PMID:16913330

Reich, S. M. (2010). Adolescents' sense of community on MySpace and Facebook: A mixed-methods approach. *Journal of Community Psychology*, *36*(6), 688–705. doi:10.1002/jcop.20389

Rosen, L. D., Whaling, K., Rab, S., Carrier, L. M., & Cheever, N. A. (2013). Is Facebook creating "iDisorders"? The link between clinical symptoms of psychiatric disorders and technology use, attitudes and anxiety. *Computers in Human Behavior*, *29*(3), 1243–1254. doi:10.1016/j.chb.2012.11.012

Ross, C., Orr, E. S., Sisic, M., Arseneault, J. M., Simmering, M. G., & Orr, R. R. (2009). Personality and motivations associated with Facebook use. *Computers in Human Behavior*, *25*(2), 578–586. doi:10.1016/j.chb.2008.12.024

Ruder, T. D., Hatch, G. M., Ampanozi, G., Thali, M. J., & Fischer, N. (2011). Suicide announcement on Facebook. *Crisis*, *32*(5), 280–282. doi:10.1027/0227-5910/a000086 PMID:21940257

Ryan, T., & Xenos, S. (2007). Who uses Facebook? An investigation into the relationship between the big five, shyness, narcissism, loneliness, and Facebook usage. *Computers in Human Behavior*, *27*(5), 1658–1664. doi:10.1016/j.chb.2011.02.004

Seder, P. J., & Oishi, S. (2009). Ethnic/racial homogeneity in college students' Facebook friendship networks and subjective well-being. *Journal of Research in Personality*, *43*(3), 438–443. doi:10.1016/j.jrp.2009.01.009

Selfhout, M. H. W., Brantje, S. J. T., Delsing, M., ter Bogt, T. F. M., & Meeus, W. H. J. (2009). Different types of internet use, depression, and social anxiety: The role of perceived friendship quality. *Journal of Adolescence*, *32*(4), 819–833. doi:10.1016/j.adolescence.2008.10.011 PMID:19027940

Shapira, N., Barak, A., & Gal, I. (2007). Promoting older adults' well-being through internet training and use. *Aging & Mental Health*, *11*(5), 477–484. doi:10.1080/13607860601086546 PMID:17882585

Sheldon, P. (2008). The relationship between unwillingness-to-communicate and students' facebook use. *Journal of Media Psychology*, *20*(2), 67–75. doi:10.1027/1864-1105.20.2.67

Simoncic, T. E. (2012). *Facebook depression revisited: The absence of an association between Facebook use and depressive symptoms*. Unpublished thesis. Retrieved from http://deepblue.lib.umich.edu/bitstream/handle/2027.42/91787/teagues.pdf?sequence=1

Skues, J. L., Williams, B., & Wise, L. (2012). The effects of personality traits, self-esteem, loneliness, and narcissism on Facebook use among university students. *Computers in Human Behavior*, *28*(6), 2414–2419. doi:10.1016/j.chb.2012.07.012

Social Media. (n.d.). In *Oxford dictionaries online*. Retrieved from http://www.oxforddictionaries.com/

Social Media Marketing, Statistics, and Monitoring Tools. (n.d.). Accessed June 23rd, 2013, from www.socialbakers.com

Special, W. P., & Li-Barber, K. T. (2012). Self-disclosure and student satisfaction with Facebook. *Computers in Human Behavior*, *28*(2), 624–630. doi:10.1016/j.chb.2011.11.008

Stack, S. (2003). Media coverage as a risk factor in suicide. *Journal of Epidemiology and Community Health*, *57*(4), 238–240. doi:10.1136/jech.57.4.238 PMID:12646535

Stefanone, M. A., Lackaff, D., & Rosen, D. (2011). Contingencies of self-worth and social-networking-site behavior. *Cyberpsychology, Behavior, and Social Networking*, *14*(1-2), 41–49. doi:10.1089/cyber.2010.0049 PMID:21329442

Steinfield, C., Ellison, N. B., & Lampe, C. (2008). Social capital, self-esteem, and use of online social network sites: A longitudinal analysis. *Journal of Applied Developmental Psychology*, *29*(6), 434–445. doi:10.1016/j.appdev.2008.07.002

Stepanikova, I., Nie, N. H., & He, X. (2010). Time on the internet at home, loneliness, and life satisfaction: Evidence from panel time-diary data. *Computers in Human Behavior*, *26*(3), 329–338. doi:10.1016/j.chb.2009.11.002

Swartz, J. (2008). Social-networking sites work to turn users into profits. *USA Today*. Retrieved from http://www.usatoday.com/tech/techinvestor/industry/2008-05-11-socialnetworking_N.htm

Valkenburg, P. M., & Peter, J. (2009). Social consequences of the internet for adolescents: A decade of research. *Current Directions in Psychological Science*, *18*(1), 1–5. doi:10.1111/j.1467-8721.2009.01595.x

Valkenburg, P. M., Peter, J., & Schouten, A. P. (2006). Friend networking sites and their relationship to adolescents' well-being and social self-esteem. *Cyberpsychology & Behavior*, *9*(5), 584–590. doi:10.1089/cpb.2006.9.584 PMID:17034326

Van der Aa, N., Overbeck, G., Engels, R. C. M. E., Scholte, R. H. J., Meerkerk, G. J., & Van den Eijnden, R. J. J. M. (2009). Daily and compulsive Internet use and well-being in adolescence: A diathesis-stress model based on big five personality traits. *Journal of Youth and Adolescence, 38*(6), 765–776. doi:10.1007/s10964-008-9298-3 PMID:19636779

van Dijck, J. (2009). Users like you? Theorizing agency in user-generated content. *Media Culture & Society, 31*(1), 41–58. doi:10.1177/0163443708098245

Vasalou, A., Joinson, A. N., & Courvoisier, D. (2010). Cultural differences, experience with social network, and the nature of "true commitment" in Facebook. *International Journal of Human-Computer Studies, 68*(10), 719–728. doi:10.1016/j.ijhcs.2010.06.002

Weisbuch, M., Ivcevic, Z., & Ambady, N. (2009). On being liked on the web and in the "real world": Consistency in first impressions across personal webpages and spontaneous behavior. *Journal of Experimental Social Psychology, 45*(3), 573–576. doi:10.1016/j.jesp.2008.12.009 PMID:20161314

Wilson, K., Fornasier, S., & White, K. M. (2010). Psychological predictors of young adults' use of social networking sites. *Cyberpsychology, Behavior, and Social Networking, 13*(2), 173–177. doi:10.1089/cyber.2009.0094 PMID:20528274

Wilson, R. E., Gosling, S. D., & Graham, L. T. (2012). A review of Facebook research in the social sciences. *Perspectives on Psychological Science, 7*(3), 203–220. doi:10.1177/1745691612442904

Yu, A. Y., Tian, A. W., Vogel, D., & Kwok, R. C.-W. (2010). Can learning be virtually boosted? An investigation of online social networking impacts. *Computers & Education, 55*(4), 1494–1503. doi:10.1016/j.compedu.2010.06.015

Zhao, S., Grasmuck, S., & Martin, J. (2008). Identity construction on Facebook: Digital empowerment in anchored relationships. *Computers in Human Behavior, 24*(5), 1816–1836. doi:10.1016/j.chb.2008.02.012

ADDITIONAL READING

Evans, L. (2010). *Social media marketing: strategies for engaging in Facebook, Twitter & other social media.* IN: Que, Indianapolis.

Kim, J., & Lee, J. E. (2011). The Facebook paths to happiness: Effects of the number of Facebook friends and self-presentation on subjective well-being. *Cyberpsychology, Behavior, and Social Networking, 14*(6), 359–364. doi:10.1089/cyber.2010.0374 PMID:21117983

Kross, E., Verduyn, P., Demiralp, E., Park, J., Lee, D. S., & Lin, N. et al. (2013). Facebook use predicts declines in subjective well-being in young adults. *PLoS ONE, 8*(8), e69841. doi:10.1371/journal.pone.0069841 PMID:23967061

Liu, C. Y., & Yu, C. P. (2013). Can Facebook use induce well-being? *Cyberpsychology, Behavior, and Social Networking, 16*(9), 674–678. doi:10.1089/cyber.2012.0301 PMID:24028138

Papathanassopoulos, S. (2011). *Media perspectives for the 21st century.* New York: Routledge.

Payette, M. J., Albreski, D., & Grant-Kels, J. M. (2013). "You'd know if you 'friended' me on Facebook": Legal, moral, and ethical considerations of online social media. *Journal of the American Academy of Dermatology, 69*(2), 305–307. doi:10.1016/j.jaad.2013.02.024 PMID:23866862

Seldman, G. (2013). Self-presentation and belonging on Facebook: How personality influences social media use and motivations. *Personality and Individual Differences, 54*(3), 402–407. doi:10.1016/j.paid.2012.10.009

Youn, S. J., Trinh, N.-H., Shyu, I., Chang, T., Fava, M., Kvedar, J., & Yeung, A. (2013). Using online social media, Facebook, in screening for major depressive disorder among college students. *International Journal of Clinical and Health Psychology*, *13*(1), 74–80. doi:10.1016/S1697-2600(13)70010-3

KEY TERMS AND DEFINITIONS

Depression: Emotional disorder characterized by intense and prolonged sadness and inability to enjoy life. Similar to unhappiness, despair, sadness, hopelessness, gloominess. Associated in the manuscript with Facebook use, psychological well-being, and suicide.

Facebook: The most popular online social networking site, launched in 2004 by Mark Zuckerberg. Also known as FB, associated in the manuscript with well-being, personality traits, narcissism, loneliness, self-esteem, and depression.

Loneliness: Unpleasant emotional response to perceived lack of quality and/or quantity of relationships with other human beings. Also known as solitariness, isolation, similar to solitude, seclusion. Associated in the manuscript with Internet use, Facebook use, psychological and social well-being.

Motivation: The driving force that causes humans to act or behave in a certain manner. Also known as reason, similar to desire, willingness, incentive, rationale. Associated in the manuscript with Facebook use.

Narcissism: An inflated self-esteem and an egotistic admiration of one's physical or mental attributes. Also known as narcissistic personality disorder, similar to arrogant pride, vanity. Associated in the manuscript with Facebook use and psychological well-being.

Online Social Networking Site: Any website that enables users to create public profiles on that website and to connect with other users of the same website. Also known as SNS, social networking service. Similar to online community, associated in the manuscript with social media, Facebook, personality traits, and well-being.

Personality: Dynamic and coherent set of characteristics of an individual, that influences his/her cognitions, behaviors, emotions, and motivations within and across situations. Also known as persona. Similar to traits, character, nature, dispositions. Associated in the manuscript with Facebook use and social networking sites.

Self-Esteem: Cognitive and emotional evaluations of one's self-worth. Also known as self-worth, similar to self-respect, self-confidence, self-regard, pride. Associated in the manuscript with Facebook use and psychological well-being.

Well-Being: The ways people experience the quality of their own lives, and includes both emotional reactions and cognitive judgments. Also known as welfare, similar to health, happiness, comfort. Associated in the manuscript with social media use and Facebook use.

Chapter 4
Information Security and Privacy in Social Media:
The Threat Landscape

Hemamali Tennakoon
Kingston University, UK

ABSTRACT

Information security and privacy are multi-faceted concepts, and earlier definitions of information security and privacy seem inadequate in the context of emerging technologies such as social media. Hence, this chapter presents an analysis of the concept of information security followed by a discussion of computer security, information security, network security, personal privacy, informational privacy, etc. Then the discussion narrows down to information security and privacy on Social Networking Sites (SNS) followed by an analysis of the consequences of information security and privacy breaches from individualistic and organizational perspectives. The lack of understanding of the complex nature of security and privacy issues are preventing businesses from gaining the full economic benefit, especially on SNS. Therefore, some solutions and recommendations are suggested towards the end of the chapter, including the need for a common legal framework. Finally, the chapter ends with suggestions for future research.

INTRODUCTION

Information security and privacy is a vital concern for organizations and individuals operating in today's digital society. Gordon et al. (2010) argue that the rise of the Internet and e-commerce has elevated the value of information as an organisational asset. However, protecting such information assets against cyber-crimes such as "denial-of-service attacks, web hackers, data breaches, identity and credit card theft, and fraud" etc. (Smith, Win-chester, Bunker, & Jamieson, 2010, p.1) is posing a major challenge to organizations operating on the web. Breaches of information security could have a significant negative effect on the value of an organization (Campbell, Gordon, Loeb,, & Zhou, 2003; Cavusoglu, Mishra, & Raghunathan 2004; Kritzinger & Smith 2008; Johnston & Warkentin, 2010), not only in terms of losing time, manpower, money and/or business opportunities (Dhillon & Moores, 2001; Whiteman & Mattord, 2003) but also in losing the trust, loyalty and goodwill of

DOI: 10.4018/978-1-4666-7401-1.ch004

their customers (Jarvenpaa, Tractinsky, & Saarinen, 2000; Miyazaki & Fernandez, 2001; Lee & Turban, 2001; McKnight, Choudhury, & Kacmar, 2002; Gefen, Karahanna, & Straub, 2003; Liu, Marchewka, Lu, & Yu, 2004; Chen & Barnes, 2007). Despite these negative consequences, many organisations, particularly those with commercial interests, have continued to use and consider the Internet as a lucrative business platform. However, in recent years, a notable change has taken place in terms of how online businesses interact with their customers, which has considerably changed traditional online business practices. This new paradigm shift involves the use of social media as a cost effective, convenient and efficient means of conducting business (Kaplan & Haenlein, 2010; Mangold & Faulds, 2009). As mentioned before, the concern for the susceptibility of information assets belonging to businesses operating on the Internet is on the rise and the emergence of online social media driven business models adds to, if not increases the concern for online security. Apart from businesses organisations, governmental and other non-profit organisations have also had their fair share of security issues in recent years. Recent incidents involving attacks on government systems using fake social media profiles is one good example (Constantin, 2013).

From an individual point of view, Symantec recently revealed consumers have high levels of trust in social media, which results in vast quantities of self-disclosed information (BusinessTech, 2013). This is not only limited to disclosure of information but extends to monetisation of social networks including the use of digital currency, purchase of virtual gifts and online credit used in services such as gaming and Voice over IP (VOIP). Cyber-criminals have taken to exploiting the information available on social media and commercial application on social media platforms. Cyber security predictions for 2013 include an increase in social media-oriented security threats such as malware attacks targeting monetary and non-monetary information, targeting both the indi-

vidual users and online businesses (BusinessTech, 2013). Recent incidents such as the Sony PlayStation information security breach (Minihane, 2011), and criticisms against Facebook apps tracking/selling personal information (Hickins, 2012) suggest there is room for further enquiry pertaining to social media security and privacy.

Bearing such issues in mind, this chapter meets three objectives. First, a brief discussion of the historical development of security is presented followed by an analysis of the meaning of security and privacy in an online context. The intention of the analysis of security and privacy definitions is to highlight the conceptual differences between the two terms. This is in response to the criticism that the term 'security' is used in a somewhat "confusing manner in the industry" and that "some people equate security for privacy" (Bergeron, 2000).

The second objective of this chapter is to develop and attempt to prove that security and privacy on social media differ from the rest of the Web. One sect of scholars argues that 'virtual criminality' is the same as 'the terrestrial crime' differing "only in terms of the medium" of technology involved (Grabosky, 2001, p.243) and it is a case of 'old wine in new bottles' (Weir, Toolan, & Smeed, 2011, p.38). The opponents of this belief argue that this is not the case (Casprini & Di Minin, 2013, p.13) mainly owing to the differences in content and connectivity between 'Web 1.0 based network economy' and 'Web 2.0 network society'. Using prior works by Schneier (2010), Rose (2011) and other information security researchers, unique attributes of Social Networking Sites (SNS) are identified and it is argued that the information security and privacy risks of social media users are different from general Web users.

Thirdly, this chapter aims to discuss information security and privacy threats and their implications from individual and organizational perspectives, with emphasis on the evolution of the threat landscape from general Web security to SNS security. Organizational issues are discussed in terms of business and public sector security and privacy threats for a comprehensive understanding. Towards the end of the chapter, solutions and recommendations for some of the security and privacy issues are discussed. In addition, directions for future research on security and privacy in the perspective of social media are suggested in the final section.

BACKGROUND

Foundation and Evolution of the Concept of Security

In the early days, security meant software and physical security of computers used for personal or business purposes (Whitman & Mattord, 2010). At the time, networking and interconnectivity of computers were not very popular and therefore, more interest was on the study of computer security. With the decentralization of information processing systems during the 1980s, networking, interconnection of personal computers became commonplace. By the 1990s, the need to connect networks of computers gave rise to the Internet and in the early stages of the use of the Internet, security was not given much priority.

Whitman and Mattord (2010) analysed some of the pioneering works in security that relate to the above-mentioned developments of computers and computer networks and found that the meaning of security has changed considerably over the years based on 'what' aspects of security have been studied (Table 1). Until the 1980s, the study of security was limited to physical security, password security and access levels etc. and did not extend to information security or network security. It is after 2000 that the study of security evolved into studies of information security, particularly the study of online information security (Whitman & Mattord, 2010). The heightened concern for online information security was attributed to the aspect of anonymity (Palme & Berglund, 2002) or 'absence of identity' (Traynor, 2003)

on the Internet that has become the root cause of a number of problems including invasion of privacy, fraudulent acts committed using stolen information etc. (Traynor, 2003).

Such background information on the foundation and evolution of the concept of security suggests that information security can be considered as a fragment of the larger domain of 'computer security', where it could be studied in multiple layers including physical security, personal security, operations security, communications security, networks security etc. However, for the purpose of this chapter, security refers to 'online information security' including the information security related to emerging technologies such as social media.

DEFINING INFORMATION SECURITY AND PRIVACY

Information Security

Kritzinger and Smith (2008, p.2) define 'Information security' as the "protection of information… where the primary goal of information security is to protect information and ensure that the availability, confidentiality and integrity of information are not compromised in any way". Whitman and Mattord (2010) take this definition a step further when they claim that information security is made up of three elements: Confidentiality, Integrity, Availability; which are also known as the CIA principles. It is further stated that identification (Landwehr, 2001) and authentication (Koved, Nadalin, Nagaratnam, Pistoia, & Shrader, 2001) should also be included in the list where identification will help distinguish who has done what, and authentication will deal with the level of authority necessary to handle information assets. Bhimani (1996, p.3) maintains that 'non-repudiation' should be a fundamental security requirement where neither of the parties involved in a transaction "should be able to deny having participated

Table 1. Comparison of early works of information security

Date	Scholar(s)	Document	Aspect of Security Studied
1968	Maurice Wilkes	Time-sharing Computer Systems	Password security
1973	Schell, Downey and Popek	Preliminary Notes on the Design of Secure Military Computer Systems	Need for additional security in military systems
1975	The federal Information Processing Standards (FIPS)	Federal Register	Digital Encryption Standards (DES)
1978	Bisbey and Hollingworth	Protection Analysis: Final Report	Discuss the Protection Analysis report by the Advance Research Project Agency (ARPA) to better understand vulnerabilities of operating systems security. Also examines the possibility of the introduction of automated vulnerability detection techniques in existing system software.
1979	Morris and Thompson	Password Security: Case History (Published by the Association of Computer Machinery-ACM)	Examines the history of a design for a password security scheme on a remotely accessed, time-sharing system.
1979	Dennis Ritchie	On the Security of UNIX and Protection of Data File Contents	Discuss about secure user ID and secure group ID.
1984	Grampp and Morris	UNIX Operating System Security	In this, the author has examined four aspects of computer security. 1. Physical control of premises and computer facilities 2. Management commitment to security objectives 3. Education of employees 4. Administrative procedures aimed at increased security.
1984	Reeds and Weinberger	File Security and UNIX System Crypt Command	Argues that no technique can be secure against the system administrator or other privilege users.

(Based on Whitman & Mattord, 2011).

in it afterwards". Dhillon and Backhouse (2000, p.128) propose an extension to the CIA principles where they argue that "responsibility, integrity, trust and ethicality (RITE) principles hold the key for successfully managing information security in the next millennium". 'Responsibility' refers to being "accountable for one's own actions". 'Trust' denotes the assurance that employees will act "in accordance with company norms and accepted and agreed patterns of behaviour, appropriate levels of confidentiality as well as ethical practice". 'Ethicality' refers to acting according to "informal norms and behaviour" which are not bound by organizational rules, while 'integrity' is explained as the trustworthiness or honesty of organizational members who handle information assets (Dhillon & Backhouse, 2000, pp.127-128). These various interpretations of 'information security' have broadened the understanding and meaning of the concept. Table 2 provides a summary of the attributes of information security discussed above.

With a view towards a broad understanding of security, Baldwin (1997, p.13) argues that it should be done "with respect to the actor whose

Table 2. Attributes of information security

Elements of Information Security	Known As	Theorist	Description
Confidentiality	CIA Principles		Ensuring information is accessible on a need-to-know basis and unauthorized access is prevented
Integrity			Data are not deleted or corrupted either accidentally or deliberately
Availability		Whitman & Mattord,2009	Ensuring that information is available when it is required and that it is able to support the organization's ability to operate and accomplish its objectives
Identification		Landwehr, 2001	To be able to distinguish who has done what to the information
Authentication		Koved et al., 2001	Understand the level of authority necessary to handle information assets
Nonrepudiation		Bhimani, 1996	Neither of the parties involved in a transaction should be able to deny having participated in it afterwards
Responsibility	RITE Principles	Dhillon & Backhouse, 2000	Being accountable for one's own actions
Integrity			The trustworthiness or honesty of organizational members who handle information assets
Trust			The assurance that employees will act in accordance with company norms and accepted and agreed patterns of behavior, appropriate levels of confidentiality as well as ethical practice
Ethicality			Acting according to informal norms and behavior which are not bound by organizational rules

values are to be secured, the values concerned, the degree of security, the kinds of threats, the means for coping with such threats, the costs of doing so, and the relevant time period". Even though Baldwin's paper discusses the universal meaning of 'security', he maintains that "economic security, environmental security, identity security, social security, and military security are different forms of security, not fundamentally different concepts" (Baldwin, 1997, p.19) and that each can be specified in terms of actors involved, value or risk associated with loss of security, level of security and others. .

Another aspect of security includes network security, systems security, and cyber security to name but a few. Further analysis of literature reveals that some scholars use the terms 'network security' and 'cyber-security' interchangeably (Bishop, 2003). For instance, in a computer systems point of view, Gollmann (1999) describes security as techniques used to ensure security within a computer system. From the perspective of network security and the Internet communication, Essinger (2001) argues that security prevails when information can be transmitted across the internet without any disturbances from unauthorized parties interfering with it.

The plethora of scholarly discussions on security can be confusing at times. Viewing security through a theoretical or a philosophical lens may enhance the understanding of online security (Alaboodi, 2007). For instance, the Information

Security Maturity Model (ISMM) describes security as the concepts, techniques, technical measures, and administrative measures used to protect information assets from deliberate or inadvertent unauthorized acquisition, damage, disclosure, manipulation, modification, loss, or use (McDaniel, 1994). Further, the Information Security Retrieval and Awareness model (ISRA) divides security issues into two categories; Technical Information Security issues (such as Firewalls, Intrusion detection, Encryption, Password Protection, Access Control) and Non-Technical Information Security issues [human related Issues] (such as Security Policies, Legal aspects, Ethics, Password Protection, Information Security Culture) (Kritzinger & Smith, 2008, p.3). This denotes that security can be explained in relation to 'security threats'; that is, the absence or lack of security. In some studies, security threats are defined as "incidents that can directly or indirectly lead to system vulnerabilities" (Im & Baskerville, 2005, p.2), including direct intentional threats such as hacking, computer viruses, computer theft or indirect, accidental ones such as natural disasters, human errors etc. Im and Baskerville (2005) further argue that intentional threats are becoming a severe problem while the other threats such as human error and threats caused by natural disasters are largely ignored in information security research. Unfortunately, "security is still widely regarded as a technical issue, not a business issue, resulting in technology solutions without supporting business processes" (Hinde, 2002, p.3) which may account for the increase in human-related security breaches.

From a philosophical perspective, Dhillon and Backhouse (2001) suggest that information systems security should be classified into four paradigms using the Burrell and Morgan framework. The four paradigms segment information security literature into functionalist, interpretive, radical humanist and radical categories. Functionalists are concerned with the 'regulation' and control of all organizational affairs. They have an objective point of view towards studying information systems security. Interpretive paradigm literature 'believes in a subjective analysis of the social world'. Radical humanists view society as anti-human and look into structural conflicts and modes of domination in society, while radical structuralists believe in radical change which can generate conflicts and even disrupt the status quo (Dhillon & Backhouse, 2001, p.4).

Discussed above are some of the means by which scholars have attempted to define security. However, the debate about how best to define security is a long-standing one. Katsikas (2006, p.531) points out that "even after many years of debates, information security has not found a worldwide definition" but agrees with previously mentioned scholars that its historic definition centres on 'confidentiality, integrity, availability and responsibility'. Thus, one may conclude that 'information security' is a construct of many attributes and the definition of security is context specific. At a basic level, confidentiality, integrity, and availability can provide a common basis for assessing presence or absence of security, but a major criticism for such rudimentary definitions is in the absence of a means by which to measure confidentiality, integrity and availability (Anderson, 2003). This indicates the need for a contemporary and comprehensive definition of information security addressing security in the era of Web 2.0.

Privacy

Bergeron (2000) contends that security is a fundamental necessity in order for privacy to prevail, but transactional or communication activities can take place in secure environments that are not private. It is apparent security and privacy are related but separate terms. Bergeron (2000, p.1) further claims, "Privacy is about informational self-determination--the ability to decide what information about you goes where. Security offers the ability to be confident that those decisions are respected".

This doubtful understanding of the meaning of privacy has led to much debate. Powers (1996, p.369) points out that the subject of individual privacy has been the focus of considerable public and academic controversy and has been able to analyse several definitions of privacy. To illustrate this point, several definitions of privacy are listed in Table 3.

It is interesting to note that the definitions of privacy in Table 3 refer not only to 'personal privacy' but also to 'information privacy'. They are undoubtedly interrelated and one cannot have personal privacy if the privacy of personal information is violated. Further extension privacy is 'online privacy', which stems from the general definition of privacy. Thus, online privacy is described as "'the sum of all private rights', 'the right to be let alone' or 'to be free from unwanted intrusion', to be secreted and secretive; a right to be unknown ("incognito"), free from unwanted information about oneself in the hands of others', unwanted scrutiny, unwanted 'publicity' or a right to be free from physical, mental, or spiritual violation" (Henkin, 1974, p.11). It is clear that personal privacy, information privacy and online privacy are interrelated. If so, this promotes the

question 'what is considered as personal information or information about oneself?' The meaning of 'personal information' may differ from one individual to another. This creates a problem to information collectors as well as information providers if one cannot distinguish between what kind of information is safer to collect/give and what is considered as 'private' (in which case requesting such information may be in violation of fundamental human rights).

The issues of what information constitutes as private and what is public is a unique feature in online privacy debate. It is argued that one fundamental difference between 'online privacy' and 'privacy' in the physical world is the nature of 'anonymity' in the two different environments. A customer purchasing goods/services from a shop in a traditional shopping environment gives the marketer only limited room for observation and data gathering. The information thus gathered may help the marketer to understand customer buying behaviour to some extent. One might not consider this form of information gathering as an invasion of privacy since the shop is a public place. It is also assumed that the information gathered will not be linked to individual customers (unless a customer uses/does not use store cards/loyalty cards, which could be used to record information), thus maintaining a sense of anonymity. However,

Table 3. Definitions of privacy

Theorist	Definition of Privacy
Alan Westin	Claim of individuals, groups, or institutions to determine for themselves, when, how and to what extent information about them is communicated to others
Samuel Warren and Louis Brandei	Privacy consists in being let alone
W.A. Parent	A condition of not having undocumented personal information about oneself known by others
Ferdinand Schoeman	Person has privacy to the extent that others have limited access to information about him, limited access to the intimacies of his life, or limited access to his thoughts or his body
Anita Allen	Personal privacy as a condition of inaccessibility of the person, his or her mental states, or information about the person to the senses or surveillance devices of others
Ruth Gavison	Definition identifies solitude, secrecy, and anonymity as components of privacy

(Powers, 1996).

customers lose privacy through obscurity in an online environment. In online transactions, the items purchased can be linked to customers. Purchasing patterns, repeat purchases, payment methods and numerous amounts of other information can be collected that can later be used for consumer profiling and target advertising. This is done in the course of legitimate business transaction with the consent and awareness of the customer. However, some unscrupulous online businesses gather sensitive information from unsuspecting online consumers using cookies, opt-in/opt-out messages etc. (Caudill & Murphy, 2000). This is referred to as "'second exchange' where consumers also make a non-monetary exchange of their personal information for value such as higher quality service, personalized offers, or discounts when they visit and interact with Web sites" (Milne & Culnan, 2004, p.2). Breaches of privacy such as the above in online transaction environments are mainly due to the unique nature of the medium (i.e. the Internet) used in the exchange process (Glazer, 1991; Milne & Gordon, 1993).

Further, Goodwin (1991) argues that 'online privacy' is a 'subset of privacy', which involves two dimensions: privacy of individuals' physical space and their information. In terms of privacy of personal information, Foxman and Kilcoyne (1993) suggest that this depends on the individual. Depending on personal characteristics, perceptions and prior experience, individuals rank the value of their personal information. In addition to the understanding of the worth of personal information and privacy threats, the amount of control individuals have over personal information dictates information disclosure behaviour of consumers (Foxman & Kilcoyne, 1993). Control over information refers to whether individuals have authority over the amount and depth of information collected. This is determined by their understanding of how information is collected, and how it is being used. Dinev and Hart (2004) add to the discourse of privacy control by introducing two underlying antecedents to privacy concerns,

namely perceived vulnerability (the belief that information will be used in an unfair manner resulting in negative consequences) and perceived ability to control submitted personal information when using the Internet.

References to privacy are found in 'Digital Rights Management' (DRM) literature in the form of 'Intellectual Privacy' (IP). Cohen (2003, p.577) states that IP "include not only rights of bodily integrity and other corporeal rights, but also rights over one's own thoughts and personality. Surveillance and compelled disclosure of information about intellectual consumption threaten rights of personal integrity". Further, it is argued that "for these reasons, in circumstances where records of intellectual consumption are routinely generated—libraries, video rental memberships, and cable subscriptions—society has adopted legal measures to protect these records against disclosure" (Cohen, 2003, p.578). As mentioned previously, surveillance of online customer shopping behaviour is a popular tool used by e-businesses as part of their market intelligence gathering and according to the above notion of 'Intellectual Privacy', such actions might be deemed as violating the IP rights of individuals.

Moor (1997) brings a theoretical angle to privacy when introducing the 'Control/Restricted access theory' where it is argued that "privacy is best understood in terms of a control/restricted access account....that is, give individuals as much control (informed consent) over personal data as realistically possible" (p.31). This implies that individuals may be restricted from accessing their own information (if it proves to be unrealistic as the theory suggests), which seems to oppose the argument that "one has privacy if and only if one has control over information about oneself" (Tavani, 2000). Such contradictory viewpoints confirm the conclusion reached by Powers (1996), which is that there is no single definition of privacy that could fit into all situations, but that it depends on the context in which it is discussed.

The need for a clear definition of 'online privacy' is important in an economic perspective, especially at a time when online businesses can benefit from low cost technological solutions such as social media platforms for conducting virtual businesses. Organisations who understand the importance of privacy to online users have developed the practice of displaying privacy notices and policies on websites (Gauzente, 2004). These practices vary across countries. Bellman, Johnson, Kobrin, & Lohse (2004) found that privacy practices are different between UK and the US and that online users have a different understanding of privacy in the two countries. The differences are fuelled by regulatory standards governing Internet privacy. For instance, in the UK (as part of the EU), Internet privacy is formally enforced and overseen by the government agency the Information Commission (IC), but in the US it is the industry that regulates privacy standards via voluntary compliance and norms developed by civic organisations such as TRUSTe (Jamal, Maier, & Sunder, 2005). In the UK, the aim of privacy/security notices on websites is part of regulatory compliance (in the UK) rather than a trust building mechanism. Contrarily, in the US, companies who want to make a better impression on their customers (and to increase customers' trust in the vendor) purchase web seals such as TRUSTe or BBB from independent providers and display them on their sites (in the UK, the market for web seals is underdeveloped) (Jamal et al., 2005).

However, the problem is whether the customers read such privacy policies or not (Milne & Culnan, 2004). The lack of industry standards and the variations in privacy protection mechanisms across the Web signify that regulatory bodies should develop a unified framework for online privacy, particularly for industries such as health care where the nature of the information gathered is highly sensitive (Jensen & Potts, 2004).

SOCIAL MEDIA SECURITY AND PRIVACY: OLD WINE IN NEW BOTTLES?

Acquisti and Grossklags (2003) state that Internet users profess to have high privacy concerns yet behave with less caution when online. Dumas (2013, p.94) argues that the Internet is "an inherently porous system" and therefore vulnerable to information security breaches. Once information is released on the Internet or on a Social Networking Site (SNS), it has a life of its own and the boundary between private and public information is somewhat unclear. Particularly for SNS, the threat of loss of information security and privacy goes beyond purposeful intrusions and is often the result of lax procedures (Dumas, 2013) and poor design of privacy policy plug-ins (Coopamootoo & Ashenden, 2011). For instance, third-party application developers can add their 'apps' to SNS such as Facebook (with limited validation and quality assurance) and such apps can gain full access to user profiles and sensitive personal information. A recent report[1] suggests that users are willing to trust social media sites and are prepared to provide financial/personal information for purchasing game credit or buying virtual gifts. In doing so, they become more susceptible to malware attacks that could compromise the security of financial/personal information. Further evidence suggests that most SNS users are ignorant of the need for online security and unwittingly become targets of Phishing frauds, identity theft and loss of private data while endangering others who belong in their social network (Shelke & Badiye 2013, p.4). Understanding the unique set up of social media sites is important at this point to differentiate them from the rest of the Web. As mentioned in the introduction, there are two schools of thought on technology-related crime such as security and privacy attacks. One set of scholars argue that online versus offline crime differ only to the extent of the medium in which crime is committed (Grabosky, 2001; Weir et al.,

2011). The opponents of this belief argue that this is not the case (Casprini & Di Minin 2013, p.13), owing to the differences in content and connectivity between 'Web 1.0 based network economy' and 'Web 2.0 network society'. For instance, Schneier (2010) argues that to better understood user security and privacy on SNS, content or data should be classified according to his taxonomy of social networking data (Table 4).

Schneier (2010, p.88) contends that 'Behavioural Data' is "the critical part of a social networking site's business model" because such data is used for targeted and customized advertising and, in less favorable circumstances, sold to third parties. This aspect of SNS set them apart from the rest of the Web and information security and privacy becomes an issue depending on the control users have over each data type.

Another unique aspect of social media relates to how SNS facilitates the creation and dissemination of user-generated content (Kaplan & Haenlein, 2010). Marwick (2011, p.16) see such connectivity and information exchange as a 'many-to-many model' and the actors involved as the 'networked audience'. It is true that elsewhere on the Web individuals generate content that are shared with others. For example, e-business users generate content such as product reviews on sites

such as eBay or Amazon.com, but the content has limited media richness and the users are often less connected to others users in comparison to social networks (Agichtein, Castillo, Donato, Gionis, & Mishne, 2008).

Further, the content generated on social networks such as Twitter happen in real-time, and is therefore time-sensitive. Content on social media sites also tend to follow a 'Push—Push—Pull communication' style (Kaplan & Haenlein 2011, p.107) meaning that content posted by one user can be re-posted and gradually "cascade down from one user's follower network to another's". If for instance the initial message was posted by a social media business, the cascading effect will allow it to reach a considerable audience (compared to e-businesses). Unless the information is confidential or can give negative publicity to the business (e.g. a faulty product recall notice), the wider reach and speed of information dissemination is advantageous to a business. The boundary between public and private information is a blur in some SNS (Shi, Rui, & Whinston, 2011) and information can become public knowledge in a matter of minutes of publication making them the "perfect environment for virtual exhibitionism and voyeurism" (Kaplan & Haenlein 2011, p.108). Therefore, the cascading effect may not

Table 4. Taxonomy of social networking data

Data Types	Description
Service Data	The data provided to SNS in order to join and use the sites. e.g. Legal name, age, date of birth
Disclosed Data	Data posted on one's own social media pages. e.g. Photographs, status updates, messages
Entrusted Data	Data posted by you on other people's social media pages. Different to 'Disclosed Data' in the sense that you lose control over entrusted data once posted.
Incidental Data	What other people post about you. e.g. A friend tagging a picture of you. Similar to 'Disclosed Data' but you do not have control over the data and the data was not created by you.
Behavioural Data	Data collected by the SNS about your habits and behaviour on the site. e.g. What pages you like, games you play
Derived Data	Data derived about you from all the other data using data aggregation.

(Schneier, 2010).

be a favourable option in some instances and can even raise questions about information privacy and security.

Rose (2011, p.35) maintains that social media is "the most dominant features on the Internet during the growth of the interactive (Web 2.0) Internet"…and on "a traditional web site, the content is delivered to the end user but they are not allowed to update or participate in the creation of the content on the web site. In social media, people are communicating, sharing, networking and interacting with others". Rose (2011) further explains that the unique set up of a SNS and resulting security and privacy issues can be viewed in Table 5.

From Table 5, and the rest of the discussion in this section, two things are apparent. First, the analysis of the distinctive attributes of SNS confirms the notion that security and privacy issues on SNS are different to that of the general Web. This supports the school of thought that social media security and privacy is not a case of 'old wine in new bottles'. Secondly, it is evident that the security and privacy risks are not applicable only to individual SNS users but also to commercial and other organizations. Based on this

latter discovery, the next section of the chapter provides a further analysis of social media security and privacy threats and their implications from an individual and an organizational perspective (including commercial/business organizations and public sector organizations).

IMPACT OF INFORMATION SECURITY AND PRIVACY ON INDIVIDUALS AND ORGANIZATIONS

Individual

Individuals may be the worst affected victims of information security breaches. Their personal information may be susceptible to attacks. For instance, due to the ignorance or lack of caution by the individuals themselves, their personal information may be the target of attackers on the web and on SNS. Further, the organizations that collect and hold information on individuals (e.g. SNS) may further be the victim of a security attack, thus compromising the safety of the information of individuals they possess. Recently, the online retailer Play.com, selling music, videos and games

Table 5. Security and privacy issues rising from the unique attributes of SNS

Attributes of SNS	Description	Example
Location Based Information	Sharing location information in real-time via social media sites or apps connected to social media sites.	Latitude on Google Maps, Foursquare, Google Buzz
Oversharing	Disclosing too much information about themselves on social media sites that may or may not give users right to control the privacy of the information published.	On interconnected social platforms such as Foursquare and Twitter, there is a blurred boundary between public and private information.
Information Aggregation	Web crawlers and other data aggregation methods can collate information published by users on various social media sites and create a profile of the individual that can be used for commercial or even unlawful purposes.	Targeted advertising on Facebook based on pages 'liked' by users and messages posted.
Risks through Direct Disclosure	Disclosing sensitive information about an organization such as trade secrets leading can lead to a security breach.	In 2010, the Israel Defense Force had to call off a raid after a soldier disclosed confidential information about the operation on his Facebook page.
Risk by Design	Security and privacy settings build into the SNS can determine the extent of privacy and security possible on the site.	Apps on Facebook can access most of the information on user profiles.

(Based on Rose, 2011).

warned its customers about "'being vigilant' after a security breach led to some personal information being compromised" (BBC News, 2011). This corresponds to the type of security breaches of personal information mentioned before. Even though the company assured that no payment details were stolen, the warning was meant as a precaution against spam e-mails that might lead to personal data breaches eventually. Security experts warn that personal information could be compromised in a number of ways in an online environment. Studies indicate that more than 200,000 malicious programs are in existence with most of them aimed at Windows operating system users (Ward, 2006). The attacks could come disguised as an e-mail message, Instant Messenger (IM), via the internet connection or though the web browser if certain websites were to be visited.

Similar incidents of breaches of personal information security on SNS were reported in media in a number of occasions. For example, in October 2010, it was reported that an application on the Social Networking site 'MySpace' has been leaking user data such as user ID, name, gender, photographs etc. from user profiles. However, the company responsible declared that the leaked user IDs could only give access to information that has already been made public (self-declared) by the user (Gastaldo, 2010a). While this was happening, it was also reported that the social networking site 'Facebook' has also been transmitting identity information to several companies. The matter went so far as to grab the attention of the U.S. Congress who pointed out that the incident is a "series of breaches of consumer security and privacy" (Gastaldo, 2010b).

According to a Kaspersky Lab security report, the social networking site 'Facebook' is the favourite site of phishers while it was also revealed that "half of phishing attacks masquerade as PayPal links, followed by eBay, HSBC, and Facebook" (Mills, 2010). Geographically speaking, the report reveals that Asia is the leading source of spam and

U.S., India, and Russia are among the other top sources. In another report, Eurostat released data on Internet security in the EU region containing data pertaining to 27 member states. It was revealed that "computers of one-third of the Internet users were affected with some or other form of virus" with highest number of incidents reported from Bulgaria, Malta and Slovakia. The lowest number of incidents was reported from Austria, Ireland, and Finland. Computer viruses were identified as the key security threat causing loss of information (PRLog Press Release, 2011).

Some of the incidents of security breaches raise questions about the demarcation between individual versus personal responsibilities in protecting personal information online. For instance, large establishments such as universities, health care institutes, government organizations etc. collect quantities of personal information and in a number of occasions such information has been reported as stolen or compromised. In March 2011, the University of York (U.K) reported a breach of 17,000 student records which had been published online by accident (Leyden, 2011). These records included personal details such as the names, contact details, and previous educational qualifications of students. A similar incident occurred at Eastern Michigan University (U.S) where two student employees accessed personal information of 45 students and provided it to a third party (Stafford, 2011). These are examples of vulnerabilities attributable to information access and storage. Thus, one could argue that the issue of an individual's information security is related, in part, to organizational information security. Victimisation through an online information security breach is possible due to one's own actions or because of disclosing information to trusted third parties in the course of online interactions/transactions. In either case, the repercussions could be serious and therefore more caution should be exercised when handling personal information, individually or as an organization.

Business Organizations

'Organizations' is a broad term and could be used to describe public, private, profit or non-profit organizations. This section focuses on profit making organizations that use the revenue generating potential of the Internet for business purposes. Teo and Choo (2001, p.1) maintain that the Internet is important for businesses "as an information-rich resource and an inter-organizational communications tool which has transformed the way that firms gather, produce and transmit competitive intelligence". On the other hand, in a marketing standpoint, whether it is for consumer marketing (Peterson, Balasubramanian, & Bronnenberg, 1997) or international marketing (Quelch & Klein, 1996), the profit making potential through e-commerce and e-business models (Mahadevan, 2000) is vast. In recent research, it is suggested that companies who can influence their customers to disclose personal information online are likely to have greater opportunities to leverage the online channel to increase revenues (Gupta, Iyer, & Weisskirch, 2010). However, research also indicates that issues of security and the use of appropriate security measures to protect customer information affect the success of e-commerce practices (Brown & Muchira, 2004; Ranganathan & Ganapathy, 2002). As previously argued, there is the risk of customer information being stolen or misused by unauthorised third parties that will lead to the loss of a customer's trust and goodwill. Such an incident occurred at Nasdaq where the company "revealed that they found "suspicious files" on its US computer servers, but denies that the access or acquisition of customer data by hackers or that its trading platforms were affected." (Computer Business Review, 2011a). The information was released to the media with the intention of gaining the confidence of the investors, but whether the attempt was successful or not is at question. In March, 2011, the "security vendor RSA admitted that its internal anti-hacking technologies have been hacked" (Latif, 2011). RSA is the security division of EMC, one of the largest enterprise data storage companies. The company's clientele includes the military, governments, banks, medical facilities, and insurance firms. They claim that the knowledge of the breach is "embarrassing" but refuse to acknowledge what type of data and how much information was stolen.

Other than unauthorized access of business information by outsiders, some businesses are accused of breaching online security by gathering information from customers without their prior consent. The case of Google is such where the company admitted to having collected "data about websites people visited on unprotected WiFi networks" (Gastaldo, 2010c) by 'accident' using their Street View cars. However, Reuters reported that other than the data about websites people visited, "personal data including complete emails and passwords" (Oreskovic, 2010) were also gathered in this instance.

Losing customers' trust is disadvantageous to business and in addition to these intangible forms of losses, businesses suffer financial losses as well due to lack of online information security (case of Softbank of Japan, February 2004; Timothy Lloyd case at Omega Engineering, U.S. in May 2000; University of California, San Francisco (UCSF) Medical Center case, October 2002). In recent years, several countries including the U.K. reported financial losses due to "phishing, pharming and misuse of payment cards such as credit and debit cards" (PRLog Press Release, 2011). A survey conducted by Symantec in 2011 revealed that cybercrimes has cost the UK economy £1.9 billion and that nearly a third of the population is affected by cyber-crimes (Brettabz, 2011). One cannot quantify the damages that can be caused by the loss of goodwill and trust of organizational stakeholders due to such incidents, and the money that has to be spent to recover from security breaches is substantial.

Research suggests managing information assets and protecting them from unauthorised access is one of the main obstacles to realizing the Internet's fullest potential in the e-Commerce (Bettman, Luce, & Payne, 1998; Miyazaki & Fernandez, 2001; Brown & Muchira, 2004). When comparing small, medium and large-scale businesses, small businesses are identified as more vulnerable to security attacks due to lack of expertise and resource constraints (Gupta & Hammond, 2005; Walczuch, Van Braven, & Lundgren, 2000; Poon & Swatman, 1999; Purao & Campbell, 1998). It has also ben argued that small and medium scale businesses have a false sense of security (McAfee, 2013). Small/medium business security breaches may not make headlines. Nonetheless, it is important to take precautions where security is concerned because unlike large organisations, small/medium businesses may not have the resource strength to recover from a cyber-attack, leading to long- term risk of business continuity (Infosecurity, 2013).

Public Sector Organizations

Public sector organizations include governments, profit or non-profit organizations or regulatory bodies. With the emergence of the concepts of 'e-politics', 'cyber-terrorism' and 'cyber-warfare', government organisations are increasingly becoming concerned about the security of the information collected and stored in government information systems and databases. A classic case to illustrate this point would be the first reported 'cyber-terrorist' launched against Estonia by Russia over a political dispute. Estonia's digital infrastructure was "bombarded by a flood of data from an unknown source" (Gaines & Miller 2009, p.574) destroying almost all Estonian government websites, nearly bringing the country's largest bank to a closure.

In a similar incident, a group of online hackers called 'Anonymous' attacked government websites in Egypt and Tunisia. The latest target of their DDoS (Distributed Denial of Service) attack is the Italian government website (Computer Business Review, 2011b). On March 23rd 2011, the European Commission and the European External Action Service acknowledged experiencing a cyber-attack of a "particularly serious nature" and that there was a risk of "unauthorised information disclosure" (Vogel, 2011).

Other public sector organizations such as aid organizations are also among the victims of information security breaches. After the recent earthquake and tsunami destruction in Japan, cyber criminals posing as non- profit aid organizations took to the Internet to fraudulently gather money from unsuspecting donors who thought they were donating money to legitimate organizations (Kaplan, 2011). Such fraudulent activities discourage the public from using online payment methods for monetary donations to aid agencies in times of national and global crisis. There are more incidents than can be recounted here pertaining to public sector information security breaches and this unfortunate trend seems only to continue. This may account for the recent interest governments have taken in online security. The Cabinet Office of the UK released their 'Strategic Defence and Security Review' (Cabinet Office, 2010) in October 2010 as part of the UK National Security Strategy where they have identified "cyber-attack as a Tier 1 threat — the highest level of risk, alongside international terrorism, international military crises and major accidents or natural hazards" (Calder, 2011). The report further states that organizations should treat information security seriously and that they should prepare themselves against security breaches by conducting penetration testing, careful planning etc. to reduce risks of data thefts and breaches of confidentiality. The importance of complying with the 'International information security standard ISO/IEC 27001' is highlighted in the report as a recommendation to organisations as part of their information security management practices.

Reports from Australia bring news of the "Australian government's decision to accede to the Council of Europe Convention on Cybercrime, the only binding international treaty on cybercrime" (Wong, 2011) which comes as no surprise considering the recent information security breaches that occurred in Australia (Cases: Virgin Blue, Commonwealth Bank, National Australian Bank (NAB) and the Australian stock exchange). Meanwhile, in the U.S, the Cyber Security Operations Centre (CERT) conducted a six month study "of data breaches across five nations between September 2009 and March 2010.... and found that 44 per cent of cases involved a malicious or criminal attack that resulted in loss or theft of personal information." (Wong, 2011). This exponential growth of information security issues seems to have awakened the public to the reality that the time has come to seriously look at online information security as an emerging global issue.

The above analysis of the impact of information security on individuals and organizations illustrates the complex nature of online security. One should keep in mind that the above issues are prevalent in varying contexts. A few years ago, reports on individual and organizational security breaches were predominantly related to Web or Internet security. The threat landscape has become increasingly diverse of late, particularly in terms of security on social media. Some of the incidents discussed in the previous sections support the argument that Internet and Web security versus social media security can no longer be viewed through the same lens. Therefore, in the next section, some practical solutions and recommendations are provided to confront issues of information security through a holistic perspective.

SOLUTIONS AND RECOMMENDATIONS

Treating Security and Privacy as Multi-Dimensional Constructs

One of the limitations of this chapter is that it only focuses on information security and privacy. Further, it was earlier mentioned that there are definitional ambiguities between information security and privacy. Nevertheless, by dissect-

ing the meaning of the two terms in a historical, evolutionary perspective, it was illustrated that privacy and security are two separate but interrelated terms, which is supported by Bergeron (2000). Further systematic reviews of literature reveal that information security and privacy are not stand-alone concepts but are linked to several other constructs that reflect the presence or absence of security. One such factor is 'behavioral intention', an outcome variable influenced by several other antecedents (e.g. trust, risk etc.) (McKnight et al., 2002; Parasuraman & Zinkhan, 2002; Ranganathan & Ganapathy, 2002). Behavioral intention is further divided in e-commerce/Web-usage studies into two main categories: online buying behaviour (Miyazaki & Fernandez, 2001; Chen & Barnes, 2007; McKnight et al., 2002; Parasuraman & Zinkhan, 2002; Ranganathan & Ganapathy, 2002) and online information disclosure behaviour (Fogel & Nehmad, 2009; Hoffman, Novak, & Peralta, 1999). As mentioned previously, other factors such as privacy perceptions, trust, risk perception, national culture and individual characteristics act as antecedents, which in turn determine the behavioural intention of Internet users (Brown & Muchira, 2004; Anderson & Agarwal, 2010; Cho, 2010; Jarvenpaa et al., 2000; Fogel & Nehmad, 2009). This signifies the need to study information security and privacy as a multi-dimensional concept. Some researchers have argued that introducing security and privacy notices such as Verisign and TRUSTe could promote trust; reduce users risk and privacy perception, consequently affecting their behavioral intention (Hu, Wu, Wu, & Zhang, 2010). This could be recommended as a solution to increasing the popularity and usage of emerging social media-based business models.

Need for a Common Legal Framework

Although over the past decade there have been extensive developments of legislative frameworks aimed at prevention and eradication of information security threats, internet legislation varies from country to country and still has significant shortcomings. Over the years, laws have not evolved sufficiently to act effectively against information security threats and it is debatable whether law enforcement has responded adequately to cyber security issues (Katyal, 2001). Even though the media has reported a number of instances where law enforcement agencies across the globe were able to detain offenders suspected of committing information security threats (BBC, 2012; Lighty & Wong, 2012; Ciccarelli, 2012), the conviction rate remains rather low due to the evasive nature of digital evidence. There is much dispute about the competency of global legal systems in dealing with online security and privacy.

From the legal perspective, privacy and security of user information collected for commercial purposes is seen as a distinctive right of the consumer (Goodwin, 1991; Caudill & Murphy, 2000; Culnan, 2000; Petty, 2000). There exist many legal instruments applicable for commercial purposes that are used to protect individual rights to privacy and security. In addition, there are also the industry standards addressing privacy and security issues. The United Nations Declaration of Human Rights, the International Covenant on Civil and Political Rights and the 95/46 European Union directive on the protection of individuals concur: privacy and security of an individual is as a fundamental human right (Gritzalis, 2004). Most of these legal instruments were developed during the time when the internet was in its infancy and before terms such as 'digital natives' or 'cyber communities' had emerged. Today individuals' rights for security and privacy extend far beyond the physical world and into the virtual environments, whilst criminologists are debating the earlier ideologies on privacy and security. Legal frameworks by their nature are country specific, which present well-known and immediate challenges in the networked society, where information can no longer be given

a specific spatial location as the earlier theories in criminology assumed (Yar, 2005). In addition, from the legal perspective, understanding of privacy varies from country to country. Particularly in the UK, the right to privacy is vaguely defined and is given limited recognition. Treatment of privacy is situation dependent and individuals are afforded a reasonable expectation of privacy. As Walker (2006) put it, English courts have upheld the respect for individual privacy "whenever the circumstances are such as to give rise to a reasonable expectation of privacy". The problem is that the test of the circumstances is so wide that it is subject to controversial interpretations (including the semantic ambiguities between the terms 'privacy' and 'security' mentioned previously (Bergeron, 2000)). Certainly, the legal interpretation of 'security' is country and circumstance dependent. We are faced with the fact that the types of information security threats are expanding. While the law is vague in terms of applicability at national rather than international levels, new threats identical to traditional crimes (e.g. theft, assault, etc.) are developing, perpetrated with means of new technology (Yar, 2005).

Information security threats are a rapidly evolving area, representing high commercial, terrorist and personal risks. Legislation in all countries is struggling to keep up with the challenges posed by cybercriminals. In order to understand how to legally counter information security threats, first we need a clear understanding of their nature. Thus, it is recommended that a unified legislative body should develop a clear legal definition of security and privacy. Further, when legislative frameworks are developed to safeguard privacy and security, policy makers could focus on technology – independent legal solutions which would provide a solution for applicability of legal instruments, irrespective of geographic boundaries of the Internet.

FUTURE RESEARCH DIRECTIONS

Since social networking is a recent phenomenon, the information security and privacy threat landscape pertaining to SNS has not been fully explored. Organizations of varying types and sizes are taking to the Internet to explore the emerging social technologies. For instance, e-business models are being replaced by social media business models, websites are being replaced by social media pages and storefronts (Safko, 2010; Berger & Thomas, 2014; Kumar & Rao, 2014; McCarthy, Rowley, Ashworth, & Pioch, 2014). Studies of such trends could provide insights about the future of information security and privacy threat landscape. Therefore, several future research opportunities within the domain of online information security and privacy are highlighted in this section.

Exploring Security and Privacy Issues in A Cross Cultural Perspective

Zakaria, Stanton, & Sarkar-Barney (2003, p.11) point out that "cultural differences seem to play a role in determining what information is transmitted, who receives the information, and the allowable circumstances under which different types of communication can occur. Furthermore, issues of personal privacy, workplace privacy, physical and social space, monitoring and surveillance, autonomy, and intimacy also vary from culture to culture." Therefore, it would be fair to assume that culture has some impact on individuals in the course of information exchange. A number of studies have looked into the effects of culture on willingness to disclose information, trust, and an individual's risk-taking behaviour (Hsee & Weber, 1999; Park & Jun 2003; Yamagishi & Yamagishi, 1994; Teo & Liu, 2007 etc.). Various cultural models capture some elements of security and privacy in a broader sense of the terms. For example, in Kluckholn and Strodtbeck's Six Dimensions of Culture, one dimension is 'privacy

of space' expressing the view that individuals should have their own space where they should have personal privacy. Within this space, what the individuals do is their own responsibility. Edward T. Hall classifies culture based on three factors: context, time and space. Similar to the Kluckholn and Strodtbeck's classification, the 'space' is described as a territory the individuals declare around them in which they own material things. People with 'high territoriality' would be more concerned about their personal boundaries and invasion of privacy and security of those boundaries. Richard D. Lewis also introduced a cultural model in 1990 with three classifications: Linear active, multi active and reactive cultures. He argues that people in linear active cultures are more concerned about privacy, are more task-oriented and individualistic (Lewis, 2006). Finally, in Trompenaars and Hampden-Turner's 'individualism versus Communitarianism' is one of the seven dimensions of culture where rights of the individual are discussed against the rights of a group or society. Privacy and security are considered as 'rights of individuals and groups'. The most popular of all is Hofstede's classifications of national culture, which is also the most criticized (Berry, Guillén, & Zhou, 2010). His model contains four cultural classifications: Power Distance, Uncertainty Avoidance, Individualism versus Collectivism, and Masculinity versus Femininity (McSweeney, 2002), and is the most often used cultural classification in research studies to study national culture. For instance, research reveals that collectivist cultures tend to choose riskier options than those in individualist cultures (Hsee & Weber, 1999). In other words, "in individualist cultures like America, a person is expected to bear the consequences of his or her decision but as opposed to this, collectivism acts as a cushion against possible losses" (Park & Jun 2003, p.15), allowing individuals in such cultures to take higher risks. In another study by Yamagishi and Yamagishi (1994) it was discovered that collectivists (e.g., Chinese) are less trusting than those in individualistic cultures. However, Tsikriktsis (2002) used the Hofstede's model to study customers' attitudes towards Web banking services and website quality expectations. 'Trust' was one of the elements that were studied. The respondents were form U.S, Europe and Australasia (Individualistic cultures) and results showed that there is lack of association between any of the cultural dimensions and trust. Further, a study by Jarvenpaa, Tractinsky, & Saarinen (1999) between online customers from Australia and Israel found that Australian (Individualistic) customers show higher trust and lower risk perception towards online businesses than those from Israel. Moreover, Teo and Liu (2007) found that there is a strong negative relationship between consumer trust and their risk perception across countries. They used samples from the United States, Singapore, and China for their study. More studies reveal that culture is a strong influencer of trust in consumer adaptation of e-commerce. It is evident that national culture is an important determinant of individual perceptions towards information security and privacy. However, some of the findings are contradictory and others are confirmatory in nature. Current findings are limited to trust, risk (risk taking and risk perception), and behavioural intention (Information disclosure and purchase intention). The majority of the research conducted looks at only one cultural dimension in the Hofstede's classification; the dimension of individualism versus collectivism and other cultural dimensions of Hofstede's have not being explored. In brief, there are several research gaps in cross-cultural studies pertaining to information security and privacy with room for future research.

Demographic Variables and Security and Privacy

Demographic variables and personal factors such as gender (Albert & Hersinta, 2013) and attitude towards SNS (Constantinides & Lorenzo-Romero, 2013) have been considered as important in re-

cent social media security research. Albert and Hersinta (2013) found that the buying behaviour of young Facebook male shoppers is affected by site security and reliability. Constantinides and Lorenzo-Romero (2013) found positive attitudes towards SNS increase site usage. Online security and privacy studies frequently make use of convenient samples of college students (Lenhart, Purcell, Smith, & Zickuhr, 2010), but whether such samples reflect the behaviour of general Web populations is suspect. Some of the questions that would interest future researchers include; 'is age an important factor in studying security and privacy?' (Particularly on SNS where the user population consists mainly of teenagers and young adults (Ellison, Steinfield, & Lampe, 2007), 'does the generation gap affect senior citizens using the Internet and SNS more compared to tech savvy youngsters?', 'does lack of understanding of technology increase victimisation of Internet and SNS users?'. It also raises the question of how non-users of the Internet and SNS perceive information security and privacy. Currently, there is limited understanding of information security to a non-user perspective (Hargittai, 2007). Thus, there is room for future research to investigate the role played by demographic variables such as level of education, technical efficacy, age, and gender in understanding information security and privacy.

The Psychological Damage Due To Loss of Privacy and Security

Loss of information security and privacy are not always straightforward and are often coupled with other cyber-threats. Online crimes range from attacks against software and hardware to non-technical threats targeting individuals (e.g. social engineering). Any illegal actions which are profit seeking (e.g. stealing credit card information) and non-monetary offences (e.g. cyber stalking) fall into the cyber threat spectrum. Katyal (2001, p.1004) describes cyber threat as a broad term covering "all sorts of crimes committed with computers-from viruses to Trojan horses; from hacking into private e-mail to undermining defense and intelligence systems; from electronic thefts of bank accounts to disrupting web sites". Katyal (2001) further contends that technology becomes a vehicle for committing traditional crimes (e.g. terrorism, stalking, bullying, etc.). Another common cyber offence is identity theft, which involves offenders using the internet in order to steal personal data from unsuspecting users. The popular means for this offence are phishing or pharming through directing users to illegitimate websites in order to disclose their security sensitive information, which falls into the hands of cyber criminals. With the proliferation of online Social Networking came yet another array of cyber threats including but not limited to cross-site scripting, clickjacking, identity theft, data mining and shortened URL linked to fraudulent sites (SOPHOS security trends report, 2013). In cross-site scripting or 'Self-XSS' attacks, users are tricked into cutting and pasting a malicious JavaScript code into their browser's address bar and the JavaScript is able to install malware into the users' computer in stealth mode. 'Clickjack-ing', 'likejacking' or 'UI redressing' involves manipulating the users into clicking a button (e.g. 'like' button on Facebook) in a social media site that will then install malware. Data mining is a security threat for social networking sites such as LinkedIn. The information found on such sites are used to launch spearphishing attacks, social engineering attacks and for identity theft. On sites like Twitter, where there is a 140 character limit, cybercriminals shorten URLs to malicious sites using bit.ly. The shortened URL may look legitimate since there is no indication of the site name but when clicked, it will redirect the user to fraudulent websites. Moitra (2005) states that the volatile nature of cyber threats hinders the development of taxonomies for cyber threats, and a lack of understanding of cyber threats will prevent us from developing effective policies to control them. Research has been conducted on

the psychological impact of some cyber threats such as cyber-staling and bullying (Willard, 2007; McLoughlin, Meyricke, & Burgess, 2009), but the psychological outcomes of victimization by loss of online information security and privacy has not been fully explored. Users' understanding about the darkside of social networking, the Internet and the study of technostress related to security and privacy are some of the niches not addressed in current security/privacy research.

CONCLUSION

This chapter covered several topics under the broader theme of information security and privacy. These include the foundations of the concept of information security, definitional ambiguities in distinguishing security and privacy and the lack of progress in developing a more suitable defini-tion suited to security and privacy of emerging technologies such as SNS. Further, this chapter reveals strong evidence supporting the argument that security and privacy issues are inherently different depending on the context. Therefore, suggestions have been made to encompass unique attributes that are typical to certain contexts such as SNS in future security and privacy research, to fully understand the antecedents and consequences of privacy and security or the lack of it.

PAPER HIGHLIGHTS
AND KEY POINTS

The key focus of this chapter is the rise of social media technologies and the security and privacy threats pertaining to social media platforms. Un-doubtedly, the technological landscape is changing and the nature and intensity of information secu-rity and privacy threats are evolving parallel to such technological changes. As such, this chapter highlights several key points for the attention of academics, practitioners and policy makers.

One such key point is how the concept of security has evolved over the years. In the early part of this chapter, it was highlighted that information security is a fragment of a lager domain with no clear definition of what constitutes 'information security'. There is no consensus on 'what' to protect or secure in an online environment, particularly in emerging technological environments such as social networking sites.

Secondly, this chapter highlights that similar to information security, privacy is also a less understood term. There seems to be a confusion regarding the relationship between privacy and security, where some use the terms interchangeably while others have treated them as related but separate concepts. Further discussion of the extents of privacy reveal that it is a multi-dimensional concept that should be studied with caution.

Another key point revealed in this chapter is the importance of studying security and privacy from the perspective of individuals and organizations. There can be noticeable changes in the threat landscape depending on the target, i.e. the victim of the security or privacy breach.

Finally, the chapter ends by highlighting the importance of developing a common legal framework to address security and privacy issues across geographic boundaries, that is able to safeguard individuals and organizations operating in cyberspace. It is suggested that academics and practitioners incorporate cultural, demographic and psychological aspects of security and privacy into future research so that the threat landscape can be better understood.

REFERENCES

Acquisti, A., & Grossklags, J. (2003, May). Losses, gains, and hyperbolic discounting: An experimental approach to information security attitudes and behavior. In *Proceedings of 2nd Annual Workshop on Economics and Information Security-WEIS* (Vol. 3). Academic Press.

Agichtein, E., Castillo, C., Donato, D., Gionis, A., & Mishne, G. (2008). Finding high-quality content in social media. In *Proceedings of the 2008 International Conference on Web Search and Data Mining* (pp. 183-194). ACM.

Alaboodi, S. S. (2007). *Towards evaluating security implementations using the information security maturity model*. ISMM.

Albert, A., & Hersinta, H. (2013). Shopping on social networking sites: A study on Facebook consumers' psychological characteristics. *Journal Communication Spectrum*, 2(2).

Anderson, C. L., & Agarwal, R. (2010). Practicing safe computing: A multi method empirical examination of home computer user security behavioral intentions. *Management Information Systems Quarterly*, 34(3).

Anderson, J. M. (2003). Why we need a new definition of information security. *Computers & Security*, 22(4), 308–313. doi:10.1016/S0167-4048(03)00407-3

Baldwin, D. A. (1997). The concept of security. *Review of International Studies*, 23(01), 5–26. doi:10.1017/S0260210597000053 PMID:10164688

BBC. (2012). *Arrest over 'cyber-attack' on Theresa May and home office*. Retrieved March 20, 2014, from http://www.bbc.co.uk/news/uk-20217968

Bellman, S., Johnson, E. J., Kobrin, S. J., & Lohse, G. L. (2004). International differences in information privacy concerns: A global survey of consumers. *The Information Society*, 20(5), 313–324. doi:10.1080/01972240490507956

Berger, H., & Thomas, C. (2014, January). SMEs: Social media marketing performance. In *Proceedings of the 8th International Conference on Knowledge Management in Organizations* (pp. 411-422). Springer Netherlands.

Bergeron, E. (2000). The difference between security and privacy. In *Proceedings of Joint Workshop on Mobile Web Privacy WAP Forum & World Wide Web Consortium*. Retrieved March 23, 2014, from http://www.w3.org/P3P/mobile-privacy-ws/papers/zks.html

Berry, H., Guillén, M. F., & Zhou, N. (2010). An institutional approach to cross-national distance. *Journal of International Business Studies, 41*(9), 1460–1480. doi:10.1057/jibs.2010.28

Bettman, J. R., Luce, M. F., & Payne, J. W. (1998). Constructive consumer choice processes. *The Journal of Consumer Research, 25*(3), 187–217. doi:10.1086/209535

Bhimani, A. (1996). Securing the commercial Internet. *Communications of the ACM, 39*(6), 29–35. doi:10.1145/228503.228509

Bishop, M. (2003). What is computer security? *IEEE Security & Privacy, 1*(1), 67–69. doi:10.1109/MSECP.2003.1176998

Brettabz. (2011). Company 'held to ransom' by cyber hacker. *All Media Scotland*. Retrieved August 25, 2014, from http://www.allmediascotland.com/media_releases/28899/held-to-ransom

Brown, M. R., & Muchira, R. (2004). Investigating the relationship between internet privacy concerns and online purchase behavior. *Journal of Electronic Commerce Research, 5*(1), 62–70.

BusinessTech. (2013). *Cyber security predictions 2013*. Retrieved August 8, 2014, from http://businesstech.co.za/news/columns/27669/cyber-security-predictions-2013/

Cabinet Office. (2010). *A strong Britain in an age of uncertainty: The national security strategy*. Retrieved August 25, 2014 from http://www.cabinetoffice.gov.uk/sites/default/files/resources/national-security-strategy.pdf

Calder, A. (2011). Sharpen penetration tests to foil cybercrime. *ZDNet*. Retrieved August 25, 2014 from http://www.zdnet.co.uk/news/security-management/2011/03/20/sharpen-penetration-tests-to-foil-cybercrime-40092180/

Campbell, K., Gordon, L. A., Loeb, M. P., & Zhou, L. (2003). The economic cost of publicly announced information security breaches: Empirical evidence from the stock market. *Journal of Computer Security, 11*(3), 431–448.

Casprini, E., & Di Minin, A. (2013). *The social media revolution: Strategies and attitudes towards the rise of an enabling technology* (No. 201302). Academic Press.

Caudill, E. M., & Murphy, P. E. (2000). Consumer online privacy: Legal and ethical issues. *Journal of Public Policy & Marketing, 19*(1), 7–19. doi:10.1509/jppm.19.1.7.16951

Cavusoglu, H., Mishra, B., & Raghunathan, S. (2004). The effect of internet security breach announcements on market value: Capital market reactions for breached firms and internet security developers. *International Journal of Electronic Commerce, 9*(1), 70–104.

Chen, Y. H., & Barnes, S. (2007). Initial trust and online buyer behaviour. *Industrial Management & Data Systems, 107*(1), 21–36. doi:10.1108/02635570710719034

Cho, H. (2010). Determinants of behavioral responses to online privacy: The effects of concern, risk beliefs, self-efficacy, and communication sources on self-protection strategies. *Journal of Information Privacy & Security, 6*(1).

Ciccarelli, S. (2012). Russian arrested for cyberattacks on Amazon. *NBC News*. Retrieved March 20, 2014, from http://www.nbcnews.com/id/48291470/ns/technology_and_science-security/t/russian-arrested-cyberattacks-amazon/

Cohen, J. E. (2003). DRM and privacy. *Communications of the ACM, 46*(4), 46–49. doi:10.1145/641205.641230

Computer Business Review. (2011a). *Nasdaq confirms security breach, denies customer data leak.* Retrieved February 10, 2014, from http://security.cbronline.com/news/nasdaq-confirms-security-breach-denies-customer-data-leak-070211

Computer Business Review. (2011b). *Italian government site attacked: ANSA.* Retrieved February 10, 2014, from http://www.cbronline.com/news/italian-government-site-attacked-ansa-070211

Constantin, L. (2013). Fake social media ID duped security-aware IT guys. *IT World.* Retrieved January 04, 2014, from http://www.pcworld.com/article/2059940/fake-social-media-id-duped-securityaware-it-guys.html

Constantinides, E., & Lorenzo-Romero, C. (2013). Social networking sites as business tool: A study of user behavior. In *Business process management* (pp. 221–240). Springer Berlin Heidelberg. doi:10.1007/978-3-642-28409-0_9

Coopamootoo, P. L., & Ashenden, D. (2011). Designing usable online privacy mechanisms: What can we learn from real world behaviour? In Privacy and identity management for life (pp. 311-324). Springer Berlin Heidelberg.

Culnan, M. J. (2000). Protecting privacy online: Is self-regulation working? *Journal of Public Policy & Marketing, 19*(1), 20–26. doi:10.1509/jppm.19.1.20.16944

Dhillon, G., & Backhouse, J. (2000). Technical opinion: Information system security management in the new millennium. *Communications of the ACM, 43*(7), 125–128. doi:10.1145/341852.341877

Dhillon, G., & Backhouse, J. (2001). Current directions in IS security research: Towards socio-organizational perspectives. *Information Systems Journal, 11*(2), 127–153. doi:10.1046/j.1365-2575.2001.00099.x

Dinev, T., & Hart, P. (2004). Internet privacy concerns and their antecedents-measurement validity and a regression model. *Behaviour & Information Technology, 23*(6), 413–422. doi:10.1080/01449290410001715723

Dumas, M. B. (2012). *Diving into the bitstream: Information technology meets society in a digital world.* Routledge.

Ellison, N. B., Steinfield, C., & Lampe, C. (2007). The benefits of Facebook "friends": Social capital and college students' use of online social network sites. *Journal of Computer-Mediated Communication, 12*(4), 1143–1168. doi:10.1111/j.1083-6101.2007.00367.x

Essinger, J. (2001). *Internet trust and security: The way ahead.* Addison-Wesley.

Fogel, J., & Nehmad, E. (2009). Internet social network communities: Risk taking, trust, and privacy concerns. *Computers in Human Behavior, 25*(1), 153–160. doi:10.1016/j.chb.2008.08.006

Foxman, E. R., & Kilcoyne, P. (1993). Information technology, marketing practice, and consumer privacy: Ethical issues. *Journal of Public Policy & Marketing,* 106–119.

Gaines, L. K., & Miller, R. L. (2009). *Criminal justice in action* (5th ed.). Thomson Wadsworth.

Gastaldo, E. (2010a). *MySpace leaks user data, too: But, apparently, it's not quite as bad as Facebook.* Retrieved February 10, 2014, from http://www.newser.com/story/103626/myspace-leaks-user-data-too.html

Gastaldo, E. (2010b). *Congress has some questions for Zuckerberg: Two representatives get involved in the latest privacy breach.* Retrieved February 10, 2014, from http://www.newser.com/story/103258/congress-has-some-questions-for-zuckerberg.html

Gastaldo, E. (2010c). *Google: We accidentally grabbed emails, passwords: Street view privacy flap worse than reported.* Retrieved February 10, 2014, from http://www.newser.com/story/103636/google-we-accidentally-grabbed-emails-passwords.html

Gauzente, C. (2004). Web merchants' privacy and security statements: How reassuring are they for consumers? A two-sided approach. *Journal of Electronic Commerce Research, 5*(3), 181–198.

Gefen, D., Karahanna, E., & Straub, D. W. (2003). Trust and TAM in online shopping: An integrated model. *Management Information Systems Quarterly, 27*(1), 51–90.

Glazer, R. (1991). Marketing in an information-intensive environment: Strategic implications of knowledge as an asset. *Journal of Marketing, 55*(4), 1–19. doi:10.2307/1251953

Gollmann, D. (1999). *Computer security.* John Wiley & Sons.

Goodwin, C. (1991). Privacy: Recognition of a consumer right. *Journal of Public Policy & Marketing*, 149–166.

Gordon, L. A., Loeb, M. P., & Sohail, T. (2010). Market value of voluntary disclosures concerning information security. *Management Information Systems Quarterly, 34*(3), 567–594.

Grabosky, P. N. (2001). Virtual criminality: Old wine in new bottles? *Social & Legal Studies, 10*(2), 243–249.

Gritzalis, S. (2004). Enhancing web privacy and anonymity in the digital era. *Information Management & Computer Security, 12*(3), 255–287. doi:10.1108/09685220410542615

Gupta, A., & Hammond, R. (2005). Information systems security issues and decisions for small businesses: An empirical examination. *Information Management & Computer Security, 13*(4), 297–310. doi:10.1108/09685220510614425

Gupta, B., Iyer, L. S., & Weisskirch, R. S. (2010). Facilitating global e-commerce: A comparison of consumers' willingness to disclose personal information online in the US and in India. *Journal of Electronic Commerce Research, 11*(1), 41–52.

Hargittai, E. (2007). Whose space? Differences among users and non-users of social network sites. *Journal of Computer-Mediated Communication, 13*(1), 276–297. doi:10.1111/j.1083-6101.2007.00396.x

Harrison McKnight, D., Choudhury, V., & Kacmar, C. (2002). The impact of initial consumer trust on intentions to transact with a web site: A trust building model. *The Journal of Strategic Information Systems, 11*(3), 297–323. doi:10.1016/S0963-8687(02)00020-3

Henkin, L. (1974). Privacy and autonomy. *Columbia Law Review, 74*(8), 1410–1433. doi:10.2307/1121541

Hickins, M. (2012). *The morning download: How Facebook could kill your business.* Retrieved April 21, 2014, from http://blogs.wsj.com/cio/2012/04/09/the-morning-download-how-facebook-could-kill-your-business/

Hinde, S. (2002). Security surveys spring crop. *Computers & Security, 21*(4), 310–321. doi:10.1016/S0167-4048(02)00404-2

Hoffman, D. L., Novak, T. P., & Peralta, M. (1999). Building consumer trust online. *Communications of the ACM, 42*(4), 80–85. doi:10.1145/299157.299175

Hsee, C. K., & Weber, E. U. (1999). Cross-national differences in risk preference and lay predictions. *Journal of Behavioral Decision Making, 12*(2), 165–179. doi:10.1002/(SICI)1099-0771(199906)12:2<165::AID-BDM316>3.0.CO;2-N

Hu, X., Wu, G., Wu, Y., & Zhang, H. (2010). The effects of web assurance seals on consumers' initial trust in an online vendor: A functional perspective. *Decision Support Systems, 48*(2), 407–418. doi:10.1016/j.dss.2009.10.004

Im, G. P., & Baskerville, R. L. (2005). A longitudinal study of information system threat categories: The enduring problem of human error. *ACM SIGMIS Database, 36*(4), 68–79. doi:10.1145/1104004.1104010

Infosecurity. (2013). *Thanks to a false sense of security, small businesses are skipping cyber-protection.* Retrieved August 25, 2014, from http://www.infosecurity-magazine.com/view/35374/thanks-to-a-false-sense-of-security-small-businesses-are-skipping-cyberprotection/

Jamal, K., Maier, M., & Sunder, S. (2005). Enforced standards versus evolution by general acceptance: A comparative study of e-commerce privacy disclosure and practice in the United States and the United Kingdom. *Journal of Accounting Research, 43*(1), 73–96. doi:10.1111/j.1475-679x.2004.00163.x

Jarvenpaa, S. L., Tractinsky, N., & Saarinen, L. (1999). Consumer trust in an internet store: A cross-cultural validation. *Journal of Computer-Mediated Communication, 5*(2).

Jarvenpaa, S. L., Tractinsky, N., & Saarinen, L. (2000). Consumer trust in an internet store: A cross-cultural validation. *Journal of Computer-Mediated Communication, 5*(2).

Jensen, C., & Potts, C. (2004, April). Privacy policies as decision-making tools: An evaluation of online privacy notices. In *Proceedings of the SIGCHI Conference on Human Factors in Computing Systems* (pp. 471-478). ACM. doi:10.1145/985692.985752

Johnston, A. C., & Warkentin, M. (2010). Fear appeals and information security behaviors: An empirical study. *Management Information Systems Quarterly, 34*(3), 549–566.

Kaplan, A. M., & Haenlein, M. (2010). Users of the world, unite! The challenges and opportunities of social media. *Business Horizons, 53*(1), 59–68. doi:10.1016/j.bushor.2009.09.003

Kaplan, D. (2011). Earthquake and tsunami breed web scams, malware. *SC Magazine*. Retrieved August 25, 2014 from http://www.scmagazineus.com/earthquake-and-tsunami-breed-web-scams-malware/article/198195/

Katsikas, S. K. (2006). Information security. In *Proceedings of 9th International Conference.* ISC.

Katyal, N. K. (2001). Criminal law in cyberspace. *University of Pennsylvania Law Review, 149*(4), 1003–1114. doi:10.2307/3312990

Koved, L., Nadalin, A., Nagaratnam, N., Pistoia, M., & Shrader, T. (2001). Security challenges for enterprise java in an e-business environment. *IBM Systems Journal, 40*(1), 130–152. doi:10.1147/sj.401.0130

Kritzinger, E., & Smith, E. (2008). Information security management: An information security retrieval and awareness model for industry. *Computers & Security, 27*(5), 224–231. doi:10.1016/j.cose.2008.05.006

Kumar, K. A., & Rao, D. C. B. N. (2014). Impact of social media marketing on business world. *International Journal of Logistics & Supply Chain Management Perspectives*, *2*(4), 504–508.

Landwehr, C. E. (2001). Computer security. *International Journal of Information Security*, *1*(1), 3–13. doi:10.1007/s102070100003

Latif, L. (2011). Anti-hacking firm RSA gets hacked. *The Inquirer*. Retrieved August 25, 2014, from http://www.theinquirer.net/inquirer/news/2035368/anti-hacking-firm-rsa-hacked?WT.rss_f=&WT.rss_a=Antihacking+firm+RSA+gets+hacked

Lee, M. K., & Turban, E. (2001). A trust model for consumer internet shopping. *International Journal of Electronic Commerce*, *6*, 75–92.

Lenhart, A., Purcell, K., Smith, A., & Zickuhr, K. (2010). *Social media & mobile internet use among teens and young adults. millennials*. Pew Internet & American Life Project.

Lewis, R. D. (2006). *When cultures collide: Leading, teamworking and managing across the globe*. Nicholas Brealey.

Leyden, J. (2011). York Uni exposes students' private info. *The Register*. Retrieved August 25, 2014, from http://www.theregister.co.uk/2011/03/16/york_uni_student_data_breach/

Lighty, T., & Wong, W. (2012). Chicago man, 27, charged in cyber attack. *Chicago Tribune*. Retrieved March 20, 2013, from http://articles.chicagotribune.com/2012-03-06/business/chi-chicago-raid-linked-to-hacking-arrests-20120306_1_cyber-attack-lulzsec-antisec

Liu, C., Marchewka, J. T., Lu, J., & Yu, C. S. (2004). Beyond concern: A privacy–trust–behavioral intention model of electronic commerce. *Information & Management*, *42*(1), 127–142. doi:10.1016/j.im.2004.01.002

Mahadevan, B. (2000). Business models for internet based e commerce: ananatomy. *California Management Review*, *42*(4), 55–69. doi:10.2307/41166053

Mangold, W. G., & Faulds, D. J. (2009). Social media: The new hybrid element of the promotion mix. *Business Horizons*, *52*(4), 357–365. doi:10.1016/j.bushor.2009.03.002

Marwick, A. E., & boyd, . (2011). I tweet honestly, I tweet passionately: Twitter users, context collapse, and the imagined audience. *New Media & Society*, *13*(1), 114–133. doi:10.1177/1461444810365313

McAfee. (2013). McAfee finds majority of small business owners have false sense of security. *McAfee for Business*. Retrieved August 25, 2014 from http://www.mcafee.com/uk/about/news/2013/q4/20131030-01.aspx

McCarthy, J., Rowley, J., Ashworth, C. J., & Pioch, E. (2014). Managing brand presence through social media: The case of UK football clubs. *Internet Research*, *24*(2), 181–204. doi:10.1108/IntR-08-2012-0154

McDaniel, G. (1994). *IBM dictionary of computing*. McGraw-Hill, Inc.

McLoughlin, C., Meyricke, R., & Burgess, J. (2009). Bullies in cyberspace: How rural and regional Australian youth perceive the problem of cyberbullying and its impact. *Improving Equity in Rural Education*, 178.

McSweeney, B. (2002). Hofstede's model of national cultural differences and their consequences: A triumph of faith-a failure of analysis. *Human Relations*, *55*(1), 89–118. doi:10.1177/0018726702055001602

Mills, E. (2010). *Study: Facebook joins PayPal, eBay as popular phishing target*. Retrieved February 10, 2011, from http://news.cnet.com/8301-27080_3-20004819-245.html

Milne, G. R., & Culnan, M. J. (2004). Strategies for reducing online privacy risks: Why consumers read (or don't read) online privacy notices. *Journal of Interactive Marketing, 18*(3), 15–29. doi:10.1002/dir.20009

Milne, G. R., & Gordon, M. E. (1993). Direct mail privacy-efficiency trade-offs within an implied social contract framework. *Journal of Public Policy & Marketing*, 206–215.

Minihane, J. (2011). *New PlayStation security breach: 93,000 accounts hit.* Retrieved November 27, 2010, from http://www.t3.com/news/new-playstation-security-breach-93000-accounts-hit

Miyazaki, A. D., & Fernandez, A. (2001). Consumer perceptions of privacy and security risks for online shopping. *The Journal of Consumer Affairs, 35*(1), 27–44. doi:10.1111/j.1745-6606.2001.tb00101.x

Moitra, S. D. (2005). Developing policies for cybercrime. *European Journal of Crime Criminal Law and Criminal Justice, 13*(3), 435–464. doi:10.1163/1571817054604119

Moor, J. H. (1997). Towards a theory of privacy in the information age. *Computers & Society, 27*(3), 27–32. doi:10.1145/270858.270866

BBC News. (2011). *Play.com warns of customer e-mail security breach.* Retrieved August 8, 2014, from http://www.bbc.co.uk/news/technology-12819330

Oreskovic, A. (2010). *Google says its cars grabbed emails, passwords.* Retrieved February 19, 2011, from http://www.reuters.com/article/2010/10/22/us-google-idUSTRE69L4KW20101022

Palme, J., & Berglund, M. (2002). *Anonymity on the internet.* Academic Press.

Parasuraman, A., & Zinkhan, G. M. (2002). Marketing to and serving customers through the internet: An overview and research agenda. *Journal of the Academy of Marketing Science, 30*(4), 286–295. doi:10.1177/009207002236906

Park, C., & Jun, J. K. (2003). A cross-cultural comparison of internet buying behavior: Effects of internet usage, perceived risks, and innovativeness. *International Marketing Review, 20*(5), 534–553. doi:10.1108/02651330310498771

Peterson, R. A., Balasubramanian, S., & Bronnenberg, B. J. (1997). Exploring the implications of the internet for consumer marketing. *Journal of the Academy of Marketing Science, 25*(4), 329–346. doi:10.1177/0092070397254005

Petty, R. D. (2000). Marketing without consent: Consumer choice and costs, privacy, and public policy. *Journal of Public Policy & Marketing, 19*(1), 42–53. doi:10.1509/jppm.19.1.42.16940

Poon, S., & Swatman, P. (1999). An exploratory study of small business Internet commerce issues. *Information & Management, 35*(1), 9–18. doi:10.1016/S0378-7206(98)00079-2

Powers, M. (1996). A cognitive access definition of privacy. *Law and Philosophy, 15*(4), 369–386. doi:10.1007/BF00127211

PRLog Press Release. (2011). *Eurostat releases figures on internet security.* Retrieved August 23, 2014, from http://www.prlog.org/11285632-eurostat-releases-figures-on-internet-security.html

Purao, S., & Campbell, B. (1998). Critical concerns for small business electronic commerce: Some reflections based on interviews of small business owners. In *Proceedings of Americas Conference on Information Systems* (AMCIS). Academic Press.

Quelch, J. A., & Klein, L. R. (1996). The internet and international marketing. *Sloan Management Review*, *37*(3).

Ranganathan, C., & Ganapathy, S. (2002). Key dimensions of business-to-consumer web sites. *Information & Management*, *39*(6), 457–465. doi:10.1016/S0378-7206(01)00112-4

Rose, C. (2011). The security implications of ubiquitous social media. *International Journal of Management & Information Systems*, *15*(1).

Safko, L. (2010). *The social media bible: Tactics, tools, and strategies for business success*. John Wiley & Sons.

Schneier, B. (2010). A taxonomy of social networking data. *IEEE Security & Privacy*, *8*(4), 88–88. doi:10.1109/MSP.2010.118

Shelke, P., & Badiye, A. (2013). Social networking: Its uses and abuses. *Research Journal of Forensic Sciences*, *1*(1), 2–7.

Shi, Z., Rui, H., & Whinston, A. B. (2014). Content sharing in a social broadcasting environment: Evidence from twitter. *Management Information Systems Quarterly*, *38*(1), 123–142.

Smith, S., Winchester, D., Bunker, D., & Jamieson, R. (2010). Circuits of power: A study of mandated compliance to an information systems security de jure standard in a government organization. *Management Information Systems Quarterly*, *34*(3), 463–486.

SOPHOS Security Trends Report. (2013). *Social networking security threats*. Retrieved March 20, 2013, from http://www.sophos.com/en-us/security-news-trends/security-trends/social-networking-security-threats/twitter-linkedin-and-google-plus.aspx

Stafford, K. (2011). University keeps quiet on recent data heist. *The Eastern Echo*. Retrieved August 25, 2014, from http://www.easternecho.com/index.php/article/2011/03/university_keeps_quiet_on_recent_data_heist

Tavani, H. T. (2000). *Privacy and the internet*. Retrieved March 24, 2011, from http://www.bc.edu/bc_org/avp/law/st_org/iptf/commentary/content/2000041901.html

Teo, T. S., & Choo, W. Y. (2001). Assessing the impact of using the Internet for competitive intelligence. *Information & Management*, *39*(1), 67–83. doi:10.1016/S0378-7206(01)00080-5

Teo, T. S., & Liu, J. (2007). Consumer trust in e-commerce in the United States, Singapore and China. *Omega*, *35*(1), 22–38. doi:10.1016/j.omega.2005.02.001

Traynor, M. (2003). Anonymity and the internet. In *Patents, copyright, trademarks, and literary property course handbook series*, (pp. 993-998). Academic Press.

Tsikriktsis, N. (2002). Does culture influence web site quality expectations? An empirical study. *Journal of Service Research*, *5*(2), 101–112. doi:10.1177/109467002237490

Vogel, T. (2011) Cyber attacks launched on EU computer systems. *European Voice*. Retrieved August 25, 2014 from http://www.europeanvoice.com/article/cyber-attacks-launched-on-eu-computer-systems/

Walczuch, R., Van Braven, G., & Lundgren, H. (2000). Internet adoption barriers for small firms in The Netherlands. *European Management Journal*, *18*(5), 561–572. doi:10.1016/S0263-2373(00)00045-1

Walker, R. (2006). *The English law of privacy - An evolving human right*. Retrieved March 27, 2013, from http://www.supremecourt.gov.uk/docs/speech_100825.pdf

Ward, M. (2006). *Tips to help you stay safe online*. Retrieved March 25, 2011, from http://news.bbc.co.uk/1/hi/technology/5414992.stm

Weir, G. R., Toolan, F., & Smeed, D. (2011). The threats of social networking: Old wine in new bottles? *Information Security Technical Report*, *16*(2), 38–43. doi:10.1016/j.istr.2011.09.008

Whitman, M., & Mattord, H. (2010). *Principles of information security*. Cengage Learning.

Willard, N. E. (2007). *Cyberbullying and cyberthreats: Responding to the challenge of online social aggression, threats, and distress*. Research Press.

Wong, A. (2011). *Attacking a growing cyber terrorism threat*. Retrieved March 24, 2011, from http://www.theaustralian.com.au/australian-it/attacking-a-growing-cyber-terrorism-threat/story-e6frgakx-1226025058588

Yamagishi, T., & Yamagishi, M. (1994). Trust and commitment in the United States and Japan. *Motivation and Emotion*, *18*(2), 129–166. doi:10.1007/BF02249397

Yar, M. (2005). The novelty of 'cyberthreat': An assessment in light if routine activity theory. *European Journal of Criminology*, *2*(4), 407–427. doi:10.1177/147737080556056

Zakaria, N., Stanton, J. M., & Sarkar-Barney, S. T. (2003). Designing and implementing culturally-sensitive IT applications: The interaction of culture values and privacy issues in the Middle East. *Information Technology & People*, *16*(1), 49–75. doi:10.1108/09593840310463023

ADDITIONAL READING

Al-Dwairi, R. M. (2013). E-Commerce Web Sites Trust Factors: An Empirical Approach. *Contemporary Engineering Sciences*, *6*(1), 1–7.

Aral, S., Dellarocas, C., & Godes, D. (2013). Introduction to the Special Issue—Social Media and Business Transformation: A Framework for Research. *Information Systems Research*, *24*(1), 3–13. doi:10.1287/isre.1120.0470

Benassi, P. (1999). TRUSTe: An online privacy seal program. *Communications of the ACM*, *42*(2), 56–59. doi:10.1145/293411.293461

Byramjee, F., & Korgaonkar, P. (2013). A review of the role of consumers' transaction costs in the traditional and online shopping environments. *Review of Business Research*, *13*(3), 41–46.

Choi, K. (2008). Computer crime victimisation an integrated theory: an empirical assessment. *International Journal of Cyber criminology*, *2*, 308-333.

Delafrooz, N., Paim, L. H., & Khatibi, A. (2011). Understanding consumer's internet purchase intention in Malaysia. *African Journal of Business Management*, *5*(3), 2837–2846.

Dumas, B. M. (2012). *Diving Into the Bitstream: Information Technology Meets Society in a Digital World*. Routledge.

Eastin, M. S., & LaRose, R. (2000). Internet Self-Efficacy and the Psychology of the Digital Divide. *Journal of Computer-Mediated Communication*, *6*(1).

Greunen, D. V., Herselman, M. E., & Niekerk, J. V. (2010). Implementation of regulation-based e-procurement in the Eastern Cape provincial administration. *African Journal of Business Management*, *4*(17), 3655–3665.

Guitton, C. (2013). Cyber insecurity as a national threat: Overreaction from Germany, France and the UK? *European Security*, *22*(1), 21–35. doi:1 0.1080/09662839.2012.749864

Hutchings, A. (2013). Hacking and Fraud Qualitative Analysis of Online Offending and Victimization. *Global Criminology: Crime and Victimization in a Globalized Era*, 93.

Joinson, A. (Ed.). (2007). *Oxford handbook of internet psychology*. Oxford University Press.

Mansell, R. (Ed.). (2007). *Handbook of Information and Communication Technologies*. Oxford Handbooks Online.

Mark. Sauter, & Carafano, J. J. (2005). *Homeland security: a complete guide to understanding, preventing, and surviving terrorism*. McGraw-Hill.

Mitnick, K. (2011). *Ghost in the Wires: My Adventures as the World's Most Wanted Hacker*. Hachette Digital, Inc.

Mitnick, K. D., & Simon, W. L. (2001). *The art of deception: Controlling the human element of security*. Wiley.com.

Odom, M. D., Kumar, A., & Saunders, L. (2002). Web assurance seals: How and why they influence consumers' decisions. *Journal of Information Systems*, *16*(2), 231–250. doi:10.2308/jis.2002.16.2.231

Orito, Y., Murata, K., & Fukuta, Y. (2013). Do online privacy policies and seals affect corporate trustworthiness and reputation? *International Review of Information Ethics*, *19*, 52–65.

Pedneault, A., & Beauregard, E. (2013). Routine activities and time use: A latent profile approach to sexual offenders' lifestyles. *Sexual Abuse*, *26*, 1–24. PMID:23434572

Peikari, H. R. (2010). Does nationality matter in the B2C environment? Results from a two nation study. *Communications in Computer and Information Science*, *92*, 149–159. doi:10.1007/978-3-642-15717-2_17

Rauch, J. E. (2001). Business and social networks in international trade. *Journal of Economic Literature*, *39*(4), 1177–1203. doi:10.1257/jel.39.4.1177

Sia, C. L., Lim, K. H., Leung, K., Lee, M. K., Huang, W. W., & Benbasat, I. (2009). Web strategies to promote internet shopping: Is cultural-customization needed? *Management Information Systems Quarterly*, *33*(3), 491–512.

KEY TERMS AND DEFINITIONS

Business Organizations: Organizations existing for profit making purposes.

Information Security: Protection of information.

Legal Frameworks: Laws dictating boundaries within which individuals/organizations can operate.

National Culture: Values, beliefs, and norms of people belonging to a geographic region.

Non-Profit Organizations: Organizations whose main purpose does not involve generating profits.

Online Information Privacy: Right to keep personal and organizational information private and inaccessible by unauthorized parties.

Online Users: Individuals or organizations using the Internet and the World Wide Web.

Social Networking Sites (SNS): Collection of individuals using the internet and online technologies to interact.

Chapter 5
Abuse of the Social Media Brain:
Implications for Media Producers and Educators

Fritz Kohle
University of Edinburgh, UK

Sony Jalarajan Raj
MacEwan University, Canada

ABSTRACT

Despite the criticism in the mainstream press regarding the use and abuse of digital and social media, its use has been increasingly encouraged and supported in schools and universities. This chapter examines the social media behaviour of techy-savvy undergraduate students at NHTV, University of Applied Sciences, Breda, The Netherlands, from the perspective of an independent documentary producer and educator, to determine whether any correlation between the amount of time spent online and the use of cognitive functions exists. Media producers require an audience capable of critical thought, and teachers educate future audiences to acquire the necessary cognitive skills. Hence, the chapter analyses how the viewer's cognitive functions impaired by the use of social and digital media affects the reception of media products. This further leads to a more critical concern about the educators' response to the challenges provided by social and digital media.

INTRODUCTION

In some recent research articles, Kohle and Cuevas (Kohle, 2012; Kohle & Cuevas, 2012; 2010) demonstrated that digital natives have and continue to adapt their viewing habits to social and digital media, challenging traditional content development, production and distribution methods. Social media marketing has become a buzz word—users, companies, charities and governments, all are exploring the use of social media. As happened during previous 'information revolutions', social media users and content creators are still in the process of developing the social media narrative. They are not only learning how to access social media networks (SNS), they are increasingly developing the capability to critically process online information, becoming social media liter-

DOI: 10.4018/978-1-4666-7401-1.ch005

ate. For example, social media has become and remains instrumental in movements such as the Occupy movement and the Arab Spring. The digital and social media revolution has become a game-changer on a global scale and is the most recent in the evolution of previous 'information explosions', such as the invention of broadcasting and print technologies, the invention of the alphabet, and language itself.

Recently, the negative aspects of social media moved into the focus of the mainstream press. Surveillance of social and digital media was highlighted once more by Edward Snowden (Branigan, 2013). Agencies such as SS8 (2011) and Glimmerglass (2011) are well described regarding their data collection activities on behalf of government and private clients. Intelligence Support Systems for Lawful Interception (ISS, 2013) offer a platform for companies such as SS8 and Glimmerglass to present their latest social media tools in intelligence gathering. Conferences take place across the globe and services offered include, but are not limited to: cyber security and lawful interception of data, as well as submarine cable landing stations, offering access to submarine optical cables that support millions of voice calls and internet traffic. SS8 specializes in 'accurate reconstruction of intercepted voice, text and internet activity' and the 'correlation of intelligence from Internet Protocol Data and Call Detail Records to full communications content' (SS8, 2013). How this can be done without violating the 1st amendment of the US constitution is debatable, not to mention international and national law for the rest of the world.

The topic of social media surveillance abuse on its own requires further investigation, but this would go beyond the scope of this paper, which does not focuses on social media surveillance and security issues, but on the impact of social media on the development of cognitive skills of digital natives and place it into a historical as well as social theory context.

BACKGROUND

This paper is relevant to media producers who continue to work in their profession and who have an interest in teaching. Familiarity with Marshall Mcluhan's (1995) media theory and Briggs & Burke's (2009) history of media is recommended. Macluhan argues that the "medium is the message". It is the media system itself which transforms society. Evidence suggests that the use and abuse of social media also has a detrimental impact on the development of cognitive skills among digital natives and immigrants alike. (Spitzer, 2012) At the same time digital natives are challenged to acquire new skills to navigate social and digital media; skills needed to become literate in the use of a new media technology, which in itself is influencing user behavior and the way content is produced. Data suggests that not only behavior is affected; the brain itself also undergoes significant changes.

Social media is not only the latest 'information explosion' in a series of evolutionary steps, since the invention of language (Kohle, 2013); it differs considerably from previous information explosion events, such as print and broadcast technologies in speed of information dissemination. This was discussed by Mcluhan, though the speed with which this new technology evolves and the extent to which it encompasses previous media technologies is beyond the scope envisaged by Mcluhan. Social and digital media are a paradigm shift when compared to previous information explosions, such as the invention of writing and the alphabet.

History teaches us that the introduction of new technology also brings with it undesirable side effects. Social media is no exception to this: it not only challenges the way media productions are developed, produced and distributed – evidence suggests social media is also playing a role in the way audiences develop their cognitive skills. With regards to content for social and digital media, we take into account Mcluhan's idea on how content for new media originates from yesterday's technology. For example: content for TV is print; content for print is writing. We take a closer look at Mcluhan and examine his ideas within the context of social media. We then conclude this paper exploring uses and abuses of social media among digital natives from the perspective of a media producer and educator.

Research Methods

We critically examined the impact social and digital media has on cognitive functions among a group of digital natives and undergraduate students aged 18-22 at NHTV, University of Applied Sciences, Breda, Netherlands. A group of 77 undergraduate students was surveyed using a multiple-choice questionnaire to investigate their social media behaviour. The survey was designed to provide insight into the use of cognitive functions such as memory and orientation. All 77 students completed the survey.

We conducted a literature review of the arguments provided by critics, such as neuro-surgeon Prof. Dr. Manfred Spitzer (2012), as well as claims by South Korean researchers who have found evidence suggesting a correlation between the early onset of dementia among South Korean digital natives and the use of digital and social media. We further investigate phenomena such as cyber bullying and Facebook depression by reviewing relevant papers in the field. We then compare the outcome of our survey to arguments presented by critics, discuss the implications for documentary filmmakers within the context of Mcluhan's ideas on media theory, and summarize our findings accordingly.

Survey Results

The author of this study observed viewing habits of digital natives since 2009, following the Occupy movement, Arab Spring, describing the impact social media have had on digital natives

and immigrants alike, as the ultimate information explosion. Abuse of social and digital media did not escape the authors' attention, i.e. use of social and digital media by agencies such as the NSA. In this chapter, we discuss the outcome of our survey, research into the impact of social media on cognitive functions and media theory. The classical definition of dementia is based on the loss of cognitive functions, memory and orientation (WHO ICD-10 Classification of Mental and Behavioral Disorders, 1992). Survey questions were designed to explore memory relating to literature read, news headlines noted, documentaries seen, and the ability to relate the campus location of NHTV to the Breda city centre. Our survey focused on the claims students made without judging the validity of the content of their claims. For example, it was not important for the survey outcome if students claimed they remembered the news headline: "Obama stops clandestine NSA internet surveillance", even if this news headline at the time of writing this paper was factually incorrect. The survey only captured the student's claim that they remembered something. We also added a control question, such as "What did you have for lunch yesterday?". If students were dement at the time of taking the survey, the answer to that question would more likely than not elude survey participants.

Only 4 out of 77 students participating in the survey stated that they spent less than 2 hours per day online. This small group claimed that they had the least difficulty staying focused during class and staying off-line during lectures. In stark contrast, 7 students claimed to spend 10 hours or more online per day: 6 students from this group stated that they had difficulties staying off-line during class and tutorials. 3 of the 4 of students claimed to spend less than 2 hours online and remembered the last documentary they saw. Only 4 of the 7 students claiming to spend 10 or more hours a day online remembered the last documentary they saw. Data suggests that more online time using social media does not correlate with improved memory.

However, not all results were this clear. 6 of the 7 students from the group that spent 10 hours online, stated that they remembered news headlines, compared to 3 out of 4 students who claimed to spend 2 hours or less online per day. In this case the 10-hour online group's results were similar to that of the 2-hour online group. This could be due to a number of reasons, such as size of the sample group and cultural differences within an international setting. Another reason could be that students 'skim' news headlines using various sources, meaning that they are aware of newsworthy events but without do not have deeper knowledge of them. It would be desirable to repeat this survey on a larger scale to investigate these two groups in more detail. We did not observe a statistically significant difference between sexes.

45 out of the 77 students stated that they spend between 3-5 hours online every day. 47% claim that they experience difficulties staying offline during lectures and tutorials. 35% do not remember the last documentary they saw, 88% do not remember the last day they spent without internet access, 71% do not remember the title of the last book they read, and 40% could not place the location of the university in relation to the city center of Breda. Based on the above, nearly half of the students in this group could be diagnosed with a mild form of dementia: a degree of memory loss interfering with every day activities, the main function affected being the learning of new material (WHO ICD-10 Classification of Mental and Behavioral Disorders, 1992).

Having said all that, 97% of students remembered their lunch the day before, an indication that dementia is not yet an issue for digital natives between the ages of 18-22. But it is debatable whether students are exercising and further developing their cognitive skills considering the survey outcomes. Data suggests that retention of literature recently read, daily news and events or documentaries seen, is not improving among this group of students by means of social and digital media. A small group of students who spent less than 2 hours online a day read more, are better informed, more focused and less distracted by social media in the classroom when compared to students who are online longer. Control questions indicate that students are not dement, but distraction from social media poses a real problem: the majority of students who are online between 3-5 hours a day find it difficult to remain offline during lectures, remain focused, remember news events, literature and documentaries seen, or even when they were last offline.

MAIN FOCUS OF THE CHAPTER

Cognitive Functions: Effects of Social and Digital Media on the Brain

Manufacturers of tablets and mobile devices are keen to expand their market reach, increasingly targeting children and teenagers for their products as existing markets reach saturation. Sandvik, Smordal and Osterud (2012) argue that the use of tablets improved language learning in a kindergarten setting. Their data suggests that digital tools such as iPads provide an opportunity for 'children to engage in useful language interaction', though it remains unclear how the use of tablets at such an early age influences brain development. Similar studies claim that children aged 3-5 developed considerable vocabulary and phonological awareness (Chiong & Shuler, 2010). Still, even proponents of digital tools claiming benefits in the development of language among 3-5 year olds are cautious and recommend further studies regarding this topic (Sandvik, Smordal & Osterud 2012).

Critics such as Manfred Spitzer (2012) and Psychiatrist Dr. Kim Dae-jin (Some teens are exhibiting signs of 'digital dementia', 2013) have described the early onset of dementia among social media users. They claim that digital and social media are hindering the normal development of cognitive functions in teenagers and adolescents.

Similar articles have appeared in other mainstream papers, highlighting concerns over the use of social and digital media (Digital Dementia on the rise, 2013; Ryall, 2012). Social and digital media may not only hinder the physical development of the brain, if used inappropriately; researchers in the field of education examined online social aggression and abusive behavior in Australia (Burgess & Mcloughlin, 2011). They claim that the consequences of cyber-bullying can be more severe than face-to-face bullying because the physical separation of victim and aggressor does not lead to an end of bullying. The recent increase in cyber-bullying and the consequent suicide of a number of teenagers brings this issue once again into the public domain (Gadkari, 2013; Arkin, 2013; Ensor, 2013; Warren & Quigley, 2013). The psychological aspects of online social aggression warrant further investigation.

If true, a growing number of digital natives are at risk of not being able to fully develop their cognitive skills, exposing them to the onset of dementia at an early age. Society as a whole will need to bear the moral and financial costs associated with an increase of dement citizens in the future. Media producers rely on audiences equipped with well-developed cognitive skills in order to encourage and stimulate critical thought on the topic presented.

Spitzer (2012) argues that the indiscriminate introduction of mobile devices and digital media into the classroom at an early age and during adolescence has a detrimental impact on the development of cognitive functions. As a neuro-scientist and brain surgeon, he found a spot in the German public highlight as one of the more vocal critics of social and digital media. His writing style can be construed as polarizing; nevertheless, he provides a well-constructed argument, not entirely against social and digital media per se.

Instead, he advocates a more thoughtful and responsible use of social media. We know too little about the impact of social media use in the class room and in kindergarten. Media use combined (TV, music, games, computer, books and cinema) averaged at 7:38 hours per day in the US in 2009 (Rideout, 2010). Consequences of this amount of media consumption are not frequently examined by industry-funded researchers for obvious reasons. The London School of Economics surveyed 25000 9-16 year olds from 25 European countries (Livingstone, Olafsson, & Staksrund, 2013). They concluded that digital natives frequently visit sites inappropriate for their age, lacking the skills to navigate SNS's safely.

In response to these considerable threats to the safety of young people and teenagers, the industry has responded with self-imposed strategies that aim to minimize these risks, though little is known about the effectiveness of these strategies. Strasburger, Jordan and Donnerstein (2010) published similar results, making concrete recommendations to schools, the entertainment and advertising industries, as well as researchers and government bodies, on how to deal with the consequences of social and digital media 'abuse'.

The importance of well-developed cognitive functions is also highlighted by Woollett and Macguire (2006, 2011) in their investigation into the role of the hippocampus, a part of the brain associated with memory. Taxi drivers who regularly studied to memorize London street maps to pass the London taxi driver exam showed a measurable increase in the size of the hippocampus. Critics such as Spitzer claim that social and digital media makes it too easy to not practice and develop cognitive functions. Spitzer explains that the descent into dementia at a later age is very much determined by how well an individual's brain developed during early, formative years: a person with well developed cognitive functions at his or her disposal is more likely to descend into dementia later in his or her life. Data suggests that lesser developed cognitive functions result in the early onset of dementia, though clearly more research is needed in this area.

His arguments are supported by reports from South Korean psychiatrists such as Kim Dae-Jin at Seoul's St. Mary's hospital (Baek Il-Hyun & Park Eun-Jee, 2012). South Korea's mobile device penetration is among the highest in the Western world (Media Trend Watch, 2012). Practitioners such as Kim Dae-Jin have noticed an increase in cases described as 'digital dementia': the deterioration of cognitive abilities not normally associated with the age group of digital natives. According to Baek Il-Hyun and Park Eun-Jee (2012), the South Korean Health Insurance Review & Assessment service also reported a significant increase in people suffering from cognitive problems since 2008. This increase correlates with the rise of the sale and use of mobile digital devices in South Korea.

Further evidence is provided by Zhou et al (2011), who measured the effects of internet addiction on the brain. Individuals addicted to being online are shown to have a different brain structure. After 50 hours of internet gaming, Lee Seung Seop collapsed and died of heart failure. Christakis (2010) concludes that parents and teachers are too complacent in dealing with this issue, and terms the separation of digital immigrants and natives the 'digital divide'. Those who need most guidance, namely digital natives, are cared for by digital immigrants who are unaware of the negative aspects of social and digital media.

Critics argue that social media discourages digital natives from developing their cognitive skills. The impact of learning on the brain and the consequent development of the hippocampus were already described by Wollett and Mcguire (2006, 2011). Digital natives are prone to 'outsource' information into the 'cloud' (Mell & Grance, 2011), their computer, laptop or mobile device, and it is reasonable to argue that they are not training their brain. For example, London taxi drivers could use a GPS based navigation system guiding them via the most suitable route to their destination. In turn, however, their hippocampus would be less developed, which, as critics claim, increases the likelihood of developing dementia earlier rather than later.

Data from our survey suggests that social and digital media do not improve cognitive functions, memory and orientation, especially when essential information is kept in a cloud instead of the brain. Social and digital media are part of a transformation process in society, and are physically measurable: South Korean and German researchers find that abuse of social and digital media have detrimental effects on the development of the brain (Spitzer, 2012).

The Medium is the Message: Or is It?

Social media can be compared to Mcluhan's famous light bulb analogy: the light bulb in itself does not have any content, but at night it illuminates an otherwise dark space for social activity. The internet, social, and digital media function very much in the same way: on their own, they have no content, but they have enabled users on an unprecedented, global scale to access and participate in a virtual space. It is reasonable to argue that this new online world is evolving into a global online collective consciousness.

Society is being transformed from a non-virtual world to encompass a virtual state, providing postmodern content via the social and digital media domain, which in itself is constantly changing: a key characteristic of post-modernity. Users no longer need to study and memorize a roadmap. This is accomplished by the mobile device instead. Perhaps this is the next evolutionary step. Dunbar (2003) describes the human brain's limitation in dealing with more than 200 social contacts, when compared to the brain of other hominids. Watkins (2010) submits that it became necessary for early man to overcome this limitation by cultural means; for example, monumentalism and storytelling. The development of language also had a major impact on the brain's structure (Corbalis, 2009)—it increased in size and led to the development of episodic memory as humans developed the ability for 'mental time travel' (Tulving, 2002). Language allowed us to tell stories that required an understanding of time: past, present and future. Or in narrative terms: a beginning, middle and end.

Briggs, Burke and Mcluhan teach us that previous media technologies played a significant role in the transformation of society and culture. We also learn that with the introduction of each new technology the human brain underwent significant changes. For example learning the London roadmap results in an increased hippocampus for London taxi drivers, a significant and measurable outcome attributed to practicing memory as a cognitive skill. Critics are also quick to highlight negative aspects regarding cyber bullying, Facebook suicides, internet addiction and their observations on the development of cognitive functions and the brain. But what if that is all part of a natural evolutionary cycle? What if we are supposed to 'outsource' information onto a cloud and share it with the world? What if the next evolutionary step for Homo Sapiens Sapiens is to develop a global collective consciousness located in the cloud? On the other hand, if dementia occurs as a result of under-developed cognitive skills as Spitzer claims, what kind of society are we looking forward to? How will outsourcing crucial information to the virtual cloud world prevent the onset of early dementia?

Mcluhan (1995) argues that the 'medium is the message'. He submits that it is the medium that transforms society rather than the message it carries. It is debatable whether or not media is causing transformation, or if it correlates regarding change. His ideas describe the transformative effect of media on cultural and social aspects of society. Evidence suggests that a correlation exists between the development of the brain and the way users engage with media. Jung's (1981) ideas on synchronicity could provide another perspective on media and 'Zeitgeist'. It is therefore reasonable to argue that the "medium being the message" not only plays a role in the transformation of society, but also a causal or correlative function in the development of the brain, a topic that warrants further investigation.

Mcluhan understood very well the nature of the beast. For example, he advised his son Eric not to expose his granddaughter Emily to "hours and hours of TV", as he considered TV to be a "vile drug which permeates the nervous system, especially the young" (Morrison, 2013). Spitzer and his South Korean counterparts present evidence that suggests that not only TV but social and digital media in particular have a detrimental effect on audiences. Jacobs (2011) points out that Mcluhan was prone to make popular statements such as this, using a variety of media platforms such as print and TV – the medium he despised so much. Jacobs rightly questions Mcluhan's credibility if on the one hand he claims that media as 'the extensions of man's consciousness …. [hold] the potential for realizing the anti-christ", yet in the same discussion proposes that "we're standing on the threshold of a liberating and exhilarating new world". How could anyone take Mcluhan seriously after such a 180 degree turnabout?

Nevertheless, many of Mcluhan's assertions are visible within the social and digital media domain. There is a case to support his claim that 'yesterday's technology' provides content in the social and digital media domain. For example, Mcluhan describes the message of the moving image as a transition from lineal connections to configurations. Previous information explosions such as print transformed a feudal society into a linear and conform society, which in turn paved the way for the French Revolution. He argues that content distributed by each new technology has its origins in the previous medium, for example the content of writing is speech that of print is writing, and so on. The key difference with social and digital media though is that it encompasses all previous forms of media in a virtual space: language, writing, print, film and interactivity.

For example, Jencks (2009) concludes that 'branded terrorism' could be considered a postmodern pre-announcement of murder, after discussing Lyotard (1992). Lyotard describes the characteristics of modernity vs. postmodernity in graphic detail. Auschwitz as a death camp was a highly structured mass-production place of murder, well organized, a well-kept secret, the epiphany of a modern, totalitarian society. G. W. Bush's pre-announced attack on Iraq, on the other hand, could be described as branded terrorism, the post-modern equivalent. Current events in Syria and the Obama administration's justification to intervene also fit this category. Mcluhan also observed that the introduction of each new technology speeds up cultural and social processes in society. The speed with which social and digital media has invaded real and virtual spaces confirm this. In fact, the speed with which social media evolves is such that by the time this paper is published, it may already be outdated. It is not surprising to observe an increase of 'old' messages being distributed via digital and social media, such as social aggression in the form of bullying, aptly named cyber-bullying as it takes place online.

Mcluhan provides a reasonable theory explaining how previous media technologies provide content for new ones. With the arrival of electronic media he foresaw the 'global village'. Social and digital media move beyond the scope of his vision; all pervasive content is reaching a global audience at an ever increasing speed, yet messages have remained the same. Previously, teenagers and adolescents were bullied at school and at home, either in person or by means of an anonymous note or letter.

Cyber-Bullying and Facebook Depression

The latest fashion among bullies today is to bully peers online. 'Facebook depression' and 'Cyber bullying' are known online phenomena. Moreno at al (2011) observe that out of some 200 students surveyed, 25% displayed depressive symptoms. 2.5% met the criteria for a major depressive episode (MDE).

Hannah Krasnova of the Institute of Information Systems, Berlin, surveyed 600 individuals to find that one in three felt worse after visiting a social networking site (SNS) (Krasnova et al, 2013; Sifferlin, 2013). Krasnova describes how Facebook users experience envy when visiting sites of peers and comparing their own lives accordingly. Krasnova demonstrates that users frequently perceive Facebook as a stressful environment. The post-modern online world is constantly changing and thus challenging users and content creators to continuously update and apply their social media skills.

Moreno's group provides further insight regarding Facebook users who decide to go public with their depression, which may not be rooted in the use of a SNS alone, but other circumstances. His group comes to a positive conclusion in their evaluation of Facebook as a platform for users to express depression: social networking sites could become a tool in dealing with depression, though this would require more regulation of SNS's. Pediatricians too have noticed the negative impact of SNS's in the lives of children. Schergin and Clarke-Pearson (2011) investigated this problem and have made specific recommendations to pediatricians dealing with the negative effects of social and digital media. Still, cases of Facebook suicide are on the increase and make headlines, with calls from concerned parents and consumer watchdogs to review and improve existing legislation regarding social media abuse and cyber bullying.

FUTURE RESEARCH DIRECTIONS

Social media and internet use has been a major issue as social space has been taken over by the virtual world. This research not only opens further consideration into the cognitive process of social media use, but the role of social media in the educational spectrum. The new learning curriculum incorporating digital technologies and virtual learning, pose challenges both to the students as well as the teachers. For a viable and effective teaching and learning module, understanding the (adverse) effect of social media use and student's concentration level is important. Hence this research initiates a humble step towards it. The date can be further used and explored in a wider scale for further indulgence into the social media research.

CONCLUSION

Why is this important to media producers and educators? Media producers need to be aware of the social media narrative developing among digital natives in order to develop, produce and distribute content to the appropriate target audience, using ethically justifiable methods. Social and digital media as a new medium implies that content of previous technologies provides content for it, according to Mcluhan. This is essential knowledge producers need in order to develop, produce and distribute content via social and digital media.

Educators, though working in a different environment, need to understand social and media technology equally well to meet their educational mandate. They develop a different kind of narrative for an audience consisting of students. Most of them are digital natives in the process of becoming versed in social media. Producers, educators nor society as a whole can afford to only note and apply the advantages of social and digital media, such as crowd-funding, social media marketing and self-distribution. Motivation to investigate the negative side of digital and social media is not coming from industry and remains neglected. Society as a whole will have to bear the costs of the negative effects of social and digital media regarding the development of an individual's cognitive function.

Though tempting, not all content should be marketed via social media and apps to younger audiences. The guidelines are not yet available to all stakeholders, though the calls to review and regulate social media practices are increasing. Industry funded research is not likely to accomplish this on its own. A media market based on generating revenues alone is not likely to implement anything else but voluntary guidelines regarding the use, implementation and marketing of social and digital media tools aimed at digital natives at home and in the classroom. Educators are advised to critically evaluate the benefits of social and digital media, and put in place guidelines that protect users and require them to practice their cognitive skills until more research in this field shows otherwise.

Our survey shows that social and digital media has become an integral part in the lives of digital natives; increasingly, digital immigrants find it difficult to escape this new technology as well. Students are using social and digital media to deal with the information tsunami they are faced with on a daily basis. For many, including digital immigrants, it has become impossible to process the amount of information presented online and via traditional media in any other way. As a consequence, information is no longer processed at a deeper level, but absorbed superficially instead. Critics argue that using social and digital media in this way does not improve the development of cognitive skills, making it even more difficult for students to acquire new knowledge and retain it in the long-term.

Producers need to carefully consider the means that should be used to develop, produce and distribute their programme to avoid unwitting support regarding the use of technology unsuitable for the intended target audience. There is a need to better understand the new emerging digital native culture. Understanding and critically examining Mcluhan's ideas in this area helps obtain the big picture. Reaching an audience is a challenge for the best of producers, but even more so without an understanding of the narrative unfolding among digital natives and digital immigrants alike.

Teachers are equally challenged when communicating with their students via SNS's, while producers are constantly searching for new ways to engage with their audience online. Expectations of online content and viewing behavior have changed significantly. In 2010, the average YouTube video, selected from among 2.5 million video clips, analysed was 4 minutes and 12 seconds in length (Inside YouTube Videos, 2010). Understanding this emerging narrative among digital natives provides numerous challenges to producers, such as length of programme, gamification, interaction and participation, format, i.e. short-form webisodes, and/or traditional long-form formats. The Scottish Film Institute is exploring new ways to meta-tag content, provide audience interaction and distribute their catalogue using technologies such as Popcorn and Distrify (Wistreich, 2012; Kempas, 2012).

New job descriptions are emerging, such as the Producer of Marketing and Distribution, social and digital media being one of the tools to develop, distribute, market their product and engage with audiences. Teachers are frequently challenged in the classroom, populated by students who are texting, skyping and facebooking. Almost half of the students in our survey stated that they found it difficult to stay offline during class. The negative effects of multi-tasking have been described in the literature, and educators are struggling to deal with the consequences of social and digital media in the classroom. Producers are dealing with this new reality by exploring new ways to reach audiences in the multi-screen-verse.

The unfolding social media narrative is increasingly making headlines because of tragic events, such as the death of a 17-year-old teenager in the UK (Teenager's death sparks cyber-blackmailing probe, 2013). According to Barbara Brams (2013), 75% of adolescents have a social network profile, which is accessed by more than half of them every day. They increasingly share private information online, disregarding privacy and safety concerns (Madden et al, 2013). Even though they still prefer face-to-face contact over social media, digital natives are increasingly exposed to cyber-bullying, resulting in depression, social isolation and suicidal thoughts (Hinduja & Patchin, 2010). Educators are challenged to pay more attention to social media; though for many, this technology is scary and unknown territory. Nevertheless, if parents fail to spot suicidal thoughts, the teacher may be the next in line to deal with the problem, but not if she or he disengaged from the social media narrative.

Bullying and suicide are not new to mankind; the social media phenomena has developed into a global platform, with its own culture, language, narrative and interaction that is not well understood by digital immigrants, such as parents, teachers, social workers, government bodies and media professionals themselves. While digital natives are exposed to the good and bad of social media, digital immigrants are trying to figure out how to deal with this new technology, leaving digital natives to deal with the consequences of social media with little or no guidance.

Social media has taken on its own dynamic pace and the rest of the world is lagging behind trying to work out how to react to his new global challenge. Viewing social and digital media from Mcluhan's perspective, we recognize the post-modern content in a post-post-modern technology. Constant change has become the norm, one might even argue that we are observing the death of post-modernity—whereas the pre-announced attack on Iraq based on branded terrorism was still effective, taking into account the weapons of mass destruction lie presented by the Bush administration, the current US administration is facing a great deal more resistance when applying the same kind of post-modern strategy to deal with Syria. Social media offers greater transparency to all stakeholders, though it will only have any benefits if users are still in control of their cognitive skills.

The Occupy and Wall Street movements demonstrate all too well how digital natives and immigrants alike have understood social media and its post-modern content. It shows how users of social and digital media have developed a new form of media literacy for this new medium, accelerating the transformation from a post-modern into a post-post-modern society. Mcluhan's ideas on media encompass this process; though social and digital media are not only encompassing the post-modern 'Zeitgeist', they contain all previous media technologies at an ever increasing speed.

Producers need to understand Mcluhan's ideas better to fully appreciate the transformation, social and digital media is facilitating for society and at an individual level. The world is in the midst of this process, audiences, users and producers are becoming media literate in this new technology. Institutions, organizations and governments are adapting swiftly to this new challenge and they are learning their lessons, reacting in typical post-modern fashion to the challenges online. Producers are more likely to adapt quickly in order to reach their target audience during this transformation. Small and medium-sized businesses are better suited to act and react to these challenges. Due to their size, they are able to act and react faster when compared to their large, modern and post-modern counterparts.

Educators, on the other hand, are required to work within hierarchies that managed to survive centuries of transformation, i.e. the introduction of print and broadcast technologies. This paper itself is a testament to the positive aspects of social media in such an environment: i.e. access to libraries and online sources, as well as the potential to collaborate at the research level with scholars across the globe made it possible to discuss and exchange new knowledge via this new virtual space. Educators are advised to actively become part of the social media narrative and provide clear guidelines on the use of social media in the classroom.

Note: Conflict of interests; the authors of this paper declare that their research has been entirely self-funded.

REFERENCES

Arkin, D. (2013). Canada charges two in teen cyber-bullying suicide case. *NBC News*. Retrieved August 20, 2013, from http://www.bbc.co.uk/news/world-us-canada-23752923

Baek, I.-H., & Park, E.-J. (2012). Digital dementia is on the rise. *Korean Joongan Daily*. Retrieved June 24, 2013, from http://koreajoongangdaily.joins.com/news/article/article.aspx?aid=2973527&cloc=joongangdaily%7Chomop

Branigan, T. (2013). Edward Snowden vows not to hide from justice amid new hacking claims. *The Guardian*. Retrieved December 6, 2013, from http://www.theguardian.com/world/2013/jun/12/edward-snowden-us-extradition-fight?INTCMP=SRCH

Briggs, A., & Burke, P. (2009). *A social history of media* (3rd ed.). Malden, MA: Polity Press.

Chiong, C., & Shuler, C. (2010). *Learning: Is there an app for that? Investigations of young children's usage and learning with mobile devices and apps*. New York: The Joan Ganz Cooney Center at Sesame Workshop.

Christakis, D. A. (2010). Internet addiction: A 21st century epidemic? *BMC Medicine*, 8(1), 61–63. doi:10.1186/1741-7015-8-61 PMID:20955578

Corbalis, M. (2009). The evolution of language. *Annals of the New York Academy of Sciences*, 1156(1), 19–43. doi:10.1111/j.1749-6632.2009.04423.x PMID:19338501

Digital Dementia on the Rise as Young People Increasingly Rely on Technology Instead of Their Brain. (2013, June 24). *Mail Online*. Retrieved June 8, 2013, from http://www.dailymail.co.uk/health/article-2347563/Digital-dementia-rise-young-people-increasingly-rely-technology-instead-brain.html

Ensor, J. (2013). Family of Skype suicide teen calls on David Cameron to tackle cyber bullying. *The Telegraph*. Retrieved August 20, 2013, from http://www.telegraph.co.uk/technology/news/10248058/Family-of-skype-suicide-teen-calls-on-David-Cameron-to-tackle-cyber-bullying.html

European Travel Commission. (2013). *New media trend watch*. Retrieved December 8, 2013, from http://www.newmediatrendwatch.com/markets-by-country/11-long-haul/63-south-korea

Gadkari, P. (2013). Ask.fm unveils changes to safety policy. *BBC News*. Retrieved August 20, 2013, from http://www.bbc.co.uk/news/world-us-canada-23752923

Glimmerglass: Optical Cyber Solutions. (2012). Retrieved October 1, 2012, from http://www.glimmerglass.com

Hinduja, S., & Patchin, W. (2010). Bullying, cyberbullying, and suicide. *Archives of Suicide Research*, *14*(3), 206–221. doi:10.1080/138111 18.2010.494133 PMID:20658375

Jacobs, A. (2011, Spring). Why bother with Marshall McLuhan? *New Atlantis (Washington, D.C.)*, *31*, 123–135.

Jung, C. (1981). *The archetypes and the collective unconscious*. New York: Princeton University Press.

Kempas, B. (2009). Maximising distrify, the PMD's top ten tips. *Scottish Documentary Institute*. Retrieved August 7, 2013, from http://blog.scottishdocinstitute.com/maxifying_distrify

Kohle, F. (2012). The Arab Spring and the Wall Street Movement: Challenges and implications for documentary filmmakers and social media. In *Proceedings of London Film & Media Conference*. NHTV University of Applied Sciences. Retrieved July 23, 2013, from http://www.thelondonfilmandmediaconference.com/registered-speakers-2012-a-to-k/

Kohle, F., & Cuevas, A. (2010). A case study in using YouTube and Facebook as social media tools in enhancing student centered learning and engagement. In *Proceedings of 3rd International Conference of Education, Research and Innovation*. Madrid, Spain: Academic Press.

Kohle, F., & Cuevas, A. (2012). Social media: Changing the way we teach and changing the way we learn. In *Proceedings of 6th International Technology, Education and Development Conference*. Valencia, Spain: Academic Press.

Krasnova, H., Wenninger, H., Widjaja, T., & Buxmann, P. (2013). *Envy on Facebook: A hidden threat to users' life satisfaction?*. Paper presented at the International Conference on Wirtschaftsinformatik (WI) / Business Information Systems 2013, Leipzig, Germany.

Lee, H. W., Choi, J.-S., Shin, Y.-C., Lee, J.-Y., Jung, H. Y., & Kwon, J. S. (2012, July). Impulsivity in internet addiction: A comparison with pathological gambling. *Cyberpsychology, Behavior, and Social Networking*, *15*(7), 373–377. doi:10.1089/cyber.2012.0063 PMID:22663306

Livingstone, S., Olafsson, K., & Staksrund, E. (2013). Risky social networking practices among 'under-age' users: Lessons for evidence-based policy. *Journal of Computer-Mediated Communication*, *18*(3), 303–320. doi:10.1111/jcc4.12012

Lyotard, J. (1992). *The postmodern explained to children, correspondence 1982–1985*. Turnaround.

Madden, M., Lenhart, A., Cortesi, S., Gasser, U., Duggan, A. S., & Beaton, M. (2013). Teen, social media and privacy. *The Berkman Center for Internet & Society at Harvard University*. Retrieved September 12, 2013 from http://pewinternet.org/Reports/2013/Teens-Social-Media-And-Privacy/Summary-of-Findings/Teens-Social-Media-and-Privacy.aspx

McLuhan, M. (1994). *Understanding media: The extensions of man*. Cambridge, MA: MIT press.

Mcluhan, M. (1995). *Essential McLuhan*. House of Anansi Press.

Mell, P., & Grance, T. (2011). *The NIST definition of cloud computing*. NIST. Retrieved July 23, 2013, from http://csrc.nist.gov/publications/nistpubs/800-145/SP800-145.pdf

Moreno, M. A., Jelenchick, L. A., Egan, K. G., Cox, E., Young, H., Gannon, K. E., & Becker, T. (2011). Feeling bad on Facebook: Depression disclosures by college students on a social networking site. *Depression and Anxiety*, *28*(6), 447–455. doi:10.1002/da.20805 PMID:21400639

Morrison, J. (n.d.). *Marshall McLuhan: Beyond the ivory tower: Academic discourse in the age of popular media*. Massachusetts Institute of Technology. Retrieved May 9, 2013, from http://www.mit.edu/~saleem/ivory/

Mrs. Davison's Kindergarten [blog]. (2013) Retrieved August, 8, 2013, from http://davison-kindergarten.blogspot.nl/p/what-we-are-doing-with-ipads.html

Ryall, J. (2012). Surge in digital dementia. *The Telegraph*. Retrieved June 8, 2012, from http://www.telegraph.co.uk/news/worldnews/asia/southkorea/10138403/Surge-in-digital-dementia.html

SS8. (n.d.). Retrieved October 1, 2012, from http://www.ss8.com/products-overview.php, http://www.ss8.com/industries/law-enforcement-agencies-0

Sandvik, M., Smordal, O., & Osterud, S. (2012). Universitetsforlaget. *Nordic Journal of Digital Literacy*, *7*(03), 204–220.

Schurgin O'Keefe, G., & Clarke-Pearson, K. (2011). The impact of social media on children, adolescents, and families. *Pediatrics*, *127*(4), 800–804. doi:10.1542/peds.2011-0054 PMID:21444588

Sifferlin, A. (2013). Why Facebook makes you feel miserable. *TIME.com*. Retrieved August 25, 2013, from http://healthland.time.com/2013/01/24/why-facebook-makes-you-feel-bad-about-yourself/

Some Teens are Exhibiting Signs of 'Digital Dementia'. (2013). *UPI.com*. Retrieved November 8, 2013, from http://www.upi.com/Science_News/Technology/2013/06/26/Some-teens-in-South-Korea-exhibiting-digital-dementia/UPI-69441372251061/

Spitzer, M. (2012). Digitale Demenz. Droemer Verlag.

Strasburger, V., Jordan, A., & Donnerstein, E. (2010). Health effects of media on children and adolescents. *Pediatrics*, *125*(4), 756–767. doi:10.1542/peds.2009-2563 PMID:20194281

Sysomos, Inc. (2010, February). *Inside YouTube videos: Exploring YouTube videos and their use in blogosphere - Michael Jackson and health care dominate.* Retrieved August 20, 2013, from http://www.sysomos.com/reports/youtube

Teenager's Death Sparks Cyber-Blackmailing Probe. (2013, August 13). *BBC News Scotland.* Retrieved August 16, 2013, from http://www.bbc.co.uk/news/uk-scotland-23723169

Warren, L., & Quigley, R. (2013). Police confirm 12 year old girls suicide note said she was being cyber-bullied as her sister reveals she knew about abuse but was sworn to secrecy. *Daily Mail.* Retrieved August 20, 2013, from http://www.dailymail.co.uk/news/article-2331670/Gabrielle-Molina-Police-confirm-12-year-old-girls-suicide-note-said-cyber-bullied-sister-reveals-knew-abuse-sworn-secrecy.html

Watkins, T. (2010). New light on Neolithic revolution in south-west Asia. *Antiquity, 84*(325), 621–634.

Wistreich, N. (2009). Have some popcorn with your documentary. *Scottish Documentary Institute.* Retrieved August 21, 2013, from http://blog.scottishdocinstitute.com/popcorn_with_your_documentary_2

Woollett, K., & Maguire, E. (2011). Acquiring the knowledge of London's layout drives structural brain changes. *Current Biology, 21*(24-2), 2109-2114. Retrieved October 1, 2013, from http://www.ncbi.nlm.nih.gov/pmc/articles/PMC3268356/

World Health Organisation. (1992). *The ICD-10 classification of mental and behavioural disorders.* Retrieved July 9, 2013, from http://www.who.int/classifications/icd/en/GRNBOOK.pdf

ISS World Training. (2013). Retrieved February, 9, 2013, from http://www.issworldtraining.com/

Zhou, Y., Lin, F.-, Du, Y.-, Qin, L.-, Zhao, Z.-, Xu, J.-, & Lei, H. (2011, July). Gray matter abnormalities in Internet addiction: A voxel-based morphometry study. *European Journal of Radiology, 79*(1), 92–95. doi:10.1016/j.ejrad.2009.10.025 PMID:19926237

ADDITIONAL READING

Agichtein, E., et al. (2008). Finding High-Quality Content in Social Media. WSDM '08 Proceedings of the 2008 International Conference on Web Search and Data Mining, pp. 183-194 doi:10.1145/1341531.1341557

Bosch, T. E. (2009). Using online social networking for teaching and learning: Facebook use at the University of Cape Town. *Communication: South African Journal for Communication Theory and Research, 35*(2), 185–200.

Dabbagh, N., & Kitsantas, A. (2012). Personal Learning Environments, social media, and self-regulated learning: A natural formula for connecting formal and informal learning. *The Internet and Higher Education, 15*(1), 3–8. doi:10.1016/j.iheduc.2011.06.002

DeAndrea, D. C., Ellison, N. B., LaRose, R., Steinfield, C., & Fiore, A. (2012). Serious social media: On the use of social media for improving students' adjustment to college. *The Internet and Higher Education, 15*(1), 15–23. doi:10.1016/j.iheduc.2011.05.009

Duffy, P (2008). Engaging the YouTube Google-Eyed Generation: Strategies for Using Web 2.0 in Teaching and Learning. *Electronic Journal of e-Learning.* 6(2), 119-129

Ellison, N. B., Steinfield, C., & Lampe, C. (2007). The Benefits of Facebook "Friends:" Social Capital and College Students' Use of Online Social Network Sites. *Journal of Computer-Mediated Communication*, *12*(4), 1143–1168. doi:10.1111/j.1083-6101.2007.00367.x

Greenhow, C., Robelia, B., & Hughes, J. E. (2009). Learning, Teaching, and Scholarship in a Digital Age. *Educational Researcher*, *38*(4), 246–259. doi:10.3102/0013189X09336671

Joosten, T. (2010). *Social Media for Educators: Strategies and Best Practices.* San Francisco: Wiley Imprint.

Kelm, O. R. (2011). Social Media It's What Students Do. *Business and Professional Communication Quarterly*, *74*(4), 505–520. doi:10.1177/1080569911423960

Kietzmann, J. H., Hermkens, K., McCarthy, I. P., & Silvestre, B. S. (2011). Social media? Get serious! Understanding the functional building blocks of social media. *Business Horizons*, *54*(3), 241–251. doi:10.1016/j.bushor.2011.01.005

Kushin, M., & Yamamoto, M. (2010). Did Social Media Really Matter? College Students' Use of Online Media and Political Decision Making in the 2008 Election. *Mass Communication & Society*, *13*(5), 608–630. doi:10.1080/1520543 6.2010.516863

Moody, M. (2010). Teaching Twitter and Beyond: Tips for Incorporating Social Media in Traditional Courses. *Journal of Magazine & New Media Research*, *11*(2), 1–9.

Pempek, T. A., Yermolayeva, Y. A., & Calvert, S. L. (2009). College students' social networking experiences on Facebook. *Journal of Applied Developmental Psychology*, *30*(3), 227–238. doi:10.1016/j.appdev.2008.12.010

Quan-Haase, A., & Young, A. L. (2010). Uses and Gratifications of Social Media: A Comparison of Facebook and Instant Messaging. *Bulletin of Science, Technology & Society*, *30*(5), 350–361. doi:10.1177/0270467610380009

Sacks, M. A., & Graves, N. (2012). How Many "Friends" Do You Need? Teaching Students How to Network Using Social Media. *Business and Professional Communication Quarterly*, *75*(1), 80–88. doi:10.1177/1080569911433326

Silius, K., et al. (2010). Students' Motivations for Social Media Enhanced Studying and Learning. *Knowledge Management & E-Learning: An International Journal (KM&EL)*, 2(1). Retrieved January 11, 2014, from http://www.kmel-journal. org/ojs/index.php/online-publication/article/ viewArticle/55

Thompson, J. B. (1995). *Media and Modernity: A Social Theory of the Media.* Cambridge: Polity Press.

Valenzuela, S., Park, N., & Kee, K. F. (2009). Is There Social Capital in a Social Network Site?: Facebook Use and College Students' Life Satisfaction, Trust, and Participation. *Journal of Computer-Mediated Communication*, *14*(4), 875–901. doi:10.1111/j.1083-6101.2009.01474.x

Wankel, C. (2010). Cutting-edge Social Media Approaches to Business Education. USA: IAP (Information Age Publishing Inc)

Wankel, L. (2011). *Higher Education with Social Media*. Bingley: Emerald Group Publishing Limited.

KEY TERMS AND DEFINITIONS

Cognitive Skill: It refers to the human capacity of processing the thoughts like memorizing, differentiating, learning, speaking and understanding information/data.

Cyber-Bullying: It's synonymous to digital abuse whereby anyone with the aid of digital technologies harass and threaten other users.

Dementia: Impaired intellectual faculty like lack of memory, concentration and judging power.

Digital Abuse: The use of digital technologies like social networking sites and digital gadgets (through SMSs, photographs or online messages) to bully and harass anyone.

Digital Natives: It represents a generation who are born or bought up in a digital era who are well-versed in the technological aspect and whose daily endeavor revolves around these technologies.

Social Media: It is a virtual medium through which the users can communicate, interact and share information with the fellow-users and indulge in a social networking. Facebook, YouTube, Second Life, Twitter etc. are some examples.

Virtual Space: It is a computer simulated environment where people interact.

Chapter 6
Social Networking:
A Retrospective into the Trust Formation and Threats

Vladlena Benson
Kingston Business School, Kingston University, UK

ABSTRACT

As the social technology matured in recent years, so did the threat landscape of the online medium. Fears about breaches of privacy and personal information security seem to dominate the list of concerns of social media users described in literature. Popular press continually reports cases of inadvertent and malicious information disclosure and breaches, cyberbullying, and stalking. Yet, social networking sites proliferated into all areas of human activity. The factor causing this phenomenon lies in the trusted nature of networks and the sense of trustworthiness of this easy-to-use technology. The formation of trust into social technology has attracted much attention, and this chapter offers an overview of the trust predictors in social settings. It continues with a retrospective into the threat landscape and the use of personalisation by social networking services to counter some of these threats. Further research directions are discussed.

BACKGROUND

I wrote a chapter on the role of personalisaton in Web 2.0 user protection half a decade ago. Five years in technology terms is a long time span. Much has change in the landscape of Web 2.0, and the social media group of internet applications has become more established, absorbing more and more internet tools which employ social technology features. Social Networking Services have gained a more defined distinction into professional and private categories, while Facebook, Linkedin, Twitter and Pinterest acquired the leading status of social networks. As we were conducting a study investigating purchase intention and risk propensity of social media users, trust and trustworthiness of social networks appeared to have a significant influence over user behaviour. This prompted me to take another look at the trust building methods, such as personalisation, employed currently on the Web 2.0 group of Internet applications, including social networking services.

The notion of *trust* spans from the social context to human computer interactions. Much research

DOI: 10.4018/978-1-4666-7401-1.ch006

(e.g. Beudoin, 2008; Jiang, Jones & Javie, 2008) now recognises the importance of understanding trust and trust-building in online communication, transactions and systems. Online interactions involve various types of risks and entail the presence of trust between communicating parties as well as in the applications used for these interactions (Riegelsberger, Sasse & McCarthy, 2003). Social networking sites (SNS) provide a straightforward, user-friendly and convenient way to connect and share information with other users online. This explains the growing popularity of such SNS as Facebook, which counts more than 1.23 billion active users. Over 700 million people made logging into Facebook a daily routine and the amount of content shared through the site reached billions (including web links, stories, blogs posts, photos, etc.) each week (Facebook Statistics, 2013). Features for customising personal profile and privacy settings, peer based rating systems and a sense of a secure environment for sharing personal information and content made SNS immensely popular.

Trust on Social Media and Its Predictors

Research suggests that individuals with a lower perception of risk display higher trustworthiness (McKnight & Chervany, 2002; Cheung & Lee, 2003). However, these conclusions have not been confirmed in the social media environment. Moreover, the relationship between the perception of risk by individual users and trustworthiness does not materialise on Facebook as shown by Nor et al., (2013). Another element of risk, namely risk propensity or the determinant of behaviour where one decides to take or to avoid risk (Sitkin & Pablo, 1992), is impacted by trustworthiness. It has been shown that in e-commerce, how much trustworthiness in an online vendor a user has influences their inclination to take or avoid risk (Xu et al., 2005). This further extends to the purchase intention, the area much researched in online behaviour, still scarce in social media settings. The association of

the online user's trust and behavioural intentions for e-commerce firms is known to be significant and trust has been shown to serve as a characteristic of 'relationship quality' (Newel et al., 1998). In social networks trust also plays an important role in purchase intention (Nor et al., 2013; Pentina et al., 2013) but such studies are rare at present as Web 2.0 monetisation opportunities are just starting to gain acceptance.

One of the areas amply explored in e-commerce literature but yet to be extended to social media lies in the investigation of the role of technological artefacts in indicating security measures, in the formation of trust in the consumer. With the view to bolster users' confidence that their activity online is safeguarded ecommerce firms employed 'self-regulatory transparency mechanisms' (Acquisti et al., 2013). 'Notices' or 'notifications', as these mechanisms are generally termed, comprise of privacy statements and security seals. Notices inform users about what data is collected and how their personal information is handled by a website (Liu et al., 2004). Information security artefacts such as privacy seals (e.g. TRUSTe, VeriSign Trusted sign) serve to play the role of acquiring user's trust online by serving as 'contextual' reinforcement. Third party 'seals of approval' such as that provided by Verisign, eTRUST, etc., have been used successfully by online vendors for years. Technology artefacts serving as proofs of the online vendor legitimacy appear to improve the level of trust in its users, specifically influencing the user's behaviour in online transactions (Wang & Benbasat, 2005). Technology artefacts also have been shown to encourage online users to disclose personal information (Hui et al., 2007; Hu et al., 2010). Personalisation serves as such an artifact which links to the access controls for user accounts. Privacy seals or security artefacts have been shown to lead to different levels of information disclosure (John et al., 2011).

The nature of social interactions online forms the basis for trust building and trust-transfer between users of social networks. Online interactions are possible only when not only users trust each other, but also when they have enough faith in the systems they use to transact as well as the organisations which provide them (Riegelsberger et al., 2005). Trust in e-commerce applications has attracted significant research attention (Golbeck, 2008), the concept of trust has been linked to security and used in the context of privacy, identity and authorisation. Research efforts have been directed at establishing factors influencing trust in online applications. For example, Dutton and Shepherd (2006) argue that trust on the Internet has been based on two indicators: net-confidence and net-risk. Perceptions of confidence in the Internet technology has been expressed through the level of reliability of information on the Internet, trust in the institutions running the Internet and the confidence in people with whom they conduct online communication and transactions. Net-risk was defined as the perceived exposure to risks or user perceived vulnerability to threats while using the Internet.

Earlier studies showed that those people who use the Internet more tend to gain more trust in technology. Dutton and Shepherd (2006) highlighted that education and experience determine formation of trust among Internet users. They also showed that reinforcement of the digital divides, including life stage factors, social gaps and proximity to the Internet, translates into significant differences in levels of trust developed by people. Based on these arguments and data reported in the 2007 OxIS Survey (Dutton & Helsper, 2008) it is possible to infer that higher levels of trust are developed by individuals aged between 18 and 24 that intensively use social media and have the closest proximity to technology.

Monitoring the threats from Internet criminals has been the centre of attention of major information security solution providers, e.g. Symantec, MessageLabs, SANs and others. However, research literature demonstrates a lack of sustained research into how social networking users are affected by cybercrime and how they respond to the existing threats. This chapter helps fill the gap in the literature by a) providing an analysis of factors influencing the formation of trust in technology in online social networks, b) identifying factors which make social networking users vulnerable to cybercrime and c) provoking a discussion on the reliability of personalisation as the mitigation instrument against social networking vulnerabilities.

The structure of the rest of the chapter is organised as follows: Section 2 provides an overview of trust theory further linked to the discussion of trends in cybercrime in section 3. Section 4 describes scenarios of Internet attacks perpetrated through social networking sites. Section 5 summarises the factors which influence formation of trust among users of online social networks and examines the aspects of behaviour which make their users vulnerable to cybercrime. The article concludes with a discussion about whether personalisation is the silver bullet to combat cyber threats on social networks. Further research directions are discussed.

1. CRITICAL CONCEPTS IN TRUST THEORY

Social Exchange Theory provides a framework defining trust and helps to explain the formation of trust in interpersonal and exchange relationships. A general definition can be given for trust as a "psychological state comprising the intentions to accept vulnerability based upon positive expectations of the intentions or behaviour of another" (Rousseau et al., 1998, p.395). Sociological connotations of trust commonly comprise of two elements: confidence and willingness to act based on this confidence (Stompka, 1999). Generally, social trust relationships are viewed as positive in social and collaborative web technology. This is the case for user-generated content, where social trust helps users wade through overwhelming amounts of information, often deceiving, inaccurate and of questionable origin. Social trust helps users find trusted information resources and identify useful content (Ziegel & Golbeck, 2006). Similarity of opinions has been widely used as a practical metric for establishing a trustworthy source of content on the web. However, the basic component of social trust, i.e. willingness to act upon belief, is what makes this type of trust unsuitable in the context of privacy, confidentiality and secure transactions. In fact, in online communication and exchanges, generally termed as transactions, trust makes transaction parties vulnerable to malicious acts. Although many definitions of online trust exist, most of them include this element of vulnerability. For instance, online trust is viewed as "...willingness to accept vulnerability in an online transaction based on positive expectations regarding future behaviours..." of transaction parties (Kimery & McCord, 2002). The metrics of interpersonal trust, "the lubricant of the inevitable frictions of social life" (Putnam, 2000, p.235), has been expressed and measured as 'trusting others'. Studies have measured interpersonal trust through expectations of behaviour of others in certain community situations or with questions about others trying to take advantage of you, people being helpful and being trustworthy (Brehm & Rahn, 1997). Beaudoin (2008) concluded that the greater the Internet use, the greater the interpersonal trust. This conclusion supports earlier findings that trust becomes a function of experience of technology. Dutton and Shepherd (2006) in a survey of the UK population use of new media found that trust on the Internet (its technology, resources and applications) is higher among more experienced users. The authors established that the more time people spend on the Internet, the more trustful they become.

Golbeck (2008) addressed six factors which encourage users to develop social trust. The first two are specific to experience and concur with Corritore, Kracher, and Wiedenbeck, (2003), the last four are related to reputation in a sense that they reflect the influence of opinions from others. The following factors are identified that encourage development of social trust:

- **Prior Lifetime of History and Events Affecting Psychological Factors:** Although generally related to previous experience, this factor is relevant to past events which affected the psychology of a user in a positive or negative way.
- **Past Experience with a Person and with Their Friends:** Users are likely to be more trustful if they had positive social experiences.
- **Rumour:** Although not always a trustworthy source of information, rumours can influence formation of social trust. If a person is aware of a negative rumour about someone or something, that person is less likely to trust the other.
- **Opinions of the Actions Undertaken by a Person:** Having knowledge of positive actions, which characterise someone, encourages social trust in others.
- **Influence of Other People's Beliefs:** Negative judgments about a person by other people are likely to discourage trust in that individual and vice versa.
- **Extending Trust to Gain Something:** If there is an incentive or interest to gain an advantage people are more likely to trust others.

Finding a way to determine how much one social networking user can trust the other represents a significant challenge to the application of social trust (Golbeck, 2008). Hundreds of social network users are unlikely to form interpersonal trust based on face to face contact. Instead, a trust transfer process from one trusted user to a new entity occurs. Estimating trust between users of social networks has been a popular discussion topic in recent literature (e.g. Massa & Avesani, 2007). Algorithms based on network structure and similarity measures among users of social networks have been developed (Avesani, Massa and Telia, 2005). Exploring community structure (Girvan & Newman, 2002) and other complex system approaches derived from probabilistic reasoning and artificial intelligence (Mitchell, 2006) are emerging for the computation of trust and prediction of its dynamics in social networks. Simpler general applications of trust formation have been widely used on the Internet for years. Including recommender systems (i.e. Amazon pioneered suggestions of shopping items based on profiles), and rating and review approaches are widely used in e-commerce. Email message filtering based on measurement of trust in sender origin is another example of trust application (Golbeck & Hendler, 2004). Social networks are enabled by peer-to-peer systems of trust building and rely on trustworthy members. The approach of rating members by peers improves the method of identifying trustworthy users but these rating are useless for third party applications as this information cannot be shared (Golbeck, 2007).

Much research, especially in the early days of e-commerce, has been conducted to understand what encourages people to trust websites. Significant attention has been placed on understanding trust in e-commerce websites as they involve monetary transactions. According to Corritore, Kracher, and Wiedenbeck, (2003) three factors affecting trust online include: perception of credibility, risk and ease of use. A large study of formation of trust in e-commerce (Wang & Emurian, 2005) had similar results. In a survey of users of e-commerce websites six major factors that encouraged people to think that a website was trustworthy were identified. While the first two features are specific to perceptions of reputation, the last four factors deal with design and implementation of the website. The factors that impact trust in online environments were identified as:

- **Brand:** Outside reputation of a company independent of its website affects users' willingness to trust website content.
- **Seal of Approval:** Trust is fostered through the evidence of third party certification and security measures.

- **Navigation:** Users are less likely to trust a website if they find it difficult to navigate through its pages.
- **Fulfillment:** Users tend to build more trust as a result of successful order processing, or form loose trust as a result of negative order fulfillment.
- **Presentation:** Layout and presentation of a website encourages users to trust a website.
- **Technology:** The technologies used for website development and operation have a significant impact on how much users trust a website.

Overall, all of the above factors are related to the three features identified in Corritore, Kracher, and Wiedenbeck, (2003). In addition, according to Golbeck, (2008) trust is developed over time. The more time users spend on a website, the more informed their decision regarding whether to trust a website becomes. The work by Beudoin (2008) follows up on these conclusions relating trust and Internet use over time. The study suggests that Internet use, including social networking, is influenced by user motivation to build social resources, ranging from social contacts and connections to social interactions.

2. MOTIVATION[1]

While the volume of online social networks-based communication and transactions is steadily rising (e.g. Golbeck, 2008), concerns of online users about the security of information stored and transmitted online continue to deepen. The findings of the Internet in Britain Report (Dutton, Helsper and Gerber, 2009) showed that a growing proportion of UK society go online to reinforce the networks of family and existing social connections, as well as to meet and be introduced to new people. Internet users, particularly those using a range of communication facilities, are likely to see online social communication as enabling them to be more productive at work and to enhance their personal, financial and economic well-being. It is not surprising that over the past several years online social network users have become targets of cybercrime. Attacks on online communities, especially based upon reputation, have been categorised by Hoffman, Zage and Nita-Rotaru, (2009). Attackers are motivated by selfish or malicious intent. In this survey attackers were classified into the following types:

- **Insider or Outsider:** Based on location of the attacker;
- **Loner or a Part of a Coalition:** Depending on whether an attacker acts as a part of an organised criminal group or alone;
- **Active or Passive Attacker:** Based on the type of attacks perpetrated.

In the context of this chapter we will focus on active malicious attackers and attack strategies since any form of attack perpetrated via or aimed at a social networking site requires interaction with the system. The next section provides an overview of attacks perpetrated using SNS.

3. THREATS ON SOCIAL NETWORKS

The underpinning technology of social media driven by peer to peer interactions becomes an easy mechanism for hackers to target large numbers of users. Here we will consider the following types of active attacks perpetrated through social networks, bearing in mind that they are not mutually exclusive and multiple threat vectors can be used to perpetrate an attack:

Sybil Attack

The problem of obtaining multiple legitimate accounts and identities at a very low cost have received significant attention (Friedman et al. 2007) enabling malicious entities to become an internal part of a social network. An adversary can then post malicious content, overhear communication between other entities, and harvest valuable personal data.

Malware Attacks

Are not only specific to social network but are increasingly low tech to execute by attaching malicious content to sharable multimedia or text. The 'clickjacking' attack on Twitter in 2009 was just one of many examples of these online threats.

Social Engineering Attacks

Social networks are an ideal ground for social engineering, which is an act of luring unsuspecting users into disclosing confidential information by exploiting interpersonal trust. Over the past few years we have seen a growing trend of social engineering attacks propagating through social networks targeting end users with the single purpose of financial gain. Tailored to the nature of social networks, such social engineering attacks as Koobface virus and Scareware links on Digg.com have spread through Facebook with considerable security threats attached. Cyberbullying and stalking also belong to this type of attacks. While no financial gain is involved directly in the motivation of attackers, these offenses on social media are treated no different than in traditional forms from legal perspective.

Hijacking Attacks

By using brute force attacks or other means of retrieving or guessing user passwords an adversary can gain access to a legitimate user's account. The reason criminals seek to abuse social networking accounts is that messages from friends have a better chance of being treated as legitimate by other users.

While not exploiting any particular vulnerability in technology most of these threats require very little expertise and are based on pure social engineering. As discussed by a number of authors (e.g. Galagher 2009, Goldman, 2009) because of the trusted nature of social networks, they are extremely attractive to Internet criminals. Catching user attention by messages such as 'don't click me', 'view my video' or 'look at my profile', threats spreading through social media take users to a completely different site, install malware on the victim's computer to steal their personal data and/or propagate further through the network.

All of the attacks discussed so far are spread by phishing messages which have an appearance of legitimacy when masqueraded as originating through a social network. According to the Internet Threats Report 2008 (Symantec Enterprise Security, 2009), 'Phishing is an attempt by a third party to solicit confidential information from an individual, group, or organization by mimicking (or spoofing) a specific brand, usually one that is well known, often for financial gain'. Phishing criminals try to hoax Internet users into disclosing sensitive information and use it in identity theft crimes. Phishing usually requires an end user to input their credentials into an online form. Information targeted by phishers includes personal data, such as credit card numbers, online banking credentials, etc.

You can probably recognise phishing messages arriving to email boxes worldwide. By the time an unsuspecting user clicks on the link in the message content the drive-by malware attack has already happened and phishing messages to the victim's trusted friends are on the way.

A successful phishing attack may use a number of methods (e.g. Ollman, 2008) to deceive social networking users into revealing their data or do something with their server and web content. The most widespread methods are described below:

Man-in-the-Middle

The attacker positions between a legitimate user and the web based social networking site and proxies the communication stream between the systems. This is one of the most successful methods of gaining control of user information and resources through observing and recording transactions between unsuspecting parties.

URL Obfuscation

By means of a phishing message seemingly originating from a trusted social networking site an adversary lures a user into clicking on a malicious hyperlink (URL) leading to an attacker's server. The ways to hide or obscure the destination of a hyperlink are many and are freely available on the web. Some of the common methods are third party's shortened URLs, bad domain names and cross-site scripting. While the in-depth discussion of this type of attack is beyond the scope if this chapter, we will draw attention to the Cross-Site Scripting attack. It exploits the trusted nature of social networks by disguising a malicious web page under a familiar URL. For example, a user receives a message from a friend on a social network and follows a URL: http://mysocialnetwork. com/login?URL=http://malicious_site.com/ phishing_page.htm. The user thinks that he is directed to his trusted social network. However, by exploiting coding vulnerabilities on the social site, the adversary has managed to refer the user to a falsified login page on the attacker's server. The unsuspecting user has no way of distinguishing the malicious URL masqueraded as legitimate and the adversary gains the user's login credentials.

Preset Session

It is an attack perpetrated by means of a phishing message containing a link to a legitimate application server. Many online applications implementing poor style session management allow user connections to define a SessionID. Users need to be authenticated before proceeding to the restricted page. The adversary's system continuously polls the restricted page of a social network site waiting for the user to click on the phishing message link containing the SessionID predefined by the adversary. The unsuspecting user authenticates and the hacker can carry out an attack.

End-User Vulnerabilitie

They are increasing exploited by criminals as web based social networking sites run application on the client side. Social sites run in web browsers and enable multimedia sharing through applications which are constantly being probed for vulnerabilities by Internet criminals. Software manufacturers constantly monitor applications for known vulnerabilities and issue patches and updates for any identified weaknesses. However, unless client side applications are patched and updated regularly, computers of social networking users are open to attacks even if a single unpatched vulnerability remains.

4. FACTORS AFFECTING FORMATION OF SOCIAL TRUST

Recent surveys of Internet users in the UK (Dutton & Helsper, 2007; Duton, Helsper & Gerber, 2009) suggest that users have developed a certain degree of tolerance to risks associated with information conveyed through the Internet. It appears that previous experience of internet use and perceived competence in technology are the most influential factors in building trust on the Internet (Dutton & Shepherd, 2006). While users are becoming more aware about phishing and other social engineering attacks, social networking sites are being more proactive about scanning downstream sites and isolating malicious content. However, two factors make the quest for safety an ongoing battle: sheer numbers of social networking traffic and reliance on end users to distinguish trusted from malicious content. Many social networking sites have increased their security defences and take technical measures to identify potential phishing attacks. However the shear amount of user generated content makes the task resource intensive and labour intensive, therefore SNS rely on customer awareness to identify and report potential offenses. The Antiphishing Working Group (2009) puts personalisation of communication as the first line of defence against phishing attacks. They recommend that the personalisation may range from an inclusion of user names, or references to previous communication or some other piece of unique information into messages. Examples include:

"Dear Amily Smith" instead of "Dear Sir/Madame" or "Hi there!"

Surprisingly enough, social networking user education hardly goes beyond the 'don't click' principle. Regular publications of social media safe practices (e.g. VanWyk, 2009) reiterate a set of similar recommendations, including:

- Don't click on encoded URL's if you are in doubt.
- **Adjust Browser Settings:** (Even though browsers are vulnerable to a significant security issues). By allowing active content to run in the browser, users trust third party content to run on their computers.
- **Choose Your Friends Wisely:** I.e., accept connections or content from people you know directly.

- Avoid running third party applications on social networking platforms, especially new ones.
- Turn up privacy controls and limit the number of people who can view one's personal information.
- **Shut Down Other Applications:** I.e., restart the browser and close down other applications before logging on to your favourite social networking site.

All of the precautions discussed earlier are certainly valuable and, as suggested by the authors, will help people to use social media 'in a reasonably safe way' (Van Wyck, 2009). It seems doubtful that putting the safety of social networking into the trusting hands of end users is the only way to mitigate cybercrime which exploits social trust. An alternative solution derives from the experience of the e-commerce sector and their efforts to build consumer trust through third party certification (Jiang, Jones & Javie, 2008). Online social networks are based on social trust and reputation that inform user decisions regarding what information to share with others and deal with information incoming from other users. However, online social networks are wide-ranging and the information needed to decide whether an unknown person or shared content is trustworthy is hardly available. More research attention is needed in understanding, managing and verifying trust on social networks.

The basic component of social trust, i.e. willingness to act upon belief, is what makes this type of trust unsuitable in the context of privacy, confidentiality and secure transactions. Whereas social trust helps users find trusted resources online based on profile setting and similarity of opinions (Ziegel &Golbeck, 2006) it makes the nature of social networking prone to cybercrime threats. It is imperative to look for ways in which trust is forged in the ICT development context.

Arguably, the development of future personalisation for social media must build upon the body of knowledge of secured transactions focusing on confidentiality and integrity principles. Factors encouraging trust from consumers to e-commerce websites, such as seal of approval, branding, navigation, presentation, technology and fulfillment (Corritore, Kracher & Wiedenbeck, 2003) can prove applicable in the context of social networking sites. Therefore, more research attention is necessary to address the issues of social trust being a lubricant of content-based transactions on social networks. One of the pressing issues to consider is moving from peer-to-peer formation of trust to third party validation processes. However, the challenge of systematically understanding when trust is needed and works best in online networks still exists. The success of third party trust-based assurance depends on additional research and ICT development efforts in the context of social networks. This article argues for the necessity of further research into the development of entities and identities on social networks. As more and more users, as well as businesses, flock to social networking to interact, communicate and conduct business, it is important to understand the risks and threats involved.

6. CONCLUSION

Users easily develop trust in social media applications, this in turn leads to higher information disclosure behaviour (Elmi et al., 2012). In earlier research trust has been long associated with propensity towards information disclosure online, this behaviour extends to social media. With the proliferation of social technologies into every area of human activity, this user friendly and high quality technology, as perceived by its users, leads to the development of higher levels of trust (Rose, 2011). Self selection of the network membership, and trust of the fellow network members promotes higher levels of personal information disclosure and threatens privacy. Although user awareness of threats posed by personalised messages and phishing in particular has been improved, much remains to be done by the social networking service providers to ensure security of personal information accumulated through them. This chapter argues that social media users need to have better knowledge about the privacy protection mechanisms and the use of personal information by social networking services as they are more inclined to reveal private information in this trusted setting. We hope that the next five years of the advances in technology and information security will bring the solution to the continuous rise of exploitation of the trusted nature of social networking services by cybercriminals.

REFERENCES

Acquisti, A., Adjerid, I., & Brandimarte, L. (2013). Gone in 15 seconds: The limits of privacy transparency and control. *IEEE Security and Privacy*, *11*(4), 72–74. doi:10.1109/MSP.2013.86

Adler, P., & Kwon, S. (2002). Social capital: Prospects for a new concept. *Academy of Management Review*, *27*, 17–40.

Anti-Phishing Working Group. (2009). Retrieved from http://www.antiphishing.org

Avesani, P., Massa, P., & Tiella, R. (2005). A trust-enhanced recommender system application: Moleskiing. In *Proceedings of the 2005 ACM Symposium on Applied Computing (SAC)* (pp. 1589-1593). ACM. doi:10.1145/1066677.1067036

Beudoin, C. E. (2008). Explaining the relationship between internet use and interpersonal trust: Taking into account motivation and information overload. *Journal of Computer-Mediated Communication*, *13*(3), 550–568. doi:10.1111/j.1083-6101.2008.00410.x

Brehm, J., & Rahn, W. (1997). Individual-level evidence for the causes and consequences of socialcapital. *American Journal of Political Science*, *41*(3), 999–1024. doi:10.2307/2111684

Cheung, C. M., & Lee, M. K. (2006). Understanding consumer trust in internet shopping: A multidisciplinary approach. *Journal of the American Society for Information Science and Technology*, *57*(4), 479–492. doi:10.1002/asi.20312

Corritore, C., Kracher, B., & Wiedenbeck, S. (2003). On-line trust: Concepts, evolving themes, a model. *International Journal of Human-Computer Studies*, *58*(6), 737–758. doi:10.1016/S1071-5819(03)00041-7

Dutton, W. H., & Helsper, E. (2007). *Oxford internet survey 2007 report: The internet in Britain*. Oxford, UK: Oxford Internet Institute.

Dutton, W. H., Helsper, E. J., & Gerber, M. M. (2009). *Oxford internet survey 2009 report: The internet in Britain*. Oxford Internet Institute, University of Oxford.

Dutton, W. H., & Shepherd, A. (2006). Trust in the internet as an experience technology. *Information Communication and Society*, *9*(4), 433–451. doi:10.1080/13691180600858606

Ellison, N. B., Steinfield, C., & Lampe, C. (2007). The benefits of Facebook 'friends': Social capital and college students' use of online social network sites. *Journal of Computer-Mediated Communication*, *12*.

Facebook Statistics. (2013). *Facebook data science*. Retrieved from: https://www.facebook.com/data/notes

Friedman, M., Resnick, P., & Sami, R. (2007). *Algorithmic game theory*. Cambridge, UK: Cambridge University Press.

Galagher, S. (2009). Social networks a magnet for malware. In *IT management ebook*. WebMediaBrands.

Girvan, M., & Newman, M. E. J. (2002). Community structure in social and biological networks. *Proceedings of the National Academy of Sciences of the United States of America*, 99(12), 8271–8276. doi:10.1073/pnas.122653799 PMID:12060727

Golbeck, J. (2007). The dynamics of web-based social networks: Membership, relationships, and change. *First Monday*, 12(11). doi:10.5210/fm.v12i11.2023

Golbeck, J. (2008). *Trust on the world wide web: A survey*. Hanover, MA: NowPublishers.

Golbeck, J., & Hendler, J. (2004). Reputation network analysis for email filtering. In *Proceedings of the First Conference on Email and Anti-Spam*. Academic Press.

Goldman, A. (2009). Businesses lack social media policies. In *IT manager's guide to social networking*. WebMediaBrands.

Hoffman, D. L., & Novak, T. P. (2009). Flow online: Lessons learned and future prospects. *Journal of Interactive Marketing*, 23(1), 23–34. doi:10.1016/j.intmar.2008.10.003

Hoffman, K., Zage, D., & Nita-Rotaru, C. (2009). A survey of attack and defence techniques for reputations systems. *ACM Computing Surveys*, 42(1), 1–16. doi:10.1145/1592451.1592452

Jiang, P., Jones, D., & Javie, S. (2008). How third party certification programs relate to consumer trust in online transactions: An exploratory study. *Psychology and Marketing*, 25(9), 839–858. doi:10.1002/mar.20243

Kimery, K. M., & McCord, M. (2002). Third-party assurances: Mapping the road to trust in e-retailing. *Journal of Information Technology Theory and Application*, 4(2), 64–82.

Liu, C., Marchewka, J. T., Lu, J., & Yu, C. S. (2004). Beyond concern: A privacy–trust–behavioral intention model of electronic commerce. *Information & Management*, 42(1), 127–142. doi:10.1016/j.im.2004.01.002

Lynch, P. D., Robert, J. K., & Srinivasan, S. S. (2001). The global internet shopper: Evidence from shopping tasks in twelve countries. *Journal of Advertising Research*, 41, 15–23.

Massa, P., & Avesani, P. (2007). Trust metrics on controversial users: Balancing between tyranny of the majority and echo chambers. *International Journal on Semantic Web and Information Systems*, 3(2).

McKnight, D. H., & Chervany, N. L. (2002). What trust means in e-commerce customer relationships: An interdisciplinary conceptual typology. *International Journal of Electronic Commerce*, 6, 35–60.

Mitchell, M. (2006). Complex systems: Network thinking. *Artificial Intelligence*, 170(18), 1194–1212. doi:10.1016/j.artint.2006.10.002

Naraine, R. (2009). When web 2.0 becomes security risk 2.0. In *Real business real threats*. Kaspersky Lab.

Nor, D. K. M., Nazarie, W. N. W. M., & Yusoff, A. A. A. M. (2013). Factors influencing individuals' trust in online purchase through social networking sites. *International Journal of Information Science and Management*, 1-16.

Ollman, G. (2008). *The phishing guide*. Accessed at: http://logman.tech.officelive.com/Documents/The%20Phishing%20Guide.pdf

Pentina, I., Zhang, L., & Basmanova, O. (2013). Antecedents and consequences of trust in a social media brand: A cross-cultural study of Twitter. *Computers in Human Behavior*, *29*(4), 1546–1555. doi:10.1016/j.chb.2013.01.045

Putnam, R. D. (2000). *Bowling alone*. New York: Simon and Schuster.

Riegelsberger, J., Sasse, M. A., & McCarthy, J. D. (2003). The researcher's dilemma: Evaluating trust in computer-mediated communication. *International Journal of Human-Computer Studies*, *58*(6), 759–781. doi:10.1016/S1071-5819(03)00042-9

Riegelsberger, J., Sasse, M. A., & McCarthy, J. D. (2005). The mechanics of trust: A framework for research and design. *International Journal of Human-Computer Studies*, *62*(3), 381–422. doi:10.1016/j.ijhcs.2005.01.001

Rose, C. (2011). The security implications of ubiquitous social media. *International Journal of Management & Information Systems*, *15*(1).

Rousseau, D. M., Sitkin, S. B., Burt, R. S., & Camerer, C. (1998). Not so different after all: Across-discipline view of trust. *Academy of Management Review*, *23*(3), 393–404. doi:10.5465/AMR.1998.926617

Sitkin, S. B., & Pablo, A. L. (1992). Reconceptualising the determinants of risk behaviour. *Academy of Management Review*, *17*, 9–38.

Stompka, P. (1999). *Trust*. Cambridge, UK: Cambridge University Press.

Symantec Enterprise Security. (2009). *Internet security threat report* (vol. 14). Symantec Press.

Urban, G. L., & Sultan, F. (2000). Placing trust at the center of your Internet strategy. *Sloan Management Review*, *42*(1), 39–48.

Van Wyck, K. (2009). How to use Facebook safely. In *IT manager's guide to social networking*. WebMediaBrands.

Wang, W., & Benbasat, I. (2005). Trust and adoption of online recommendation agents. *Journal of the AIS*, *6*(3), 72–101.

Wang, Y. D., & Emurian, H. (2005). An overview of online trust: Concepts, elements, and implications. *Computers in Human Behavior*, *21*(1), 105–125. doi:10.1016/j.chb.2003.11.008

Xu, H., Teo, H.-H., & Tan, B. C. Y. (2005). Predicting the adoption of location-based services: The role of trust and perceived privacy risk. In *Proceedings of the 26th International Conference on Information Systems* (ICIS 2005). Las Vegas, NV: ICIS.

Yousafzai, S., Pallister, J., & Foxall, G. (2005). E-banking-A matter of trust: Trust-building strategies for electronic banking. *Psychology and Marketing*, *22*(2), 181–201. doi:10.1002/mar.20054

Ziegler, C., & Golbeck, J. (2006). Investigating correlations of trust and interest similarity. *Decision Support Systems*, *43*(2).

KEY TERMS AND DEFINITIONS

Security Measures: Means employed to protect system, application or data from breaches and minimise security threats.

Security Notices: In e-commerce context, regulatory transparency means. These mechanisms comprise of privacy statements and security seals. Notices inform users about what data is collected and how their personal information is handled by a website.

Threat: In computing context refers to the possibility/danger of exploitation of a vulnerability in a system or application aimed to cause harm/destruction or breach of confidentiality.

Trust: In human relations context, associated with establishing trustworthiness of another person. In computing terms refers to the ability to establish confidence into or validity of another party in the computer transaction (e.g. communication, monetary, information sharing, etc.).

ENDNOTES

[1] The discussion of the threat landscape has been presented in Benson, V. (2011). Social Networking and Trust: Is Personalisation the Only Defence Technique?. In M. Lytras, P. Ordóñez de Pablos, & E. Damiani (Eds.) *Semantic Web Personalization and Context Awareness: Management of Personal Identities and Social Networking* (32-41). Hershey, PA: Information Science Reference, and further developed for this chapter.

Chapter 7
Reflections on the Impact of Social Technologies on Lecturers in a Pathway Institution

Donna M Velliaris
Eynesbury Institute of Business and Technology, Australia

Craig R Willis
Eynesbury Institute of Business and Technology, Australia

Paul B Breen
Greenwich School of Management, UK

ABSTRACT

Education has evolved over time from face-to-face teaching to computer-supported learning, and now to even more sophisticated electronic tools. In particular, social technologies are being used to supplement the classroom experience and to ensure that students are becoming increasingly engaged in ways that appeal to them. No matter how educationally beneficial, however, new technology is affected by its users. To investigate this, lecturers at the Eynesbury Institute of Business and Technology (EIBT)—a Higher Education pathway provider—were surveyed to determine their perception and application of social technolog(ies) in their personal, but predominantly 'professional' lives. Utilising a qualitative and autoethnographic approach, one author provides an insight into their own attitude toward social technologies, coupled with responses to three open-ended questions. Thereafter, the same questions were posed to EIBT academic staff to understand their willingness or reluctance to use social technologies in their practice as part of their first-year pathway course(s).

INTRODUCTION

Educators have been using technologies for decades i.e., resources that range from 'textbooks to overhead projectors, from typewriters in English language classrooms to charts of the periodic table on the walls of laboratories' (Mishra & Koehler, 2006, p. 1023). Herein, 'technology/ technologies' will refer to artefacts and tools of the Web 2.0 era and beyond. The 'information age' is characterised by the diffusion of Information and Communications Technologies (ICTs) and

DOI: 10.4018/978-1-4666-7401-1.ch007

an increased demand for educational approaches that foster 'lifelong learning' (Fischer & Konomi, 2007). Slaoti, Motteram and Onat-Stelma (2013, p. 78) referred to this phenomenon as the 'technologification' of [adult] learning. As far back as Laurillard (1993), there was a desire to make greater use of the affordances of new technologies, which has since expanded exponentially as the physical terrain of study itself has become increasingly digital (Beard & Dale, 2010). Emerging social technologies offer new opportunities, otherwise referred to as 'participatory media' and/or 'relationship technologies' (Greenhow, Robelia, & Hughes, 2009). In the present landscape of Higher Education (HE) and technological change, important transformations are underway in terms of how students study.

BACKGROUND

Eynesbury Institute of Business and Technology

The Eynesbury Institute of Business and Technology (EIBT) is one of a growing number of private providers linking up with partner universities to establish programs that aim to improve the academic performance and language skills of international students and simultaneously create opportunities to promote Australian HE in a global market. EIBT students are almost exclusively international and the main objective is to secure their tertiary destination prior to them meeting entry requirements. EIBT aims to matriculate international students to 'target' institutions (Martin, 2014, p. 5) by offering diplomas that comprise the exact same courses that constitute the first-year of a bachelor degree in Business, Information Technology or Engineering at the *University of Adelaide* or the *University of South Australia*.

Though EIBT is accessible to local students, recruitment is predominantly directed towards full fee-paying international students who:

1. Have completed Year 11 high school in Australia and would prefer to continue their studies in a different academic context;
2. Have completed Year 12 high school in Australia, but did not obtain an ATAR [Australian Tertiary Admission Rank] sufficient for direct entry into university;
3. Have graduated from high school abroad, but whose English language proficiency did not meet the minimum requirement for direct entry into university; or
4. Are above 20 years of age with a relevant employment history.

EIBT diploma programs benefit from the discipline-specific expertise and academic rigour the universities apply to their own curriculum (Velliaris & Willis, 2014). Cross-institutional lecturers—PhD candidates, experienced academics and/or business professionals—deliver approximately 40 courses across three back-to-back trimesters. The pathway university moderates diploma delivery and grants advanced standing for courses if students achieve the minimum entry-level score upon graduation.

Impact of Social Technologies

In a seminal article, Putnam (1995) documented a broad decline in civic engagement and social participation in the United States (US) over a 35 year period, and also argued that social disengagement was affecting individual lives and the social fabric of the US at two levels. First, at the *individual* level, disengagement was contributing to a poorer quality of life and diminished physical and psychological health. That is, when people have more social contact, they tend to be both physically and mentally happier and healthier. Second, at the *societal* level, disengagement was seen to be associated with a more corrupt and less efficient government, as well as increased crime. Putnam (1995) claimed that when citizens are involved in civic life, schools operate more efficiently, politicians are more responsive, and streets are safer.

In terms of HE, there has been a shift in the view(s) of the purpose of education. There is growing emphasis on the need to enable and support not only the acquisition of knowledge, but also to develop the skills and resources necessary for students to engage with technologies (Owen, Grant, Sayers, & Facer, 2006). Essentially, technologies of the past were:

1. Specific;
2. Stable; and
3. Transparent,

whilst new technologies are:

1. Protean;
2. Unstable; and
3. Opaque (Koehler & Mishra, 2009, p. 60).

Relatedly, Hooper and Rieber (1995, p. 161) outlined the critical difference between 'educational technology' and mere 'technology in education' with the argument that 'guidance for designing effective technology-based classrooms should be grounded in the literature on effective pedagogy in general'. The aim of improving HE quality, invites such questions as—*To what extent can social technologies improve the overall standard of teaching and learning?*

Since the introduction of computing into society, both scholars and technologists have pondered its impact (e.g., Bell, 1973; Jacobson & Roucek, 1959; Leavitt & Whisler, 1958) and the degree to which technology itself has contributed to a shift

in the nature of education (McGrath, Karabas, & Willis, 2011; Motteram, 2013). Scholars who advocate for the positive and beneficial impact of using social technologies are many (Snow, 2012; Spires, Wiebe, Young, Hollebrands, & Lee, 2012; Trilling & Fadel, 2009). The timeline of this can be traced to Warschauer's (2003, 2007) vast portfolio of works, as well as studies conducted by Salmon (2005), and Motteram and Sharma (2009).

On the other hand, there exists a certain scepticism and apprehension by other HE educators concerning its use (e.g., Garrison & Kanuka, 2004). Some scholars warn against uncritical adoption of tools such as social networking sites, including Alvesson and Sandberg (2013, p. 20) who discussed the contextual factor of 'fashion and fads in society' and warned against embracing something because it is a 'hot' topic today, yet is in danger of going 'cold' tomorrow. In addition, Selwyn (2011, p. 108) suggested that technology involves 'the deskilling of lecturers and their students, engendering a tool mentality where technology is used to yield mechanical tasks and situations of social disconnect'.

Lea and Jones (2011, p. 391) pointed out that 'in a fast-moving technological world, applications being heralded by learning technologists in HE are constantly being overtaken by new ones'. A culture of 'instability' is inevitable around environments of rapid change and comes about as a consequence of the pace at which new technologies are improved and disseminated. Accordingly, the knowledge required to use digital technologies is never static. Koehler and Mishra (2009, p. 61) reviewed the differences in standardised and specified technologies of the past, such as microscopes and chalkboards, and those of the increasingly digital in the present time.

Predominantly, a reluctance to integrate technology applies to the newer generation of social networking sites, namely Chirp, Conversations, Flayvr, Medium, Pheed and Thumb. Educators may be unfamiliar with many of them and somewhat reluctant to cross social boundaries, thus merging parts of their personal and professional worlds (Schwartz, 2009).

At the heart of effective teaching with technology—together with the interactions/relationships between/among them—are three core components:

1. Content;
2. Pedagogy; and
3. Technology.

These interactions occur differently across contexts and account for wide variations seen in the extent and quality of educational technology integration. Koehler and Mishra (2009, p. 60) introduced a framework for teacher knowledge and for technology integration called Technologi-cal Pedagogical Content Knowledge (originally TPCK, but now TPACK or Technology-Pedagogy-and-Content-Knowledge, refer to Figure 1). They stressed that it 'built on Lee Shulman's construct of Pedagogical Content Knowledge (PCK) to include technology knowledge'. Through the interaction of these bodies of knowledge—practically and theoretically—there is creation of the flexibility 'needed to successfully integrate technology use into teaching' and a description of how understanding of educational technologies and PCK interact to produce 'effective teaching' (Koehler & Mishra, 2009, p. 62).

Teaching and learning occurs in a sociocultural system where various tools and forms of interaction create collective activity that may be supported by technological affordances, an argument supported by Chapelle (2010) and Motteram (2013).

Figure 1. TPACK framework and its knowledge components (Koehler & Mishra, 2009, p. 63).

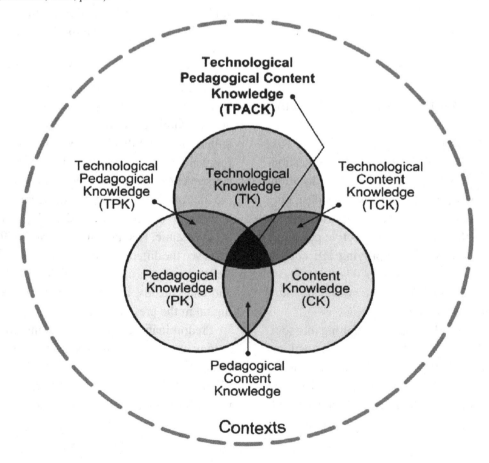

Besides being a resource manager, increasingly lecturers need to become a 'partner in learning' rather than a facilitator. That is, HE lecturers need to view students as contributors of knowledge and thus allow them to participate in the creation of content (Beldarrain, 2006, p. 149). It would seem advantageous, therefore, to better understand how students today use and make sense of social technologies. Such an understanding may provide essential information for educators who employ social networks to communicate with them and/ or those who are contemplating integrating such tool(s) in the future (Blattner & Lomicka, 2012).

Although questions need to be considered at an institutional level, there are many questions that need to be addressed at a 'personal' level regarding academics' own practice and commitment to utilising social technologies in the delivery of their course(s). The central focus of this chapter was to explore if, how and/or why academics use social technologies, which may reveal the mediating relationship among content, pedagogy, and technology as well as issues related to their professional identit(ies) (Coldron & Smith, 1999, p. 711).

Though the many challenges facing HE in the digital age strongly suggest that the university will change or that it must change, there appears to be no suggested prototype for the 'university of the future'. In closing, 'the risks of doing nothing are higher than the risk of doing something. Universities typically take too long to adopt new technologies. Institutional inertia can be a significant barrier to adoption' (J. Armstrong & Franklin, 2008).

RESEARCH PROCESS

Autoethnographic Methodology

A qualitative and autoethnographic methodology has increasingly become a preference for teacher-researchers aiming to examine the multiplicity of social, cultural and educational factors that may have contributed to their professional identity (Ellis & Bochner, 2000b). Throughout this chapter, the term 'autoethnography' will refer to the research genre that associates the personal with the social, cultural and educational. Writing begins with a descriptive narrative of events and associated activities that unfolded, and then develops into a reflective analysis of those occurrences.

Ellis and Bochner (2000a) characterised autoethnography as 'autobiographies that self-consciously explore the interplay of the introspective, personally engaged self with cultural descriptions mediated through language, history, and ethnographic explanation'. They offered an insightful triadic model to illustrate the complexity of autoethnographic nomenclature. They explained how autoethnographers can vary in their emphasis across the dimensions of:

1. The self [*auto*];
2. The culture [*ethno*]; and
3. The research process [*graphy*] and may therefore, align anywhere along the continuum of these three axes.

Similarly, Chang (2008) emphasised how autoethnography should be:

1. Autobiographical in its content orientation;
2. Cultural in its interpretive orientation; and
3. Ethnographical in its methodological orientation. Accordingly, self-reflective writings devoid of one of these three ingredients may fail to be a true *auto-ethno-graphy*.

Rooney (2005) referred to an autoethnographic method as 'insider' research, whereby the concept of validity may be problematic due to the teacher's own involvement with the subject of study. This methodology allows teacher-researchers to access primary data from its genesis, as the prime source of data stems from themself. As a methodology that is primarily interested in excavating the formation of identity, Austin and Hickety (2007) claimed that autoethnography holds significant potential for the development of critically reflexive and genuinely emancipatory professional practice for educators. Indeed, autoethnographers are privileged with an intimate and holistic perspective on their 'familiar' data; a familiarity that provides advantages to them in relation to collection, analysis and interpretation (Velliaris & Willis, 2014). For example, teachers 'situate their selves in their own teaching and in their students' learning; and students situate their learning in their selves and their teacher's teaching' (P. Armstrong, 2008).

As Polkinghorne (1988, p. 161) noted, autoethnography through narrative inquiry and 'life' go together, and in the sharing of a personal narrative, one shares their journey. The attraction of an autoethnographic approach is its capacity to render life experiences in relevant and meaningful ways (Connelly & Clandinin, 1990, p. 10); unravelling them and the causal links among events uncovered. Hence, this type of insider research can facilitate: authenticity; closer relationships; ease of access; informed knowledge; and richer data (Arksey & Knight, 1999; Rooney, 2005). In other words, it has considerable benefits in terms of generating a fuller description of the study and its setting (Creswell, 2008).

This methodology is often described as 'reader-friendly' because a narrative style of writing tends to be more engaging than conventional scholarly writing (Chang, 2008). According to Nash (2004, p. 28), 'scholarly personal narratives liberate researchers from abstract, impersonal writings and touch readers' lives'. Gergen and Gergen (2002, p. 14) contended that 'in using oneself as an [auto] ethnographic exemplar, the researcher is freed from the traditional conventions of writing'. Autoethnography thus enables one's unique voice—inclusive of colloquialisms, reverberations and emotional expressiveness—to be valued. This process may generate new insights and enhance sensitivity towards the knowledge gained (Velliaris & Willis, 2014).

Qualitative Survey Method

To better understand the complex and rapidly changing nature of social technologies in the first-year 'pathway' experience, the researchers were interested in EIBT academics' use of social technologies. For the purpose of this study, a brief questionnaire was disseminated via EIBT's online portal to academic lecturers with ten (n=10) individuals contributing. Data collection consisted of one source in the form of an 'open-ended' survey (Creswell, 2008; Kaufman, Guerra, & Platt, 2006; Neuman, 2004). The intention was to elicit personal responses to three research questions that would help to display multiple layers of autoethnographic consciousness and that were arranged in a somewhat chronological order in terms of past, present and future contexts.

- **Past:** What, if any, social technologies have you used/attempted to use in business, IT or engineering courses? And, what positive and/or negative experiences have you faced?
- **Present:** Do you use social media in your personal life? What, how and why?
- **Future:** How would you respond to the statement, 'ICTs will continue to affect teaching and learning profoundly, no matter what the response of traditional higher education institutions'?

Academic staff remained anonymous and were assigned a Respondent Number (RN1-RN10) for identification purposes. No narrative style or way of articulating the content of responses was established. This was motivated by a desire for the writing to be a trial process; a 'pilot' study or 'small scale version or trial run, undertaken in preparation for the major study' (Polit, Beck, & Hungler, 2001, p. 467). Further, the age and gender of respondents was unidentifiable since the emphasis was on qualitative features and issues of relevance to the research purpose (Patton, 1990, p. 169).

While it is acknowledged that there are countless social technologies that may support educational activities in HE, this study did not focus on any particular 'type'. This was an 'exploratory' study (Neuman, 2004, p. 15) that involved becoming familiar with a new setting and its particular features, gathering a range of data from a small community, and creating a preliminary picture of contributors' professional viewpoints to be able to generate ideas for future research-informed action. The three overarching objectives were:

1. To acknowledge the value of one's experiences and understand how educators are themselves a rich source of description and insight;
2. To employ the reading and writing of self-narratives as a window through which self and others can be examined and understood; and
3. To share and value the narratives for EIBT teaching and learning improvement.

In order to set the scene, the narratives commence with one author's own personal stories. For Ellis and Bochner (2000, p. 738), the primary aim of autoethnography is to 'come to understand [one]self in deeper ways and with understanding yourself comes understanding others'.

REPORTED NARRATIVES

Autoethnography

As teaching and learning intrinsically define who I am, I felt compelled to embark on this autoethnographic journey to investigate my teacher-learner self. My personal narrative has been drawn together as a compilation of anecdotal, scholarly, and autobiographical writing. Organised chronologically, I attempt to link my personal motivation to pursue this study as it was

the 'process of opening inward that allow[ed] me to reach outward toward understanding' (Berger, 2001, p. 515).

Crossing time, I (re)visit and (re)construct seminal events in my life using knowledge—gleaned in intervening years—to see how my past experiences may have informed, guided and influenced me today. What follows is my story; insight and interpretation of experiences that may have contributed to my professional identity as an academic in the Australian HE sector. In purposefully completing this narrative, I 'attempt to take you as the reader into the intimacies of my world. I hope to do this in such a way that you are stimulated to reflect upon your own life in relation to mine' (Sparkes, 1996, p. 467).

I matriculated from high school in 1988. I had little choice of subjects and definitely no computing or computer-related studies. I am not entirely sure what year that subject was introduced into South Australian high schools, indeed I did not have the luxury of 'rapid editing, instantaneous cut-and-paste... and unlimited perfectibility... infinitely re-editable and instantly distributable [assignments]' (Land & Bayne, 2008, p. 676). My handwriting regularly changed and hand cramps were inevitable after a long school day.

Following matriculation in the late 1980s, I applied to be an international exchange student. I spent one year abroad in Tokyo, and similarly, my Japanese host families and high school did not have Internet facilities. My mother and I always maintained a close relationship and writing letters became our primary source of communication as phone calls incurred astronomical charges. During those days, the walk to the mailbox was filled with anticipation. I would leave the house to amble to the post box, savouring the cherry blossoms blowing in the breeze and pondering: 'What stamp did my mother choose? What type of stationery? What travels did this letter take from my mother's hands to mine?'

I became increasingly gratified that she had taken the time to put pen to paper—to sit down perhaps as I often did with a cup of [green] tea—to write a letter especially for me. It took up to 10 days for mail to be sent and received between Australia and Japan and hence, I learnt firsthand that patience was a virtue. What was frustrating in the beginning, became a cathartic process; finding private spaces to foster contemplation and deliberation. My mother and I kept all our letters and today, they remain in a treasured folder.

During my exchange student days, I recall occasions spent at landmarks such as *Hachiko Square* in *Shibuya* or *Almond* on the corner of *Roppongi Crossing* and making forays to a payphone to check for messages with my host families. Indeed, mobile phones have revolutionised the experience of arranging meetings in urban space. After many travels to and from Japan, one significant difference in the use of mobile phones for social interactions in Adelaide (Australia) versus Tokyo (Japan) is apparent. In Adelaide, it seems almost impossible to arrange a meeting point and somehow become lost. The terrain is flat, the landmarks are big and bold, and with a population density of only three persons (or less) per square kilometre—'Who needs a mobile phone to coordinate a simple meeting? How has such an uncomplicated event become complicated?'

In enormous contrast, there are at least 12 million persons in Tokyo or approximately 350 persons per square kilometre, so it is not surprising that one rather 'desperately' requires a mobile phone. Tokyoites today, initially agree on a general time and place and exchange 10+ messages that progressively narrow in on and eventually enable persons to converge in a 'coordinated dance through the urban jungle' (Ito, 2003, p. 2). While I used a mobile phone in Tokyo for many years, I only recently succumbed to getting one in Australia.

I became a school teacher in my early 20s and email quickly evolved from a novel way of communicating to a full-blown business tool that without careful management could become a real-time sponge. Undoubtedly, email is a powerful communications tool, but one that also has the potential for deep impact on relationships and 'mood' in the workplace. For most emailers, sloppy, shady or chit-chat email habits carry few consequences, but for others, sending inappropriate content and mishandling/misuse can be disastrous. Communicating at such a fast pace via email or other social application gives individuals the potential to engage in 'incivility'; communicative behaviour exhibited in computer-mediated interactions that violate workplace norms of mutual respect (Lim & Teo, 2009, p. 419). In agreement with Lindley, Harper and Sellen (2009, p. 1701), oftentimes emailing 'discourages the possibility of ruminating before sending a reply and it limits self-reflection'.

Younger workers represent the generation to have grown-up with the Internet and various social technologies. They are comfortable sending emails pertaining to many and varied events, including: birth notices; invitations to weddings; marriage/divorce announcements; thank you notes; condolences; and job inquiries/applications. HE student recruitment, marketing, alumni relations, and even 'admissions' have begun to send out decisions via email (Fallows, 2002). As an educator, my attitude presents a contrast to that of younger generations for whom communication is frequently constant (i.e., peripheral, pervading, transient and short-lived). Unlike electronic communication, a handwritten letter engages the totality of my heart and senses. Subscribing to Davis (2009), 'in a small but significant fashion, the act of writing to another person gives us the opportunity to engage in the healing and repairing of our fractured world, as two individuals are able to reach out, connect, acknowledge, and celebrate one another'.

In 2000, I completed my Master's thesis on Computer Assisted Language Learning (CALL) for Japanese language teaching and learning in Australia. Japanese consists of three scripts:

Hiragana, Katakana and Kanji. The first two are called 'syllabaries' because each symbol is a syllabic unit, while *Kanji* [Chinese] characters are ideographic symbols. While Romaji [Romanised Japanese] is not entirely foreign to native speakers of Japanese, this script is used on limited occasions, such as writing their name on a passport. It is not an integral part of their native orthography and is not often mixed with the other scripts and importantly, Romaji does not always transcribe the spoken language in a grapheme-phoneme match. Japanese has traditionally suffered from a shortage of orthographically well-designed CALL programs (Okuyama, 2007, p. 357). Hence, while my French and Italian teaching colleagues were able to implement online 'social' letter writing/chat activities with foreign students abroad, while I failed to see the advantage of promoting un-authentic Japanese.

While I acknowledge that social technologies play an important role in present and future teaching and learning processes, efforts should be made to monitor the effects/affects on the writing skills of HE students (Omar & Miah, 2013). Chronologically, Tapscott (1999) put forward the notion of the 'net generation', while social commentators coined the term 'millennials' as a generational label (Howe & Strauss, 2000). In 2001, Prensky suggested that HE (undergraduate) students could be characterised as 'digital natives' (i.e., young, fast, technologically avid, into graphics, texting and gaming, experiment with trial and error) due to their exposure to digital technologies while growing up. Subsequently, a proliferation of less widely used epithets have surfaced, each attempting to capture the essence of the same phenomenon (e.g., Generation C, Google Generation, and the Nintendo Generation). Conversely, their mature lecturers can be characterised as 'digital immigrants' (i.e., older, less familiar and somewhat uncomfortable with technology, preferring to carefully read hardcopies offline).

As a HE lecturer, I can identify with being a digital immigrant as well as a 'reluctant adopter'; realise technology is a part of today's world and try to engage with it, but it feels alien and unintuitive… While they possess a basic cell phone, they do not text if they can help it… check their emails intermittently and perhaps have surrendered to online banking' (Zur & Zur, 2011). Moreover, I am a 'minimalist'. That is, I try to engage with technology minimally and only when necessary… Google for information if they have to and purchase online only if they cannot do so in a local store. While they may have a Facebook account, they may check it once a day or every couple of days. They will ask for directions to a friend's house instead of checking Google maps. If absolutely necessary, they will use Skype, but they are not eager to do so' (Zur & Zur, 2011).

As a minimalist-reluctant-adopter-&-digital-immigrant, 'netspeak' language register (or blargo, cyberslang, cyberterms, digichat, digitalk, e-lingo, geekspeak, leetspeak, net lingo, textspeak, and my personal favourite 'textese') is not my preference. Transformations (mostly mutations) of the English language in the hands of technology has been rapid and affected large number of users (Kinsella, 2010). Features such as: an absence of apostrophes e.g., don't = dont, can't = cant; random capitalisation to express deeper emotion e.g., I AM ANGRY or GRRRR; exaggerated punctuation e.g., what = whaaaat?!, please = pleassse; countless shorthand/acronyms/initialisms for brevity e.g., Absent From Keyboard = AFK, Be Right Back = BRB, Got To Go Parent Over Shoulder = GTGPOS, Laughing Out Loud = LOL, Oh My God = OMG; special symbols to intensify feelings e.g., I **love** you; and linguistic shortcuts enabled by emoticons e.g.,:-D:o may be acceptable among friends, however, I must decode emails from students who commonly use this style.

One random website (not worth citing), claimed that lecturers who recognise that netspeak is 'different' and not deficient, can find ways to harness this language enroute to improving students' academic writing. My response to that proposition is 'witwct'.

Question 1: What, if any, social technologies have you used/attempted to use in business, IT or engineering courses? And, what positive and/or negative experiences have you faced?

I feel uneasy answering this question and affirm that I have never used social technolog(ies) in the classroom. I concede that social networking sites are undeniably engaging for HE students, who fall within the 18-24 demographic, but I remain hesitant. The underlying debate relates to whether or not the 'popularity' of social networking systems can be the impetus for effective integration into my teaching. I am not referring to the simple tasks of uploading a course syllabi, showing YouTube clips in class (Is YouTube a social technology?) or other simple and minimally expected teacher tasks. I am referring to actual formative and summative assessment tasks that incorporate more advanced applications.

Using social media may move discussions and interactions that are private (i.e., happening in a secure classroom), into a public space. Stories abound about students posting images and comments on Facebook that have later come back to curse them when submitting a job application or employees being dismissed because of comments made in what they thought was a private space… Class-created content and online commentary can be stored and archived by anyone with access, which creates the potential for them to resurface at a later stage. 'Will this public learning space inhibit risk-taking and instead foster a reluctance to share ideas with a broader audience for fear that these things will come back to haunt ME later?'

In a study conducted by Ajjan and Hartshorne (2008, p. 73) based on HE faculty decisions to implement Web 2.0 social technologies, they defined 'attitude' as the degree to which individuals favour a certain behaviour. They explicated three attitudinal types, namely, perceived:

1. Usefulness;
2. Ease of use; and
3. Compatibility.

First, 'usefulness' was identified as the degree to which an individual believed that technology would improve their job performance; the higher the perceived usefulness the more likely an individual would adopt that new technology. Second, 'ease of use' represented the degree to which an innovation was easy to understand and operate; technologies perceived to be less complex have higher possibility of acceptance and use by potential users. And third, 'compatibility' was described as the degree to which technology fit with the existing values and experiences. With this in mind, my main hurdle appears to be Attitudinal Type (1).

New technologies must be introduced in a curricular properly and not randomly (e.g., evidence to suggest that they will enhance rather than detract from the teaching and learning). First, however, I have a duty to uncover the mass of social technologies to make a selection suitable for my educational purposes because, the more things I could teach, the greater the need to make my students responsible and effective/efficient partners in the learning process. By understanding which social technologies are more apt for supporting specific activities in teaching and learning, I will be in a better position to make an informed decision i.e., to deploy or otherwise and invest in such resources.

Question 2: Do you use social media in your personal life? What, how and why?

As I perused the Internet, I found a list of the top ten social networking sites in the world, namely:

1. Facebook;
2. Twitter;
3. Ozone;
4. Google+;
5. Sina Weibo;
6. Habbo;
7. Renren;
8. Linkedin;
9. Vkontakte; and
10. Bebo (Bhabwat, Omre, & Chand, 2013).

From this list, I have used one and heard of only three of these sites. Others not on this particular listing include: Ask.fm; Care2; Classmates; Cyworld, del.icio.us; digg; flickr; Friendster; Hi5; Instagram; Last.fm; LiveJournal; MeetMe; Meetup; MyLife; MySpace; Ning; Orkut; Pinterest; Stumpleupon; Tagged; Travellerspoint; Tumblr; VK; and Xanga, from which I am familiar with a mere two.

In 2007, I decided to join Facebook as I was a frequent traveller and it appeared to be the most convenient method of documenting my adventures with few words and lots of photos. I regularly composed lengthy emails CC'ed to family and friends, but I found Facebook an enjoyable medium for visually sharing my global ventures. Today, I still have my account, but my list of 'friends' is entirely comprised of family and 'strong' friendships. I have chosen to maintain the highest level of privacy, as I do not want colleagues and students to see too much of my personal life. My concerns over becoming too dependent on this media relates to: cyber bullying; identity theft; misuse of information for less than savoury purposes; privacy issues; stalking; taking things out of context; virtual integrity; and issues relating to intellectual property and copyright. While I acknowledge that this may be interpreted as having something to 'hide', on the contrary, I use Facebook for my closest relations.

In 2011, in a small lecture theatre, one student announced that they could not find me on Facebook. I casually laughed and responded that I thought it was inappropriate to have students linked to my account, when I wanted to answer, 'You cannot find me for a reason'. Many students interpreted my response as meaning 'no current students', because at the conclusion of the course, they asked me again. As previously stated, Facebook users are predominantly 18-24 years, a life stage sometimes called 'emerging adulthood' (Bumgarner, 2007), which is a transitory period between adolescence and adulthood when they are probably experiencing freedom by living on their own for the first time and not yet having a family and/or a stable career. If Facebook had been introduced in my 20s, I may have had hundreds of friends, potentially including my former students.

As a final point, I tend to use Facebook when I am entirely alone; a time when I can coordinate a meeting with a friend, post photos of the kids or a 'selfie' for laughs.

Question 3: How would you respond to the statement, 'IT will continue to change teaching and learning profoundly, no matter what the response of traditional higher education institutions'?

I mused over Levine's (2000, p. 2) distinction between 'brick universities' (i.e., traditional HE institutions) and 'click universities' (i.e., virtual HE institutions) or the 'brick and click universities' that offer a combination of the two. With reference to the 'click' type scenario, once faculty and courses go online, administrators gain greater direct control over faculty performance and course content, and thus the potential for administrative scrutiny, supervision, regimentation, discipline and even censorship may increase dramatically. At the same time, the use of technology entails an inevitable extension of working time and an intensification of work as faculty struggle at all hours of the day *and* night to stay on top of that technology and respond (via chatrooms, virtual office hours, and email) to 'everyone' with whom they have now become instantly and continuously accessible.

While many students appreciate the ease and freedom of online services, they may also appreciate a face-to-face physical space where they can interact with others and obtain expert advice. An interesting metaphor for future [HE] educators is that of the teacher as 'concierge' (Bonk, 2010, p. 64); the notion of a teacher shifting from a deliverer of content to that of an educational concierge who finds and/or suggests resources as learners need them. Additionally and in agreement with Levine (2000, p. 4), I imagine that to a certain extent—in the future—an individual's education will occur in a cornucopia of settings and geographic locales via a plethora of educational providers.

It is clear that societal needs will continue to dictate great changes in the knowledge it expects from universities. As traditional degrees lose importance, there may be the need to establish a central database to record an individual's educational achievements (i.e., however and wherever they were gained) and to store supporting documentation. Such an educational 'passport' will file a student's lifetime educational history. It is difficult to imagine the roles society will ask the university to play in the century ahead; one can only be certain they will be different from the roles HE educators and students play today.

Participant Responses

Herein, data stemming from survey responses are shared. Excerpts provide an insight into respondents' lives, but should be conceived as a subjective process realised in a specific historical context. Readers should, therefore, make their own judgments about the extent to which commonalities/dissimilarities could potentially inform their own practices.

In response to the first research question: 'What, if any, social technologies have you used/attempted to use in business, IT or engineering courses? And, what positive and/or negative experiences have you faced?' an almost equal number of respondents have/have not attempted to use social technologies in their courses. First, those who have attempted to use some form of social technology have implemented 'limited' techniques as noted below:

- "I have used Facebook and Twitter (not as much)."
- "I have not used any social media applications within any of my classes, only discussion boards, chat and web/video conferencing within the Learning Management Systems (LMS) of the organisations that I have worked for."
- "Fairly limited in some institutions; mainly interactive discussion boards and live chats. However, some Facebook interactions in one or two university courses."
- "Only discussion forums. These appear to be more relevant to students' desire to use when external (fully online) students are involved. Students who physically attend classes appear to still want to undertake face-to-face discussion especially when their language skills are poor and work involves complex calculations."

On the other hand, respondents who have yet to incorporate social technolog(ies) have either chosen not to or were opposed to this type of resource.

- "None. These students are people I teach, not my personal friends. I should not need to consistently entertain them."
- "None. It is a waste of time. A soon-to-be published paper in a recognised academic journal will attest to this."
- "None. I have not personally used any social technologies to support my teaching. The primary reason for this is the perceived additional workload associated with incorporating them into my teaching and learning environment. At present, I do not have the time."
- "No, workload creep is something many professionals in HE deal with. Many academics play multiple roles and struggle to stay afloat. Adding social media into the mix can become time intensive. There needs to be a strategic reason and plan in place to use social media, otherwise why bother?"

As an extension to the first survey question, respondents were asked to elucidate both 'positive' and 'negative' experience(s) of utilising a social technolog(ies) in their teaching courses. Again, there was a clear divide among those who were 'open' to exploring this type of media and those who strongly opposed continued use or exploration of social media stemming from negative personal experiences. First, in terms of the 'positive', several respondents commented that:

- "Within the Learning Management Systems (LMS), the chat, discussion boards and web conferencing have been beneficial from a review of material perspective and in fact created some offline student interaction where they formed study groups of their own following these sessions."
- "Facebook in an Open Universities Australia (OUA) site and in a university course. This connects students (well some students who like it); often generational

and not all students. It met the needs of those who like this type of interaction and community building. A part enables social connection for them and gives me as coordinator the chance to read their discussions in terms of what is needed and what they understand, however, it is not a substitute for academic discussion boards."
- "I set up a class Facebook account once so that students could communicate with each other in class and externally, as not all wanted to be friends with each other but still found the ability to chat useful. A moderated forum discussion would be just as useful but at the time Moodle did not allow for an effective one and to some of the students Facebook was a novelty and they were keen to find out what it was all about."
- "I wouldn't say there were any negative experiences. The main issues are: (1) being confident in the application yourself; (2) being clear on the purpose for including the use of the application from a teaching and learning perspective; and (3) finding out if students are willing to use their social media accounts for educational purposes or whether they want separate educational accounts. I think this is one benefit of having these tools within the Learning Management System (LMS) as a single sign-on function."

In stark contrast, the following comments highlight several respondents' rather staunch opposition to social technologies in the HE classroom having experienced a 'negative' event in their career.

- "Too many problems to discuss individually!"
- "None. All negative i.e., 60 students found guilty of sharing information on Facebook for an assessment."

- "Inappropriate comments which require me to set the standards re: behaviours. Also, students setting up Facebook sites from which I am excluded (I do not mind that...) however, on these sites there may be sharing of work which crosses the line of 'own work' even if in the end it does not show up as plagiarism."

Three respondents offered more pedagogically-based reasons for avoiding social media.

- "I think the biggest is ability to communicate appropriately. Many who use the forums make the mistake of assuming the reader understands shorthand. I do not. Is that an indication of my abilities or a lack of desire to communicate in what I believe is a 'lazy' way? My thinking in this regard has been formed by my commercial working experience where clarity in communication can spell the difference between a good and bad decision."
- "Often students end up going on Facebook etc. and lose track as to why they are in front of the computer during class. I found a few students addicted to the various popular games on Facebook and trying to play in class (e.g., Farmville and Candy Crush). It has slowed down somewhat over the past couple of years. Facebook is no longer the social media of choice for many of them. They use Snapchat and other 'closed' apps. In addition, while EIBT can limit the availability of websites that can be viewed on their network, students may find links that have somehow passed through the system. There may be times when students are not accessing the Internet through a monitored network."
- "A perfect example of the loss of control relates to blogs and their 'comments' feature. In HE, having a blog to begin with can be controversial and opening up the comments feature to allow two-way dialog can be frightening. While this feature can easily be turned off that begs the question—Why even use the blog format to begin with?"

In response to the second question: 'Do you use social media in your personal life? What, how and why?' the spread of responses was across a broad range of the spectrum. At one end were a couple of respondents who commented that they did use some form of social technology in their personal life, but did not identify what type, although the how and/or why was stated.

- "Yes. To keep in touch with my friends across the world."
- "Yes, it is easy to use and connect to friends and overseas family. It allows for a greater interconnectedness and effectively reduces the tyranny of distance. It also allows for direct contact with companies. Often you do not feel like a voice in the desert if there are others who can read your comments."

One respondent indicated that they personally used social media for academic purposes; creating a type of synergy among scholars across the globe.

- "I belong to special interest groups in the areas of research I am interested in, which keeps me connected with around-the-world research, conferences, and people. I am able to connect with other researchers throughout South-East Asia, Europe, Africa and parts of India. It is a great builder of both social and human capital."

Few lecturers claimed to use some form social media in their personal life, but at a minimal level and as a matter of necessity rather than preference. Some examples of those responses included:

- "Rarely. Only to contact friends, but I prefer email."
- "Not interested, though I have been 'persuaded' to have a LinkedIn account which I seldom use. After accessing multiple course databases and discussion forums the 'thrill' of doing it in my own environment is limited."
- "Yes, in the first instance just to see what all the hype was about and then slowly finding some social usages such as networking; being able to be found by people I went to high school or university with or previous work colleagues. It is also useful for sharing photos easily and keeping in touch with family overseas. I am not a significant user, but the applications I use are Facebook (I may log in once a month and read, but rarely post anything), Skype (approximately once every 4-6 week) and while I have a Twitter account and follow various people/organisations, I have never tweeted."
- "The advent of social media has created so many forms of media that those who follow blogs, Twitter friends, Facebook friends, MySpace friends, etc., can easily find themselves overloaded now when trying to keep up with 'traditional media' such as email, print publications, and instant messaging."

At the opposite end of the spectrum was one respondent who declared:

- "No, it is a waste of time!!"

In response to the third question: 'How would you respond to the statement, 'IT will continue to change teaching and learning profoundly, no matter what the response of traditional higher education institutions'?' an array of responses were recorded. Four respondents believed—to differing degrees—that change(s) were inevitable.

- "Agreed. While IT is unlikely to overtake on-campus studies to become the sole form of teaching and learning, it is an integral part of the blended-learning environment, and therefore an essential part of the student experience. Student learning has always been directly influenced by the level of engagement and feedback, consequently social technologies can be used to assist students, especially those at risk, in addition to the face-to-face component of their studies."
- "I think IT will continue to change teaching and learning but I think traditional HE institutions may find themselves in difficulty if they ignore the changes and do not attempt to 'get on board' so to speak. Of course, a huge part of this is the culture of teaching and learning which strangely enough is not embedded in HE institutions. Generally, the teaching lecturers do not do research and vice versa, which essentially leads to teaching lecturers being stuck in their (at times) antiquated, anti-technology ways because they do not experience anything else."
- "I totally agree that the ship is sailing towards us and we can either get on and sail forward or get left behind. In the process, if we do not embrace it our education, learning communities and student engagement will not reach the new benchmarks that students expect, whether written down or not. In the longer term, I am sure research will show that institutions that have included social media and other e-learning educational tools into their teaching and learning strategies will have performed better, and also to have feedback that the experience for students is more engaging, exciting, connecting and caring. My experience in Open Universities Australia (OUA) shows that new technologies offer great ways to reach and connect with students and for

them to attain synergy by connecting with each other. Virtual communities and virtual learning is both the current and new wave of education, and needs to be embraced not just to ensure keeping abreast of competitors but is like old machine technology where the decision to use a pedal sewing machine or move to an electronic sewing machine with many options is the choice. The answer? Well there is only one choice = move forward."

- "Of course IT will change! In and of itself, IT is a service tool and will respond to changes in the general community. In due course, those changes will filter into education. The issue we usually miss when we use the letters 'IT' is that we often view it as 'electronic'. We need to view IT as 'information technology', otherwise Why are we not still using wax tablets with stone stylus to write?"

Two respondents sat somewhat on the fence.

- "Hmmmm... Good question. Students are the main clients of the university and directly or indirectly the main source of income. Their characteristics and needs steer the university in its programs and approaches. As higher numbers of non-traditional students, such as working people, require new services from the university, their influence will be a substantial component in the change process. Parallel to them, the faculty in the institution are another critical variable affecting change. Instructors bring with them their own histories with respect to change and technology in teaching and learning, which in turn influences their willingness or capacity to adopt new forms of educational delivery. Thus, student and instructor characteris-

tics are both critical baseline conditions for the choice of a dominant scenario for the institution."

- "I do not think it will change teaching and learning profoundly, as good teaching practice should be the focus and IT developments will provide a greater range of tools to achieve effective teaching and learning outcomes. As for the response from traditional HE institutions, while it may range from a rapid and innovative response through to a very slow and evolutionary change, the reality is that as student demands and expectations change so too will the institutions' uses of these tools."

The final four respondents were those who believed that teaching and learning in HE will not be affected by social technologies.

- "Not really. Overall it seems that HE institutions do not expect revolutionary change as a result from or related to the use of IT. In general, there is not really a concern about being 'forced' to change by external influences or developments. Rather, a 'business as usual' approach is taken."
- "Disagree. It will not change it profoundly. The media simply gives people an excuse to research it and to become experts in an area."
- "No. Smart phones are now commonplace, tablets are replacing or substituting computers and laptops, and social media has become second nature. The rapid and widespread adoption of these technological innovations has completely changed the way people conduct their daily lives, including how knowledge is digested and taught in our classrooms. But is it a positive change? IT will continue to change elements of teaching, but ultimately, it cannot change

the core business which remains human interaction; technology is not a magic wand, merely a tool."

- "Probably not. I recall the so-called 'e-education bubble' between 1997-2000 that 'online learning' would quickly and fundamentally rupture the conventional campus-based model of HE. However, online learning has had relative impact on-campus and on distance education. A fundamental move away from on-campus provision has not materialised. Despite the tremendous public attention given to technology, it seems that the majority of academics across the country have not 'dramatically' transformed their teaching methods or redesigned their programs/ courses. To do so is time-consuming. Importantly, such activities have not yet been rewarded in promotion and tenure review the way scholarly publications have been. The disincentives of the current academic reward structure may account for the notable absence of burgeoning educational technology in HE."

FINDINGS AND IMPLICATIONS

Supportive Findings

Narrative data from this exploratory study suggests that while there are a number of advantages in using social technologies in HE, there are also pitfalls that warrant consideration. First, positive attributes and considerations for using social technologies came across in a number of the following ways.

Social technologies appear to have become a natural extension of the way that many people are already using the web rather than a completely new departure and therefore, they could be seen to bring the outside world into the classroom. Social technologies can create opportunities for collaborative work. 'Authentic' engagement

with wider communities of learning, especially for professional development, can draw on the expertise of external persons. Lecturers can invite peers—physically and/or virtually—from other universities and from outside academia to contribute to the educative process.

The narratives further suggest that for social technologies to work effectively, there may be a requirement for a new paradigm of learning; though not one so radical as that espoused by Prensky (2001). Rather, it should be based on networking, connecting, and community which are philosophies driving the use of social software, underpinned by the theories of constructivism and connectives, and that these require a rethinking of pedagogies and practices. This is supported by Spires et al., (2012, p. 5) who stated that 'in a social constructivist learning environment, effective learning happens through interactive processes of discussion, negotiation, and sharing'. The meaningful integration of social technologies can empower students as partners in the learning process. This can engender a mindset where students are increasingly viewed as contributors of knowledge and allowed to participate in its creation, as in Beldarrain (2006, p. 149) who viewed lecturers and students as 'partners' in the learning process. The narratives suggest that it is not enough to simply have knowledge of social technologies. Importantly, there is the need to be knowledgeable about how to integrate appropriate technologies with traditional pedagogic strategies and thereby, make the resulting content meaningful to the lives of students. For this to occur, a theoretical framework such as TPACK can play a major role.

Though from the narratives themselves there are no specific instances of TPACK, the findings have provided a sense of where lecturers are in terms of their developmental continuum and how TPACK could be integrated into their teaching philosophy and resultant practice. Further to this, there has been the creation of new possibilities for encouraging learners to contribute, rather than passively consume content. The affordances of new technologies are being assimilated and integrated into existing virtual learning environments and are widely available elsewhere because there is already significant take-up of at least some technologies. This claim is supported in both the narratives and in the literature by Spires et al., (2012) who argued that 'educational systems have to stay abreast of the changes in online research, communication, and social media in order for students to be prepared for 21st Century work and citizenship'.

Despite email sometimes being a 'real time sponge' it can also serve as a useful tool for communication, record-keeping, and instant addressing of problems. From actions that teachers have claimed to be a part of their practice, social technologies can have major benefits in terms of course management, particularly in terms of storage, dissemination and submission. Such evolution and integration of new spaces can support life-long learning by providing places where teachers and learners can access their resources even after leaving university. Historically, once teachers and students depart a university they may effectively lose access to their peers, HE resources and many of the works that they created during that time.

Critical Findings

Despite the positive features and opportunities associated with social technologies, it is equally important to capture the voices and arguments of those who are critical of the adoption of new technological tools. On their own, they do not provide any real evidence of a shift in traditional forms of education, and indeed may make some lecturers feel inhibited by their presence in the classroom.

Among some academics, there appears to be an expectation that they should be using these technologies in their teaching, even if they do not feel entirely comfortable/confident with them. This goes against the values of a conceptual framework such as TPACK where the emphasis is on the natural integration of technologies, rather than forced delivery. Pressure may invoke anxiety amongst lecturers to not disadvantage students by expecting them to engage in innovative practices that may not benefit their learning. This is supported by Koehler and Mishra (2009) who described how social and contextual factors can complicate relations between teaching and technology. Social and institutional contexts are often unsupportive of lecturers' efforts to integrate the use of technology into their work. Lecturers often have inadequate/inappropriate experience with using digital technologies for instructional purposes. Further to this, acquiring a new knowledge-base and skill-set can be challenging, particularly if it is a time-intensive activity that must fit into an already demanding schedule (Koehler & Mishra, 2009).

Continuing the theme of teaching norms, there is a fear that traditional frameworks for the development of academic knowledge do not sit comfortably with the speed of information sharing and production that exists via the Internet. The rapid expansion of information accessible through the web coupled with tools that can be used to repurpose and create new knowledge online, are forming an entirely 'different' and potentially undesirable HE environment. Hence, there is apprehension that the traditional knowledge-base of teaching itself is changing as a result of the perceived need for the integration of technology or technological 'fads' that have little lasting impact and/or are unproven in terms of their effectiveness.

Further, there is a sense of technology not only changing the physical shape and appearance of the classroom, but also the nature of people's identities in the world outside the classroom. The sociocultural shift in the way people share and access information has introduced new challenges for educators regarding the intersecting of personal and professional boundaries. In addition, social technologies may challenge current notions of authority, as lecturers find that their expertise is questioned. Students may explore alternative sources of information and (re)construct knowledge in other ways.

CONCLUSION

Part of the impetus for this research was the recognition that although there are demonstrable benefits of integrating social tools in HE, and specifically within EIBT, there are some challenges that prevent their enthusiastic integration. For social technologies to expand and flourish in HE, it was necessary to investigate academics' conceptions and gain deeper insight into why they may or may not incorporate social technologies into their course(s).

The use of an autoethnographic approach could be criticised for capturing only instances of espoused actions and not actual practice. It was, however, suited to this study, which was deemed to be exploratory from the outset. Indeed, all methodologies have strengths and weaknesses; autoethnography is an intriguing and promising qualitative method that offers a way of giving voice to personal experience for the purpose of extending sociological understanding. A professional life story expresses a particular sense of self and a perspective on membership of a group, which in this case was EIBT. These reflections perhaps do not show the process followed in producing these texts, but reveal decisions and tensions of the 'self' in understanding how one may apply social technologies to shape their own personal and professional selves.

As presented, there is a wide range of perspectives about technology and its impact on HE, from one extreme in which it is viewed as an exogenous variable driving all progress, to another where the risks and menaces for academics abound. The findings here may be used as a guide for other academics and/or educational designers to improve pedagogical practices in HE settings. This also raises interesting questions related to how social media might be incorporated into theoretical frameworks such as TPACK. Perhaps to achieve this, lecturers need to feel more confident about their existing pedagogical and content knowledge, and its relationship with technological knowledge, which should be seen as interlocking rather than separate. Nevertheless, sizeable challenges remain for researchers, lecturers and learners in a HE environment progressively more informed by the digital.

This chapter sought to enrich the current literature on the use of social technologies for HE teaching and learning that is still emerging. It is hoped that this work will contribute to practice by providing empirical and authentic evidence of the challenges faced by EIBT lecturers. HE educators should be attuned to the ever-changing and often diverse characteristics of students and let this be an important and/or guiding factor in informing how technological tools can help augment and enrich the educational environment.

REFERENCES

Ajjan, H., & Hartshorne, R. (2008). Investigating faculty decisions to adopt web 2.0 technologies: Theory and empirical tests. *The Internet and Higher Education*, *11*(2), 71–80. doi:10.1016/j.iheduc.2008.05.002

Alvesson, M., & Sandberg, J. (2013). *Constructing research questions: Doing interesting research*. Sage.

Arksey, H., & Knight, P. (1999). *Interviewing for social scientists*. London: Sage.

Armstrong, J., & Franklin, T. (2008). A review of current and developing international practice in the use of social networking (web 2.0) in higher education (September 2008 ed.). Franklin Consulting.

Armstrong, P. (2008). *Toward an autoethnographic pedagogy*. Paper presented at the 38th Annual SCUTREA Conference, Edinburgh, UK.

Austin, J., & Hickety, A. (2007). *Autoethnography and teacher development*. Common Ground.

Beard, J., & Dale, P. (2010). Library design, learning spaces and academic literacy. *New World Library*, *111*(11/12), 480–492. doi:10.1108/03074801011094859

Beldarrain, Y. (2006). Distance education trends: Integrating new technologies to foster student interaction and collaboration. *Distance Education*, *27*(2), 139–153. doi:10.1080/01587910600789498

Bell, D. (1973). *The coming of post-industrial society: A venture in social forecasting*. Basic Books.

Berger, L. (2001). Inside out: Narrative autoethnography as a path toward rapport. *Qualitative Inquiry*, *7*(4), 504–218. doi:10.1177/107780040100700407

Bhabwat, S., Omre, R., & Chand, D. (2013). Development of social networking sites and their role in online share trading and business with special reference to facebook. *International Journal of Business Management & Research*, *3*(2), 31–52.

Blattner, G., & Lomicka, L. (2012). Facebook-ing and the social generation: A new era of language learning. *Alsic Apprentissage des Langues et Systèmes d'Information et de Communication*, *15*(1). doi:10.4000/alsic.2413

Bonk, C. J. (2010). How technology is changing school. *Educational Leadership*, *67*(7), 60–65.

Bumgarner, B. A. (2007). You have been poked: Exploring the uses and gratifications of Facebook among emerging adults. *First Monday*, *12*(11). doi:10.5210/fm.v12i11.2026

Chang, H. (2008). *Autoethnography as method*. Left Coast Press.

Chapelle, C. A. (2010). Invited commentary research for practice: A look at issues in technology for second language learning. *Language Learning & Technology*, *14*(3), 27–30.

Coldron, J., & Smith, R. (1999). Active location in teachers' construction of their professional identities. *Journal of Curriculum Studies*, *31*(6), 711–726. doi:10.1080/002202799182954

Connelly, F. M., & Clandinin, D. J. (1990). Stories of experience and narrative inquiry. *Educational Researcher*, *19*(5), 2–14. doi:10.3102/0013189X019005002

Creswell, J. W. (2008). *Educational research: Planning, conducting, and evaluating quantitative and qualitative research* (3rd ed.). Pearson Education.

Davis, G. J. (2009). The joys of a handwritten letter. *Journal of American Amateur Press Association*, *78*, 46–61. Retrieved from http://www.greenapple.com/~aapa/ejournals/Whippoorwill_E-Comment/n0078.pdf

Ellis, C., & Bochner, A. P. (2000a). Autoethnography, personal narrative, and personal reflexivity. In N. Denzin & Y. Lincoln (Eds.), *Handbook of qualitative research* (2nd ed.; pp. 645–672). Sage.

Ellis, C., & Bochner, A. P. (2000b). *Autoethnography, personal narrative, reflexivity: Researcher as subject* (Vol. 2). Sage.

Fallows, D. (2002). *Email at work: Few feel overwhelmed and most are pleased with the way email helps them do their jobs*. Pew Internet & American Life Project.

Fischer, G., & Konomi, S. (2007). Innovative socio-technical environments in support of distributed intelligence and lifelong learning. *Journal of Computer Assisted Learning*, *23*(4), 338–350. doi:10.1111/j.1365-2729.2007.00238.x

Garrison, D. R., & Kanuka, H. (2004). Blended learning: Uncovering its transformative potential in higher education. *The Internet and Higher Education, 7*(2), 95–105. doi:10.1016/j.iheduc.2004.02.001

Gergen, M., & Gergen, K. (2002). Ethnographic representation as relationship. In A. Bochner & C. Ellis (Eds.), *Ethnographically speaking: Autoethnography, literature, and aesthetics* (pp. 11–33). Altamira.

Greenhow, C., Robelia, B., & Hughes, J. E. (2009). Learning, teaching, and scholarship in a digital age web 2.0 and classroom research: What path should we take now? *Educational Researcher, 38*(4), 246–259. doi:10.3102/0013189X09336671

Hooper, S., & Rieber, L. P. (1995). Teaching with technology. In A. C. Ornstein (Ed.), *Teaching: Theory into practice* (pp. 154–170). Allyn & Bacon.

Howe, N., & Strauss, W. (2000). *Millennials rising: The next great generation*. Vintage Books.

Ito, M. (2003). Mobiles and the appropriation of place. *Receiver: Mobile Environment Magazine, 8*, 1–3.

Jacobson, H. B., & Roucek, J. S. (1959). *Automation and society*. Philosophical Library.

Kaufman, R. A., Guerra, I., & Platt, W. A. (2006). *Practical evaluation for educators: Finding what works and what doesn't*. Corwin Press. doi:10.4135/9781412990189

Kinsella, N. (2010). *BTW it's just netspeak LOL* (Vol. 3). Queensland, Australia: Griffith Working Papers in Pragmatics and Intercultural Communication.

Koehler, M., & Mishra, P. (2009). What is technological pedagogial content knowledge (TPACK)? *Contemporary Issues in Technology & Teacher Education, 9*(1), 60–70.

Land, R., & Bayne, S. (2008). Social technologies in higher education: Authorship, subjectivity and temporality. In *Proceedings of the 6th International Conference on Networked Learning*. Academic Press.

Laurillard, D. (1993). *Rethinking university teaching: A framework for the effective use of educational technology*. Routledge.

Lea, M. R., & Jones, S. (2011). Digital literacies in higher education: Exploring textual and technological practice. *Studies in Higher Education, 36*(4), 377–393. doi:10.1080/03075071003664021

Leavitt, H. J., & Whisler, T. L. (1958). Management in the 1980s. *Harvard Business Review*, (Nov-Dec), 41–48.

Levine, A. E. (2000). The future of colleges: 9 inevitable changes. *The Chronicle of Higher Education, 47*(9), 1–5.

Lim, V. K. G., & Teo, T. S. H. (2009). Mind your e-manners: Impact of cyber incivility on employees' work attitude and behavior. *Information & Management, 46*(8), 419–425. doi:10.1016/j.im.2009.06.006

Lindley, S. E., Harper, R., & Sellen, A. (2009, 4-9 April). *Desiring to be in touch in a changing communications landscape: Attitudes of older adults*. Paper presented at the SIGCHI Conference on Human Factors in Computing Systems, Boston, MA. doi:10.1145/1518701.1518962

Martin, P. (2014). Teachers in transition: The road to EAP. In P. Breen (Ed.), *Cases on teacher identity, diversity and cognition in higher education* (pp. 287–317). IGI Global. doi:10.4018/978-1-4666-5990-2.ch012

McGrath, J. E., Karabas, G., & Willis, J. (2011). From TPACK concept to TPACK practice: An analysis of the suitability and usefulness of the concept as a guide in the real world of teacher development. *International Journal of Technology in Teaching and Learning*, 7(1), 1–23.

Mishra, P., & Koehler, M. J. (2006). Technological pedagogical content knowledge: A framework for integrating technology in teacher knowledge. *Teachers College Record*, 108(6), 1017–1054. doi:10.1111/j.1467-9620.2006.00684.x

Motteram, G. (Ed.). (2013). *Innovations in learning technologies for English language teaching*. London: The British Council.

Motteram, G., & Sharma, P. (2009). Blending learning in a web 2.0 world. *International Journal of Emerging Technologies & Society*, 7(2), 83–96.

Nash, R. J. (2004). *Liberating scholarly writing: The power of personal narrative*. Teachers College Press.

Neuman, W. L. (2004). *Basics of social research: Qualitative and quantitative approaches*. Pearson Education Incorporated.

Okuyama, Y. (2007). CALL vocabulary learning in Japanese: Does Romaji help beginners learn more words? *CALICO Journal*, 24(2), 355–379.

Omar, A., & Miah, M. (2013). Digital evolution of the written language. In *Proceedings of the Information Systems Educators Conference ISSN (Education Special Interest Group of the AITP)*. San Antonio, TX: ISSN.

Owen, M., Grant, L., Sayers, S., & Facer, K. (2006). Social software and learning. Bristol, UK: Academic Press.

Patton, M. (1990). *Qualitative evaluation and research methods*. Sage.

Polit, D. F., Beck, C. T., & Hungler, B. P. (2001). *Essentials of nursing research: Methods, appraisals and utilization* (5th ed.). Lippincott Williams & Wilkins.

Polkinghorne, D. (1988). *Narrative knowing and human science*. University of New York Press.

Prensky, M. (2001). Digital natives, digital immigrants. *On the Horizon*, 9(5), 1–6. doi:10.1108/10748120110424816

Putnam, R. (1995). Bowling alone: America's declining social capital. *Journal of Democracy*, 6(1), 65–78. doi:10.1353/jod.1995.0002

Rooney, P. (2005). *Researching from the inside - Does it compromise validity? A discussion.* Dublin Institute of Technology ARROW@DIT Articles: Learning, Teaching & Technology Centre.

Salmon, G. (2005). Flying not flapping: A strategic framework for e-learning and pedagogial innovation in higher education institutions. *Research in Learning Technology*, 13(3), 201–218. doi:10.1080/09687760500376439

Schwartz, H. L. (2009). 'Facebook: The new classroom commons?'. *The Chronicle Review*, 56(6), B12–B13.

Selwyn, N. (2011). *Education and technology: Key issues and debates*. Bloomsbury.

Slaoti, D., Motteram, G., & Onat-Stelma, Z. (2013). *Innovations in learning technology for English language teaching* (G. Motteram, Ed.). London: The British Council.

Snow, C. (2012). *Orientations towards using social media, digital and mobile technologies to improve literacy skills among diverse students in urban schools*. Harvard University Press.

Sparkes, A. C. (1996). The fatal flaw: A narrative of the fragile body-self. *Qualitative Enquiry*, *2*(4), 463–494. doi:10.1177/107780049600200405

Spires, H., Wiebe, E., Young, C., Hollebrands, K., & Lee, J. (2012). Towards a new learning ecology: Professional development for teachers in 1:1 learning environments. *Contemporary Issues in Technology & Teacher Education*, *12*(2), 232–254.

Tapscott, D. (1999). Educating the net generation. *Educational Leadership*, *56*(5), 6–11.

Trilling, B., & Fadel, C. (2009). *21st century skills: Learning for life in our times*. John Wiley & Sons.

Velliaris, D. M., & Willis, C. R. (2014). Getting personal: An autoethnographic study of the professional identit(ies) of lecturers in an Australian pathway institution. In P. Breen (Ed.), *Cases on teacher identity, diversity, and cognition in higher education* (pp. 87–110). IGI Global. doi:10.4018/978-1-4666-5990-2.ch004

Warschauer, M. (2003). Demystifying the digital divide. *Scientific American*, *289*(2), 42–47. doi:10.1038/scientificamerican0803-42 PMID:12884537

Warschauer, M. (2007). The paradoxical future of digital learning. *Learning Inquiry*, *1*(1), 41–49. doi:10.1007/s11519-007-0001-5

Zur, O., & Zur, A. (2011). *On digital immigrants and digital natives: How the digital divide affects families, educational institutions, and the workplace*. Retrieved 11 March 2014, from Zur Institute: http://www.zurinstitute.com/digital_divide.html

ADDITIONAL READING

Alsup, J. (2005). *Teacher identity discourses: Negotiating personal and professional spaces*. NY: Routledge.

Belbase, S., Luitel, B. C., & Taylor, P. C. (2013). Autoethnography: A method of research and teaching for transformative education. *The Journal of Educational Research*, *1*, 86–95.

Burgess, A., & Ivanič, R. (2010). Writing and being written: Identity issues across timescales. *Written Communication*, *27*(2), 228–255. doi:10.1177/0741088310363447

Coulter, C. A. (2009). Response to comments: Finding the narrative in narrative research. *Educational Researcher*, *38*(8), 608–611. doi:10.3102/0013189X09354124

du Preez, J. (2008). Locating the researcher in the research: Personal narrative and reflective practice. *Reflective Practice*, *9*(4), 509–519. doi:10.1080/14623940802431499

Duncan, M. (2008). Autoethnography: Critical appreciation of an emerging art. *International Journal of Qualitative Methods*, *3*(4), 28–39.

Dyson M. (2007). My story in a profession of stories: Autoethnography - An empowering methodology for educators. *Australian Journal of Teacher Education, 32*(1): Article 3.

Franklin Klinker, J., & Todd, R. H. (2007). Two autoethnographies: A search for understanding of gender and age. *Qualitative Report*, *12*(2), 166–183.

Granger, C. A. (2011). *Silent moments in education: An autoethnography of learning, teaching, and learning to teach*. Toronto: University of Toronto Press.

Mitchell, C., O'Reilly-Scanlon, K., & Weber, S. (Eds.). (2013). *Just who do we think we are? Methodologies for autobiography and self-study in education*. NY: Routledge.

Starr, L. J. (2010). The use of autoethnography in educational research: Locating who we are in what we do. *Canadian Journal for New Scholars in Education*, *3*(1).

Wall, S. (2008). An autoethnography on learning about autoethnography. *International Journal of Qualitative Methods*, *5*(2), 146–160.

KEY TERMS AND DEFINITIONS

Autoethnography: Autobiographies that self-consciously explore the interplay of the introspective and personally engage 'self' with cultural descriptions mediated through language and history. This methodology can vary depending on the relative importance placed on its three components: the self [*auto*]; the culture [*ethno*]; and the research process [*graphy*].

EIBT: The Eynesbury Institute of Business and Technology offers full fee-paying pre-university pathways for predominantly international students entering one of two South Australian HE institutions: *The University of Adelaide* or *University of South Australia*.

ICT: Information and Communications Technology (ICT) is often used as an extended synonym for Information Technology (IT), but is a more specific term that stresses the role of unified communication i.e., any product that will store, retrieve, manipulate, transmit or receive information electronically in a digital form.

Pathway Provider: Educational institutions that offer students alternative forms of entry into university programs. Applicants may include: early school leavers; those that have not achieved the academic and/or English requirements to obtain direct entry; or students looking to return to study after a period of absence.

Web 2.0: The term given to describe a second generation of the World Wide Web that is focused on the ability for people to collaborate and share information online.

Chapter 8
Facebook and Moodle as Classroom Extensions:
Integrating Digital Technologies in the Curriculum

Nuria Pons Vilardell Camas
Federal University of Paraná, Brazil

Maysa Brum Bueno
Catholic University of Dom Bosco, Brazil

Neli Maria Mengalli
Catholic University of São Paulo, Brazil

Renata Aquino Ribeiro
Federal University of Ceará, Brazil

Monica Mandaji
Paulista University of São Paulo, Brazil

ABSTRACT

This chapter analyses how autonomy, collaboration, and cooperation are built in a class designed to use digital technologies for a teacher development syllabus. For the purpose of this chapter, data was collected using an empirical-qualitative approach through active observation in participative action, using a questionnaire and Moodle e-portfolio that addressed learning in several virtual tools including Facebook. The final analysis demonstrates that it is possible to understand the autonomous and collaborative teaching and learning process when online tools such as social networks are used, and it is also possible to determine students' participation through authorship. However, such acknowledgment requires that participants be prepared in terms of methodology, including teachers, and have the means to consider accepting new ways of teaching through the cooperation enabled by social networks and virtual learning environments.

INTRODUCTION

Communication and information technologies, especially collaborative software available on the web, are part of the young generation's routine (Patrício & Gonçalves, 2010). According to

Capobianco (2010), such tools offer resources to enhance educational processes, thus opening new possibilities to improve traditional education.

Some college students already use social network sites (SNS), as reported in national and international research (Patrício & Gonçalves,

DOI: 10.4018/978-1-4666-7401-1.ch008

2010; Capobianco, 2010; Cain, 2008; Muñoz & Towner, 2011). Even when students do not want to mix studies and virtual spaces used for leisure, they have a way of using such tools for learning, thus facilitating the exploration of their resources (Patrício & Gonçalves, 2010) in the classroom.

Many studies show that simply accessing the web does not mean using its sites, nor does reading webpages mean their readers learn, question, or even share what they learned, including getting to develop authorship skills (Camas, 2008; 2012; Costa, 2012). This study agrees with these findings, and aims to develop a dialogue with 35 college students enrolled in the undergraduate education program at the Federal University of Paraná, located in Curitiba, Brazil. This study, developed throughout 2012, was about the use of different tools available on the web, such as YouTube, Wikipedia, blogs, SNSs, and their association with Learning Management Systems (LMS) at graduate level education.

In Brazil there are relatively few studies that address the need to analyse such tools in the pedagogical process, since many teachers and students are still inhibited to use them for a lack of a better understanding of their features.

There is a need to have a pedagogical framework to help include these users in the digital culture, as well as to guide students who are enrolled in the education program to become teachers so that the critical use of current and future digital technologies can be part of the curricular narrative (Goodson, 2005: 2007).

In education, we understand that for a teacher to include his students in the cyberculture and be enabled to reflect upon cybersociety, first there is the need to be prepared in advance by understanding that simply accessing a social network or LMS to perform an assigned task will not change any educational system nor will it be considered educational innovation. Access to web tools must be linked to pedagogical goals, or else the methodologies which employ technology will not

meet the class objectives and enable the students' education (Costa, 2012).

The Ministry of Education in Brazil introduced, as part of the process to transform national educational bases, the PCN (National Curricular Parameters, in English) to guide syllabi selection and pedagogical procedures for teachers' classroom goals. In the PCN, there is a chapter dedicated to the use of technologies in the book "References of Languages, Codes and their Technologies".

A closer look into the Brazilian syllabi matrix reveals that technology was included to transform the teachers' perception of languages and how they can be used, enabling educators to experience new possibilities, which go beyond the traditional oral and written forms provided that teachers are trained to use technology and move from functional literacy to world awareness.

Essentially, this means that the role of universities to train future teachers has occasionally neglected the critical training of undergraduate students in education regarding the use of technology.

As other studies have proposed (Camas 2008; 2012; Camas & Mengali, 2011), it is essential in our country that technology is a subject in undergraduate courses so that teachers can understand and include new technologies as classroom tools, promoting debates about the impact caused by their use in the structure of our cognitive activity.

Given the possibilities provided by digital technologies, and the search for conscious, collaborative and autonomous professional and social development for educators, a few questions can be raised. First, are we teaching and learning with the mediation of digital tools (LMS, SNS, among others), which are characterized by the Web 2.0 convergence and mobility? If so, does such learning use digital media and their cybercultural aspects, i.e., are students the creators and co-creators in the learning process? And, do students use social software as a support for educational activities at undergraduate level?

The quest to answer the questions above led to the setting of the research goals of this study, which were to design and observe a course at the Federal University of Paraná, Brazil. We decided not to make the course a requirement for the degree, because we believed that students who chose to attend it would do so either due to curiosity about the course or through the motivation to learn.

In the elective course designed for this study, entitled "Digital Culture and Teacher Development", a total of 60 hours for the course was divided into 30 hours of on-campus attendance with the teacher-researcher and the students, and 30 hours online, which could be done through an LMS (Moodle) and social networks among other software.

Secondary goals included:

1. Enable the use of several digital tools (Google Drive, Youtube, Blogger, Twitter etc.) throughout the 60 hours of the course;
2. Develop critical thinking (autonomy, collaboration and cooperation);
3. Observe and analyse throughout the course term the way students used digital media for sharing (Dias, 2008), understanding in its broader dimension which includes collaborating and cooperating (Belloni & Gomes, 2008) to develop autonomy (Freire 1997) in the learning process; and
4. Learn the importance of recording data by students as future teachers in the environments used in this research (Moodle, Facebook, Google Drive, and traditional classrooms).

Empirical-qualitative methodology included active observation (Freire, 1983b; Ludke & André, 1986) in participative action (Freire, 1983b; Chizzotti, 2006). This approach helped understand the social and cultural aspects of what was being experienced as a group, and as the teacher-researcher in a course that made the dialogical-collaborative practice the confirmation of pedagogical planning.

We must emphasize that this is empirical research, which focused on practices rather than the university educational structure. Therefore, what is established in this study is dependent upon the context of the course scenario, focused on the participants' choice of the use of technology.

The choice to work on empirical action research following Freire (1983b) implied the researcher had to participate, to be included in the social space covered by the study, and, as such, this is a research model which is performed live, while sharing experiences with the research participants.

We also assume that planning disciplines for online courses in virtual environments in traditional education directly implies a new teaching and curricular organization of information, contents and activities to be developed, which aim at knowledge construction through collaboration, cooperation and autonomy of the participants: teacher and learners.

The research will discuss the theoretical references adopted, thus contributing by revising methodologies and theories. It will then recall the situation experienced with a methodological approach, and analyse the data collected. It will also present research fields that can be further investigated beyond this study. Finally, the conclusion of the experience will be presented.

TO EDUCATE IN THE DIGITAL ERA

Every educational project should seek to promote the educator's reflection about various theoretical tendencies, so that the coexistence of diverse pedagogical approaches can be understood. It should also help new approaches which are needed for developing the concept of education in the digital era. The aim is to seek out the best practices in new learning contexts.

The teacher's intentional actions should be extensively planned and constantly reassessed for the possibility of reconstructing the actions (Almeida, 2004) since education is committed to contributing to cognitive, emotional, social and human development as well as to ethics.

Under this perspective, it is possible to conclude that a course based on learning concepts that emphasize critical thinking, research, autonomous learning (Freire, 1997) and knowledge-building implies learning processes focused on mediation (Vygotsky,1989).

In an online context, mediation is also made possible by interaction (Silva, 2001) among course participants (teachers and students alike), by course material and information sources to which meaning is attributed, and by reflective and/or creative activities that prioritize research, creation, and student production in various media and technologies.

We agree with Valente (1999, 2005) and Almeida (2005) that the teacher will have to observe and give meaning to the characteristics of virtuality, which are present through the use of the many available tools and interfaces. The teacher will also need to develop research and organize information; use synchronous and asynchronous communication media, and have a minimum understanding of the LMS in use, or the web tools he uses with his students.

However, it is necessary to understand that the pedagogical and critical use of digital tools require knowledge of the various languages and media to represent content and learning; hence, the importance of focusing on teacher development.

Our students are already inserted in cyberculture, even the so-called digital natives, but this does not mean they can use technologies in the classroom integrated into the curriculum (Camas & Mengalli, 2011).

One of our duties as developers of future teachers is to focus on teaching our students to be critical, autonomous and participants of their time. One of the university's duties and of all those educational developers must be to reflect on the challenges that students face or will face in their profession and their lives in a century laden with changes.

Education is also responsible in developing students for current social requirements so as to embrace education as a dialogical practice (Freire, 1983a), to understand the new, to develop critical thinking, researching, recording and creating autonomously, and therefore, with critical competency (Freire, 1997).

Future teachers should be developed to have autonomous research competency and critical thinking to solve problems, resorting to information and communication technology to engage in a cultural and educational transformation so that such learning can raise questions and seek social transformation.

Brazil still follows the conservative paradigm of transmission of fragmented information which has been known as the "banking education concept" (Freire, 1997, p.66), which implies that the teacher's knowledge is to be deposited in the student, and it is the only way of teaching to be understood and required by the learner in search of what is believed to be formal education.

This educational pattern of receiving information previously treated by other minds - generally the teacher's - ensures the comfort zone for both the transmitting teacher and the receiving students. Students and teachers need to be aware of this transformational process so they can play their historic role (Freire, 1997) in the evolution of education, a sought after achievement we have yet to reach in our country.

Using a Learning Management System (LMS) together with different Web 2.0 tools can help build a new way of learning, and can result in several increases in quality of education since the future teacher who learns the various areas of knowledge (Horton Jr., 2008) using digital artefacts from the start of his development can bring a new practice to his profession, a new look to education, regardless of the educational modality one chooses.

We agree with Almeida (2005, 328-331) when she points out that as we use an LMS to teach in an interactive manner, we are also teaching how to organize different learning situations. This means teachers also have to set the example by using the LMS. However, we believe that regardless of the digital tool used, including SNS, teachers should also set the example of the kind of use to be made, as pointed out by Muñoz & Towner (2011).

Reflection can be created in the classroom by a teacher who works as a mediator, seeking to identify the students' thought representations, providing relevant information, encouraging the search for diverse sources of information and performing experiments. This process will enhance students' experience of meaningful and critical learning without neglecting the important development of creation, a natural movement of the Web 2.0.

Social Networks and Education

Considering the term 'social networks' as tools that allow social relationships to happen online, some of those tools were discussed with participants of this study, such as Twitter, Facebook, LinkedIn, Google+ among others.

The participants in this research selected Facebook because it is used by a third of Brazil's population (65 million total) (Congo, 2013). Facebook can be explored as an important pedagogical tool, mainly in promoting collaboration in the educational process and also allowing the critical and reflective construction of information and knowledge (Fernandes, 2011). Our study will explore this idea.

Collaboration, Cooperation, and Autonomy as Enablers of Creation

Learning and using digital technology means understanding new ways of seeing and performing in education. Learning theories that have supported us so far, while still valid, "cannot alone handle the complexity of the theme that we deal with" (Belloni & Gomes 2008, p.15) when we teach today.

In Brazil, it is now common to use the terms "collaboration", "cooperation", "creativity" and "autonomy" when referring to digital and educational technologies, similarly to what happened around the year 2000 with the term "interaction", which was profoundly researched by Silva (2001), but which can still be a source of confusion. Our interest is mainly on collaborative and cooperative work in the teaching practice regarding the use of LMS and social networks (Facebook). Therefore, we agree with research performed by Belloni & Gomes (2008) in revisiting Papert (1994); Valente (1999; 2005); Fernando Almeida & Fonseca (2000); Perriault (2002) and Almeida (2005, 2004) who pointed out the fact that cooperation goes beyond collaborating, and once adopted, it enables the development of the group practicing it.

We agree with Belloni & Gomes (2008, p. 732) in that "there is collaboration even when there is no commitment to developing a joint project" and that "cooperation starts when there is a common task linked to the success of a joint project" (p.732). Therefore, the LMS can enhance "student-student-teacher interaction in a network of cooperative and collaborative relations which are highly conducive to learning" (Belloni & Gomes, 2008, p. 732).

Using digital technological devices requires critical understanding, which translates into overcoming the educational fragmentation we face today, and promoting ethics, dialogical empowerment, and commitment and respect to cooperation in the collective and individual learning. It also requires record-keeping - a key factor to consider for learning environments in formal education - which should go beyond the compulsory reproduction of what the teacher wants, and move on to educate for actions also in the digital culture.

Without becoming hostages of electronic devices, but being aware of the need to virtualize the educational process, we follow Lemos (2002) in regarding cyberculture as the post-massive reading-and-writing culture, i.e., the culture which allows for creation and co-creation of our students, who are still used to accepting what their teachers broadcast in class and to providing the answers their teachers think are the best.

Freire (1997) enables us to better understand this post-massive culture when he reminds us of the need of a new education, calling it "autonomous pedagogical development", which comes to life due to the need to have critical-thinking men and women. Criticism is born out of doubts we bring up, the questionings of what we should do, the need to research and to act not like simple passive receivers, but like "critical emitter-receivers" (Camas, 2012, p.53).

The kind of autonomy that enables the individual to be an emitter-receiver is given by emancipation (Freire 1983a 1997). By focusing on the concept of dialogue, which "is the encounter of world-mediated men to name the world" (Freire,1983 p.107), it is implied that by reflecting upon the practice and acting on it to transform it, we need communication to happen through listening, reading, analysis, acknowledgment, mistakes, reflection, acceptance and change.

Dialogue is the word, as it enables acting and thinking as a subject in history. It means overcoming the culture of silence and alienation, unveiling a subject and creator of one's own historic existence. This is true because "to exist humanly is to phrase the world, to change it. The phrased world then returns as problematized to the phrasers, demanding a new phrase from them" (Freire, 1983, p.78), and, as a result, creation and co-creation are understood as being performed by emitter-receiver individuals both in an LMS and in an SNS, such as Facebook.

Freire proposes the dialogue for the building of intersubjectivity in history making, and not only as a spectator. Therefore, he suggests we develop a different way of understanding when facing processes which are "prominent in modern culture" (Zitkoski, 2003).

Schools should actually be a public space to access knowledge, able to interact communicatively with the various sectors that compose society's structure. This is something still lacking in Brazil.

Findings in our study support Vygotsky (1989) by establishing that language promotes mediation between subjects and knowledge, as well as between the situations where knowledge is created. It is through language that teacher and student become aware of themselves in the world and of their knowledge, which can be mediated to and by each other.

METHODOLOGICAL PATH: SOME NECESSARY EXPLANATIONS

This study used Freire's (1983b) empirical research in action approach. Empirical methodology in participative action presumes that teacher development means experiencing social emancipation, rising of awareness and transformation (Freire, 1983b; Chizzotti 2006).

Bringing the contribution of Paulo Freire's theory to empirical methodologies implies reflection of the relation established between subject and object in research, overcoming the common notion that the researcher acts upon research participants unilaterally and vertically.

It also implies thinking about interactions between the researcher and the researched subjects from a different perspective and in the horizontal direction of this relation. Both are different because they come from different social places, have different kinds of knowledge and have lived unique experiences, but this does not mean the researcher is any better or superior to the participant. As such, the former teaches and learns with those being studied and the latter also teaches and learns with the researcher.

In our data collection procedures, the participants were not reduced to the condition of mere research subjects. More than a vertical process of gathering information, the researcher's relationship with the research participants becomes an educational act, according to Freire's (1983b) methodological understanding and concept.

Active and participative observations (Ludke & André, 1986) were used for the research strategy since the researcher was in contact with the studied phenomenon so that data collection would be done in a natural context and with the studied group's help.

For a deeper understanding of social reality, a questionnaire was applied as the initial data collection tool. It consisted of a hierarchical series of questions, which means a semi-structured questionnaire that could be answered in writing, and uploaded to the LMS by the students (Marconi & Lakatos, 2003)

Research Field

The studied university is the University of Paraná (UFPR), located in the state of Paraná, Brazil, more precisely in its capital, Curitiba. It has over 25,531 students at on-campus undergraduate levels, and 112 professional development courses (data collected at the vice chancellor's office for planning affairs, p. 11, 2011). The university also belongs to the Brazilian Open University System (UAB - UFPR, as in the Portuguese acronym), which is a system oriented towards courses in distance education, undergraduate bachelor's degrees, specialization and graduate levels in the state of Paraná with hybrid in-class and on-line courses with over 2,000 students.

Out of the university's total, a sample of 35 regularly enrolled students was selected of which 20 were attending Pedagogy and 15 students were attending a pre-service, grant-funded program for teaching (PIBID - CAPES, in Portuguese) which is part of a broader project entitled "Digital Technologies and Teacher Development: curriculum integration of diverse tools for learning at Elementary Level".

A virtual classroom was created in an LMS - Moodle (http://moodle.ufpr.br) for the course "Digital Culture and Teacher Development", which would be integrated with on-site activities.

At the first on-site meeting, the course guidelines and schedule were presented. To be coherent with Paulo Freire's methodology (1983b), there was the proposition of a dialogue to understand the students' world knowledge and to stimulate collective knowledge, so as to enable the construction of autonomy, and the creation of a collective project that enabled collaboration, cooperation and emitter-receiver individuals' participation.

Clarification on Researched Experience

The researcher, who is also a teacher at UFPR Faculty of Education - Pedagogy course, created the course "Digital Culture and Teacher Development" in 2012 with a total number of 60 class-hours, out of which 30 were held on-site at the university campus and 30 were conducted on the LMS and other tools like Google Drive, Facebook and YouTube.

The elective course had as its goals:

- To approach the professional development required from future teachers to use different digital tools at the schools in which they would work;
- To conceptualize and understand in pedagogical terms what is collaboration, cooperation, sharing, and autonomy in educational contexts;
- To understand and use different digital tools for classroom activities.

As it is an empirical experience in a formal education environment, the formal rules of log-entering, number of accesses and privacy required by the university's regiment were followed and, as such, the choice was made for Moodle as it is the university's official LMS and all collected data were recorded by the students in the e-portfolio tool "Diário" (Diary, in English) and in the LMS forums.

This study, then, presents:

1. The analysis of the applied questionnaire to know the participants;
2. The researcher's experience reported in her mobile diary;
3. The analysis of data collected in 24 e-portfolios that constitute the learning marks by the participants; and
4. Messages written in the LMS learning forums.

We analysed the categories of autonomy and emancipation, creation and co-creation, collaboration and cooperation, besides those which emerged in the process such as acceptance of the established, development of critical thinking, and learning occurred during the educational process.

It is important to remember that this study counted on the researcher's participation working full time with the students, which explains the need to include co-authors. The inherent depth of action research required the participation of these fellow researchers to help develop a deeper understanding of observations, and ensures the required ethics in the daily routine with participants, as well as in interpreting data so that it would faithfully translate research facts.

Before classes started, participants were asked to sign the Free and Conscious Authorization term, since the course would generate the present study. On the same day, enrolled students received the questionnaire, defined as "field knowledge about the class". The questionnaire application was meant to provide profile data of the sample population with questions about age, sex, internet access from home, mobile technologies owned,

places used to access the internet, social software they knew of and used on a daily basis, teaching-learning experiences they had, and whether they used LMS in other courses.

Aiming at learning more about the educational context, analysis of the responses showed the reality which these college students experienced.

The 35 participants had computers at home with broadband internet access; all had cell phones, 5 students had tablets, 20 students had notebooks which they would bring to college; 29 students had never used virtual learning environments (LMS) for communication and sharing of educational content; 6 students used LMS in other courses; 30 students used Facebook for leisure such as games, reading and chatting with classmates, as well as to articulate course assignments; 5 had no access to social networks such as Facebook or Twitter, and were not interested in using them.

All 35 participants used Google on content searches for academic assignments and personal interests, such as looking for a job, among others. All participants believed in the possibility of learning by using LMS and social networks, although they also claimed they would not be able to do so without learning pedagogical and methodological actions focused on learning goals.

The Questionnaire and Its Evidences of Pedagogical Action

The questionnaire responses showed that using communication and information technologies is related to internet access. The participants are familiar with, and use software like Paint, Power Point, Word, and Excel. A total of 60% navigated on social networks, and 100% have personal email and use Google for content searches.

All learners stated that digital technologies are important for life in society, with 73% of them claiming that knowing and being able to use digital technologies are critical for life and to get a job. All participants answered that they would not know how to use digital technologies in the classroom when they became teachers.

Supported by these answers, some strategies were developed before the course started, bearing in mind that public education policies aim at modernization to overcome the unsatisfactory stage faced by Brazilian education according to public policies. Even though, they do not always offer options to develop improvements on educational performance. Therefore, it is the university's role to provide this answer to society.

The reality of infrastructure in some of the Brazilian public universities sometimes brings the discomfort and the problem of not having internet access, added to the fact that computers are not always available in all the classrooms. With this in mind, and guided by the data collected in the questionnaire, all in-campus classes were conducted in a classroom equipped with Wi-Fi and a few computers or tablets available since not all the students had notebooks or personal tablets.

The Researcher's Analysis and Report: Experiencing the Discoveries

In the first class, students were asked to talk about the lesson plan that teachers are supposed to deliver, in compliance to school rules. The researcher-teacher's first action was to do away with the printed version of the course contents, and invite students to log on to Moodle and download the Lesson Plan to be read on the screen.

The first reaction was sheer surprise on students' faces. I asked which of them had already used a virtual environment in class - even though I had this information in the questionnaire - and the answer was that the majority had not used it before and that would be the first time that 30 of the participants would be logging in to an LMS.

I invited them to fill out the individual profile on Moodle, with a brief academic curriculum, their experience, the networks they belonged to, their hobbies and also to add their photos and read their classmates' profiles so as to know each other, and have a first exploration of the LMS and additional networks that they might share.

Following this session, which I called initial recognition and presentation of different tools available on Moodle for classroom activities, the students were invited to research different themes within the field of digital culture and the elementary teacher's role, using several digital technologies during the following week. Within a week they started their personal portfolios in the LMS assigned to the course, making accessible what they thought was significant to them.

I suggested that the course's final assignment should be based on class cooperation. I explained there would be no formal tests to assess them, and evaluation would be done based on their participation in the themes discussed in the classroom and others that proved to be necessary for both collective and individual learning. The e-portfolio created on Moodle was weekly checked by me, and would work as a guide for the students' autonomy and learning.

The e-portfolio was divided into different files, and one of them was to address the question "what are your expectations regarding the course "Digital Culture and Teacher Development?" Students were also told that question would be answered throughout the course's first week and should be revised every fifteen days until the end of the course. This would allow for checking the concepts being learned by the students and the practices brought up by the students' learning processes and the teacher's teaching processes. This way they would reflect whether their initial representation had been fulfilled or not regarding the development of future teachers in the digital culture era and the use of different social networks.

During classes, several digital environments and social networks were explored such as blogs, Google Drive, YouTube, Wikispaces, Twitter and Facebook, so that students could choose which of the networks they would like to use to improve their professional development.

After a few days of regular use of tools in the classroom, one of the students was asked by his colleagues to open a group called "Aula Virtuante" (Virtu-acting Class, in English) on Facebook. They explained to me the idea in the name was to combine the virtual with the acting, because this is how they viewed the possibilities of teacher engagement in social networks. Another student opened a Facebook page to display the actions of the 15 grant-receivers in the public funding teacher development program at undergraduate levels.

I presented the discourse analysis of the e-portfolios, with the basic ideas proposed by the participants of the study under the perspective of acceptance, collaboration and cooperation, creation, co-creation, and autonomy.

Acceptance of the Established

In the first week, twenty-four students wrote in their portfolio that their chief expectation in relation to the course was:

(...) to fulfil the required number of class hours for electives (...) (Student F, 2012).

I have to build about 200 hours in elective courses; I thought the theme was cool and getting 60 hours will be very valuable (Student G, 2012).

The excerpts above remind us of the "banking education" perspective (Freire, 1997), which ends up resulting in a non-emancipative education for the development of knowledge, and where the established is accepted and reproduced without the critical thinking that would promote personal and social development. So, if the student starts off willing to learn and develop, the answer to this expectation would not necessarily be about the number of hours to complete his education.

Some students wrote in their e-portfolio, they expected to:

(...) explore the internet (Students N, D, F, 2012).

(...) have classes in the lab, therefore a change from the usual classroom (Student C, 2012).

(...) be able to change environments and have access to the web (Student H, 2012).

(...) I thought it was cool to use the internet in class (Student K, 2012).

Here we can see that none of the students started the course fully aware of the importance of digital culture in teacher development, or in Freire's concept of autonomy (1983a, 1997), and what it would represent in research terms, and even less so about cooperation and collaboration (Belloni & Gomes, 2008). There was no mention of the possibility of dialogue that would promote creation and co-creation among students, or even the use of digital tools that enable communication among persons out of the classroom environment.

Before the initial data analysis, a proposal for pedagogical action was presented on understanding and using Moodle and other tools. The proposal - based on theory in practice - required that the students get together in small groups to address themes ranging from research and theoretical reflections of each group, to research and use of various web tools that could help teaching, as well as LMS tools. The discussions were all held on-site, and recorded in the e-portfolios and theme-oriented forums in Moodle.

Cooperation and Collaboration

Since the purpose of this course was also to observe cooperation and collaboration (Belloni & Gomes, 2008), the students were asked to discuss the course objectives that did not match their initial expectations. In a classroom discussion, which was recorded by one member of each group in the group forum, ideas regarding the aim of "developing the practice of critical thinking through research and dialogue", and how this was initially understood in relation to digital and social software were analysed. For the students,

(...) to research is to open Google and find what you want (Student Z, group forum, 2012);

(...)Teacher, for this we have Wikipedia (Student C, group forum, 2012).

Regarding group work, the majority agreed:

(...) We get together and share activities and then send them via email, someone gets everything together, print it and, there you are, job done (Student W, group forum, 2012).

Regarding digital culture and teacher development, they believed all it took was to use internet access with basic tools. Their answers:

We use email with some teachers and Google for content search (Student F, group forum, 2012).

I do have Facebook, but I don't use it for classes; at school, just email and Google for content search (Student M, group forum, 2012).

Autonomy, Creation, and Co-Creation

As in-campus classes were also planned for students to participate online via LMS and other social software, I used students' answers to understand-

ing the underlying principles of the relationships they were establishing through their collective and individual research, through dialogues posted in the forum of each module, and in the Facebook group "Virtuante".

At the start, the students had some difficulty understanding the need to read what their classmates had written, to help each other, and be committed to self-learning and helping others to learn. As classes developed and dialogues became a tangible reality with everyone's participation, students started to post their impressions about their classmates' production, besides posting references and suggestions for further readings for their colleagues in the forum:

(...) you talk about collaboration, but I found an article and understood that you can also call "uniting" collaboration, cooperation, everything we do here that we share; I'm going to insert this in our glossary and the link to the article I am referring to. You can find it in http//eft.edu.com. pt/index.php/eft/article/view/17/8. Check if you agree (Student B, Collaboration Forum, 2012.)

Student B's posting brought great excitement to the Moodle forum, leading them to conclude that:

(...)When education is done through cooperation, it ceases to be just memorization (Student RS, Collaboration Forum, 2012.)

Even though it was understood that:

(...) We can't always give up memorization, like in Botany; otherwise there is no way to remember (Student C, Collaboration forum, 2012.)

The forum discussion was continued, which allowed students to understand that including the use of different software in pedagogical activities in order to work on the curriculum helped different competencies:

Yes, but if you set the kids to memorize in a different way, I don't know, I even think memorization stops being just memorization. See, make the kids draw, paint, create an e-book...Wouldn't they learn better and more? (Student A1, collaboration forum, 2012.)

We can video-record it, ask students to take photos or video-record fruits/leafs, - I don't know, I am into Physics (laughs) -that they find nearby school or home, teach them to edit it, throw it in YouTube; wouldn't it be an awesome class? (Student R, collaboration forum, 2012.)

During an in-campus class, the group used student A's questions to suggest that the best way would be to have each group develop one activity in the areas which required memorization tasks being done in other tools and later have each group report their experience.

Student autonomy was practiced and understood as using knowledge to transform their world (Freire, 1997):

When we started, I'd always open pages. Slowly, I started to move away from them to discover new sources of curiosities, but the kind that would help me in my development, my work and my studies. One of the best classes was about using Google and taking this learning to Moodle; it was incredible to understand everybody's collaboration. I've used it for other assignments in other courses, and I taught my friends and really approved of it (Student E, e-portfolio, 2012.)

Student E refers to the collaborative use they had in class concerning Google Docs, in which they learned to write collectively, respecting everybody and, besides this, the possibility of group writing in software, and how to upload their work on to the LMS. This meant they had a practical experience that an LMS should not be seen as an institutional straitjacket, and that it is

possible and healthy for students to share various tools, but also to understand that each institution's rules must be respected.

In Student F's report, his statement about being able to understand little by little indicates that he had the time to understand the use of the several tools presented in the classroom and in the social network:

Today, as I am writing, I remember our classes and I can notice the difference these months made: my maturity regarding discoveries and how much this was and will always be useful. I could understand, little by little, what the internet will always offer. All the classes will be in positive spots, every one of them changed attitudes related to the way I use the internet, and in every class I was able to learn different things, which made every class a valuable one. In our last meeting, I can say it was indeed a pleasure to turn good attitudes into an addiction. The learning will stay not only in the computer room, but also in my professional development and so forth. (Student F, e-portfolio, 2012.)

As students had reported in the classroom that they did not know what creation and cocreation meant - often reporting the use of copying and pasting texts in their practice - I suggested the reading and discussion of Lemos (2002), and a chapter in the book Comunicação ou Extensão (Communication or Extension, Freire, 1983a), and also made available on the LMS web library the link for them to watch Paulo Freire talking about his theories.

After these activities, students were asked to choose the tools with which to write about their ideas of creation and co-creation. The groups chose Wiki, the group's collaborative glossary in Moodle, Google Drive and YouTube.

Nobody chose Twitter or Facebook. I asked why they would not use Facebook, since they already had a private group there. Their collected answers, in class, were as follows: six students did not elect social networks for formal education, twelve claimed they got side-tracked by parallel chats that disturbed participation, two students did not answer, and four claimed the log records were lost and the Facebook environment did not represent the real creation, which did not motivate them for educational activities. This fact drew the researcher's attention, as Facebook was well-known by the students and practically all of them had access to it.

Even in a small sample of thirty-five students, it can be noticed that once they use digital tools in a critical manner they are able to choose those that would best translate their learning expectations. This comes to reinforce Freire's belief that action for emancipation and educational dialogue for learning enables creation and co-creation.

However, because students had created the Virtuante profile on Facebook and decided not to choose it for the pedagogical actions, one can relate this to the need to develop a greater learning for both students and teachers, as according to Towner & Muñoz (2011). Their study concludes that many students also do not grasp the academic potential of SNS, even though they have the opportunity to use them as a formal learning tool (Muñoz &Towner, 2011.) We noticed that our students are not able to give meaning to SNS as an educational tool; these are still considered social agents, as opposed to an opportunity to share information, collaborate and learn about colleagues and teachers, as can be depicted in the students' e-portfolio entries:

I could not provide meaning to FB, even with Virtuante as an organized form of learning, it seems that things get lost, and whatever else is in my profile draws a lot more of my attention than the class (Student G, e-portfolio, 2012.)

Teacher, I don't like either Twitter or Facebook; I even had a peek, but I wouldn't use it in class (Student N, e-portfolio, 2012.)

Critical Thinking Development

Students worked with different tools such as You-Tube, Google Translator, Hot Potatoes, Webquest, Wikipedia, blogs, podcasts, Facebook, and Google Drive. Thinking about the non-instructional learning, they developed activities related to fields of knowledge and interest that are part of schools' syllabi and of their specific areas, searching through other tools to experience the concepts that were discussed. They always updated their learning on the LMS, sometimes via forums, sometimes using their individual portfolios. They also brought over their achievements to the in-campus class, explaining them to their colleagues, questioning and learning with their mistakes.

We agree with Belloni & Gomez (2008) that cooperation developed within a shared project; the creation of lessons that transformed their participative practices and the understanding that memorizing took a different direction, by using tools other than the course book or the paper notebook.

At the end of the course, students were asked to return to the question presented at the beginning of the term, "initial expectations", and reflect upon it, by reading the activities and learning achieved in their e-portfolios. They would answer whether there had been any improvement in their learning and whether the tool Moodle, used as a classroom extension, had helped their learning.

During one week (data collected in Moodle stats), students - surprisingly - revisited their actions in Moodle and answered that:

When I started this elective I had expectations and they are far more than fulfilled! I remember the first day, when I said what I expected from this elective and I can see it went far beyond. It is interesting to see that its flexibility did not hinder message it wanted to convey; it really changed my view about digital tools. I found the discussions to be very interesting (Student S, individual e-portfolio, June 2012.)

I acquired a critical view about this and a position regarding its importance. I enjoyed participating in our classes and did not know what sharing and cooperation meant. I learned how to use tools I couldn't use before, and saw how simple and important they are. I also learned that I didn't know how to work in a group (Student P, e-portfolio, 2012.)

Today I can teach how to use certain tools for those who don't know how and I had a great idea: I'll make a cool blog in my area of knowledge to teach this stuff. Moodle is not visually appealing, but I didn't even care after I learned how to participate in it (Student A, e-portfolio, 2012.)

Learning happened through dialogue (Freire, 1983a) and as a critical professional development even when confronted with new difficulties. The conscious practices of learning promote the will to help others, thus confirming pedagogical actions for change and understanding of the class' context.

(...) Digital culture allowed me to contact another reality, different from that of biological scientificism. It allowed the connectivity with people of other areas of knowledge here, and outside the classroom. Such connectivity allowed me to understand the role of social networks in the construction of modern knowledge and the importance of knowing how to use digital culture for academic development. It was really great. The teacher obviously knows a lot, has clear thinking, and enabled us to break free from the right-or-wrong idea, and instead develop our own ideas to contribute for us to construct our collectivity in learning (Student G, e-portfolio, 2012.)

I really enjoyed making reflections about videos. That cognitive development tool is not usually used by our teachers in other courses. I had contact with many tools that expanded the possibilities and the easiness of group work, such as Google Docs, Moodle, Facebook. Also, the questionnaire

tool, which can be a scientific work tool that will reduce time and paper use. Using Hot Potatoes to create assessment tools in virtual classrooms. Also the creation of animated videos for educational purposes.

The only extra thing I'd like to have explored in the course would be how to build a virtual classroom in Moodle. (Student B, e-portfolio, 2012.)

In the testimonials presented in the e-portfolio, there is a notion of learning with one's mistakes, with questionings, and with research that generates exchange and knowledge (Freire, 1997), collaboration, cooperation and sharing (Dias, 2008). Students found all this out by themselves and understood through a collective way of learning, in alignment with studies by Vygotsky (1989), Freire, (1970, 1997), Belloni & Gomes (2008) which state that they went beyond what was already known. As Student B points out, as future teachers they should be able to create a course using the same tool they did as a learner of the world (Freire, 1997).

We can also notice that some students understand the use of SNS aligned with the use of an LMS and that one should not necessarily replace the other, as each has its function and learning goals, as suggested by Muñoz &Towner (2011).

Learning Performed during the Educational Process

The access to and critical use of a medium are different situations that must be learned by individuals, but such learning must be mediated (Vygosky, 1989) so that it is enabled in its authentic form, which is the possibility of understanding theory in practice.

I used to love using the internet, but I hadn't realized that I used less than 1% of what it could offer me. Facebook, Twitter and blogs were not even close to what awaited me. Even though I liked these sites, I missed doing something useful on the internet. The elective course was key for me to discover, with my colleagues' help, ways to explore everything that our classes had to offer. (Student D, e-portfolio, 2012).

In the past, the way I used the internet to study was very simple: I used Google to find out about a subject (which was usually already on Wikipedia), and absorbed everything I needed from that source, or at least what I thought I needed. Thanks to your classes, I could realize what sites had the best quality; I hadn't seen anything like it before in terms of didactic content on the internet. Group work online proved to be much more dynamic than what I thought it could be before, with the use of simple applications such as Google Drive and Moodle, Facebook and our Virtuante group. All this, together with the fact I met lots of great people, will always be with me in my academic life. I hope I can live more of this in the future (Student C, e-portfolio, 2012).

All the classroom activities were mediated, and had their evaluation criteria thoroughly discussed with the students. A significant fact is that there were no absences throughout the term. When asked about not skipping classes, students unanimously responded that having access to theory in teaching practice motivated them to participate.

All the final testimonials reassured that it is possible to go a step beyond the transmission-based education, inherited from the banking education (Freire, 1997). The kind of education where dialogue, autonomy, collaboration and cooperation are possible when the teacher understands reconstruction of pedagogical actions, as proposed by Almeida (2004; 2005). However, it is necessary to master the means (Valente, 1999; 2005), the science, and the competencies - understood as information literacy (Horton, 2008), required for teaching in the 21st century.

It is important, at this point, to reflect upon the barriers to the adoption of social technologies in the educational context, also within the Brazilian context. There are a number of issues which prevent teachers from adopting technologies in their classes as well as planning the pedagogical use of social networks. Authors point out, however, that these barriers are in conflict with the reality of everyday greater use of technology by students and the society.

When discussing the use of social networks in school is it important to remember the debate which has been happening for a while in education about the different views about innovation in society. It is a fact that teachers and education policy experts connected to schools tend to resist technological innovation and they do express difficulties in moving forward, theoretically and practically, towards more technologically enhanced courses, a condition which may be even more complicated when one discusses social technologies.

According to Libâneo (1996) this fact happens because, in Brazil, the association between education and technological development has suffered from an excessively technical perspective, during the military dictatorship, which resulted in a political resistance to technology other than, of course, cultural and social reasons such as an undetermined fear against machines and electronic equipment, fear of the lack of personal identity and being replaced by computers, cultural and scientific education with flaws or professional training which does not include technology. To that one may add the visibility and instantaneous capability of information dissemination in social networks.

To Vazquéz Gómez (1994), there is a need to work on initial and continuous training of teachers to the integration of information and communication technology in the curriculum, as well as developing cognitive and operational skills for the use of media and education towards career management and technological innovation in general, as nowadays one cannot state that the school is the only thing responsible for social transformations.

Today, this task goes through multiple actors and multiple scenarios and it is not possible to argue against the increasingly important role of social networks. Considering this reality, the school has the commitment to help students become intellectual subjects, able to build categories for comprehension and critical analysis of the reality (Libâneo, 1996).

A time for a greater challenge has, therefore, been reached. It is the time for responding to the new demands which the growing use of technology stimulates, it is necessary that the teacher is able to adjust the teaching to the new possibilities of society, of knowledge, of the student, of the several cultural universes, the media and whatever demands that this professional amplifies the general knowledge, developing communicative skills other than having the domain of informational language and social networks within an articulated plan with their classes.

According to Kenski (1996) students are used to learning through sound, colors, images such as in photos or movies; their world is multisound and multicolor. It has plenty of colors, images and sounds which sets it apart from the almost exclusively one-toned, one-sounded space that the school usually offers.

Such a fact is a worse reality when the discussion is about social networks, which enable the possibility of media convergence, especially for kids and young people as if it was an extension of their own actions.

FUTURE RESEARCH DIRECTIONS

In the course of the present study we identified a growing evolution in students' development in relation to understanding and using internet tools on a daily basis. However, in terms of educational performance we must motivate them by extending the traditional classroom as a place to incorporate digital technology.

In this perspective, this study is placed in the scope of exploring answers to the following questions:

- What methodologies should be developed to handle the integration of various tools and SNS for our students' learning development?
- What methodologies should be applied to confirm that we are emitter-receivers in the digital era?
- How can we include the use of digital technologies at college curriculum level for elementary school teacher professional development with a critical view on technology as a learning improvement?

Many other questions should emerge in the next year, since this empirical research was designed to help us explore technologies in the classroom, and start a movement within the university to promote the use of tools that can help learning development in both students and teachers.

CONCLUSION

It was a happy surprise to be able to change both our students' and our own initial expectations as participants of an action research through the permanent example of theory-in-practice.

Teaching and learning together with the students, studying the curation of content compatible with class goals as well as organizing them in an LMS was a one of a kind opportunity. The LMS served not only as a place to access PDF texts, or links to webpages, but also helped reflection and reconstruction of students' practice by online and in-class interaction, so as to encourage formal education without creating the straitjacket of a single digital tool for learning.

Restrictions in the experience were essentially due to lack of infrastructure in the classroom, and often for lack of access to the internet in class. This issue will be addressed through the federal grant assigned to the project for academic development (FDA - UFPR in Portuguese) for the forthcoming years, which has already provided thirty-three tablets, and also with the aid received by another local foundation (Fundação Araucária) in the state of Paraná for a project accepted in February 2013 for the development and continuation of this research.

The tools used in this study (LMS, SNS, etc.) did not represent any problems for students to learn how to perform, and did not replace people at any given time. They became helpers in a new teaching-learning process between teacher and students, constructing a curricular path of collaboration.

The experience allowed for understanding that lesson-planning should integrate educational knowledge and virtual features, which characterized the context of the course, and the students' context and experience. This experience allowed for the construction of a new curricular narrative on a new learning path to rethink classes and the incorporation of technologies in student development.

Not all students are becoming more familiar with various digital tools; however, if we fail to incorporate the latter at college level education, we might be neglecting the critical development for their classroom use.

From this experience, a new research path was opened to design teaching methodologies focused on digital culture and how to articulate new digital learning for citizenship development.

REFERENCES

Almeida, F. J., & Fonseca, F. M. Jr. (2000). *Projetos e ambientes inovadores*. Brasília, DF: MEC/SEED.

Almeida, M. E. B. (2004). *Inclusão digital do professor: Formação e prática pedagógica*. Editora Articulação – Universidade Escola.

Almeida, M.E.B., & Prado, M.E.B.B. (2005). *Integração de tecnologias, linguagens e representações*. Brasília: TV Escola, SEED-MEC.

Belloni, M. L., & Gomes, N. G. (2008). Infância, mídias e aprendizagem: Autodidaxia e colaboração. *Educ. Soc.*, *29*(104), 717-746. Retrieved from http://www.cedes.unicamp.br

Camas, N. P. V. (2012). A literacia da informação na formação de professores. In Tecendo os fios na educação: Da informação nas redes à construção do conhecimento mediada pelo professor. Curitiba: CRV.

Camas, N. P. V., & Mengalli, N. M. (2012). Use of digital interfaces as an extension of school attendance. *Publication of IEEE Technical Committee on Learning Technology*, *13*, 66–69.

Capobianco, L. (2010). *Comunicação e literacia digital na internet – Estudo etnográfico e análise exploratória de dados do programa de inclusão digital acessaSP – PONLINE: Dissertação (mestrado em ciências da comunicação)*. Escola de Comunicação e Artes, Universidade de São Paulo.

Chizzotti, A. (2006). *Pesquisa qualitativa em ciências humanas e sociais*. Petrópolis, RJ: Vozes.

Congo, M. (2013). *Um terço dos brasileiros tem Facebook: País se torna o 2º em número de usuários*. Available at http://blogs.estadao.com.br/radar-tecnologico/2013/01/23/um-terco-dosbrasileiros-tem-facebook-pais-se-torna-o-2o-em-numero-de-usuarios/

Dias, P. (2008). Da e-moderação à mediação colaborativa nas comunidades de aprendizagem. *Educação Formação & Tecnologias*, *1*(1), 4–10.

Extensão ou Comunicação. (1979). Rio de Janeiro: Paz e Terra.

Freire, P. (1983a). *Educação como prática da liberdade*. Rio de Janeiro: Paz e Terra.

Freire, P. (1983b). Criando métodos de pesquisa alternativa. In *Pesquisa participante, 3ª edição*. São Paulo: Brasiliense.

Freire, P. (1997). *Pedagogia da autonomia*. Rio de Janeiro: Paz e Terra.

Gómez, V. (1994). Gonzalo: Tecnologías avanzadas y educación. In *Teoría de la educación*. Madrid: Taurus Universitaria.

Goodson, I. (2007). Currículo, narrativa e o futuro social. Revista Brasileira de Educação, 12(35), 241 – 252.

Grinspun, M. P. S. Z. (1999). Educação e tecnologia, desafios e perspectivas. São Paulo, Ed. Cortez.

Horton, F. Jr. (2008). *Introduction à la maîtrise de l'information*. Paris: UNESCO.

Kenski, V. M. (1996). O ensino e os recursos didáticos em uma sociedade cheia de tecnologias. In *Didática: O ensino e suas relações*. Campinas: Papirus.

Learning Curriculum, and Life Politics. (2005). London: Routledge.

Lemos, A. (2002). *Cibercultura: Tecnologia e vida social na cultura contemporânea*. Porto Alegre: Sulina.

Lévy, P. (1999). *Cibercultura*. São Paulo: Editora 34 Ltda.

Libâneo, J. C. (1996). Didática: Pedagogia e modernidade: Presente e futuro da escola. In *Infância, escola e modernidade*. São Paulo: Cortez.

Lüdke, M., & André, M. E. D. A. (1986). *Pesquisa em educação: Abordagens qualitativas*. São Paulo: EPU.

Marconi, M. A., & Lakatos, E. M. (2003). *Fundamentos de metodologia científica*. São Paulo: Atlas.

Muñoz, C., & Towner, T. (2011). Back to the "wall": How to use Facebook in the college classroom. *First Monday, 16*(12). doi:10.5210/fm.v16i12.3513

Papert, S. (1994). *A máquina das crianças*. Porto Alegre: ARTMED.

Patrício, M. R. V., & Gonçalves, V. M. B. (2010). Utilização educativa do facebook no ensino superior. In *Proceedings of Conference Learning and Teaching in Higher Education. Universidade de Évora*. Retrieved from http://bibliotecadigital.ipb.pt/bitstream/10198/2879/4/7104.pdf

Perriault, J. (2002). *Éducation et nouvelles technologies*. Paris: Nathan.

Silva, M. (2001). *Sala de Aula Interativa*. Editora Quartet.

Silva, M. (2010). Educar na cibercultura: Desafios à formação de professores para docência em cursos online. *Revista Digital de Tecnologias Cognitivas*, (3), 36-51.

Valente, J. A. (1999). *O computador na sociedade do conhecimento: Cadernos informática para a mudança em educação*. Brasília, DF: MEC/SEED.

Valente, J. A. (2005). *A espiral da espiral de aprendizagem: O processo de compreensão do papel das tecnologias de informação e comunicação na educação. Tese (Livre Docência) – Instituto de Artes*. Campinas: UNICAMP.

Vygotsky, L. S. A. (1989). *A formação social da mente*. São Paulo: Martins Fontes.

Zitkoski, J. J. (2003). Educação popular e emancipação social: Convergências nas propostas de freire e habermas. ANPED 26. Reunião, GT 6, Caxambu.

KEY TERMS AND DEFINITIONS

Classroom Extensions: An extra space where pedagogical practices occur and, as well, a flipped classroom practice, anticipating or postponing content and activities which may contribute to learning. An expansion of the classroom as well, as it ignites and improves the possibilities for learning without the constraints of the formal concrete classroom space.

Coauthorship: The ability to identify, create an interact pedagogical content and practices in a technology enhanced educational setting. In addition, the possibility to master and resample educational ideas in a collaborative way.

Curriculum: Everyday pedagogical content and practices in education, constantly rebuilt and incorporating changes as to meaningful for the students' context.

Cyberculture in Digital Culture: In this study the notion developed by Silva (2005), Lemos (2002), and Levy (1999). They define cyberculture as the lifestyle and behaviors assimilated and transmitted in the "historical and daily experience marked by information technologies" (Silva, 2010, p.38). We underscore that mediation in Internet-based communication and information is different than the centralized emission in both communicational and informational terms in the format used by traditional means such as radio, television, and books and magazines. In what is defined as cyberspace, message emission, and reception coexist as they rely on hypertext, interactivity, virtuality, among other features.

Emitter-Receiver: Given the possibility provided by emission and transmission on the Web 2.0, the author defines the subject who inhabits digital tools to be different from those in the remaining information technologies. The cyberspace inhabitant has the potential ability of not receiving a message passively, as well as to participate in the construction of a newly discussed message, regardless of time and physical space that exist between emitter and receiver, as both can be emitter-receivers on the Web 2.0.

Learning Management System: A virtual space where teaching and learning occur and which can be integrated with Web 2.0 spaces as well as further developments of the semantic web and other newer technologies. A space which can be reorganized and recontextualized by the teacher with the contribution of the students.

Social Networks: Virtual spaces of connectivity through networks of relationships, allowing to create interest-specific groups for a defined purpose educational or professional.

Chapter 9

Measuring the Social Impact:
How Social Media Affects Higher Education Institutions

Vladlena Benson
Kingston Business School, Kingston University, UK

Stephanie Morgan
Kingston Business School, Kingston University, UK

ABSTRACT

Effective social media usage has particular challenges for HE institutions. The many opportunities afforded by social media, increasingly demanded by students, have negative potential. Social technology requires substantial investment to do well, and in particular, it can be very hard to measure its performance. In this chapter, the authors focus on how aligning with strategic objectives can reduce the risk and enhance the effectiveness of social media use throughout the student lifecycle. They also consider the risks which social media investment entails in HE. Using a case study of a UK university, the authors identify common themes for social media adoption in educational settings. They offer practical recommendations and key areas to consider before launching or enhancing a social media strategy in the field of HE.

1. INTRODUCTION[1]

The significance of social networking is no longer contested; it is viewed by many as a game-changing innovation set to transform the face of higher education. Social media is on its way to earning a distinctive position amongst educational technologies, attracting the attention of academic and industry researchers. The adoption of social media for academic purposes became inevitable with the wide acceptance of the tool by end-users. Social media in higher education took on a multi-faceted role: serving as networking enabler, marketing and recruitment tool, collaboration, teaching and learning tool as well as a medium presenting career management and entrepreneurship opportunities (Benson & Morgan, 2014). Extant literature offers rich accounts of the integration of social media in educational settings; the positive impact of this technology outweighs the negative potential. However, this area requires further exploration. We hope that this chapter will provide a balanced

DOI: 10.4018/978-1-4666-7401-1.ch009

view which will be helpful for the use of social media within university strategy while raising the awareness of the challenges presented by this technology. .

Earlier research (see for review Benson, Morgan & Tennakoon, 2012) opened up a discussion of how universities adopt social media, not only for marketing but for relationship building, career management and learning and teaching purposes. Conole and Alevizou (2010) systematically reviewed literature on the benefits and challenges presented by the integration of web 2.0 technologies into higher education. They emphasise the widely accepted benefit of enabling new communication channels and media sharing with a specific emphasis on content generation (in the case of video sharing through YouTube, and virtual interaction e.g. on SecondLife). The rich picture of the uses of social technologies emerges as a means for content production, collaboration and communications. Serving not only as a new communication mechanism, social technologies also changed the mode of communication, - as well as synchronous communication new forms of asynchronous connections delivered by blogging and micro-blogging sites and various social networking services have been developed. Perhaps one of the earliest applications of social media - community enablement, has found its potential in the HE context. Support for existing communities and facilitating the formation of new ones through social media reflects the earlier ideas of the Community of enquiry framework (Garrison et al, 2000) and offers opportunities for instructors to move away from the didactic to student-led, constructivist approaches in their practice (Garrison & Arbaugh, 2007). However, the opportunities presented by social media have significant challenges associated with them in the HE context. For example, the shift of control in a social networking environment towards students who are more accustomed to leading communication virtually and the impact of user generated content and its validity present only some of the emerging challenges

(Conole & Alevizou, 2010). This chapter focuses on the implications of social media channels for universities, not only from the measurement of success, but also from the challenges presented by the 'dark side' of social technology which are yet to be fully understood. Multiple stakeholders are involved in the integration of social media by universities: students, instructors, alumni, support staff, marketers, industry, etc. By employing social media universities may find themselves charting the unknown waters of technology with yet to be defined principles for data handling, privacy and information protection, cognitive and behavioural implications, and more. We provide insights into the dual-edged sword of the social technology: enable Higher Education Institutions (HEIs) to get a step closer to being able to define their goals for social media effectiveness and at the same time keep the challenges of social media in sight, for example privacy, information security, psychological implications and other challenges. This will enable HEIs to establish a successful, as well as efficient, social media communication strategy and to be in a position to measure the effectiveness of the new technology investment, enabling effective decision making regarding investment and approach. Further, it will help HE institutions in identifying the 'pain points' of social media and addressing the needs of internal and external stakeholders.

We discuss a case of an established multi channel social media strategy at a UK university and offer insights from academic staff into the benefits and challenges presented by the social technology in learning and teaching. We also present the dimensions of social media uses in an HE context and open the discussion on the set of metrics necessary for measuring the effectiveness of social media adopted in line with the goals of HEIs. Literature on business marketing provides plenty of metrics for social media analysis (Fodor & Hoffman, 2010), however the HE context is rather different. To address these differences we suggest a framework for aligning strategic objectives of HEIs along with possible social media strategies to achieve them. These strategies are applicable in various stages of the student lifecycle, which differs markedly in terms of university goals, students' expectations and the objectives /involvement of a wide variety of external stakeholders. This case is of a successful application of a mature social media strategy at a UK university, which is located in the London metropolitan area and has a network of international links. The social media strategy has been facilitating internal and external communication of the HEI with a wide range of stakeholders. The paper proposes a framework for aligning social media practices with university goals, taking into account the characteristics of individual higher education institutions. It is argued that student recruitment, engagement, achievement and employability can be improved through the integration of social media in higher education. We hope that the article will help in bringing HEIs closer to solving the dilemma of being able to justify investment into social media and to measure effectiveness (or the lack of thereof) of the technology, which is itself continually changing. The article concludes with a practical social media strategy matrix for the adoption of social media, based on strategic objectives which can be tailored to individual HEIs.

2. SOCIAL NETWORKING AND HIGHER EDUCATION

We live in a digital world where social media touches every aspect of the whole student lifecycle, from initial search, pre-entry, the education itself, job search and as alumnus. HE organizations have incorporated social media into the education process as well as its marketing communication channels, often without fully understanding the impact this may have on their operation or their students. The nature of students is changing (and perhaps, being changed) by technology and the increasingly large, always-on community which

is enabled through social media. Today's Digital Natives are used to 'bite-sized, on-demand' learning, but also are increasingly collaborative and experienced in global communications. Many years have passed from the time Prensky (2001) originally came up with the term 'digital natives', the technology is ubiquitous and continually changing, impacting on the learning landscape on a global scale.

There has been substantial academic research on the application of social media technology to learning and teaching. Online social media allows learners to communicate and collaborate across national and cultural boundaries, generate academic content, and become active participants in the learning process. The use of social media has increased across a range of disciplines, as wide ranging as medical, architecture, marketing, and business as well as communications studies. With the proliferation of mobile devices social networking in higher education is likely to continue its successful adoption (Benson & Morgan 2012, Morgan & Benson 2014). However the implications of such devices for student learning are still unclear.

Employability is increasingly important in education and as businesses increase their own use of social media it becomes even more important to encourage students to make appropriate use of these. Employers are increasingly expecting such skills and will discuss these capabilities in job interviews. However Tuten & Marks (2012) suggest that even in marketing education these tools are not yet much used. Barriers cited by staff include lack of time and issues with adjusting to the quantity of tools available. HE institutions need to invest in staff time and support to enable them to make effective use of tools, however this can be hard to justify without a clear strategy linked to the specific HEI employability objectives.

The concept of fully integrating social media into coursework and teaching is increasingly gaining attention. George & Dellasega (2011) discuss this in the specialist area of medical education.

They argue that this integration helps students to acquire the skills needed for problem solving and collaboration using technology required in the 21st century. Student feedback has been excellent supporting the value of this approach. Staff will need support however in understanding how this integration can be achieved.

A range of studies suggest that this integration into teaching and learning does have many benefits, and is worth the investment in training and time that faculty will require to achieve true integration. Okoro (2012) suggests that social media improves the quality of student learning outcomes however also emphasises the importance of selective use of the medium. Blaschke (2012) shows that social media can encourage self determined learning to develop autonomy and capability to learn. Although aimed at distance learning, these aspects can be applied to more traditional learning environments. McCarthy (2010) used Facebook within a blended delivery model and found that today's digital natives engage readily with this approach. The first year experience of students was considerably enhanced in this case. In a Taiwanese study, Hung & Yuen (2010) found that the use of social media enhanced student's sense of community, giving a strong feeling of social connectedness which improved their learning experience. Okoro, Hausman & Washington (2012) found use of social media encourages active engagement, collaboration, and participation in class activities. Whilst they agree that social media can be a distraction for students, effective use was shown to sustain quality instruction and skills development. A number of studies support the view that the use of social media increases student independence and autonomy, enabling them to learn methods of assimilating information, and suiting the learning styles of today's 'digital natives'.

However, there are many other potential negatives with distraction being only one of the minor considerations. Hrastinski & Aghaee (2012) found evidence of 'digital dissonance' (the divide between personal and educational use, see Clark et al. 2009) although the majority of students in this small study did use Facebook to initiate contact with peers and found social media useful to facilitate groupwork. They rightly emphasise the importance of ensuring there is a teaching strategy in place. Friesen & Lowe (2012) argue against the claim that social media places the learner at the centre of a network of knowledge and expertise. They argue for the questionable promise of the use of this in learning as in their view social media constrains debate, and therefore learning. Kurkela (2011) emphasised the potential for unintended, usually negative, consequences of this technique and argued for the need for a systematic understanding of the purpose of the use of social media. There have been suggestions that digital natives have reduced empathy or emotional intelligence due to the over-focus on communicating online (Kuss et al., 2013), although this is controversial and requires further research it could have a major impact on social media use in education. Issues with privacy, data security and trust have been highlighted in a number of studies (see this book chapters 1, 4, 5 and 7) and the impact on well-being, including increases in loneliness and depression and the potential to normalise the use of alcohol and drugs, has been demonstrated (see chapters 2 and 3). There has been some research focusing on the impact on those required to teach online, with issues of time and concerns about over-use of technology being prominent (e.g. this book chapter 9). Some studies suggest that young people are particularly prone to over-use of social media to the stage of addiction, where it begins to impact on their private and educational lives (Beard &

Wolf, 2001, see also Kuss et al, 2013). It is possible that by encouraging social media use within the learning environment educators could make this more likely. Finally there is still insufficient understanding of the actual impact on learning, with some suggesting that the use of social media will encourage superficial approaches to learning (Cifuentes, 2011).

Many positives have been found, suggesting that as long as there is a clear strategic use of social media it can have benefits. For example, Laire, Castelyn & Mottart (2012) demonstrated that using social media such as Storify (which collects content from multiple social networks, and creates the possibility for students to write their own memorable story by adding text) increased student engagement and improving student performance in EFL writing instructions. Ravenscroft et. al. (2012) give an overview of the issues involved and strategies that may be needed to integrate informal and formal learning, and these are taken up in their special issue on social media in learning (Journal of Computer Assisted Learning, Volume 28, issue 3, 2012).

Nyangau & Bado (2012) offer a full review of the literature on marketing through social media in HE and found many HE organizations are using this increasingly for student recruitment, although it was still unclear whether social media actually influences student decision making. Benson et al. (2012) outline the advantages of integrating the strategy for marketing and educational use of social media throughout the student lifecycle. We suggest that the use of social media for marketing, if strategically integrated with use in the curriculum, may increase student awareness of social media and use within coursework, and thereby reduce digital dissonance. It is clear from the above, that social media in HE has a number of positive and negative possibilities. We will argue that taking a strategic approach to the use of social media will reduce risk and enhance effectiveness, however to develop a strategy does require an understanding

of the different types of social media that may be used, as they have different issues. We offer below some categorisations that should prove helpful.

3. CATEGORIES OF SOCIAL MEDIA APPLICATIONS

From the early days of social networking research attempts were made to classify social networks. Curiously early typologies recognised the informal nature of social networks and suggested a dichotomous classification of social networking services into personal and professional (Dutta & Fraser, 2009; Benson, Morgan & Fillipaious, 2010). Social networking sites providing a way to connect, communicate, and share content with friends and family, e.g. Bebo, MySpace, vContacte and others have been considered personal social networks. On the other hand, networks enabling business connections or set up to offer commercial services have been coined as professional. LinkedIn has been a de rigueur example of professional social networks set up solely for business activity. However, with the proliferation of social media into every area of life the delineation between personal and professional social platforms began to blur. A prominent example of this process is the innovation of the Facebook platform. Started as a network for leisure use only, it eventually encompassed professional networking, as well as enabled business and commercial interactions and opportunities. Similar trends are characteristic of other social media. Both YouTube and Instagram started off as multimedia self publishing and sharing networks, but eventually turned into effective media communication channels serving varied purposes from marketing to career portfolio management tools. Therefore we argue that the classification into personal and professional social networks is now obsolete, as many social platforms effectively serve dual purposes and new entrants into the social media arena continue to appear.

Another stream of attempts to categorise social networks was based on their functionality. While the research studies were conducted in a variety of settings, from tourism to marketing, their findings tend to cluster around a finite number of categories. Xiang & Gretzel (2010) analysed Google search queries on social media and classified the types of social media included in the search results by their frequency. According to the researchers, the majority of the social media landscape is used as virtual community enablers (40%), followed by the review platforms (27%), bloggs (15%), social networking (9%), media sharing sites (7%) and other category. Kaplan & Haenlein (2010) offer another functional classification of social platforms including: Blogs, Collaborative Projects (e.g. Wikipedia), Social Networking Sites (e.g. Facebook), Content Communities (e.g. YouTube), Virtual Social Worlds (e.g. Second Life) and Virtual Game Worlds (e.g. WarCraft). This classification also introduces self-Presentation/self-Disclosure and Media - richness/Social presence. According to this classification blogs and collaborative projects have a low media-richness and social presence factor, as they are text-based and enable relatively simple exchange, unlike technically sophisticated Virtual worlds, for example. On the other hand Content Communities score low on self disclosure, while social networks (e.g. Facebook) naturally offer a higher level of self-presentation opportunities. The functional perspective on social media provides the rationale for the categorisation presented by Fodor & Hoffman (2010). They discern the following types: Blogs and microblogging (e.g. Twitter), Cocreation (e.g. NikeiD), Social Bookmarking (e.g. StumbleUpon), Forums and Discussion Boards (e.g. Google Groups), Product Reviews (e.g. Amazon), Social Networks (e.g. LinkedIn) and Media Sharing sites (e.g. Flickr, YouTube). Depending on the purpose of the social media channel, the measurement of its performance changes accordingly.

4. MEASURING THE EFFECTIVENESS OF SOCIAL MEDIA

Commercial presence on social media has facilitated the rise of social technologies over the last few years. Projections for the growth of social marketing are extremely positive, facilitated by the expansion of applications, rise of mobile device capabilities and diversification of mobile networks (Woodhouse, 2012). Woodhouse also cites statistics of the top most popular internet sites, which include Facebook, Twitter and LinkedIn amongst the top 12 most visited in the world. The organic growth of social media marketing and convergence of social networking sites offers opportunities for consolidated marketing. Assessing the success of a social media investment has always presented difficulties in the business world. Coming into the next stage of maturity, social technology is moving away from the phase of inflated expectations and is now expected to deliver real return on investment (Blanchard 2011). Holistic evolutions of social media ROI on the basis of "We have members, so we think it works..." are no longer sufficient to answer management level questions, such as "Social marketing is everywhere, but how can we justify the ROI?" Social return on investment is notoriously difficult to calculate (Anderson 2012). Recent statistics suggest that only a small proportion of companies can measure their social media channel effectiveness; 80% of those investing in social media marketing have no idea of how to measure their ROI. The same study reports that nearly half of marketing managers, for whom social marketing is a priority, are under pressure to report on the ROI of their corporate social channel and quantify the outcomes (Lenskold 2012). These findings indicate the developing trend of social media channel turning from a 'nice-have' into a 'must-have', while proven quantifiable KPIs appear unavailable. Work by Fodor & Hoffman (2010) presents three dimensions of social media evaluation objectives, including brand awareness, brand engagement and word of mouth. They base their evaluation metrics on easily accessible statistics, such as unique visits, number of retweets, number of likes and references. While the list offered by Fodor & Hoffman (op cit) is very extensive, not all of them are applicable in the context of applications other than marketing.

Sales focused firms integrate social engagement into their sales processes. This type of social activity is centred round the metrics of 'social conversation' rate in the context of the sales cycle (Anderson 2012). Social conversation rate, measurable through virtually any social networking site, is obtained from the number of replies and comments per post. This helps to measure whether what the firm is saying to customers translates into business value. Those firms who set brand awareness as their business goal for social media investment, cultivate trust as the basis of their customer relationships and loyalty building, and employ social engagement metrics for community building. For example the number of members or followers and the community growth rate could serve as indicators of increasing brand awareness and expansion of reach on social media. Responses to posts, likes and retweets are treated as social effects which reflect brand influence and therefore have measurable business value (Shaefer 2012). Finally, amplification rate, so called 'spreading the word' through the network in the form of retweets and shares per post, and applause rate, knowing what your audience 'likes', are another set of measurements which are argued to measure ROI of a social media channel.

Organizations are not focused on achieving just a single business objective through their social media channels. Very often a combination of objectives drives the choice of social media strategy, necessitating a mix of effective metrics for social media channels (Gallaugher & Ransbotham 2010). The business rate on marketing investment has historically been calculated through econometric analysis of spending and sales, as well as competitor comparison. As higher education would have different objectives for social media strategies, it is difficult to extend commercial firms' approaches to measuring HE marketing effectiveness. Aligning a firm's business goals and social media objectives, as well as estimation of available resources are paramount for identifying the right mix of metrics for social investment evaluation. Having a clear view of user/customer journey through the firms' or HEI's social channels will help increase understanding of customer expectations and ways to meet them through social engagement.

Earlier technology had an incremental influence on learning and teaching innovation. The advent of blogs, electronic assessment, wikis, gamification, etc. has had a significant impact on higher education as new tools became available to instructors (Pimmer, Linxen, & Grohien, 2012). New ways of doing traditional things meant that technology represented incremental innovation. Since the emergence of the Internet social media is the key technology which now has a pervasive influence on the educational sector (see Benson et al., 2010).

Social media is a cross-disciplinary field. A substantial body of research on social networking research has been accumulated in the areas of psychology and sociology (Wilson, Gosling, & Graham, 2012), criminology (Conger, Pratt, & Loch, 2013) and marketing (Fodor & Hoffman, 2010), social capital theory (Valenzuela, Park, & Kee, 2009) and information systems research (Smith, Dinev, & Xu, 2011). Social media includes Facebook, LinkedIn, Twitter, blogs, virtual worlds such as Second Life, YouTube, vlogs, etc. These various media are increasingly used by students throughout their time in Higher Education and beyond, while academics including from the fields not directly related to technology are beginning to embrace social media adoption.

We now turn to our case study of social media integration to further the discussion of potential ways of measuring effectiveness.

5. THE CASE OF A UK UNIVERSITY: SOCIAL MEDIA CHANNEL INTEGRATION[2]

Kingston University established its presence on social media over seven years ago, and has been using a range of social applications to interact with various stakeholders. Twitter and Facebook are key, with LinkedIn being used particularly with the Business School. Since 2010 specific pages were set up on Facebook to target students considering joining the University. This aspect has been developed in scope over time and now covers a full range of support and communication at every stage of the selection, admission and induction process. The main Facebook page has over 25,500 'likes', now, increasing by 10,000 in the last 12 months and demonstrating a strong acceptance of the social networking site in this area. Twitter has been used for five years and the main 'tweet' hashtag has just over 22,300 followers, up by 4,000 in the last six months. Many of the 'followers' on twitter are journalists, alumni and indeed other Universities. As HE becomes more competitive globally, it is increasingly important to track activities of others in the sector and understand the competitive environment.

The central communications team started to integrate the use of social media channels into the communication strategy in a formal way about two years ago, and at first this was slow to take-off. This is fairly typical of early entrants to new media. Careful consideration had to be given to balance the conflicting needs to make the channel meaningful to the student (e.g. by having an area dedicated to a specific course) whilst having sufficient activity to make the area appealing and give the feel that the site is worth regular return visits.

In the past eighteen months a much more strategic approach has been taken, with a new member of staff employed centrally, along with additional support in faculties, with a main part of the role to work on the schedule of campaigns linked to pre-application, post application, joining and then during their time at the University. Important links are also being made with alumni. Clearly this has taken commitment (and resources) but it is starting to succeed in Kingston's aims of encouraging relationship development.

Adding multimedia seems to enhance social engagement; graduation pictures for example are always popular. Videos are also increasingly used on social networking sites and are the most popular aspects of the course pages. Being able to see and hear other students and the teaching staff talking about the experience of studying at Kingston appears to be very important to potential students. It is vital to tie in to the recruitment cycle and student life-cycle and ensure a coherent and integrated approach. The use of social media cannot just be passive, setting up initial pages is just the first step in a long process, and the integration of the different media needs careful thought throughout.

Not all of the work has to be done by University staff. One of the most successful social media sites we run was started on Facebook (with staff blessing) by Kingston students to enable students to easily raise issues and offer ideas to their course representatives, who can then feed this back to the relevant staff. The group has over 450 members, with hundreds of posts and the course teams have learnt a great deal about student views from this. Furthermore they can respond immediately if necessary rather than have to wait for the more formal student committees or feedback forms. However this does require a good relationship with the students who set up the space, as twice so far inaccurate statements have been made and we have requested that these statements be deleted or modified and responded to 'offline'. Without a level of trust and engagement with the students, this could cause difficulties.

Social media is being used increasingly in teaching and coursework. The use of Facebook, blogs, wikis and indeed twitter has enabled staff and students to collaborate and develop communities of practice. Staff in all faculties have set up blogs, wikis and Facebook pages, and many are now encouraging students to use their mobiles in class to access these pages, in an attempt to increase usage. As always, these staff tend to be the 'early adopters', who are comfortable with technology and are willing to invest time in developing a clear strategy for the use of social media, ensuring this is meaningful to the students. Analysis so far indicates that the benefits proposed in the literature cited above are being found, with students engaging fully in the tasks and commenting that they feel more confident regarding the use of social media for their discipline.

Blogs are also being used to increase collaboration between students and staff outside the standard learning situation. For example the University Student Academic Development Research Associate Scheme (SADRAS) brings together staff and students to research in areas that will improve the student experience, and all create blogs to record their collaboration as part of the process. This is helping to ensure that staff and students reflect on their work together, and facilitates evaluation of the scheme.

Social technologies have successfully proven themselves as pedagogical tools. However as the innovation and changes to communication medium brought around by social media are spreading through society, these sweeping changes force HE institutions to embrace social innovation in more areas than learning and teaching. A qualitative pilot study of the technology adoption by business instructors helped shed some light on the perceptions of social technologies by academic staff at the research site[3]. The general view of instructors is that pedagogy drives technology adoption, not vice versa. The quote from one of the study participants summarises the role of technology in their practices follows:

One of the things that is quite interesting is how sometimes you don't actually have to think about technology; it sort of emerges in because it's just the way of the world.

Indeed social technologies weaved themselves into the fabric of everyday life, then proliferated into professional areas and applications, such as learning and teaching, alumni and recruitment, student support and many other HE areas. While examples of the integration of social media in teaching were reported by all participants, the range of techniques varied. They included the extensive use of interactive discussion capabilities on various social networks - e.g. to escape the 'four walls' confinement of the classroom in Twitter; rich use of blogs - from project management to e-commerce implementation; study social presence of organization, on Second Life or other networks; explore how business leverage and operate on social media. The objective of keeping teaching interesting and engaging, immersing students into the environment they are comfortable with emerged as a leading driver for social technology adoption among interviewed academic staff. Strategies of social technologies have been mentioned by all participants and instructors measured how effective the strategy was by its effect on students. For example, empowerment of individual learners was achieved in the following setting:

….I tried to start a trending discussion where people in the classroom were responding to a blog comment from a lecturer at Oxford about recruitment. So that really encouraged them and made them think that their opinions are valuable.

Releasing the control of the classroom to students was reported to have a positive impact on student participation in self organising environment as the following example illustrates:

We have a student Facebook group which is intended just for student feedback amongst themselves so it's student led, student run, student populated group. I quite often participate in that just to clarify issues.

While alumni relationship were one of the earliest manifestations of social media applications in HE, student networking and career management opportunities have since been extended to benefit current students as well as the following quote illustrates:

I set up an alumni group on LinkedIn for graduates of our specialist degrees both the undergraduates and the postgraduates and now we have extended it so we allow the current students to join the group as well[…] using social media to help network and help them find jobs for each other, research opportunities and so on.

Social technologies have also been reported as a trouble-shooting mechanism in case of unforeseen circumstances, for instance:

We had a wonderful example of using a discussion board when we had to cancel a class, so we ran the lecture on a discussion board so we had this sort of the community spirit[…] it's a good fall back.

While the benefits of social technologies for student learning have been widely acknowledged in the University, drawbacks have been also voiced. For example staff were concerned about the reliability of technology or lack thereof, especially in the case of third party social networking sites or learning management systems plugins. Some mentioned that 'three out of four times' something goes terribly wrong when teaching with technology. Others voiced students' expectations for immediate feedback and lecturer's availability 24/7, as the following quote illustrates:

I'm sure there's quite an expectation that if students put something on the discussion board at 2 o'clock in the morning, there's almost an expectations that they will get a reply very soon.

Finally, fluency with social media seemed to be the determinant factor towards its adoption in the class room. As one of the interviewees, a younger member of academic staff, said:

…I am generation Y. I don't really remember life before mobile phones and so on.

Technical skill acquisition for staff also surfaced as self-taught rather than owing to formal staff development activities. Some of technically savvy instructors mentioned that there are academics who ' would not touch technology with a barge pole, while others are very much into it'.

The social dimension of media seemed to have had in impact on the diffusion of teaching innovation as instructors genuinely interested in technology formed interest groups where they 'self-support each other'. Interestingly enough this presented a challenge for 'traditionalists' venturing out into the social technologies field:

The only difficulties there are if you're forced to do it [using social technology] and you are out of your comfort zone. I think frankly if people are happy with technology then they can see a great role for it and it works for students, go for it every time. This Twitter idea from one of my colleagues is fantastic. But I don't think we all should do the same thing anyway. I really do believe that we should have a whole portfolio of innovations that we own.

Ultimately, it was the effect of social media foot print on students which raised instructors' concerns:

It's something that we talk to students a lot about, because we're all passionate about employability and telling students to be terribly careful about what they put about themselves online and on social media, maintaining the integrity of their Facebook sites and not divulging too much [information]...

Aiming to meet student expectations and include a popular communication channel into their communication strategy, universities have incorporated social networking into the marketing of their courses, learning and teaching strategy, maintaining alumni connections, and other areas. However, universities remain unclear about the effectiveness of their social media channels, and are even less aware about the resources which social media management requires. HEIs are making ad hoc attempts to employ social media without the appropriate tools or metrics for measuring the effectiveness of their social media communication channels.

Through the exploratory study of social media adoption at this UK University we identified five areas of social media influence in HE. These dimensions of the social platform are: learning and teaching objectives, development of social capital and career management skills among students, social creativity and innovation space for students, university social marketing and student recruitment strategy, and finally areas of privacy in information handling compliance. The challenge of measuring effectiveness in each of these domains remains, however below we give some pointers:

- **Learning and Teaching:** Measuring effectiveness here is complex, and clearly more research is needed. However analysis of the quantity and quality of student uptake of social media linked directly to their learning should be undertaken, along with more qualitative evaluation of student engagement and approaches to social media,

and assessment of links to and achievement of learning outcomes. If staff have been alerted to potential negative aspects of using social media there is potential to reduce these, and again many of these can be measured (for example, student self-esteem, reported feelings of isolation etc.).

- **Social Capital and Career Management:** Analysis could be undertaken of the number of students using social media to initiate and maintain contacts related to their chosen careers, and the extent of their interactions with their network. The number of alumni members, their levels of activity, and their links to students and other alumni, as well as monitoring of success (e.g. promotions, salary etc.) can also be analysed. However, students need to be aware that their social activity may become public due to inadvertent or intentional actions of themselves and others. Their skills in managing their social profiles for professional vs personal purposes need to be developed at the university level or earlier.
- **Space for Creativity and Innovation:** The quantity of items uploaded or discussed linked to new ideas, creativity and innovation could be counted, and the number of items successfully launched (e.g. as a business or submissions for copyright, patents etc.). However we would argue for a more qualitative approach as well, assessing student and staff evaluations of the levels of creativity and innovation generated.
- **Marketing and Recruitment:** Here more typical measurements such as number of visits, 'likes', re-tweets and so on could be used, in a similar way to many other organizations assess social media ROI as highlighted above. Ideally longitudinal analysis should be made of which students engage before joining, how they progress through their time in the HEI, and their engagement as alumni, to assess patterns over

time. While social media can significantly enhance recruitment and marketing campaigns, universities must have crisis management strategies in place. Social media has served as a fruitful platform for spreading information damaging reputation of many organizations. Universities should think about putting reputation management plans in place and their online profile monitoring.

- **Privacy and Compliance Considerations:** Here we are often looking for absence rather than presence. We would hope that educating students and staff successfully about privacy and good practice would lead to an absence of negative press stories, students not losing jobs due to social media exposure, and low levels of complaints or non-compliance.

Social media has created a paradigm shift in the way universities interact with students and a variety of stakeholders, from industry to government. The communication between the university and its students is no longer one way, but is transforming into a mutual and powerful dialogue empowering the voice of stakeholders in shaping up the future of higher education.

6. DISCUSSION

Starting a new social media strategy for an HEI is not an easy task and many factors need to be taken into account, including allocation of resources and an in depth analysis of external and internal needs and drivers. Taking a more strategic approach will enable HEIs to increase their understanding of the return they receive for their investment, and reduce the potential negative consequences of social media use. Below we give some suggestions based on the literature and our own research.

6.1 Key Areas to Consider before Launching Your Social Media Strategy

1. **Focus on Relationship Building Rather than Sales:** Whilst the position of social marketing has recently gained a lot more clarity and understanding, it has yet to deliver the expected benefits as a sales channel, while delivering effectively as a relationship realisation tool.

2. **Multi Social Networking Site Presence:** Marketing strategists make assumptions that with the growth and diversification of the social media landscape and intensification of use over time, presence in social media becomes vital to any organization. The social media landscape changes rapidly; therefore the choice of the social platform may be a short term decision rather than a long-term strategy.

3. **Aligning Resources to Stakeholder Needs:** Starting a social media strategy is often associated with initiating multiple profiles on as many social networks as possible. Social media presence should be driven by business objectives and alignment of resources according to the strategy, including the choice of social platform(s).

4. **Single Channel Social Marketing:** Choosing one social marketing platform, e.g. LinkedIn or Facebook, offers some advantages, while limiting marketing opportunities. The popularity of social sites tends to vary geographically. While Facebook, Google, etc. have originated in the West and retain popularity in English speaking countries, the emerging markets, e.g. Russia and China, give preference in popularity to other social networking sites, virtually unknown to the rest, such as China's Renren (Vincos 2012). Also, stable social networking sites

have become a platform for fierce competition of developed brands as well as emerging ones. Investigating competitors' presence on social marketing channels should be the initial point for assessment of new social marketing initiatives and identifying whether you can measure up and/or compete with the existing successful brands.

5. **Short Term vs. Long Term Campaigns:** Social media facilitates relationship building, when deciding on the social strategy marketers need to be aware that a social channel as a successful conversation-based engagement tool for all stakeholders is difficult to realise, and requires persistence and appropriate resources. However, this ambitious, resource intensive endeavour has the promise to deliver long term strategic objectives, unlike short term campaigns that help test feasibility and determine effectiveness of social channels. Integrating the student lifecycle will also offer benefits; students who interact on social media during their courses are more likely to remain active as alumni.

6. **The Promise of Social Mobile:** The long term plans of many social networking sites, including Facebook and LinkedIn, emphasise the future development of the mobile dimension of social networking. The evolution of social marketing onto the mobile platform is on the mind of marketers worldwide. The outlook for mobile social marketing presents a logical progression from web based to a more convenient on-the-go platform, and is anticipated to go mainstream in the next year or so, further strengthening the current standing of social mobile applications (Benson & Morgan 2012).

6.2 Strategic Alignment

Assessment of the effectiveness of the social media investment has been notoriously problematic for organizations in public and private sectors alike. Social media has been widely adopted by higher education institutions looking for innovative communication channels with their stakeholders. However, social media management requires continuous investment, persistent engagement and monitoring of its effectiveness. Strategic business goals commonly sought through the introduction of social media which are emerging in private sector companies fall into the categories of brand management and sales. KPIs emerging in social media marketing comprise social traffic, social engagement, amplification rate, applause rate and social response rate. However, metrics for social media effectiveness differ markedly in the higher education area. While quantifiable monetary outcomes are a high priority in the private sector, higher education draws largely intangible benefits from social media presence. The strategic objectives of social media investment in HE may include benefits such as life-long learning, alumni engagement, wider community stakeholder management, research interest group community formation and growth, as well as relationship building with and between learners. In order to help universities establish and prioritise their strategic objectives within social media we attempted to summarise key benefits which social media may deliver in the HE sector. These include marketing as well as learning and teaching goals, some of which may serve dual roles in the HE context.

Those HEIs who are looking to 'test the waters' of social media must conduct an in-depth analysis of stakeholders, any party that is likely to play a role or be impacted by social media channels, and establish metrics for social effectiveness. It is important to establish KPI monitoring strategy against which the effectiveness of the social media channel for the specific HEI is continually assessed. When the goals of the social media investment for a university focus on stakeholder engagement, for example student, business and research community interactions are a priority, then stakeholder analysis needs to drive the HEI communication plan, supported by the diffusion of innovation strategy engaging not only innovators, but also cautious adopters, into the social dialogue. Formation of special interest groups, as in the case described earlier, promotes growth of the conversation rate and serves as a natural platform for community building. Alumni management is a specific example of relationship management. Well established or professionally oriented social networking sites tend to provide a common platform connecting individuals for professional and leisure purposes, while fostering a sense of belonging to their 'alma mater'.

A common driver for social media investment becomes a necessity to keep up with competitors, i.e. 'they have it, so it should work for us too' approach. This goal is the most risky and may see a university plunge into the social media waters with presence on multiple social networking sites but either lacking resources or a clear strategy. The risk of negative posts overwhelming the marketing team is also possible if the resources are not there to monitor and deflect negatives (a good social media approach will include 'service recovery' strategies that can turn negative chatter into positives). Allocating a social media manager and monitoring of the social channel performance are key actions in this case to avoid this risk. In the study of the views of academic staff towards adoption of social technologies we found that personal interest in technology itself and having supportive colleagues play an important role in the successful integration of social media tools into practice. The main driver behind the decision to adopt social technology is student engagement and development of the rapport with learners using social technology they can't do without. In the evaluation of effectiveness of technology intervention such indicators as student motivation, attendance, learner (and lecturer) satisfaction played a significant part.

In a similar way to commercial firms, universities are concerned about building stronger brand awareness amongst their current and prospective students, as well as for maintaining their business image and research reputation with external stakeholders, including employers, alumni and other Universities. Brand awareness as a result of social media integration helps build trust as the basis of customer relationships and loyalty building; therefore it is paramount to employ social engagement metrics for community building. This includes the number of members or followers, and the community growth rate. Responses to posts, likes and retweets are considered to have social impact which demonstrates brand influence and therefore have measurable business value.

7. CONCLUSION

Over the past few years organizations in the public and private sectors have turned to social media in the hope of establishing an effective communication channel with their customers, suppliers and other stakeholders. Following this trend, Higher Education Institutions (HEI) have adopted social media channels for a variety of purposes. Accounts about HEIs' use of social media are plentiful in academic literature (see for a review Conole & Alevizou, 2010). Aiming to meet student expectations and include a popular channel into their communication strategy, universities have incorporated social networking into the marketing of their courses, learning and teaching strategy, maintaining alumni connections, and other areas. However, universities remain unclear about the effectiveness of their social media channels, and are even less aware about the resources which social media management requires. HEIs are making ad hoc attempts to employ social media without the appropriate tools or metrics for measuring its value.

In this chapter we discussed a case of a multi-channel social strategy applied at a UK HEI for the past seven years. The metrics used for the analysis of the channel effectiveness comprises of marketing, and learning and teaching goals. Through the exploratory study of the university efforts around social media adoption, five dimensions critical to the implementation of social strategy have been identified. They are learning and teaching objectives, development of social capital and career management skills among students, social creativity and innovation space for students, university social marketing and student recruitment strategy, and finally areas of privacy in information handling compliance. We also listened to the voice of the academic staff on social media adoption in learning and teaching, community building and alumni relationship management. While student motivation, engagement and interest in the subject surfaced as the key metrics of successful social media integration into pedagogy, instructors were concerned about students' privacy and personal information handled through social sites - a third party in the instructor-learner information exchange. An overall view of the inevitability of social technology entering the learning and teaching process has emerged as younger generation of lecturers represent generation Y.

Whether the primary objective of an HEI social media strategy becomes alumni engagement or marketing of its courses, it is important to consider key issues in the specific context before launching or during re-assessment of the effectiveness of a social media strategy. The choice between a single social networking service and multi-channel marketing strategy is down to the specific institution and its objectives and resources available. Consequently, a specific set of KPIs must be established by HEIs reflecting their individual needs and strategic goals. We argue that student recruitment, engagement, achievement and employability can be improved by higher education institutions opening a strategic social media communication channel. In a similar way, the potential risks involved with the increased use of social media can be reduced.

REFERENCES

Anderson, B. (2012). Cracking the social ROI code: Social media performance indicators demystified. *Cambridge Marketing Review*, (4), 12-15.

Beard, K. W., & Wolf, E. M. (2001). Modification in the proposed diagnostic criteria for Internet addiction. *Cyberpsychology & Behavior*, *4*(3), 377–383. doi:10.1089/109493101300210286 PMID:11710263

Benson, V., Filippaios, F., & Morgan, S. (2010). Online social networks: Changing the face of business education and career planning. *International Journal of Business and Management*, *4*(1), 20–33.

Benson, V., & Morgan, S. (2012). Student experience and learning management systems: Issues of wireless access and cloud deployment. In *Proceedings of the International Conference on Wireless Information Networks and Systems (WINSYS)*. Rome, Italy: Academic Press.

Benson, V., Morgan, S., & Tennakoon, H. (2012). A framework for knowledge management in higher education using social networking. *International Journal of Knowledge Society Research*, *3*(2), 44–54. doi:10.4018/jksr.2012040104

Blanchard, O. (2011). *Social media ROI: Managing and measuring social media efforts in your organization*. Indianapolis, IN: QUE Publishing.

Blaschke, L. M. (2012). Heutagogy and lifelong learning: A review of heutagogical practice and self-determined learning. *International Review of Research in Open and Distance Learning*, *13*(1), 56–71.

Cifuentes, L., Xochihua, O. A., & Edwards, J. (2011). Learning in web 2.0 environments: Surface learning and chaos or deep learning and self-regulation? *Quarterly Review of Distance Education*, *12*(1).

Clarke, T., & Clarke, E. (2009). Born digital? Pedagogy and computer-assisted learning. *Education + Training*, *51*(5–6), 395–407. doi:10.1108/00400910910987200

Conole, G., & Alevizou, P. (2010). *A literature review on the use of web 2.0 tools in higher education*. York, UK: Higher Education Academy.

Dutta, S., & Fraser, M. (2009). When job-seekers invade Faceebok. *The McKinsey Quarterly*, *2009*(March). Available online at http://www.mckinsey.com/insights/high_tech_telecoms_internet/when_job_seekers_invade_facebook

Fodor, M., & Hoffman, D. (2010). Can you measure the ROI of your social marketing? *MIT Sloan Review*, *52*(11), 40–50.

Friesen, N., & Lowe, S. (2011). The questionable promise of social media for education: Connective learning and the commercial imperative. *Journal of Computer Assisted Learning*, *28*(3), 183–194. doi:10.1111/j.1365-2729.2011.00426.x

Gallaugher, J., & Ransbotham, S. (2010). Social media and customer dialog management at Starbucks. *Management Information Systems Quarterly Executive Journal*, *9*(4), 197–211.

Hrastinski, S., & Aghaee, N. (2012). How are campus students using social media to support their studies? An explorative interview study. *Education and Information Technologies*, *17*(4), 451–464. doi:10.1007/s10639-011-9169-5

Hung, H. T., & Yuen, S. C. (2010). Educational use of social networking technology in higher education. *Teaching in Higher Education*, *15*(6), 703–714. doi:10.1080/13562517.2010.507307

Kaplan, A., & Haenlein, M. (2010). Users of the world, unite! The challenges and opportunities of social media. *Business Horizons*, *53*(1), 59–68. doi:10.1016/j.bushor.2009.09.003

Kurkela, L. (2011). Systemic approach to learning paradigms and the use of social media in higher education. *International Journal of Emerging Technologies in Learning*, *6*(1), 14–20.

Kuss, D. J., van Rooij, A. J., Shorter, G. W., Griffiths, M. D., & van de Mheen, D. (2013). Internet addiction in adolescents: Prevalence and risk factors. *Computers in Human Behavior*, *29*(5), 1987-1996.

Laire, D., Casteleyn, J., & Mottart, A. (2012). Social media's learning outcomes within writing instruction in the EFL classroom: Exploring, implementing and analyzing storify. *Procedia: Social and Behavioral Sciences*, *69*, 442–448. doi:10.1016/j.sbspro.2012.11.432

Lenskold, J., & Qaqish, D. (2012). *Lead generation marketing effectiveness study*. LenskoldGroup. Retrieved from http://www.lenskold.com/content/LeadGenROI_2012.html

McCarthy, J. (2010). Blended learning environments: Using social networking sites to enhance the first year experience. *Australasian Journal of Educational Technology*, *26*(6), 729–740.

Nyangau, J.Z., & Bado, N. (2012). Social media and marketing of higher education: A review of the literature. *Journal of the Research Center for Educational Technology*, *8*(1), 38-51.

Ofcom. (2012). *Adults media use and attitudes report 2012*. Retrieved from http://stakeholders.ofcom.org.uk/

Okoro, E. (2012). Social networking and pedagogical variations: An integrated approach for effective interpersonal and group communications skills development. *American Journal of Business Education.*, *5*(2), 219–224.

Okoro, E. A., Hausman, A., & Washington, M. C. (2012). Social media and networking technologies: An analysis of collaborative work and team communication. *Contemporary Issues in Education Research.*, *5*(4), 295–299.

Onlinemba.com. (2012). *Social demographics: Who's using today's biggest networks*. Retrieved from http://mashable.com/2012/03/09/social-media-demographics/

Ravenscroft, A., Warburton, S., Hatzipanagos, S., & Conole, G. (2012). Designing and evaluating social media for learning: Shaping social networking into social learning? *Journal of Computer Assisted Learning*, *28*(3), 177–182. doi:10.1111/j.1365-2729.2012.00484.x

Shaefer, M. W. (2012). *ROI (return on influence): The revolutionary power of Klout, social scoring, and influence marketing*. McGrawHill.

Tuten, T., & Marks, M. (2012). The adoption of social media as educational technology among marketing educators. *Marketing Education Review*, *22*(3), 201–214. doi:10.2753/MER1052-8008220301

Vincos. (2012). *World map of social networks*. Retrieved from http://vincos.it/world-map-of-social-networks/

Woodhouse, P. (2012). Global social networking version 2.0. *Cambridge Marketing Review*, (4).

Xiang, Z., & Gretzel, U. (2010). Role of social media in online travel information search. *Tourism Management*, *31*(2), 179–188. doi:10.1016/j.tourman.2009.02.016

KEY TERMS AND DEFINITIONS

Categorisation of Social Networking Services: Types of social media services according to various characteristics, such as purpose (e.g. personal/professional), functionality (e.g. microblogging or virtual communities).

Social Engagement: A special metrics applicable to social media which measures the level of active involvement of user with the brand/network/community. It is suggested that likes, comments and shares on social media sites are indicators of social engagement of users with the social media site.

Social KPI: A set of metrics which help monitor and evaluate performance of a social media channel. For example, number of members, registration rate or even salary level in a University LinkedIn alumni group.

Social Return on Investment (ROI): The economic principle of calculating the extra value in relation to the original invested resources; based on the cost-benefit analysis, in the context of social media it measures the value provided to the organization through the employment of social media channels. These costs and benefits may be tangible (e.g. savings/costs) or intangible (e.g. satisfying stakeholder expectations).

Social Strategy: A set of formulated strategic objectives towards social media use and social tools to implement organizational goals.

Student Experience: Measurement of how universities cater to students based on various criteria, ranging from campus environment and student welfare to helpfulness of staff and class sizes.

Student Lifecycle: Process of becoming, being a student and entering the alumnus stage. Includes aspirations rising, pre-application and application support, university entry, learning, assessment and support, alumni relations and life-long learning stages.

ENDNOTES

[1] This is an updated and extended version of a chapter that appeared in the 2014 book *Cutting Edge Technologies and Social Media Use in Higher Education* also published by IGI Global.

[2] This case has been presented earlier at the ICEL 2013 conference and has been further developed for this chapter.

[3] The study was conducted internally as a part of a wider research into the longitudinal insights into technology adoption by business academics conducted as a part of an MA dissertation. We would like to thank Bernadette Delaney for her valuable contribution to this research.

Chapter 10

The Prevalence, Effects, and Reactions to Use of Short Message Services in University Settings in South West Nigeria

Amos A. Alao
Covenant University, Nigeria

Taiwo O. Abioye
Covenant University, Nigeria

Kikelomo I. Evbuoma
Covenant University, Nigeria

ABSTRACT

This chapter focuses on the extent of the usage of Short Message Services (SMS) in three universities in Southwest Nigeria, with 243 participants drawn from Covenant University, Bells University, and Lagos State University, who responded to a questionnaire on SMS. Data generated from the study confirmed the high usage of SMS among subjects in general and males in particular, within the age range of 31 to 40 years; a large number of subjects, especially those in administrative positions, were affected by the usage of SMS; most of the subjects are more tolerant when the messages are related to religion, are work-related, or are from family members. Subjects expressed concern when the contents of the SMS are related to adverts, when SMS are used when there are network problems, and the possible exploitation of recipients. Steps to minimize the disadvantages of the use of SMS are discussed.

INTRODUCTION

The general goal of technology is to assist man to accomplish tasks faster and with high productivity, and to accomplish a task better and with ease. While acknowledging the positive effects of technology, it is equally important to be conscious of any negative effects of its use. The awareness of any discomfort in usage can enable the user to maximize benefits and minimize possible harmful effects. The recognition of possible dangers inherent in the use of any technological tool can

DOI: 10.4018/978-1-4666-7401-1.ch010

boost confidence in its usage, assist in appreciating the beneficial effects, and highlight any possible negative consequences.

Sheldon (2012) noted that news of cybercrimes such as bullying, extortion and pornography and other forms of fraud are reported daily, sensitizing everyone to the good and bad sides of web sites. According to him, this is the key to navigating the internet in today's fast paced technological society. Sheldon (2012) also refers to the generation born between 1980 and 1994 as ''digital natives'' or the "Net generation", with their lives immersed in technology; surrounded by cell phones, computers, video games, digital music players and video cameras. She further asserted that "we need to understand not just how they use these new tools but how they are attached to them" (Sheldon, 2012).

Lickerman (2010) reiterates that the general effect of technology and the various forms of electronic ways we connect with each other have not come without cost. It has been noted that the recent explosion in electronic and wireless communication technology has revolutionized the way we send messages via e-mail, mailing list, text messaging, "tweets," Facebook, blogs and vlogs, chat rooms, and video conferencing in addition to the use of face-to-face interactions (Weiten, Hammer & Dunn,2012).

The short message service "SMS" has been described as a miniature and abridged style of transmitting information (Taiwo, 2009). Various names have also been given to this style of sending messages such as text or texto in North America, an SMS in the United Kingdom and most of Europe, TMS in the Middle East, Asia and Australia (Ochonogor, Alakpodia & Achugbue, 2012). Short message services or short message systems (SMS) are frequently used to send short messages in preference to e-mail which are longer and where internet services are required. Short messages could be relayed from anywhere, and

one may not need the elaborate equipment usually utilized when communicating by e-mail, especially for those who do not have e-mail services on their mobile phones.

Electronically mediated communication that takes place via technology such as cellphones, computers and hand held devices are available today and a new type of slang ("net lingo") has been developed to facilitate quick and easy use in text messaging (Weiten, Hammer, & Dunn, 2012). The SMS style of communication is fast becoming a universal phenomenon commonly used (Njemanze, 2012). In developed countries and to a lesser extent in developing countries, all ages are affected by the recent developments in media technology.

Today, media technology has reached the nooks and crannies of rural settings in the developing world. In rural settings in Nigeria for example, it is not uncommon to see market women display cell phones, and they answer calls and send SMS with excitement. However, users with low levels of education are likely to be susceptible to fraudulent acts, perpetuated through the short message service (SMS). The short message service for example was observed to have become prominent in Nigeria during the introduction and advent of mobile phones (handsets/GSM), and the explosion of the use of SMS to the licensing of two GSM service providers in the country in 2001, namely MTN and ECONET (Chiluwa, 2008;Taiwo, 2007, 2008, 2009, 2010).

Within a year of the introduction of GSM in Nigeria, Awonusi (2004, p. 47) noted that there were almost 1 million subscribers. Today, other functional service providers such as GLOBACOM and ETISALAT are available. The SMS style of communication was used for many different communication purposes in Nigeria, such as exchanging information, for events, invitation to religious, social, political and academic meetings, making business contacts and sending goodwill messages (Taiwo, 2009, p.102). The spread of text messaging in Nigeria has also been observed to be due to its being a cost–effective and creative way for people to communicate, and also because it is asynchronous in nature in terms of response (Abioye, 2012).

BACKGROUND

Various studies have focused on the use of SMS. Some have concentrated on the socio-linguistics of SMS (Abioye, 2012; Chiluwa, 2008; Höfich, & Gebhardt, 2005; Kasesniemi, 2003; Ling, 2001, 2005; Njemanze, 2012; Ochonogor, Alakpodia & Achugbue, 2012; Yousaf & Ahmed, 2003). Crystal (2001) noted that the short messaging system (SMS) has triggered the emergence of new forms of written text. The important features of SMS were observed to be in the economy of words and effectiveness of the message (Abioye, 2012). Nevertheless, it has been observed that the higher the exposure to the use of SMS, the more the negative effect on the writing skills of university students (Yousaf & Ahmed, 2003).

Other studies have explored the social and psychological effects of SMS (Crabtree, Nathan, & Roberts, 2003; Reid & Reid, 2004, 2007; Taylor, 2002; Yau-hau-Tse, 2011). Psychologically, it has been pointed out that texting to some people instills more of a feeling of ever-lasting contact than voice calls (Yousaf& Ahmed, 2003), whilst texters by texting messages can create a better interpersonal relationship and make people feel better linked and supported by their friends and families (Crabtree, Nathan, & Roberts, 2003). The main objectives of this chapter are to explore the prevalence of usage of short message services (SMS) among subjects, determine the effects of SMS on users and reactions of subjects to SMS. The benefits and possible consequences of SMS are explored and suggestions on how to minimize risks of use are made.

Specifically, this chapter is to:

1. Determine the prevalence of SMS usage.
2. Explore if the use of SMS affects recipients.
3. Identify the prevalence of unsolicited SMS.
4. Examine the reactions of subjects to SMS on various issues, namely
   a. Religious messages,
   b. Work-related information,
   c. Downloading of a particular tone and music,
   d. Messages from family members, and
   e. Different adverts.
5. Find out if SMS usage is considered beneficial.
6. Determine how sending of SMS to others is perceived.
7. Investigate the perception of SMS usage with reference to
   a. Use of abbreviations in messages,
   b. Unsolicited messages,
   c. Likelihood of exploitation of users of SMS by service providers,
   d. Control of SMS usage in the workplace, and
   e. SMS usage when network connection is poor.
8. Ascertain what affected subjects negatively after receiving and reading an SMS.

METHODOLOGY

Population

To investigate the use of SMS and explore its challenges in a university setting, subjects were purposively selected from three institutions of learning, namely Lagos State University in Lagos State, Covenant University and Bells University of Technology both in Ogun State of Nigeria. All three institutions are located in the South West of Nigeria.

Instrument

A survey questionnaire called Telephone Short Messages Service Questionnaire (TSMSQ) was designed for the purpose of this study and it was piloted on a few subjects at Covenant University to check its validity and reliability. Some ambiguous statements pointed out during the pilot stage were reworded and the expert opinions of professionals were also sought in refining the questionnaire. The open-ended items were explored to elicit additional information from subjects. The instrument was in two parts; the background information which collected the demographic variables of subjects, and the section on the perceived effects of the use of SMS and the reactions of subjects to varying types and contents of SMS.

Procedure

A coordinator for data collection was appointed for each institution after interactions, and respondents were informed of what the study concerned and the rationale behind it. To ensure confidentiality and privacy of subjects, their names were not required in responding to the questionnaire and participation was voluntary.

RESULTS

Background Information of Subjects

This study comprised 243 subjects drawn from three universities from Ogun and Lagos states of Nigeria, namely Covenant University (98 participants or 40.3%), The Bells University of Technology (80 participants or 32.9%) and Lagos State University (65 participants or 26.7%). There were one hundred and thirty (130) male participants and one hundred and thirteen (113) female participants. One hundred and eight (108) subjects were in the administrative staff category and seventy one (71) subjects were in the academic staff category, and nineteen (19) subjects belonged to the other category. The subjects were mainly drawn from administrative and academic departments.

The Prevalence of Text Messages Received

The data in Table 1 show the prevalence of text messages received by subjects.

The data reveal that most of the subjects (210) or (86.4%) receive text messages daily compared to few subjects (22) or (9.1%) that receive text

Table 1. Prevalence of text messages received

| PSMS | Gender | | | | Total | |
| | Male | | Female | | | |
	F	%	F	%	F	%
Daily	114	46.91	96	39.51	210	86.4
Every Other Day	12	4.94	10	4.12	22	9.1
Once a Week	2	.82	3	1.23	5	2.1
Rarely	2	.82	4	1.65	6	2.5
Total	130	53.50	113	46.50	243	100.0

messages every other day. Only 5 and 6 subjects or 2.1% and 2.5% respectively indicated receiving messages once a week and rarely. This confirms that the daily use among subjects is high.

With reference to gender, 114 (46.91%) male subjects and 96(39.51%) female subjects receive text messages daily.

As shown in Table 2, the daily text messages being received was highest among the age group 31-40 years with 83 subjects (34.16%), followed by age group 21-30 years with 68 subjects (27.98%) in this category, while subjects in the age range 41-49 years with 38 subjects (15.64%) received text messages daily. Less daily text messages were received by the age group 50years and above with 14 subjects (5.7%), and the age group 15-20 years with 7 subjects (2.88%) received the least text messages in the group.

The data in Table 3 show that the prevalence of text messages received daily is highest among administrative staff compared to academic staff and other categories of staff. One hundred and four (104) administrative staff, i.e. (42.80%), 83 or (34.16%) academic staff, and 23 or (9.47%) other categories of staff received text messages daily.

Effects of the Use/Reading of SMS One Time and Another

Data from the study also indicate that a high number of the subjects, 198 (81.5%), have been affected one way or another after using or reading an SMS compared to 45 subjects (18.5%) who indicated the contrary.

Table 2. Prevalence of messages received according to age

	Age											
	15-20 Yrs.		21-30 Yrs.		31-40 Yrs.		41-49 Yrs.		50 Yrs. and Above		Total	
PSMS	F	%	F	%	F	%	F	%	F	%	F	%
Daily	7	2.88	68	27.98	83	34.16	38	15.64	14	5.76	210	86.4
Every Day	1	.41	3	1.23	9	3.70	8	3.29	1	.41	22	9.1
Once a Week	0	.00	2	.82	1	.41	0	.00	2	.82	5	2.1
Rarely	0	.00	2	.82	4	1.65	0	.00	0	.00	6	2.5
Total	8	3.29	7	30.86	97	39.92	46	18.93	17	7.00	243	100.0

Table 3. Prevalence of text messages received according to nature of duty

	Academic Staff		Administrative Staff		Others		Total	
PSMS	F	%	F	%	F	%	F	%
Daily	83	34.16	104	42.80	23	9.47	210	86.4
Every Other Day	4	1.65	16	6.58	2	.82	22	9.1
Once a Week	1	.41	4	1.65	0	.00	5	2.1
Rarely	2	.82	4	1.65	0	.00	6	2.5
Total	90	37.04	128	52.67	25	10.29	243	100.0

Effects of SMS One Way or Another According to Nature of Duty

Data generated from the study indicate that subjects have been affected one way or another after receiving and reading an SMS. One hundred and eight (108) subjects (44.44%) in the administrative category indicated that they have been affected one way or another after receiving and reading an SMS. This represents seventy one, (71) or (29.22%) of the subjects in the academic staff category and nineteen (19) or (7.82%) of subjects in the "others" category.

Receiving Unsolicited Text Messages

The study has revealed that most of the subjects, 223 (91.8%) have also received unsolicited text messages compared to 20 subjects (8.2%) who indicated that they have never received unsolicited text messages.

Reactions to the nature and type of messages received by respondents

Table 4 explores the reactions of subjects with reference to the following messages, namely:

1. Religious messages,
2. Work-related messages and information, and
3. Requests to download a particular tone or music.

Religious Messages

As shown in Table 4, the majority of subjects, 191 or 78.60%, were indifferent to receiving or reading religious messages. The respondents were indifferent irrespective of gender when receiving or reading religious messages on SMS. One hundred and nine (109) or 44.86% male subjects and 82 or 33.74% of female subjects were indifferent. Only 25 subjects or 8.46% expressed negative feelings of being a little bit irritated, very irritated or annoyed. Expressions captured in the "others" category includes words and statements such as "I am blessed", "happy", "feels comforted".

Work-Related Messages

As indicated in Table 4, 177 or 72.84% of subjects were indifferent to receiving and reading SMS messages related to work information. Twenty-six subjects or 10.73% were irritated. With reference to gender, a majority of the subjects (both male and female) were indifferent to receiving messages or information related to their work. One hundred and two male subjects (41.98%) and 75 female subjects (30.86%) were indifferent. Only 6 or 2.47% were annoyed.

Downloading a Particular Tone or Music

As indicated in Table 4, with reference to receiving and reading SMS regarding the downloading tone

Table 4. Reactions to religious messages, work-related messages, and downloading tones/music

	Religious Messages				Work Related Messages				Downloading Tone and Music			
	Males		Females		Males		Females		Males		Females	
	Fr.	%	Fr.	%	Fr.	%	Fr.	%	Fr.	%	Fr.	%
Indifferent	109	44.86	82	33.74	102	41.98	75	30.86	60	24.96	32	13.17
A little bit irritated	7	2.88	7	2.88	8	3.29	10	4.12	26	10.70	30	12.35
Very Irritated	2	.82	1	.41	4	1.65	4	1.65	23	9.47	22	9.05
Annoying	2	.82	4	1.65	4	1.65	2	.82	19	7.82	20	8.23
Others	10	4.12	19	7.82	12	4.94	22	9.05	2	.82	2	.82

or music, overall 92 subjects or 37.86% were indifferent. One hundred and one subjects or 41.57% were irritated. That is, fifty six (56) or 23.05% were a little bit irritated while 45 or 18.52%, were very irritated. Thirty nine (39) subjects or 16.05%, were annoyed. The negative reactions expressed seem to show more disaffection in this area compared to receiving/reading religious messages or reading/receiving work related information. With reference to gender, especially among the female subjects, sixty male subjects (24.69%) were indifferent to the downloading of tone or music, while 26 male subjects (10.70%) were a little bit irritated, 23 male subjects (9.47%) were very irritated and 19 male subjects (7.82%) were very annoyed.

The reactions of female subjects showed more disaffection to downloading tones or music. While 32 female subjects (13.17%) were indifferent, almost an equal number of 30 female subjects (12.35%) were a little bit irritated. About the same number of female subjects, 22 (9.05%) and 20 subjects or (8.23%) were very irritated or annoyed respectively

Reactions of Subjects to Messages on Qualification of an Award, Messages from Family Members and Messages on Different Adverts

The various reactions of subjects to SMS information regarding the winning of awards, messages from family members and messages on different adverts are highlighted in Table 5.

Winning an Award

Data in Table 5 show that more negative reactions were expressed by subjects in general after receiving an SMS that their telephone number has won an award. A total of 81 subjects (33.34%) indicated that they were annoyed, 70 subjects (28.81%) were very irritated and 37 subjects (15.22%) were a little bit irritated, whilst 42 subjects (17.29) indicated that they were indifferent.

With reference to gender, about the same number of 43 females (17.7%) and 38 males (15.64%) were annoyed. More males, 44 (18.11%), com-

Table 5. Reactions to messages on award, messages from family members, and adverse reactions after receiving/reading SMS

Description	SMS on Qualification for Award				Family Members				Different Adverts Effects			
	Male		Female		Male		Female		Male		Female	
	Fr.	%	Fr.	%	Fr.	%	Fr.	%	Fr.	%	Fr.	%
Indifferent	10	4.12	32	13.17	102	41.98	48	19.75	60	24.69	21	8.654
A little bit irritated	28	11.52	9	3.70	7	2.88	9	3.70	24	9.88	36	14.81
Very irritated	44	18.11	26	10.70	2	0.82	5	2.06	30	12.35	14	5.76
Annoyed	38	15.64	43	17.70	1	0.41	2	0.82	10	4.12	40	16.46
Others	10	4.12	3	1.23	18	7.41	48	19.75	6	2.47	2	0.82
Total	130	53.50	113	46.50	130	53.5	113	46.50	130	53.50	113	46.5

pared to 26 females (10.70) were very irritated. More male subjects, 28 (11.52%), compared to 9 (3.70%) female subjects were a little bit irritated and more female subjects, 32 (13.17%), compared to 10 (4.12%) of male subjects were indifferent.

SMS from Family Members

Data in Table 5 reveal the reactions of subjects when they received and read SMS from family members. One hundred and five (105) subjects (50.73%) were indifferent, 16 subjects (3.78%) felt a little bit irritated, 7 subjects (2.88%)were very irritated, and 3 subjects (1.23%) were annoyed whilst 66 subjects (27.16%) indicated other reactions. Along gender lines, more male subjects, 102 (41.98%) compared to 48 female subjects (19.75%) were indifferent. More female subjects, 48 (19.75%) compared to 18 male subjects (7.41%) expressed other reactions outside of being indifferent, a little bit irritated, very irritated, or annoyed. Very few subjects indicated being a little bit irritated, very irritated or annoyed.

SMS on Adverts

As shown in Table 5, 81 subjects (33.33%) were indifferent to receiving adverts by SMS, 60 subjects (24.69%) were a little bit irritated,

44 subjects (18.11%) were very irritated and 50 subjects (20.58%) were annoyed. With reference to gender, more male subjects, 60 (24.69%), compared to 21 female subjects (8.64%) were indifferent to receiving adverts by SMS. More female subjects, 36 (14.81%), compared to 24 male subjects (9.88%) were a little bit irritated and more male subjects, 30 (12.35%), compared to 14 female subjects (5.76%) were very irritated. A larger number of female subjects, 40 (16.46%) compared to 10 male subjects (4.12%) were annoyed about receiving adverts from SMS.

Perceived Benefits of SMS

As indicated in Figure 1, the majority of the respondents, 156 (64.2%), perceived the use of SMS to be sometimes beneficial while 62 subjects (25.5%) perceived its use to be always beneficial, and 16 subjects (6.6%) were not sure.

Perception on Sending of SMS to Others

From the data generated, the sending of SMS to others is considered to be a legitimate enquiry by 120 subjects (49.4%), while 49 subjects (20.2%) described it as an invasion of one's privacy.

Figure 1. Perceived benefits of SMS

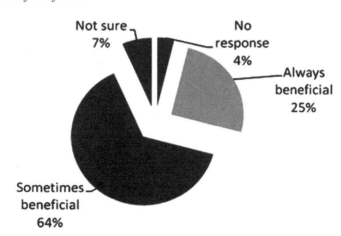

Reactions to the Use of Abbreviations in SMS and Position on Unsolicited SMS

Table 6 provides responses of subjects on the use of abbreviations in SMS and positions on unsolicited SMS.

- **Use of Abbreviations in SMS and Possible Distortion of Information:** As shown in Table 6, close to half of the subjects, 117 (48.1%), agreed that the use of different abbreviations in SMS may distort the message being sent, while 66 subjects (27.2%) strongly agree with the statement.
- **Use of Abbreviations and Grammatical Expression:** Data in Table 6 reveal that ninety four (94) subjects (38.7%) strongly agreed, and the same number agreed that the use of SMS with abbreviations encourages poor grammatical expressions.
- **Discouraging the Use of Abbreviations in SMS:** From Table 6, it is observed that 78 (32.1%) of the subjects wanted the use of SMS with many abbreviations to be discouraged while 70 (28.8%) of the subjects in the study also strongly agreed with this position.

- **Discouraging Unsolicited SMS:** Table 6 also shows that one hundred and five (105, or 43.2%) of the subjects strongly agreed that unsolicited SMS should be discouraged while 83 (34.2%) of the respondents agreed with discouraging unsolicited SMS.

Exploitation of Recipients of SMS, Bothering of Customers with SMS, Use of SMS in the Workplace, and Reliability of SMS When Network is Bad

Data shown in Table 7 explored the likelihood of exploitation of people through SMS, ascertained whether service providers bother customers with SMS, and explored the position of subjects on the control of the use of SMS in the workplace, and the reliability of the use of SMS when there are network challenges.

- **SMS Usage and Exploitation:** The data in Table 7 reveal that 84 (34.6%) of the respondents strongly agreed that recipients of SMS could easily be exploited while 76 subjects (31.3%) agreed that recipients could easily be exploited.

Table 6. Responses of subjects on the use of abbreviations in SMS and positions on unsolicited SMS

	Abbreviation Used in SMS Distort Information Sent		Use of SMS with Abbreviations Encourage Poor Grammatical Expression		Use of Abbreviation in SMS Should Be Discouraged		Unsolicited SMS to Be Discouraged	
	Frequency	%	Frequency	%	Frequency	%	Frequency	%
No Response	3	1.2	3	1.2	3	1.2	6	2.5
Strongly Agree	66	27.2	94	38.7	70	28.8	105	43.2
Agree	117	48.1	94	38.7	78	32.1	83	34.2
Not Sure	24	9.9	22	9.1	40	16.5	34	14.0
Disagree	27	11.1	27	11.1	48	19.8	12	4.9
Strongly Disagree	6	2.5	3	1.2	4	1.6	3	1.2
Total	243	100.0	243	100.0	243	100.0	234	100.0

Table 7. Responses of subjects on exploitation, bothering of customers, control of use of SMS in work places, and reliability of SMS during network problems

	Recipients of SMS Can Easily Be Exploited		Service Providers Are Bothering Customers with SMS		Use of SMS to Be Controlled in the Workplace		SMS Usage May Not Be Reliable during Network Problem	
	Frequency	%	Frequency	%	Frequency	%	Frequency	%
No Response	7	2.9	8	3.3	6	2.5	6	2.5
Strongly Agree	84	34.6	139	27.2	53	21.8	111	45.7
Agree	76	31.3	67	27.6	91	37.4	82	33.7
Not Sure	46	18.9	18	7.4	31	12.8	23	9.5
Disagree	23	9.5	7	2.9	44	18.1	14	5.8
Strongly Disagree	7	2.9	4	1.6	18	7.4	7	2.9
Total	243	100.0	243	100.0	243	100.0	243	100.0

- **Bothering of Customers with SMS by Service Providers:** In Table 7, the data reveal that about half of the respondents, 139 (57.2%), strongly agreed that service providers are bothering customers with SMS while 67 subjects (27.6%) agreed that service providers are bothering customers.
- **Use of SMS in the Workplace:** From Table 7, about one third of the respondents, 91 subjects (37.4%), agreed that the use of SMS be controlled in the workplace, while 53 subjects (21.8%) strongly agreed, 44 subjects (18.1%) disagreed, 31 subjects (18.1%)were not sure and 18 subjects (7.4%) strongly disagreed that the use of SMS be controlled in the workplace.
- **Reliability of SMS during Network Challenges:** Table 7 shows the reliability of SMS usage when there are network problems. One hundred and eleven (111, or 45.7%) of the respondents strongly agreed, while 82 subjects (33.7%) agreed that SMS usage may not be reliable when there are network problems.

Experience of Negative Effects of SMS at One Time or Another

In response to the item on the questionnaire prompting the subjects to indicate whether they have ever been affected negatively after receiving SMS, 142 subjects (58.4%) said yes while 93 subjects (38.3%) said no.

What Affected Subjects Negatively After Receiving/Reading SMS

Table 8 provides information on what affected respondents negatively after receiving and reading SMS. Forty one (41, or16.9%) of the respondents

Table 8. What affected respondents negatively after receiving/reading SMS

		Frequency	Percent
Valid	No response	51	21.0
	Loud sound	32	13.2
	Odd hour	17	7.0
	Unsolicited content	41	16.9
	High number of messages	5	2.1
	Multiple reasons	97	39.9
	Total	243	100.0

indicated the unsolicited content of the message being what affected them negatively, followed by 32 subjects (13.2%) indicating the loud sound accompanying the message and 17 subjects (7.0%) indicating the odd hour the message was received. A lower number of the subjects, 5 (2.1%), indicated the high number of messages received. It is noteworthy that 97 subjects (39.9%) indicated multiple reasons which affected them negatively.

DISCUSSION

Prevalence of SMS Usage

There is good daily usage of SMS among subjects as revealed in the study which was overwhelming compared to usage every other day, once a week or rarely. This confirms the wide acceptance of SMS as a means of communication in an academic environment. It is also evident that the prevalence of text messages received is higher among male compared to female subjects. The age range of people receiving SMS was mainly among subjects who are forty years old and below compared to subjects above this age.

It is noted from the study that subjects under 40 years of age received more text messages compared to subjects above this age range. Fewer messages were received by subjects in the age bracket of 20 years and below and those in the age bracket of 50 years and above.

Effects of the Use of SMS on Recipients

We naturally react to messages either positively or negatively. Since a significant percentage of subjects (81.5%) had indicated being affected one way or the other, it is important to determine if the effect is positive or negative and to explore ways to address the concerns expressed.

Unsolicited Messages

The number of subjects (91.8%) receiving unsolicited text messages is high.

These unsolicited messages have been a source of concern to subjects. While it is expected that service providers' intentions are to make money, the frequency of unsolicited messages needs to be minimized so that customers are not forced to seek other service providers who are less intrusive on their customers.

Reactions to Contents of Messages

- **Religious Messages:** The subjects seem to be largely indifferent to receiving religious messages as majority of them (191 or 78.6%) were in this category, with much smaller percentages being a little bit irritated, very irritated, or annoyed. The tolerance for religious music can be said to be apparent among subjects.
- **Work-Related Messages:** The findings suggest that most of the subjects were indifferent to receiving work-related messages. This may be due to their expectation of receiving work-related information while at work and also considering the amount of time spent at work.
- **Downloading Tones or Music:** More negative reactions were displayed by subjects to downloading tones or music compared to receiving or reading religious messages or receiving/reading SMS on work-related information. The negative reactions expressed seem to show more disaffection in this area compared to the others. More than half of the subjects (57.62%) indicated a combination of a little bit irritated, irritated, or annoyed after receiving or reading SMS to download tones or music. Less tolerance was displayed in this area.

- **Qualification for an Award:** The subjects expressed strong disapproval when an SMS is received expressing that their telephone number has qualified for an award. About one-third of the subjects (33.34%) were annoyed, while close to one-third again were equally very irritated. Close to one-sixth (15.22%) were a little bit irritated, whilst another one sixth (17.29%) indicated that they were indifferent. The fraudulent intention implied in the message (since the subscribers did not enter any form of contest for these implied rewards) seemed to have accounted for the strong negative reactions expressed by subjects.

- **Messages Relating to Family Members:** The family as a unit plays diverse roles and acts as a support to its members. The findings in this study indicate that about half of the subjects are indifferent to SMS relating to family members. This indifference may not connote lack of concern for each other. It has been observed that close to one third of the subjects, 66 (27.16%), indicated other reactions when SMS relating to family members were received and read, which included these words in the following order; "happy", "excited", "interested", "feels good", "feels OK", "attentive", and "curious". As expected, in a healthy family, there were no threats in the communication between members.

- **Messages Concerning Adverts:** About one third (81 subjects or 33.33%), were indifferent to receiving adverts by SMS. It is significant to note that about a quarter of the subjects (60, or 24.69%) were a little bit irritated. Close to one fifth of the subjects (44 subjects or 18.11%) were very irritated, and about the same proportion (50 or 20.58%) were annoyed. This observation

translates to about two-thirds of the subjects expressing discomfort with receiving adverts via SMS.

Perceived Benefits of SMS

There is the general recognition of the usefulness and benefits of SMS. Generally, the use of any technological tool, including the use of telephones to send SMS has been observed to depend on a number of factors, especially access, utility and motivation. The study by Alao, Ojo and Forcheh (2007) on Computer Technology (CT) conducted to determine the nature, extent and predictors of CT adoption in Botswana, considered among other factors perceived usefulness as a predictor of PC use. Perceived Usefulness (PU) was defined by Davis (1987) as "the degree to which a person believes that using a particular system would enhance his or her job performance".

The advantages or the relevance and possible disadvantages or shortcomings of the use of SMS have been discussed in other literature. While appreciating the advantages of SMS, it is equally important to be aware of its possible shortcomings.

Individuals have utilized SMS sometimes when they do not want verbal dialogue with the recipient or when the recipient cannot be reached when called on the telephone. Lickerman (2010) noted that the use of SMS makes confrontation easier when one is afraid of face-to face confrontation. Weiten, Hammer and Dunn (2012) noted the advantages of the use of cellphones (also for non-text conversation) as a convenient way to keep in touch, provide a sense of security and summon aid in an emergency.

Perception of Sending of SMS

Sending of SMS to others is considered to be a legitimate enquiry by about half of the subjects

(120 subjects or 49.4%), possibly because of the perceived usefulness and benefits. It is not surprising that about one fifth of the subjects (49 subjects or 20.2%) described it as an invasion of one's privacy. The reactions of subjects to unsolicited messages and the various adverts received via SMS could inform the perception of intrusion on privacy.

Use of Different Abbreviations in SMS and Poor Grammatical Expression

Data in Table 6 reveal that overwhelming numbers (94, 38.7%) of respondents strongly agreed, and the same number agreed that the use of SMS with abbreviations encourages poor grammatical expressions. This supports earlier findings in sociolinguistic studies (Abioye, 2012; Chiluwa, 2008; Höfich, & Gebhardt 2005; Kasesniemi, 2003; Ling, 2001, 2005; Njemanze, 2012; Ochonogor, Alakpodia & Achugbue, 2012; Yousaf & Ahmed, 2003).

Discouraging Use of Many Abbreviations in SMS

The data in Table 6 indicate that about one third of the subjects (78 or 32.1%) agreed that the use of SMS with many abbreviations should be discouraged. Close to one third of the subjects (70 or 28.8%) also strongly agreed with this position.

This seems to suggest that most of the subjects are weary of SMS with many abbreviations. Such abbreviations may sometimes pose problems and recipients are perhaps occasionally unable to decode some of the abbreviations. This finding is in line with the observations of Lickerman (2010).

Discouraging Unsolicited SMS

Table 6 reveals that a high percentage of the respondents are concerned with unsolicited SMS. More than three quarters of the subjects (188 or 77.4%) in the "agree" and "strongly agree" categories want

unsolicited SMS to be discouraged. Since most of the unsolicited messages usually come from the service providers, consumer advocacy with regards to preventing unsolicited messages from service providers may need to be explored. While one expects service providers to make money, it is equally important for the respective service providers not to be intrusive while serving their customers

Easy Exploitation of SMS Recipients

The findings in Table 7 indicate the subjects are in accord that recipients of SMS could easily be exploited. The subjects had previously expressed dissatisfaction to messages such as "your number has qualified for an award", to which some recipients may respond to and give away vital information about themselves which could be used against them in the future.

Service Providers Bothering Customers with SMS

There is general agreement that service providers are bothering customers with SMS given the high percentage indicating this position. About two thirds of the subjects (160 or 65.9%) in the "strongly agree" and "agree" categories expressed this position. There appears to be a need to sensitize service providers about this concern expressed by customers.

Controlling the Use of SMS in the Workplace

The study reveals that more than half of the subjects (144 or 59.2%) indicated that the use of SMS in the workplace should be controlled. About one third of the respondents, 91 (37.4%), agreed that the use of SMS be controlled in the workplace, while 53 subjects (21.8%) strongly agreed, 44 subjects (18.1%) disagreed, 31 (18.1%) are not sure, and 18 subjects (7.4%) strongly disagreed that the use of SMS be controlled in the workplace.

The use of SMS by management to reach employees in work places is not uncommon. This style of communication is meant to reach employees faster irrespective of their location. The SMS is also present to serve as a prompt reminder of meetings and assignments to be submitted, to mention but a few. There is need to explore further the rationale for the control of SMS usage in the workplace as indicated by about half of the subjects.

Reliability of SMS Usage and Network Problems

More than three-quarters of the subjects (193 or 79.4%) indicated that the usage of SMS may not be reliable when there are network problems. Specifically, 111 (45.7%) of the respondents strongly agreed, while 82 (33.7%) agreed that SMS usage may not be reliable when there are network problems. If network is not available or when there is congestion, the possibility of not being able to send a message or the other party receiving the message late or not at all is likely. Consequently, there may be the need to rely on other methods of communication between management and employees or between one party or another, and ensuring that the use of SMS is not the sole method of communication but rather a supplement.

If Subject Has Ever Been Affected Negatively after Receiving SMS

Despite the usefulness of SMS over other telephone methods of communications, people have expressed discomfort with its usage. Exploitation of an individual is possible if one reacts carelessly to a text message by giving out vital information about oneself. It will be simplistic to assume that every SMS/alert received is meant for the good of the recipient. However, there are some fraudsters willing to take advantage of unsuspecting

recipients of such messages. Consequently, short message services should be treated with caution; they are to be read carefully, they are to be shared and discussed with others for information or advice when the motives of the contents are in doubt or a possible diabolical intention is suspected. Cybercrimes, extortion and different forms of fraud happen daily to unsuspecting recipients and when it sounds ''too good'', sometimes it may not be good. Lickerman (2010) noted the danger of subtly substituting electronic relationships for physical ones or mistaking our electronic relationships for physical ones. Making our meaning clear electronically, when using SMS, presents extra challenges. For example, Lickerman (2010) indicated that when we write things like "LOL" and "LMAO" to describe our laughter, they are no real substitutes for hearing people laugh, which has the power to lift up our spirits when we are feeling low.

In this study, more than half of the subjects (142 58.4%) said "yes" to having been negatively affected after receiving SMS, while 93 subjects (38.3%) said "no". This percentage indicating "yes" suggests the need to explore what negative effects were present.

What Affected Subjects Negatively after Receiving SMS

In exploring what has affected subjects negatively after receiving and/or reading the SMS, the subjects gave reasons according to severity as follows:

1. Multiple reasons by 97 subjects (39.9%),
2. Forty one (41) subjects (16.9%) indicated the unsolicited content of the message,
3. 32 subjects (13.2%) indicated the loud sound accompanying the message,
4. 17 subjects (7.0%) indicated the odd hour the message was received, and
5. 5 subjects (2.1%) indicated the high number of messages received.

When asked to indicate other things which affected subjects negatively on receiving/reading the SMS, multiple reasons provided include comments like: the sender of the message, persistence of the sender and abusive content of the message.

FUTURE RESEARCH DIRECTION

Communication is essential in interpersonal relationships, among family members, between groups, and within organizations. The style of communication, the medium of communication and the contents of the message will continue to elicit different reactions and feelings from recipients of messages.

The use of SMS as a means of communication is now being utilized both at the individual and corporate levels. This means of communication is also being adopted in work settings to achieve a paperless office. Consequently, future research will need to address the various and possible negative effects of this nonverbal communication and how to ameliorate such effects. From this study, concerns have been raised on the possibility of exploitation of customers by service providers. Hence, focus may be on consumer rights for individuals who are exploited, and protection from undue invasion of privacy.

At the socio-cultural and psychological levels, in a country like Nigeria, the mobile phone is not just a symbol of technological ornamentation, but also an indication of the users' literacy skills which serves as a source of enhancing their self-esteem. Smith (2006, p. 500) concludes that:

… new linguistic turns of phrase and innovative social practices that have evolved with the proliferation of cell phone technology … also indicate the degree to which cell phone culture has taken root in everyday life.

Knowing that the SMS provides the opportunity for the functionally literate to exercise their reading and writing skills particularly using pidgin and Nigerianisms in such messages is an advantage. Thus, investigating how the SMS has been able to enhance literacy skills of the functional literate and, by implication, their self-esteem would be a worthwhile venture. Also, it would be beneficial to determine to what extent the SMS culture has been embedded into our communication culture as a nation. A new paradigm might be to look critically at SMS "language" in the Nigerian context as a form/level of attainment of literacy.

At the educational level, the concern of the use of abbreviation in SMS and the consequent negative effect on grammar will need to be examined. SMS usage is common not only in the work setting but also in educational settings. Teaching pedagogy in the use of words and construction of messages may need to be continually emphasized to ensure proper usage and meaningful communication.

CONCLUSION

This study has established the relevance of SMS as a means of communication that is beneficial, and its use has been shown to be more prevalent among the age group of 40 years and below compared to the age 40 years and above. Its usage is more prevalent among administrative staff compared to academic staff in a university setting.

Many users of SMS have shown tolerance to messages related to family members which have elevated their moods by being happy, excited and feeling good after receiving or reading SMS that are family-related. While subjects seem to be generally indifferent to religious messages and work related information or the request to download a tune or music, subjects have expressed strong disaffection to messages that express they have qualified for an award, and messages concerning different adverts.

While recognizing the general usefulness and benefits of SMS as a mean of communication, concern has been expressed on its effects in encouraging poor grammatical expressions and the possibility of distorting the message sent, especially when abbreviations cannot be correctly decoded or interpreted by the recipient. Some have indicated that the use of abbreviations in SMS should be discouraged.

It is recognized generally that even though the sending of SMS from one person to another can be taken as legitimate inquiry, the privacy of the recipient needs to be respected and preserved. Unsolicited messages need to be discouraged and service providers need to respect the rights to privacy of customers by reducing the number of these messages.

The use of SMS in the workplace can be beneficial if it is used as a supplement to other forms of communication. Subjects are in agreement that the use of SMS may not be reliable when there are network problems. It has been established that the use of SMS can have a negative effect on both the sender and the receiver. Some of the negative effects include but not limited to:

1. Receiving unsolicited messages,
2. Distractions which accompany an incoming message when the phone is in a loud mode, and
3. The odd hour when some messages may be received.

Possible Strategies to Minimize These Negative Effects of SMS

The study has revealed that the time of the day the text message is received and the frequency of the text messages received may have negative effects, especially when the telephone is set at "loud" receiving mode. Some subjects have indicated being "startled", when a loud text message was received in meetings after they have been told to switch their phones off. Others considered the loud sound as a source of disturbance especially when received at night when they are asleep or when the text message comes unexpectedly.

It May Be Helpful to Follow Some of These Steps to Minimize Some of the Negative Effects

- Not taking telephones to important meetings.
- Adhering promptly to messages that phones be switched off if displayed or announced.
- Putting telephones in the silent or vibrate only mode in the sound profile at meetings, to avoid embarrassment of its ringing loudly then or when sleeping or resting.
- Putting the telephone in a place you can feel or see it vibrate.
- Deleting immediately any message which is suspicious or whose motive is not clear or when it appears to be an unsolicited message.
- Aside from these proactive steps, it can be dangerous to read or reply to text messages when driving. Sending text messages requires concentration which should not be competing with the concentration required for driving. Reading text messages when driving also requires visual attention which should not compete with the visual attention needed for driving.

The use of SMS in communication can be enjoyable but every user needs to be aware of its possible demerits or shortcomings and take appropriate steps to minimize its disadvantages.

REFERENCES

Abioye, T. (2012). A stylistic analysis of emerging paradigms and prominent features in Nigeria SMS discourse. In R. Taiwo & I. Chiluwa (Eds.), *Computer-mediated discourse in Africa* (pp. 55–67). New York, NY: Nova Science Publishers.

Alao, A. A., Ojo, S. O., & Forcheh, N. (2009). Using computer technology for educational and occupational information. In R. Roth, C. Hiew, & A. L. Comunian (Eds.), *Peace, hope, and well-being across the cultures* (pp. 191–201). Shaker Verlag, Aachen.

Awonusi, V. O. (2004). 'Little' Englishes and the law of energetic: A sociolinguistic study of SMStext messages as register and discourse in Nigerian English. In S. Awonusi & E. A. Babalola (Eds.), *The domestication of English in Nigeria: A festschrift for Abiodun Adetugbo at 65* (pp. 45–62). Lagos: University of Lagos Press.

Bargh, J. A., & Mc Kenna, K. Y. A. (2004). The internet and social life. *Annual Review of Psychology, 55*(1), 573–590. doi:10.1146/annurev.psych.55.090902.141922 PMID:14744227

Boase, J., & Wellman, B. (2006). Personal relationships on and off the internet. In A. L. Vangelistic & D. Perlman (Eds.), *The Cambridge handbook of personal relationships.* New York, NY: Cambridge University Press. doi:10.1017/CBO9780511606632.039

Chiluwa, I. (2008). SMS text messaging and the Nigerian Christian context: Constructing values and sentiments. *International Journal of Language. Society and Culture, 24,* 11–20.

Crystal, D. (2001). *Language and the internet.* Cambridge, UK: Cambridge University Press. doi:10.1017/CBO9781139164771

Davis, F. D. (1987). Perceived usefulness, perceived ease of use and user acceptance of information technology. *Management Information Systems Quarterly, 13*(3), 319–340. doi:10.2307/249008

Höfich, J., & Gebhardt, J. (2005). Changing cultures of written communication: Letter – email–SMS. In R. Harper, L. Palen, & A. Taylor (Eds.), *The inside text: Social, cultural and design perspectives on SMS* (Vol. 4, pp. 9–32). Dordrecht, The Netherlands: Springer. doi:10.1007/1-4020-3060-6_2

Kasesniemi, E. (2003). *Mobile messages: Young people and a new communication culture.* Tempere, Finland: Tampere University Press.

Lickerman, A. (2010). The effect of technology on relationships: The risks of internet addiction. *Psychology Today, 8.*

Ling, R. (2004). *The mobile connection: The cell phone's impact on the society.* Amsterdam: Morgan Kaufmann Publishers.

Ling, R. (2005). The socio-linguistics of SMS: An analysis of SMS use by a random sample of Norwegians. In R. S. Ling & P. E. Pedersen (Eds.), *Mobile communications: Re-negotiation of the social sphere* (pp. 335–350). London: Springer. doi:10.1007/1-84628-248-9_22

Njemanze, Q. U. (2012). The "SMS" style of communication: Implication on language usage among Nigerian university students. *Journal of Communication, 3*(1), 17–23.

Reid, D. J., & Reid, F. J. (2004). *Insights into the social and psychological effects of SMS text messaging.* Retrieved from http://www.160characters.org/

Reid, D. J., & Reid, F. J. (2005). Textmates and text circles: Insights into the social ecology of SMS text messaging. In A. Lasen & L. Hamill (Eds.), *Mobile world, past, present and future* (pp. 105–118). London: Springer. doi:10.1007/1-84628-204-7_7

Rogers, C. B. (1951). *Client centred therapy: Its current practice, implications and theory.* Boston: Houghton Mifflin Company.

Sheldon, P. (2012). *Psychologist examines effects of technology society.* University of Huntsville.

Smith, D. J. (2006). Cell phones, social inequality, and contemporary culture in Nigeria. *Canadian Journal of African Studies, 40*(3), 496–523.

Taiwo, R. (2007). Tenor in electronic media Christian discourse in South Western Nigeria. *Nordic Journal of African Studies, 16*(1), 75–89.

Taiwo, R. (2008). Linguistic forms and functions of SMS text messages. In S. Kelsey & K. St Armant (Eds.), *The handbook of research in computer mediated communication* (pp. 969–982). IGI Global. doi:10.4018/978-1-59904-863-5.ch068

Taiwo, R. (2009). The use of socio-cultural elements for creativity in Nigeria SMS texts. *Journal of Linguistic Association of Nigeria, 12*, 99–108.

Taiwo, R. (2010). *"The thumb tribe" and innovative English usage: Creativity and social change in the context of SMS messages in Nigeria.* Paper presented at the 3rd European Conference on African Studies, Leipzig, Germany.

Weiten, W., Hammer, E.Y., & Dunn, D.S. (2012). *Psychotherapy and contemporary life, human adjustment.* Wasdsworth, MA: Cengage Learning.

Yau-Hau Tse, A. (2011). *Social and psychological impacts of SMS texting on Malaysian university students.* Solls: INTECT.

Yousaf, Z., & Ahmed, M. (2013). Effects of SMS on writing skills of the university students in Pakistan: A case study of University of Gujrat. *Asian Economic and Financial Review, 3*(3), 389–397.

ADDITIONAL READING

Brown, A. (1998). Encountering misspellings and spelling performance. Why wrong isn't right. *Journal of Educational Psychology, 80*(4), 488–495. doi:10.1037/0022-0663.80.4.488

Car, J., & Gurol-Urganci, I., Jongh, T de., Vodopivec-Jamsek, V, & Atun, R. (2012). Mobile phone messaging reminders for attendance at healthcare appointments. *Cochrane Database of Systematic Reviews, 7*, CD007458. PMID:22786507

Coomes, C. M., Lewis, M. A., Uhrig, J. D., Furberg, R. D., Harris, J. L., & Bann, C. M. (2012). Beyond reminders: A conceptual framework for using short message service to promote prevention and improve healthcare quality and clinical outcomes for people living with HIV. *AIDS Care, 24*(3), 328–357. doi:10.1080/09540121.2011.608421 PMID:21933036

Drouin, M., & Davis, C. (2009). R u txting? Is the use of text speak hurting your literacy? *Journal of Literacy Research, 41*(1), 4. doi:10.1080/10862960802695131

Hang, S., Meyer, C., Dymalski, A., Lippke, S., & John, U. (2012). Efficacy of a text messaging (SMS) based smoking cessation intervention for adolescents and young adults: Study protocol of a cluster randomized controlled trial. *BMC Public Health, 12*(1), 51. doi:10.1186/1471-2458-12-51 PMID:22260736

Hardy, H., Kumar, V., Doros, G., Farmer, E., Drainoni, M., & Rybin, D. et al. (2011). Randomized Controlled Trial of a personalized Cellular phone reminder system to enhance Adherence to Antiretroviral therapy. *AIDS Patient Care and STDs, 25*, 153–161. PMID:21323532

Igarashi, T., Takai, J., & Yoshida, T. (2005). Gender differences in social network development via mobile phone text messages: A longitudinal study. *Journal of Social and Personal Relationships, 22*(5), 691–713. doi:10.1177/0265407505056492

Kegg, S., Nata, M., Lau, R., & Pakianathan, M. (2004). Communication with patients: Are e-mail and text messaging the answer? *International Journal of STD & AIDS, 15*, 46.

Lewandowski, G., & Harrington, S. (2006). The influence of phonetic abbreviations on evaluation of student performance. *Current Research in Social Psychology*, *11*(15), 215–226.

Lim, M., Hocking, J., Hellard, M., & Aitkem, C. (2008). SMS STI: A review of the uses of mobile phone text messaging in sexual health. *International Journal of STD & AIDS*, *19*(5), 287–290. doi:10.1258/ijsa.2007.007264 PMID:18482956

Lopresti-Goodman, S. M., Rivera, A., & Dressel, C. (2012). Practicing Safe Text: The Impact of Texting on Walking Behavior. *Applied Cognitive Psychology*, *26*(4), 644–648. doi:10.1002/acp.2846

Mao, Y., Zhang, Y., Zhang, Y., & Zhai, S. (2008). Mobile phone text messaging for Pharmaceutical care in a hospital in China. *Journal of Telemedicine and Telecare*, *14*(8), 410–414. doi:10.1258/jtt.2008.080406 PMID:19047450

Militello, L. K., Kelly, S. A., & Melynk, B. M. (2012). Systematic Review of Text-Messaging Intervention to promote healthy behaviours in pediatric and adolescent populations: Implications for clinical practice and research. *Worldviews on Evidence-Based Nursing*, *9*(2), 66–77. doi:10.1111/j.1741-6787.2011.00239.x PMID:22268959

Nasar, J., Hecht, P., & Wener, R. (2008). Mobile telephones, distracted attention, and pedestrian Safety. *Accident; Analysis and Prevention*, *40*(1), 69–75. doi:10.1016/j.aap.2007.04.005 PMID:18215534

Nickels, A., & Dimov, V. (2012). Innovations in technology: Social media and mobile technology in the care of adolescents with asthma. *Current Allergy and Asthma Reports*, *12*(6), 607–612. doi:10.1007/s11882-012-0299-7 PMID:22976493

Obadare, E. (2004). The Great GSM (Cell Phone) Boycott: Civil Society, Big Business and The State in Nigeria. *Dark Roast* (Occasional Paper Series, No. 18). Cape Town, South Africa: Isandla Institute.

Piester, B., Wood, C., & Bell, V. (2008). Text Msg in school literacy. Does texting and knowledge of abbreviations adversary affect children's literacy attainment? *Literacy*, *42*(3), 137–144. doi:10.1111/j.1741-4369.2008.00489.x

Schwebel, D., Byington, K. W., & Schwebel, D. C. (2011). Distracted walking: Cell phones increase injury risk for college pedestrians. *Journal of Safety Research*, *42*(2), 101–107. doi:10.1016/j.jsr.2011.01.004 PMID:21569892

Schwebel, D., Stavrinos, D., Byington, K., Davis, T., O'Neal, E., & de Jong, D. (2012). Distraction and pedestrian safety: How talking on the phone, texting, and listening to music impact crossing the street. *Accident; Analysis and Prevention*, *45*, 266–271. doi:10.1016/j.aap.2011.07.011 PMID:22269509

Shuter, R., & Chattopadhyay, S. (2010). Emerging Interpersonal Norms of Text Messaging in India and the United States. *Journal of Intercultural Communication Research*, *29*(2), 123–147. doi:10.1080/17475759.2010.526319

Smith, D. J. (2006). Cell Phones, Social Inequality, and Contemporary Culture in Nigeria. *Canadian Journal of African Studies / Revue Canadienne des Études Africaines,* 40 (3), 496-523.

Stavrinos, D., Byington, K. W., & Schwebel, D. C. (2011). Distracted walking: Cell phones increase injury risk for college pedestrians. *Journal of Safety Research*, *42*(2), 101–107. doi:10.1016/j.jsr.2011.01.004 PMID:21569892

Thurlow, C., & Poff, M. (2011). The language of text messaging. In S. C. Herring, D. Stein, & T. Virtanen (Eds.), *Handbook of the Pragmatics of CMC*. Berlin, New York: Mouton de Gruyter.

Uchiyama, M., Demura, S., & Natsuhori, E. (2012). Changes in gait properties during texting messages by a cell phone. Attention and gait control. *Gazzetta Medica Italiana Archivioper le Scienze Mediche, 171*(3), 331–340.

Wood, C., Meachem, S., Bowyer, S., Jackson, E., Tarczynski-Bowles, M. L., & Plester, B. (2011). A longitudinal study of children's text messaging development and literacy develop. *British Journal of Psychology, 102*(3), 431–442. doi:10.1111/j.2044-8295.2010.02002.x PMID:21751998

KEY TERMS AND DEFINITIONS

Anger: An emotion laden with tension and hostility resulting from perceived injustice or unfair treatment.

Annoyance: A state of displeasure sometimes characterized with furry and dissatisfaction.

Effects: Consequences or outcomes of an event, action, or situation.

Indifference: A position of neutrality, not eliciting a positive or negative action or reaction to a situation.

Intrusion: Unwanted, unexpected, or invasion of one's privacy.

Irritated: A sensitivity bothering on annoyance or disgust.

Odd hour: An uncomfortable time for an individual for example when an SMS is received at a meeting, when asleep or any situation when such a message is not expected.

Prevalence: Frequency of occurrence or existence of an event, or total number of cases at a given time.

Privacy: The right to be left alone, undisturbed, and to control other's access to one's physical and psychological world.

Short Message Services (SMS): This is an abridged style of communication which is sometimes called text or texto or simply SMS.

Chapter 11

The Role of Social Media in Creating and Maintaining Social Networks Including its Impact on Enhancing Competitive Positioning within the Education Sector

Adam Raman
Kingston University, UK

ABSTRACT

Social media is being increasingly utilised within society as an interactive communication platform. It has revolutionised the manner in which organisations communicate with their stakeholders, from the old way of simply designing messages and transmitting them across a desired medium, described as a static, one-way communication channel. Communications are the means by which organisations achieve their strategic goals through influencing their stakeholders. Social media allows stakeholders to connect to one another in relational, interactional networks. This means that stakeholders can now interact with organisations and each other and have a greater influence on the outcomes of communication strategies, which was impossible with traditional media. Organisations have less power dictating communications to stakeholders who in turn have more power in co-creating communication with each other. Social media is likely to have a major competitive impact on higher education institutions and these institutions should be accounting for these changes in their future strategy development. This chapter explores how social media is being utilized in organisations.

DOI: 10.4018/978-1-4666-7401-1.ch011

INTRODUCTION

Social media is being extensively utilised by organisations including those in higher education to raise awareness, build and maintain their reputation, as well as create demand for their courses. It is also being used to effectively communicate and engage with other stakeholders such as motivating and retaining current as well as attracting prospective students and employees. It can also be used to raise the profile of a university amongst its board of governors, research & funding bodies and local community. Social Media can be seen as a communication and promotional platform but a major question arises as to the extent to which this new platform is similar or different to previous platforms utilised in the past. For example is it the same as advertising or public relations (PR) or is it significantly different? This question is pertinent in the sense that the traditional methods utilised in strategic communications planning (developing and transmitting messages) tend to rely on single transactional communications between a supplier (education provider) and a consumer (student) where interaction between the two is not seen as being important. Therefore, students are subject to static on-line and off-line brochures including advertorials and third party publications endorsing the institutions or the academic staff working for them. The only interactions that any potential new student may have with an academic institution are dyadic communications between themselves and course directors, administrators, recruitment staff and current students when they either phone, email or visit the institution. Social media on the other hand is different as it allows interactions between multiple stakeholders who are embedded in social network communities. This calls for a different sort of strategic communication planning and Higher Education establishments who are not considering this factor could be inappropriately developing their social media strategies, leading to a detrimental situation of being ineffective and possibly losing their competitive position to other establishments who are planning more appropriately and effectively.

ISSUES RELATING TO THE STRATEGIC PLANNING OF SOCIAL MEDIA WITH HIGHER EDUCATION INSTITUTIONS

Parallel to the changes occurring in the fields of strategic management and marketing strategy, there has been a shift from a reliance on traditional media (print and television for example) to the widespread inclusion of social media (Hanna, Rohm, and Crittenden, 2011; Andrew and Galak, 2012) within integrated marketing communication strategies. Classical approaches to strategy are believed to be driving the planning of newer digital and social media strategies within organisations. Executives are believed to be explicitly or subconsciously using older, outmoded strategy frameworks for planning their social media or worse still, they are not using any strategy techniques at all and are simply being tactical. Several executives are also likely to be outsourcing their strategy development to external communication agencies who themselves are likely to be implementing outmoded approaches.

Although there are some theoretical suggestions regarding social media strategy (Kaplan and Haenlein, 2010; Weinberg and Pehlivan, 2011; Hanna, Rohm, Crittenden, 2011; Kietzmann et al., 2011), at present there appears to be no research into the appropriateness of the social media strategies that firms are actually creating and implementing.

This chapter will evaluate the applicability of newer emergent strategy perspectives to social media strategy development with theories being linked from the relational and interactional network theoretical marketing literature (Håkansson, 1982; Håkansson & Johanson, 1992; Håkansson & Snehota, 1995) as well as the customer – supplier value co-creation literature (Vargo & Lusch, 2004; 2008). These perspectives will then be used to explore how some firms operating within the Pet Industry in the United States are planning and implementing their social media strategies. In particular we will explore whether firms are incorporating social media as simply one element of a traditional Integrated Marketing Communications (IMC) promotional mix, therefore employing social media as a tactic aimed at increasing purchase behavior (Weinberg and Pehlivan, 2011; Mintzberg and Waters, 1985; Kumar and Mirchandani, 2012), or conversely whether firms are creating more appropriate strategies, based on the principles of marketing's interactional, relational and co-creation of value (Håkansson, 1982; Håkansson & Johanson, 1992; Håkansson & Snehota, 1995; Vargo and Lusch, 2004).

THE IMPORTANCE AND RELEVANCE OF SOCIAL MEDIA IN HIGHER EDUCATION

Social media can no longer be ignored and not using it will deny an institution access to its potential source of students and employees as well as adversely affect its corporate reputation and future performance. Students and other stakeholders should no longer be viewed as single unconnected individuals not influencing each other who can be influenced using mass communications. Historically when this was the case the source of competitive advantage of a university would be its historic reputation, the current reputation of its academics achieved through publication, the perceived relevance of its courses and the resources that it deployed to its media budget communicating its reputation. Today the first three are still relevant but a university will need to build their competitive advantage by building social capital, which is defined as the relational links between communities (networks) of students and stakeholders interacting with each other. Social media is a highly effective tool in developing social capital. Higher Education institutions should think of social media in two ways, the first being that using social media is only the entry ticket for institutions to access the new competitive game and the second is working more appropriately

and effectively with the new media. It is not simply the technology but the application of the technology with the appropriate resources, mind set and processes.

The purpose of this chapter will be the conceptual evaluation of reviewing and applying established network theories to developing and implementing more appropriate and effective social media strategies within the context of Higher Education, in order to improve the longer competitive positioning of the institutions embedded within this sector.

DEFINING COMPETITIVE ADVANTAGE WITHIN THE CONTEXT OF HIGHER EDUCATION

The competitive advantage of a higher education academic institution can be described using theories from the strategic management literature. Several theories exist from the classical to the contemporary perspectives of business strategy. These theories were originally developed within the context of profit making organisations but it is important to note that they are adaptable and applicable to non for profit organisations such as universities. There exists a tendency to reject theory developed in the profit making sector that could potentially be applied in the non for profit sector with the result of reinventing theory and frameworks that already exist. However, it is important that one considers the specific context in which the theory was originally developed including the new context in which it is being applied. Extending theoretical applications without extending the theory so that it is appropriate and applicable can be fraught with errors which can increase risk and uncertainty, severely impacting strategic decision making. Appropriate measures will be taken to ensure that any theory that is extended from a different context is modified to match its new environment.

The fact that strategic business concepts such as competitive advantage are only applicable to profit making organisations is a misnomer, as non for profit organisations still need to generate an incremental economic value or deliver their products or services within an agreed externally funded budget. The only major difference between the different types of organisations is that the ultimate existence and strategic goal for a non for profit organisation is not simply to make a profit for profit's sake, which is the case for profit making organisations. Non for profits make a profit in order to be used to achieve other non–financial goals. Therefore non for profit organisations still need to have very efficient business operational processes to raise money, as inefficient processes will tend to consume cash in order to run the operations required to raise funds and leave very little funding to achieve the non-financial aims of the organisation.

One perspective of competitive advantage is that it can be thought of as consisting of the primary and secondary operational activities supporting the primary activities that a higher education institution must undertake, in order to deliver value to its students and other stakeholders (Porter, 1985). If a university can deliver the same offering, as perceived by the students and other stakeholders, as competing institutions using fewer activities, it will incur less cost generating greater profits and therefore have a greater source of competitive advantage relative to the competition. Therefore competitive advantage can be thought of as achieving an efficient, optimal operational configuration, described as its value chain, that matches its value proposition (Porter, 1980) offered to students and funding institutions. This is the reason why some institutions can still make a profit by charging less for their courses, but their value chain processes will be designed to incur less costs. Other institutions charging higher fees will need to justify to potential students why this is the case and usually this will be justified by a strong reputation. Stronger reputed institu-

tions can have fewer students and more inefficient value chains as their excessive costs are likely to be covered by the higher fees.

In addition to operational processes (the value chain – Porter, 1985) universities can develop their sources of competitive advantage by being distinctive. By developing distinctive capabilities (Kay, 1993) for an institution that are considered valuable, rare, non-substitutable and inimitable relative to competing institutions (Barney 1991), these institutions can therefore be described as possessing a greater source of competitive advantage relative to the competition. Specifically distinctiveness can be achieved through having developed a better reputation, a unique regulatory or legal position, being continuously innovative and regularly reinventing oneself and finally through developing unique relationships between yourself and your suppliers. Institutions can be thought of as competing on distinctiveness through either one or more of the attributes described.

Strategic activities occur within institutions to build or exploit distinctive competitive positioning. To understand how social media can enhance the competitive positioning of higher education institutions one needs to consider the likely different models of strategic decision making within universities.

DELIBERATE AND EMERGENT STRATEGY FORMULATION WITHIN HIGHER EDUCATION INSTITUTIONS

Strategic decision making within organisations tends to occur as a deliberate planning process (Mintzberg, 1985) where higher education institutions will plan their strategic objectives and identify the initiatives required to achieve their goals. The initiatives will be carried out as planned and the results obtained will also occur as expected. This model follows a hierarchical chain of command approach, where senior managers plan the strategies and middle to lower managers implement them without question. Senior management will identify whether strategies have been through implementing financial and operational control measures. There is no opportunity for lower management to adapt the strategy through a learning process. Alternatively management can follow an emergent strategy process (Mintzberg, 1985), where plans are initially developed but are continuously adapted during the implementation process as management learn from changes occurring within the environment. Strategic decision making is therefore an emergent process requiring flexible resources to continuously adapt to the environment.

Deliberate strategic planning processes tend to occur in organisations operating in stable environments whereas emergent strategies are more suitable for organisations operating in turbulent and changeable environments. Conventionally, communication strategies within organisations including higher education institutions have tended to be planned using traditional, deliberate approaches of strategy.

TRADITIONAL MODELS OF COMMUNICATION PLANNING

Integrated communication strategies involve the complete development and implementation of an organisation's communication strategies across a number of media platforms designed to meet the needs of different stakeholders being targeted (Fill, 2002). Strategic communication goals are developed in line with the overall corporate goals of the institution and aligned to the goals of different units or faculties within the HE institution such as Medicine, Business, Science and Law. These goals are also aligned to the overall goals of the individual courses being run within each faculty. Overall strategic goals can be considered as either financial, environmental, or social as well as goals relating to increasing awareness,

interest, desire or call for action, including handling post adoption stress caused through post cognitive dissonance surrounding whether the right course or the right institution has been selected by the student.

Having identified the overall corporate, faculty and individual course objectives specific communication goals are identified relating to the desired change required of the stakeholders. It could be that stakeholders simply need to be informed, or be made aware of the differentiated offerings, or remind stakeholders of attributes and offerings or finally to persuade them to take action. Different communication tools such as advertising, sales promotion, personal selling and public relations are then utilised to achieve desired objectives with market research being used to assess strategic goals and verify whether communication goals have been achieved.

Traditional communication strategic frameworks are linear and static frameworks with the exception of personal selling which is dyadic and interactional. All other communication tools tend to be one-sided transactional communications which involve identifying the message required to achieve specific communication goals with the specific stakeholders. This is followed with transmitting the message using a specific communication medium which is finally received by the stakeholder along with numerous other messages from competing sources. The institution needs to ensure that it achieves "the greatest share of the voice" to beat the competition. The traditional communication strategies have been the mainstay of communication within HE and the most appropriate way of deploying communications was to out-promote the competition by having a bigger promotional budget. Traditional communications linked with word of mouth and attracting good academics were sufficient to attract funds and build an effective competitive positioning.

THE CURRENT WEAKNESSES OF TRADITIONAL COMMUNICATION MEDIA IN HIGHER EDUCATION

Traditional models of strategic planning tend to be used in traditional communication planning. Traditional communication media rely on strategy processes which are considered transactional and developed and implemented according to the traditional classical methods of strategic planning. Current communication strategies are developed using what Mintzberg (1994, 1998) describes as the planning school frameworks of strategy. Mintzberg (1994, 1998) describes the development and evolution of strategy within the literature as composing of ten different schools consisting of the design, planning, positioning, entrepreneurial, cognitive, learning, and power, cultural, environmental and the configuration schools representing the different ways that strategies are believed to be being developed within organisations. These frameworks can be described as one-sided transactional strategy, "closed system" frameworks where organisations develop strategy based on scanning the needs of their external and internal environments followed by developing and implementing strategies at a distance of their customers. The strategies that are developed are based on what senior academics feel are appropriate and important to their stakeholders and not what the stakeholders themselves feel are important. Limited opportunities exist for students and organisations to interact with HE institutions in order to co-develop value offerings and communications. Organisations using these rational classical frameworks tend not to wish to develop direct relationships with their customers and stakeholders. Organisations prefer for their stakeholders to develop relationships with the reputation of their brand rather than establishing long term relationships with the organisations themselves. Finally, performance measurements as to whether strategies have been successful or not are once again measured at a distance where organisa-

tions will monitor sales from customers through internal records or through market research using outsourced external agencies. Strategy is therefore a one way directional process from the corporate centre directed throughout the organisation with limited interaction between external and internal stakeholders. Communication strategies within marketing departments of organisations including communication agencies have adopted these strategic planning approaches.

The process is circular with thinking, learning and adapting strategy being the privilege of only the senior management team with them being the only ones allowed to make strategic decisions regarding positioning and promotional initiatives. Strategy in this type of organisation is described as a "top down" (Earl, 1989) or "outside in" (Dewit & Meyer, 1994) process where senior management think and decide whilst junior staff simply do as they are told. Alternative strategies include what the same author describes as "bottom up" (Earl, 1989) approaches where strategy is developed at the "coal face" by the staff and the role of senior management is ensuring that their staff are appropriately resourced to carry out their duties. Finally "inside out" (Earl, 1989) approaches involve the strategizing process resulting in a complete transformation of the existing organisation. It should be noted that Dewit & Meyer (1994) also refer to "inside out" strategy development but they use it to describe the "bottom up" strategic approach instead whereas Earl (1989) uses the term to describe transformational strategy development. It is very common in the strategy literature for similar terms to have different meanings, hence the importance to define or explain all the terms being used. Although Fill (1995) states that his Integrated Communications framework is supposed to be used in an "open systems" interactive approach, considered as a more contemporary perspective of strategy development, its actual usage, in terms of practice as well as how the framework has been taught in numerous communication courses, has been more of a stepwise classical planning approach. Classical strategy perspectives are believed to be redundant with newer more modern theoretical processes involving experiential, learning, flexibility and adaptability emergent rather than command and control (Mintzberg, 1985).

LIMITATION OF CLASSICAL STRATEGY AND COMMUNICATIONS FRAMEWORKS

The traditional models of strategy and communications development rely on the assumptions originally developed in classical economics. Under these assumptions purchasers and suppliers were seen as independent entities where no relational or cooperation was thought to exist between different customers and competing suppliers as well as between customers and suppliers. Customers were thought to act independently from each other and competed against each other by wanting the best (cheapest) prices. Suppliers on the other hand wanted to gain the highest possible price and assumed limited communications with customers amongst themselves comparing prices. Transactions between suppliers and customers were deemed to be the most useful unit of analysis in strategic purchasing behaviour research and all activities during transactions were evaluated and any activities occurring prior and after the transactions were considered irrelevant. These frameworks were not seen as appropriate for businesses doing business with each other as it failed to provide an appropriate explanation of actual business behaviour which relied on interactions and relationships between suppliers and customers. These Business to Business (B2B) transactions were seen as being different to Business to end consumer transactions (B2C) because B2B transactions were affected by historical relationships between supplier and customer and future transactions were also likely to be affected by historic and current interactions during the transactions.

Relationships were seen as the most appropriate unit of analysis in business research and transaction approaches were confined to B2C environments. It is important to note that service businesses also showed a lack of conformity to transactional frameworks with relationships being seen as more important than the transactions. Additionally, relationship approaches were initially developed and adopted by the Europeans, particularly the Nordic countries. The North Americans initially resisted relational aspects of strategy development as being the predominant strategy perspective a number of times, but are now appreciating its value. Within B2B and Service industries, purchasing is influenced by interactions between parties who have previous experience through historic relationships between the relevant parties as well as being influenced by third parties embedded in an interactional relational network. In recent times with the increasing use of social media where stakeholders are forming relational ties in large networks over the internet, the differential gap between B2C and B2B is narrowing with both fields being described as converging (Vargo & Lusch, 2011; Ellis, 2010). Higher Education involves end consumers - students as well as a number of business customers; public funding bodies as well as other stakeholders. These classical approaches to strategy are believed to be a major driver for planning the newer digital and social media strategies. Executives within organisations are either explicitly using these frameworks or are subconsciously driven towards these approaches in their social media strategy planning. These planning frameworks are suitable for use in stable and predictable business environments but are poor at predicting outcomes in complex, turbulent and unpredictable environments where newer strategy perspectives are recommended. The weakness of classical promotional strategies in social media strategizing is emphasised by Kaplan & Haenlein (2010:P60) who state that "historically, companies were able to control the information available about them through strategically placed press announcements and good public relations managers. Today, however, firms have been increasingly relegated to the sidelines as mere observers, having neither the knowledge nor the chance - or, sometimes, even the right - to alter publicly posted comments provided by their customers." Social media is believed to be disruptive to existing business environments therefore creating increased complexity therefore rendering traditional frameworks useless. Therefore executives are believed to be either adopting outdated modes of strategizing their social media, or worse that they are not using any strategy techniques and simply being tactical. Finally some executives are likely to be outsourcing their strategizing to external agencies who are themselves implementing outmoded approaches.

The HE institutions are also service based, therefore considering the B2B and service elements traditional communications which have been used extensively historically are not appropriate. With the introduction and increased usage of social media, students are creating social networks meaning that newer interactional/relational network perspectives of strategy behaviour are required to model influencers and adoption behaviour within HE.

SOCIAL MEDIA AND SOCIAL CAPITAL IN HIGHER EDUCATION

Social media can be considered as all the current web technologies which allow end stakeholders to interact with organisations and institutions by adding content. Social media allows different stakeholders (actors), including other customers and third parties, as well as staff from an organisation, to interact with one another and form interactional social networks. Social media can be thought of as consisting of bespoke organisational sites which consist of stakeholders being recruited and exposed to content, for which said stakeholders are invited to comment as well

as add their own content. Specific social media sites such as Facebook and LinkedIn differ from bespoke sites as they allow different organisations and individuals to connect. Content sites such as Youtube allow students and academics to create and upload content relating to academia as well as share content uploaded from other academics and students relating to academic topics and events. To date social media has been used in HE as a platform to enhance the teaching experience in lectures as well as allowing students access to material outside of lectures. Until recently HE institutions had considerable power over their students, who were attracted to the reputation of a university made known to them through advertising or word of mouth through friends, family and links with former students. Social media over the internet has provided students and other stakeholders with considerable power to interact with a large number of other students and stakeholders in a relational network, providing them with the power of co-creating reputational value of the HE in a short space of time.

THE UTILISATION OF SOCIAL CAPITAL IN HIGHER EDUCATION

Capital can be defined as the investment of resources with the expected return of an economic profit (Lin, 2002). With regards to HE capital can be seen as producing resources such as knowledge, materials and reputation followed by utilising that knowledge, material and reputation to secure grants and generate profits from selling courses. HE institutions had used social capital historically; capital derived from the unique relational ties with their academics and students through ties with schools and other organisations. Nowadays social media offers the opportunity to create unique relational network ties globally at great speeds and can enhance or damage the reputation of HE institutions in a matter of hours. Social media through social capital through accessing networks can affect long term competitive advantage. Historically theories of competitive advantage focussing on B2C marketing did not recognise the importance of networks which are now being recognised as being vital, through the rise of social media which involves the creation of networks.

DEVELOPING A NETWORK THEORY OF THE FIRM

Network approaches are increasingly being used to gain a better understanding of business behaviour (Johanisson, 1995). They have been described as being the fabric of human interactions (Jackson, 2006). They are relationally based affecting the way people regularly relate to one another through sharing information and favours in varied settings, including influencing decisions taken inside organisations across the world. Networks affect how and with whom organisations conduct business (Jackson, 2006). The regularities regarding network structures across many disciplines make the "scientific study" of networks a possibility (Jackson, 2006: P1) and the depth and impact that networks have on human behaviour make such studies "a necessity" (Jackson, 2006: P1). Network analysis has been described as a "fundamental intellectual tool for the study of social structures (as) social structures can be represented as networks" (Wellman and Berkowitz 1988: 4). Within the social sciences network theory has been a goldmine and has provided explanations for social phenomena in a wide variety of disciplines ranging from psychology to economics (Borgatti et al, 2009). Networks have also proved to be useful in exploring complex organizational phenomena such as power and influence, organising efforts, strategic alliances, multinational corporations and inter-firm competition (Borch & Arthur, 1995).

Network theory in the form of Social Network Analysis (SNA) has a long and complex history (Durland & Fredericks, 2005). The origins of Network theory in the social sciences occurred during the 1930s where it stayed as a social science tool until the 1950s when it was linked with graph theory and mathematics by Cartwright and Harary (1956). Networks as a scientific pursuit were originally developed in sociology over a hundred years ago and became established as a central field within the same subject area over the last fifty years (Jackson, 2006). The mathematical research into networks has progressed over the same period with regards to the structure of random graphs with intermittent links to sociology (Jackson, 2006) and resulted in the array of contemporary and conventional network models. Network theory includes "small worlds" models, also known as "six degrees of separation" since, in the social network of the world, any person turns out to be linked to any other person by roughly six connections. Small world networks are founded on fairly complex mathematics even though the principles are straightforward to understand. Despite the complexity of the subject it is very popular, and has established itself in many different fields ranging from computer networks, to biological ecosystems, to business management.

Network theory can be described as still being in a period of rapid development even though a significant literature has accumulated in the field and new articles are appearing on regular basis. Borgatti et al (2009) express the increasing interest in network research as "an explosion of interest" in the subject within the physical and social sciences (P892).

Over the years, networks have been independently researched by a diverse group of scientists, including mathematicians, physicists, computer scientists, sociologists, and biologists who have been building the new field of network theory or the "science of networks" (Barabási 2002; Buchanan 2002; Watts 2004). Economists have shown little interest in the field but over the last decade the amount of research relating to the game theoretic and economic perspectives has mushroomed (Jackson, 2006). The rise of network research in physics and computer science has only occurred recently. They are distinct in their approaches and methods and have a different literature and are beginning to become more aware of each other, including acknowledging and sharing experiences with each other. There has been a significant amount of "reinventing the wheel" between network theory developed in the physical and social sciences, with the physical sciences not acknowledging or taking into account the original findings from social sciences.

Network theory originated in mathematics and was adopted in sociology. Graph theory over the decades has spread beyond the domain of pure mathematics to applications in engineering (Ahuja et al. 2014), operations research (Nagurney 1993), and computer science (Lynch 1996). However it has found a welcome home in sociology, where it has been extensively present for a number of years, with sociology also being the first of the social sciences to adopt it.

Network analyses have been used in management to develop understandings of job performance, innovation, promotion, creativity and unethical behaviour and are also ever increasingly being utilised in management consultancy as diagnostics and prescriptive tools (Borgatti and Halgin, 2011). In the field of marketing, business networks have been used to research internationalisation, technological development, purchasing, services, new product development and marketing strategy (McCloughlin & Horan, 2000; Welch, 2000).

Networks involve the interaction of actors. Actors can be people but can also consist of groups, organisations and societies with links occurring at the macro social-structural level as well as the micro level (Ritzer, 2011).

Network approaches, according to Burt (1982) and Granovetter (1985), are different to "atomistic" and "normative" approaches to sociology. Modern day organisations should no longer be viewed by a firm existing within a distinctive boundary enclosing its internal environment and separat-

ing it from the external environment. Instead organisations should be viewed as a collection of intra-organisational and inter-organisational relational networks all interacting with one another (Achrol, 1997). These intra and inter organisational networks can also be linked to additional network structures to form nets (Mintzberg & Van Der Heyden, 1999), or if these networks link different levels of analysis across society, organisations, groups and individuals, as they are most likely to do, these will result in "nested networks" (Moliterno & Mahony, 2011:P444).

Networks of organisations by themselves do not create superior competitive advantages for focal firms located within them, but it is the manners in which they are developed and effectively managed as well as utilised that potentially yield competitive benefits and value (Huston & Sakkab, 2006)

Networks are the means by which new ventures are mainly created in so-called "voluntaristic settings" (Johannison, 1995:P215). Networks have the potential of being both restrictive, potentially hampering innovative ideas on the one hand, as an enabler for creating new ventures depending on whether they are being used in deterministic paradigmatic context or in "voluntaristic settings" (Johannisson, 1995).

DEFINING NETWORK CONCEPTS AND NETWORK THEORY IN MARKETING

Strategic networks are defined as firms investing in co-operative relationships between themselves in order to exchange or share information and/or resources (Borch & Arthur, 1995). Economic exchanges between firms are seen by the authors Borch & Arthur (1995) as a central part of network research where social bonds are believed to create a basis for trust, reciprocity and commitment among network firms.

Although social network analysis is not a new area, its application to marketing particularly the practitioner applications can be regarded as novel (Doyle, 2007). The introduction of network theory into the understanding of markets and marketing can be said to have occurred in 1982, in Sweden with the publication of two books; Hagg and Johanson, 1982; and Hammarkvist et al., 1982. These publications were perceived as being distinctive as they were a departure from current perspectives as they viewed markets as networks (Mattsson & Johanson, 2004). The first publication; "Firms in Networks: A New View on Competitiveness", contributed to the contemporary discussions regarding what constituted international competitiveness of Sweden's industry. The authors rejected the "micro economic perspective on markets with its focus on relative production costs, the market price as the coordinating mechanism, disregard of marketing and negative attitude to relationships in the market. They argued for a network perspective on industrial markets with focus on relationships between firms in a market as the mechanism for coordination and development and as a valid base for discussions about competitiveness of Swedish industry" (P259). The second publication "Marketing for Competitiveness", contributed to the discussion of the role of marketing and market orientation relating to the success of Swedish industrial firms in international markets. It presented a network perspective on markets and argued against the marketing mix perspective which was seen to have a focus on sellers' "means of competition" and had a disregard for interactions between sellers and buyers and its role in inter-firm cooperation (Mattsson & Johanson, 2004: P260). These publications according to the authors were simply "a small step" in the development of network theory in marketing, but they have great significance in the fact that they were first publications that "explicitly argued for a network view" (P260).

NETWORKS AS AN ADDITIONAL CONTRIBUTION TO THE MACRO/MICRO PERSPECTIVES IN SOCIAL SCIENCES

Research within social sciences have traditionally tended to focus either on studying individuals at the micro level being affected by attributes, or at the macro level where all individual behaviours are combined and measured as a single aggregate where the impacts of attributes on aggregate behaviour is studied. Whether research is focussing on the attribute effects on aggregate or individual behaviour, there exists an underlying assumption that all individuals are acting independently of each other and there are no relational interactions linking them. Networks provide a suitable alternative to view and study social science settings as they allow the study of combined relational units interacting with each other and embedded within a relational network structure. The network environment is different to the macro and micro environments usually used to describe social science setting, as it describes a new environment perspective that consists of relational links between specific actors in networks that cuts across both the macro and micro settings.

RELEVANT NETWORK THEORIES

There are several articles relating to social and business networks available across a wide spectrum of different disciplines. Two network theoretical approaches in particular, the Industrial Marketing (IMP) Group (http://www.impgroup. org/about.php - accessed April 2013) approach developed within the B2B marketing arena and the Service Dominant Logic approach (Vargo & Lusch, 2004; 2008) could provide insights as to how competitive advantages of HE institutions can be achieved using social media. The IMP approach identified that most business transactions were affected by interactions (Håkansson, 1982; Turnbull & Valla, 1986) between suppliers and customers, where customers were co-creators of value in the interaction. Transactions only tended to occur if there were pre-existing relationships between customer and supplier groups. Interactions involved the formation of actor bonds between different parties within the different organisations as well as the sharing of activity links and resource ties. This is called the Actor, Resources and Activity (ARA) IMP model. In later IMP studies (Håkansson & Johanson, 1992; Håkansson & Snehota, 1995) it was shown that the specific dyadic interactions were also affected by further dyads interactions within a wider network.

Individuals within HE organisations consisting of existing and historic students can form relationships and share informational resources and activities over social media sites, with the specific interactions contributing to specific relational ties which can therefore create distinctive capabilities which lead to a sustainable competitive advantages.

SERVICE DOMINANT LOGIC: STRATEGY AS "OPERANT AND OPERAND" RESOURCES AND CUSTOMERS AND SUPPLIERS BEING CONSIDERED AS EQUAL PARTNERS IN CO-CREATING VALUE

Although developed within marketing, a newer controversial strategy perspective can be considered as being introduced in 2004 focussing on the area of service rather than services marketing. This new theoretical perspective called Service Dominant Logic - SDL (Vargo & Lusch, 2004; 2008) has contributed to the marketing and strategic management debate by linking the ideas of services marketing, relationship marketing, market orientation, network perspectives, integrated marketing communications (IMC) and the resource

based view of the firm (Lusch & Vargo, 2006) in a novel approach that has created a holistic "service logic" for marketing practice. Vargo & Lusch (2004 & 2008) claim that SDL represents a paradigm shift in the way that we should think about marketing. According to the authors we should move away from a paradigm that emphasises goods (Goods Dominant Logic - GDL) to one that considers service (Service Dominant Logic - SDL) as all goods are bought for their service application. Value in the SDL paradigm is co-created through using the product or service (value in use) rather than value in exchange and embedded value through manufacturing which are concepts from GDL (sdlogic.net homepage - http://www.sdlogic.net/ - accessed April 2013).

SDL is based on ten foundational premises (FPs), 8 of which were proposed in the 2004 Vargo & Lusch Journal of Marketing article and an additional two which were introduced in their 2008 article in the Academy of Marketing Science. The FPs consists of:

1. Service is the fundamental basis of exchange;
2. Indirect exchange masks the fundamental basis of exchange;
3. Goods are a distribution mechanism for service provision;
4. Operant resources are the fundamental source of competitive advantage;
5. All economies are service economies;
6. The customer is always a co-creator of value;
7. The enterprise cannot deliver value, but only offer value propositions;
8. A service-centred view is inherently customer oriented and relational;
9. All social and economic actors are resource integrators; and
10. Value is always uniquely and phenomenologically determined by the beneficiary.

SDL's major contribution to strategy involves the conceptualisation and actions of two types of organisational resources that potentially yield competitive advantage. Organisations consist of tangible operand resources which include tangible buildings, people and cash and they are acted upon by intangible operant resources which include skills, competences and capabilities, values, attitudes and beliefs. The manner in which organisations leverage the combined effects of their operand and operant resources often characterises their strategizing approaches. Intangible resources can be considered to add value to achieving a sustainable differential competitive advantage within organisations and often it is the intangible resources that give to the heterogeneity, inimitability, rare and valuable resources (Barney 1991) described in the RBV perspectives of strategy that are difficult to copy and substitute.

SDL and the RBV of strategy can be said to share similar perspectives with SDL providing additional detail of what constitutes valuable, rare, inimitable, non-substitutable (VRIN) resources. The view that intangible assets or resources add value to organisations has been considered a controversial issue, particularly in financial accounting where intangibles such as brands are often not included as a specific asset on the balance sheet and are at best only represented as goodwill. Doyle (2009) suggests that with the exception of patents, developing strong relationships and brand reputations through promotional efforts are the best ways of securing a sustainable differential competitive advantage. Finally Hunt & Madhavaram (2006) discuss that the Resource Advantage (RA) theory would be an ideal integrative theory across the different areas of strategic management and strategic marketing. SDL according to authors (ibid) is perfectly accounted for in RA theory. Therefore SDL can be thought of as an appropriate theory to evaluate issues regarding strategic marketing and management, which includes how social media strategies are developed and implemented within organisations.

An additional important area of contribution of SDL to strategic marketing and management, particularly in relation to social media strategiz-

ing, is the fact that "the customer is always a co-creator of value" (FP6 Vargo & Lusch, 2004) and "all social and economic actors are resource integrators" (FP9 Vargo & Lusch, 2008). Value co-creation and all actors being resource integrators in SDL are similar and related concepts to the interaction of actors in the IMP B2B business networks literature. These two foundational premises clearly demonstrate that value co-creation and resource integration leading to a sustainable differential competitive advantage is reliant on the fact that organisations allow customers and other stakeholders to freely interact and build networked relationships. Social media can be considered as an enabler to creating interactional, relational dynamic networks. Therefore classical transactional marketing communication frameworks are unlikely to be appropriate. This sentiment is shared by Kaplan & Haenlein (2010:P65); "Yet, whatever the ultimate decision——to buy, make, or both—— it is vital that there is an understanding of the basic idea behind Social Media. It's all about participation, sharing, and collaboration, rather than straightforward advertising and selling."

In relation to HE institutions SDL provides the perfect theoretical platform in explaining how social media can develop competitive advantage. The interaction and co-creation of value using operand and operant resources provides a suitable explanation for B2B interactions (HE institution and funding body), B2C interactions (HE institution and students) and finally C2C (students interacting with other students).

MANAGERIAL IMPLICATIONS FOR SOCIAL MEDIA STRATEGIZING IN HE

The traditional approaches to strategic and promotional planning provided managers with greater control over the strategy process and ultimately the strategic outcome. Managers within HE will often have little or no control over the outcomes with emergent perspectives of strategy, particularly those involving the co-creation of communications with end customers and stakeholders, as it is with using social media. Managers should realise that customers are affected by the quality, credibility and legitimacy of communication messages (Fill, 2002), with promotional messages created by organisations and their agencies being considered the least credible and having the lowest legitimacy. As evidenced through word of mouth research studies, legitimacy and credibility of communications are highest amongst peer group members, therefore allowing these groups to freely communicate on the social media sites is very important. Within social media end customers and stakeholders are unlikely to want organisations to communicate with them using one way communication approaches as they do with traditional advertising. Organisations will need to be excluded or considered as being equal partners (actors) in the dialogue embedded in an interactional, relational network. "Wikipedia, for example, expressly forbids the participation of firms in its online community" (Kaplan & Haenlein, 2010:P60). Howard Schultz, the chairman of Starbuck's who's confidential memo about the current situation of the organisation at the time was leaked and widely discussed on social media sites and rapidly diffused to mainstream news sites, remarked that everyone outside the company had an opinion about the intention of the Starbucks memo as well as Schultz as an effective leader. He also remarked that nothing was confidential relating to the internet and noted that Starbuck's voice was nowhere to be found in these discussions; they had been excluded (Gray & Vander Val, 2012). This has major implications for HE institutions.

Several managers will not be accustomed to democratic styles of management that rely on relinquishing control of communications to their end customers and stakeholders, as described in the following sentence; "Yet, not overly many firms seem to act comfortably in a world where consumers can speak so freely with each other and businesses have increasingly less control over the information available about them in cyberspace" (Kaplan & Haenlein, 2010:P59). Managers should also not be tempted to interfere with negative comments by trying to delete messages on social network sites managed by their organisations as this can have disastrous effects. Actors linked together and interacting within networked systems can amplify effects. Small disturbances such as a decision to delete a dialogue within a site is likely to cause greater disturbances through amplification as it travels through the system using a process of positive feedback. This is commonly known as the "Butterfly effect" (Lorenz, 2000) where a butterfly flapping its wings on one continent can cause tornadoes on another continent due to interconnected weather systems. This effect in social media is described in the following sentence from an interview with Muhtar Kent, CEO of Coca Cola; "[Question]: That's the challenge: To what extent do you control the message? Coke has had to deal with things like those viral videos that show people putting Mentos in Diet Cokes and creating giant fountains. Do these things cause concern? Or do you try to embrace them? [Answer]: It's not just that you can't control it—when you try, it backfires. You have to understand consumers: They would like to be heard. It's a question of co-creating content. Five years ago social media was 3% of our total media spend. Today it's more than 20% and growing fast" (Ignatius, 2011:P96).

CONCLUSION AND RECOMMENDATIONS

Social media is not like any other media that has previously existed as it allows interactions across B2B, B2C and C2C and networked relationships to be formed across different stakeholders. It is a revolutionary form of communication as it does not use technology simply to improve the efficiency of processes that were previously undertaken, but uses technology to revolutionise how communication takes place between an organisation and its stakeholders. This means that it is a disruptive medium which enhances the power of end customers and stakeholders to enter a dialogue regarding organisations and their offerings. A different emergent strategy approach is required in planning social media strategies and the theoretical foundations from network theory and Service Dominant Logic can offer significant insight and should be adopted by managers to develop and implement their social media strategies. Managers within HE institutions need to think very carefully about how they engage and plan HE's future social media strategies, as these can affect both social capital and competitive advantage.

FUTURE RESEARCH AGENDA

This is a conceptual article and empirical research is required to verify the propositions developed from this critical review of social media strategizing in HE institutions. These propositions include:

- Traditional static models of strategic planning and communications planning are inappropriate for planning an HE's organisation's social media strategies.
- The realised strategies relating to social media planning within HE are likely to be emergent rather than deliberate.
- Dynamic, relational, interactional and networked perspectives are considered more appropriate to evaluating how social media strategies are formulated and implemented within HE.
- Service Dominant Logic and the Resource Based View (RBV) also provide a better

perspective on understanding how social media strategies should be planned and implemented within HE.

- Managers within HE are either planning and implementing their social media strategies on inadequate traditional communication planning mind-sets, or outsourcing their SM strategies to communication agencies who are using outdated thinking, or finally they may be simply being tactical in developing their SM initiatives.
- Social media is an environment which primarily allows organisations to build and manage relationships and establish their reputation amongst their customers and other stakeholders.
- Organisations should audit and maximise and align their technological, design & managerial capabilities to enhance their relational, reputational, interactional capabilities with their end customers and stakeholders.
- A different managerial style is required with social media strategizing and managers need to apply a democratic style rather than an autocratic command and control style.
- The impact of social media on selling goods and services is a secondary effect of having established appropriate relationships and reputation.
- End customers and stakeholders do not wish for organisations to communicate with them on social media sites using a traditional one way mechanism as they do with advertising; customers want organisations to participate in a dialogue as an equal actor interacting in a relational social network.
- Due to amplification effects caused in network systems caused by positive feedback

mechanisms, organisations should refrain from the temptation of deleting and stopping chats amongst interacting stakeholders as this is likely to cause a backlash which is likely to severely impact upon an organisation's reputation.

- Organisations that are establishing successful social media strategies are consciously or subconsciously applying emergent, relational, interactional strategies.

REFERENCES

Achrol, R. S. (1997). Changes in the theory of interorganizational relations in marketing: Toward a network paradigm. *Journal of the Academy of Marketing Science*, 25(1), 56–71. doi:10.1007/BF02894509

Ahuja, R. K., Magnanti, T. L., & Orlin, J. B. (2014). *Network flows: Theory, algorithms, and applications*. Harlow, UK: Pearson Education Limited.

Andrew, S., & Galak, J. (2012). The effects of traditional and social earned media on sales: A study of a microlending marketplace. *JMR, Journal of Marketing Research*, 49(5), 624–639. doi:10.1509/jmr.09.0401

Barabasi, A. L. (2002). *Linked: The new science of networks*. Cambridge, MA: Perseus.

Barney, J. (1991). Firm resources and sustained competitive advantage. *Journal of Management*, 17(1), 99–120. doi:10.1177/014920639101700108

Borch, O. J., & Arthur, M. B. (1995). Strategic networks among small firms: Implications for strategy research methodology. *Journal of Management Studies*, 32(4), 419–441. doi:10.1111/j.1467-6486.1995.tb00783.x

Borgatti, S. P., & Halgin, D. S. (2011). On network theory. *Organization Science*, 22(5), 1168–1181. doi:10.1287/orsc.1100.0641

Borgatti, S. P., Mehra, A., Brass, D. J., & Labianca, G. (2009). Network analysis in the social sciences. *Science*, 323(5916), 892-895.

Buchanan, M. (2003). *Nexus: Small worlds and the groundbreaking theory of networks*. New York, NY: WW Norton & Company.

Burt, R. S. (2001). Structural holes versus network closure as social capital. *Social Capital: Theory and Research*, 31-56.

Cartwright, D., & Harary, F. (1956). Structural balance: A generalization of Heider's theory. *Psychological Review*, 63(5), 277–293. doi:10.1037/h0046049 PMID:13359597

Dewitt, B., & Meyer, R. (1994). *Strategy: Process, content, context*. St Paul, MN: West Publishing.

Doyle, P. (2009). *Value-based marketing: Marketing strategies for corporate growth and shareholder value*. Chichester, UK: Wiley.

Doyle, S. (2007). The role of social networks in marketing. *Journal of Database Marketing & Customer Strategy Management*, 15(1), 60–64. doi:10.1057/palgrave.dbm.3250070

Durland, M. M., & Fredericks, K. A. (2005). An introduction to social network analysis. *New Directions for Evaluation*, 2005(107), 5–13. doi:10.1002/ev.157

Earl, M. J. (1989). *Management strategies for information technology*. Upper Saddle River, NJ: Prentice-Hall, Inc.

Ellis, N. (2010). *Business to business marketing: Relationships, networks and strategies*. Oxford, UK: OUP.

Fill, C. (1995). *Marketing communications*. Harlow, UK: Prentice-Hall.

Fill, C. (2002). *Marketing communications: Contexts, strategies, and applications* (3rd ed.). Harlow, UK: Financial Times Prentice Hall.

Granovetter, M. (1985). Economic action and social structure: The problem of embeddedness. *American Journal of Sociology*, *91*(3), 481–510. doi:10.1086/228311

Gray, D., & Vander Wal, T. (2012). *The connected company*. North Sebastopol, CA: O'Reilly Media, Inc.

Hägg, I., & Johanson, J. (1982). *Företag i nätverk-ny syn på konkurrenskraft. Stockolm*. Academic Press.

Håkansson, H. (1982). *International marketing & purchasing of industrial goods: An interaction approach*. Chichester, UK: John Wiley & Sons.

Håkansson, H., & Johanson, J. (1992). A model of industrial networks. In B. Axelson & G. Easton (Eds.), *Industrial networks a new view of reality*. London, UK: Routledge.

Håkansson, H., & Snehota, I. (1995). *Developing relationships in business networks*. London, UK: Routledge.

Hammarkvist, K. O., Håkansson, H., & Mattsson, L. G. (1982). Marknadsföring för konkurrenskraft. Liber Ekonomi.

Hanna, R., Rohm, A., & Crittenden, V. (2011). We're all connected: The power of the social media ecosystem. *Business Horizons*, *54*(3), 265–273. doi:10.1016/j.bushor.2011.01.007

Hunt, S. D., & Madhavaram, S. (2006). The service – dominant logic of marketing – Theoretical foundations, pedagogy, and resource-advantage theory. In *The service-dominant logic of marketing: Dialog, debate, and directions*. Armonk, NY: ME Sharpe Inc.

Huston, L., & Sakkab, N. (2006). Connect & develop. *Harvard Business Review*, *84*(3), 58–66.

Ignatius, A. (2011). Shaking things up at Coca-Cola - An interview with Muhtar Kent by Adi Ignatius. *Harvard Business Review*, (October), 94–99.

Jackson, M. O. (2006) The economics of social networks. In Advances in economics and econometrics: Volume 1: Theory and applications. Cambridge University Press.

Johannisson, B. (1995). Paradigms and entrepreneurial networks–Some methodological challenges. *Entrepreneurship & Regional Development*, *7*(3), 215-232.

Johanson, J., & Mattsson, L. G. (1994). *The markets-as-networks tradition in Sweden*. Springer.

Kaplan, A. M., & Haenlein, M. (2010). Users of the world, unite! The challenges and opportunities of social media. *Business Horizons*, *53*(1), 59–68. doi:10.1016/j.bushor.2009.09.003

Kay, J. (1993). *Foundation of corporate success: How business strategies add value*. Oxford, UK: Oxford University Press.

Kietzmann, J., Hermkens, K., McCarthy, I., & Silvestre, B. (2011). Social media? Get serious! Understanding the functional building blocks of social media. *Business Horizons*, *54*(3), 241–251. doi:10.1016/j.bushor.2011.01.005

Kumar, V., & Mirchandani, R. (2012). Increasing the ROI of social media marketing. *Sloan Management Review*, *54*(1), 55–61.

Lin, N. (2002). *Social capital: A theory of social structure and action* (Vol. 19). New York: Cambridge University Press.

Lorenz, E. (2000). *The butterfly effect: The chaos avant-garde: Memories of the early days of chaos theory*. Singapore: World Scientific Publishing.

Lynch, N. A. (1996). *Distributed algorithms*. San Francisco, CA: Morgan Kaufmann.

Mcloughlin, D., & Horan, C. (2000). The production and distribution of knowledge in the markets-as-networks tradition. *Journal of Strategic Marketing, 8*(2), 89–103. doi:10.1080/096525400346196

Mintzberg, H. (1994). *Rise and fall of strategic planning*. New York: Free Press.

Mintzberg, H., Ahlstrand, B. W., & Lampel, J. (1998). *Strategy safari: The complete guide trough the wilds of strategic management*. London, UK: Financial Times Prentice Hall.

Mintzberg, H., & Van der Heyden, L. (1999). Organigraphs: Drawing how companies really work. *Harvard Business Review, 77,* 87–95. PMID:10621269

Mintzberg, H., & Waters, J. A. (1985). Of strategies, deliberate and emergent. *Strategic Management Journal, 6*(3), 257–272. doi:10.1002/smj.4250060306

Moliterno, T. P., & Mahony, D. M. (2011). Network theory of organization: A multilevel approach. *Journal of Management, 37*(2), 443–467. doi:10.1177/0149206310371692

Nagurney. (1993). *Network economics: A variational inequality approach*. Boston: Kluwer Academic Publishers.

Porter, M. E. (1980). *Competitive strategy*. New York: Free Press.

Porter, M. E. (1985). *Competitive advantage*. New York: Free Press.

Ritzer, G. (2011). *Sociological theory* (7th ed.). New York: McGraw Hill, International.

Turnbull, P. W., & Valla, J. P. (1986). Strategic planning in industrial marketing: An interaction approach. *European Journal of Marketing, 20*(7), 5–20. doi:10.1108/EUM0000000004652

Vargo, S. L., & Lusch, R. F. (2004). Evolving to a new dominant logic for marketing. *Journal of Marketing, 68*(1), 1–17. doi:10.1509/jmkg.68.1.1.24036

Vargo, S. L., & Lusch, R. F. (2008). Service-dominant logic: Continuing the evolution. *Journal of the Academy of Marketing Science, 36*(1), 1–10. doi:10.1007/s11747-007-0069-6

Vargo, S. L., & Lusch, R. F. (2011). It's all B2B… and beyond: Toward a systems perspective of the market. *Industrial Marketing Management, 40*(2), 181–187. doi:10.1016/j.indmarman.2010.06.026

Watts, D. J. (2004). *Six degrees: The science of a connected age*. New York: WW Norton & Company.

Weinberg, B., & Pehlivan, E. (2011). Social spending: Managing the social media mix. *Business Horizons, 54*(3), 275–282. doi:10.1016/j.bushor.2011.01.008

Welch, C. (2000). The archaeology of business networks: The use of archival records in case study research. *Journal of Strategic Marketing, 8*(2), 197–208. doi:10.1080/0965254X.2000.10815560

Wellman, B., & Berkowitz, S. D. (Eds.). (1988). *Social structures: A network approach*. Cambridge, UK: Cambridge University Press.

KEY TERMS AND DEFINITIONS

Actor: A term specifically used in network theory which is synonymous with stakeholder but can also include organisations, resources and activities that can be linked to create value for HE institutions.

Industrial Marketing and Purchasing (IMP) Group: A group of academics who subscribe to the belief that economic and social outcomes of organisations are a result of their interactions with other organisations linked together in relational networks. Positive outcomes can only occur by the sharing of resources and activities between individuals in different organisations located within and between networks. Their theory provides the means to explain why social media can affect the competitive position of HE institutions through the multiple communication interactions of students with each other regarding the quality of an HE institution's offering.

Integrated Marketing Communications: Planned communication strategies developed by HE institutions ensuring that their advertising, public relations, professional selling, sales promotional, digital marketing strategies are fully integrated and aligned with the institutions overall marketing and corporate strategies.

Network Theory: A group of theories developed independently in mathematics, social and natural sciences that focus on evaluating phenomena based on the relational interactions between variables rather than considering them as being simply dependent and independent.

Network: A collection of interacting stakeholders connected to each other through social media and having influence over educational institutions and potentially impacting upon their reputation and competitiveness.

Operant and Operand Resources: The tangible and intangible resources possessed by an HE institution that drives competitiveness. The competitive positioning of HE institutions is based on the way that they develop and exploit their unique and rare intangible processes, skills, leadership styles and systems on their tangible asset resources. It is the interaction between these tangible and tangible resources which give rise to competitive advantage.

Service Dominant Logic (SDL): A theory that explains that students are important integrators of value with suppliers of higher education and that HE institutions need to co-create the manner in which they promote their offerings with the direct involvement of students using social media.

Social Media: External global independent electronic platform allowing stakeholders to connect as well communicate to one another.

Strategy Formulation and Implementation: Concerns how strategy is developed and implemented within HE. Strategy within HE institutions should be viewed as identifying and implementing activities to exploit opportunities to increase student satisfaction and eliminate threats that could reduce it relative to the competition. It is imperative that competition should be viewed as collaborative to raise the profile for the whole sector and competitive to differentiate the merits of different institutions at dealing with HE issues.

Chapter 12
The Impact of Social Media on Cultural Tourism

Evangelia Marinakou
Royal University for Women, Bahrain

Charalampos Giousmpasoglou
Bahrain Polytechnic, Bahrain

Vasileios Paliktzoglou
University of Eastern Finland – Joensuu, Finland

ABSTRACT

Social networks have become very popular recently in the tourism sector. This chapter presents the use of social media and more specifically Trip Advisor in reference to reviews of cultural attractions and their potential influence on the development of cultural tourism in Bahrain. The findings propose that people use Trip Advisor to collect information about a destination and share experiences with other community members. They also suggest that cultural tourism has a potential to grow in the region; however, there should be more information available. The cultural attractions should be more organized, offer more information, and enhance the cultural experience. This chapter recommends that social networks and Trip Advisor should be used by the local tourism authorities for the development and promotion of cultural tourism in Bahrain. Finally, the attraction websites should be further enhanced and other social media could be used to communicate with visitors in Bahrain.

INTRODUCTION

The Internet has become the most significant phenomenon today. Moreover, the development of Information and Computer Technology (ICT) during the last decades has provided new opportunities to the whole tourism industry (Buhalis, 2003). The diffusion of the interactive Web 2.0 features and applications has offered tourism markets the potential to have real conversations (Milano, Baggio & Piattelli, 2011). Internet marketing has also impacted on both marketers and consumers, influencing and changing consumer behaviour in tourism as well. Hence, consumers nowadays take part in the communication of products including tourism products, and in many

DOI: 10.4018/978-1-4666-7401-1.ch012

cases via online social networks they decide what information to share, how the information may be used, creating many challenges for marketers and other stakeholders (Stewart & Pavlov, 2002). Therefore, these new consumer demands have created new consumer needs, which means that organisations have to start rethinking the ways they operate and they communicate with their consumers. Social media has not only changed the communication with the customer, but have also made information easier to access anytime. At the same time they are a very good source of information on customer needs, demands and reviews on products and services, social media "are taking an important role in travellers' information search and decision-making behaviours'" (Yoo, Gretzel & Zach, 2011, p.526). For example, TripAdvisor is "the leader among travel related consumer review websites, as 50 million users per month seek advice about their travel plans" (Fotis, Buhalis & Rossides, 2012, p.15). The research objective of this study is to identify the potential to develop further cultural tourism via social networks and reviews on TripAdvisor on the various attractions and cultural sites in the Kingdom of Bahrain.

LITERATURE REVIEW

Tourism in Bahrain

The Middle East offers a wide collection of centers of touristic appeal, and many rank these attractions among the most important places to visit (Knowles, Diamantis & El-Mourhabi, 2004). As the flow of oil income has been decreasing, the GCC members have turned their attention to other economies and sources of income and have been following the path of economic diversification through the development of tourism (Karolak, 2012). For example, tourism accounted for 16.6% of UAE GDP in 2010, making UAE a global leader

in the higher-end leisure market (WTTC, 2011, p.19). Tourism in the region is considered as a major source of foreign exchange, and is important to the Arab countries economy. Tourism is also a crucial generator of employment to many of these countries including Bahrain. Bahrain has a strong financial sector, contributing 30% to GDP, and is making an effort to liberalize the economy by encouraging the government with positive results. Tourism in this context is seen as a growing market that may contribute 8% of the country's GDP (Amado, 2011).

The challenge in the region is to identify the potential of cultural tourism development, as well as to further develop the infrastructure and services to enrich and extend tourist arrivals (Knowles, Diamantis & El-Mourhabi, 2004, p.299). Although, Bahrain offers various events such as the F1, the competition is high from its neighbours such as Abu Dhabi, hence should focus on additional sources of international tourism income, such as cultural tourism. In terms of culture and heritage, Bahrain offers a rich history of religious, Hellenic, Roman and Ottoman sites. For example, Manama was the 2013 Capital of Arab Tourism, as part of UNESCO's programme to promote culture capitals across the world. There are also a number of cultural festivals taking place every year such as the Cultural Spring Festival and the Bahrain Summer Festival. With a blend of music, theatre, poetry, art exhibitions and dance performances, these attract tourists from the Gulf Cooperation Council (GCC) mainly (www.multivu.com).

Due to these cultural and heritage sites Bahrain, among other countries in the GCC, has attracted the attention as a center for tourism from international bodies and companies. According to Knowles, Diamantis & El-Mourhabi (2004, p.304) "the country is increasingly encouraging investment in the tourism sector". At the same time it has become attractive to business and leisure visitors. In 2010, almost 9 million people visited Bahrain (Figure 1).

Figure 1. Non-Bahraini visitor arrivals (2001-2012)
Source: Central Informatics Organisation, Ministry of Culture.

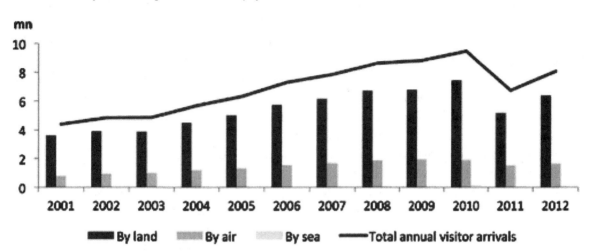

It is estimated that in 2015 the tourist arrivals in Bahrain will be 11.459 million and in 2020, 12.198 million (Alpen Capital, 2011, p.4). However, Bahrain has been attracting visitors mainly from Saudi Arabia who are in search for entertainment, as well as business, and not culture.

As Bahrain is an island, new technologies such as social networks including TripAdvisor can enhance the development of cultural tourism as they simplify access attracting new tourists via the information provided on relevant websites.

Web 2.0 and Social Media

During the last years different authors (Alexander, 2006; Zimmer, 2008; O'Reilly, 2008) have tried to define Web 2.0 from many different viewpoints. Despite the fact that almost all the definitions are debatable, none of them exclude one another. In a recent work (Junco, Heiberger & Loken, 2011), it was stated that social media are a collection of Internet websites, services and practices that support collaboration, communication, participation and sharing. On the other hand, Web 2.0 has been defined as "an ambiguous concept - a

conglomeration of folksonomies and syndication, wikis and mashups, social networks and reputation, ubiquitous content and perhaps even kitchen sinks" (Lindstrom, 2007, p.6).

Bryer and Zavatarro (2011) define social media as new technologies that aid social interaction and collaboration whilst also enabling deliberation amongst stakeholders. These technologies include blogs, wikis, media (audio, photo, video, text) sharing tools, networking platforms (Facebook and Twitter) and virtual worlds.

Some Web 2.0 technologies and services that are contributing to the Higher Education domain are blogs, microblogs, wikis, multimedia sharing services and content syndication through RSS, podcasting and content tagging services, social networking sites and other social software. At the same time, Web 2.0 has been widely used in tourism (i.e. Tourism 2.0 a touristic version of Web 2.0), is an important tool for tourists, as it affects the image and the business of destinations, companies and other organisations (Milano et al., 2011).

Many of these applications are relatively mature and they have been used for many years. On the other hand, new features and capabilities are being added regularly. In the next section we will discuss the features of main Web 2.0 services.

Blogs

Jorn Barger was the first person who introduced the term 'blog' in 1997. He was referring to a simple webpage which consisted of a few brief paragraphs (containing personal opinions), information and personal diary entries which were called 'posts.' All these posts were arranged chronologically, with the most recent placed first (Doctorow et al., 2002). Most of the blogs allow visitors to add comments below the posts.

Wikis

According to Ebersbach, Glaser and Heigle (2006) a *wiki* is a webpage or a set of web pages which anyone, who has been allowed access, can easily edit. Wikipedia became very popular because the concept of the wiki as a collaborative tool that facilitates the production of group work, is widely understood and upheld. With wikis we can share ideas, receive updates to and live coverage of events and we can build and trust a community. They can also be used for student projects, collaborating on ideas and organizing documents and resources from individuals and groups of students.

Tagging and Social Bookmarking

A 'tag' is a keyword that refers to a digital object (e.g. a website, picture or video clip) which it helps to describe, but it cannot actually be used as part of a formal classification system.

Social bookmarking systems help to share a number of common features (Millen, Feinberg, & Kerr, 2005). The users are allowed to create lists of 'bookmarks' or 'favorites' and to store these on a remote service (rather than within the client browser) which can later be shared with other us-

ers of the system. These bookmarks can also be tagged with keywords. Social bookmarking can further be used to create a set of resources which can be accessed from any computer connected to the internet. With bookmarking we can conduct research and share it with peers. We can also rate and review bookmarks to help students decide on the usefulness of resources.

Social Networking

Social Networks are professional and social networking sites which can be used for meeting people, finding like minds and sharing content (Cobb 2010). The examples of social networking sites are numerous to list but the most popular include Facebook, Twitter, Ning, Flickr, Tumblr, Utterz, NPR, WWWEDU.

RSS and Syndication

RSS is a group of formats that allows users to access content updates from RSS-enabled websites and blogs without the need to visit the related sites. The information from the different websites is collected within a feed (usually using the RSS format) and it is then shown to the user in a process known as syndication. With RSS feeds we can replace email lists and reduce emailing. Finally, we can keep the course specific WebPages relevant and current.

Google Educational Applications

Google Apps can be characterized as one of the most powerful communication and collaboration tools. It can be accessed via the web, so everyone can connect with everyone else, no matter where they are. It is very flexible, easy to use and web-based so there is no need for hardware maintenance or software installation. It is a suite of applications that includes Gmail, Google Calendar (shared calendaring), Google Drive (store and

Table 1. Characteristics of Google Apps

Google Apps	Characteristics
Gmail	Google Apps offer 25GB of storage per user. It also offers powerful spam filtering and a 99.9% uptime SLA. All these are hosted by Google and there is no cost and no advertisements for students, faculty or staff.
Google Calendar	Helps teachers and faculties to organize their time. Anyone can easily schedule lessons and meetings. Multiple calendars can be overlaid to see when people are available - a great way to manage staff schedules (can send invitations and manage RSVPs).
Drive	Provides a storage place for up-to-date versions of files from anywhere. Educators can share individual files or whole folders with specific people or an entire team. Can facilitate the creation of and reply to comments on files in order to get feedback or add ideas.
Docs	With Google Docs anyone can create rich documents with images, tables, equations, drawings, links and more. Gather input and manage feedback with social commenting.
Sheets	Google Sheets can keep and share lists, track projects, analyze data and track results with the spreadsheet editor. There are some very useful tools like advanced formulas, embedded charts, filters and pivot tables to help get new perspectives on data.
Slides	Helps in the creation of slides with presentation editor, which supports features like embedded videos, animations and dynamic slide transitions. The presentations can be published on the web so anyone can view them, or they can be shared privately.
Sites	Sites are shared workspaces for classes and faculties. The students can build their own project sites without the need to write in code. It is as easy as writing a document. There are many pre-designed templates. In addition, Google Site provides a system and site-level security controls.
Vault	Google vault is an added archiving and e-discovery feature to Google Apps for Education. It is optional and adds archiving, e-discovery and information governance capabilities. With vault anyone can define retention policies, place legal holds on users as needed, and can run reports on user activity and actions in the archive.

share), Google Talk (instant messaging and voice over IP), Google Docs, Spreadsheets and Slides (online document hosting and collaboration), Google Sites (team site creation and publishing), Google Vault (Add Archiving and e-discovery to Google Apps for Education), Start Page (a single customizable access point for all applications), Google Video and Google Security and Compliance. Google Apps is causing quite a stir in the academic environment.

Some other useful Apps from Google include Google Moderator (for creating a series about a discussion topic to which students can submit questions, ideas and suggestions), YouTube (for sharing and accessing videos with educational content), Google Maps, Picasa (for sharing and exploring photos), Scholar (for searching academic literature across many sources) and Blogger.

Kaplan & Haenlein (2010) proposed a taxonomy that classifies social media types according to their level of social presence, media richness and level of self-presentation, self-disclosure as they are presented in Table 2.

This chapter presents social media use in tourism and more specifically consumer review and ratings website, TripAdvisor as consumer blogs

Table 2. Social media taxonomy

Type	Examples
Social networking websites	Facebook, Linkedin
Blogs, Content communities	YouTube, Flickr, Slideshare, Scrib
Collaborative projects	Wikipedia, Wikitravel
Virtual social worlds	Second life
Virtual game worlds	World of Warcraft
Microblogs	Twitter
Consumer review and rating websites	TripAdvisor, Epinions
Internet fora	Fodor's Travel Travel Talk

and reviews have emerged as one of the most prominent themes in research in social media in travel and tourism. Buhalis (2003) claims that e-tourism is a process of digitalization of all processes and chains of value in the tourism sector as it is discussed in the following section.

Social Networks in Tourism

The internet and the on-line social networks have become very popular in recent times and have changed the way people communicate and search for information (Twumasi & Adu-Gyamfi, 2013). As Miguens, Baggio & Costa (2008) state these websites are the epitome of the phenomenon known as Web 2.0, as the website is no longer a static page but a dynamic platform where people exchange views and opinions. Tourism has been one of the most important components of online commerce, which has actually changed the structure of the industry. For example, in Europe tourism on the internet represented almost 19.4% of the total market in 2007 (Miguens et al., 2008). Web 2.0 provides user generated content, and access to consumers to comment on products and services, leading to shift from Business-to-consumer marketing to a peer-to-peer model (Miguens et al., 2008). Social media is also influenced by Web 2.0 applications. Especially, social networks have opened new features of social reality (Wang & Fesenmaier, 2002). In addition, virtual communities are growing and are becoming influential in tourism, as consumers as well as bloggers share information and experiences with other members. Social networks allow their members to interact without restrictions in time and space. Nowadays, there are many different types of social networking sites such as Facebook, MySpace, Twitter, and TripAdvisor, or lonelyplanet for tourism related reviews. Social networking has changed consumer behaviours as at the same time many tourism companies and providers also operate online to support these type of consumers who are seeking for in-

formation and even buy their tourism products via the internet. The more these communities increase the higher the potential for tourism companies and tourism destinations to benefit as the internet and social networks provide an effective medium to communicate (Twumasi & Adu-Gyamfi, 2013). According to Buhalis & Law (2008) "ICT plays a critical role for the competitiveness of tourism organisations and destinations, as well as for the entire industry as a whole" (p.609). Some criticize the use of Web 2.0 technology in tourism, as they claim that "the boundaries between information producers and users is blurred, and the concepts of authority and control are radically changed" (Milano et al., 2011, p.3). According to Buhalis (2003) the Internet has become the primary way used by Destination Management Organizations (DMO) to communicate with prospective tourists. For example, destinations like visitlondon.com are reacting to the content in the website created by users and are incorporating User Generated Contents (UGC) as part of their websites (Inversini & Buhalis, 2009). The Tourism British Council was the first to introduce UGC contents, to include blogs (Miguens et al., 2008). Additionally, the Florence Official Tourist Office embraces geo-referenced contents regarding tourism attractions through GoogleMaps (Miguens et al., 2008, p.2).

Tourism providers are understanding that "ICT if managed properly, can generate tremendous positive value for their organisations" (Marchiori, Dedekind & Cantoni, 2010, p.326). In view to this, Milano (2010, in Milano et al., 2011) proposes three phases that are influencing in the travel experience formation process:

- **Pre-Experience:** Built on other people's travel stories, before travelling;
- **Experience during Travel or Stay:** With real time shared experiences mainly via mobile phones;
- **Post-Experience:** Which disseminates comments, evaluations, emotions.

In addition, Inversini & Buhalis (2009) propose that destinations are providing information to travelers in a factual way. Many tourist companies have started changing the way they approach their customers and present their businesses online (Au, 2010). Xiang & Gretzel (2010) state that there are official destination and attraction websites such as cultural heritage attraction websites, as well as unofficial sources of information such as blogs, online communities, social networks, personal websites etc. The latter are significantly contributing to the massive growth of information on destinations on the web. The hotel industry is also seeing hotel bookings via Facebook increasing; in fact, they have surpassed the hotel bookings made by TripAdvisor (Astburry, 2011).

Studies have also been conducted on the effects of ICT tools on the image and the popularity of the destinations or other tourism operators, mainly in the hospitality sector (Sigala, 2010; Burgess et al., 2009). In general, these studies propose that tourism operators have not fully understood the importance of technology in tourism. Moreover, there are credibility issues as the information provided online especially visitors' comments, may be forged for particular interests by unscrupulous competitors. In other cases there is overload of useless information (Milano et al., 2011). These have created some tension between the tourism providers and users, for example Xiang and Gretzel (2010, p.186) state:

Social media websites are ubiquitous in online travel information search in that they occur everywhere [...] no matter what search keywords a traveler uses. Certain social media websites, which can be considered more comprehensive and travel-specific websites, are becoming increasingly popular and are likely to evolve into primary online travel information sources. The results confirm that tourism marketers can no longer ignore the role of social media in distributing travel-related information without risking to become irrelevant.

Nevertheless, social networks referred to as 'electronic word-of-mouth' (Litvin, Goldsmith & Pan, 2008), have widely been used by users as means to provide online feedback, communicate and share information with potential travelers about a wide range of topics, such as products, services and events. These comments have been found to contribute to the web reputation of these organisations or destinations. Dellarocas (2003) proposes that the consumers' ability to understand the credibility of reviews has developed by analyzing the consistency and ratings. Chen, Cheung, Luo & Sia (2009) suggest that this should wary marketers as they should manage this word-of-mouth. In view to this, Inversini (2009) suggests that this 'online reputation' can be managed by destinations with the use of Web 2.0 in order to attract more tourists. Tourism offers services and products that are intangible, perishable, inseparable and heterogenous (Cooper, 2012), hence tourism organisations should invest more on their reputation and developing their image (Buhalis, 2003). Many hospitality and tourism products are considered as high risk purchases, hence the emotional risk of reference group evaluation is an important aspect of the decision making process, raising marketing stress levels for providers (Litvin et al., 2008). For example, 67% of US travelers used the Internet to search for information on destinations or check prices and schedules (Travel Industry Association of America (2005 in Litvin et al., 2008, p. 8). Moreover, loyal customers are encouraged to post links to tourism provider's website, in order to nurture a community of interest in which tourists talk about the destination. Monitoring these reviews and uploads allows managers to post responses to critical comments; they may even identify popular bloggers that appeal to their customers and coordinate and cooperate with them. For example they may invite them to the destination for a complimentary visit. This marketing strategy may contribute to the reputation of the organization. Further, Marchiori et al. (2010) claim that tourists are keen on selecting tourism service providers upon their reputation. The study of online word of mouth is important to support and enhance the reputation of destinations. Lee, Law & Murphy (2011) propose that the credibility of an opinion leader can be ascertained through analyzing their rating and the consistency of their reviews. Their main objective is to help others make better decisions, but at the same time they enjoy posting their experiences. Moreover, expert websites such as TripAdvisor are perceived to be more trustworthy and useful (Bronner, Ridder, Neijens & Willemsen, 2011), hence marketers should closely monitor them. In addition, "when the amount of positive reviews outweigh negative reviews it is considered credible" (Stead, 2012, p.5). Chen et al. (2009) also propose that a comparison of reviews of the same product/service in other sources may contribute to the assessment of credibility. They add the timeliness of the review, as the closer the review is written to the experience the more fresh is in the consumer's mind, hence the more credible. The lack of negative reviews may show evidence that the website is filtered by other sources. Finally, anonymous postings are not considered credible, on the other side, personally identified reviewers are considered to be more credible and genuine (Stead, 2012). According to TripAdvisor reviewers on their site are trusted members of the travel community, although an investigation from the UK's Advertising Standards Agency proved that in some cases there were some fake reviews. This result forced TripAdvisor to change the site for hotel listings from 'Reviews you can trust' to 'Reviews from our community' as it was found that some hotels had hired freelancer reviewers to comment on their establishments (Stead, 2012). Nevertheless, consumers are more positively influenced by consumer-generated reviews (Buhalis & Law, 2008). A study by Stead (2012) reveals that negative TripAdvisor reviews have stronger effect on the consumer. She also adds that assessing the consistency between large amounts of reviews is the most commonly used technique to ascertain

review credibility by participants in her study. She concludes that consumers approach TripAdvisor in a critical way which makes their reviews more credible. The effective management of such social media can facilitate tourism managers (DMOs, hotels, or any other tourism company) to market effectively their own organization online.

Although there are conflicting opinions about the use and the impact of UGC in tourism, the importance of Web 2.0 cannot be ignored for the survival and the success of tourism companies (Scorrano, 2011). Hence, social networks facilitate interactivity and promote the formation of communities that share content for tourism products and services. As Scorrano (2011) claims "they are also generators of image of the destination" (p.950). The development of social networks has also attracted the attention of governments, and has changed the way provide online information and services as well as the way they interact with stakeholders. Danis et al. (2009) claim that governments can use social media to procure and position resources and local knowledge, monitor and resolve problems and engage their constituents in a cooperative atmosphere. They can be used by governments to rejuvenate their services and products, hence to rejuvenate or develop tourism. Mergel, Schweik & Fountain (2009) also suggest that specific ministries and entities could use blogs to communicate with public hearings, wikis and RSS feeds to coordinate work, and wikis to internally share expertise. Social networks provide governments with information on tourists, which when filtered is capable of conveying important tourist flows (Scorrano, 2011). They may use the reviews and information available via social networks to highlight the destination's services and factors of attractiveness, and therefore offer respective products and services that may attract more visitors.

TripAdvisor is considered as a place that travelers may leave their comments and give advice to other consumers; it provides information on destinations, flights, hotels and other tourist services (Stead, 2012). It also provides users a forum to add their personal opinion on the products and services they consumed. According to TripAdvisor LLC (2011) the TripAdvisor Media Group websites generated $486 million revenue. TripAdvisor facilitates the reviewing of tourism products and services around the world and brings together individuals in discussion forums, as well as it allows interactions between peers. It also provides a powerful platform for experts in tourism to interact with the users and consult their comments and posted views (Buhalis & Law, 2008). Hennig-Thurau & Walsh (2003) claim that consumers are reading such views and they use them in a way to save time in decision-making in choosing a tourist product, service and/or destination. In fact, TripAdvisors users in January 2011 were 4.6 million (Cochrane, 2011). Interestingly, TripAdvisor launched in 2007 a new feature called the Traveler Network, which "allows users to add acquaintances to their travel maps, by connecting to pre-existing sources" (Miguens et al., 2008, p.2).

Although the impact of the internet and social networks is growing, there is very little research on the influence of these social networks such as Trip Advisor, on the buying behavior of travel consumers, and how their views and expressed shared opinions may provide an indication of further tourism enhancement and development. According to Zaugg (2006 in Twumasi & Adu-Gyamfi, 2013, p.106) the issue of online travellers' buyer behaviour has received limited attention. Therefore, the purpose of this research is to present the potential to develop and promote cultural tourism with the use of comments from TripAdvisor, who are the immediate consumers of the tourist product.

RESEARCH METHODOLOGY

This study attempted to explore the impact of online travel communities in TripAdvisor in the decision making for developing cultural tourism in Bahrain. The nature of the study demanded that a qualitative approach be used. Secondary data of visitors' reviews from Tripadvisor.com has been collected. TripAdvisor is a company established by Expedia in 2000 and has been chosen for this study due to its large scale of coverage on travel destinations and accommodation reviews (Twumasi & Adu-Gyamfi, 2013). TripAdvisor has been chosen as it is considered to be amongst the most successful social networking communities in tourism, and provides a powerful platform for interaction between peers (Buhalis & Law, 2008). On Sunday 6th April 2014, a review of the website showed 563 topics under the Bahrain Travel Forum section available at http://www.tripadvisor. com/ShowForum-g293996-i3669-Bahrain.html. At the same time there were 1.507 forum posts from members who are knowledgeable about the destination. From Sunday 6th until Sunday 13th April 2014, under the section 'Things to do in Manama', there were 19 attractions identified and in total 192 reviews (see Table 2). Fifty (50) cases were purposively selected and analysed for the study. According to Twumasi & Adu-Gyamfi (2013, p.106) 'the obstructive measures used in the data collection are frequently used by sociologists and psychologists in their studies of group behaviours and interactions'. Instead of actually interviewing all these people, the researchers observed the participants behavior and used raw data of the communication that people produced.

Content analysis was performed to the data, on the complaints, advice and reviews from people using the website. The grounded theory approach was used with keywords analysis, which provided four main categories experience, facilities, customer service and recommend the attraction. Content analysis is used for this study, as it 'allows researchers to study written, visual, or aural data to understand what they mean to people and what information is conveyed' (Hvass & Munar, 2012, p.96). Content analysis of social media or travel is used by other studies such as Wenger (2008) who analysed the content of blog postings and Xiang & Gretzel (2010) who studied social media and its role as an information travel search. All the postings were read and their content was analysed to identify the key themes that emerged in the reviews. Firstly the overall evaluation of the site was identified and then the main themes that emerged were the facilities, the service, the additional information (i.e. brochures) and directions. All were evaluated and discussed as follows.

RESULTS AND DISCUSSION

Description of the Sample

The characteristics of the individuals that provide reviews on TripAdvisor are important in order to understand their decision making process and their background. Prior to analyzing the data, the researchers explored the characteristics of the participants. According to Um & Crompton (1997) the travellers' characteristics influence their decision making process and they are widely used to explain and predict their destination choice. These characteristics are mainly socio-demographic including age, education, income and marital status, as well as psychological, for example whether those with low income are less likely to pursue travel arrangement involving expensive airfares and hotels than those who are more worthy.

For the purpose of this study, pre-determined variables designed by TripAdvisor were used, which included the location, the self-description of the members, their travel style, when they are travelling, their age and gender. In addition, the final participants were chosen based on the date (the most recent, from November 2013 until April 2014) they posted their reviews in order to have the most updated data. The majority of the participants did not meet all the above mentioned criteria, therefore the researchers decided to include those reviews from people who met the following criteria gender, age, location and time of posting the review as shown in Table 3.

Most of the participants were male (76%) and 24% were female, between the age of 10-25 (66%), from the UK, US, UAE and Saudi Arabia, as most of the visitors in Bahrain are from neighbouring countries (Wells, 2011). The sample characteristics also showed evidence that there are no geographical boundaries of online communities, members are from all over the world who visit the site to comment, seek advice, share travel information and purchase travel products and services. In addition, these demographics were in line with Buhalis' (2003) claim that 78% of worldwide internet users are in USA and UK.

The Impact of Social Networking Site Reviews on TripAdvisor on Cultural Tourism in Bahrain

Cultural heritage tourism is defined as "a form of tourism that highlights the cultural heritage and

Table 3. The characteristics of Bahrain forum sample members (n=50)

Variables Used	N=50	%
Gender		
Male	38	76
Female	12	24
Age		
20-25	33	66
26-35	11	22
36-50	3	6
50+	3	6
Location		
UK	12	24
USA	13	26
Saudi Arabia	13	26
UAE	9	18
Other	3	6
Time of Posting		
March 2014	24	48
April 2014	26	52

artistic aspects of a destination or experiences and activities for tourism" (Douglas, Douglas & Derrett, 2001, p.17). The participants in the study provided reviews on various cultural attractions and events in Bahrain (Table 4).

The attractions that mainly refer to sports tourism i.e. Bahrain International Circuit or entertainment i.e. Wahoo Waterpark were not included in the study as they do not form part of cultural tourism as per the definition provided above. The reviews of the above cultural and heritage attrac-

tions in Bahrain provide adequate data on the sites and on visitors' views on the availability, opening hours, customer service, available information and overall experience, as well as whether they recommend the attraction.

Most of the participants in the study commented on the availability of tourism attractions in Bahrain. They claimed that there are few to very little available attractions, and even less cultural attractions. This indicates that there should be more sightseeing developed in the country. In addition, they suggested that there are limited food and beverage facilities, and where available they do not have adequate service. They positively however, commented on the quality of the food. In reference to the facility itself, the comments varied. For some attractions like the Al-Fatih Mosque, the Bahrain National Museum and the Ahmed Al Fateh Islamic Center, the comments were encouraging as they commented very well on the building and the exhibits. For other the comments were very negative for example Bab Al Bahrain souq were people were not happy and satisfied with the planning, buildings and atmosphere. They found the place too crowded and busy. One reviewer stated that "the Bab el Bahrain really isn't a proper souk. All the shops are housed in a modern shopping arcade'. Another also added that 'the narrow alleys of the souk behind the Gateway to Bahrain is overcrowded".

Moreover, all the participants commented negatively to the available printed material on the sites. There is limited information on some sites, and in other cases there is no information, hence the tourists had to wander around and asked local people about the location of the attraction or to find some relevant information, although it was mentioned on the Ministry of culture website. More specifically, one of the reviewers said:

Table 4. Cultural, heritage, and leisure sites in TripAdvisor (Bahrain)

Type of Attraction/Event	No. of Reviews (Total= 1238)	No. of Reviews Chosen for the Study (N=50)
Cultural and Heritage Sites		
Al-Fatih Mosque	191	12
Qalat Al Bahrain	167	5
Ahmed Al Fateh Islamic Center	4	1
Ad Diraz Temple	2	1
Bahrain National Museum	215	11
Beit Al Qur'an	20	2
Bab al Bahrain Souk	120	8
Mohammed Bin Faris House of Sout Music	1	1
Tree of Life	121	6
Oil Museum and First Oil Well	4	1
Museum of Pearl Diving	2	1
Bait Shaikh Salman Historic Palace	1	1
Leisure Attractions		
Wahoo Water Park	65	0
Al Dar Islands Bahrain	57	0
Adhari Park	29	0
Bahrain International Circuit	126	0
Lost Paradise of Dilmun Water Park	93	0
Viva Karting Bahrain	19	0
Wahoo Waterpark	1	0

Source: TripAdvisor (2014).

This venue is situated in Muharraq; the best way to locate it is to ask around -- but bear in mind that you may have to approach several people before you find it, as many locals didn't know it when we enquired, although it's in the middle of the neighbourhood. It seems to be an old building in which a new performance space has been built.

Research shows that negative reviews have a stronger effect on consumers (East, Hammond & Lomax, 2008).

Nevertheless, the majority of the reviewers commented positively on the customer service and the friendliness of staff, as well as on the opportunity to learn a lot about the culture, the history of Bahrain and the attraction itself. For example one of the reviewers stated about Al-Fatih Mosque:

They were very welcoming and our tour guide was wonderful. We were helped to learn about Islam in a very non-threatening way and got to learn about their beliefs and faith!

Another added:

I've been on several mosque tours and while this mosque may not be the most beautiful or the biggest, it certainly had the nicest people running the tours.

Whereas one more stated:

Exceptional tour with the best staff. Very friendly and amazing experience.

Finally, most of the reviewers claimed that the majority of the attractions were a good experience for the whole family. All were happy that they were allowed to take videos and pictures. White (2010) suggests that photos taken by tourists and posted on social networks such as Facebook generate interest to viewers and can easily become part of the viewer's travel plans. Many have challenged the credibility of such sources, however research shows that they can be reliable tools for evaluation (Mack, Blose & Pan, 2008). Table 5 exhibits the reviewers' overall evaluation of the attractions used for the purpose of this study.

It is evident from the above that the reviewers rated the overall experience as excellent, very good and in some cases average. The attractions that were not well evaluated were Ad Diraz temple, the Museum of Pearl Diving and the Oil Museum, however the comments were very limited to provide a significant view.

Table 5. Evaluation of sites

N	Site	Excellent	Very Good	Average	Poor	Terrible
191	Al-Fatih Mosque	106	65	16	3	1
215	Bahrain National Museum	99	94	15	5	2
167	Qalat Al Bahrain	71	72	20	4	0
20	Beit Al Qur'an	10	8	2	0	0
120	Bab al Bahrain Souk	32	46	29	9	4
4	Ahmed Al Fateh Islamic Center	2	1	1	0	0
1	Mohammed Bin Faris House of Sout Music	0	0	0	0	0
121	Tree of Life	9	24	50	25	13
4	Oil Museum and First Oil Well	1	2	0	1	0
2	Museum of Pearl Diving	0	0	2	0	0
2	Ad Diraz Temple	0	0	1	0	1
1	Bait Shaikh Salman Historic Palace	0	0	0	0	0

Source: TripAdvisor (2014).

Bahrain has been promoted as a cultural venue in the Arabian Gulf, and there has been an increased investment in culture in the region (Alpen Capital, 2011). However, there are many challenges as they have been identified in the above. Although, "the region's challenge now is to drive the next wave of innovation that emphasizes, celebrates and promotes Middle Eastern cultures, heritage and tradition" (GlobalFutures & Foresight, 2007, p.3), the authorities should consider the above comments not only for the promotion of Bahrain as a cultural destination, but also for the future development of tourism in the country.

Despite attempts to revitalize tourism growth in Bahrain, there are several challenges that may arise in the future. As Bahrain is trying to market itself as a luxury destination and diversify the pool of tourists it attracts, it is necessary to conduct a thorough branding analysis in order to assess the impact of initiatives undertaken in recent years. In addition, in the context of ever-growing competition, place marketing creates "uniqueness in order to improve the competitive position of the place marketed" (Kavaratzis & Ashworth, 2010, p.2). As Dowling (2001) proposes destinations should focus on developing their image and reputation. Consequently, destinations such as Bahrain that are able to attract tourism and foreign investments, should consider consumers' views on the tourist product, and according to Milano, Baggio & Piattelli (2011) social media could add to the dissemination of information on cultural and other tourism attractions and products. Chua & Banerjee (2013) similarly support this view and claim that "TripAdvisor is recognized as an important information source among users for travel planning" (p.3).

CONCLUSION

This chapter contributes to the current literature on the use of social media (TripAdvisor) on cultural tourism planning and development. This study shows that communication via social media can be effective for tourism destinations and cultural tourism. Online communities have strong influence on consumer behavior, and consequently on the image of the attraction or the destination. Websites like TripAdvisor can be a valuable monitoring medium to explore the views of visitors to various attractions. If these reviews are monitored effectively they provide reliable information on the cultural attractions and the potential for further development of cultural tourism in Bahrain. Advantages and challenges are usually discussed within these reviews providing an overview of the performance of the attractions and potential comments and ideas may be provided to enhance the tourist product and services. Tourism companies and other organisations are faced with new consumers who can easily find information on the product or the destination, and they can share their views, make comments and provide suggestions in an informal collaborative way, increasing their influence to other consumers' decision-making. All tourism businesses should identify the need to implement strategies and tools using UGC to incorporate new technologies to enrich their presence online and enhance their image and reputation. The information provided on the destinations or the attractions' websites should have an extensive representation of photos and graphics in order to provide a tangible image or experience to potential visitors. This tangible experience may contribute to the image of the cultural sites and hence to further development of this form of tourism in the country.

The findings suggest that there are not many cultural attractions available in Bahrain. Those that exist should be further developed to enhance the tourist experience. Further information should be provided on the cultural attractions, more photos and videos, travel maps and other multimedia elements should be added to provide potential visitors with further information. A successful website should consider customer's interest and preferences in order for this information to provide personalized communication, services and adaptation to the development of cultural tourism.

In addition, it is important to realize the potential of tourism and the need for collaboration among tourism agencies and authorities as well as for collaboration with other countries with mature tourism sectors. Bahrain is not the only country looking for a sound strategy to attract a steady flow of international leisure tourists in the coming years. The search for a right balance and a variety of activities is essential to keep up with the competition of Bahrain's neighbors. The branding or rebranding of tourism and cultural tourism in the country is a complex process, and depends on the country's unique political, economic and social conditions. As a result the local authorities, including the Ministry of Culture, and the travel community should consider the reviews available on TripAdvisor in reference to the development of cultural attractions. Social media and TripAdvisor are potential tools to shape behaviours, influence the travel decision and can be trusted for decision making especially in planning and developing tourism products. By using the Internet as a marketing tool, tourism organisations in Bahrain may gain a distinct advantage in customer retention, they can create themes and routes that interest this particular segment and increase the tourism demand in the country.

LIMITATIONS OF RESEARCH

A few limitations were identified in this research. This study is of an exploratory nature and the results cannot be generalized without further studies on larger samples. The convenience sampling method used to select the participants may not be representative of the population. However, the chosen sample served the purpose of this paper. The secondary data is collected from TripAdvisor only for Bahrain and may be considered as not reliable and trustworthy. Further research

can extended to other travel websites and refer to other attractions for a more complete view. Finally, other factors may be considered such as location, language, city or country of origin to make further analysis on the reviews.

REFERENCES

Alexander, B., & Levine, A. (2008). Web 2.0 storytelling: Emergence of a new genre. *EDUCAUSE Review*, *43*(6), 40–56.

Alpen Capital. (2011). *GCC hospitality industry*. Retrieved April 5, 2014, from http://www.alpencapital.com/ downloads/GCC-Hospitality-Report-13-April-%202011.pdf

Amado, F. R. (2011). *Cultural master plan for Bahrain: Parametric models in urban planning*. Retrieved April 9, 2014, from https://fenix.tecnico.ulisboa.pt/downloadFile/395142732371/Resumo.pdf

Assael, H. (2003). *Consumer behavior: A strategic approach*. Boston: Houghton Mifflin.

Astburry, M. (2011). Hotel booking through facebook? *Daily Planet Dispatch*. Retrieved April 15, 2014, from http://dailyplanetdispatch.com/?p=7629

Au, A. (2010). *Adoption of web 2.0 by tourism businesses in NSW (research reports)*. Sydney: Tourism New South Wales. Retrieved April 26, 2014, from http://corporate.tourism.nsw.gov.au/Sites/SiteID6/objLib40/Adoption-of-Web%20 2Jan10.pdf

Bahrain Economic Development Board. (2009). *Tourism sector performance*. Manama: BEDB. Retrieved March 22, 2014, from http://www.bahrainedb.com/uploadedFiles/Bahraincom/Bahrain-ForBusiness/11.%20AER%20-%20Articles%20 -20Tourism%20Sector%20Performance.pdf

Balakrishnan, M. S. (2008). Dubai a star in the East: A case study in strategic destination branding. *Journal of Place Management and Development, 1*(1), 62–91.

Bronner, R., De Ridder, J. A., Neijens, P. C., & Willemsen, L. M. (2011). Highly recommended! The content characteristics and perceived usefulness of online consumer reviews. *Journal of Computer-Mediated Communication, 17*(1), 19–8. doi:10.1111/j.1083-6101.2011.01551.x

Bryer, T. A., & Zavattaro, S. M. (2011). Social media and public administration. *Administrative Theory & Praxis, 33*(3), 325–340. doi:10.2753/ATP1084-1806330301

Buhalis, D. (2003). *Etourism: Information technologies for strategic tourism management.* Harlow, UK: Prentice Hall.

Buhalis, D., & Law, R. (2008). Progress in information technology and tourism management: 20 years on and 10 years after the Internet – The state of eTourism research. *Tourism Management, 29*(4), 609–623. doi:10.1016/j.tourman.2008.01.005

Burgess, S., Sellitto, C., & Karanasios, S. (Eds.). (2009). *Effective web presence solutions for small businesses: Strategies for successful implementation.* Hershey, PA: Information Science Reference. doi:10.4018/978-1-60566-224-4

Chen, H., Cheung, M. Y., Luo, C., & Sia, C. L. (2009). Credibility of electronic word-of-mouth: Information and normative determinants of online consumer recommendations. *International Journal of Electronic Commerce, 13*(4), 9–8. doi:10.2753/JEC1086-4415130402

Chua, A. Y. K., & Banerjee, S. (2013). Reliability of reviews on the internet: The case of TripAdvisor. In *Proceedings of the World Congress on Engineering and Computer Science.* San Francisco: WCECS.

Chung, J. Y., & Buhalis, D. (2008). Web 2.0: A study of online travel community. In P. O. Connor, W. Hopken, & U. Gretzel (Eds.), *Information and communication technologies in tourism* (pp. 70–81). New York: Springer.

Cobb, J. (2010). *Learning 2.0 for associations.* Tagoras. Retrieved April 15, 2014, from http://www.tagoras.com/docs/Learning-20-Associations-2ed.pdf

Cochrane, K. (2011, 25 January). Why TripAdvisor is getting bad review. *The Guardian.* Retrieved from http://www.theguardian.com/uk

Cooper, C. (2012). *Essentials of tourism.* Harlow, UK: FT – Prentice Hall.

Danis, C., Bailey, M., Christensen, J., Ellis, J., Erickson, T., Farrell, R., & Kellogg, W. (2009). Mobile applications for the next billions: A social computing application and a perspective on sustainability. In *Proceedings of the 2nd Workshop on Innovative Mobile Technology and Services for Developing Countries* (IMTS – DC 09). Kampala, Uganda: Academic Press.

Dellarocas, S. (2003). The digitization of word of mouth: Promise and challenge of online feedback mechanisms. *Management Science, 49*(10), 1407–1424. doi:10.1287/mnsc.49.10.1407.17308

Doctorow, C., Dornfest, R., Johnson, S., Powers, S., Trott, B., & Trott, M. (2002). *Essential blogging: Selecting and using weblog tools.* Sebastopol, CA: O'Reilly.

Douglas, N., Douglas, N., & Derrett, R. (2001). *Special interest tourism: Context and cases.* New York: John Wiley & Sons.

Dowling, G. (2001). *Creating corporate reputations.* New York: Oxford University Press.

East, R., Hammond, K., & Lomax, W. (2008). Measuring the impact of positive and negative word of mouth on brand purchase probability. *International Journal of Research in Marketing*, *25*(3), 215–224. doi:10.1016/j.ijresmar.2008.04.001

Ebersbach, A., Glaser, M., & Heigl, R. (2006). *Wiki: Web collaboration*. Springer-Verlag Berlin Heidelberg.

Fotis, J., Buhalis, D., & Rossides, N. (2012). Social media use and impact during the holiday travel planning process. In M. Fuchs, F. Ricci, & L. Cantoni (Eds.), *Information and communication technologies in tourism* (pp. 13–24). Vienna: SpringerVerlag. doi:10.1007/978-3-7091-1142-0_2

Hennig-Thurau, T., & Walsh, G. (2003). Electronic word of mouth: Motives for and consequences of reading customer articulations on the internet. *International Journal of Electronic Commerce*, *8*(2), 51–74.

Hvass, K. A., & Munar, A. M. (2012). The takeoff of social media in tourism. *Journal of Vacation Marketing*, *18*(2), 93–103. doi:10.1177/1356766711435978

Inversinni, A., & Buhalis, D. (2009). Information convergence in the long trail: The case of tourism destination information. In W. Hopken, U. Gretzel & R. Law (Eds.), *Information and communication technology in tourism: Proceedings of the international conference in Lugano, Switzerland* (pp. 381-392). Wien: Springer.

Junco, R., Heiberger, G., & Loken, E. (2011). The effect of Twitter on college student engagement and grades. *Journal of Computer Assisted Learning*, *27*(2), 119–132. doi:10.1111/j.1365-2729.2010.00387.x

Kaplan, A., & Haenlein, M. (2010). Users of the world, unite! The challenges and opportunities of social media. *Business Horizons*, *53*(1), 59–68. doi:10.1016/j.bushor.2009.09.003

Karolak, M. (2012). Tourism in Bahrain: A continuous search for economic development and for preservation of cultural heritage. In *Proceedings of the 2012 Gulf Studies Conference*. Retrieved March 26, 2014 from http://www.academia.edu/1821165/Tourism_in_Bahrain_A_Continuous_Search_for_Economic_Development_and_for_Preservation_of_Cultural_Heritage

Kavaratzis, M., & Ashworth, G. J. (2010). Place branding: Where do we stand? In G. J. Ashworth & M. Kavaratzis (Eds.), *Towards effective place brand management: Branding European cities and regions and regions, Cheltenham, UK and Northampton* (pp. 1–14). Edward Elgar. doi:10.4337/9781849806398.00007

Knowles, T., Diamantis, D., & El-Mourhabi, J. B. (2004). *The globalization of tourism and hospitality: A strategic perspective* (2nd ed.). Toronto: Thomson.

Law, R., Leung, R., & Buhalis, D. (2014). Information technology application in hospitality and tourism: A review of publications from 2005 to 2007. *Journal of Travel & Tourism Marketing*, *26*(5), 599–623.

Lee, H., Law, R., & Murphy, J. (2011). Helpful reviewers in TripAdvisor, an online travel community. *Journal of Travel & Tourism Marketing*, *28*(7), 675–687. doi:10.1080/10548408.2011.611739

Lindstrom, P. (2007). *Securing "web 2.0" technologies*. Midvale, UT: Burton Group EDUCAUSE Center for Applied Research.

Litvin, S. W., Goldsmith, R. E., & Pan, B. (2008). Electronic word-of-mouth in hospitality and tourism management. *Tourism Management*, *29*(3), 458–468. doi:10.1016/j.tourman.2007.05.011

Mack, R., Blose, J., & Pan, B. (2008). Believe it or not: Credibility of blogs in tourism. *Journal of Vacation Marketing*, *14*(2), 133–144. doi:10.1177/1356766707087521

Marchiori, E., Dedekind, C., & Cantoni, L. (2010). Applying a conceptual framework to analyse online reputation of tourist destinations. In U. Gretzel, R. Law, & M. Fuchs (Eds.), *Information and communication technologies in tourism: Proceedings of the international conference in Lugano, Switzerland* (pp. 321-332). Wien: Springer.

Mergel, I., Schweik, C., & Fountain, J. (2009). *The transformational effect of web 2.0 technologies on government*. Social Science Research Network. Retrieved April 2, 2014, from http://ssrn.com/abstract=1412796

Miguens, J., Baggio, R., & Costa, C. (2008). Social media and tourism destinations: TripAdvisor case study. In *Proceedings of the IASK Advances in Tourism Research 2008*. Aveiro: ATR.

Milano, R., Baggio, R., & Piattelli, R. (2011). The effects of online social media on tourism websites. In *Proceedings of the 18th International Conference on Information Technology and Travel and Tourism*. Innsbruck, UK: Enter. doi:10.1007/978-3-7091-0503-0_38

Millen, D., Feinberg, J., & Kerr, B. (2005). Social bookmarking in the enterprise. *Queue*, *3*(9), 28–35. doi:10.1145/1105664.1105676

O'Reilly, T. (2008). *Why dell.com (was) more Enterprise 2.0 than Dell IdeaStorm*. Retrieved March 23, 2014, from http://radar.oreilly.com/2008/09/why-dell-dot-com-is-more-enterprise.html

Scorrano, P. (2011). The 2.0 marketing strategies for wine tourism destinations of excellence. *The China Business Review*, *10*(10), 948–960.

Sigala, M. (2010). eCRM 2.0 applications and trends: The use and perceptions of Greek tourism firms of social networks and intelligence. *Computers in Human Behavior*, *27*(2), 655–661. doi:10.1016/j.chb.2010.03.007

Stead, L. A. (2012). How do consumer reviews on TripAdvisor affect consumer decision making when booking an international hotel. *Hospitality Management Review Student Journal at Sheffield Hallam University*, 2. Retrieved March 27, 2014, from http://research.shu.ac.uk/domino/index.php/HMJ/article/view/21/36

Stewart, D. W., & Pavlov, P. A. (2002). From consumer response to active consumer: Measuring the effectiveness of interactive media. *Journal of the Academy of Marketing Science*, *4*(30), 376–396. doi:10.1177/009207002236912

Twumasi, A., & Adu-Gyami, K. (2013). The impact of social networking sites on the purchasing behaviours of online travel community members. *Information and Knowledge Management*, *3*(11), 105–111.

Um, S., & Crompton, J. L. (1997). Development of pleasure travel attitude dimensions. *Annals of Tourism Research*, *18*, 374–378.

Wang, Y., & Fesenmaier, D. R. (2002). Defining the virtual tourist community: Implications for tourism marketing. *Tourism Management*, *23*(4), 407–417. doi:10.1016/S0261-5177(01)00093-0

Wells, R. (2011). Reopening the door to tourism post Arab Spring. *Middle East*, 51.

Wenger, A. (2008). Analysis of travel bloggers' characteristics and their communication about Austria as tourism destination. *Journal of Vacation Marketing*, *14*(2), 169–176. doi:10.1177/1356766707087525

White, L. (2010). Facebook, friends and photos: A snapshot into social networking for generating travel ideas. In N. Sharda (Ed.), *Tourism informatics: Visual travel recommender systems, social communities, and user interface design*. Hershey, PA: IGI Global. doi:10.4018/978-1-60566-818-5.ch007

WTTC. (2011). *Travel & tourism 2011*. World Travel & Tourism Council. Retrieved March 27, 2014, from http://www.wttc.org/site_media/uploads/downloads/traveltourism2011.pdf

Xiang, Z., & Gretzel, U. (2010). Role of social media in online travel information search. *Tourism Management*, *31*(2), 179–188. doi:10.1016/j.tourman.2009.02.016

Yoo, K. H., Gretzel, U., & Zach, F. (2011). Travel opinion leaders and seekers. In R. Law, M. Fuchs, & F. Ricci (Eds.), *Information and communication technologies in tourism* (pp. 525–535). Vienna: SpringerVerlag.

Zimmer, M. (2008). Preface: Critical perspectives on web 2.0. *First Monday*, *13*(3). doi:10.5210/fm.v13i3.2137

KEY TERMS AND DEFINITIONS

Blog: A virtual log, commonly used for sharing ideas.

Cultural Heritage Tourism: Tourism that highlights the cultural heritage and artistic aspects of a destination.

Social Media: Web 2.0 web sites and applications.

Tag: A keyword that refers to a digital object.

Trip Advisor: Travel Web 2.0 website providing reviews of travel-related content.

Web 2.0: A conglomeration of folksonomies and syndication, wikis and mashups, social networks.

Wiki: A webpage or a set of web pages that can be edited by anyone.

Chapter 13
Business Networks and Public Procurement in Turkey

Tuba Bircan
Bahçeşehir University, Turkey

Esra Çeviker-Gürakar
Okan University, Turkey

ABSTRACT

In this chapter, we quantitatively analyze the role of network membership in the performance of firms within the public procurement market in Turkey. We use a unique public procurement dataset of all high-value public procurement contracts—those with a contract value worth over TL 1,000,000—awarded between 2005 and 2010. We consider two types of networks: (1) Internet-based procurement-specific networks and (2) business networks established through business associations. Internet-based procurement-specific business networks provide their members with a wide range of procurement related services, access to critical resources, and timely information. Business associations help member firms establish a strong and unified presence, effectively protect their shared interests, and thus collectively influence governmental economic policies. The findings suggest that both types of network memberships are effective in winning public procurement contracts. There is also an overlap among network memberships, with 8.4% of contracts awarded to the firms that have membership in both networks.

INTRODUCTION

Public procurement comprises a substantial part of government spending in Turkey, where one-fourth of annual public spending goes to public procurement whose share in GDP is around 8.5%. Every year around 140,000 public procurement contracts are awarded to mainly small and medium enterprises (SMEs)[1] that make up 99.9% of total enterprises and 77.9% of total employment in the country[2]. Public procurement thus serves as a major tool in supporting the relatively fragile private sector firms, whose well-being is associated with the welfare of this considerable part of the society. Therefore, one major factor in analyzing the dynamics of the public procurement market, which is among the most important areas where the state and the private sector interact, is the mechanisms that affect the performance of firms in winning government procurement contracts.

DOI: 10.4018/978-1-4666-7401-1.ch013

With the emergence and spread of electronic-government reform plans and practices, information and communication technologies have appeared to be an important instrument used by the firms operating in the public procurement market in Turkey. For instance, the Turkish Public Procurement Law mandates advertising tender notices and requirements for auctions in the Public Procurement Bulletin, the official internet-based source of tender notices in Turkey. Moreover, several private, profit-seeking, internet-based establishments have been formed to provide the members with more opportunities through various services that help them in their task of winning procurement auctions. Firms in the public procurement market, which compete for higher shares in the market, pay an annual fee to these establishments in order to benefit from a wide range of services that provide them with up to date and detailed information about the market. The internet-based procurement-related establishments collect all information about legal changes and tender notices and make it available for their members. They classify the tender notices by city, sector and procuring entity. Moreover, they provide search engines where the member firms can search for certain tender notices. A subscriber, when logged in, can see the tender notices published after its last visit to the website. Email newsletters are also sent to network members according to their interests. In addition, they collect information on procurements, which are in progress and have not yet officially been published. They also provide 24/7 online-support. Finally, the network members interact with each other through the website for collaboration (e.g. forming consortiums to bid in specific auctions of high value procurements).

Yet, despite the fact that IT-based procurement-specific networks serve as an important tool for the member firms, a large number of firms in Turkey lack the necessary skills and infrastructure to follow all the developments in the procurement market. The reason is that adoption of the improve-

ments in the information and communication technologies by Turkey's firms, 99.9% of which are SMEs, is not at desired levels. A substantial portion of SMEs either does not have the necessary information technology infrastructure or do not have enough trained employees to conduct IT based activities. Moreover, 9% of SMEs do not have internet access.[3] Therefore a significant number of firms typically suffer from a lack of timely information.

Nevertheless, in Turkey, one-quarter of the high-value public procurement contracts are awarded to members of IT-based procurement-specific networks. These results indicate a positive relationship between increased ability to reach timely procurement-specific information and the performance of member firms in auction winning. Yet, the fact that the remaining three-quarters of contracts are awarded to the firms that do not invest in IT-based procurement-specific network activities raises the question of whether there are additional mechanisms that affect the public procurement auction outcomes in Turkey. To answer this question, we expand our analysis and examine the effect of business association membership on firms' performances in the public procurement market. On this stage of the study, we build our analysis on the relatively new literature on 'politically-connected firms' (PCF) that reveals various dynamics of state private sector relations. The literature on firms' political connections generally takes into account direct connections in which a firm's board member or shareholder is a former/current politician or has kinship/friendship with incumbent politicians.

The importance of social networks in easing entry to profitable markets and channeling the allocation of corporate credits or government procurement contracts to the firms with direct political connections is empirically proven for various countries[4]. As for the relationship between political connections and allocation of public procurement contracts, a recent paper by Goldman et.al. (2014) on the effect of direct political connections on the allocation of public procurement contracts in the US demonstrates the former is important in determining the allocation of the latter. Similarly, recent research indicates that direct political connections are important in determining the allocation of concession awards as well as firm performance in Turkey (Gunduz & Ozcan, 2014). Likewise, a recent project conducted by Gurakar and Bircan (in press) on the effect of direct political connections on public procurement auctions in the construction sector finds a positive relation between direct political connections and auction winning. Yet, these studies generally deal with large corporate firms and neglect the SMEs and the indirect connections to the ruling party established through institutionally structured networks of businesses (business associations). The ties between the SMEs under specific business associations and their influence in policy-making remain relatively under-researched.

In Turkey, where 99.9% of firms are SMEs, political connections are rather complex and hence cannot be analyzed solely by direct measures. Accordingly, we make an extension to the literature on 'politically-connected firms' and quantitatively analyze the link between indirect political connections established through business associations and the performance of the member firms in the public procurement market. To investigate the role of indirect political connections established through business associations in the allocation of public procurement contracts, we categorize the contract-awarded firms into groups based on their memberships in business associations. Some of these business associations explicitly state their support to the government, whereas others are not known to have any harmonic relations with the ruling party. This information helps us to explore the value of political connections in auction outcomes through our analyses of the performances of the politically-connected and non-connected business networks. To do so, we

analyze the matches between the winning firms and their network membership appearances (connected vs. non-connected) in order to detect

1. The effect of indirect political affiliations on the allocation of government procurement contracts;
2. The effect of exclusion from a political network on the performance of firms that are members of non-connected business associations.

Furthermore, in order to analyze the value of political connections we also use legal changes in the Public Procurement Law (PPL) that increase discretion in awarding contracts. This is important for the purpose of this study as the relationship between the use of legal changes and the dynamics in political affiliation and auction winning may be a sign of the extent of the business associations' success in influencing policy making. This also lets us test the argument that the so-called connected association member firms collectively put pressure on the government to create opportunity spaces via certain measures that keep them out of the scope of the PPL[5].

Accordingly, for our quantitative analysis, we use three types of datasets:

1. A dataset that contains information about IT-based procurement-specific network membership with around seventeen thousand members in total;
2. A business network membership dataset that contains four different business associations with more than fifty thousand member firms in total; and
3. A unique public procurement dataset of all high-value public procurement contracts (around forty-one thousand contracts) – that are worth above 1.000.000 Turkish Liras (TL) – awarded between 2005 and 2010.

The public procurement dataset has detailed information on all procuring institutions (such as the Ministries and the Municipalities); firm names that are awarded with a public procurement contract; auction types (goods, services, construction); auction methods (open tender, negotiated procedure, restricted procedure, procurements made under exemptions); as well as the economic details of procurements (estimated cost, lowest bid, highest bid, winning bid, the contract price). This dataset also lets us explore various legal amendments and how these legislations increased the range of contracts that fell outside the more transparent public procurement processes, which embrace the possibility of creating opportunity spaces for some privileged firms or protects them from extensive competition.

After examining the role of two different types of networks on auction outcomes separately, we dig deeper and examine the overlaps between the two types of membership. We scrutinize if the business associations that outperform in the procurement market are indeed the ones that use IT-based networks more widely compared to the less successful ones. Such an analysis would let us better interpret the functions of business associations. Do business associations, which we assume create opportunity spaces for member firms through political networks, also provide their members with information and support for IT-based network activities? Finally, we evaluate the performance of the firms that are not included in any of these networks.

Background

Business networks are considered to be operative and useful in influencing government economic policies. As Jackson (2008, 2010) stated, networks of relationships among various firms and political organizations affect research and development, patent activity, trade patterns, and political alliances. Business networks and the resources they allow the member firms to tap into, via creation

of a beneficial setting that are not available to non-members, can serve as a source of sustainable competitive advantage for the former (Gulati et al, 2000, p. 207). These apparent economic and social benefits stand as a major motivating factor particularly for small firms for joining business networks.

Prior studies suggested that social ties could be an essential instrument for the firms to access beneficial information and resources for their survival and success (Palmer 1983; Mizruchi & Stearns 1988; Geletkanycz & Hambrick 1997; Pfeffer & Salancik 2003). Likewise, "networks" and "networking" are found to be important entrepreneurial tools that contribute to the establishment, development and growth of firms (Shaw & Conway, 2000). A network is not limited to its actors but is also a set of relationships. Former studies presented several definitions of a "business network" such as "a set of connected exchange relationships between firms" (Forsgren & Johanson, 1992) or "a group of businesses joined in a voluntary formal organization of indefinite duration having as one primary goal the enhancement of business success" (Miller et al, 2007).

In this chapter we focus on "formal," contractual relationships among organizations and businesses. Formal business networks can be defined as "voluntary arrangements between firms aimed at providing a competitive advantage for the participants" (Coviello & Munro, 1995; Fuller-Love & Thomas, 2004, p. 245). A formal business-networking group can be defined as "a formal group formed to facilitate the networking of independent members so that relationship building and relationship maintenance can take place with a view to delivering mutually beneficial community and business focused outcomes through working together" (Lake, 2004, pp. 152-3). Formal business networks which are also called "business associations" are formed with the objective of fulfilling specific goals and increasing the effectiveness of the members' business activities. The fundamental aim of business associations is facilitating the success of member businesses by offering some worthy benefits for the members who are business owners. Business associations have been shown to help small businesses in achieving success (Greve & Salaff, 2003; Davis et al, 2006) through various ways and means. For instance, firms increased the ability to collectively act under the umbrella of business networks and therefore helped them to overcome particular constraints on their way to maximizing their interests. Moreover, joining business associations can bring numerous lasting benefits to members (Dennis Jr. & William, 2003), such as access to critical resources and timely information (Hollendsen, 1998; Floyd & Wooldridge, 1999; Johnson et al, 2005; Clarke et al, 2006), alliances (Håkansson & Snehota, 1995; Fuller-Love & Thomas, 2004) and internationalization (Coviello & McAuley, 1999).

BUSINES NETWORKS AND PUBLIC PROCUREMENT IN TURKEY

Business Associations in Turkey

For every available private sector division in Turkey, all established companies and corporations are required to register as members of "Turkish Union of Chambers and Commodity Exchanges" (TOBB), which gathers many organizations of the business world under its umbrella. Since its membership is obligatory for the firms without exception, TOBB is the country's highest legal entity representing the entire private sector. The union was founded in 1950 as an umbrella organization in Ankara. TOBB is a confederation of all local chambers of commerce, industry and maritime as well as commodity exchanges in Turkey. Both it and other civil associations of business attract entrepreneurs of various characteristics and affect economic and political courses. Yet the Chambers' role under TOBB as the predominant spokesman for business in Turkey is no longer valid, as the corporatist ways of interest representation came to

a halt by the establishment of independent business associations. Below we give short information about these associations.

TÜSİAD

The biggest and the most influential interest based voluntary business association in Turkey is the Turkish Industry and Business Association (TÜSİAD) which represents major holdings and capital groups. TÜSİAD, being the first business association in Turkey founded in 1971, is composed of the CEOs and Executives of the major industrial and service companies in Turkey, including those that are among global Fortune 500 companies. TÜSİAD was formed by 12 of Turkey's largest industrial entrepreneurs and managers. By the end of the 1970s its membership increased to 165 of Turkey's largest industrial and commercial concerns. Since TÜSİAD was a voluntary organization created outside the corporatist structure, the government had no legal obligation to consult with it. Nevertheless, as Barkey (1990, p.112) notes; "since its membership consisted of the richest business enterprises, no government could ignore it." Thus the government soon accepted TÜSİAD as a legitimate representative of a section of the private sector and the association became an active participant in formulating economic policy.

TÜSİAD members are not included in our quantitative analysis because they are large industrial corporations that rarely operate in the public procurement market. Rather they are active in auctions for privatization and concession awards such as country-wide electricity and natural gas production and distribution. Thus, we will analyze the auction-winning performances of the members of a SMEs business network – TÜRKONFED – that is organically linked to TÜSİAD.

Toward the end of 1980s, the emergence of a new middle-rich class, "conservative bourgeoisie", became notable as a result of the simultaneous rise of political Islam and the evolution of new industrial centers in Anatolia. In contrast with

Eurocentric and secular characteristics of the conventional middle-rich class of the Turkish Republic, the new business elite, originating from Anatolian towns, desired to assert their provincial identity and preserve their values and traditions. The new business class established its own business associations with the purpose of exploring new market opportunities and creating business partnership networks for their own clientele (Atlı, 2011). Then in the 1990s and 2000s foundations of new businessmen's associations were set up; with socially religious outlooks and economically liberal outlooks, MÜSİAD, ASKON and TUSKON, became gate-openers for the Turkish employers' arena which had been until then dominated by TÜSİAD.

MÜSİAD

As an alternative to TÜSİAD which represents the secular business elite, the Association of Independent Industrialists and Businessmen – Müstakil Sanayici ve İşadamları Derneği (MÜSİAD) – was founded in 1990 by religiously-devout entrepreneurs with ties to Prime Minister Özal or to the Islamist Necmettin Erbakan whose Welfare Party was briefly in power in 1997. MÜSİAD is an Islamic-oriented business association (see Buğra 1998, 1999, 2002; Çınar 2005; Keyman & Koyuncu 2004; Öniş 1997) and with its institutional public identity and the religiously conservative social group of large but mainly medium size enterprises that it represents, MÜSİAD is situated at the intersection of spheres of business associations and Islamic movements (Yankaya, 2009).

It currently has 66 branches with 143 contact points in 60 countries. According to figures provided on the association's website, MÜSİAD member-firms operate in each and every sector in the economy; in total, they produce 15% of the GDP and employ more than 1,500,000 people. Moreover, they also operate in the international market; their major import and export areas cover Europe, Central Asia, the Middle East and North Africa. As an interest group, its strength stems from the breadth of its social base; with headquarters in Istanbul, the association organizes more than 7,000 firms through its national structure of local branches all over Anatolia.

The founder/director of MÜSİAD Erol Yarar explicitly describes the conservative businessmen as the substantive and new "bourgeois" that directed the attention to the "new elite" and conservative business associations that they founded.

ASKON

As MÜSİAD grew as a business group, its alliance with AKP (governing Justice and Development Party) got stronger while its connections with Erbakan petered out. This fracture gave birth to a new and relatively more conservative business association that was affiliated to Necmettin Erbakan: ASKON. ASKON, which had parallel goals with MÜSİAD, was founded in 1998. Its name is a short for "Anatolian Lions Businessman Association". The association states the following as their main principles: integrity, respect for business ethics, freedom, opposition to extravagance, quality in production, fair distribution of income, and faithfulness (ASKON's publicity pamphlet, 1998). Several hundreds of MÜSİAD members – mainly comprised of small companies – left MÜSİAD to join ASKON, which counts more than 600 members today.

TUSKON

TUSKON, short for Confederation of Businessmen and Industrialists of Turkey, was formed in 2005 as a non-governmental and non-profit umbrella organization by 7 different regional business federations. TUSKON has 211 business associations and over 55,000 entrepreneurs, which makes it the largest union of employers in Turkey. Ninety percent of the TUSKON members are Small or Medium Establishments with fewer than 50 employees, though 100 of the 500 biggest Turkish companies are also TUSKON members.

As mentioned on the official website of the association, TUSKON defines its purpose as being a generous and rich resource-sharing organization, making full use of its experience and connections, which are invaluable for reaching success in international markets. What separates TUSKON from ASKON and MÜSİAD is its strength among Anatolian entrepreneurs. The absolute majority of TÜSİAD members are based in old industrial districts such as Istanbul, Ankara, and Adana, while more than fifty percent of MÜSİAD member firms are in the new industrial districts of Anatolia such as Konya, Mardin, and Kayseri. TUSKON has much fewer members from old industrial districts and more from eastern and southeastern Anatolia as well as the Black Sea Region.

To quote from an interview with the director of TUSKON, Rızanur Meral, "TUSKON is popular because we focus on the direct generation of business. In Anatolia, we have a strong production structure set up by the 'hacı babalar' (the older generation who have been on the haj pilgrimage), and now the 'kravatlı oğulları' (their western-tie-wearing sons) are keen to expand".

TÜRKONFED

TÜRKONFED (Turkish Enterprise and Business Confederation) was established in 2004 as a nation-wide confederation, representing 6 federations and 69 associations. Today, it represents 20 federations and 141 associations. It has over 11,000 members who create a business volume of over 208 billion USD annually. It was TÜSİAD who played a leading role in TÜRKONFED's establishment. Today, these two organizations conduct many projects in cooperation.

TÜRKONFED is known to have no political connections with the ruling party. The federation does not explicitly support the government. Quite the reverse, TÜRKONFED's constitution says: "Members cannot assign duties to active parliamentary deputies and public servants in their companies, subsidiaries, participations and companies in which they hold management positions; they cannot designate such persons to their management, audit or any other committee... Members and their organizations cannot manipulate their relations with political parties in line with their commercial interests and abstain from seeking personal or corporate interest through such relations. They maintain their neutrality and impartiality to political parties; they cannot take on active duties in political parties and enter into relations of seeking interest."

Operation of the Public Procurement Market in Turkey

In Turkey, 28 different public institutions, ranging from municipalities to health and education ministries, conduct procurement auctions and award contracts. Auctions are separated into three different categories with respect to type of procurement: goods, services, and construction work. The value shares of these three sectors in aggregate total are 32%, 33.2% and 34.3% respectively. In terms of yearly values, there is a significant rise in the share of the services sector from 28% in 2005 to 34.5% in 2010, while the share of goods decreased by 10%.

According to the Public Procurement Law (PPL), procurements can be made using five different methods: open auction, restricted procedure, negotiated procedure, direct procurement, and design contest.

The open procedure is the most widely used auction method. On average, three-quarters of all high-value procurements are made via open tender procedure. Yet, the PPL defines particular circumstances within which the procurement can be made under restricted procedure. Restricted procedure can be used if "open procedure is not applicable as the nature of the subject necessitates specialty and/or high technology and in procurement of works where estimated costs exceed the half of threshold value" (PPL, p.32). If the restricted procedure is determined as the procurement method, then the contracting authority carries out a pre-qualification evaluation in accordance with the qualification criteria defined in the law and invites only the firms that satisfy the criteria. Both the number and the value of contracts awarded under the restricted procedure quadrupled in 5 years, from 45 and TL 200 million to 165 and TL 871 million respectively.

The third procurement method is the negotiated procedure. Negotiated procedure is determined as the procurement method by law if

1. The estimated cost is below the pre-defined monetary limits;
2. "It is inevitable to conduct the tender procedures immediately, due to occurrence of specific events relating to defense and security";
3. Characteristics of the works, goods or services to be procured are so complex that it is impossible to define the technical and financial aspects clearly;
4. "It is inevitable to conduct the tender procedures immediately, due to unexpected and unforeseen events such as natural disasters, epidemics, risk of losing lives or properties or events that could not be predicted by the contracting authority."

One interesting aspect of this procurement method is that in 2008 a legal amendment was made to the PPL regarding removal of publicity requirements for such procurements. Accordingly, contracting entities are given the authority to invite a minimum of three firms without any publication of a notice in cases defined in (1), (2) and (4). The number of contracts awarded under the negotiated procedure and their value share in total public procurement jumped from 309 and

5% (TL 1.8 billion) in 2005 to 630 and 10% (TL 4.3 billion) in 2008. Later both the number and the value of contracts decreased to 451 and TL 2.4 billion in 2010.

The fourth procurement method is direct buying, for which advertising or establishing a tender commission or evaluation of qualification requirements is not required. This is a method used mostly for low-value procurements and hence comprises a negligible share in total high value public procurement, both in terms of value (0.004%) and the number of contracts awarded (0.03%).[6]

Finally, particular procurements are made under the article that defines the "exceptions" (Article 3). Article 3 does not define a procurement method but describes numerous types of procurements that shall be exempted from the PPL and thus the regulation of the PPA. The most important paragraph in Article 3 is Paragraph-G, which states that procurements whose estimated costs and contract prices do not exceed the threshold level stated in the law are exempted from the PPL. The importance of paragraph 3-G stems from the fact that it is the procuring entities which are involved, which calculate the estimated cost, and hence the process can well be exploited by some state bureaucrats and connected firms. Indeed, procurements made under the "exceptions" article increased both in number of contracts awarded and the yearly total values. The number of contracts awarded via this exception procedure increased threefold – from 395 in 2005 to 1177 in 2010. The value share of such procurements in total high-value procurement doubled from 6.6% in 2005 to 13.8% in 2010. This increase particularly comes from the rise in procurements made under 3-G. The number of contracts awarded under 3-G increased from 325 to 906 and their value share in total high-value procurement almost doubled from 5.5% to 10.5%.

ANALYSIS AND RESULTS

Looking at the public procurement dataset, the aggregate total of high-value government procurement is over TL 240 billion for the period between 2005 and 2010. As seen in Figure 1, the yearly total of high-value procurements increases substantially during the sample period showing that the state-private sector relationship gets gradually more extensive over time. It rises about 45% – from TL 34.3 billion in 2005 to TL 48.5 billion in 2010. Similarly, the number of high-value procurement contracts increases from 5368 in 2005 to 8738 in 2010. The increase in the number of high-value contracts indicates that the government creates opportunity spaces for the private sector via offering increasingly more projects (See Figure 1).

On average, business association member firms get 14% of all high-value procurement contracts. The 14% share is indeed very high, given that the high value procurements account for over two-thirds of all procurements. Regarding the member firms' performance over time, Figure 2 illustrates that their share in total procurement gradually

increased from 13.2% (TL 4.5 billion) in 2005 to 15% (TL 7.3 billion) in 2010. This trend is similar for the number of contracts awarded as well. The members of business associations increased their share in total number of contracts awarded from 11% (595 contracts) to 12.7% (1112 contracts) over the sample period (See Figure 2).

The bulk of the above-mentioned shares go to the members of business associations that explicitly state their support for the government. Figure 3 demonstrates that politically-connected firms get 12.7% of the total share that business associations get, whereas the non-connected associations' share is only 1.3%. The yearly performance growth of business associations is also attributed to politically-connected associations. Politically non-connected association, TÜRKONFED, could increase its share by only 0.2% over the period. Thus, politically-connected associations' shares in total high value procurements and their yearly performance are a sign of the positive effect of membership to a politically-connected business network on firms' performance in the public procurement market (See Figure 3).

Figure 1. Yearly total of high-value procurements

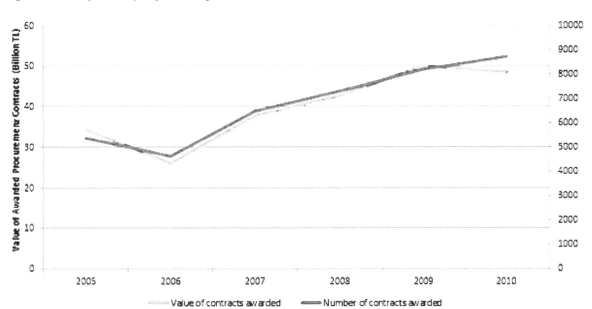

Figure 2. Share of business associations members in public procurement

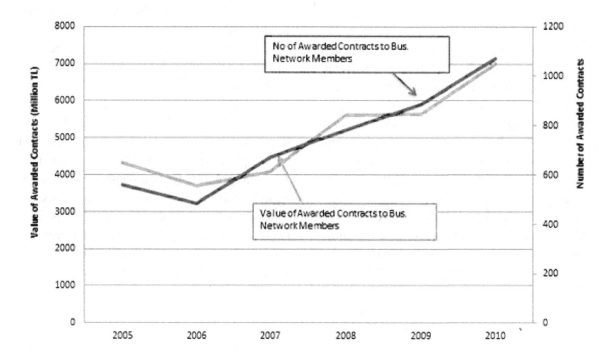

Figure 3. Politically-connected vs. non-connected firms

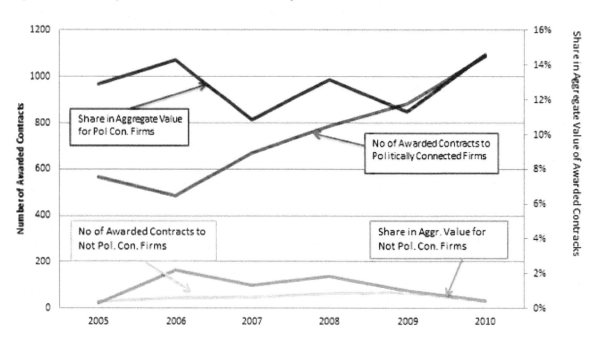

Nevertheless, politically-connected business associations not only provide their members with a strong and unified presence and thus an opportunity to effectively express themselves through political networks, but also support them to invest in and better exploit IT-based activities. As Figure 4 demonstrates politically-connected networks are more successful in using IT-based procurement networks compare to the non-connected ones.

As seen in Figure 5 and Figure 6, for the procurement methods, association members get 13.7%, 11%, 11.1% and 14.2% of high-value procurements made under open, restricted, negotiated procedures and the procurements made under the "exceptions" article respectively. Politically-connected associations' members substantially increased their share in total number of high-value contracts awarded under the restricted procedure from less than 1% to 3.6%. As indicated in Figure 6, their share in aggregate value also rose from 2.2% (TL 70 million) to 3.8% (TL 120 million). For the procurements made under the negotiated procedure, associations' shares in total value

increased from 1% to 2.6%. This rise owes itself particularly to the legal amendment of 2008 that removed the publicity requirement for procurements made under the negotiated procedure. Interestingly, around 65% of all high-value procurements made under the negotiated procedure were conducted after this legal amendment was put into place. Politically-connected associations' performances in open auctions also rose during the sample period, indicating that formal channels work also in more transparent procurement processes. While the number of high-value contracts awarded to these association members doubled during the sample period, the share of the member firms in total value of procurement made with open auction rose from 1.8% (TL 3.3 billion) in 2005 to 3.2% (TL 5.8 billion) in 2010.

In terms of procurements made under the "exceptions" article, politically-connected association members managed to increase their share in total number of contracts from a bare 0.8% in 2005 to 2.6% in 2010. The share of business association members in total value of such procurements also

Figure 4. Internet-based procurement network membership by business associations

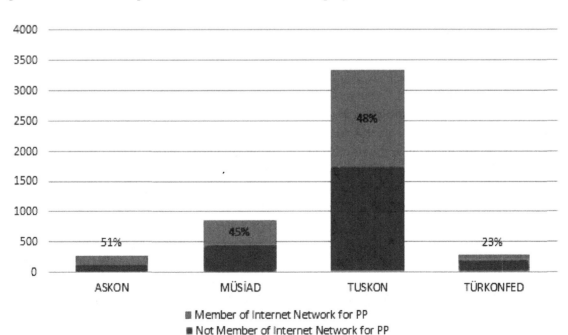

Figure 5. Amount of procurements going to the members of the politically connected associations (by procurement method)

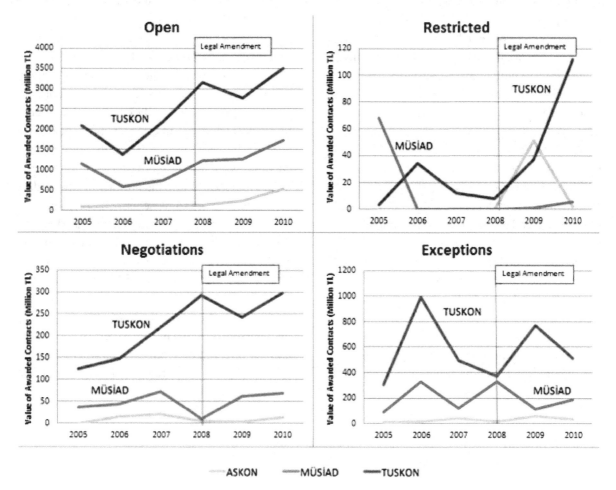

increased from 1.3% to 2.1% during the same period. This rise corresponds to a 75% increase in absolute value – from TL 403 million to TL 702 million. These upsurges owe largely to association shares in procurement made under the article 3-G which creates room for procuring entities and the firms for exploiting their connections via moving the procurements, with estimated costs below the pre-determined threshold level out of the scope of the PPL. In addition, member firms' performance in municipal procurements about restoration, restitution and conservation projects of cultural heritage made under the exceptions article (3-I)

also rose significantly – almost fifteen fold – indicating associations' successes in forming relations at the local level.

Referring to Figure 5 again, members of TÜRKONFED, which is not known to have any political connections with the ruling party, on the other hand, are awarded with the procurement contracts mostly made under the open auction procedure (on average 85%). There is one exceptional year – 2010 – in which 51% of the public procurement contracts awarded to TÜRKONFED members were not won through open auctions but under the *exceptions* article. The year of 2010

Figure 6. politically connected business associations' share in total procurements (by procurement method)

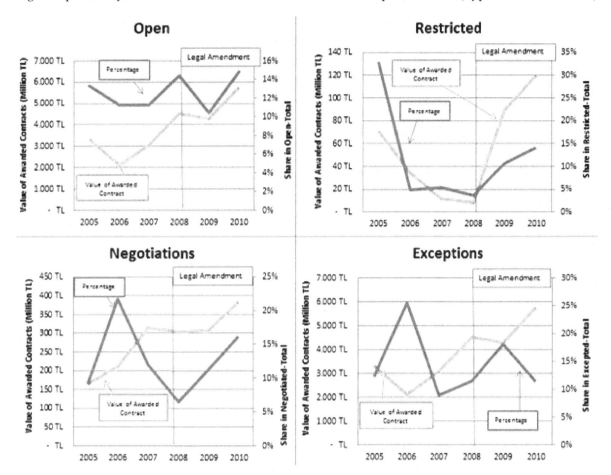

indeed coincides with politically non-connected business associations' attempts to develop their relations with the politically-connected associations. In this year TÜSİAD made a visit to TUSKON. This was followed by TÜRKONFED's visit to TUSKON.

Overall, our results suggest that membership to a politically-connected business association has a positive effect on a firm's performance in the public procurement market, particularly for procurements that are contracted under less transparent methods. Yet, not all politically-connected associations perform equally successfully. TUSKON by far performs better than the other associations. It gets the lion's share – 65% – from the associations' pie, while MÜSİAD accounts for the largest part

of the rest. ASKON's share on the other hand, though tripled during the sample period, does not even reach 10% of the total procurement contracts awarded to the business associations.

TUSKON is particularly successful in getting the contract awards in procurements auctioned under the restricted procedure. As demonstrated in Figure 5, it increased its share in total government procurement made under restricted procedure from a mere 1% (TL 3 million) in 2005 to 13% (TL 110 million) in 2010. TUSKON's successful performance in procurements made under the restricted procedure is particularly important given that these auctions, in contrast to open auctions, were made among the invited firms. ASKON had not been awarded any contracts for such procurements until 2009. By 2009, a legal amendment that indicates that restricted procedure can be used in procurement of construction works where estimated costs exceed the half of the pre-determined threshold value was put into force. After this change in PPL, ASKON managed to be awarded contracts worth TL 51 million. Such legal amendments indeed create opportunity spaces for the procuring state entities and the connected firms, since the former can calculate the estimated cost of procurement in a way that can be made under the restricted procedure so that only the invited firms can bid. Yet, the data demonstrates that this legal amendment was not exploited by MÜSİAD, whose share drastically reduced from 30% to almost null. Nevertheless, underperformance of MÜSİAD firms in such procurements does not mean that MÜSİAD as the second most powerful business association in Turkey is unsuccessful in benefiting from its connections with the current government. On the contrary, as it is emphasized elsewhere in the literature (e.g. Gunduz & Ozcan, 2014; Meyersson, 2014; Gurek, 2008), MÜSİAD firms are big enough to benefit from the public-private partnership movement and compete for more profitable auctions, the most important ones being the concession awards for which there are no comprehensive legal frameworks and hence political connections work even more extensively.

TUSKON's comparative performance in Figure 5 is also significant for the procurements made under the negotiated procedure, for which procuring entities are not obliged to publish a notice of the planned procurement. TUSKON managed to increase its share in high-value procurements made under negotiated procedure almost threefold. TUSKON's share is almost five times and twenty times higher than the shares of MÜSİAD and ASKON respectively. Nonetheless, MÜSİAD members also increased their share by 90%. ASKON's share on the other hand does not follow any regular pattern for this type of high-value procurements.

Regarding the high-value procurements made under the exceptions article TUSKON again gets much higher shares – almost three-fourth of such types of procurements – compared to the other two politically-connected business associations. In terms of these associations' performance over time in Figure 5, TUSKON's share rose by 60% while MÜSİAD's and ASKON's shares grew by 45% and 32% respectively.

As stated above, the associations' performance rose also in open auctions, which is considered to be a more transparent means of public procurement. Regarding the open auctions, TUSKON that increased its share from 8% (TL 2 billion) to 10% (TL 3.5 billion) again gets the highest share among the three associations. Several reasons can be suggested for TUSKON's success. For instance the number of its member firms is by far higher than what the other three associations have in total. More importantly, TUSKON members are geographically more widely distributed compared to the members of the other politically-connected associations.

CONCLUSION

The twentieth century witnessed an expansion of new literature and the development of a notable body of knowledge about the fundamental dimensions of social networking. With the Information Age, the internet and social networking became irrevocable elements of daily and business life.

In this chapter we argue that in Turkey IT-based procurement-specific networks, which provide their members with a wide range of procurement related services, help those member firms in their task of auction winning given that the one-fourth of the high-value public procurement contracts are indeed awarded to the members of these networks. However, we also show that adoption of such IT-based activities by Turkey's firms, 99.9% of which are SMEs, is in fact not at desired levels.

This is confirmed by the fact that the remaining three-quarters of contracts are awarded to the firms that do not invest in IT-based procurement-specific network activities.

Accordingly, with an aim to discover further networking mechanisms, we focus on business associations that relate closely to business such as civic club or trade/business association groups. Firms value forming or joining business associations highly, as these networks enable them to keep their autonomy and also provide them with resilience for pulling together their resources to compete in the market.

Our findings support our argument that business associations are effective in performance development in winning government procurement contracts. Although the share of the formal networks of business associations in high-value procurements is around 14%, this share is indeed significant given the fact that the procurement auctions analyzed are the high-value contracts which are worth more than TL 1,000,000. The high-value procurements indeed account for 80% of all procurements in terms of value despite the fact they form only 10% of all contracts awarded in terms of number.

Yet our results also suggest that membership to a politically-connected business association provides greater advantages to member firms in winning public procurement auctions than membership to a non-connected business association. This fact is demonstrated via showing how the government creates some "opportunity spaces" for indirectly affiliated business networks in public procurement auctions. Nonetheless, connected business associations not only help their members through the political networks they create, but also support them to invest in and better exploit IT-based activities. Indeed, politically-connected networks are more successful in using IT-based procurement networks compared to the non-connected ones.

FUTURE RESEARCH DIRECTIONS

This research paves the way for two future research topics.

First of all, as our results suggest one-quarter of all high-value procurement contracts go to internet-based procurement specific business networks while one-eighth of them are awarded to the members of business associations. There is also an overlap among network memberships. That is 8.4% of contracts awarded to the firms that have membership in both networks. The remaining contracts, however, are awarded to the firms that are not included in any type of these formal networks. These findings raise the question of whether the informal social networks established through kinship/friendship with incumbent politicians play a significant role in auction winning in a developing country like Turkey. Answering this question, however, requires extensive research and data construction since contrary to formal networks a dataset on informally-connected firms naturally does not exist. The role of informal institutional structures and relations are important in answering many questions in Turkey. Thus, we believe that a significant part of the remaining awarded contracts could be explained using such data once it is collected.

Second, in this chapter we analyze the influence of business network membership on performance of member-firms using only high-value procurements in order to find signs of upward mobilization. Yet, although the high-value procurements account for 80% of the total value of contracts awarded during the sample period, they constitute merely 10% of the number of contracts awarded. This finding necessitates exploring the performance of SME networks for procurements worth below 1,000,000 since the market of low-value procurements is the main area of competition for the majority of network-member SMEs, which normally lack the necessary capital to compete in the high-value procurement auctions. Moreover, expansion of such an analysis through examining the significance of the relationship between discretionary legal measures and allocation of low-value public procurement contracts would also let us explore the extent of power of the SME-based business networks in economic policy making. For instance we could not analyze 'direct buying' as it is valid for low-value procurements. Yet, procurements made through direct buying indeed accounts for 14% of all procurements. Thus, exploring the dynamics of state private sector relations for low-value procurements is of importance.

REFERENCES

Atlı, A. (2011). Businessmen as diplomats: The role of business associations in Turkey's foreign economic policy. *Insight Turkey*, *13*(1), 119–128.

Buğra, A. (1998). Class, culture, and state: An analysis of interest representation by two Turkish business associations. *International Journal of Middle East Studies*, *30*(04), 521–539. doi:10.1017/S0020743800052545

Buğra, A. (1999). *Islam in economic organizations*. Istanbul: TESEV.

Buğra, A. (2002). Labor, capital, and religion: Harmony and conflict among the constituency of political Islam in Turkey. *Middle Eastern Studies*, *2*(38), 187–204. doi:10.1080/714004454

Clarke, J., Thorpe, R., Anderson, L., & Gold, J. (2006). It's all action, it's all learning: Action learning in SMEs. *Journal of European Industrial Training*, *30*(6), 441–455. doi:10.1108/03090590610688825

Coviello, N. E., & McAuley, A. (1999). Internationalization and the small firm: A review of contemporary empirical research. *Management International Review*, *39*(3), 223–237.

Coviello, N. E., & Munro, H. (1995). Growing the entrepreneurial firm. *European Journal of Marketing*, *29*(7), 49–61. doi:10.1108/03090569510095008

Davis, A. E., Renzulli, L. A., & Aldrich, H. E. (2006). Mixing or matching? The influence of voluntary associations on the occupational diversity and density of small business owners' networks. *Work and Occupations*, *33*(1), 42–72. doi:10.1177/0730888405281914

Faccio, M. (2006). Politically connected firms. *The American Economic Review*, *96*(1), 369–386. doi:10.1257/0002828067761577704

Floyd, S. W., & Wooldridge, B. (1999). Knowledge creation and social networks in corporate entrepreneurship: The renewal of organizational capability. *Entrepreneurship Theory and Practice*, 123-143.

Forsgren, M., & Johanson, J. (1992). Managing internationalization in business networks. In M. Forsgren & J. Johanson (Eds.), *Managing networks in international business*. Philadelphia: Gordon and Breach.

Fuller-Love, N., & Thomas, E. (2004). Networks in small manufacturing firms. *Journal of Small Business and Enterprise Development*, *11*(2), 244–253. doi:10.1108/14626000410537182

Geletkanycz, M. A., & Hambrick, D. C. (1997). The external ties of executives: Implications for strategic choice and performance. *Administrative Science Quarterly*, *42*(4), 654–681. doi:10.2307/2393653

Goldman, E., Rocholl, J., & So, J. (2013). Politically connected boards of directors and the allocation of procurement contracts. *Review of Finance*, *17*(5), 1617–1648. doi:10.1093/rof/rfs039

Greve, A., & Salaff, J. W. (2003). Social networks and entrepreneurship. *Entrepreneurship Theory and Practice*, *28*(1), 1–23. doi:10.1111/1540-8520.00029

Gulati, R., Nohria, N., & Zaheer, A. (2000). Strategic networks. *Strategic Management Journal*, *21*(3), 203–215. doi:10.1002/(SICI)1097-0266(200003)21:3<203::AID-SMJ102>3.0.CO;2-K

Gunduz, U., & Ozcan, G. B. (2014). Political connectedness and business performance: Some evidence from Turkish industry rankings. *Business and Politics*, *16*(4), 1469–3569.

Gurakar, E. C., & Bircan, T. (in press). Political connections and public procurement in Turkey: Evidence from construction work contracts. In *Political economy determinants of private sector dynamism in the ERF region*. Economic Research Forum.

Håkansson, H., & Snehota, I. (1995). *Developing relationships in business networks*. London: Routledge.

Hedström, P., & Stern, C. (2008). Rational choice and sociology. In The new Palgrave dictionary of economics (pp. 872–877). Basingstoke, UK: Palgrave Macmillan.

Hollendsen, S. (1998). *The network model from global marketing: A market-responsive approach*. Prentice Hall Europe.

Horton, J., Millo, Y., & Serafeim, G. (2011). Resources or power? Implications of social networks on compensation and firm performance. *Journal of Business Finance & Accounting*, *39*(3-4), 399–426. doi:10.1111/j.1468-5957.2011.02276.x

Jackson, M. O. (2008). *Social and economic networks*. Princeton, NJ: Princeton Univ. Press.

Jackson, M. O. (2010). An overview of social networks and economic applications. In The handbook of social economics. Elsevier Press.

Jacoby, T. (2004). *Social power and the Turkish state*. London: Frank Cass.

Johnson, G., Scholes, K., & Whittington, R. (2005). *Exploring corporate strategy: Text and cases*. London: Pearson Education.

Keyman, F., & Koyuncu, B. (2004). AKP, MÜSİAD, Ekonomik kalkınma ve modernite. *Düsünen Siyaset*, *19*, 125–145.

Kıvanç, Ü. (1997). İslamcılar ve para-pul: Bir dönüsüm hikayesi. *Birikim*, *99*, 39–58.

Lake, P. W. (2004). *Business networks in a regional industrial cluster*. (Unpublished DBA Dissertation). University of Southern Queensland.

Miller, N., Besser, T., & Malshe, A. (2007). Strategic networking among small business in small US communities. *International Small Business Journal*, *25*(6), 631–665. doi:10.1177/0266242607082525

Mizruchi, M. S., & Stearns, L. B. (1988). A longitudinal study of the formation of interlocking directorates. *Administrative Science Quarterly*, *33*(2), 194–210. doi:10.2307/2393055

Öniş, Z. (1997). The political economy of Islamic resurgence in Turkey: The rise of the welfare party in perspective. *Third World Quarterly*, *18*(4), 743–766. doi:10.1080/01436599714740

Palmer, D. (1983). Broken ties: Interlocking directorates and intercorporate coordination. *Administrative Science Quarterly*, *28*(1), 40–55. doi:10.2307/2392384

Pfeffer, J., & Salancik, G. R. (2003). *The external control of organizations: A resource dependence perspective*. Stanford, CA: Stanford University Press.

Silverman, R. (2012). *Justice and development in the marketplace: Business and politics in AKP-era Turkey*. (Unpublished master's thesis). University of Washington.

Sönmez, M. (2010). *Türkiye'de iş dünyasının örgütleri ve yönelimleri.* Istanbul: Friedrich Ebert Stiftung. Retrieved March 6, 2014, from http://www.tuskon.org/?p=content&cl=kurumsal&i=3

Yankaya, D. (2009). The Europeanization of MÜSIAD: Political opportunism, economic Europeanization, Islamic Euroscepticism. *European Journal of Turkish Studies*, 9, 1–18.

ADDITIONAL READING

Birley, S. (1985). The role of networks in the entrepreneurial process. *Journal of Business Venturing*, *1*(1), 107–117. doi:10.1016/0883-9026(85)90010-2

Buğra, A. (1998). Class, culture, and state: An analysis of interest representation by two Turkish business associations. *International Journal of Middle East Studies*, *30*(04), 521–539. doi:10.1017/S0020743800052545

Buğra, A. (1999). *Islam in economic organizations.* Istanbul: TESEV.

Buğra, A. (2002). Labor, capital, and religion: Harmony and conflict among the constituency of political Islam in Turkey. *Middle Eastern Studies*, 2(38), 187–204. doi:10.1080/714004454

Greve, A., & Salaff, J. W. (2003). Social networks and entrepreneurship. *Entrepreneurship Theory and Practice*, *28*(1), 1–23. doi:10.1111/1540-8520.00029

Håkansson, H., & Snehota, I. (1995). *Developing relationships in business networks.* London: Routledge.

Jackson, M. O. (2008). *Social and economic networks.* Princeton, NJ: Princeton Univ. Press.

Miller, N., Besser, T., & Malshe, A. (2007). Strategic networking among small business in small US communities. *International Small Business Journal*, *25*(6), 631–665. doi:10.1177/0266242607082525

KEY TERMS AND DEFINITIONS

Business Associations: Business Associations help member firms in establishing a strong and unified presence, effectively protect their shared interests and thus collectively influence economic policy making process.

Internet-Based Public Procurement Networks: Private, profit-seeking, internet-based establishments that provide the subscriber firms with a wide range of procurement related services, access to critical resources and timely information that help them in participating and winning procurement auctions.

Political Economy: An approach that examines how politics shape developments in the economy and how economy shapes politics. It particularly looks at the interaction of political institutions and economic institutions.

Public Procurement: The procurement of goods, services and construction works by public institutions from the private sector. Public procurement comprises a substantial part of government spending in most of the countries, accounts for a substantial part of the global economy, and is among the most important areas where the state and the private sector interact.

ENDNOTES

[1] SMEs are defined as companies with fewer than 250 employees.

[2] Turkish Statistical Institute (TUIK).

[3] These statistics are available at http://www.kobi.org.tr/index.php/tanimi/stats.

[4] See Faccio, 2006 for a panel of 47 countries; Goldman et.al., 2014 for US; Coviello, 2012 for Italy; Choi and Thum, 2007 for China; Khwaja and Mian, 2005 for Pakistan; and Checkir and Diwan, 2013 for Egypt).

[5] For the details of this argument, see Ercan and Oguz (2006).

[6] Design contest is used very rarely and thus comprises a negligible share in total public procurement both in terms of value and the number of contracts awarded.

Chapter 14
New Social Media Agendas for Teaching and Learning in Libraries

Michelle Kowalsky
Rowan University, USA

Bruce Whitham
Rowan University, USA

ABSTRACT

This chapter reviews the current literature on the types of social media practices in college and university libraries, and suggests some new strategic agendas for utilizing these tools for teaching and learning about the research process, as well as other means to connect libraries to their users. Library educators continually hope to "meet students where they are" and use social media to "push" library content toward interested or potential university patrons. One new way to improve engagement and "pull" patrons toward an understanding of the usefulness of licensed resources and expert research help is through the channels of social media. By enhancing awareness of library resources at the point of need, and through existing social relationships between library users and their friends, libraries can encourage peer interaction around new research methods and tools as they emerge, while increasing the use of library materials (both online and within the library facility) in new and different ways.

INTRODUCTION

As libraries seek the attention of users who have search engines at their fingertips and continuous connectivity with others on their mobile devices, they need to find new ways to engage their university community in resources beyond those that are free on the Web. Licensed journals and database subscriptions, as well as e-books and the services of expert research librarians, provide a window into the scholarly content on which high-level professionals, academics, and scholars base their daily work.

While many people may be content to have information served to them by their favorite media outlet or their network of friends, libraries attempt to break people out of these passive routines of consumption by providing a range of

DOI: 10.4018/978-1-4666-7401-1.ch014

resources containing alternative viewpoints and data for decision-making. Learning to interpret these resources is the primary task of any college or university student, and one which librarians believe can be facilitated by social media.

Academic libraries are undergoing rapid transformation, away from a library centric model to a user based model focused on skills, knowledge, and relationships with faculty, staff, and students. Objectives include an emphasis on ensuring students can find resource and can make informed and critical evaluations regarding quality and relevancy. Success more than ever requires methods that engage students who are highly connected to social networks.

Social media users of all ages, by their very nature, now possess an enhanced capacity to self-organize and to provide for themselves (Selwyn, 2012, p. 3). Libraries can assist users with research by capitalizing on their interest in self-reliance, or more accurately their interest in technology-reliance, by providing avenues of social media which both teach information skills and promote use of library resources. The return on investment in implementing and maintaining social media initiatives for libraries, especially in their effects on university community engagement and learning, is often priceless.

The impact of social media in libraries, according to the research, is mixed at best. Social media seems to be most useful as a strategy for increasing awareness more than a mechanism for delivering instruction or a method for achieving learning outcomes. Social media has been documented in the library literature as improving libraries' connectivity to their patrons, or users, and providing better access to targeted groups who might benefit from the library's resources or services. Yet the literature also shows that social media is not as effective for quantitative measures of assessment, especially given the numerous variables and outcome effects generated. Qualitative and anecdotal

evidence, however, is readily available for libraries using social media to expand their reach, and it is a useful way to document the scope and sequence of these activities.

This chapter aims to identify a variety of teaching and learning agendas for libraries which can be served via multiple social media tools, both now and in the future. In this way, libraries will not feel compelled to react to each new trend without critical consideration, but rather will be able to develop and categorize multiple efforts towards maximum impact in assessing library outreach as well as institutional learning about research.

BACKGROUND

Social media as understood by libraries is a broad phenomenon intimately related to widespread use of wireless Internet and handheld devices. Boyd and Ellison (2008) define social network sites as "web-based services that allow individuals to

1. Construct a public or semi-public profile within a bounded system,
2. Articulate a list of other users with whom they share a connection, and
3. View and traverse their list of connections and those made by others within the system" (p. 211).

The nature and nomenclature of these connections may vary from site to site, but their basic functions remain similar; people want to know what their friends and aspirant peers are doing, thinking, and deciding.

The Pew Research Center's Internet and American Life Project has been conducting research on topics related to Internet use since 2000, and has provided a variety of this data for review on their website. Since worldwide technology trends are often on the minds of library professionals, a type of evidence-based decision making occurs in libraries whenever new and useful trends are identified. For example, some of these recent statistics from their annual report demonstrate the importance of understanding social media from an educator's point of view:

- Social Media has increased from 8% in 2000 to 73% in 2013.
- Use of Social Media by teenagers is 81%.
- In 2012, the average teen sent 60 texts per day.
- 71% of adults have a Facebook account.
- Social Media Use is evenly distributed: 88% urban, 87% suburban, 83% rural.
- 87% of the adult U.S. population uses the Internet.
- Of those in the 18 to 29 age cohort, users constitute 97% (Pew Research, 2013).

For educators, especially those teaching at the intersection of adolescence and adulthood, these trends signify a change in the ways that people think, interact, and communicate. Librarians in higher education have embraced the idea that these trends will assist them with their missions of supporting the design of original research, training others to find and use appropriate resources for various purposes, and providing credible information on different points of view in multiple disciplines.

Libraries of many kinds use social media interaction with their users as a measure of interest, of actual use, or of community engagement. Yet empirical studies in librarianship which define effect sizes or outcome comparisons for these initiatives are elusive, since each library is at a different stage of its unique trajectory of modernization. In higher education, student uses of social media seem to change with the semester, as students gravitate toward the next popular app or the newest place to gather online. Hence, strict measurement of a library's impact on these shifts, or of a library's benefits from these shifts, is difficult to quantify. Perhaps, quantifying social media as a direct measure of student outcomes is asking the wrong question; only once a connection has been made, can learning occur.

Studies of libraries' social media practices also sometimes indicate opposing views of what students do when online. Simultaneously, the information profession has determined that students only talk to people they know in person when making references to their schoolwork, or that they seek information anonymously from perceptible online peers (Ellison, Steinfield, & Lampe, 2007, p. 1143). Therefore, getting information skills and library knowledge into students' peer circles is a possible strategy for learning, so that this information can circulate among acquaintances and utilize existing peer recognition standards. Yet some reports note that students do not want their teachers or authority figures involved in their social networks. A study of 366 freshmen at Valparaiso University "made it clear that some students will resent a library/librarian's intrusion into their private space" (Connell, 2009, p. 33). These negative reactions by students may limit any educator's chances for authentic student engagement about academics via these channels.

In order to improve dialogue given these common characterizations of today's college students, which seem to change by semester, librarians can focus on several aspects of teaching and learning which will persist over time. As they stop following each new trend in a reactive manner, information professionals can strategically plan for groups of assessment characteristics for which a variety of online social tools can provide data. Often, it is a combination of assessment data, and assessment for multiple purposes, which will reveal the most accurate and complex picture of a university's relationship to its library.

Social media is already a pervasive experience for students, and even many of their teachers. Lane and Lewis (2013), in a review of the literature on social media and education outcomes, note that today's university student will experience many kinds of engagement which include academic experience, interaction with peers and faculty, involvement in co-curricular activities, and out-of-class engagement, all as educationally-relevant activities (p. 41). Most, if not all, of these experiences include a social media component; therefore, incorporating a library-related social media component into students' lives is essential if we want them to experience the benefits of our libraries' many resources and services.

Libraries also have an obligation to reach all university students, not just those going on to research-based careers. Experiencing a learning community which engages with high-quality resources to expand and extend learning includes the experience of having conversations with other learners. Connolly (2011) believes that the advantages of social media and social networks can contribute significantly to engaging certain reluctant students; for example, shy or isolated students are able to use social media to facilitate face-to-face encounters and thus feel an enhanced sense of community (p. 130). Libraries are a natural and central place where a unique mixing of majors, ages, and backgrounds of students can take place. Once libraries also provide sites for connection online, opportunities for outreach multiply.

McCarthy (2010) notes that social media has enhanced the interactivity between local and international students. This is a natural area of collaboration for university libraries, which often have a rich compilation of materials and language professionals to assist with global learning. "Many international students saw the online environment is a perfect opportunity to engage with peers as they were able to consider their comments and critiques over a period of time rather than being put on the spot in the lecture or tutorial" (McCarthy, 2010, p. 734). Cultural or language-based inhibitions were overcome when in the online social forum, resulting in better communication overall.

Similar positive outcomes can exist for the general student population as well; they are all new—at some point in their university career—to

a discipline or major, to a group of peers in a new class, or to a professor or librarian who will judge their work. Social media can facilitate dialogue in a novel situation without bringing sensations of inadequacy or ignorance to the surface. In fact, most university students, even graduate students, may feel intimidated at the volume and density of academic literature and its accompanying complexities of access.

TARGETED USES OF SOCIAL MEDIA IN LIBRARIES

Libraries are able to use social media in targeted ways that can both help the user and also help the library as an organization. Much of the academic literature expressing opinions on social media and marketing suggests that achieving good measures is not so simple a task, yet commercial sites can offer some insight into streamlining efforts and implementation. Even a selective adoption of corporate or business experiences can be helpful. Hird (2010), for example, notes eleven points that marketers use to measure social media; several have direct applicability to libraries: an analysis of traffic, purposeful public relations, retention of users, and customer engagement (p. 2).

Traffic in libraries in the past consisted of physical counts of the people who walked through the front gates. Many library buildings are still crammed with students, but new measures to determine real traffic are now needed as much of the information provided by libraries is available 24/7 online. Database usage counts, for example, give librarians valuable information about the online resources, but it is the venue of social media to determine the quality of that traffic data and the contexts in which the traffic appears and replicates.

To do this, university library outreach efforts are engaging users through a variety of social media platforms. The message of the library must be compelling, yet it also must be seen. As an illustration, retention of returning customers is also a somewhat nebulous measure. In this sense the role the library is tied to that of institution, wherein retention of students each year until graduation is measured. But library funding is tied to demonstrable success in the delivery of service. Those who "like" the library and those that "tweet" about the library are demonstrating connecting behaviors using social media, and this As Hird and others have said, "ample data support the idea that fans are worth more than non fans" (2010, p. 2).

Social media presents a real opportunity to achieve similar success while overcoming the limitations within the physical library. A combination of social media used in conjunction with a well-planned program can offer opportunities for engagement on a far greater scale. Yet currently, there may be no particularly efficient method for assessing of social media initiatives on their own; rather their analysis should be a component of assessing a larger program. Social media may provide one aspect of a more robust strategy of awareness, engagement, or learning which, as described below, can take many forms.

Social Media for Current Awareness

Libraries in higher education are able to take advantage of constant connectivity of users in order to implement a variety of current awareness services, such as alerting users of new resources or encouraging discovery via existing resources that may have been forgotten. Delivering better value via social media—while a worthwhile goal—is difficult to quantify except in the context of learning outcomes, and even then it proves difficult.

Social media in this context can help students be self-reliant, finding things on their own, especially electronically, and show off to others what they know by either re-tweeting, pinning, or commenting on the usefulness of the suggestions made. But focusing only on students' expressions of their needs, and what they believe satisfies these needs, is also not enough; educators must make

decisions based on where students are going, not where they are currently. This complicates the process of evaluation of social media efforts merely through counts and percentages of their growth.

Tenopir, Volentine, & King (2013) found, after surveying more than 2,000 academics in the United Kingdom, that faculty who maintained blogs, taught with or created online videos, and listened to podcasts tend to read more books and other scholarly publications as well (p. 201). Hence, engagement in social media by faculty may increase their productivity or time on scholarly tasks. "The use of social media is also not replacing traditional scholarly resources, but instead they are used alongside as part of the vast amount of information sources available to scholars" (Hughes, 2013, p. 146).

Promotions of current awareness, alerting efforts, or positive reactions from users are often enough information to validate our attempts at new social media initiatives. But since most of the published research does not utilize rigorous methods of analyzing the impact of social media on various operations of scholars and their libraries, "self-reported numerical data cautiously supports that perception of success" (Heyliger, et al., 2013, p. 374).

For example, results from Subrahmanyam, et al. (2008) "show that emerging adults' offline and online worlds are connected, and they use online communication for offline issues, and to connect with people in their offline lives" (p. 432). Similarly, the next generation of these efforts should purposefully mix in-person interaction with online interaction in order to gain maximum effectiveness and impact. In the future, a "light touch" via social media may be enough to encourage in-person connectivity, to reinforce acquisition of complex information behaviors one step at a time, and to provide a confidential outlet for students' questions and their teachers' and librarians' answers.

By adopting social media, librarians offer a level of interactivity to students who already have expectations that they will contribute feedback on and critique of their education and those providing it. This can create a healthy dialogue, especially if not in a face-to-face format, and presents an affordance not available in person with today's undergraduates. Further, the role of the librarian is enhanced as librarians partner with faculty and staff to strengthen collaborative efforts toward shared goals across the campus. Any information which might improve the campus community's understanding of the many resources available to them, and get them talking about them in any fashion online, might supplement the conversation around scholarly ideas, or even start new ones.

Social Media for Community Building

Another use of social media by libraries is to facilitate connections among users with similar interests, either in reading or other activities like hobbies (e.g., gardening) or thematic interests (e.g., World War II). Social media helps create affinity groups and identify new members, so that even virtual versions of in-person groups, such as book clubs, can start and grow. At academic institutions, affinity groups around research methods (e.g., ethnographers), data analysis tools (e.g., users of statistical software *R*), disciplinary areas (e.g., geographers), or even current themes (e.g., Downton Abbey fans), can develop easily with the assistance of social media, and often will encourage interdisciplinarity.

Exchange of ideas and research in this manner may create a power inequity when in person, especially if only a few experts and many novices in the topic at hand are continually present. Philips (2011), in a library project tracking 151 college libraries' uses of Facebook, noted that "the immediacy, informality, and interactivity of Facebook offer libraries opportunities to influence how they are perceived, to demonstrate their support of students, and to reinforce the contexts they share with students" (p. 521). Particularly, the opportunity

to influence students may be at the heart of many reasons why using social media seems necessary despite few statistically significant gains for the return on investment of staff time.

Weinberg, et al. (2013) suggests taking a closer look at several aspects of social media, such as the differences between its outcomes of participation, empowerment, and contribution (p. 287). For social media to be successful for building community in and through libraries, an equal mix of participants must be present: those who participate to contribute their expertise, to learn from more experienced others, and to engage as partners in a mutual conversation. When a group comes together for a shared purpose, even if the group is fleeting, gains in instruction and information needs may increase just enough to declare the initiative a success.

Through their research, Anwyll, Chawner, & Tarulli (2013) identified three main reasons why libraries might use social media for readers' advisory services, in other words, librarians' efforts to help connect readers with (primarily fiction) books which they might enjoy. In deploying social media for this purpose of building a community of readers, libraries used social media as a way of reaching out to potential library patrons who were not daily users, as a way to promote new books and resources, and to engage in a conversation about books and ideas (Anwyll, Chawner, & Tarulli, 2013, 114).

The researchers noted that having simply a consistent numbers of "followers" or "friends" were an acceptable level of success, even if those numbers not continually growing in a linear fashion over time (Anwyll, Chawner, & Tarulli, 2013, p. 116). Since much of the library research cannot identify specific outcomes related to increased engagement, circulation, reference questions or group materials use from these types of data, any assessments must include other types of data as part of a composite strategy analysis.

Self-Regulated Learning of Research Skills

The challenge for libraries is not just one of promotion. Ultimately the library needs to engage the users in their own learning. Recent online presentations given to students in our own library measured engagement based on a pattern of instruction followed by immediate applications of what they had learned. The success rate was high and the satisfaction rate of the learners was very positive. However limited space, time, and staffing constrain such outreach on a broader scale, and limit transferability to a fully online or social media format. While certain teaching activities may not be easily transported to a technological delivery system, the idea of a pre-existing network of learners is still appealing. Nevertheless, social media may assist libraries in supporting the curriculum in a 24/7 manner, creating an improvement in library services which would be welcomed eagerly by most students.

As mentioned earlier, public services librarians, specifically those in research, reference, and instruction, have long offered guidance, both one-on-one and in lab and classroom settings classrooms. Students required an understanding of the structure of databases and the logical equations that allow relevant resource to be found. Yet social media studies such as Gikas & Grant (2013) and others have emphasized students' ongoing interest in online versions of these types of training because of the immediate access they will have to information and to others (p. 21). Our present analysis indicates that perhaps one (the online access for places to start research) can lead to the other (more in-depth and specific instruction with a librarian).

Mack, et al. (2007), for example, used a decidedly un-technological method which increased student engagement, an in-person instructional session by a librarian in cooperation with a subject-specialist faculty member. Students at Penn State asked just as many Facebook questions of the librarian as they did via email or in person during a semester, once the option was introduced as a means of communication. Ease of connectivity with a more-expert other may encourage students to ask more questions and positively reinforce this behavior with timely and targeted answers.

Web 2.0, social media, and the transformation in social networks have identified changes in the way students are approaching their education. Libraries certainly have been presented with challenge, but also an unprecedented opportunity, to engage students through collaboration. Group learning and peer instruction can easily expand when employing instructional materials delivered by the library through various social media formats. Online library tutorials are one type of instructional material which can go viral on video channels like YouTube, and which allow student feedback via a rating system visible to all. Dewald's (1999) standards for taking library instruction online translate as well to specialized social media tools which allow for sharing of video, audio, ratings systems, quiz results, and the like.

Furthermore, the phenomenon of students influencing and modifying their learning through use of social media and social networks offer libraries the further advantage of broadcasting awareness of point-of-need resources, a phenomenon marketers refer to as amplification. Learners themselves are able to amplify the usefulness of library skills to their peers by broadcasting comments on their information literacy experiences through their existing social media, which often include students from their classes, in years ahead or behind them in college or high school, or even university-age students who are not library users. Benefits of these connections may reap many rewards that are not even measurable by current processes.

Encouraging Peer Context for University Students and Faculty

Students may also benefit from learning about what their peers are doing on other college campuses across the country and around the world. Social media, both serendipitous and planned, can assist students in a type of metacognition about what it means to do research as a college student. For example, SpringShare's LibGuides is one example of a shared platform which enables students to easily find suggested resources of peer institutions, and to see what other learners are doing with their online resources. Similarly, librarians themselves can learn new ways of teaching the research process, or of showcasing useful disciplinary sources or research tools for students and faculty.

Tweets and "likes" on Facebook about successful student research projects, or particularly skillful course papers, can be included on a library's webpage to help provide targets for achievement for students. Items which use recommendation tags, even within a university library's open access repository system, are alternate ways in which libraries can use social media to encourage advanced researching behavior among students. Social learning and constructivist theories of Vygotsky (1980), the community of practice theories of Engeström (1998), and situated learning theories of Lave and Wegner (1991) all point to the necessity of learning in the context of one's peers as a modern-day approach. Social media will facilitate this, but human peers, and not just computers, will still be required for learning.

Social networks not only help students learn more about what their peers are learning at other colleges, but also can help them identify what alumni are saying is most important for getting hired or for future success. Libraries can connect campus career centers to additional resources which mitigate student weaknesses, and encourage use of information resources to build new skills. Providing the opportunity for student users to show off what they have learned via online badges (as in Santos, et al., 2013) or certificates of completion (as in Jacklin & Robinson, 2013).

Faculty are also interested in social media affordances, and librarians can help improve scholars' visibility on web, help them find new collaborators,

and enhance metadata to describe faculty research in ways that help increase indexing by search engines and social media technologies. Bar-Ilan, et al. (2012) studied faculty connections to promote their scholarship and its impact, including use of social media accounts on LinkedIn, via Google Scholar researcher profiles, citation sharing tools, and other methods. Their work confirmed the messiness of social media sources for citation impact data, and caution against misinterpretations of correlations and other online "noise" in the data from social media repostings, automatic retweets, and the like (Bar-Ilan, et al., 2012, p. 12).

For faculty members, librarians could identify possibilities for "altmetrics," or alternate methods of gauging the research impact of faculty scholarship via social media. Social bookmarking of scholarly works, via tagging systems like CiteULike or Mendeley can assist libraries in labeling and categorizing information according to ways that users understand in a particular field. Librarians often use these tools to help researchers to find relevant works or researchers in a particular discipline, and this information can lead either to a potential new collaborator or a body of work not found easily via traditional database or search engine algorithms. Online reference managers like RefWorks Zotero can help reveal a researcher's thinking and search strategies to more sophisticated users if these lists are shared. The incorporation of social media tools designed for faculty, such as OpenScholar, an open source Drupal based application, will allow faculty members to develop customizable academic websites which then connect to multiple social media tools.

Issues, Problems, Solutions

Outreach for librarians can best be described as a targeted effort to introduce tools and resources to new library users as well as to raise awareness of the library's resources and services, thereby leading to further communication and enriched contact with the audiences. When the value of unbiased, non-commercial information is questioned in society, or support for non-Googled information wanes, libraries encounter difficulties in sustaining their missions, even among educated users. Many of these issues of promotion and awareness can be solved by social media, yet many others are also created by social media.

Peters, et al. (2013) explains that social media, although ubiquitous, must be explicitly managed, and especially in four key areas: 'motives,' 'content,' 'network structure,' and 'social roles and interactions' (p. 281). Users have many reasons for engaging in online ratings, discussions, or alerts, and these behaviors are quite familiar within their current social circles. Yet library users may not always realize ways in which these behaviors may relate to interaction with their university libraries as well. Finding the time to manage these social media products, and to work to change some people's minds about the value of different types of information, is a common problem which leads often to avoidance of social media initiatives altogether.

Similarly, users who are not as familiar with library holdings or services may take out their frustrations on the library's social networks. At times, library staff may not simplify use enough for users' tastes, resulting in a disconnect between user's expectations of fast, easy, 'read-my-mind' access as misapplied to a university homework project or a complex literature search. However, Peters, et al. (2013) reminds us that both the content and context of what our institutions online have an influence on the reception of these messages by our users (p. 292). Therefore, we can and should control for disconnect by positioning information appropriately in an online environment to help reach diverse groups of users in ways which result in their most favorable reception.

Issues and problems with social media are intimately linked to issues related to the technological changes of society, and libraries are no exception. With the introduction of the Web,

library search tools moved from traditional paper formats like indexes, pathfinders, and guides into online formats like search engines, web page ranking systems, and content management tools like LibGuides. Although abstracting and indexing are finding aids that have existed since the days of paper, many users do not know that they were precursors to early databases and their searchable fields. The great disruption in the library system arrived with Google, a now-ubiquitous tool that uses indexing via word search algorithms to discover resources. Improved access to computers and easier searching methods resulted in a change in the way information is searched and viewed in the public eye, yet librarians and libraries are intimately involved in these developments even if the general population may think otherwise.

Early complaints about the quality of the materials found online, compared to the subscription resources in the library, for example, lasted for a few years. But refinements in Google's main search tool, the addition of Google Scholar, the rapid digitization of books and articles, and technologies that can authenticate legitimate users of resources have allowed subscription based resources to be indexed and accessed through Web-based search tools. The first option for research for both students and faculty has now gone online, enabling users to forget the original, vetted sources of information. Libraries have worked with publishers and search engines, such as for Google Scholar contents, so these partnerships have been fruitful in the past and will continue into the future. Hence, many difficulties for libraries in these areas have not necessarily been technological, but instead are related to public perceptions.

The rapid advance of social media tools presents users with a wide array of choices, and choosing the best tool for a given task is not always easy. Additionally, having the skill set needed to prepare pedagogically-grounded presentations that are also informative and engaging in social media requires strategic planning and implementation so that libraries will not lose opportunities to meet students where they are, and especially if they are always online.

These challenges are not impossible to overcome, as appropriate skills can be hired and developed. Partnerships with various departments on campus, such as graphic arts, studio arts, or computer science, can provide value to the process as well. The advent of social media and the rapid expansion of bandwidth for information delivery have encouraged libraries to migrate their instruction and access online in more sophisticated ways. Appropriate resources which speak to current users' sensibilities will find interested audiences ready and waiting to engage in well-designed library instruction via social channels.

The adoption of social media by libraries can contribute many solutions. Librarians have seen the evolution of databases and other search and organizing tools over time, and have adapted online practices and programs in response. Advances in so-called fuzzy technology, which helps students whose search construction is less than specific, can only bring students so far through a messy information seeking problem. More refined search skills allow for pinpoint searching, both in subscription databases and Web resources like Google Scholar, and these skills are most likely internalized via targeted instruction applied at the point of need by a skilled searcher. The right skill set makes a big difference in the quality and relevancy of results obtained by students and their faculty mentors, and increases confidence and validity in the searches completed.

Research instruction offered by librarians in classrooms and computer labs may now move into the realm of social networks when students are seeking tools to assist them in their searches. Moreover, recognizing their preference is for just-in-time, or point-of-need assistance cannot be overstated. Quick answers to immediate issues help students with their precise concerns, and they will take it from there. When librarians initiate conversations with broader teaching parameters

in mind, they are often received by students as if they were hearing the history of "how Moses came down from the mountain." These attempts at contextualization of a query are incongruous with the immediacy of student queries and often not replicated well online. In a world where students want direct, online communication, we must be able to accommodate them easily. As Murphy and Meyer (2013) suggest that "the only real way to lose at the social media game is not to play" (p. 15). Often, playing the game means using online tools in ways that are more similar to students' own patterns of engagement.

Reaching students and maintaining a connection through social media does not in itself ensure that student will stay engaged with the library. Outreach to their social network requires that library websites to be configured to function well on personal devices. Research and experience show that the mention of social networks in traditional learning environments, such as classrooms or labs, will result in increased use of library resources. We can measure the use but how do we measure the quality of, or the outcomes of, this social network interaction? Methods and results remain to be seen.

FUTURE RESEARCH DIRECTIONS

User interest varies among types of interactions, and that technologies which are popular at the time may not lend themselves to the types of communication needed, as Chen, Chu, & Xu (2012) explain. The same is true for library-based interactions; Twitter is not as useful for extended knowledge sharing, as it is for obtaining a broad spectrum of quick reactions and comments. Knowledge gathering for library program assessment solely via social network sites is also not as efficient or effective as data which represents users' behaviors or helps us draw conclusions about their opinions.

An integrated social science approach, which utilizes both quantitative and qualitative data about a variety of phenomenon in college libraries, is most likely a better choice for assessment of learning and of library performance in their outreach services. Social research methods including ethnography, phenomenology, and mixed methods including interviews, focus groups, and surveys are additional means by which libraries could identify contexts in which social media statistics can be interpreted.

Lee & Ma (2012) suggest consideration of users' intentions when implementing social media applications in various contexts. A variety of behaviors may be exhibited by social network site users for a variety of purposes, not all of them related to an intention of group collaboration or benefit, as many institutions may assume. Information seeking, status seeking, socializing, entertainment, prior experience, and intentions all play a role in the style of users' interactions with the media and the nature and frequency of what they share (Lee & Ma, 2012, p. 336).

Similarly, Nicholas, et al. (2011) agree that social media may be outside of the pervue of an academic libraries' main mission and gold standards of providing researchers with access to the best vetted, scholarly, peer-reviewed materials available. The authors argue a salient point, explaining that social media is "unlikely to have an influence or impact on library functions in any major way, other than possibly negatively, by decoupling university libraries even further from scholarly information communication and provision" (Nicholas, et al., 2011, p. 374). The authors maintain that the disintermediation of social media will again remove the library from the consciousness of users who feel they can find everything themselves online via a search engine like Google, and this remains a real threat to the work of libraries as authoritative information providers.

Nevertheless, some type of human interaction—whether it is teaching a student how to go about an advanced search, modeling an information literacy lesson for faculty, or design-

ing a cognitive apprenticeship model in which researchers watch more advanced learners (or "masters") use new resources in a discipline—will probably be an important component of learning, which social media might facilitate. Pollet, et al. (2011) explains: "Social relationships are prone to decay over time, and each relationship needs active maintenance to prevent this decay. Even if time on the Internet is spent on social media rather than on non-social activities, these media may be less effective at building and maintaining emotionally intense relationships than other types of communication" (p. 257).

Hence, finding multiple online social avenues which work in different ways for the present group of users, and which speak to many of their affiliation or status needs, may produce a robust strategy of combined online and offline outreach efforts. Similarly, plan for revisiting those avenues frequently and making adjustments would keep the channels and the content fresh in the minds of users. Simply reminding users that library resources, services, and personnel exist—within the course of their daily routines—may help those users who present more sophisticated needs to reach out to information professionals more easily. Ideally, we hope they will ask more sophisticated questions and engage in more complex conceptual problem-solving, which can't be answered via a quick click of the mouse.

CONCLUSION

Libraries have long been early adopters of technology. With each advance—mainframe computing desktop computers, the Internet and Web-based networks—library organizations have quickly adopted and internalized technological advances to improve service delivery. The library services which have been improved significantly over time include matching materials with users to fulfill their information needs, answering content and process questions during research at all levels, and building knowledge about disciplinary conventions in research design, publishing, and dissemination.

However, significant advances in bandwidth and high-speed Internet, free discovery tools, (e.g. Google and Bing) and free social network tools that have become almost traditions now (e.g. Facebook, Twitter, Tumblr, YouTube, Flickr, Pinterest) are pervasive. Today's students are connected to a digital world that allows them to communicate, to create, and to collaborate in ways that are profoundly changing the way they use and reuse knowledge. In supporting their learning at each higher level, librarians must stay well-versed in new technologies and their applications in order to assist students in navigating a world full of content created by everyone and anyone.

Students have become creators of knowledge and employ social media to influential the world in ways none of us could likely have imagined just a few decades ago. Yet fundamental aspects of critical engagement, appreciation of the multiple "ways of knowing," engaging the world ethically and recognizing diverse points of view are necessary for lifelong learning and for informed citizenship. The university library is uniquely positioned to assist users over time to develop these skills and deploy them strategically over the course of their degrees and careers.

Libraries are in a unique position to share information across disciplines, to connect questions to answers, and to leverage social media in unique ways. As information mediators and knowledge collaborators at any academic institution, university-level librarians must strive to enhance the research and development skills of its constituents in as many ways as possible. Social media as an interaction and outreach strategy for modeling library-initiated and library-facilitated academic discussions will be an agenda for the future that is both achievable and sustainable for all.

REFERENCES

Anwyll, R., Chawner, B., & Tarulli, L. (2013). Social media and readers' advisory. *Reference and User Services Quarterly*, *53*(2), 113–118. doi:10.5860/rusq.53n2.113

Bar-Ilan, J., Haustein, S., Peters, I., Priem, J., Shema, H., & Terliesner, J. (2012). *Beyond citations: Scholars' visibility on the social web*. Retrieved 2 March 2014, from http://arxiv.org/ftp/arxiv/papers/1205/1205.5611.pdf

Boyd, D. M., & Ellison, N. B. (2008). Social network sites: Definition history, and scholarship. *Journal of Computer-Mediated Communication*, *13*(1), 210–230. doi:10.1111/j.1083-6101.2007.00393.x

Chen, D. Y.-T., Chu, S. K.-W., & Xu, S.-Q. (2012). How do libraries use social networking sites to interact with users? *Proceedings of the American Society for Information Science and Technology*, *49*(1), 1–10.

Connell, R. S. (2009). Academic libraries, Facebook and MySpace, and student outreach: A survey of student opinion. *Libraries and the Academy*, *9*(1), 25–36. doi:10.1353/pla.0.0036

Connolly, M. (2011). Does social networking enhance or impede student learning? Social networking and student learning: Friends with benefits. In P. M. Magolda & M. B. Baxter (Eds.), *Contested issues in student affairs: Diverse perspectives and respectful dialogue* (pp. 122–134). Sterling, VA: Stylus Press.

Dewald, N. H. (1999). Transporting good library instruction practices into the web environment: An analysis of online tutorials. *Journal of Academic Librarianship*, *25*(1), 26–31. doi:10.1016/S0099-1333(99)80172-4

Ellison, N. B., Steinfield, C., & Lampe, C. (2007). The benefits of Facebook "friends": Social capital and college students' use of online social network sites. *Journal of Computer-Mediated Communication*, *12*(4), 1143–1168. doi:10.1111/j.1083-6101.2007.00367.x

Gikas, J., & Grant, M. (2013). Mobile computing devices in higher education: Student perspectives on learning with cellphones, smartphones & social media. *The Internet and Higher Education*, *19*, 18–26. doi:10.1016/j.iheduc.2013.06.002

Hird, J. (2011, August 1). *11 ways to measure the value of social media*. Retrieved 18 March 2014, from https://econsultancy.com/blog/7838-11-ways-to-measure-the-value-of-social-media

Hughes, A. M. (2013). Academics in the UK use social media to enhance traditional scholarly reading. *Evidence Based Library and Information Practice*, *8*(4), 145–147.

Jacklin, M. L., & Robinson, K. (2013). Evolution of various library instruction strategies: Using student feedback to create and enhance online active learning assignments. *Partnership: The Canadian Journal of Library & Information Practice & Research*, *8*(1), 1–21.

Lee, C. S., & Ma, L. (2012). News sharing in social media: The effect of gratifications and prior experience. *Computers in Human Behavior*, *28*(2), 331–339. doi:10.1016/j.chb.2011.10.002

Mack, D., Behler, A., Roberts, B., & Rimland, E. (2007). Reaching students with Facebook: Data and best practices. *Electronic Journal of Academic and Special Librarianship*, *8*(2), 4–12.

Murphy, J., & Meyer, H. (2013). Best (and not so best) practices in social media. *ILA Reporter*, *31*(6), 12–15.

Nicholas, D., Watkinson, A., Rowlands, I., & Jubb, M. (2011). Social media, academic research and the role of university libraries. *Journal of Academic Librarianship*, *37*(5), 373–375. doi:10.1016/j.acalib.2011.06.023

Peters, K., Chen, Y., Kaplan, A. M., Ognibeni, B., & Pauwels, K. (2013). Social media metrics—A framework and guidelines for managing social media. *Journal of Interactive Marketing*, *27*(4), 281–298. doi:10.1016/j.intmar.2013.09.007

Pew Research Internet Project. (2013, December 30). *Social media update 2013*. Retrieved 16 March 2014, from http://www.pewinternet.org/2013/12/30/social-media-update-2013

Philips, N. K. (2011). Academic library use of Facebook: Building relationships with students. *Journal of Academic Librarianship*, *37*(6), 512–522. doi:10.1016/j.acalib.2011.07.008

Pollet, T. V., Roberts, S. G. B., & Dunbar, R. I. M. (2011). Use of social network sites and instant messaging does not lead to increased offline social network size, or to emotionally closer relationships with offline network members. *Cyberpsychology, Behavior, and Social Networking*, *14*(4), 253–258. doi:10.1089/cyber.2010.0161 PMID:21067280

Selwyn, N. (2012). Social media in higher education. In A. Gladman (Ed.), *The Europa world of learning 2012* (62nd ed.; pp. 3–7). London: Routledge.

Smith, E. (2013). User education in social media applications @ your library. *The Australian Library Journal, 62*(4), 305–313. doi:10.1080/000 49670.2013.845075

Subrahmanyam, K., Reich, S. M., Waechter, N., & Espinoza, G. (2008). Online and offline social networks: Use of social networking sites by emerging adults. *Journal of Applied Developmental Psychology, 29*(6), 420–433. doi:10.1016/j.appdev.2008.07.003

Tenopir, C., Volentine, R., & King, D. W. (2013). Social media and scholarly reading. *Online Information Review, 37*(2), 193–216. doi:10.1108/OIR-04-2012-0062

Weinberg, B. D., de Ruyter, K., Dellarocas, C., Buck, M., & Keeling, D. I. (2013). Destination social business: Exploring an organization's journey with social media, collaborative community and expressive individuality. *Journal of Interactive Marketing, 27*(4), 299–310. doi:10.1016/j.intmar.2013.09.006

ADDITIONAL READING

Bobish, G. (2011). Participation and pedagogy: Connecting the social web to ACRL learning outcomes. *Journal of Academic Librarianship, 37*(1), 54–63. doi:10.1016/j.acalib.2010.10.007

Bridges, L. (2012). Librarian as professor of social media literacy. *Journal of Library Innovation, 3*(1), 48–65.

Burhanna, K. J., Seeholzer, J., & Salem, J. Jr. (2009). No natives here: A focus group study of student perceptions of Web 2.0 and the academic library. *Journal of Academic Librarianship, 35*(6), 523–532. doi:10.1016/j.acalib.2009.08.003

DeAndrea, D., Ellison, N., LaRose, R., Steinfield, C., & Fiore, A. (2012). Serious social media: On the use of social media for improving students' adjustment to college. *The Internet and Higher Education, 15*(1), 15–23. doi:10.1016/j.iheduc.2011.05.009

Duggan, M., & Smith, A. (2014, January). Pew Research Center. Social media update 2013 [full report]. Retrieved 10 March 2014, from http://www.pewinternet.org/files/2013/12/PIP_Social-Networking-2013.pdf

Engeström, Y., & Middleton, D. (Eds.). (1998). *Cognition and communication at work.* Cambridge University Press.

Hargittai, E. (2007). Whose space? Differences among users and non-users of social network sites. *Journal of Computer-Mediated Communication, 13*(1), 276–297. doi:10.1111/j.1083-6101.2007.00396.x

Jacobson, T., & Mackey, T. (2013). Proposing a metaliteracy model to redefine information literacy. *Communications in Information Literacy, 7*(2), 84–91.

Johnson, L., Adams Becker, S., Estrada, V., & Freeman, A. (2014). *NMC Horizon Report: 2014 Higher Education Edition.* Austin, TX: New Media Consortium.

Kim, K.-S., Sin, S.-C. J., & Yoo-Lee, E. (2013, forthcoming). Undergraduates' use of social media as information sources. *College and Research Libraries* [anticipated Publication Date: July 1, 2014]. Retrieved 19 March 2014, from http://crl.acrl.org/content/early/2013/02/06/crl13-455.full.pdf

King, D. L. (2013). *Face2Face: Using Facebook, Twitter, and other social media tools to create great customer connections.* Chicago: Information Today.

Lave, J., & Wenger, E. (1991). *Situated learning: Legitimate peripheral participation.* Cambridge University Press. doi:10.1017/CBO9780511815355

Lesy, M. (2007). Visual literacy. *The Journal of American History*, *94*(1), 143–153. doi:10.2307/25094783

Mackey, T. R., & Jacobson, T. E. (2011). Reframing information literacy as a metaliteracy. *College & Research Libraries*, *72*(1), 62–78. doi:10.5860/crl-76r1

Midyette, J., Youngkin, A., & Snow-Croft, S. (2014). Social media and communications: Developing a policy to guide the flow of information. *Medical Reference Services Quarterly*, *33*(1), 39–50. doi:10.1080/02763869.2014.866482 PMID:24528263

Nández, G., & Borrego, Á. (2013). Use of social networks for academic purposes: A case study. *The Electronic Library*, *31*(6), 781–791. doi:10.1108/EL-03-2012-0031

OpenScholar website (2014). "Open scholar was created for faculty. It is an open source application built on the Drupal open source content management system and offers scholars the ability build personal or project-based academic web. Ideal for communication and collaboration." Retrieved 18 March 2014, from http://theopenscholar.org/pages/about-openscholar

Ovadia, S. (2013). When social media meets scholarly publishing. *Behavioral & Social Sciences Librarian*, *32*(3), 194–198. doi:10.1080/01639269.2013.817886

Sanderson, H. (2011). Using learning styles in information literacy: Critical considerations for librarians. *Journal of Academic Librarianship*, *37*(5), 376–385. doi:10.1016/j.acalib.2011.06.002

Santos, C., Almeida, S., Pedro, L., Aresta, M., & Koch-Grunberg, T. (2013, July). Students' perspectives on badges in educational social media platforms: The case of SAPO campus tutorial badges. In *IEEE 13th International Conference on Advanced Learning Technologies (ICALT),* (pp. 351-353).

Saw, G., Abbott, W., Donaghey, J., & McDonald, C. (2013). Social media for international students—It's not all about Facebook. *Library Management*, *34*(3), 156–174. doi:10.1108/01435121311310860

Steiner, S. K. (2012). *Strategic planning for social media in libraries (TECH SET #15).* Chicago: ALA TechSource.

Sternberg, J. (2011, September 2). Social media's slow slog into the ivory towers of academia. *The Atlantic*. Retrieved 10 March, 2014, from http://www.theatlantic.com/technology/archive/2011/09/social-medias-slow-slog-into-the-ivory-towers-of-academia/244483/

Verdier, R. L. (2009). The rise of Web 2.0 technology and its implications for democracy. Bachelors Honors Thesis, Wesleyan University. Retrieved 19 March 2014, from http://wesscholar.wesleyan.edu/etd_hon_theses/301/

Vygotsky, L. S. (1980). *Mind in society: The development of higher psychological processes.* Harvard University Press.

Witek, D., & Grettano, T. (2012). Information literacy on Facebook: An analysis. *RSR. Reference Services Review*, *40*(2), 242–257. doi:10.1108/00907321211228309

Yadagiri, S., & Sagar Thalluri, P. (2012). Information technology on surge: Information literacy on demand. *DESIDOC Journal of Library & Information Technology*, *32*(1), 64–69. doi:10.14429/djlit.32.1.1408

Yang, C. C., Brown, B. B., & Braun, M. T. (2014). From Facebook to cell calls: Layers of electronic intimacy in college students' interpersonal relationships. *New Media & Society*, *16*(1), 5–23. doi:10.1177/1461444812472486

Zhang, Y., & Leung, L. (2014). A review of social networking service (SNS) research in communication journals from 2006 to 2011. *New Media & Society*, *16*(3), 1–18.

KEY TERMS AND DEFINITIONS

Collaboration/Collaborative Learning: Engagement of multiple educators, library users and/or learners with each other, either online or inside of the library, which leads to further communication and enriched contact about the library's features.

Community Building: Efforts in gathering groups of library users, or even groups of libraries or librarians, for the purposes of shared experiences in learning, in exchange of ideas and viewpoints, and support for information services and resources.

Current Awareness: A process of keeping up-to-date in a subject field or discipline via systematic methods which include technological tools like alerts and constant contact with other professionals, organizations, and associations.

Library Instruction: A planned program which teaches a sequence of increasingly complex information literacy skills, technological skills, and reasoning skills to library users, in this case, college students and their faculty members.

Outreach: The targeted contact of, and communication with, specific audiences to promote library tools, resources, and services; a main mission and goal of most libraries.

Self-Regulated Learning: The cognitive and affective aspects of learning as propelled by one's own motivation and monitoring; considered a high level of human control important to success in formal and informal education.

Social Media: Those online tools which permit users to communicate constantly via their mobile phones and internet connections and which both encourage and display relationships among users that permits sharing news, photos, etc. in ways which permeate daily life.

Chapter 15
Educational Edifices Need a Mobile Strategy to Fully Engage in Learning Activities

Sharon L. Burton
American Meridian University, USA

Hamil R. Harris
Washington Post, USA

Darrell Norman Burrell
Florida Institute of Technology, USA

Kim L. Brown-Jackson
National Graduate School of Quality Management, USA

Dustin Bessette
National Graduate School of Quality Management, USA

Rondalynne McClintock
Claremont Graduate University, USA

Shanel Lu
National Graduate School of Quality Management, USA

Yoshino W. White
Management Consultant, USA

ABSTRACT

Research in mobile learning (m-learning) about technology and software and mobile learning's application to educationally related undertakings and a long-term sustainability remain unclear. This chapter untwines the tangled information surrounding m-learning strategy through examining the drivers and perceptions for m-learning in the 21st century. The data will unearth the value of employing diverse modalities of m-learning. Administrators will gain knowledge to develop and implement mobile strategy. Faculty will enhance their familiarity on the diverse types of m-learning tools and the value of employing m-learning in the classroom. Administrators and faculty members will gather knowledge that guides efforts to diminish barriers in support of a successful m-learning implementation. In addition, administrators will garner developed knowledge to analyze, gather requirements, develop, and then implement a strategic m-learning plan for long-term sustainability. Academics and practitioners will gain insight into understanding the balance of a mobile strategy amid economic value and the required controls.

DOI: 10.4018/978-1-4666-7401-1.ch015

INTRODUCTION

M-learning technology and software research, and m-learning's relevance to educationally linked activities is meager. This chapter will review the world of m-learning and divulge leading answers regarding the anytime, and anyplace state of learning in the mobile space. The chapter provides answers to questions such as: What are mobile devices and how are they used in education? How is the technology utilized and applied in learning? What are the different types of mobile devices used in education? What are m-learning impacts to education and learning? What are the different transformative avenues that mobile learning serves (e.g., anytime anywhere utilization) in this educational virtual environment? This work will pull forward information and data regarding functional capabilities to access learning through mobile technology, as well as assist readers to better comprehend the intricate and precipitously shifting landscape of higher education and research in this globalizing era. The researchers will sift through today's mobile learning perceptions, positives and negatives, and the definition of mobile learning and the understanding of mobile devices. Also, this work will review understanding of the future meaning of mobile learning and mobile devices as this technology's learning use continues to be re-conceptualized. Moreover, the data will unveil the performance of mobile devices for educational usage as functionality relates to how courses should be developed. Further, this work will expose emerging mobile learning application in remote locations. This chapter will result in a current understanding of mobile technology, m-learning, as well as the vital role of mobility and communication in the application and process of m-learning in the 21st century.

M-Learning Defined

Learning through mobile device technologies is broadly recognized by the overall learning community (Lan & Huang, 2011). Mobile learning (m-learning) in fact extends the reach of education in many parts of the world, not only to all social-economic levels, but also in a manner unconstrained of location and time, thus signifying the new opportunity for further development in the education industry (Allathkani, 2013). Mobile technology is a powerful trend within this information age. The internet and computers provided principle means in learners' acknowledgements and usages of fresh computer technology (Yang, 2012). M-learning has roots in a project referred to as HandLeR. This project, deemed a student project, and the first of its kind, was a technological visible expression of an idea of a personal or mobile system to sustain continuous and lifelong learning (Sharples, 2000; Sharples, Corlett, & Westmancott, 2002). As posited by Naismith and Corlett (2006), the HandleR project received funding from British Telecom and Kodak. This funding led to the growth of the United Kingdom's University of Birmingham's active m-learning community (Naismith & Corlett, 2006). Yang (2012) later described mobile learning as gaining its name through educational concentration on enabling and outspreading the scope of instructing and absorbing information.

Numerous definitions exist for m-learning. According to Pinkwart, Hoppe, Milrad, & Perez (2003), M-learning is e-learning that utilizes mobile technologies and transmissions that are wireless (2003). Per Attewell and Savill-Smith (2005), m-learning is learning through "wireless technological devices that can be pocketed and utilized wherever the learner's device can retrieve unbroken transmissions signals." Another view of m-learning is the capability to acquire or deliver educational learning objects on personal handheld devices. Educational learning objects denote digital learning assets, which comprise forms of content or media accessible on personal handheld devices.

Through the writings of Pinkwart et al. (2003), readers could garner the understanding that m-learning was thought to be a subset of e-learning. In 2000, Yacci defined e-learning, also known as distance education as "the practical subset of education that deals with instruction in which distance and time are the criterial [*sic*] attributes; that is, student and teacher (and other students) are separated by distance and/or time" (p.1). Today, e-learning's understanding has changed as it relates to m-learning. Developing in significance and distinction, m-learning is education wherein the key technology is a handheld device, as also according to (Ally, 2009).

Numerous benefits are associated with m-learning. This type of learning can be delivered anytime, and anywhere. Table 1 provides benefits of m-learning at a high level. When drilling down on m-learning benefits, numerous advantages emerge. M-learning is flexible, supports a just-in-time need, supports multiple learning styles, enhances social education and learning, supports reflection and data collection, and eliminates technological barriers. First, let us review m-learning's flexibility.

M-learning's flexibility leads to convenience. This flexibility and accessibility derives from education and training being able to be accessed anytime and anywhere. This is the precise instant that learning is necessitated. Next is the significance of m-learning.

M-learning permits education and training to be delivered at anytime and anywhere instead of being simulated. Thus, the ability to have m-learning anytime and anywhere supports education and learning at an appointed time, as well as need. This anytime and anywhere education and training lends to the relevance of the need for such education. This relevant understanding is in support of multiple learning styles – visual, auditory, and kinesthetic.

As stated by Robertson, Smeille, Wilson, and Cox, learning styles are the manners in which learners process new information (2011). Even though other series exist regarding learning, a prevailing understanding is that learners process information in diverse ways. Through m-learning, visual learners benefit from illustration through text, animation, and photographs. The visual learner can view images and have visuals in their mind. Auditory learners may benefit from m-learning through hearing and listening. This hearing and listening can be in the form of video, plus listening to and contributing to discussions. This learner remembers by listening. Next is the kinesthetic learner who may benefit from m-learning through activity. As posited by Hutton, kinesthetic learners desire to "move around and touch things" (2013, Help Kinesthetic Learners) in order to learn as best as possible.

Table 1. Benefits, challenges, and resolutions for m-learning

Benefits	Challenges	Resolutions
Access information outside of learning institutions.	Potential distractions. Data security.	Develop a mobile strategy that provides solutions to overcome challenges and promote learning.
Reach underserved populations due to the low cost of mobile technologies.	Fill teaching and learning capabilities not fully understood by educators.	Ensure faculty members and administrators are engaged in on-going education and training.
Foster collaboration.	Inability to understand the multiple technologies and share information through such technologies.	Develop communities of practice for all faculty members, administrators, and learners.
Support personalized learning.	Size of technologies and font sizes can hamper learning.	Promote continuous education and training.

Whilst m-learning supports the learning styles, it augments social education and learning. A salient presupposition of social learning is that significant communication amid collaborators can bring about amplified comprehension. Social education through m-learning encourages group effort and knowledge sharing in forums. As a result, social education through m-learning can transform educational settings, preparation, and deliveries. Through the employment of social education, social media, and contributing in on-line communities, learners can identify with certain actions and behaviors, and actively act upon learning content. Academics can perform as facilitators of the learners' interactions. As well as enhancing social education and learning, m-learning supports reflection, contemplation, plus information and data collection.

Through introspection, the observation and examination of one's own thoughts and ideas, m-learning holds a space in the process of formal and informal reflection, as well as a more formalized experimental approach. This reflection occurs through recordings of thoughts, ideas, and opinions. Introspection is derived from psychologist Wilhelm Wundt who supported experiential psychology and set the stage for behaviorism (Silverman, 2011). The voice recorder on cellular phones facilitates immediate recording of thoughts, observations, and opinions. This technology also supports evidence collection. The easy mobility of mobile technology supports ready availability used for assembling a collection of facts, data, and substantiations through audio, still, and video cameras. Additionally, m-learning bridges learning barriers.

M-learning aids the movement of learning that is contextualized and intermingled into current, practical, and real-life learning experiences. This basis of learning can be understood in adult learning, particularly in Knowles' six postulations:

1. Self-directedness,
2. Need to know,
3. Use of experience in learning,
4. Readiness to learn,
5. Orientation to learning, and
6. Internal motivation (Taylor & Kroth, 2009).

Also, m-learning removes technological barriers in learning through the use of mobile devices. In cases when individuals are using personal mobile devices, they are readily accustomed to the technology. More, m-learning's capability to reach learners anytime and anyplace supports the functionality to reach underrepresented populations. Developed using mobile authoring tools, m-learning permits a single design to permeate traverse platforms to diverse mobile technologies.

M-learning is ubiquitous learning that engages learners and mobile technologies. This learning type influences ever-present mobile technology for the acceptance, growth, and implementation of knowledge, skills, abilities, and competencies. M-learning's influence infuses through an education and training, or performance foundation even though the location of the learners may be liberated from time, location, and space. Recognizing the electrified advances in wireless and mobile technologies, learning now occurs far beyond classroom walls into the anytime and anywhere environment. M-learning turned a pivotal development point when it became the investiture of a conference for learning. Within the 21st century is now a conference dedicated to m-learning. This annual conference is appropriately named mLearn.

M-learning emerged from its project status and is cornering its position in mainstream education. Through traversing educational models, and telecommunications, and then becoming a valid revenue stream, m-learning is a force to be reckoned with. Benefits and challenges exist. Benefits are revealed through the capability to deliver education through an anytime and anyplace model. Challenges remain in the details of technological understanding, and application. The resolution for such benefits and challenges at institutions of higher learning is to design and implement a mobile strategy that can fully engage in learning activities in the mobile environment. The development of a mobile strategy should include learning considerations in each process step. An overview of these benefits and challenges are documented in Table 1.

MOBILE DEVICES PORTABILITY AND USAGE

Mobile computing technologies continue to evolve at a brisk pace. Today mobile technologies include mobile phones, smart phones, phablets, and tablet computers (Yang, 2012). Mobile software development is keeping pace with mobile technology's swiftness. The combination of the rapid growth in mobile technology and mobile software is driving global learning in the mobile learning, m-learning, space. Seppala and Alamaki postulated this trend of mobile devices would electrify educational learning because 98% of university learners owned mobile phones (2003).

The data shows that more individuals are currently using mobile applications to a larger degree than they are on the world-wide-web. According to Ally and Samaka (2013) individuals in developing countries do not have access to information and educational material through desktop computers; however, such information can be accessed through mobile devices. The 2013 International Telecommunications Union (ITU) report shows there are 6.8 billion mobile-cellular subscriptions. This is an increase over the previously reported 5.3 billion mobile-cellular subscription in the 2010 ITU report. The 2013 ITU report further establishes that mobile-cellular subscriptions are at approximately 100%. In stark contrast, 2.7 billion people are online (e-learning), this is almost 40%. The Pew Institute provides the following adult ownership information: 90% of Americans own cell phones, 58% of Americans own smart phones, 38% of Americans have e-readers, and 42% have a tablet computer (2014).

Mobile device usage is a focus of colleges and universities, as well as for profit businesses. The electrifying speed that mobile technology impacted college and university campuses is evident through companies like NV3 Technologies. NV3 Technologies installed charging stations at four institutions of higher learning (Razzak, 2011). Razzak notes these learning edifices are Auburn University in Alabama, the University of Alaska, the University of Miami in Coral Gables, Florida, and Towson State University in Maryland (2011).

Mobile devices such as laptops, iPods, tablets, and mobile phones are used in colleges and universities. Duke University's August 2004-2005 freshman class received Apple iPods containing freshman orientation information, the university's academic calendar, and the university's website for downloading academic materials (Belanger, 2005; Gawel, 2004). Encouraging innovative technology usage, Duke University provided 20GB devices equipped with Belkin Voice Recorders; however, later stopped distributing the tool, yet still encourage usage (Read, 2006). According to Seaton Hall University's website an evident feature of Seaton Hall University's technology plan is the University's Mobile Computing Program, relished as the university's adaptation of ubiquitous computing (n.d.). Further, mobile computing technologies utilized in the program are changed every two years for learners and every three years for faculty members (Seaton Hall University, n.d.). The University's website reveals a semester mobile computing fee, fulltime in addition to technology fees. The take-a-ways from mobile devices portability and usage is technological advancements, learner-driven needs, and social constructivism are constantly reshaping the manner colleges and universities, instructors, learners, and administrators conduct educational activities and focus on technologies utilized and budgeted. Mobile learning tools include digital dictionaries, DVD players, e-readers, handheld, iPods, iPads, multimedia cellular phones (e.g., Blackberries, Androids, and Phablets), and MP3 players. These portable modes, discussed in popular and academic literature as mobile, nomadic, PDAs, portable, and wireless are an integral part of society. Colleges and universities must be prepared to learn and understand the plethora of m-learning functionality, capability, application, and forward development potential.

M-LEARNING IMPACTS TO EDUCATION AND LEARNING

Technology is ubiquitous. Through technology, learners and educators can develop an overall awareness of technology as an influencer (Burton, Bessette, Brown-Jackson, & Grimm, 2013). M-learning offers an ever-present quality and enables users to gain immediate access to education and learning (Ismail, Bokhare, & Azizian, 2013). The acceptance and implementation of technology programs and practices requires examining their effectiveness in diverse educational boundaries (Prettyman, Ward, Jaulk, & Awad, 2012). Impacts to understanding in terms of learning through technology include learners' perceptions (Prettyman et al., 2012), knowledge construction (Binsaleh, S., & Binsaleh, M. 2013), collaborative learning (Rogers, Connelly, Hazelwood, & Tedesco (2010), information and exchange, and lifelong learning.

Due to the number of people with mobile-cellular subscription, this data provided an understanding of how m-learning moved into the education and learning space. M-learning wraps under the framework of distance education incorporating several elements from Knowles' adult learning model, as well as the basic learning theories (behaviorism, cognitivism, and constructivism). M-learning impacts learning at the college and university level, as well as prepares learners to move into the work world with a heightened understanding of training modalities. Businesses

must move towards a learning oriented standpoint in order to take action to market fluctuations and enhanced competition (Finch, Burrell, Walker, Rahim, & Dawson, 2010). United Technologies Corp., according to Summerfield (2005) implemented m-learning into its training modalities and supported its employees in taking online courses through Stanford University. Summerfield further posited that m-learning reduced corporate training cost in that travel costs were lessened and this time savings enabled employees to be more productive (2005). For colleges and universities to employ an m-learning strategy, these organizations must understand the changes which they experience prior to responding. It is important to understand that acting in response to change often requires businesses to seek changes in their organizational cultures (Finch, Burrell, Walker, Rahim, & Dawson, 2010).

MOBILE TECHNOLOGY TOOLS AND THE APPLICATION TO A MOBILE STRATEGY COURSE PROJECT

Multiple technology tools exist that are used in the academic realm. These tools include but are not limited to; laptops, smart phones, tablet computers, personal digital assistants. Many of these items are integrated into the rationalization of educational learning tools to assist student learners in higher education in the 21st century. The potential benefits of sustainability planning and strategic actions that focus on economic, environmental, and social gains will help to ensure the future growth and health of higher education (Burrell, Anderson, Bessette, & Dawson, 2011). Mobile technology tools can ensure that the potential benefits are gained, the sustainable plans are obtained, and learners have a better sense of communication and cognitive skills through elaborative mobile technology usages. Mobile technology is a valuable asset that is now being widely used in higher education.

Mobile technology tools are now also employed in higher educational settings. Technology is currently surrounding the everyday workforce and educational spectrum. Technology has the ability to provide compelling assistance in higher education. Borquez (2004) found that educational institutions worldwide have integrated technological solutions to enhance the learning process. These integrated m-learning solutions have numerous implications to higher education's sustainable operations solution. At this point two important questions need to be answered: "Exactly what are m-learning tools?" The other question is, "What is the history of these m-learning tools?"

Laptops

The laptop is a tool that can run from battery power or AC power; it has fewer cables than a desktop. Designed for portability and full functionality, the laptop has a built-in monitor, keyboard, functionality that act as the mouse, and speakers. Numerous laptops are designed to have the capability of a desktop. This means that a detachable mouse, bigger monitor, speakers, and other exterior technologies can to added to the laptop. Other names for the laptop are labtop, notebook, and netbooks.

History of the Laptops

The laptop has history as far back as 1979. This laptop, designed by William Moggridge, was for Grid Systems Corporation. This early laptop was used by NASA's early 1980's space shuttle program. Another designer of the laptop was Manny Fernandez. This laptop built for the executive level employee was promoted as the first laptop computer in 1983. This computer was promoted through Gavilan Computer Company. The laptop computer moved through numerous iterations by

numerous companies to include but are not limited to (i.e., Epson, Radio Shack, IBM, Compaq, NEC, Apple, Lenovo, and McIntosh) to become the technology it is today.

Smartphones

This smartphone, known also known as smart phone, is a mobile phone. This phone has more progressive computing ability and connectivity than phones with basic features. The smartphone is capable of completing many functions akin to a computer. Such functionality includes calling, email, limited to text messaging, still and video camera, MP3 player and video playback, as well as calling, and web browsing. This phone's capability includes digital voice service. Some phones have the capability to produce different voice tones, different from the voice tone of the caller.

History of the Smartphones

The telephone dates back to Alexander Graham Bell. In the 1980s, Motorola introduced cell phones to the public. Later, in 1993, IBM and BellSouth introduced the first smartphones. Smartphone capabilities continued to emerge over the years, as companies battled for position in the industry.

Tablet Computers

Tablet computers are mobile computers with display, touch capability, battery, cameras, and have finger or stylus touch. The tablet computer employs an operating system developed to employ a touch surface. Tablet computer makers deliver distinct features, advantages, and disadvantages. Applications (Apps) on tablet computers, in addition to touch screens, support the delivery of a computer usage experience that is different from that of a laptop and desktop computers. Users can use the built in keyboard or, depending upon the tablet, attach an external keyboard.

History of Tablet Computers

The tablet computer dates back to 1987 with the onset of the Linus Write-Top computer. This green screen computer enabled the functionality of a stylus. Later, in 1989, Palm delivered the Gridpad. Gridpad ran on MS-Dos. In 1993, Apple debuted the Newton, which enabled the functionality of a stylus. Then in 1997, Palm introduced the PalmPilot, a stylus enabled technology. The PalmPilot was referred to as a personal digital assistant, PDA. In 2000, Microsoft introduced a tablet personal computer to market. The term tablet pc caught the attention of the public and manufacturers of mobile technology. Later in 2010, Apple introduced the iPad. In 2012, Microsoft introduced the Surface tablet. Over the years, other companies have introduced iPads.

Mobile technology is used in higher education learning because it assists learners in many areas of cognitive perspectives. Mobile learning in general is important to the skill development and growth of students as learners in the future. The future of the educational industry is at stake based on the fact that education can provide a valued return on investment for students and learners. M-learning includes digital video that is a leading segment of mobile technology tools, which assists the virtual aspect of learning. Digital video is increasingly being used as a technology to facilitate learning experiences both within the classroom and without, e.g. (Buckingham, Issy, & Juian, 1999). Digital video encompasses the virtual cognitive portion of the communication for students to gather and group informative learning perspectives together. The popularity of m-learning and mobile technology is driving colleges, universities, and other educational edifices towards a technology strategy. However, the current strategies are very diverse.

CLOUD COMPUTING IN MOBILE LEARNING

Behind the precipitous adoption of mobile technologies in the learning domain are advances in cellular communication delivery systems, with focused emphasis on the impact of combining cloud computing with mobile devices. Cloud computing with mobile devices, referred to as mobile cloud computing, entails combining the technological advances in electronic communications with the innovations in computing hardware and software. Cloud computing enables the mobility of technology to support dispersed learning over time (El-Sofany, Al Tayeb, Alghatani, & El-Seoud, 2013). This ability is important because learning is a cumulative process across both formal and informal contexts, requiring the learner to make connections among various experiences.

Mobile cloud computing leverages the capability of mobile devices, which are inherently resource restricted, by separating the user interface from the application logic (Rao, Sasidhar, & Kumar, 2013). The separation of the interface from the application is crucial to the ability to create fast interactions of flexible content that can be accessed easily and leverage a variety of learning modalities (Naismith & Corlett, 2006). The accessibility and ease of use of audio files, streaming video, and voice over Internet protocol (VOIP) are incumbent on the separation between the user interface and the application logic as it is a main advantage in making this technology a cost effective choice for delivering learning. The advantage of mobile cloud computing centers around the ability of streamlining the processes required to deliver instruction by optimizing the capacity of the hardware while ensuring the security of the software (Rao et al., 2013). It is this optimization that allows applications to respond efficiently on mobile devices, creating an acceptable user learning experience. In fact, the separation of application software from a constrained computing platform is another key to the advantages afforded by mobile cloud computing. Thus et al. posited that "context is the most distinctive feature in mobile learning" (Thus et al., 2012). With regard to the learning context, the separation between application logic and user interface addresses latency issues that appear as transmission delays, constrained battery life, and limitations on bandwidth that can impede the learning experience.

Incorporating cloud computing into mobile learning environments advances understanding beyond enhancing the contextual nature of learning. Cloud computing reduces the costs associated with hardware, licensing, and software required to deliver learning (Rao et al., 2012) that is relevant, context aware, and reliable. The business processes required to implement mobile learning rely on the ability to leverage computing Infrastructure as a Service (IaaS), a technique that enables the organization to scale and manage applications and services as needed. In the same vein, Platforms as a Service (PaaS) make use of a centralized operating system, relational databases, and security enhanced connectivity. Additionally, Software as a Service (SasS) and Exchange Hosted Services (EHS) aid in data encryption and confidentiality for sensitive and protected information. Cloud computing in mobile learning enhances the overall learning experience by improving the performance of the learning delivery, lowering associated operating costs, and improving information access across the spectrum.

COLLABORATION AND M-LEARNING

M-learning supports cognitive psychologist, Vygotsky's, social constructivist learning wherein learners and instructors collaborate on the construction of knowledge. Social-constructivism

theory, also called socio-constructivism, and constructivism provide that information in the brain is endlessly modifying. Constructivism focuses on actively learning versus passively absorbing information (Huang & Dolejs, 2007). Through constructivism, learners systematize their knowledge and construct their experiences through personal lenses as opposed to education through pedagogy where significance is placed on the role of the teacher (Bedi, 2004; Knowles, 1980). Per (Burrell, Finch, Fisher, Rahim, & Dawson, 2011), "constructivist learning theories have sought to create learning environments that come closer to real life environments." Additionally with pedagogy, learners may have the tendency to repeat their instructors' understandings of materials. On the other hand, adult learners are identified by adult learner traits (Finch & Rahim, 2011). A better understanding of adults' traits can be gleaned in Malcolm Knowles' six adult learning postulations:

1. Self-directedness,
2. Need to know,
3. Use of experience in learning,
4. Readiness to learn,
5. Orientation to learning, and
6. Internal motivation (Chan, 2010; Forrest & Peterson, 2006; Knowles, 1985; Merriam, Caffarella, & Baumgartner, 2006).

Indication of the adult learning knowledge understanding in Knowles's model is, with McGrath's reasoning, in the difference between child and adult learners. "Adult learners need to know why they are learning new knowledge before they are willing to participate" (McGrath, 2009, p. 99).

Through these collaborative and omnipresent environments learners are capable of being involved in original, critical, and multi-faceted thinking. This collaborative thinking with ownership of efforts and technology by learners is positioned at a higher level of Bloom's Taxonomy, a learning assessment tool (Skiba, 2013), which includes evaluating, analyzing, elaborating, and problem-solving (Barrios, 2004). Through technology, learners are enclosed with chances for learning and changes in their opinions of themselves (Bebell & Kay, 2010).

MOBILE AND M-LEARNING POLICIES AT COLLEGES AND UNIVERSITIES: AN ANALYSIS

Colleges and Universities are employing mobile strategies; however, as mobile technology evolves, so is the need for a widening of mobile policies that are a part of mobile strategies. This heading, Mobile and M-learning Polices at Colleges and Universities, contains a review of multiple colleges' and universities' mobile policy strategies. In review of the information, mobile policy strategy is provided in multiple ways. Some websites provide information from the colleges' or universities' websites. Other websites provide mobile policy strategy from a general website that represents a state's colleges and universities system. This mobile strategy review is of colleges and universities across the United States. The size of the institution is not a criterion.

The first institution is Berea College, which is located in Berea, KY. Berea College's policy provides the following mobile technology information:

Mobile telephones or other portable wireless devices may be issued to college employees who have a frequent need for remote telephone access or for use in the event of an emergency. College-owned portable wireless devices and service category breakouts are to be acquired following the College policy and procedures. (Berea College, 2013, Portable Wireless Devices)

Berea College's (2013) website provides information such as suggested personal voice plans, and suggested group voice plans, supported data plans, and suggested handheld wireless devices. Additional information includes utilization of handheld wireless devices, and how individuals should apply for wireless service. Next is Carlton College located in Northfield, MN.

Carlton College's policy provides the following mobile technology information:

This policy governs the use of mobile devices to conduct college business or to access college data. Accessing college email and calendaring are considered to be conducting college business, and is therefore included in this policy. Carleton College has adopted this policy to safeguard the college's investments and data and to comply with various regulations. This policy applies to both college-owned and personally-owned mobile devices which connect to the Carleton network. Mobile devices include any portable device that allows access to college information and data. (Carlton College, 2012, College Data on Mobile Devices)

Carlton Colleges' (2012) website provides information such as policy centered on the configuration of college and personally owned mobile technologies aimed at protecting susceptible data. Additional documented website policy procedures include securing mobile technologies and disposal, in addition to and how to handle breaches in security. The Minnesota State Colleges and Universities' system has a website that provides an overall mobile learning and m-learning policy.

Minnesota State Colleges and Universities' system (2014) provides information in numerous headings, with its mobile strategy being no exception. These headings include: mobile strategy on purpose of the electronic communication, definitions, criteria for cellular device, mobile computing device, or other wireless communication service plans, technology approval and annual assessment, individual employee accountability, and cellular technologies. Instead of providing a general policy statement, the Minnesota State

Colleges and Universities' does not give a single paragraph on the purpose of its mobile strategy. Instead, the mobile strategy policy is broken down in the multiple headings.

The University of Washington (2012) located in Seattle, WA provides its mobile strategy policy information in numerous headings. Topic generalized information includes university-issued technologies, personal handheld devices utilized for business purposes, accountability for mobile technology, employee accountability, and non-entitled people regarding the mobile strategy. A heading for additional information is also listed. The University of Washington's mobile strategy purpose statement is as follows:

The University of Washington's policy provides the mobile technology following:

This policy governs the use of, and payment for, mobile device technologies (such as smart phones and tablets) required for business purposes by the University of Washington (UW). This policy applies when a department head determines that an employee holds a position [,] which requires that the employee be regularly available to respond to business-related communication via phone, email, text, etc. This policy addresses mobile devices issued by the UW and personal mobile devices used for business purposes. This policy applies to all units and individuals at the UW including all campuses, colleges, schools, departments, centers, hospitals, clinics and other units. (University of Washington, 2012, Purpose)

Next is the University of Texas, in College Station, Texas.

The University of Texas' website provides policy information under numerous headings. A generalization of these headings includes a position statement, a strategy statement, and recommendations. Under recommendations are several topics. This information includes website design, stand-a-lone websites, and mobile applications.

The University of Texas' mobile strategy includes a comparison between responsive website, mobile website, and mobile applications (University of Texas, 2012). The University of Texas' mobile strategy purpose statement is as follows:

Texas A&M University supports mobile web technologies that simplify keeping pace with a rapidly evolving mobile landscape. These technologies must be:

- **Device Agnostic:** Compatible with any web-capable mobile device.
- **Platform Independent:** Usable by applications written in any language and on any environment.
- **Easy to Use:** Simple to deploy and maintain (Texas A & M University, 2012, Texas A&M's Mobile).

An analysis of the mobile strategies for Berea College, Carlton College, Minnesota State College, the University of Washington, and the University of Texas – Texas A & M University provide a variety of information. Through the review of colleges and universities' mobile strategies, the diversity of such strategies can be understood. Berea College's site notes the need for remote telephone access or for use in the event of an emergency. This terminology is not used in any of the other institutions of higher learning. On the other hand, Berea refers to plans and devices the college deems appropriate to use. Carlton College gives an overall policy that governs the use of mobile devices to perform the business of the college to include accessing college data.

Similar, yet different is the information provided by the Minnesota State Colleges and Universities' system, and the University of Washington, and the University of Texas – Texas A & M University. All three provide the mobile strategy through topic headings. These headings detail specified policy and procedure information that supports the overall mobile strategy. The headings are similar, though different. The Minnesota State Colleges and Universities' system does not give a general statement; however, the University of Washington does provide a mobile strategy purpose statement. The essential features are that all of the colleges, universities, and systems provide information regarding a mobile strategy. The relationship of the information is that it supports aspects of the overall mobile strategy. An overall point to understand is that each mobile strategy has different aspects, some more detailed than the others. If this chapter were to provide a proposition by supposing the aspects of a mobile policy, and then work backward by reviewing numerous college and university systems, there is the opportunity to gather multiple headings that could be used to cross-reference a business requirement for a mobile strategy.

MOBILE AND M-LEARNING SURVEY RESULTS

The determination for a mobile strategy to engage fully in learning activities required further investigation to include the voice of the customer. The customer includes users of mobile technology on the campuses of institutions of higher learning. A survey of 11 questions was conducted regarding m-learning and technologies. The survey was placed on educational and professional sites for data collection. The survey facilitated data collection of demographic aspects of participants, in addition to their understanding and participation in m-learning and mobile technology. Survey participants were asked to complete the survey and did not have to self-identify. It should be understood that demographic information is indicated by gender, age, role, and graduation date range. None of the participants are known by the research team. The researchers reviewed the data for themes. Descriptive statistical data is given, along with a qualitative summary of the survey questions.

RESULTS AND DATA FINDINGS

Eleven (11) research questions were used to collect data. Eighty-two (82) individuals responded in all cases. Survey questions are referred to using the letter "Q" and the number of the questions is as ordered on the survey. Demographic questions include questions Q1 through Q4. The use of demographic questions allows for the cross tabulation of data if required. A built-in assumption was that survey participants would have familiarity with the subject. The results are provided as follows.

Q1: What is your age?

Age groups were divided into seven (7) groups. All 82 survey participants responded to all questions. The disc shows the breakdown of the age groups. Three (3.66%) percent of the respondents are represented in the 18-24 age range. Fourteen (17.07%) percent of the respondents are represented in the 25-34 age range. Thirteen (15.05%) percent of the respondents are represented in the 35-44 age range. Twenty-six (31.71%) percent of the respondents are represented in the 45-54 age range. Eighteen (23.17%) percent of the respondents are represented in the 55-64 age range. Seven (8.64%) percent of the respondents three are represented in the 65-74 age range. None of the respondents were in the 75 or older range.

The data showed that the 45-54 age range had the highest participation in this survey. The 55-64 age range had the second highest responses. The third highest responses were with the 25-34 age range.

Review Figure 1 for details.

Q2: What is your gender?

Distribution of participants in terms of gender is not equal. Sixty-three (76.83%) are female. Nineteen (23.17) are male. No responses were skipped. The survey was not prone to either gender. Review Figure 2 for details.

Figure 1. What is your age?

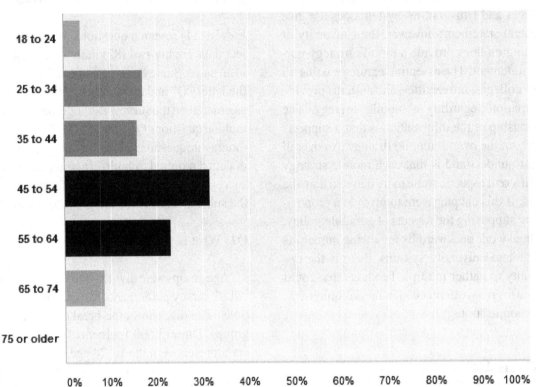

Figure 2. What is your gender?

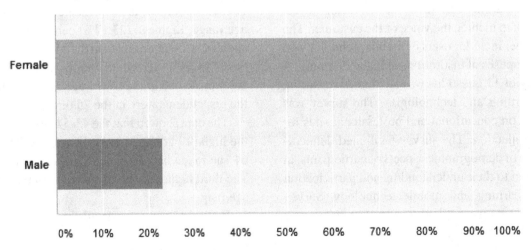

Q3: Select your position at the last institution of higher learning in that you were associated.

Positions were divided into in four (4) groups and all 82 participants responded in question three

(3). The data shows the breakdown of the position groups. Two (2.44%) percent of the respondents are represented in the "Other" category. Eighteen (21.95%) percent of the respondents are represented in the "Instructor" category. Fifty-five

(67.07%) percent of the respondents are represented in the "Learner/Student" category. Seven (8.54%) percent of the respondents are represented in the "Non-applicable" category.

The data showed that the "Learner/Student" category had the highest participation in this survey question. The "Instructor" category had the second highest participation. The third highest responses were with the "Non-applicable" category.

Four of the "Other" category participants chose to provide the name of their positions. The positions are Administrator, Parent, President of a University, and Researcher.

Review Figure 3 for details.

Q4: In what year do you expect to graduate, or select the year you last graduated?

The graphic displays the given number of years provided as the selection list. The responses column provides the number of respondents per category and their representative percentages. The data showed that the "2011-2015" category had the highest participation in this survey question. The "2006-2010" category had the second highest participation. The third highest responses tied at

the number 9 and include the following categories, "1980-1984," "2000-2005," and "2016-2020."

The data shows that the respondents graduated throughout a wide range of years.

Review Figure 4 for details.

Q5: Does your institution of higher learning support mobile technology in the face-to-face classroom environment?

This question had three answer categories. All 82 participants responded in Q5. The data shows the breakdown. Fifty-two (63.41%) of the respondents are represented in the "Yes" category. Twenty (24.39%) of the respondents are represented in the "Unsure" category. Ten, (12.20%) of the respondents are represented in the "No" category.

Review Figure 5 for details.

The results of this question shows a pattern of mobile technology being in the classroom between "1980-1984". The trend decreased, and then returned to the 1980-1984 date ranges between "2000-2005". The "2006-2010" and "2011-2015" shows an upward spiral. The "2016-2020" year range shows a return to the earlier spurt, "1980-1984".

Figure 3. Select your position at the last institution of higher learning in that you were associated.

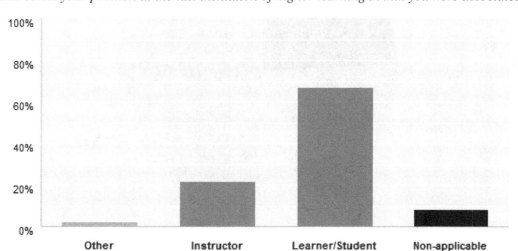

Figure 4. In what year do you expect to graduate, or select the year you last graduated?

Answer Choices	Responses	
Did not graduate	3.66%	3
1965-1969	2.44%	2
1970-1974	3.66%	3
1975-1979	2.44%	2
1980-1984	10.98%	9
1985-1989	6.10%	5
1990-1994	4.88%	4
1995-1999	8.54%	7
2000-2005	10.98%	9
2006-2010	13.41%	11
2011-2015	21.95%	18
2016-2020	10.98%	9
Total		82

Figure 5. Does your institution of higher learning support mobile technology in the face-to-face class-room environment?

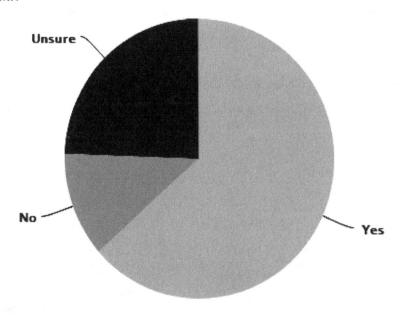

Q6: If your institution of higher learning supports mobile technology in the face-to-face classroom, have you used such technology to support studies inside the classroom?

Categories were divided into in three (3) groups and all 82 participants responded in Q6. The bar chart shows the breakdown as follows. Forty-three (52.44%) of the respondents are represented in the "Yes" category. Twelve (14.63%) of the respondents are represented in the "No" category. Twenty-seven (32.93%) of the respondents are represented in the "N/A" category.

The fact that Twenty-seven, (32.93%) of the respondents are represented in the "N/A" category provides a point of further study.

Review Figure 6 for details.

Q7: Select your academic major, area you teach, or are associated with.

Twenty-two different academic major categories were provided. The highest number of responses was received by the "Medical (All Areas)" category at a total of 23 (28.05%). The

second highest number of responses was received by "Other" category at a total of 14 (17.07%). The third highest number of responses was received by the "Business" category at a total of 13 (15.85%). Six academic majors were not selected by any respondents. The complete listing of respondents and percentages were noted in the chart.

Seven of the "Other" category participants chose to provide the name of their positions. The academic major categories are Communications, Social Work, Mental Health Counseling, Human Resources, and Nursing. Nursing was listed three times. One respondent noted that nursing is not the same as medical.

Review Figure 7 for details.

Q8: Select the top mobile learning activities in which you participated during college.

Seven mobile learning activities were provided. One mobile learning activity was not selected by any respondents. The highest number of responses was received by the "Laptop" category at a total of 41 (50.00%). The second highest number of responses was received by "Non-applicable"

Figure 6. If your institution of higher learning supports mobile technology in the face-to-face classroom, have you used such technology to support studies inside the classroom?

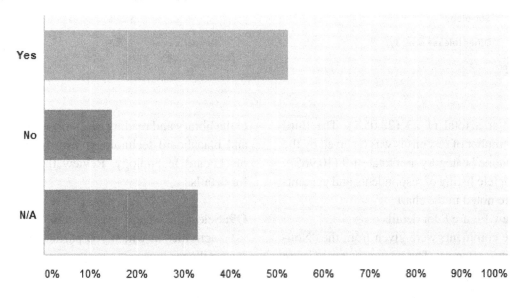

Figure 7. Select your academic major, area you teach, or are associated with

Answer Choices	Responses	
Graphic Design	0.00%	0
Accounting	1.22%	1
Art	1.22%	1
Astrology	0.00%	0
Biology	0.00%	0
Business	15.85%	13
Computer Science	1.22%	1
Criminology	1.22%	1
Criminal Justice	3.66%	3
Education	12.20%	10
Engineering	2.44%	2
Instructional Design	1.22%	1
Law	6.10%	5
Management Information Systems	3.66%	3
Mathematics	2.44%	2
Medical (All areas)	28.05%	23
Meteorology	0.00%	0
Multi-media Design	1.22%	1
Music	0.00%	0
Psychology	0.00%	0
Sociology	1.22%	1
Other (please specify) Responses	17.07%	14
Total		82

category at a total of 23 (28.05%). The third highest number of responses was received by the "Smartphone" category at a total of 9 (10.98%). The complete listing of respondents and percentages were noted in the chart.

Review Figure 8 for details.

Three comments were given from the "Non-applicable" category. The responses are "Going to the library and reading the book as I returned," and blackboard technology. Two people chose blackboard technology. Review the Q8 image for details.

Q9: Select the second most used mobile learning activities in which you participated during college.

Figure 8. Select the top mobile learning activities in which you participated during college

Answer Choices	Responses	
Digital Dictionaries	1.22%	1
e-reader	1.22%	1
Ipods	0.00%	0
Laptop	50.00%	41
Smartphone	10.98%	9
Tablet computer	8.54%	7
Non-applicable	28.05%	23
Total		82

Seven mobile learning activities were provided for the second most used. One mobile learning activity was not selected by any respondents. The highest number of responses was received by the "Non-applicable" category at a total of 29 (35.37%). The second highest number of responses was received by "Smartphone" category at a total of 22 (26.83%). The third highest number of responses was received by the "Laptop" category at a total of 13 (15.85%). The complete listing of respondents and percentages were noted in the chart.

The learning activity not selected was Digital Dictionaries.

Review Figure 9 for details.

Q10: Did the educational edifice require you to only read a mobile policy and procedure for adherence?

Categories were divided into three (3) groups and all 82 participants responded in Q10. The chart shows the breakdown as follows. Eighteen (21.95%) of the respondents are represented in the "Yes" category. Forty-three (52.44%) of the respondents are represented in the "No" category. Twenty-one (25.61%) of the respondents are represented in the "Unsure" category.

Figure 9. Select the second most used mobile learning activities in which you participated during college

Answer Choices	Responses	
Digital Dictionaries	0.00%	0
e-reader	6.10%	5
Ipods	2.44%	2
Laptop	15.85%	13
Smartphone	26.83%	22
Tablet computer	13.41%	11
Non-applicable	35.37%	29
Total		82

Review Figure 10 for details.

Q11: Did the educational edifice require you to read and sign a mobile policy and procedure for adherence?

Categories were divided into three (3) groups and all 82 participants responded in Q11. The chart shows the breakdown as follows. Nineteen (23.17%) of the respondents are represented in the "Yes" category. Forty-eight (58.54%) of the respondents are represented in the "No" category. Fifteen (18.29%) of the respondents are represented in the "Not Sure" category.

Review Figure 11 for details.

MOBILE AND M-LEARNING STRATEGIES AT COLLEGES, UNIVERSITIES, AND EDUCATIONAL EDIFICES: AN ANALYSIS

What did the survey participants say about mobile technology usage? Understanding from the analysis described seems to show that a mobile strategy is needed in colleges, universities, and educational edifices. The diversity of the strategies noted under the heading 'Mobile and M-learning Strategies at Colleges, Universities, and Educational Edifices: An Analysis', leads to the supposition that the current strategies are not consistent. Additionally, prior to input of a strategy, leaders and administrators need to demonstrate that they understand that in order to get the best work out of a mobile strategy, they must develop a requirements document that includes the voice of the customer. Further, support of the strategy needs to have a top down effect (Burton, 2007). The leadership and faculty must be urged to become and then remain competent in the understanding of mobile technologies. A consistent and updated strategy must be sustained to ensure all users are aware of the institution's usage policies and procedures. Administrators should not assume that users automatically understand mobile technology usage. If a policy and procedure exists, there should not be an assumption that users understand the information or know where to locate the documents. After requirements gathering and prior to implementation, learning and understanding

Figure 10. Did the educational edifice require you to only read a mobile policy and procedure for adherence?

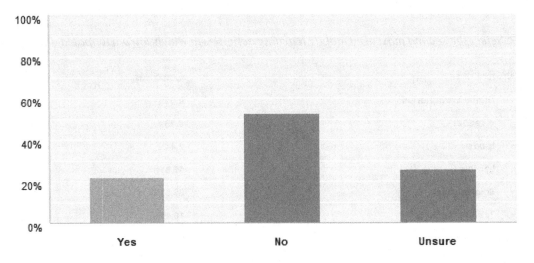

Figure 11. Did the educational edifice require you to read and sign a mobile policy and procedure for adherence?

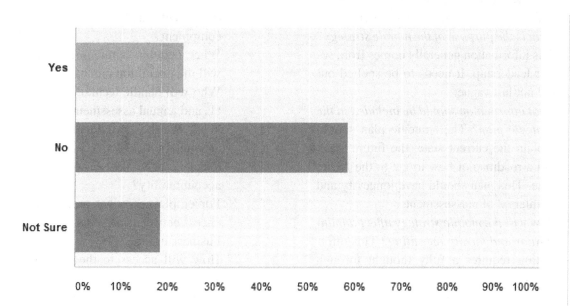

mobile technology and the associated policies and procedures can be supported through communications campaigns, in addition to education and training.

The alignment of a mobile technology strategy with institutional business strategies is significant. This alignment should flow to all users of technology at the institutions. Survey question five (5) shows 63.41% of respondents know that their institutions of higher learning support mobile technology in the face-to-face classroom environment. This percentage is over 50%; however, there is a question to be asked. The question is, 'Is 63.41% high enough or should that percentage be 75% or higher?' On the other hand, 36.59% of respondents answered negatively, in regards to their knowledge as to whether their institutions of higher learning support mobile technology in the face-to-face classroom environment. At this juncture, there is a gap in knowledge base and understanding. Further, when asked, "If your institution of higher learning supports mobile technology in the face-to-face classroom, have you used such technology to support studies inside the classroom," the number of "Non-applicable" responses was 32.93%, an unknown. This unknown could be due to learners working and educating in the online space. Then again, 32.93% of respondents answered "No." Through this data, a gap shows that there is not a uniform mobile technology strategy that spans colleges, universities, and other educational edifices. The question is, 'How does an institution ensure it has a mobile strategy in line with the 21st century?'

REQUIREMENTS FOR A MOBILE TECHNOLOGY AND STRATEGY

Administrators need to ensure a sound requirements gathering exercise to ensure their colleges, universities, and educational edifice collect all required information. The requirements gathering stage is one where a designated person meets with all stakeholders to ensure well-rounded data is gathered. Information that should be documented in the strategic plan is noted in a question and answer format.

- *Who are the stakeholders?* Stakeholders can include administrators, institutional leaders, faculty member, and students.
- *What is the purpose of the mobile strategy?* This information generally comes from senior leadership. It needs to be spelled out and not left vague.
- *What information should be included in the strategic plan?* The strategic plan should explain the current state, the future state, and a roadmap of how to get to the future state. This plan should have longevity and an interval of reassessments.
- *How will the mobile strategy affect administrator and faculty recruiting?* This information requires a fully thought through answer.
- *How will the mobile strategy affect student recruiting and retention?*

The requirements gathering document needs to include specific information. A key point to note is that if the institution decides not to use the information, this decision should be noted. A recommended format is an excel spreadsheet. Information that should be documented in the requirements gathering document are noted below.

- Questions that should be asked of stakeholders when gathering requirements. The stakeholder(s) to ask may be from a few business units, or be a combination of all stakeholders.
  - What is considered equipment usage at the institution?
  - What is the institution's approved usage of mobile technology?
  - What are the different technologies that are approved to be used?
    - What are the understood definitions of the technologies?
  - If any, what are the differences between the use of institution owned equipment and personal owned equipment?
  - What cellular communication plan will the institution purchase?
  - Who will handle technology approvals and annual assessment?
  - What is the individual employee accountability?
  - What is the non-employee accountability?
  - For employees, what are the differences between personal usage and business usage?
  - How will access to the network be provided?
  - How will personal and sensitive data be protected?
  - How will the network be advertised?
    - What will be advertised about the network?
  - How will the institution keep students abreast of the institution's policy?
  - How will abuse be dealt with by the institution?
  - How will virtual plagiarism be handled?

CONCLUSION

Determining a strategic mobile plan, and developing the appropriate policy and procedure is important for colleges, universities, and educational edifices. Developing a mobile strategy, reviewing the strategy, and tracking bandwidth pivot on mastering the understanding of the need for a strategy, and also communicating the required information to users. The expectation users have to compare to the reality of the strategy and policy in place can be costly if not handled appropriately. Even though over 63.41% of the respondents in this study know that their institution have a mobile strategy, this number, which is below 70%, could be understood as the onset of a potential security concern.

Again, an important question for the institution to establish is, 'What is the percentage of individuals who do not know the institution has a mobile strategy that includes a policy and procedure?' Another question, 'What does the 36.59% representing this suggest about the mobile strategy? Is data being accessed and used appropriately? At 36.59%, can the number of individuals not knowing or being unsure of the mobile strategy only be seen as having a negative effect on security, and strategy?' The lack of an effective strategy drills down to the capability to attract and retain competent administrators and faculty, as well as qualified students.

The comprehensive purpose of this chapter is to provide an understanding of mobile strategy as it relates to mobile usage and m-learning. Colleges, Universities, and educational edifices should ensure their mobile strategies are sound. The institutions' strategies should be understood by leaders at all levels. The lack of a sound mobile strategy with a well-developed policy and procedure could be costly. The mobile strategy needs to be clear. "Therefore, it is crucial for managements' perceptions to be clear and precise because their decision making and ultimate effectiveness depends on such precision" (Burton, 2009, p. vii). An initial reference starting point is to develop the mobile strategy encompassing Covey's second principle of personal leadership, "Begin with the End in Mind" (Covey, 1990).

REFERENCES

Allathkani, M. A. (2013). *An exploration and evaluation of the attitudes and perceptions of students towards use of mobile technology in higher education in the Kingdom of Jordan.* ProQuest Dissertations and Thesis (Order No. 3578753)

Ally, M. (Ed.). (2009). *Mobile learning: Transforming the delivery of education and training.* Athabasca, Canada: Athabasca University Press.

Ally, M., & Samaka, M. (2013). Open education resources and mobile technology to narrow the learning divide. *International Review of Research in Open and Distance Learning, 14*(2), 14–27.

Attewell, J., & Savill-Smith, C. (2005). Mobile learning anytime everywhere. London, UK: London Learning and Skills development Agency.

Barrios, T. (2004, March 22). *Laptops for learning: Final report and recommendations of the laptops for learning task force.* Retrieved from http://etc.usf.edu/l4l/report.pdf

Bebell, D., & Kay, R. (2010). One to one computing: A summary of the qualitative results from the Berkshire wireless learning initiative. *The Journal of Technology, Learning, and Assessment, 9*(2), 5–58.

Bedi, A. (2004). An andragogical approach to teaching styles. *Education for Primary Care, 15*, 93–108.

Belanger, Y. (2005, June). *Duke University iPod first year experience final evaluation report.* Retrieved from Duke University Center for Instructional Technology: http://cit.duke.edu/pdf/reports/ipod_initiative_04_05.pdf

Berea College. (2013). Phone services. *Portable Wireless Devices*. Retrieved from https://www.berea.edu/phone-services/portable-wireless-devices/

Binsaleh, S., & Binsaleh, M. (2013). Mobile learning: What guidelines should we produce in the context of mobile learning implementation in the conflict area of the four southernmost provinces of Thailand. *Asian Social Science*, 9(13), 270–281. doi:10.5539/ass.v9n13p270

Borquez, A. D. (2004). *Mobile and wireless technology: The impact in a higher education setting*. ProQuest Dissertations and Thesis (Order no. 3155384).

Buckingham, D., Issy, D., & Juian, S. D. (1999). The difference is digital? Digital technology and student media production, convergence. *Convergence (London)*, 5(4), 10–20. doi:10.1177/135485659900500402

Burrell, D., Finch, A., Fisher, J., Rahim, E., & Dawson, M. (2011). The use of engaging and experiential learning innovative teaching practices for graduate students. *Review of Higher Education & Self-Learning*, 3(11), 45–53.

Burrell, D. N., Anderson, M., Bessette, D., & Dawson, M. (2011). A contemporary evaluation of universities and sustainability strategic planning. *Review of Management Innovation & Creativity*, 4(11), 65–80.

Burton, S. L. (2007). *Quality customer service: Rekindling the art of service to customers* (2nd ed.). Lulu Publications.

Burton, S. L. (2009). *Diversity: Just what is it and why does it keep changing?* Lulu Publications.

Burton, S. L., Bessette, D., Brown-Jackson, K., & Grimm, F. (2013). Educating the educators: Retooling instructional chest of knowledge, skills, abilities, and competencies to support technological and social changes plus deliver quality results. In *Proceedings of EDU Learn 2013 Conference* (pp. 1172-1176). Academic Press.

Carlton College. (2012). College data on mobile devices. *Information Technology, Documents, & Records*. Retrieved from http://apps.carleton.edu/handbook/it/?policy_id=866001

Chan, C. (2010). Applications of andragogy in multi-disciplined teaching and learning. *Journal of Adult Education*, 39(2), 25–35.

Covey, S. R. (1989). *The 7 habits of highly effective people*. New York, NY: Simon & Schuster.

El-Sofany, H. F., Al Tayeb, A., Alghatani, K., & El-Seoud, S. A. (2013). The impact of cloud computing technologies in e-learning. *International Journal of Emerging Technologies in Learning*, 37-43. doi:10.3991/ijet.v8iS1.2344

Finch, A., Burrell, D. N., Walker, R., Rahim, E., & Dawson, M. (2010). Changing the cultures of colleges and universities to make them more adaptive. *Review of Higher Education and Self-Learning*, 3(7), 40–53.

Finch, A., & Rahim, E. (2011). Adult learning styles and technology-driven learning for online students. *Academic Leadership the Online Journal, 9*(2).

Forrest, S. P., & Peterson, T. O. (2006). It's called andragogy. *Academy of Management Learning & Education*, 5(1), 113–122. doi:10.5465/AMLE.2006.20388390

Gawel, R. (2004). Duke purchases iPods for incoming frosh. *Class Electronic Design, 52*(18), 8.

Huang, G., & Dolejs, B. (2007). Reading theatre, parents as actors: Movie production in a family literacy workshop. *Reading Improvement, 44*(2), 87–98.

Hutton, S. (2013). Helping kinesthetic learners succeed. *Education.com.* Retrieved from http://www.education.com/magazine/article/kinesthetic_learner/

International Telecommunications Union (ITU). (2010). *The world in 2010: Facts and figures.* Retrieved from http://ehis.ebscohost.com/eds/pdfviewer/pdfviewer?vid=2&sid=4a0d2ded-27e9-4428-bd8e-7c25dc2b22b2%40sessionmgr12&hid=2

International Telecommunications Union (ITU). (2013). *The world in 2013 facts and figures.* Retrieved from http://www.itu.int/en/ITU-D/Statistics/Documents/facts/ICTFactsFigures2013.pdf

Ismail, I., Bokhare, S. F., Azizan, S. N., & Azman, N. (2013). Teaching via mobile phone: A case study on Malaysian teachers' technology acceptance and readiness. *Journal of Educators Online, 10*(1).

Knowles, M. S. (1980). *The modern practice of adult education: From pedagogy to andragogy (revised and updated).* Englewood Cliffs, NJ: Cambridge Adult Education.

Knowles, M. S. (1985). Applications in continuing education for the health professions. Chapter five of andragogy in action. *MOBIUS: The Journal of Social Change, 5*(2), 80–100. PMID:10271191

Lan, Y., & Huang, S. (2011). Using mobile learning to improve the reflection: A case study of traffic violation. *Journal of Educational Technology & Society, 15*(2), 179–193.

McGrath, V. (2009). Reviewing the evidence on how adult students learn: An examination of Knowles' model of andragogy. Adult Learner: *The Irish Journal of Adult and Community Education,* 99-110.

Merriam, S. B., Caffarella, R. S., & Baumgartner, L. M. (2006). *Learning in adulthood: A comprehensive guide* (3rd ed.). San Francisco: Jossey-Bass.

Minnesota State Colleges and Universities. (2014). *Procedure 5.22.2, cellular and other mobile computing devices.* Retrieved from http://www.mnscu.edu/board/procedure/522p2.html

Naismith, L., & Corlett, D. (2006). Reflections on success: A retrospective of the mLearn conference series 2002-2005. In *Across generations and cultures, mLearn 2006 book of abstracts* (pp. 118–220). Banff, Canada: Academic Press.

Pew Research Center. (2014). *Mobile technology fact sheet.* Pew Research Internet Project. Retrieved from http://www.pewinternet.org/fact-sheets/mobile-technology-fact-sheet/

Pinkwart, N., Hoppe, H. U., Milrad, M., & Perez, J. (2003). Educational scenarios for cooperative use of personal digital assistants. *Journal of Computer Assisted Learning, 19*(3), 383–391. doi:10.1046/j.0266-4909.2003.00039.x

Prettyman, S. S., Ward, C. L., Jaulk, D., & Awad, G. (2012). *21st century learners: Voices of students in a one-to-one STEM environment.* Academic Press.

Rao, N. M., Sasidhar, C., & Kumar, V. S. (2012). Cloud computing through mobile-learning. *International Journal of Advanced Computer Science and Application, 1*(6), 42–47.

Razzak, M. (2011, October 4). Universities nationwide utilize NV3 technologies' cell-phone and tablet charging kiosks. *Bloomberg.* Retrieved from http://www.bloomberg.com/apps/news?pid=con ewsstory&tkr=ERCG:GR&sid=aEq9Fn9BsxLA

Read, B. (2006). Duke stops giving students free iPods but will continue using them in classes. *The Chronicle of Higher Education, 52*(36), A39.

Robertson, L., Smellie, T., Wilson, P., & Cox, L. (2011). Learning styles and fieldwork education: Students' perspectives. *New Zealand Journal of Occupational Therapy, 58*(1), 36–40.

Rogers, Y., Connelly, K., Hazelwood, W., & Tedesco, W. (2010). Enhancing learning: A study of how mobile devices can facilitate sensemaking. *Personal and Ubiquitous Computing, 14*(2), 111–124. doi:10.1007/s00779-009-0250-7

Seppala, P., & Alamaki, K. (2003). Mobile learning in teaching. *Journal of Computer Assisted Learning, 19*(3), 330–335.

Seton Hall University. (n.d.). About the mobile computing program. *Seton Hall University's Website.* Retrieved from http://www.shu.edu/offices/technology/about-mobile-computing.cfm

Sharples, M. (2000). The design of personal mobile technologies for lifelong learning. *Computers & Education, 34*(3-4), 177–193. doi:10.1016/S0360-1315(99)00044-5

Sharples, M., Corlett, D., & Westmancott, O. (2002). The design and implementation of a mobile learning resource. *Personal and Ubiquitous Computing, 6*(3), 220–234. doi:10.1007/s007790200021

Silverman, R. E. (2011). Is psychology a science? *Skeptic, 17*(1), 36–39.

Skiba, D. J. (2013). Bloom's digital taxonomy and word clouds. *Nursing Education Perspectives, 34*(4), 277–280. doi:10.5480/1536-5026-34.4.277 PMID:24187736

Summerfield, B. (2005). United Technologies Corp.: Learning partnerships & mobile learning. *Chief Learning Officer, 4*(2), 42.

Taylor, B., & Kroth, M. (2009). Andragogy's transition into the future: Meta-analysis of andragogy and its search for a measurable instrument. *Journal of Adult Education, 38*, 1–11.

Thus, H., Chatti, M. A., Yalcin, E., Pallasch, C., Kyryliuk, B., Mageramov, T., & Schroeder, U. (2012). Mobile learning in context. *International Journal of Technology Enhanced Learning, 4*(5), 332–344. doi:10.1504/IJTEL.2012.051818

University of Texas. (2012). *Texas A&M mobile strategy.* Retrieved from http://gomobile.tamu.edu/texas-am-mobile-strategy

University of Washington. (2012). *Mobile device use and allowance policy.* Retrieved from http://www.washington.edu/admin/rules/policies/APS/55.01.html

Yacci, M. (2000). Interactivity demystified: A structural definition for distance education and intelligent CBT. *Educational Technology, 40*(4), 5–16.

Yang, S. (2012). Exploring college students' attitudes and self-efficacy of mobile learning. *Turkish Online Journal of Educational Technology, 11*(4), 148–154.

KEY TERMS AND DEFINITIONS

Educational Technologies: Equipment and machines designed and developed from the application of scientific knowledge. For the purpose of this study, educational technology and technology will mean the same thing.

E-Learning: Electronically supported learning that takes place on the world-wide-web. It can be synchronous or asynchronous. The term is listed in numerous forms, E-Learning, elearning, and eLearning.

Information Technology (IT): Information technology staff characterized a team of individuals accountable for campus-wide or organizational-wide services, software, and support of infrastructure that manage and provide information employing data, voice and video to the community of employees, alumni, and others.

Learner: Refers to adult students who have or are currently taking a year of distance learning courses.

M-Learning: Convenient learning mobility that interacts with portable technologies.

Smartphone: Technological device that allows users to make telephone calls, and use features found on a personal digital assistant or a computer.

Tablet Computers: Hand held mobile computer, generally with a touch screen or stylus enabled surface.

Compilation of References

Abioye, T. (2012). A stylistic analysis of emerging paradigms and prominent features in Nigeria SMS discourse. In R. Taiwo & I. Chiluwa (Eds.), *Computer-mediated discourse in Africa* (pp. 55–67). New York, NY: Nova Science Publishers.

Achrol, R. S. (1997). Changes in the theory of interorganizational relations in marketing: Toward a network paradigm. *Journal of the Academy of Marketing Science*, *25*(1), 56–71. doi:10.1007/BF02894509

Acquisti, A., Adjerid, I., & Brandimarte, L. (2013). Gone in 15 seconds: The limits of privacy transparency and control. *IEEE Security and Privacy*, *11*(4), 72–74. doi:10.1109/MSP.2013.86

Acquisti, A., & Grossklags, J. (2003, May). Losses, gains, and hyperbolic discounting: An experimental approach to information security attitudes and behavior. In *Proceedings of 2nd Annual Workshop on Economics and Information Security-WEIS* (Vol. 3). Academic Press.

Adler, P., & Kwon, S. (2002). Social capital: Prospects for a new concept. *Academy of Management Review*, *27*, 17–40.

Agichtein, E., Castillo, C., Donato, D., Gionis, A., & Mishne, G. (2008). Finding high-quality content in social media. In *Proceedings of the 2008 International Conference on Web Search and Data Mining* (pp. 183-194). ACM.

Ahuja, A. K., Biesaga, K., Sudak, D. M., Draper, J., & Womble, A. (2014). Suicide on Facebook. *Journal of Psychiatric Practice*, *20*(2), 141–146. doi:10.1097/01.pra.0000445249.38801.d1 PMID:24638049

Ahuja, R. K., Magnanti, T. L., & Orlin, J. B. (2014). *Network flows: Theory, algorithms, and applications.* Harlow, UK: Pearson Education Limited.

Ajjan, H., & Hartshorne, R. (2008). Investigating faculty decisions to adopt web 2.0 technologies: Theory and empirical tests. *The Internet and Higher Education*, *11*(2), 71–80. doi:10.1016/j.iheduc.2008.05.002

Ajzen, I., & Fishbein, M. (1980). *Understanding attitudes and predicting social behavior*. Englewood Cliffs, NJ: Prentice-Hall.

Akers, R. L. (1996). Is differential association/social learning cultural deviance theory? *Criminology*, *34*(2), 229–247. doi:10.1111/j.1745-9125.1996.tb01204.x

Alaboodi, S. S. (2007). *Towards evaluating security implementations using the information security maturity model*. ISMM.

Alao, A. A., Ojo, S. O., & Forcheh, N. (2009). Using computer technology for educational and occupational information. In R. Roth, C. Hiew, & A. L. Comunian (Eds.), *Peace, hope, and well-being across the cultures* (pp. 191–201). Shaker Verlag, Aachen.

Alarcón-del-Amo, M., Lorenzo-Romero, C., & Gómez-Borja, M. (2011). Classifying and profiling social networking site users: A latent segmentation approach. *Cyberpsychology, Behavior, and Social Networking*, *14*(9), 547–553. doi:10.1089/cyber.2010.0346 PMID:21288133

Albert, A., & Hersinta, H. (2013). Shopping on social networking sites: A study on Facebook consumers' psychological characteristics. *Journal Communication Spectrum*, *2*(2).

Alexander, B. (2006). Web 2.0: A new wave of innovation for teaching and learning? *Educational Review*, *41*(2), 32–44.

Alexander, B., & Levine, A. (2008). Web 2.0 storytelling: Emergence of a new genre. *EDUCAUSE Review*, *43*(6), 40–56.

Alfonso, M., & Kaur, R. (2013). Self-injury among early adolescents: Identifying segments protected and at risk. *The Journal of School Health*, *82*(12), 537–547. doi:10.1111/j.1746-1561.2012.00734.x PMID:23151115

Allam, M. F. (2010). Excessive internet use and depression: Cause-effect bias? *Psychopathology*, *43*(5), 334. doi:10.1159/000319403 PMID:20664310

Allathkani, M. A. (2013). *An exploration and evaluation of the attitudes and perceptions of students towards use of mobile technology in higher education in the Kingdom of Jordan*. ProQuest Dissertations and Thesis (Order No. 3578753)

Ally, M. (Ed.). (2009). *Mobile learning: Transforming the delivery of education and training*. Athabasca, Canada: Athabasca University Press.

Ally, M., & Samaka, M. (2013). Open education resources and mobile technology to narrow the learning divide. *International Review of Research in Open and Distance Learning*, *14*(2), 14–27.

Almeida, M.E.B., & Prado, M.E.B.B. (2005). *Integração de tecnologias, linguagens e representações*. Brasília: TV Escola, SEED-MEC.

Almeida, F. J., & Fonseca, F. M. Jr. (2000). *Projetos e ambientes inovadores*. Brasília, DF: MEC/SEED.

Almeida, M. E. B. (2004). *Inclusão digital do professor: Formação e prática pedagógica*. Editora Articulação – Universidade Escola.

Alpen Capital. (2011). *GCC hospitality industry*. Retrieved April 5, 2014, from http://www.alpencapital.com/downloads/GCC-Hospitality-Report-13-April-%202011.pdf

Altman, I. (1975). *The environment and social behavior: Privacy, personal space, territory, crowding*. Monterey: Brooks/Cole.

Alvesson, M., & Sandberg, J. (2013). *Constructing research questions: Doing interesting research*. Sage.

Amado, F. R. (2011). *Cultural master plan for Bahrain: Parametric models in urban planning*. Retrieved April 9, 2014, from https://fenix.tecnico.ulisboa.pt/downloadFile/395142732371/Resumo.pdf

Amichai-Hamburger, Y., & Ben-Artzi, E. (2003). Loneliness and internet use. *Computers in Human Behavior*, *19*(1), 71–80. doi:10.1016/S0747-5632(02)00014-6

Amichai-Hamburger, Y., & Vinitzky, G. (2010). Social network use and personality. *Computers in Human Behavior*, *26*(6), 1289–1295. doi:10.1016/j.chb.2010.03.018

Amstrong, J., & Franklin, T. (2008). *A review of current and developing international practice in the use of social networking (web 2.0) in higher education*. Franklin Consulting. Retrieved January 4, 2014, from http://arthurmckeown.typepad.com/files/web-2.0-in-higher-education.pdf

Anderson, B. (2012). Cracking the social ROI code: Social media performance indicators demystified. *Cambridge Marketing Review*, (4), 12-15.

Anderson, P. (2007). What is web 2.0? Ideas, technologies and implications for education. *JISC Technology and Standards Watch*, 1-64.

Anderson, C. L., & Agarwal, R. (2010). Practicing safe computing: A multi method empirical examination of home computer user security behavioral intentions. *Management Information Systems Quarterly*, *34*(3).

Anderson, J. M. (2003). Why we need a new definition of information security. *Computers & Security*, *22*(4), 308–313. doi:10.1016/S0167-4048(03)00407-3

Anderson, P., De Bruijn, A., Angus, K., Gordon, R., & Hastings, G. (2009). Impact of alcohol advertising and media exposure on adolescent alcohol use: A systematic review of longitudinal studies. *Alcohol and Alcoholism (Oxford, Oxfordshire)*, *44*(3), 229–243. doi:10.1093/alcalc/agn115 PMID:19144976

Andrew, S., & Galak, J. (2012). The effects of traditional and social earned media on sales: A study of a microlending marketplace. *JMR, Journal of Marketing Research*, *49*(5), 624–639. doi:10.1509/jmr.09.0401

Anti-Phishing Working Group. (2009). Retrieved from http://www.antiphishing.org

Anwyll, R., Chawner, B., & Tarulli, L. (2013). Social media and readers' advisory. *Reference and User Services Quarterly, 53*(2), 113–118. doi:10.5860/rusq.53n2.113

Arkin, D. (2013). Canada charges two in teen cyber-bullying suicide case. *NBC News.* Retrieved August 20, 2013, from http://www.bbc.co.uk/news/world-us-canada-23752923

Arksey, H., & Knight, P. (1999). *Interviewing for social scientists.* London: Sage.

Armstrong, J., & Franklin, T. (2008). A review of current and developing international practice in the use of social networking (web 2.0) in higher education (September 2008 ed.). Franklin Consulting.

Armstrong, P. (2008). *Toward an autoethnographic pedagogy.* Paper presented at the 38th Annual SCUTREA Conference, Edinburgh, UK.

Armstrong, J., Ruttle, P., Burk, L., Costanzo, P., Strauman, T., & Essex, M. (2013). Early risk factors for alcohol use across high school and its covariation with deviant friends. *Journal of Studies on Alcohol and Drugs, 74*(5), 746–756. PMID:23948534

Arora, M., Mathur, N., Gupta, V., Nazar, G., Reddy, K., & Sargent, J. (2012). Tobacco use in Bollywood movies, tobacco promotional activities and their association with tobacco use among Indian adolescents. *Tobacco Control, 21*(5), 482–487. doi:10.1136/tc.2011.043539 PMID:21730099

Assael, H. (2003). *Consumer behavior: A strategic approach.* Boston: Houghton Mifflin.

Astbury, M. (2011). Hotel booking through facebook? *Daily Planet Dispatch.* Retrieved April 15, 2014, from http://dailyplanetdispatch.com/?p=7629

Atav, S., & Spencer, G. (2002). Health risk behavior among adolescents attending rural, suburban, and urban schools: A comparative study. *Family & Community Health, 25*(2), 53–64. doi:10.1097/00003727-200207000-00007 PMID:12010115

Atlı, A. (2011). Businessmen as diplomats: The role of business associations in Turkey's foreign economic policy. *Insight Turkey, 13*(1), 119–128.

Attewell, J., & Savill-Smith, C. (2005). Mobile learning anytime everywhere. London, UK: London Learning and Skills development Agency.

Au, A. (2010). *Adoption of web 2.0 by tourism businesses in NSW (research reports).* Sydney: Tourism New South Wales. Retrieved April 26, 2014, from http://corporate.tourism.nsw.gov.au/Sites/SiteID6/objLib40/Adoption-of-Web%202Jan10.pdf

Augner, C., & Hacker, G. W. (2012). Associations between problematic mobile phone use and psychological parameters in young adults. *International Journal of Public Health, 57*(2), 4437–4441. doi:10.1007/s00038-011-0234-z PMID:21290162

Austin, J., & Hickety, A. (2007). *Autoethnography and teacher development.* Common Ground.

Avesani, P., Massa, P., & Tiella, R. (2005). A trust-enhanced recommender system application: Moleskiing. In *Proceedings of the 2005 ACM Symposium on Applied Computing (SAC)* (pp. 1589-1593). ACM. doi:10.1145/1066677.1067036

Awonusi, V. O. (2004). 'Little' Englishes and the law of energetic: A sociolinguistic study of SMStext messages as register and discourse in Nigerian English. In S. Awonusi & E. A. Babalola (Eds.), *The domestication of English in Nigeria: A festschrift for Abiodun Adetugbo at 65* (pp. 45–62). Lagos: University of Lagos Press.

Aymerich-Franch, L. (2011). *Aulas 2.0: The use of social media as learning tools.* Paper presented at Congreso Internacional de Comunicación y Educación: Estrategias de Alfabetización Mediática, Bellaterra, Spain.

Aymerich-Franch, L., & Carrillo, M. (2014). The adoption of social media in financial journalism. In B. Çoban (Ed.), *Sosyal medya d/evrimi.* Istanbul: Yayinlari.

Aymerich-Franch, L., & Fedele, M. (2014). Students' privacy concerns on the use of social media in higher education. In V. Benson & S. Morgan (Eds.), *Cutting-edge technologies and social media use in higher education.* Hershey, PA: IGI Global. doi:10.4018/978-1-4666-5174-6.ch002

Back, M. D., Stopfer, J. M., Vazire, S., Gaddis, S., Schmukle, S. C., Egloff, B., & Gosling, S. D. (2010). Facebook profiles reflect actual personality, not self-idealization. *Psychological Science*, *20*(10), 1–3. PMID:20424071

Baek, I.-H., & Park, E.-J. (2012). Digital dementia is on the rise. *Korean Joongan Daily*. Retrieved June 24, 2013, from http://koreajoongangdaily.joins.com/news/article/article.aspx?aid=2973527&cloc=joongangdaily%7Chomop

Bahrain Economic Development Board. (2009). *Tourism sector performance*. Manama: BEDB. Retrieved March 22, 2014, from http://www.bahrainedb.com/uploadedFiles/Bahraincom/BahrainForBusiness/11.%20AER%20-%20Articles%20-20Tourism%20Sector%20Performance.pdf

Balakrishnan, M. S. (2008). Dubai a star in the East: A case study in strategic destination branding. *Journal of Place Management and Development*, *1*(1), 62–91.

Baldwin, D. A. (1997). The concept of security. *Review of International Studies*, *23*(01), 5–26. doi:10.1017/S0260210597000053 PMID:10164688

Barabasi, A. L. (2002). *Linked: The new science of networks*. Cambridge, MA: Perseus.

Bargh, J. A., & Mc Kenna, K. Y. A. (2004). The internet and social life. *Annual Review of Psychology*, *55*(1), 573–590. doi:10.1146/annurev.psych.55.090902.141922 PMID:14744227

Bargh, J. A., McKenna, K. Y. A., & Fitzsimons, G. M. (2002). Can you see the real me? Activation and expression of the "true self" on the internet. *The Journal of Social Issues*, *58*(1), 33–48. doi:10.1111/1540-4560.00247

Bar-Ilan, J., Haustein, S., Peters, I., Priem, J., Shema, H., & Terliesner, J. (2012). *Beyond citations: Scholars' visibility on the social web*. Retrieved 2 March 2014, from http://arxiv.org/ftp/arxiv/papers/1205/1205.5611.pdf

Barney, J. (1991). Firm resources and sustained competitive advantage. *Journal of Management*, *17*(1), 99–120. doi:10.1177/014920639101700108

Barrios, T. (2004, March 22). *Laptops for learning: Final report and recommendations of the laptops for learning task force*. Retrieved from http://etc.usf.edu/l4l/report.pdf

Baudrillard, J. (1983). *The precession of simulacra* (2nd ed.). New York, NY: Durham & Kellner.

BBC News. (2011). *Play.com warns of customer e-mail security breach*. Retrieved August 8, 2014, from http://www.bbc.co.uk/news/technology-12819330

BBC. (2012). *Arrest over 'cyber-attack' on Theresa May and home office*. Retrieved March 20, 2014, from http://www.bbc.co.uk/news/uk-20217968

Beard, J., & Dale, P. (2010). Library design, learning spaces and academic literacy. *New World Library*, *111*(11/12), 480–492. doi:10.1108/03074801011094859

Beard, K. W., & Wolf, E. M. (2001). Modification in the proposed diagnostic criteria for Internet addiction. *Cyberpsychology & Behavior*, *4*(3), 377–383. doi:10.1089/109493101300210286 PMID:11710263

Bebell, D., & Kay, R. (2010). One to one computing: A summary of the qualitative results from the Berkshire wireless learning initiative. *The Journal of Technology, Learning, and Assessment*, *9*(2), 5–58.

Becker, S., & Curry, J. (2014). Testing the effects of peer socialization versus selection on alcohol and marijuana use among treated adolescents. *Substance Use & Misuse*, *49*(3), 234–242. doi:10.3109/10826084.2013.824479 PMID:23965039

Bedi, A. (2004). An andragogical approach to teaching styles. *Education for Primary Care*, *15*, 93–108.

Belanger, Y. (2005, June). *Duke University iPod first year experience final evaluation report*. Retrieved from Duke University Center for Instructional Technology: http://cit.duke.edu/pdf/reports/ipod_initiative_04_05.pdf

Beldarrain, Y. (2006). Distance education trends: Integrating new technologies to foster student interaction and collaboration. *Distance Education*, *27*(2), 139–153. doi:10.1080/01587910600789498

Bell, D. (1973). *The coming of post-industrial society: A venture in social forecasting*. Basic Books.

Bellman, S., Johnson, E. J., Kobrin, S. J., & Lohse, G. L. (2004). International differences in information privacy concerns: A global survey of consumers. *The Information Society*, *20*(5), 313–324. doi:10.1080/01972240490507956

Belloni, M. L., & Gomes, N. G. (2008). Infância, mídias e aprendizagem: Autodidaxia e colaboração. *Educ. Soc.*, *29*(104), 717-746. Retrieved from http://www.cedes.unicamp.br

Bennett, S., Bishop, A., Dalgarno, B., Waycott, J., & Kennedy, G. (2012). Implementing web 2.0 technologies in higher education: A collective case study. *Computers & Education*, *59*(2), 524–534. doi:10.1016/j.compedu.2011.12.022

Benson, V., & Morgan, S. (2012). Student experience and learning management systems: Issues of wireless access and cloud deployment. In *Proceedings of the International Conference on Wireless Information Networks and Systems (WINSYS)*. Rome, Italy: Academic Press.

Benson, V., Filippaios, F., & Morgan, S. (2010). Online social networks: Changing the face of business education and career planning. *International Journal of Business and Management*, *4*(1), 20–33.

Benson, V., Morgan, S., & Tennakoon, H. (2012). A framework for knowledge management in higher education using social networking. *International Journal of Knowledge Society Research*, *3*(2), 44–54. doi:10.4018/jksr.2012040104

Berea College. (2013). Phone services. *Portable Wireless Devices*. Retrieved from https://www.berea.edu/phone-services/portable-wireless-devices/

Berger, H., & Thomas, C. (2014, January). SMEs: Social media marketing performance. In *Proceedings of the 8th International Conference on Knowledge Management in Organizations* (pp. 411-422). Springer Netherlands.

Berger, L. (2001). Inside out: Narrative autoethnography as a path toward rapport. *Qualitative Inquiry*, *7*(4), 504–218. doi:10.1177/107780040100700407

Bergeron, E. (2000). The difference between security and privacy. In *Proceedings of Joint Workshop on Mobile Web Privacy WAP Forum & World Wide Web Consortium*. Retrieved March 23, 2014, from http://www.w3.org/P3P/mobile-privacy-ws/papers/zks.html

Berger, P., & Luckmann, T. (1966). *The social construction of reality: A treatise in the sociology of knowledge*. Garden City, NY: Anchor Books.

Bergsma, L., & Carney, M. (2008). Effectiveness of health-promoting media literacy education: A systematic review. *Health Education Research*, *23*(3), 522–542. doi:10.1093/her/cym084 PMID:18203680

Berry, H., Guillén, M. F., & Zhou, N. (2010). An institutional approach to cross-national distance. *Journal of International Business Studies*, *41*(9), 1460–1480. doi:10.1057/jibs.2010.28

Bettman, J. R., Luce, M. F., & Payne, J. W. (1998). Constructive consumer choice processes. *The Journal of Consumer Research*, *25*(3), 187–217. doi:10.1086/209535

Beudoin, C. E. (2008). Explaining the relationship between internet use and interpersonal trust: Taking into account motivation and information overload. *Journal of Computer-Mediated Communication*, *13*(3), 550–568. doi:10.1111/j.1083-6101.2008.00410.x

Bevan, J. L., Pfyl, J., & Barclay, B. (2012). Negative emotional and cognitive responses to being unfriended on Facebook: An exploratory study. *Computers in Human Behavior*, *28*(4), 1458–1464. doi:10.1016/j.chb.2012.03.008

Bhabwat, S., Omre, R., & Chand, D. (2013). Development of social networking sites and their role in online share trading and business with special reference to facebook. *International Journal of Business Management & Research*, *3*(2), 31–52.

Bhimani, A. (1996). Securing the commercial Internet. *Communications of the ACM*, *39*(6), 29–35. doi:10.1145/228503.228509

Binsaleh, S., & Binsaleh, M. (2013). Mobile learning: What guidelines should we produce in the context of mobile learning implementation in the conflict area of the four southernmost provinces of Thailand. *Asian Social Science*, *9*(13), 270–281. doi:10.5539/ass.v9n13p270

Bishop, M. (2003). What is computer security? *IEEE Security & Privacy*, *1*(1), 67–69. doi:10.1109/MSECP.2003.1176998

Blanchard, O. (2011). *Social media ROI: Managing and measuring social media efforts in your organization*. Indianapolis, IN: QUE Publishing.

Blaschke, L. M. (2012). Heutagogy and lifelong learning: A review of heutagogical practice and self-determined learning. *International Review of Research in Open and Distance Learning, 13*(1), 56–71.

Blattner, G., & Lomicka, L. (2012). Facebook-ing and the social generation: A new era of language learning. *Alsic Apprentissage des Langues et Systèmes d'Information et de Communication, 15*(1). doi:10.4000/alsic.2413

Boase, J., & Wellman, B. (2006). Personal relationships on and off the internet. In A. L. Vangelistic & D. Perlman (Eds.), *The Cambridge handbook of personal relationships*. New York, NY: Cambridge University Press. doi:10.1017/CBO9780511606632.039

Bonk, C. J. (2010). How technology is changing school. *Educational Leadership, 67*(7), 60–65.

Borch, O. J., & Arthur, M. B. (1995). Strategic networks among small firms: Implications for strategy research methodology. *Journal of Management Studies, 32*(4), 419–441. doi:10.1111/j.1467-6486.1995.tb00783.x

Borders, T., & Booth, B. (2007). Rural, suburban, and urban variations in alcohol consumption in the United States: Findings from the National Epidemiologic Survey on Alcohol and Related Conditions. *The Journal of Rural Health, 23*(4), 314–321. doi:10.1111/j.1748-0361.2007.00109.x PMID:17868238

Borgatti, S. P., Mehra, A., Brass, D. J., & Labianca, G. (2009). Network analysis in the social sciences. *Science, 323*(5916), 892-895.

Borgatti, S. P., & Halgin, D. S. (2011). On network theory. *Organization Science, 22*(5), 1168–1181. doi:10.1287/orsc.1100.0641

Borquez, A. D. (2004). *Mobile and wireless technology: The impact in a higher education setting.* ProQuest Dissertations and Thesis (Order no. 3155384).

Borsari, B., & Carey, K. (2001). Peer influences on college drinking: A review of the research. *Journal of Substance Abuse, 13*(4), 391–424. doi:10.1016/S0899-3289(01)00098-0 PMID:11775073

boyd, d. m., & Ellison, N. B. (2008). Social network sites: Definition, history, and scholarship. *Journal of Computed-Mediated Communication, 13*, 210-230.

Boyd-Ball, A., Véronneau, M., Dishion, T., & Kavanagh, K. (2013). Monitoring and peer influences as predictors of increases in alcohol use among American Indian youth. *Prevention Science.* PMID:23775578

Boyd, D. M., & Ellison, N. B. (2008). Social network sites: Definition history, and scholarship. *Journal of Computer-Mediated Communication, 13*(1), 210–230. doi:10.1111/j.1083-6101.2007.00393.x

Branigan, T. (2013). Edward Snowden vows not to hide from justice amid new hacking claims. *The Guardian.* Retrieved December 6, 2013, from http://www.theguardian.com/world/2013/jun/12/edward-snowden-us-extradition-fight?INTCMP=SRCH

Brehm, J., & Rahn, W. (1997). Individual-level evidence for the causes and consequences of socialcapital. *American Journal of Political Science, 41*(3), 999–1024. doi:10.2307/2111684

Brettabz. (2011). Company 'held to ransom' by cyber hacker. *All Media Scotland.* Retrieved August 25, 2014, from http://www.allmediascotland.com/media_releases/28899/held-to-ransom

Briggs, A., & Burke, P. (2009). *A social history of media* (3rd ed.). Malden, MA: Polity Press.

Bronner, R., De Ridder, J. A., Neijens, P. C., & Willemsen, L. M. (2011). Highly recommended! The content characteristics and perceived usefulness of online consumer reviews. *Journal of Computer-Mediated Communication, 17*(1), 19–8. doi:10.1111/j.1083-6101.2011.01551.x

Brown, B., Eicher, S., & Petrie, S. (1986). The importance of peer group ("crowd") affiliation in adolescence. *Journal of Adolescence, 9*(1), 73–96. doi:10.1016/S0140-1971(86)80029-X PMID:3700780

Brown, M. R., & Muchira, R. (2004). Investigating the relationship between internet privacy concerns and online purchase behavior. *Journal of Electronic Commerce Research, 5*(1), 62–70.

Bryer, T. A., & Zavattaro, S. M. (2011). Social media and public administration. *Administrative Theory & Praxis, 33*(3), 325–340. doi:10.2753/ATP1084-1806330301

Buchanan, M. (2003). *Nexus: Small worlds and the groundbreaking theory of networks.* New York, NY: WW Norton & Company.

Buckingham, D., Issy, D., & Juian, S. D. (1999). The difference is digital? Digital technology and student media production, convergence. *Convergence (London)*, *5*(4), 10–20. doi:10.1177/135485659900500402

Buffardi, L. E., & Campbell, W. K. (2008). Narcissism and social networking web sites. *Personality and Social Psychology Bulletin*, *34*(10), 1303–1314. doi:10.1177/0146167208320061 PMID:18599659

Buğra, A. (1998). Class, culture, and state: An analysis of interest representation by two Turkish business associations. *International Journal of Middle East Studies*, *30*(04), 521–539. doi:10.1017/S0020743800052545

Buğra, A. (1999). *Islam in economic organizations*. Istanbul: TESEV.

Buğra, A. (2002). Labor, capital, and religion: Harmony and conflict among the constituency of political Islam in Turkey. *Middle Eastern Studies*, *2*(38), 187–204. doi:10.1080/714004454

Buhalis, D. (2003). *Etourism: Information technologies for strategic tourism management*. Harlow, UK: Prentice Hall.

Buhalis, D., & Law, R. (2008). Progress in information technology and tourism management: 20 years on and 10 years after the Internet – The state of eTourism research. *Tourism Management*, *29*(4), 609–623. doi:10.1016/j.tourman.2008.01.005

Burgess, S., Sellitto, C., & Karanasios, S. (Eds.). (2009). *Effective web presence solutions for small businesses: Strategies for successful implementation*. Hershey, PA: Information Science Reference. doi:10.4018/978-1-60566-224-4

Burngarner, B. A. (2007). You have been poked: Exploring the uses and gratifications of Facebook among emerging adults. *First Monday*, *12*(11).

Burrell, D. N., Anderson, M., Bessette, D., & Dawson, M. (2011). A contemporary evaluation of universities and sustainability strategic planning. *Review of Management Innovation & Creativity*, *4*(11), 65–80.

Burrell, D., Finch, A., Fisher, J., Rahim, E., & Dawson, M. (2011). The use of engaging and experiential learning innovative teaching practices for graduate students. *Review of Higher Education & Self-Learning*, *3*(11), 45–53.

Burt, R. S. (2001). Structural holes versus network closure as social capital. *Social Capital: Theory and Research*, 31-56.

Burton, S. L. (2007). *Quality customer service: Rekindling the art of service to customers* (2nd ed.). Lulu Publications.

Burton, S. L. (2009). *Diversity: Just what is it and why does it keep changing?* Lulu Publications.

Burton, S. L., Bessette, D., Brown-Jackson, K., & Grimm, F. (2013). Educating the educators: Retooling instructional chest of knowledge, skills, abilities, and competencies to support technological and social changes plus deliver quality results. In *Proceedings of EDU Learn 2013 Conference* (pp. 1172-1176). Academic Press.

Burton, S., Dadich, A., & Soboleva, A. (2013). Competing voices: Marketing and counter-marketing alcohol on Twitter. *Journal of Nonprofit & Public Sector Marketing*, *25*(2), 186–209. doi:10.1080/10495142.2013.787836

BusinessTech. (2013). *Cyber security predictions 2013*. Retrieved August 8, 2014, from http://businesstech.co.za/news/columns/27669/cyber-security-predictions-2013/

Cabinet Office. (2010). *A strong Britain in an age of uncertainty: The national security strategy*. Retrieved August 25, 2014 from http://www.cabinetoffice.gov.uk/sites/default/files/resources/national-security-strategy.pdf

Cain, J. (2008). Online social networking issues within academia and pharmacy education. *American Journal of Pharmaceutical Education*, *72*(1), 1–7. doi:10.5688/aj720110 PMID:18322572

Calder, A. (2011). Sharpen penetration tests to foil cybercrime. *ZDNet*. Retrieved August 25, 2014 from http://www.zdnet.co.uk/news/security-management/2011/03/20/sharpen-penetration-tests-to-foil-cybercrime-40092180/

Camas, N. P. V. (2012). A literacia da informação na formação de professores. In Tecendo os fios na educação: Da informação nas redes à construção do conhecimento mediada pelo professor. Curitiba: CRV.

Camas, N. P. V., & Mengalli, N. M. (2012). Use of digital interfaces as an extension of school attendance. *Publication of IEEE Technical Committee on Learning Technology*, *13*, 66–69.

Campbell, K., Gordon, L. A., Loeb, M. P., & Zhou, L. (2003). The economic cost of publicly announced information security breaches: Empirical evidence from the stock market. *Journal of Computer Security, 11*(3), 431–448.

Capobianco, L. (2010). *Comunicação e literacia digital na internet – Estudo etnográfico e análise exploratória de dados do programa de inclusão digital acessaSP – PONLINE: Dissertação (mestrado em ciências da comunicação)*. Escola de Comunicação e Artes, Universidade de São Paulo.

Carlton College. (2012). College data on mobile devices. *Information Technology, Documents, & Records*. Retrieved from http://apps.carleton.edu/handbook/it/?policy_id=866001

Cartwright, D., & Harary, F. (1956). Structural balance: A generalization of Heider's theory. *Psychological Review, 63*(5), 277–293. doi:10.1037/h0046049 PMID:13359597

Casprini, E., & Di Minin, A. (2013). *The social media revolution: Strategies and attitudes towards the rise of an enabling technology* (No. 201302). Academic Press.

Cassidy, J. (2006, May 15th). *Me media: How hanging out on the internet became big business*. Accessed on May 23rd, 2013, from The New Yorker Website: http://www.newyorker.com/archive/2006/05/15/060515fa_fact_cassidy

Caudill, E. M., & Murphy, P. E. (2000). Consumer online privacy: Legal and ethical issues. *Journal of Public Policy & Marketing, 19*(1), 7–19. doi:10.1509/jppm.19.1.7.16951

Cavusoglu, H., Mishra, B., & Raghunathan, S. (2004). The effect of internet security breach announcements on market value: Capital market reactions for breached firms and internet security developers. *International Journal of Electronic Commerce, 9*(1), 70–104.

Center for Disease Control and Prevention. (2012). *Fact sheets - Binge drinking*. Retrieved December 5, 2013 from http://www.cdc.gov/alcohol/fact-sheets/binge-drinking.htm

Chan, C. (2010). Applications of andragogy in multi-disciplined teaching and learning. *Journal of Adult Education, 39*(2), 25–35.

Chang, H. (2008). *Autoethnography as method*. Left Coast Press.

Chapelle, C. A. (2010). Invited commentary research for practice: A look at issues in technology for second language learning. *Language Learning & Technology, 14*(3), 27–30.

Chen, D. Y.-T., Chu, S. K.-W., & Xu, S.-Q. (2012). How do libraries use social networking sites to interact with users? *Proceedings of the American Society for Information Science and Technology, 49*(1), 1–10.

Chen, H., Cheung, M. Y., Luo, C., & Sia, C. L. (2009). Credibility of electronic word-of-mouth: Information and normative determinants of online consumer recommendations. *International Journal of Electronic Commerce, 13*(4), 9–8. doi:10.2753/JEC1086-4415130402

Chen, S.-Y., & Tzeng, J.-Y. (2010). College female and male heavy internet users' profiles of practices and their academic grades and psychosocial adjustment. *Cyberpsychology, Behavior, and Social Networking, 13*(3), 257–262. doi:10.1089/cyber.2009.0023 PMID:20557244

Chen, Y. H., & Barnes, S. (2007). Initial trust and online buyer behaviour. *Industrial Management & Data Systems, 107*(1), 21–36. doi:10.1108/02635570710719034

Cheung, C. M., Chiu, P.-Y., & Lee, M. K. (2011). Online social networks: Why do students use Facebook? *Computers in Human Behavior, 27*(4), 1337–1343. doi:10.1016/j.chb.2010.07.028

Cheung, C. M., & Lee, M. K. (2006). Understanding consumer trust in internet shopping: A multidisciplinary approach. *Journal of the American Society for Information Science and Technology, 57*(4), 479–492. doi:10.1002/asi.20312

Child, J. T., Haridakis, P., & Petronio, S. (2012). Blogging privacy rule orientations, privacy management, and content deletion practices: The variability of online privacy management activity at different stages of social media use. *Computers in Human Behavior, 28*(5), 1859–1872. doi:10.1016/j.chb.2012.05.004

Child, J. T., Pearson, J. C., & Petronio, S. (2009). Blogging, communication, and privacy management: Development of the blogging privacy management measure. *Journal of the American Society for Information Science and Technology, 60*(10), 2079–2094. doi:10.1002/asi.21122

Child, J. T., & Petronio, S. (2011). Unpacking the paradoxes of privacy in CMC relationships: The challenges of blogging and relational communication on the internet. In K. Wright & L. Webb (Eds.), *Computer-mediated communication in personal relationships* (pp. 21–40). New York: Peter Lang.

Chiluwa, I. (2008). SMS text messaging and the Nigerian Christian context: Constructing values and sentiments. *International Journal of Language. Society and Culture*, *24*, 11–20.

Chiong, C., & Shuler, C. (2010). *Learning: Is there an app for that? Investigations of young children's usage and learning with mobile devices and apps*. New York: The Joan Ganz Cooney Center at Sesame Workshop.

Chizzotti, A. (2006). *Pesquisa qualitativa em ciências humanas e sociais*. Petrópolis, RJ: Vozes.

Cho, H. (2010). Determinants of behavioral responses to online privacy: The effects of concern, risk beliefs, self-efficacy, and communication sources on self-protection strategies. *Journal of Information Privacy & Security*, *6*(1).

Christakis, D. A. (2010). Internet addiction: A 21st century epidemic? *BMC Medicine*, *8*(1), 61–63. doi:10.1186/1741-7015-8-61 PMID:20955578

Christofides, E., Muise, A., & Desmarais, S. (2009). Information disclosure and control on Facebook: Are they two sides of the same coin or two different processes? *Cyberpsychology (Brno)*, *12*(3). PMID:19250020

Christofides, E., Muise, A., & Desmarais, S. (2012). Hey mom, what's on your facebook? Comparing Facebook disclosure and privacy in adolescents and adults. *Social Psychological & Personality Science*, *3*(1), 48–54. doi:10.1177/1948550611408619

Chua, A. Y. K., & Banerjee, S. (2013). Reliability of reviews on the internet: The case of TripAdvisor. In *Proceedings of the World Congress on Engineering and Computer Science*. San Francisco: WCECS.

Chung, J. Y., & Buhalis, D. (2008). Web 2.0: A study of online travel community. In P. O. Connor, W. Hopken, & U. Gretzel (Eds.), *Information and communication technologies in tourism* (pp. 70–81). New York: Springer.

Ciccarelli, S. (2012). Russian arrested for cyberattacks on Amazon. *NBC News*. Retrieved March 20, 2014, from http://www.nbcnews.com/id/48291470/ns/technology_and_science-security/t/russian-arrested-cyberattacks-amazon/

Cifuentes, L., Xochihua, O. A., & Edwards, J. (2011). Learning in web 2.0 environments: Surface learning and chaos or deep learning and self-regulation? *Quarterly Review of Distance Education*, *12*(1).

Clarke, J., Thorpe, R., Anderson, L., & Gold, J. (2006). It's all action, it's all learning: Action learning in SMEs. *Journal of European Industrial Training*, *30*(6), 441–455. doi:10.1108/03090590610688825

Clarke, T., & Clarke, E. (2009). Born digital? Pedagogy and computer-assisted learning. *Education + Training*, *51*(5–6), 395–407. doi:10.1108/00400910910987200

Cobb, J. (2010). *Learning 2.0 for associations*. Tagoras. Retrieved April 15, 2014, from http://www.tagoras.com/docs/Learning-20-Associations-2ed.pdf

Cochrane, K. (2011, 25 January). Why TripAdvisor is getting bad review. *The Guardian*. Retrieved from http://www.theguardian.com/uk

Cohen, J. E. (2003). DRM and privacy. *Communications of the ACM*, *46*(4), 46–49. doi:10.1145/641205.641230

Coldron, J., & Smith, R. (1999). Active location in teachers' construction of their professional identities. *Journal of Curriculum Studies*, *31*(6), 711–726. doi:10.1080/002202799182954

Computer Business Review. (2011a). *Nasdaq confirms security breach, denies customer data leak*. Retrieved February 10, 2014, from http://security.cbronline.com/news/nasdaq-confirms-security-breach-denies-customer-data-leak-070211

Computer Business Review. (2011b). *Italian government site attacked: ANSA*. Retrieved February 10, 2014, from http://www.cbronline.com/news/italian-government-site-attacked-ansa-070211

Congo, M. (2013). *Um terço dos brasileiros tem Facebook: País se torna o 2° em número de usuários*. Available at http://blogs.estadao.com.br/radar-tecnologico/2013/01/23/um-terco-dosbrasileiros-tem-facebook-pais-se-torna-o-2o-em-numero-de-usuarios/

Connell, R. S. (2009). Academic libraries, Facebook and MySpace, and student outreach: A survey of student opinion. *Libraries and the Academy, 9*(1), 25–36. doi:10.1353/pla.0.0036

Connelly, F. M., & Clandinin, D. J. (1990). Stories of experience and narrative inquiry. *Educational Researcher, 19*(5), 2–14. doi:10.3102/0013189X019005002

Connolly, M. (2011). Does social networking enhance or impede student learning? Social networking and student learning: Friends with benefits. In P. M. Magolda & M. B. Baxter (Eds.), *Contested issues in student affairs: Diverse perspectives and respectful dialogue* (pp. 122–134). Sterling, VA: Stylus Press.

Conole, G., & Alevizou, P. (2010). *A literature review of the use of web 2.0 tools in higher education.* Higher Education Academy, The Open University, UK. Retrieved December 12, 2013, from http://www.heacademy.ac.uk/assets/documents/subjects/bioscience/event-report-2009-leicester-literature-review.pdf

Conole, G., & Alevizou, P. (2010). *A literature review on the use of web 2.0 tools in higher education.* York, UK: Higher Education Academy.

Constantin, L. (2013). Fake social media ID duped security-aware IT guys. *IT World.* Retrieved January 04, 2014, from http://www.pcworld.com/article/2059940/fake-social-media-id-duped-securityaware-it-guys.html

Constantinides, E., & Lorenzo-Romero, C. (2013). Social networking sites as business tool: A study of user behavior. In *Business process management* (pp. 221–240). Springer Berlin Heidelberg. doi:10.1007/978-3-642-28409-0_9

Coopamootoo, P. L., & Ashenden, D. (2011). Designing usable online privacy mechanisms: What can we learn from real world behaviour? In Privacy and identity management for life (pp. 311-324). Springer Berlin Heidelberg.

Cooper, C. (2012). *Essentials of tourism.* Harlow, UK: FT – Prentice Hall.

Corbalis, M. (2009). The evolution of language. *Annals of the New York Academy of Sciences, 1156*(1), 19–43. doi:10.1111/j.1749-6632.2009.04423.x PMID:19338501

Corbett, P. (2011). *Facebook demographics and statistics including federal employees and gays in the military.* Retrieved on October 5, 2013 from http://istrategylabs.com/2011/01/2011-facebook-demographics-and-statistics-including-federal-employees-and-gays-in-the-military

Corritore, C., Kracher, B., & Wiedenbeck, S. (2003). On-line trust: Concepts, evolving themes, a model. *International Journal of Human-Computer Studies, 58*(6), 737–758. doi:10.1016/S1071-5819(03)00041-7

Costa, P. T., & McCrae, R. R. (1992). Normal personality assessment in clinical practice: The NEO personality inventory. *Psychological Assessment, 4*(1), 5–13. doi:10.1037/1040-3590.4.1.5

Cotton, S. R., Ford, G., Ford, S., & Hale, T. M. (2012). Internet use and depression among older adults. *Computers in Human Behavior, 28*(2), 496–499. doi:10.1016/j.chb.2011.10.021

Covey, S. R. (1989). *The 7 habits of highly effective people.* New York, NY: Simon & Schuster.

Coviello, N. E., & McAuley, A. (1999). Internationalization and the small firm: A review of contemporary empirical research. *Management International Review, 39*(3), 223–237.

Coviello, N. E., & Munro, H. (1995). Growing the entrepreneurial firm. *European Journal of Marketing, 29*(7), 49–61. doi:10.1108/03090569510095008

Coyne, S., Padilla-Walker, L., Day, R., Harper, J., & Stockdale, L. (2013). A friend request from dear old dad: Associations between parent-child social networking and adolescent outcomes. *Cyberpsychology, Behavior, and Social Networking*, 2152–2723. PMID:23845157

Creswell, J. (2009). *Research design: Qualitative, quantitative, and mixed methods approaches* (3rd ed.). Thousand Oaks, CA: Sage Publications, Inc.

Creswell, J. W. (2008). *Educational research: Planning, conducting, and evaluating quantitative and qualitative research* (3rd ed.). Pearson Education.

Crisan, D. (2013). *To the Romanian Facebook user: May your life be as awesome as you describe it on your Facebook profile* [translated from Romanian]. Unpublished thesis.

Cristakis, D. A., Moreno, M. M., Jelenchick, L., Myaing, M. T., & Zhou, C. (2011). Problematic internet usage in US college students: A pilot study. *BMC Medicine, 9*(77). http://www.biomedcentral.com/content/pdf/1741-7015-9-77.pdf PMID:21696582

Crocker, J., Luhtanen, R. K., Cooper, M., & Bouvrette, A. (2003). Contingencies of self-worth in college students: Theory and measurement. *Journal of Personality and Social Psychology, 85*(5), 894–908. doi:10.1037/0022-3514.85.5.894 PMID:14599252

Crystal, D. (2001). *Language and the internet*. Cambridge, UK: Cambridge University Press. doi:10.1017/CBO9781139164771

Culnan, M. J. (2000). Protecting privacy online: Is self-regulation working? *Journal of Public Policy & Marketing, 19*(1), 20–26. doi:10.1509/jppm.19.1.20.16944

Danis, C., Bailey, M., Christensen, J., Ellis, J., Erickson, T., Farrell, R., & Kellogg, W. (2009). Mobile applications for the next billions: A social computing application and a perspective on sustainability. In *Proceedings of the 2nd Workshop on Innovative Mobile Technology and Services for Developing Countries* (IMTS – DC 09). Kampala, Uganda: Academic Press.

Datu, J. A., Valdez, J. P., & Datu, N. (2012). Does Face-booking make us sad? Hunting relationship between Facebook use and depression among Filipino adolescents. *International Journal of Research Studies in Educational Technology, 1*(2), 83–91. doi:10.5861/ijrset.2012.202

Davey, G., & Zhao, X. (2012). 'A real man smells of tobacco smoke'—Chinese youth's interpretation of smoking imagery in film. *Social Science & Medicine, 74*(10), 1552–1559. doi:10.1016/j.socscimed.2012.01.024 PMID:22445156

Davila, J., Hershenberg, R., Feinstein, B. A., Gorman, K., Bhatia, V., & Starr, L. R. (2012). Frequency and quality of social networking among young adults: Associations with depressive symptoms, rumination, and co-rumination. *Psychology of Popular Media Culture, 1*(2), 72–86. doi:10.1037/a0027512 PMID:24490122

Davis, A. E., Renzulli, L. A., & Aldrich, H. E. (2006). Mixing or matching? The influence of voluntary associations on the occupational diversity and density of small business owners' networks. *Work and Occupations, 33*(1), 42–72. doi:10.1177/0730888405281914

Davis, F. D. (1987). Perceived usefulness, perceived ease of use and user acceptance of information technology. *Management Information Systems Quarterly, 13*(3), 319–340. doi:10.2307/249008

Davis, G. J. (2009). The joys of a handwritten letter. *Journal of American Amateur Press Association, 78,* 46–61. Retrieved from http://www.greenapple.com/~aapa/ejournals/Whippoorwill_E-Comment/n0078.pdf

DeHaan, S., Kuper, L., Magee, J., Bigelow, L., & Mustanski, B. (2013). The interplay between online and offline explorations of identity, relationships, and sex: A mixed-methods study with LGBT youth. *Journal of Sex Research, 50*(5), 421–434. doi:10.1080/00224499.2012.661489 PMID:22489658

Dellarocas, S. (2003). The digitization of word of mouth: Promise and challenge of online feedback mechanisms. *Management Science, 49*(10), 1407–1424. doi:10.1287/mnsc.49.10.1407.17308

Dewald, N. H. (1999). Transporting good library instruction practices into the web environment: An analysis of online tutorials. *Journal of Academic Librarianship, 25*(1), 26–31. doi:10.1016/S0099-1333(99)80172-4

Dewitt, B., & Meyer, R. (1994). *Strategy: Process, content, context.* St Paul, MN: West Publishing.

Dhillon, G., & Backhouse, J. (2000). Technical opinion: Information system security management in the new millennium. *Communications of the ACM, 43*(7), 125–128. doi:10.1145/341852.341877

Dhillon, G., & Backhouse, J. (2001). Current directions in IS security research: Towards socio-organizational perspectives. *Information Systems Journal, 11*(2), 127–153. doi:10.1046/j.1365-2575.2001.00099.x

Dias, P. (2008). Da e-moderação à mediação colaborativa nas comunidades de aprendizagem. *Educação Formação & Tecnologias, 1*(1), 4–10.

Diener, E. (1984). Subjective well-being. *Psychological Bulletin*, *95*(3), 542–575. doi:10.1037/0033-2909.95.3.542 PMID:6399758

Diener, E., Emmons, R. A., Larsen, R. J., & Griffin, S. (1985). The satisfaction with life scale. *Journal of Personality Assessment*, *49*(1), 71–75. doi:10.1207/s15327752jpa4901_13 PMID:16367493

Digital Dementia on the Rise as Young People Increasingly Rely on Technology Instead of Their Brain. (2013, June 24). *Mail Online*. Retrieved June 8, 2013, from http://www.dailymail.co.uk/health/article-2347563/Digital-dementia-rise-young-people-increasingly-rely-technology-instead-brain.html

Dinev, T., & Hart, P. (2004). Internet privacy concerns and their antecedents-measurement validity and a regression model. *Behaviour & Information Technology*, *23*(6), 413–422. doi:10.1080/01449290410001715723

Doctorow, C., Dornfest, R., Johnson, S., Powers, S., Trott, B., & Trott, M. (2002). *Essential blogging: Selecting and using weblog tools*. Sebastopol, CA: O'Reilly.

Dolcini, M., & Adler, N. (1994). Perceived competencies, peer group affiliation, and risk behavior among early adolescents. *Health Psychology*, *13*(6), 496–506. doi:10.1037/0278-6133.13.6.496 PMID:7889904

Dong, G., Lu, Q., Zhou, H., & Zhao, X. (2011). Precursor or sequela: Pathological disorders in people with internet addiction disorder. *PLoS ONE*, *6*(2), 1–5. doi:10.1371/journal.pone.0014703

Douglas, N., Douglas, N., & Derrett, R. (2001). *Special interest tourism: Context and cases*. New York: John Wiley & Sons.

Dowling, G. (2001). *Creating corporate reputations*. New York: Oxford University Press.

Doyle, P. (2009). *Value-based marketing: Marketing strategies for corporate growth and shareholder value*. Chichester, UK: Wiley.

Doyle, S. (2007). The role of social networks in marketing. *Journal of Database Marketing & Customer Strategy Management*, *15*(1), 60–64. doi:10.1057/palgrave.dbm.3250070

Duggan, M., & Brenner, J. (2013). *The demographics of social media users, 2012* (Vol. 14). Pew Research Center's Internet & American Life Project.

Dumas, M. B. (2012). *Diving into the bitstream: Information technology meets society in a digital world*. Routledge.

Durland, M. M., & Fredericks, K. A. (2005). An introduction to social network analysis. *New Directions for Evaluation*, *2005*(107), 5–13. doi:10.1002/ev.157

Dutta, S., & Fraser, M. (2009). When job-seekers invade Faceebok. *The McKinsey Quarterly*, *2009*(March). Available online at http://www.mckinsey.com/insights/high_tech_telecoms_internet/when_job_seekers_invade_facebook

Dutton, W. H., & Helsper, E. (2007). *Oxford internet survey 2007 report: The internet in Britain*. Oxford, UK: Oxford Internet Institute.

Dutton, W. H., Helsper, E. J., & Gerber, M. M. (2009). *Oxford internet survey 2009 report: The internet in Britain*. Oxford Internet Institute, University of Oxford.

Dutton, W. H., & Shepherd, A. (2006). Trust in the internet as an experience technology. *Information Communication and Society*, *9*(4), 433–451. doi:10.1080/13691180600858606

Earl, M. J. (1989). *Management strategies for information technology*. Upper Saddle River, NJ: Prentice-Hall, Inc.

East, R., Hammond, K., & Lomax, W. (2008). Measuring the impact of positive and negative word of mouth on brand purchase probability. *International Journal of Research in Marketing*, *25*(3), 215–224. doi:10.1016/j.ijresmar.2008.04.001

Ebersbach, A., Glaser, M., & Heigl, R. (2006). *Wiki: Web collaboration*. Springer-Verlag Berlin Heidelberg.

Ellis, C., & Bochner, A. P. (2000a). Autoethnography, personal narrative, and personal reflexivity. In N. Denzin & Y. Lincoln (Eds.), *Handbook of qualitative research* (2nd ed.; pp. 645–672). Sage.

Ellis, N. (2010). *Business to business marketing: Relationships, networks and strategies*. Oxford, UK: OUP.

Ellison, N. B., Steinfield, C., & Lampe, C. (2007). The benefits of Facebook "friends": Social capital and college students' use of online social network sites. *Journal of Computer-Mediated Communication, 12*(4), 1143–1168. doi:10.1111/j.1083-6101.2007.00367.x

Ellison, N. B., Steinfield, C., & Lampe, C. (2011). Connections strategies: Social capital implications of Facebook-enabled communication practices. *New Media & Society, 13*(6), 873–892. doi:10.1177/1461444810385389

El-Sofany, H. F., Al Tayeb, A., Alghatani, K., & El-Seoud, S. A. (2013). The impact of cloud computing technologies in e-learning. *International Journal of Emerging Technologies in Learning*, 37-43. doi:10.3991/ijet.v8iS1.2344

Ensor, J. (2013). Family of Skype suicide teen calls on David Cameron to tackle cyber bullying. *The Telegraph*. Retrieved August 20, 2013, from http://www.telegraph.co.uk/technology/news/10248058/Family-of-skype-suicide-teen-calls-on-David-Cameron-to-tackle-cyber-bullying.html

Espinoza, G., & Juvonen, J. (2011). The pervasiveness, connectedness, and intrusiveness of social network site use among young adolescents. *Cyberpsychology, Behavior, and Social Networking, 14*(12), 705–709. doi:10.1089/cyber.2010.0492 PMID:21668346

Essinger, J. (2001). *Internet trust and security: The way ahead*. Addison-Wesley.

European Travel Commission. (2013). *New media trend watch*. Retrieved December 8, 2013, from http://www.newmediatrendwatch.com/markets-by-country/11-long-haul/63-south-korea

Extensão ou Comunicação. (1979). Rio de Janeiro: Paz e Terra.

Faccio, M. (2006). Politically connected firms. *The American Economic Review, 96*(1), 369–386. doi:10.1257/000282806776157704

Facebook Help Center. (2014). Retrieved from https://www.facebook.com/help/384834971571333

Facebook Newsroom. (2012). One billion people on Facebook. *Facebook*. Retrieved September 20, 2013, from http://newsroom.fb.com/News/457/One-Billion-People-on-Facebook

Facebook Statistics. (2013). *Facebook data science*. Retrieved from: https://www.facebook.com/data/notes

Fallows, D. (2002). *Email at work: Few feel overwhelmed and most are pleased with the way email helps them do their jobs*. Pew Internet & American Life Project.

Feinstein, B. A., Hershenberg, R., Bhatia, V., Latack, J. A., Meuwly, N., & Davila, J. (2013). Negative social comparison on Facebook and depressive symptoms: Rumination as a mechanism. *Psychology of Popular Media Culture, 2*(3), 161–170. doi:10.1037/a0033111

Fernando, A. (2008). Baby steps in web 2.0 education. *Communication World, 25*(3), 8–9.

Fiellin, L., Tetrault, J., Becker, W., Fiellin, D., & Hoff, R. (2012). Previous use of alcohol, cigarettes, and marijuana and subsequent abuse of prescription opioids in young adults. *The Journal of Adolescent Health, 52*(2), 158–163. doi:10.1016/j.jadohealth.2012.06.010 PMID:23332479

Fill, C. (2002). *Marketing communications: Contexts, strategies, and applications* (3rd ed.). Harlow, UK: Financial Times Prentice Hall.

Fill, C. (1995). *Marketing communications*. Harlow, UK: Prentice-Hall.

Finch, A., & Rahim, E. (2011). Adult learning styles and technology-driven learning for online students. *Academic Leadership the Online Journal, 9*(2).

Finch, A., Burrell, D. N., Walker, R., Rahim, E., & Dawson, M. (2010). Changing the cultures of colleges and universities to make them more adaptive. *Review of Higher Education and Self-Learning, 3*(7), 40–53.

Fischer, G., & Konomi, S. (2007). Innovative socio-technical environments in support of distributed intelligence and lifelong learning. *Journal of Computer Assisted Learning, 23*(4), 338–350. doi:10.1111/j.1365-2729.2007.00238.x

Floyd, S. W., & Wooldridge, B. (1999). Knowledge creation and social networks in corporate entrepreneurship: The renewal of organizational capability. *Entrepreneurship Theory and Practice*, 123-143.

Fodor, M., & Hoffman, D. (2010). Can you measure the ROI of your social marketing? *MIT Sloan Review, 52*(11), 40–50.

Fogel, J., & Nehmad, E. (2009). Internet social network communities: Risk taking, trust, and privacy concerns. *Computers in Human Behavior, 25*(1), 153–160. doi:10.1016/j.chb.2008.08.006

Forest, A., & Wood, J. (2012). When social networking is not working individuals with low self-esteem recognize but do not reap the benefits of self-disclosure on Facebook. *Psychological Science, 23*(3), 295–302. doi:10.1177/0956797611429709 PMID:22318997

Forrest, S. P., & Peterson, T. O. (2006). It's called andragogy. *Academy of Management Learning & Education, 5*(1), 113–122. doi:10.5465/AMLE.2006.20388390

Forsgren, M., & Johanson, J. (1992). Managing internationalization in business networks. In M. Forsgren & J. Johanson (Eds.), *Managing networks in international business*. Philadelphia: Gordon and Breach.

Fotis, J., Buhalis, D., & Rossides, N. (2012). Social media use and impact during the holiday travel planning process. In M. Fuchs, F. Ricci, & L. Cantoni (Eds.), *Information and communication technologies in tourism* (pp. 13–24). Vienna: SpringerVerlag. doi:10.1007/978-3-7091-1142-0_2

Fournier, A., & Clarke, S. (2011). Do college students use facebook to communicate about alcohol? An analysis of student profile pages. *Cyberpsychology (Brno), 5*(2), 1–12.

Foxman, E. R., & Kilcoyne, P. (1993). Information technology, marketing practice, and consumer privacy: Ethical issues. *Journal of Public Policy & Marketing*, 106–119.

Freire, P. (1983a). *Educação como prática da liberdade*. Rio de Janeiro: Paz e Terra.

Freire, P. (1983b). Criando métodos de pesquisa alternativa. In *Pesquisa participante, 3ª edição*. São Paulo: Brasiliense.

Freire, P. (1997). *Pedagogia da autonomia*. Rio de Janeiro: Paz e Terra.

Friedman, M., Resnick, P., & Sami, R. (2007). *Algorithmic game theory*. Cambridge, UK: Cambridge University Press.

Friesen, N., & Lowe, S. (2011). The questionable promise of social media for education: Connective learning and the commercial imperative. *Journal of Computer Assisted Learning, 28*(3), 183–194. doi:10.1111/j.1365-2729.2011.00426.x

Fuller-Love, N., & Thomas, E. (2004). Networks in small manufacturing firms. *Journal of Small Business and Enterprise Development, 11*(2), 244–253. doi:10.1108/14626000410537182

Gadkari, P. (2013). Ask.fm unveils changes to safety policy. *BBC News*. Retrieved August 20, 2013, from http://www.bbc.co.uk/news/world-us-canada-23752923

Gaines, L. K., & Miller, R. L. (2009). *Criminal justice in action* (5th ed.). Thomson Wadsworth.

Galagher, S. (2009). Social networks a magnet for malware. In *IT management ebook*. WebMediaBrands.

Gallaugher, J., & Ransbotham, S. (2010). Social media and customer dialog management at Starbucks. *Management Information Systems Quarterly Executive Journal, 9*(4), 197–211.

Garas, A., Garcia, D., Skowron, M., & Schweitzer, F. (2012). Emotional persistence in online chatting communities. *Scientific Reports, 2*(204), 402. PMID:22577512

Garrison, D. R., & Kanuka, H. (2004). Blended learning: Uncovering its transformative potential in higher education. *The Internet and Higher Education, 7*(2), 95–105. doi:10.1016/j.iheduc.2004.02.001

Gastaldo, E. (2010a). *MySpace leaks user data, too: But, apparently, it's not quite as bad as Facebook*. Retrieved February 10, 2014, from http://www.newser.com/story/103626/myspace-leaks-user-data-too.html

Gastaldo, E. (2010b). *Congress has some questions for Zuckerberg: Two representatives get involved in the latest privacy breach*. Retrieved February 10, 2014, from http://www.newser.com/story/103258/congress-has-some-questions-for-zuckerberg.html

Gastaldo, E. (2010c). *Google: We accidentally grabbed emails, passwords: Street view privacy flap worse than reported*. Retrieved February 10, 2014, from http://www.newser.com/story/103636/google-we-accidentally-grabbed-emails-passwords.html

Gauzente, C. (2004). Web merchants' privacy and security statements: How reassuring are they for consumers? A two-sided approach. *Journal of Electronic Commerce Research, 5*(3), 181–198.

Gawel, R. (2004). Duke purchases iPods for incoming frosh. *Class Electronic Design, 52*(18), 8.

Gefen, D., Karahanna, E., & Straub, D. W. (2003). Trust and TAM in online shopping: An integrated model. *Management Information Systems Quarterly*, *27*(1), 51–90.

Geletkanycz, M. A., & Hambrick, D. C. (1997). The external ties of executives: Implications for strategic choice and performance. *Administrative Science Quarterly*, *42*(4), 654–681. doi:10.2307/2393653

Gergen, M., & Gergen, K. (2002). Ethnographic representation as relationship. In A. Bochner & C. Ellis (Eds.), *Ethnographically speaking: Autoethnography, literature, and aesthetics* (pp. 11–33). Altamira.

Gibbs, J. L., Ellison, N. B., & Heino, R. D. (2006). Self-presentation in online personals: The role of anticipated future interaction, self-disclosure, and perceived success in internet dating. *Communication Research*, *33*(2), 152–177. doi:10.1177/0093650205285368

Gikas, J., & Grant, M. (2013). Mobile computing devices in higher education: Student perspectives on learning with cellphones, smartphones & social media. *The Internet and Higher Education*, *19*, 18–26. doi:10.1016/j.iheduc.2013.06.002

Girvan, M., & Newman, M. E. J. (2002). Community structure in social and biological networks. *Proceedings of the National Academy of Sciences of the United States of America*, *99*(12), 8271–8276. doi:10.1073/pnas.122653799 PMID:12060727

Glazer, R. (1991). Marketing in an information-intensive environment: Strategic implications of knowledge as an asset. *Journal of Marketing*, *55*(4), 1–19. doi:10.2307/1251953

Glimmerglass: Optical Cyber Solutions. (2012). Retrieved October 1, 2012, from http://www.glimmerglass.com

Goffman, E. (1959). *The presentation of self in everyday life*. New York: Doubleday.

Golbeck, J. (2007). The dynamics of web-based social networks: Membership, relationships, and change. *First Monday*, *12*(11). doi:10.5210/fm.v12i11.2023

Golbeck, J. (2008). *Trust on the world wide web: A survey*. Hanover, MA: NowPublishers.

Golbeck, J., & Hendler, J. (2004). Reputation network analysis for email filtering. In *Proceedings of the First Conference on Email and Anti-Spam*. Academic Press.

Goldman, A. (2009). Businesses lack social media policies. In *IT manager's guide to social networking*. WebMediaBrands.

Goldman, E., Rocholl, J., & So, J. (2013). Politically connected boards of directors and the allocation of procurement contracts. *Review of Finance*, *17*(5), 1617–1648. doi:10.1093/rof/rfs039

Gollmann, D. (1999). *Computer security*. John Wiley & Sons.

Gómez, V. (1994). Gonzalo: Tecnologías avanzadas y educación. In *Teoría de Ia educación*. Madrid: Taurus Universitaria.

Gonzales, A. L., & Hancock, J. T. (2011). Mirror, mirror on my Facebook wall: Effects of exposure to Facebook on self-esteem. *Cyberpsychology, Behavior, and Social Networking*, *14*(1-2), 79–83. doi:10.1089/cyber.2009.0411 PMID:21329447

Goodson, I. (2007). Currículo, narrativa e o futuro social. Revista Brasileira de Educação, 12(35), 241 – 252.

Goodwin, C. (1991). Privacy: Recognition of a consumer right. *Journal of Public Policy & Marketing*, 149–166.

Gordon, L. A., Loeb, M. P., & Sohail, T. (2010). Market value of voluntary disclosures concerning information security. *Management Information Systems Quarterly*, *34*(3), 567–594.

Gowen, K., Deschaine, M., Gruttadara, D., & Markey, D. (2012). Young adults with mental health conditions and social networking websites: Seeking tools to build community. *Psychiatric Rehabilitation Journal*, *35*(3), 245–250. doi:10.2975/35.3.2012.245.250 PMID:22246123

Grabosky, P. N. (2001). Virtual criminality: Old wine in new bottles? *Social & Legal Studies*, *10*(2), 243–249.

Granovetter, M. (1985). Economic action and social structure: The problem of embeddedness. *American Journal of Sociology*, *91*(3), 481–510. doi:10.1086/228311

Gray, D., & Vander Wal, T. (2012). *The connected company*. North Sebastopol, CA: O'Reilly Media, Inc.

Greenhow, C., Robelia, B., & Hughes, J. E. (2009). Learning, teaching, and scholarship in a digital age web 2.0 and classroom research: What path should we take now? *Educational Researcher, 38*(4), 246–259. doi:10.3102/0013189X09336671

Grenard, J., Dent, C., & Stacy, A. (2013). Exposure to alcohol advertisements and teenage alcohol-related problems. *Paediatrics, 131*(2), e369–e379. doi:10.1542/peds.2012-1480 PMID:23359585

Greve, A., & Salaff, J. W. (2003). Social networks and entrepreneurship. *Entrepreneurship Theory and Practice, 28*(1), 1–23. doi:10.1111/1540-8520.00029

Griffiths, R., & Casswell, S. (2010). Intoxigenic digital spaces? Youth, social networking sites and alcohol marketing. *Drug and Alcohol Review, 29*(5), 525–530. doi:10.1111/j.1465-3362.2010.00178.x PMID:20887576

Grinspun, M. P. S. Z. (1999). Educação e tecnologia, desafios e perspectivas. São Paulo, Ed. Cortez.

Gritzalis, S. (2004). Enhancing web privacy and anonymity in the digital era. *Information Management & Computer Security, 12*(3), 255–287. doi:10.1108/09685220410542615

Gulati, R., Nohria, N., & Zaheer, A. (2000). Strategic networks. *Strategic Management Journal, 21*(3), 203–215. doi:10.1002/(SICI)1097-0266(200003)21:3<203::AID-SMJ102>3.0.CO;2-K

Gunduz, U., & Ozcan, G. B. (2014). Political connectedness and business performance: Some evidence from Turkish industry rankings. *Business and Politics, 16*(4), 1469–3569.

Gupta, A., & Hammond, R. (2005). Information systems security issues and decisions for small businesses: An empirical examination. *Information Management & Computer Security, 13*(4), 297–310. doi:10.1108/09685220510614425

Gupta, B., Iyer, L. S., & Weisskirch, R. S. (2010). Facilitating global e-commerce: A comparison of consumers' willingness to disclose personal information online in the US and in India. *Journal of Electronic Commerce Research, 11*(1), 41–52.

Gurakar, E. C., & Bircan, T. (in press). Political connections and public procurement in Turkey: Evidence from construction work contracts. In *Political economy determinants of private sector dynamism in the ERF region*. Economic Research Forum.

Haferkamp, N., & Krämer, N. (2011). Social comparison 2.0: Examining the effects of online profiles on social-networking sites. *Cyberpsychology, Behavior, and Social Networking, 14*(5), 309–314. doi:10.1089/cyber.2010.0120 PMID:21117976

Hägg, I., & Johanson, J. (1982). *Företag i nätverk-ny syn på konkurrenskraft. Stockolm.* Academic Press.

Håkansson, H. (1982). *International marketing & purchasing of industrial goods: An interaction approach.* Chichester, UK: John Wiley & Sons.

Håkansson, H., & Johanson, J. (1992). A model of industrial networks. In B. Axelson & G. Easton (Eds.), *Industrial networks a new view of reality*. London, UK: Routledge.

Håkansson, H., & Snehota, I. (1995). *Developing relationships in business networks*. London, UK: Routledge.

Hammarkvist, K. O., Håkansson, H., & Mattsson, L. G. (1982). Marknadsföring för konkurrenskraft. Liber Ekonomi.

Hanna, R., Rohm, A., & Crittenden, V. (2011). We're all connected: The power of the social media ecosystem. *Business Horizons, 54*(3), 265–273. doi:10.1016/j.bushor.2011.01.007

Harghittai, E. (2008). Whose space? Differences among users and non-users of social network sites. *Journal of Computer-Mediated Communication, 13*(1), 276–297. doi:10.1111/j.1083-6101.2007.00396.x

Harrison McKnight, D., Choudhury, V., & Kacmar, C. (2002). The impact of initial consumer trust on intentions to transact with a web site: A trust building model. *The Journal of Strategic Information Systems, 11*(3), 297–323. doi:10.1016/S0963-8687(02)00020-3

Hedström, P., & Stern, C. (2008). Rational choice and sociology. In The new Palgrave dictionary of economics (pp. 872–877). Basingstoke, UK: Palgrave Macmillan.

Henkin, L. (1974). Privacy and autonomy. *Columbia Law Review, 74*(8), 1410–1433. doi:10.2307/1121541

Hennig-Thurau, T., & Walsh, G. (2003). Electronic word of mouth: Motives for and consequences of reading customer articulations on the internet. *International Journal of Electronic Commerce, 8*(2), 51–74.

Hewitt, A., & Forte, A. (2006). *Crossing boundaries: Identity management and student/faculty relationships on the Facebook.* Paper presented at the CSCW Conference, Canada.

Hew, K. F. (2011). Students' and teachers' use of Facebook. *Computers in Human Behavior, 27*(2), 662–676. doi:10.1016/j.chb.2010.11.020

Hickins, M. (2012). *The morning download: How Facebook could kill your business.* Retrieved April 21, 2014, from http://blogs.wsj.com/cio/2012/04/09/the-morning-download-how-facebook-could-kill-your-business/

Hinde, S. (2002). Security surveys spring crop. *Computers & Security, 21*(4), 310–321. doi:10.1016/S0167-4048(02)00404-2

Hinduja, S., & Patchin, W. (2010). Bullying, cyberbullying, and suicide. *Archives of Suicide Research, 14*(3), 206–221. doi:10.1080/13811118.2010.494133 PMID:20658375

Hird, J. (2011, August 1). *11 ways to measure the value of social media.* Retrieved 18 March 2014, from https://econsultancy.com/blog/7838-11-ways-to-measure-the-value-of-social-media

Hoffman, E. W., Pinkleton, B. E., Austin, E. W., & Reyes-Velázquez, W. (2014). Exploring college students' use of general and alcohol-related social media and their associations to alcohol-related behaviors. *Journal of American College Health.* Retrieved from http://www.tandfonline.com/doi/abs/10.1080/07448481.2014.9028 37#.U3Tk0PldV8E

Hoffman, D. L., & Novak, T. P. (2009). Flow online: Lessons learned and future prospects. *Journal of Interactive Marketing, 23*(1), 23–34. doi:10.1016/j.intmar.2008.10.003

Hoffman, D. L., Novak, T. P., & Peralta, M. (1999). Building consumer trust online. *Communications of the ACM, 42*(4), 80–85. doi:10.1145/299157.299175

Hoffman, K., Zage, D., & Nita-Rotaru, C. (2009). A survey of attack and defence techniques for reputations systems. *ACM Computing Surveys, 42*(1), 1–16. doi:10.1145/1592451.1592452

Höfich, J., & Gebhardt, J. (2005). Changing cultures of written communication: Letter – email– SMS. In R. Harper, L. Palen, & A. Taylor (Eds.), *The inside text: Social, cultural and design perspectives on SMS* (Vol. 4, pp. 9–32). Dordrecht, The Netherlands: Springer. doi:10.1007/1-4020-3060-6_2

Hollendsen, S. (1998). *The network model from global marketing: A market-responsive approach.* Prentice Hall Europe.

Hooper, S., & Rieber, L. P. (1995). Teaching with technology. In A. C. Ornstein (Ed.), *Teaching: Theory into practice* (pp. 154–170). Allyn & Bacon.

Horton, F. Jr. (2008). *Introduction à la maîtrise de l'information.* Paris: UNESCO.

Horton, J., Millo, Y., & Serafeim, G. (2011). Resources or power? Implications of social networks on compensation and firm performance. *Journal of Business Finance & Accounting, 39*(3-4), 399–426. doi:10.1111/j.1468-5957.2011.02276.x

Howe, N., & Strauss, W. (2000). *Millennials rising: The next great generation.* Vintage Books.

Hrastinski, S., & Aghaee, N. (2012). How are campus students using social media to support their studies? An explorative interview study. *Education and Information Technologies, 17*(4), 451–464. doi:10.1007/s10639-011-9169-5

Hsee, C. K., & Weber, E. U. (1999). Cross-national differences in risk preference and lay predictions. *Journal of Behavioral Decision Making, 12*(2), 165–179. doi:10.1002/(SICI)1099-0771(199906)12:2<165::AID-BDM316>3.0.CO;2-N

Huang, C. (2010). Internet use and psychological well-being: A meta-analysis. *Cyberpsychology, Behavior, and Social Networking, 13*(3), 241–249. doi:10.1089/cyber.2009.0217 PMID:20557242

Huang, G., & Dolejs, B. (2007). Reading theatre, parents as actors: Movie production in a family literacy workshop. *Reading Improvement, 44*(2), 87–98.

Huang, G., Unger, J., Soto, D., Fujimoto, K., Pentz, M., Jordan-Marsh, M., & Valente, T. (2013). Peer influences: The impact of online and offline friendship networks on adolescent smoking and alcohol use. *The Journal of Adolescent Health*, 1–7. PMID:24012065

Hughes, A. M. (2013). Academics in the UK use social media to enhance traditional scholarly reading. *Evidence Based Library and Information Practice, 8*(4), 145–147.

Hum, N. J., Chamberlin, P. E., Hambright, B. L., Portwood, A. C., Schat, A. C., & Bevan, J. L. (2011). A picture is worth a thousand words: A content analysis of Facebook profile photographs. *Computers in Human Behavior, 27*(5), 1826–1833. doi:10.1016/j.chb.2011.04.003

Hung, H. T., & Yuen, S. C. (2010). Educational use of social networking technology in higher education. *Teaching in Higher Education, 15*(6), 703–714. doi:10.1080/13562517.2010.507307

Hunt, S. D., & Madhavaram, S. (2006). The service – dominant logic of marketing – Theoretical foundations, pedagogy, and resource-advantage theory. In *The service-dominant logic of marketing: Dialog, debate, and directions*. Armonk, NY: ME Sharpe Inc.

Huston, L., & Sakkab, N. (2006). Connect & develop. *Harvard Business Review, 84*(3), 58–66.

Hutton, S. (2013). Helping kinesthetic learners succeed. *Education.com*. Retrieved from http://www.education.com/magazine/article/kinesthetic_learner/

Hu, X., Wu, G., Wu, Y., & Zhang, H. (2010). The effects of web assurance seals on consumers' initial trust in an online vendor: A functional perspective. *Decision Support Systems, 48*(2), 407–418. doi:10.1016/j.dss.2009.10.004

Hvass, K. A., & Munar, A. M. (2012). The takeoff of social media in tourism. *Journal of Vacation Marketing, 18*(2), 93–103. doi:10.1177/1356766711435978

Ignatius, A. (2011). Shaking things up at Coca-Cola - An interview with Muhtar Kent by Adi Ignatius. *Harvard Business Review*, (October), 94–99.

Im, G. P., & Baskerville, R. L. (2005). A longitudinal study of information system threat categories: The enduring problem of human error. *ACM SIGMIS Database, 36*(4), 68–79. doi:10.1145/1104004.1104010

Infosecurity. (2013). *Thanks to a false sense of security, small businesses are skipping cyber-protection.* Retrieved August 25, 2014, from http://www.infosecurity-magazine.com/view/35374/thanks-to-a-false-sense-of-security-small-businesses-are-skipping-cyberprotection/

International Telecommunications Union (ITU). (2010). *The world in 2010: Facts and figures.* Retrieved from http://ehis.ebscohost.com/eds/pdfviewer/pdfviewer?vid=2&sid=4a0d2ded-27e9-4428-bd8e-7c25dc2b22b2%40sessionmgr12&hid=2

International Telecommunications Union (ITU). (2013). *The world in 2013 facts and figures.* Retrieved from http://www.itu.int/en/ITU-D/Statistics/Documents/facts/ICTFactsFigures2013.pdf

Inversinni, A., & Buhalis, D. (2009). Information convergence in the long trail: The case of tourism destination information. In W. Hopken, U. Gretzel & R. Law (Eds.), *Information and communication technology in tourism:Proceedings of the international conference in Lugano, Switzerland* (pp. 381-392). Wien: Springer.

Ismail, I., Bokhare, S. F., Azizan, S. N., & Azman, N. (2013). Teaching via mobile phone: A case study on Malaysian teachers' technology acceptance and readiness. *Journal of Educators Online, 10*(1).

ISS World Training. (2013). Retrieved February, 9, 2013, from http://www.issworldtraining.com/

Ito, M. (2003). Mobiles and the appropriation of place. *Receiver: Mobile Environment Magazine, 8*, 1–3.

Jacklin, M. L., & Robinson, K. (2013). Evolution of various library instruction strategies: Using student feedback to create and enhance online active learning assignments. *Partnership: The Canadian Journal of Library & Information Practice & Research, 8*(1), 1–21.

Jackson, M. O. (2006) The economics of social networks. In Advances in economics and econometrics: Volume 1: Theory and applications. Cambridge University Press.

Jackson, M. O. (2010). An overview of social networks and economic applications. In The handbook of social economics. Elsevier Press.

Jackson, M. O. (2008). *Social and economic networks.* Princeton, NJ: Princeton Univ. Press.

Jacobs, A. (2011, Spring). Why bother with Marshall McLuhan? *New Atlantis (Washington, D.C.), 31,* 123–135.

Jacobson, H. B., & Roucek, J. S. (1959). *Automation and society.* Philosophical Library.

Jacoby, T. (2004). *Social power and the Turkish state.* London: Frank Cass.

Jamal, K., Maier, M., & Sunder, S. (2005). Enforced standards versus evolution by general acceptance: A comparative study of e-commerce privacy disclosure and practice in the United States and the United Kingdom. *Journal of Accounting Research, 43*(1), 73–96. doi:10.1111/j.1475-679x.2004.00163.x

Jarvenpaa, S. L., Tractinsky, N., & Saarinen, L. (1999). Consumer trust in an internet store: A cross-cultural validation. *Journal of Computer-Mediated Communication, 5*(2).

Jaya, R. (2008). Advantages of learner-centered approach to learning English. *Language in India, 8*(12), 40–45.

Jelenchick, L. A., Eickhoff, J. C., & Moreno, M. A. (2013). ''Facebook depression?'' Social networking site use and depression in older adolescents. *The Journal of Adolescent Health, 52*(1), 128–130. doi:10.1016/j.jadohealth.2012.05.008 PMID:23260846

Jenkins, H. (2006). *Convergence culture: Where old and new media collide.* Cambridge, MA: MIT Press.

Jensen, C., & Potts, C. (2004, April). Privacy policies as decision-making tools: An evaluation of online privacy notices. In *Proceedings of the SIGCHI Conference on Human Factors in Computing Systems* (pp. 471-478). ACM. doi:10.1145/985692.985752

Jiang, P., Jones, D., & Javie, S. (2008). How third party certification programs relate to consumer trust in online transactions: An exploratory study. *Psychology and Marketing, 25*(9), 839–858. doi:10.1002/mar.20243

Johannisson, B. (1995). Paradigms and entrepreneurial networks–Some methodological challenges. *Entrepreneurship & Regional Development, 7*(3), 215-232.

Johanson, J., & Mattsson, L. G. (1994). *The markets-as-networks tradition in Sweden.* Springer.

Johnson, G., Scholes, K., & Whittington, R. (2005). *Exploring corporate strategy: Text and cases.* London: Pearson Education.

Johnson, J. A. (1981). The "self-disclosure" and "self-presentation" views of item response dynamics and personality scale validity. *Journal of Personality and Social Psychology, 40*(4), 761–769. doi:10.1037/0022-3514.40.4.761

Johnston, L. D., O'Malley, P. M., Bachman, J. G., & Schulenberg, J. E. (2012). *Monitoring the future, national survey results on drug use, 1975-2012, volume 1: Secondary school students.* Retrieved from http://www.monitoringthefuture.org//pubs/monographs/mtf-vol1_2012.pdf

Johnston, A. C., & Warkentin, M. (2010). Fear appeals and information security behaviors: An empirical study. *Management Information Systems Quarterly, 34*(3), 549–566.

Joinson, A. N. (2008). Looking at, looking up or keeping up with people? Motives and use of Facebook. In *Proceedings of CHI '06* (pp. 1027–1036). New York: ACM.

Jones, N., Blackey, H., Fitzgibbon, K., & Chew, E. (2010). Get out of MySpace! *Computers & Education, 54*(3), 776–782. doi:10.1016/j.compedu.2009.07.008

Jones, S., & Waite, R. (2013). Underage drinking: An evolutionary concept analysis. *The Nursing Clinics of North America, 48*(3), 401–413. doi:10.1016/j.cnur.2013.05.004 PMID:23998767

Junco, R., Heiberger, G., & Loken, E. (2011). The effect of Twitter on college student engagement and grades. *Journal of Computer Assisted Learning, 27*(2), 119–132. doi:10.1111/j.1365-2729.2010.00387.x

Jung, C. (1981). *The archetypes and the collective unconscious.* New York: Princeton University Press.

Jung, C. G., & Franz, M.-L. (1978). *Man and his symbols.* London: Pan Books.

Kalpidou, M., Costin, D., & Morris, J. (2011). The relationship between Facebook and the well-being of undergraduate college students. *Cyberpsychology, Behavior, and Social Networking, 14*(4), 183–189. doi:10.1089/cyber.2010.0061 PMID:21192765

Kaplan, D. (2011). Earthquake and tsunami breed web scams, malware. *SC Magazine*. Retrieved August 25, 2014 from http://www.scmagazineus.com/earthquake-and-tsunami-breed-web-scams-malware/article/198195/

Kaplan, A. M., & Haenlein, M. (2010). Users of the world, unite! The challenges and opportunities of Social Media. *Business Horizons, 53*(1), 59–68. doi:10.1016/j.bushor.2009.09.003

Karolak, M. (2012). Tourism in Bahrain: A continuous search for economic development and for preservation of cultural heritage. In *Proceedings of the 2012 Gulf Studies Conference*. Retrieved March 26, 2014 from http://www.academia.edu/1821165/Tourism_in_Bahrain_A_Continuous_Search_for_Economic_Development_and_for_Preservation_of_Cultural_Heritage

Kasesniemi, E. (2003). *Mobile messages: Young people and a new communication culture*. Tempere, Finland: Tampere University Press.

Katsikas, S. K. (2006). Information security. In *Proceedings of 9th International Conference*. ISC.

Katyal, N. K. (2001). Criminal law in cyberspace. *University of Pennsylvania Law Review, 149*(4), 1003–1114. doi:10.2307/3312990

Kaufman, R. A., Guerra, I., & Platt, W. A. (2006). *Practical evaluation for educators: Finding what works and what doesn't*. Corwin Press. doi:10.4135/9781412990189

Kavaratzis, M., & Ashworth, G. J. (2010). Place branding: Where do we stand? In G. J. Ashworth & M. Kavaratzis (Eds.), *Towards effective place brand management: Branding European cities and regions and regions, Cheltenham, UK and Northampton* (pp. 1–14). Edward Elgar. doi:10.4337/9781849806398.00007

Kay, J. (1993). *Foundation of corporate success: How business strategies add value*. Oxford, UK: Oxford University Press.

Kempas, B. (2009). Maximising distrify, the PMD's top ten tips. *Scottish Documentary Institute*. Retrieved August 7, 2013, from http://blog.scottishdocinstitute.com/maxifying_distrify

Kennedy, G., et al. (2009). *Educating the net generation: A handbook of findings for practice and policy*. Australian Learning and Teaching Council. Retrieved December 12, 2013, from http://www.netgen.unimelb.edu.au/downloads/handbook/NetGenHandbookAll.pdf

Kenski, V. M. (1996). O ensino e os recursos didáticos em uma sociedade cheia de tecnologias. In *Didática: O ensino e suas relações*. Campinas: Papirus.

Keyman, F., & Koyuncu, B. (2004). AKP, MÜSİAD, Ekonomik kalkınma ve modernite. *Düsünen Siyaset, 19*, 125–145.

Kietzmann, J., Hermkens, K., McCarthy, I., & Silvestre, B. (2011). Social media? Get serious! Understanding the functional building blocks of social media. *Business Horizons, 54*(3), 241–251. doi:10.1016/j.bushor.2011.01.005

Kimery, K. M., & McCord, M. (2002). Third-party assurances: Mapping the road to trust in e-retailing. *Journal of Information Technology Theory and Application, 4*(2), 64–82.

Kim, J., LaRose, R., & Peng, W. (2009). Loneliness as the cause and the effect of problematic internet use: The relationship between internet use and psychological well-being. *Cyberpsychology & Behavior, 12*(4), 451–455. doi:10.1089/cpb.2008.0327 PMID:19514821

Kim, J., & Lee, J. (2011). The Facebook paths to happiness: Effects of the number of Facebook friends and self-presentation on subjective well-being. *Cyberpsychology, Behavior, and Social Networking, 14*(6), 359–364. doi:10.1089/cyber.2010.0374 PMID:21117983

Kinsella, N. (2010). *BTW it's just netspeak LOL* (Vol. 3). Queensland, Australia: Griffith Working Papers in Pragmatics and Intercultural Communication.

Kirkpatrick, G. (2005). Online 'chat' facilities as pedagogic tool. *Active Learning in Higher Education, 6*(2), 145–159. doi:10.1177/1469787405054239

Kıvanç, Ü. (1997). İslamcılar ve para-pul: Bir dönüsüm hikayesi. *Birikim, 99*, 39–58.

Knowles, M. S. (1980). *The modern practice of adult education: From pedagogy to andragogy (revised and updated)*. Englewood Cliffs, NJ: Cambridge Adult Education.

Knowles, M. S. (1985). Applications in continuing education for the health professions. Chapter five of andragogy in action. *MOBIUS: The Journal of Social Change, 5*(2), 80–100. PMID:10271191

Knowles, T., Diamantis, D., & El-Mourhabi, J. B. (2004). *The globalization of tourism and hospitality: A strategic perspective* (2nd ed.). Toronto: Thomson.

Koehler, M., & Mishra, P. (2009). What is technological pedagogial content knowledge (TPACK)? *Contemporary Issues in Technology & Teacher Education, 9*(1), 60–70.

Kohle, F. (2012). The Arab Spring and the Wall Street Movement: Challenges and implications for documentary filmmakers and social media. In *Proceedings of London Film & Media Conference*. NHTV University of Applied Sciences. Retrieved July 23, 2013, from http://www.thelondonfilmandmediaconference.com/registered-speakers-2012-a-to-k/

Kohle, F., & Cuevas, A. (2012). Social media: Changing the way we teach and changing the way we learn. In *Proceedings of 6th International Technology, Education and Development Conference*. Valencia, Spain: Academic Press.

Kohle, F., & Cuevas, A. (2010). A case study in using YouTube and Facebook as social media tools in enhancing student centered learning and engagement. In *Proceedings of 3rd International Conference of Education, Research and Innovation*. Madrid, Spain: Academic Press.

Koved, L., Nadalin, A., Nagaratnam, N., Pistoia, M., & Shrader, T. (2001). Security challenges for enterprise java in an e-business environment. *IBM Systems Journal, 40*(1), 130–152. doi:10.1147/sj.401.0130

Krämer, N. C., & Winter, S. (2008). Impression management 2.0: The relationship of self-esteem, extraversion, self-efficacy, and self-presentation within social networking sites. *Journal of Media Psychology, 20*(3), 106–116. doi:10.1027/1864-1105.20.3.106

Krasnova, H., Wenninger, H., Widjaja, T., & Buxmann, P. (2013). *Envy on Facebook: A hidden threat to users' life satisfaction?*. Paper presented at the International Conference on Wirtschaftsinformatik (WI) / Business Information Systems 2013, Leipzig, Germany.

Kraut, R., Kiesler, S., Boneva, B., Cummings, J., Helgeson, V., & Crawford, A. (2002). Internet paradox revisited. *The Journal of Social Issues, 58*(1), 49–74. doi:10.1111/1540-4560.00248

Kraut, R., Patterson, M., Lundmark, V., Kiesler, S., Mukopadhyay, T., & Scherlis, W. (1998). Internet paradox: A social technology that reduces social involvement and psychological well-being? *The American Psychologist, 53*(9), 1017–1031. doi:10.1037/0003-066X.53.9.1017 PMID:9841579

Kritzinger, E., & Smith, E. (2008). Information security management: An information security retrieval and awareness model for industry. *Computers & Security, 27*(5), 224–231. doi:10.1016/j.cose.2008.05.006

Kross, E., Verduyn, P., Demiralp, E., Park, J., Lee, D., & Lin, N. et al. (2013). Facebook use predicts declines in subjective well-being in young adults. *PLoS ONE, 8*(8), 1–6. doi:10.1371/journal.pone.0069841 PMID:23967061

Kujath, C. L. (2011). Facebook and MySpace: Complement or substitute for face-to-face interaction? *Cyberpsychology, Behavior, and Social Networking, 14*(1-2), 75–78. doi:10.1089/cyber.2009.0311 PMID:21329446

Kumar, S. (2009). Undergraduate perceptions of the usefulness of web 2.0 in higher education: Survey development. In: D. Remenyi (Ed.), *Proceedings of 8th European Conference on E-learning* (pp. 308-314). Academic Press.

Kumar, K. A., & Rao, D. C. B. N. (2014). Impact of social media marketing on business world. *International Journal of Logistics & Supply Chain Management Perspectives, 2*(4), 504–508.

Kumar, V., & Mirchandani, R. (2012). Increasing the ROI of social media marketing. *Sloan Management Review, 54*(1), 55–61.

Kurkela, L. (2011). Systemic approach to learning paradigms and the use of social media in higher education. *International Journal of Emerging Technologies in Learning*, *6*(1), 14–20.

Kuss, D. J., van Rooij, A. J., Shorter, G. W., Griffiths, M. D., & van de Mheen, D. (2013). Internet addiction in adolescents: Prevalence and risk factors. *Computers in Human Behavior*, *29*(5), 1987-1996.

Laire, D., Casteleyn, J., & Mottart, A. (2012). Social media's learning outcomes within writing instruction in the EFL classroom: Exploring, implementing and analyzing storify. *Procedia: Social and Behavioral Sciences*, *69*, 442–448. doi:10.1016/j.sbspro.2012.11.432

Lake, P. W. (2004). *Business networks in a regional industrial cluster*. (Unpublished DBA Dissertation). University of Southern Queensland.

Lampe, C., Ellison, N., & Steinfield, C. (2006). A Face(book) in the crowd: Social searching vs. social browsing. In *Proceedings of the 2006 20th Anniversary Conference on Computer Supported Cooperative Work* (pp. 167-170). New York, NY: ACM Press.

Lampe, C., Ellison, N., & Steinfield, C. (2006). A Face(book) in the crowd: Social searching vs. social browsing. In *Proceedings of CSCW-2006*. ACM. doi:10.1145/1180875.1180901

Land, R., & Bayne, S. (2008). Social technologies in higher education: Authorship, subjectivity and temporality. In *Proceedings of the 6th International Conference on Networked Learning*. Academic Press.

Landwehr, C. E. (2001). Computer security. *International Journal of Information Security*, *1*(1), 3–13. doi:10.1007/s102070100003

Lan, Y., & Huang, S. (2011). Using mobile learning to improve the reflection: A case study of traffic violation. *Journal of Educational Technology & Society*, *15*(2), 179–193.

Latif, L. (2011). Anti-hacking firm RSA gets hacked. *The Inquirer*. Retrieved August 25, 2014, from http://www.theinquirer.net/inquirer/news/2035368/anti-hacking-firm-rsa-hacked?WT.rss_f=&WT.rss_a=Antihacking+firm+RSA+gets+hacked

Laurillard, D. (1993). *Rethinking university teaching: A framework for the effective use of educational technology*. Routledge.

Law, R., Leung, R., & Buhalis, D. (2014). Information technology application in hospitality and tourism: A review of publications from 2005 to 2007. *Journal of Travel & Tourism Marketing*, *26*(5), 599–623.

Lea, M. R., & Jones, S. (2011). Digital literacies in higher education: Exploring textual and technological practice. *Studies in Higher Education*, *36*(4), 377–393. doi:10.1080/03075071003664021

Learning Curriculum, and Life Politics. (2005). London: Routledge.

Leavitt, H. J., & Whisler, T. L. (1958). Management in the 1980s. *Harvard Business Review*, (Nov-Dec), 41–48.

Lee, C. S., & Ma, L. (2012). News sharing in social media: The effect of gratifications and prior experience. *Computers in Human Behavior*, *28*(2), 331–339. doi:10.1016/j.chb.2011.10.002

Lee, H. W., Choi, J.-S., Shin, Y.-C., Lee, J.-Y., Jung, H. Y., & Kwon, J. S. (2012, July). Impulsivity in internet addiction: A comparison with pathological gambling. *Cyberpsychology, Behavior, and Social Networking*, *15*(7), 373–377. doi:10.1089/cyber.2012.0063 PMID:22663306

Lee, H., Law, R., & Murphy, J. (2011). Helpful reviewers in TripAdvisor, an online travel community. *Journal of Travel & Tourism Marketing*, *28*(7), 675–687. doi:10.1080/10548408.2011.611739

Lee, M. K., & Turban, E. (2001). A trust model for consumer internet shopping. *International Journal of Electronic Commerce*, *6*, 75–92.

Lehavot, K., Ben-Zeev, D., & Neville, L. E. (2012). Ethical considerations and social media: A case of suicidal postings on Facebook. *Journal of Dual Diagnosis*, *8*(4), 341–346. doi:10.1080/15504263.2012.718928

Lemos, A. (2002). *Cibercultura: Tecnologia e vida social na cultura contemporânea*. Porto Alegre: Sulina.

Lenhart, A., Purcell, K., Smith, A., & Zickuhr, K. (2010). *Social media & mobile internet use among teens and young adults. millennials*. Pew Internet & American Life Project.

Lenskold, J., & Qaqish, D. (2012). *Lead generation marketing effectiveness study.* LenskoldGroup. Retrieved from http://www.lenskold.com/content/LeadGenROI_2012.html

Levine, A. E. (2000). The future of colleges: 9 inevitable changes. *The Chronicle of Higher Education, 47*(9), 1–5.

Lévy, P. (1999). *Cibercultura.* São Paulo: Editora 34 Ltda.

Lewis, K., Kaufman, J., & Christakis, N. (2008). The taste for privacy: An analysis of college student privacy settings in an online social network. *Journal of Computer-Mediated Communication, 14*(1), 79–100. doi:10.1111/j.1083-6101.2008.01432.x

Lewis, K., Kaufman, J., Gonzales, M., Wimmer, A., & Cristakis, N. (2008). Taste, ties, and time: A new social network dataset using Facebook.com. *Social Networks, 30*(4), 330–342. doi:10.1016/j.socnet.2008.07.002

Lewis, R. D. (2006). *When cultures collide: Leading, teamworking and managing across the globe.* Nicholas Brealey.

Leyden, J. (2011). York Uni exposes students' private info. *The Register.* Retrieved August 25, 2014, from http://www.theregister.co.uk/2011/03/16/york_uni_student_data_breach/

Libâneo, J. C. (1996). Didática: Pedagogia e modernidade: Presente e futuro da escola. In *Infância, escola e modernidade.* São Paulo: Cortez.

Lickerman, A. (2010). The effect of technology on relationships: The risks of internet addiction. *Psychology Today, 8.*

Lighty, T., & Wong, W. (2012). Chicago man, 27, charged in cyber attack. *Chicago Tribune.* Retrieved March 20, 2013, from http://articles.chicagotribune.com/2012-03-06/business/chi-chicago-raid-linked-to-hacking-arrests-20120306_1_cyber-attack-lulzsec-antisec

Lim, V. K. G., & Teo, T. S. H. (2009). Mind your e-manners: Impact of cyber incivility on employees' work attitude and behavior. *Information & Management, 46*(8), 419–425. doi:10.1016/j.im.2009.06.006

Lindley, S. E., Harper, R., & Sellen, A. (2009, 4-9 April). *Desiring to be in touch in a changing communications landscape: Attitudes of older adults.* Paper presented at the SIGCHI Conference on Human Factors in Computing Systems, Boston, MA. doi:10.1145/1518701.1518962

Lindstrom, P. (2007). *Securing "web 2.0" technologies.* Midvale, UT: Burton Group EDUCAUSE Center for Applied Research.

Ling, R. (2004). *The mobile connection: The cell phone's impact on the society.* Amsterdam: Morgan Kaufmann Publishers.

Ling, R. (2005). The socio-linguistics of SMS: An analysis of SMS use by a random sample of Norwegians. In R. S. Ling & P. E. Pedersen (Eds.), *Mobile communications: Re-negotiation of the social sphere* (pp. 335–350). London: Springer. doi:10.1007/1-84628-248-9_22

Lin, N. (2002). *Social capital: A theory of social structure and action* (Vol. 19). New York: Cambridge University Press.

Lin, N. (2005). A network theory of social capital. In D. Castiglione, J. Van Deth, & G. Wolleb (Eds.), *The handbook of social capital.* Oxford University Press.

Litt, D. M., & Stock, M. L. (2011). Adolescent alcohol-related risk cognitions: The roles of social norms and social networking sites. *Psychology of Addictive Behaviors, 25*(4), 708–713. doi:10.1037/a0024226 PMID:21644803

Litvin, S. W., Goldsmith, R. E., & Pan, B. (2008). Electronic word-of-mouth in hospitality and tourism management. *Tourism Management, 29*(3), 458–468. doi:10.1016/j.tourman.2007.05.011

Liu, C., Marchewka, J. T., Lu, J., & Yu, C. S. (2004). Beyond concern: A privacy–trust–behavioral intention model of electronic commerce. *Information & Management, 42*(1), 127–142. doi:10.1016/j.im.2004.01.002

Livingstone, S., Olafsson, K., & Staksrund, E. (2013). Risky social networking practices among 'under-age' users: Lessons for evidence-based policy. *Journal of Computer-Mediated Communication, 18*(3), 303–320. doi:10.1111/jcc4.12012

Lorant, V., Nicaise, P., Soto, V., & D'Hoore, W. (2013). Alcohol drinking among college students: College responsibility for personal troubles. *BMC Public Health, 13*(615), 1–6. PMID:23805939

Lorenz, E. (2000). *The butterfly effect: The chaos avantgarde: Memories of the early days of chaos theory.* Singapore: World Scientific Publishing.

Lüdke, M., & André, M. E. D. A. (1986). *Pesquisa em educação: Abordagens qualitativas.* São Paulo: EPU.

Lu, X., Watanabe, J., Liu, Q., Uji, M., Shono, M., & Kitamura, T. (2011). Internet and mobile phone text-messaging dependency: Factor structure and correlation with dysphoric mood among Japanese adults. *Computers in Human Behavior, 27*(5), 1702–1709. doi:10.1016/j.chb.2011.02.009

Lynch, N. A. (1996). *Distributed algorithms.* San Francisco, CA: Morgan Kaufmann.

Lynch, P. D., Robert, J. K., & Srinivasan, S. S. (2001). The global internet shopper: Evidence from shopping tasks in twelve countries. *Journal of Advertising Research, 41,* 15–23.

Lyotard, J. (1992). *The postmodern explained to children, correspondence 1982–1985.* Turnaround.

Mack, D., Behler, A., Roberts, B., & Rimland, E. (2007). Reaching students with Facebook: Data and best practices. *Electronic Journal of Academic and Special Librarianship, 8*(2), 4–12.

Mack, R., Blose, J., & Pan, B. (2008). Believe it or not: Credibility of blogs in tourism. *Journal of Vacation Marketing, 14*(2), 133–144. doi:10.1177/1356766707087521

Madden, M., Lenhart, A., Cortesi, S., Gasser, U., Duggan, A. S., & Beaton, M. (2013). Teen, social media and privacy. *The Berkman Center for Internet & Society at Harvard University.* Retrieved September 12, 2013 from http://pewinternet.org/Reports/2013/Teens-Social-Media-And-Privacy/Summary-of-Findings/Teens-Social-Media-and-Privacy.aspx

Madge, C., Meek, J., Wellens, J., & Hooley, T. (2009). Facebook, social integration and informal learning at university: 'It is more for socialising and talking to friends about work than for actually doing work'. *Learning, Media and Technology, 34*(2), 141–155. doi:10.1080/17439880902923606

Mahadevan, B. (2000). Business models for internet based e commerce: an anatomy. *California Management Review, 42*(4), 55–69. doi:10.2307/41166053

Maimon, D., & Browning, C. (2012). Underage drinking, alcohol sales and collective efficacy: Informal control and opportunity in the study of alcohol use. *Social Science Research, 41*(4), 977–990. doi:10.1016/j.ssresearch.2012.01.009 PMID:23017864

Mangold, W. G., & Faulds, D. J. (2009). Social media: The new hybrid element of the promotion mix. *Business Horizons, 52*(4), 357–365. doi:10.1016/j.bushor.2009.03.002

Marchiori, E., Dedekind, C., & Cantoni, L. (2010). Applying a conceptual framework to analyse online reputation of tourist destinations. In U. Gretzel, R. Law, & M. Fuchs (Eds.), *Information and communication technologies in tourism: Proceedings of the international conference in Lugano, Switzerland* (pp. 321-332). Wien: Springer.

Marconi, M. A., & Lakatos, E. M. (2003). *Fundamentos de metodologia científica.* São Paulo: Atlas.

Margulis, S. (2011). Three theories of privacy: An overview. In S. Trepte & L. Reinecke (Eds.), *Privacy online: Perspectives on privacy and self-disclosure in the social web.* Berlin: Springer.

Martin, P. (2014). Teachers in transition: The road to EAP. In P. Breen (Ed.), *Cases on teacher identity, diversity and cognition in higher education* (pp. 287–317). IGI Global. doi:10.4018/978-1-4666-5990-2.ch012

Marwick, A. E., & boyd, . (2011). I tweet honestly, I tweet passionately: Twitter users, context collapse, and the imagined audience. *New Media & Society, 13*(1), 114–133. doi:10.1177/1461444810365313

Massa, P., & Avesani, P. (2007). Trust metrics on controversial users: Balancing between tyranny of the majority and echo chambers. *International Journal on Semantic Web and Information Systems*, *3*(2).

Matsueda, R. (1988). The current state of differential association theory. *Crime and Delinquency*, *34*(3), 277–306. doi:10.1177/0011128788034003005

Mayer, A., & Puller, S. L. (2008). The old boy (and girl) network: Social network formation on university campuses. *Journal of Public Economics*, *92*(1-2), 329–347. doi:10.1016/j.jpubeco.2007.09.001

Mazer, J. P., Murphy, R. E., & Simonds, C. J. (2007). 'I'll see you on 'Facebook': The effects of computer-mediated teacher self-disclosure on student motivation, affective learning, and classroom climate. *Communication Education*, *56*(1), 1–17. doi:10.1080/03634520601009710

Mazer, J. P., Murphy, R. E., & Simonds, C. J. (2009). The effects of teacher self-disclosure via Facebook on teacher credibility. *Learning, Media and Technology*, *34*(2), 175–183. doi:10.1080/17439880902923655

McAfee. (2013). McAfee finds majority of small business owners have false sense of security. *McAfee for Business*. Retrieved August 25, 2014 from http://www.mcafee.com/uk/about/news/2013/q4/20131030-01.aspx

McAndrew, F. T., Bell, E. K., & Garcia, C. M. (2007). Who do we tell and whom do we tell on? Gossip as a strategy for status enhancement. *Journal of Applied Social Psychology*, *37*(7), 1562–1577. doi:10.1111/j.1559-1816.2007.00227.x

McAndrew, F. T., & Milenkovic, M. A. (2002). Of tabloids and family secrets: The evolutionary psychology of gossip. *Journal of Applied Social Psychology*, *32*(5), 1064–1082. doi:10.1111/j.1559-1816.2002.tb00256.x

McAndrew, F. T., & Sun Jeong, H. (2012). Who does what on Facebook? Age, sex, and relationship status as predictors of Facebook use. *Computers in Human Behavior*, *28*(6), 2350–2365. doi:10.1016/j.chb.2012.07.007

McCarthy, J. (2010). Blended learning environments: Using social networking sites to enhance the first year experience. *Australasian Journal of Educational Technology*, *26*(6), 729–740.

McCarthy, J., Rowley, J., Ashworth, C. J., & Pioch, E. (2014). Managing brand presence through social media: The case of UK football clubs. *Internet Research*, *24*(2), 181–204. doi:10.1108/IntR-08-2012-0154

McCreanor, T., Lyons, A., Griffin, C., Goodwin, I., Barnes, H., & Hutton, F. (2013). Youth drinking cultures, social networking and alcohol marketing: Implications for public health. *Critical Public Health*, *23*(1), 110–120. doi:10.1080/09581596.2012.748883

McDaniel, G. (1994). *IBM dictionary of computing*. McGraw-Hill, Inc.

McGrath, V. (2009). Reviewing the evidence on how adult students learn: An examination of Knowles' model of andragogy. Adult Learner: *The Irish Journal of Adult and Community Education*, 99-110.

McGrath, J. E., Karabas, G., & Willis, J. (2011). From TPACK concept to TPACK practice: An analysis of the suitability and usefulness of the concept as a guide in the real world of teacher development. *International Journal of Technology in Teaching and Learning*, *7*(1), 1–23.

McKnight, D. H., & Chervany, N. L. (2002). What trust means in e-commerce customer relationships: An interdisciplinary conceptual typology. *International Journal of Electronic Commerce*, *6*, 35–60.

McLoughlin, C., Meyricke, R., & Burgess, J. (2009). Bullies in cyberspace: How rural and regional Australian youth perceive the problem of cyberbullying and its impact. *Improving Equity in Rural Education*, 178.

Mcloughlin, D., & Horan, C. (2000). The production and distribution of knowledge in the markets-as-networks tradition. *Journal of Strategic Marketing*, *8*(2), 89–103. doi:10.1080/096525400346196

McLuhan, M. (1994). *Understanding media: The extensions of man*. Cambridge, MA: MIT press.

Mcluhan, M. (1995). *Essential McLuhan*. House of Anansi Press.

McSweeney, B. (2002). Hofstede's model of national cultural differences and their consequences: A triumph of faith-a failure of analysis. *Human Relations*, *55*(1), 89–118. doi:10.1177/0018726702055001602

Mehdizadeh, S. (2010). Self-presentation 2.0: Narcissism and self-esteem on Facebook. *Cyberpsychology, Behavior, and Social Networking, 13*(4), 357–364. doi:10.1089/cyber.2009.0257 PMID:20712493

Mell, P., & Grance, T. (2011). *The NIST definition of cloud computing.* NIST. Retrieved July 23, 2013, from http://csrc.nist.gov/publications/nistpubs/800-145/SP800-145.pdf

Mergel, I., Schweik, C., & Fountain, J. (2009). *The transformational effect of web 2.0 technologies on government.* Social Science Research Network. Retrieved April 2, 2014, from http://ssrn.com/abstract=1412796

Merriam, S. B., Caffarella, R. S., & Baumgartner, L. M. (2006). *Learning in adulthood: A comprehensive guide* (3rd ed.). San Francisco: Jossey-Bass.

Metlife Foundation. (2013). *Partnership attitude tracking study.* Retrieved from http://www.drugfree.org/tag/partnership-attitude-tracking-study

Meyrowitz, J. (1985). *No sense of place.* Oxford, UK: Oxford University Press.

Miguens, J., Baggio, R., & Costa, C. (2008). Social media and tourism destinations: TripAdvisor case study. In *Proceedings of the IASK Advances in Tourism Research 2008.* Aveiro: ATR.

Milano, R., Baggio, R., & Piattelli, R. (2011). The effects of online social media on tourism websites. In *Proceedings of the 18th International Conference on Information Technology and Travel and Tourism.* Innsbruck, UK: Enter. doi:10.1007/978-3-7091-0503-0_38

Millen, D., Feinberg, J., & Kerr, B. (2005). Social bookmarking in the enterprise. *Queue, 3*(9), 28–35. doi:10.1145/1105664.1105676

Miller, N., Besser, T., & Malshe, A. (2007). Strategic networking among small business in small US communities. *International Small Business Journal, 25*(6), 631–665. doi:10.1177/0266242607082525

Mills, E. (2010). *Study: Facebook joins PayPal, eBay as popular phishing target.* Retrieved February 10, 2011, from http://news.cnet.com/8301-27080_3-20004819-245.html

Milne, G. R., & Culnan, M. J. (2004). Strategies for reducing online privacy risks: Why consumers read (or don't read) online privacy notices. *Journal of Interactive Marketing, 18*(3), 15–29. doi:10.1002/dir.20009

Milne, G. R., & Gordon, M. E. (1993). Direct mail privacy-efficiency trade-offs within an implied social contract framework. *Journal of Public Policy & Marketing*, 206–215.

Minihane, J. (2011). *New PlayStation security breach: 93,000 accounts hit.* Retrieved November 27, 2010, from http://www.t3.com/news/new-playstation-security-breach-93000-accounts-hit

Minnesota State Colleges and Universities. (2014). *Procedure 5.22.2, cellular and other mobile computing devices.* Retrieved from http://www.mnscu.edu/board/procedure/522p2.html

Minocha, S. (2009). A case study-based investigation of students' experiences with social software tools. *New Review of Hypermedia and Multimedia, 15*(3), 245–265. doi:10.1080/13614560903494320

Mintzberg, H., Ahlstrand, B. W., & Lampel, J. (1998). *Strategy safari: The complete guide trough the wilds of strategic management.* London, UK: Financial Times Prentice Hall.

Mintzberg, H. (1994). *Rise and fall of strategic planning.* New York: Free Press.

Mintzberg, H., & Van der Heyden, L. (1999). Organigraphs: Drawing how companies really work. *Harvard Business Review, 77*, 87–95. PMID:10621269

Mintzberg, H., & Waters, J. A. (1985). Of strategies, deliberate and emergent. *Strategic Management Journal, 6*(3), 257–272. doi:10.1002/smj.4250060306

Mishra, P., & Koehler, M. J. (2006). Technological pedagogical content knowledge: A framework for integrating technology in teacher knowledge. *Teachers College Record, 108*(6), 1017–1054. doi:10.1111/j.1467-9620.2006.00684.x

Mitchell, M. (2006). Complex systems: Network thinking. *Artificial Intelligence, 170*(18), 1194–1212. doi:10.1016/j.artint.2006.10.002

Miyazaki, A. D., & Fernandez, A. (2001). Consumer perceptions of privacy and security risks for online shopping. *The Journal of Consumer Affairs*, *35*(1), 27–44. doi:10.1111/j.1745-6606.2001.tb00101.x

Mizruchi, M. S., & Stearns, L. B. (1988). A longitudinal study of the formation of interlocking directorates. *Administrative Science Quarterly*, *33*(2), 194–210. doi:10.2307/2393055

Moitra, S. D. (2005). Developing policies for cybercrime. *European Journal of Crime Criminal Law and Criminal Justice*, *13*(3), 435–464. doi:10.1163/1571817054604119

Moliterno, T. P., & Mahony, D. M. (2011). Network theory of organization: A multilevel approach. *Journal of Management*, *37*(2), 443–467. doi:10.1177/0149206310371692

Moor, J. H. (1997). Towards a theory of privacy in the information age. *Computers & Society*, *27*(3), 27–32. doi:10.1145/270858.270866

Moran, M., Seaman, J., & Tinti-Kane, H. (2011). *Teaching, learning, and sharing: How today's higher education faculty use social media*. The Babson Survey Research Group, and Converseon.

Moreno, M. A., Briner, L. R., Williams, A., Brockman, L., Walker, L., & Christakis, D. A. (2010). A content analysis of displayed alcohol references on a social networking web site. *The Journal of Adolescent Health: Official Publication of the Society for Adolescent Medicine*, *47*(2), 168–175. doi:10.1016/j.jadohealth.2010.01.001 PMID:20638009

Moreno, M. A., Jelenchick, L. A., Egan, K. G., Cox, E., Young, H., Gannon, K. E., & Becker, T. (2011). Feeling bad on Facebook: Depression disclosures by college students on a social networking site. *Depression and Anxiety*, *28*(6), 447–455. doi:10.1002/da.20805 PMID:21400639

Moreno, M., Christakis, D., Egan, K., Brockman, L., & Becker, T. (2012). Associations between displayed alcohol references on Facebook and problem drinking among college students. *Archives of Pediatrics & Adolescent Medicine*, *166*(2), 157–163. doi:10.1001/archpediatrics.2011.180 PMID:21969360

Moreno, M., Parks, M., Zimmerman, F., Brito, T., & Christakis, D. (2009). Display of health risk behaviors on MySpace by adolescents: Prevalence and associations. *Archives of Pediatrics & Adolescent Medicine*, *163*(1), 27–34. doi:10.1001/archpediatrics.2008.528 PMID:19124700

Morrison, J. (n.d.). *Marshall McLuhan: Beyond the ivory tower: Academic discourse in the age of popular media*. Massachusetts Institute of Technology. Retrieved May 9, 2013, from http://www.mit.edu/~saleem/ivory/

Morrison, C., & Gore, H. (2010). The relationship between excessive internet use and depression: A questionnaire-based study of 1,319 young people and adults. *Psychopathology*, *43*(2), 121–126. doi:10.1159/000277001 PMID:20110764

Motteram, G. (Ed.). (2013). *Innovations in learning technologies for English language teaching*. London: The British Council.

Motteram, G., & Sharma, P. (2009). Blending learning in a web 2.0 world. *International Journal of Emerging Technologies & Society*, *7*(2), 83–96.

Mrs. Davison's Kindergarten [blog]. (2013) Retrieved August, 8, 2013, from http://davisonkindergarten.blogspot.nl/p/what-we-are-doing-with-ipads.html

Mundt, M., Mercken, L., & Zakletskaia, L. (2012). Peer selection and influence effects on adolescent alcohol use: A stochastic actor-based model. *BMC Pediatrics*, *12*(115), 1–10. PMID:22867027

Muñoz, C., & Towner, T. (2011). Back to the "wall": How to use Facebook in the college classroom. *First Monday*, *16*(12). doi:10.5210/fm.v16i12.3513

Murphy, J., & Meyer, H. (2013). Best (and not so best) practices in social media. *ILA Reporter*, *31*(6), 12–15.

Myslín, M., Zhu, S., Chapman, W., & Conway, M. (2013). Using Twitter to examine smoking behavior and perceptions of emerging tobacco products. *Journal of Medical Internet Research*, *15*(8), e174. doi:10.2196/jmir.2534 PMID:23989137

Nadkarni, A., & Hofmann, S. G. (2012). Why do people use Facebook? *Personality and Individual Differences*, *52*(3), 243–249. doi:10.1016/j.paid.2011.11.007 PMID:22544987

Nagurney. (1993). *Network economics: A variational inequality approach*. Boston: Kluwer Academic Publishers.

Naismith, L., & Corlett, D. (2006). Reflections on success: A retrospective of the mLearn conference series 2002-2005. In *Across generations and cultures, mLearn 2006 book of abstracts* (pp. 118–220). Banff, Canada: Academic Press.

Naraine, R. (2009). When web 2.0 becomes security risk 2.0. In *Real business real threats*. Kaspersky Lab.

Nash, R. J. (2004). *Liberating scholarly writing: The power of personal narrative*. Teachers College Press.

National Institute on Alcohol Abuse and Alcoholism (NIAAA). (2013). *College drinking*. Retrieved on October 5, 2013 from http://pubs.niaaa.nih.gov/publications/CollegeFactSheet/CollegeFactSheet.pdf

National Institute on Drug Abuse. (1998). National survey results on drug use from the monitoring the future study, 1975-1997 (Vol. 1). Rockville, MD: Author.

Neuman, W. L. (2004). *Basics of social research: Qualitative and quantitative approaches*. Pearson Education Incorporated.

Newport, F. (2010, July 30). U.S. drinking rate edges up slightly to 25-year high. *Gallup Well-Being*. Retrieved December 5, 2013, from http://www.gallup.com/poll/141656/drinking-rate-edges-slightly-year-high.aspx

Nicholas, D., Watkinson, A., Rowlands, I., & Jubb, M. (2011). Social media, academic research and the role of university libraries. *Journal of Academic Librarianship*, *37*(5), 373–375. doi:10.1016/j.acalib.2011.06.023

Nishimura, S., Hishinuma, E., & Goebert, D. (2013). Underage drinking among Asian American and Pacific Islander adolescents. *Journal of Ethnicity in Substance Abuse*, *12*(3), 259–277. doi:10.1080/15332640.2013.805176 PMID:23967886

Njemanze, Q. U. (2012). The "SMS" style of communication: Implication on language usage among Nigerian university students. *Journal of Communication*, *3*(1), 17–23.

Nor, D. K. M., Nazarie, W. N. W. M., & Yusoff, A. A. A. M. (2013). Factors influencing individuals' trust in online purchase through social networking sites. *International Journal of Information Science and Management*, 1-16.

Nosko, A., Wood, E., & Molema, S. (2010). All about me: Disclosure in online social networking profiles: The case of Facebook. *Computers in Human Behavior*, *26*(3), 406–418. doi:10.1016/j.chb.2009.11.012

Nyangau, J.Z., & Bado, N. (2012). Social media and marketing of higher education: A review of the literature. *Journal of the Research Center for Educational Technology, 8*(1), 38-51.

O'Brien, S., & Bierman, K. (1988). Conceptions and perceived influence of peer groups: Interviews with preadolescents and adolescents. *Child Development*, *59*(5), 1360–1365. doi:10.2307/1130498 PMID:3168646

O'Reilly, T. (2008). *Why dell.com (was) more Enterprise 2.0 than Dell IdeaStorm*. Retrieved March 23, 2014, from http://radar.oreilly.com/2008/09/why-dell-dot-com-is-more-enterprise.html

O'Dea, B., & Campbell, A. (2011). Healthy connections: Online social networks and their potential for peer support. *Studies in Health Technology and Informatics*, *168*, 133–140. PMID:21893921

Ofcom. (2012). *Adults media use and attitudes report 2012*. Retrieved from http://stakeholders.ofcom.org.uk/

Ohannessian, C. M. (2009). Media use and adolescent psychological adjustment: An examination of gender differences. *Journal of Child and Family Studies*, *18*(5), 582–593. doi:10.1007/s10826-009-9261-2 PMID:21359124

Okoro, E. (2012). Social networking and pedagogical variations: An integrated approach for effective interpersonal and group communications skills development. *American Journal of Business Education.*, *5*(2), 219–224.

Okoro, E. A., Hausman, A., & Washington, M. C. (2012). Social media and networking technologies: An analysis of collaborative work and team communication. *Contemporary Issues in Education Research.*, *5*(4), 295–299.

Okuyama, Y. (2007). CALL vocabulary learning in Japanese: Does Romaji help beginners learn more words? *CALICO Journal*, *24*(2), 355–379.

Ollman, G. (2008). *The phishing guide.* Accessed at: http://logman.tech.officelive.com/Documents/The%20 Phishing%20Guide.pdf

Omar, A., & Miah, M. (2013). Digital evolution of the written language. In *Proceedings of the Information Systems Educators Conference ISSN (Education Special Interest Group of the AITP).* San Antonio, TX: ISSN.

Ong, E. Y., Ang, R. P., Ho, J. C., Lim, J. C., Goh, D. H., Lee, S., & Chua, A. Y. (2011). Narcissism, extraversion and adolescents' self-presentation on Facebook. *Personality and Individual Differences, 50*(2), 180–185. doi:10.1016/j.paid.2010.09.022

Öniş, Z. (1997). The political economy of Islamic resurgence in Turkey: The rise of the welfare party in perspective. *Third World Quarterly, 18*(4), 743–766. doi:10.1080/01436599714740

Onlinemba.com. (2012). *Social demographics: Who's using today's biggest networks.* Retrieved from http://mashable.com/2012/03/09/social-media-demographics/

Oreskovic, A. (2010). *Google says its cars grabbed emails, passwords.* Retrieved February 19, 2011, from http://www.reuters.com/article/2010/10/22/us-google-idUSTRE69L4KW20101022

Organisation for Economic Cooperation and Development. (2007). *Participative web: User-created content.* OECD Committee for Information, Computer and Communications Policy Report, April. Retrieved from http://www.oecd.org/internet/ieconomy/38393115.pdf

Orr, E. S., Sisic, M., Ross, C., Simmering, M. G., Arseneault, J. M., & Orr, R. R. (2009). The influence of shinness on the use of Facebook in an undergraduate sample. *Cyberpsychology & Behavior, 12*(3), 337–340. doi:10.1089/cpb.2008.0214 PMID:19250019

Owen, M., Grant, L., Sayers, S., & Facer, K. (2006). Social software and learning. Bristol, UK: Academic Press.

Palme, J., & Berglund, M. (2002). *Anonymity on the internet.* Academic Press.

Palmer, D. (1983). Broken ties: Interlocking directorates and intercorporate coordination. *Administrative Science Quarterly, 28*(1), 40–55. doi:10.2307/2392384

Pantic, I., Damjanovic, A., Todorovic, J., Topalovic, D., Bojovic-Jovic, D., & Ristic, S. et al. (2012). Association between online social networking and depression in high school students: Behavioral physiology viewpoint. *Psychiatria Danubina, 24*(1), 90–93. PMID:22447092

Papert, S. (1994). *A máquina das crianças.* Porto Alegre: ARTMED.

Parasuraman, A., & Zinkhan, G. M. (2002). Marketing to and serving customers through the internet: An overview and research agenda. *Journal of the Academy of Marketing Science, 30*(4), 286–295. doi:10.1177/009207002236906

Park, C., & Jun, J. K. (2003). A cross-cultural comparison of internet buying behavior: Effects of internet usage, perceived risks, and innovativeness. *International Marketing Review, 20*(5), 534–553. doi:10.1108/02651330310498771

Patrício, M. R. V., & Gonçalves, V. M. B. (2010). Utilização educativa do facebook no ensino superior. In *Proceedings of Conference Learning and Teaching in Higher Education. Universidade de Évora.* Retrieved from http://bibliotecadigital.ipb.pt/bitstream/10198/2879/4/7104.pdf

Patton, M. (1990). *Qualitative evaluation and research methods.* Sage.

Peluchette, J., & Karl, K. (2008). Social networking profiles: An examination of student attitudes regarding use and appropriateness of content. *Cyberpsychology & Behavior, 11*(1), 95–97. doi:10.1089/cpb.2007.9927 PMID:18275320

Peluchette, J., & Karl, K. (2010). Examining students' intended image on Facebook: What were they thinking?! *Journal of Education for Business, 85*(1), 30–37. doi:10.1080/08832320903217606

Pempek, T., Yermolayeva, Y., & Calvert, S. (2009). College students' social networking experiences on Facebook. *Journal of Applied Developmental Psychology, 30*(3), 227–238. doi:10.1016/j.appdev.2008.12.010

Pentina, I., Zhang, L., & Basmanova, O. (2013). Antecedents and consequences of trust in a social media brand: A cross-cultural study of Twitter. *Computers in Human Behavior, 29*(4), 1546–1555. doi:10.1016/j.chb.2013.01.045

Perkins, H., Meilman, P., Leichliter, J., Cashin, J., & Presley, C. (1999). Misperceptions of the norms for the frequency of alcohol and other drug use on college campuses. *Journal of American College Health, 47*(6), 253–258. doi:10.1080/07448489909595656 PMID:10368559

Perriault, J. (2002). *Éducation et nouvelles technologies.* Paris: Nathan.

Peters, K., Chen, Y., Kaplan, A. M., Ognibeni, B., & Pauwels, K. (2013). Social media metrics—A framework and guidelines for managing social media. *Journal of Interactive Marketing, 27*(4), 281–298. doi:10.1016/j.intmar.2013.09.007

Peterson, R. A., Balasubramanian, S., & Bronnenberg, B. J. (1997). Exploring the implications of the internet for consumer marketing. *Journal of the Academy of Marketing Science, 25*(4), 329–346. doi:10.1177/0092070397254005

Petronio, S. (2002). *Boundaries of privacy: Dialectics of disclosure.* State University of New York.

Petronio, S., & Caughlin, J. (2006). Communication privacy management theory: Understanding families. In D. Braithwaite & L. Baxter (Eds.), *Engaging theories in family communication: Multiple perspectives.* Thousand Oaks, CA: Sage. doi:10.4135/9781452204420.n3

Petty, R. D. (2000). Marketing without consent: Consumer choice and costs, privacy, and public policy. *Journal of Public Policy & Marketing, 19*(1), 42–53. doi:10.1509/jppm.19.1.42.16940

Pew Research Center. (2014). *Mobile technology fact sheet.* Pew Research Internet Project. Retrieved from http://www.pewinternet.org/fact-sheets/mobile-technology-fact-sheet/

Pew Research Center's Internet & American Life Project. (2013). *72% of online adults are social networking site users* (Report). Retrieved December 5, 2013 from http://pewinternet.org/Reports/2013/social-networking-sites.aspx

Pew Research Center's Internet & American Life Project. (2013). *The demographics of social media users – 2012* (Report). Retrieved December 5, 2013 from http://pewinternet.org/~/media/Files/Reports/2013/PIP_SocialMediaUsers.pdf

Pew Research Internet Project. (2013, December 30). *Social media update 2013.* Retrieved 16 March 2014, from http://www.pewinternet.org/2013/12/30/social-media-update-2013

Pfeffer, J., & Salancik, G. R. (2003). *The external control of organizations: A resource dependence perspective.* Stanford, CA: Stanford University Press.

Philip, R., & Nicholls, J. (2009). Group blogs: Documenting collaborative drama processes. *Australasian Journal of Educational Technology, 25*(5), 683–699.

Philips, N. K. (2011). Academic library use of Facebook: Building relationships with students. *Journal of Academic Librarianship, 37*(6), 512–522. doi:10.1016/j.acalib.2011.07.008

Pincus, A. L., Ansell, E. B., Pimentel, C. A., Cain, N. M., Wright, A. C., & Levy, K. N. (2009). Initial construction and validation of the pathological narcissism inventory. *Psychological Assessment, 21*(3), 365–379. doi:10.1037/a0016530 PMID:19719348

Pinkwart, N., Hoppe, H. U., Milrad, M., & Perez, J. (2003). Educational scenarios for cooperative use of personal digital assistants. *Journal of Computer Assisted Learning, 19*(3), 383–391. doi:10.1046/j.0266-4909.2003.00039.x

Pirkis, J., Blood, R. W., Beautrais, A., Burgess, P., & Skehan, J. (2006). Media guidelines on the reporting of suicide. *Crisis, 27*(2), 82–87. doi:10.1027/0227-5910.27.2.82 PMID:16913330

Polit, D. F., Beck, C. T., & Hungler, B. P. (2001). *Essentials of nursing research: Methods, appraisals and utilization* (5th ed.). Lippincott Williams & Wilkins.

Polkinghorne, D. (1988). *Narrative knowing and human science.* University of New York Press.

Pollet, T. V., Roberts, S. G. B., & Dunbar, R. I. M. (2011). Use of social network sites and instant messaging does not lead to increased offline social network size, or to emotionally closer relationships with offline network members. *Cyberpsychology, Behavior, and Social Networking, 14*(4), 253–258. doi:10.1089/cyber.2010.0161 PMID:21067280

Poon, S., & Swatman, P. (1999). An exploratory study of small business Internet commerce issues. *Information & Management, 35*(1), 9–18. doi:10.1016/S0378-7206(98)00079-2

Porter, M. E. (1980). *Competitive strategy.* New York: Free Press.

Porter, M. E. (1985). *Competitive advantage.* New York: Free Press.

Powers, M. (1996). A cognitive access definition of privacy. *Law and Philosophy, 15*(4), 369–386. doi:10.1007/BF00127211

Prensky, M. (2001). Digital natives, digital immigrants. *On the Horizon, 9*(5), 1–6. doi:10.1108/10748120110424816

Prettyman, S. S., Ward, C. L., Jaulk, D., & Awad, G. (2012). *21st century learners: Voices of students in a one-to-one STEM environment.* Academic Press.

PRLog Press Release. (2011). *Eurostat releases figures on internet security.* Retrieved August 23, 2014, from http://www.prlog.org/11285632-eurostat-releases-figures-on-internet-security.html

Purao, S., & Campbell, B. (1998). Critical concerns for small business electronic commerce: Some reflections based on interviews of small business owners. In *Proceedings of Americas Conference on Information Systems* (AMCIS). Academic Press.

Putnam, R. (1995). Bowling alone: America's declining social capital. *Journal of Democracy, 6*(1), 65–78. doi:10.1353/jod.1995.0002

Putnam, R. D. (2000). *Bowling alone.* New York: Simon and Schuster.

Quelch, J. A., & Klein, L. R. (1996). The internet and international marketing. *Sloan Management Review, 37*(3).

Quinn, S., & Oldmeadow, J. (2013). Is the igeneration a 'we' generation? Social networking use among 9-to 13-year-olds and belonging. *The British Journal of Developmental Psychology, 31*(1), 136–142. doi:10.1111/bjdp.12007 PMID:23331112

Ranganathan, C., & Ganapathy, S. (2002). Key dimensions of business-to-consumer web sites. *Information & Management, 39*(6), 457–465. doi:10.1016/S0378-7206(01)00112-4

Rao, N. M., Sasidhar, C., & Kumar, V. S. (2012). Cloud computing through mobile-learning. *International Journal of Advanced Computer Science and Application, 1*(6), 42–47.

Ravenscroft, A., Warburton, S., Hatzipanagos, S., & Conole, G. (2012). Designing and evaluating social media for learning: Shaping social networking into social learning? *Journal of Computer Assisted Learning, 28*(3), 177–182. doi:10.1111/j.1365-2729.2012.00484.x

Razzak, M. (2011, October 4). Universities nationwide utilize NV3 technologies' cell-phone and tablet charging kiosks. *Bloomberg.* Retrieved from http://www.bloomberg.com/apps/news?pid=conewsstory&tkr=ERCG:GR&sid=aEq9Fn9BsxLA

Read, B. (2006). Duke stops giving students free iPods but will continue using them in classes. *The Chronicle of Higher Education, 52*(36), A39.

Reboussin, B., Song, E., & Wolfson, M. (2012). Social influences on the clustering of underage risky drinking and its consequences in communities. *Journal of Studies on Alcohol and Drugs, 73*(6), 890–898. PMID:23036206

Reich, S. M. (2010). Adolescents' sense of community on MySpace and Facebook: A mixed-methods approach. *Journal of Community Psychology, 36*(6), 688–705. doi:10.1002/jcop.20389

Reid, D. J., & Reid, F. J. (2004). *Insights into the social and psychological effects of SMS text messaging.* Retrieved from http://www.160characters.org/

Reid, D. J., & Reid, F. J. (2005). Textmates and text circles: Insights into the social ecology of SMS text messaging. In A. Lasen & L. Hamill (Eds.), *Mobile world, past, present and future* (pp. 105–118). London: Springer. doi:10.1007/1-84628-204-7_7

Ricardo, C., & Chavarro, A. (2010). El uso de Facebook y Twitter en la educación. *Instituto de Estudios en Educación, 11*, 1–9.

Ridout, B., Campbell, A., & Ellis, L. (2012). 'Off your face(book)': Alcohol in online social identity construction and its relation to problem drinking in university students. *Drug and Alcohol Review, 31*(1), 20–26. doi:10.1111/j.1465-3362.2010.00277.x PMID:21355935

Riegelsberger, J., Sasse, M. A., & McCarthy, J. D. (2003). The researcher's dilemma: Evaluating trust in computer-mediated communication. *International Journal of Human-Computer Studies, 58*(6), 759–781. doi:10.1016/S1071-5819(03)00042-9

Riegelsberger, J., Sasse, M. A., & McCarthy, J. D. (2005). The mechanics of trust: A framework for research and design. *International Journal of Human-Computer Studies, 62*(3), 381–422. doi:10.1016/j.ijhcs.2005.01.001

Ritzer, G. (2011). *Sociological theory* (7th ed.). New York: McGraw Hill, International.

Robertson, L., Smellie, T., Wilson, P., & Cox, L. (2011). Learning styles and fieldwork education: Students' perspectives. *New Zealand Journal of Occupational Therapy, 58*(1), 36–40.

Roblyer, M. D., McDaniel, M., Webb, M., Herman, J., & Witty, J. V. (2010). Findings on Facebook in higher education: A comparison of college faculty and student uses and perceptions of social networking sites. *The Internet and Higher Education, 13*(3), 134–140. doi:10.1016/j.iheduc.2010.03.002

Rogers, C. B. (1951). *Client centred therapy: Its current practice, implications and theory.* Boston: Houghton Mifflin Company.

Rogers, Y., Connelly, K., Hazelwood, W., & Tedesco, W. (2010). Enhancing learning: A study of how mobile devices can facilitate sensemaking. *Personal and Ubiquitous Computing, 14*(2), 111–124. doi:10.1007/s00779-009-0250-7

Rooney, P. (2005). *Researching from the inside - Does it compromise validity? A discussion.* Dublin Institute of Technology ARROW@DIT Articles: Learning, Teaching & Technology Centre.

Rose, C. (2011). The security implications of ubiquitous social media. *International Journal of Management & Information Systems, 15*(1).

Rosen, L. D., Whaling, K., Rab, S., Carrier, L. M., & Cheever, N. A. (2013). Is Facebook creating "iDisorders"? The link between clinical symptoms of psychiatric disorders and technology use, attitudes and anxiety. *Computers in Human Behavior, 29*(3), 1243–1254. doi:10.1016/j.chb.2012.11.012

Ross, C., Orr, E., Sisic, M., Arseneault, J., Simmering, M., & Orr, R. (2009). Personality and motivations associated with Facebook use. *Computers in Human Behavior, 25*(2), 578–586. doi:10.1016/j.chb.2008.12.024

Rousseau, D. M., Sitkin, S. B., Burt, R. S., & Camerer, C. (1998). Not so different after all: Across-discipline view of trust. *Academy of Management Review, 23*(3), 393–404. doi:10.5465/AMR.1998.926617

Ruder, T. D., Hatch, G. M., Ampanozi, G., Thali, M. J., & Fischer, N. (2011). Suicide announcement on Facebook. *Crisis, 32*(5), 280–282. doi:10.1027/0227-5910/a000086 PMID:21940257

Ryall, J. (2012). Surge in digital dementia. *The Telegraph.* Retrieved June 8, 2012, from http://www.telegraph.co.uk/news/worldnews/asia/southkorea/10138403/Surge-in-digital-dementia.html

Ryan, T., & Xenos, S. (2007). Who uses Facebook? An investigation into the relationship between the big five, shyness, narcissism, loneliness, and Facebook usage. *Computers in Human Behavior, 27*(5), 1658–1664. doi:10.1016/j.chb.2011.02.004

Safko, L. (2010). *The social media bible: Tactics, tools, and strategies for business success.* John Wiley & Sons.

Salmon, G. (2005). Flying not flapping: A strategic framework for e-learning and pedagogial innovation in higher education institutions. *Research in Learning Technology, 13*(3), 201–218. doi:10.1080/09687760500376439

Sandvik, M., Smordal, O., & Osterud, S. (2012). Universitetsforlaget. *Nordic Journal of Digital Literacy, 7*(03), 204–220.

Santor, D. A., Deanna Messervey, D., & Kusumakar, V. (2000). Measuring peer pressure, popularity, and conformity in adolescent boys and girls: Predicting school performance, sexual attitudes, and substance abuse. *Journal of Youth and Adolescence, 29*(2), 163–182. doi:10.1023/A:1005152515264

Schneier, B. (2010). A taxonomy of social networking data. *IEEE Security & Privacy, 8*(4), 88–88. doi:10.1109/MSP.2010.118

Schulte, M., Ramo, D., & Brown, S. (2009). Gender differences in factors influencing alcohol use and drinking progression among adolescents. *Clinical Psychology Review*, *29*(6), 535–547. doi:10.1016/j.cpr.2009.06.003 PMID:19592147

Schurgin O'Keefe, G., & Clarke-Pearson, K. (2011). The impact of social media on children, adolescents, and families. *Pediatrics*, *127*(4), 800–804. doi:10.1542/peds.2011-0054 PMID:21444588

Schwartz, H. L. (2009). 'Facebook: The new classroom commons?'. *The Chronicle Review*, *56*(6), B12–B13.

Scorrano, P. (2011). The 2.0 marketing strategies for wine tourism destinations of excellence. *The China Business Review*, *10*(10), 948–960.

Seder, P. J., & Oishi, S. (2009). Ethnic/racial homogeneity in college students' Facebook friendship networks and subjective well-being. *Journal of Research in Personality*, *43*(3), 438–443. doi:10.1016/j.jrp.2009.01.009

Selfhout, M. H. W., Brantje, S. J. T., Delsing, M., ter Bogt, T. F. M., & Meeus, W. H. J. (2009). Different types of internet use, depression, and social anxiety: The role of perceived friendship quality. *Journal of Adolescence*, *32*(4), 819–833. doi:10.1016/j.adolescence.2008.10.011 PMID:19027940

Selwyn, N. (2011). *Education and technology: Key issues and debates*. Bloomsbury.

Selwyn, N. (2012). Social media in higher education. In A. Gladman (Ed.), *The Europa world of learning 2012* (62nd ed.; pp. 3–7). London: Routledge.

Semiocast. (2012). Twitter reaches half a billion accounts. *Semiocast*. Retrieved September 20, 2013, from http://semiocast.com/en/publications/2012_07_30_Twitter_reaches_half_a_billion_accounts_140m_in_the_US

Seppala, P., & Alamaki, K. (2003). Mobile learning in teaching. *Journal of Computer Assisted Learning*, *19*(3), 330–335.

Seton Hall University. (n.d.). About the mobile computing program. *Seton Hall University's Website*. Retrieved from http://www.shu.edu/offices/technology/about-mobile-computing.cfm

Shaefer, M. W. (2012). *ROI (return on influence): The revolutionary power of Klout, social scoring, and influence marketing*. McGrawHill.

Shapira, N., Barak, A., & Gal, I. (2007). Promoting older adults' well-being through internet training and use. *Aging & Mental Health*, *11*(5), 477–484. doi:10.1080/13607860601086546 PMID:17882585

Sharples, M. (2000). The design of personal mobile technologies for lifelong learning. *Computers & Education*, *34*(3-4), 177–193. doi:10.1016/S0360-1315(99)00044-5

Sharples, M., Corlett, D., & Westmancott, O. (2002). The design and implementation of a mobile learning resource. *Personal and Ubiquitous Computing*, *6*(3), 220–234. doi:10.1007/s007790200021

Sheldon, P. (2008). The relationship between unwillingness-to-communicate and students' facebook use. *Journal of Media Psychology*, *20*(2), 67–75. doi:10.1027/1864-1105.20.2.67

Sheldon, P. (2012). *Psychologist examines effects of technology society*. University of Huntsville.

Shelke, P., & Badiye, A. (2013). Social networking: Its uses and abuses. *Research Journal of Forensic Sciences*, *1*(1), 2–7.

Shi, Z., Rui, H., & Whinston, A. B. (2014). Content sharing in a social broadcasting environment: Evidence from twitter. *Management Information Systems Quarterly*, *38*(1), 123–142.

Sifferlin, A. (2013). Why Facebook makes you feel miserable. *TIME.com*. Retrieved August 25, 2013, from http://healthland.time.com/2013/01/24/why-facebook-makes-you-feel-bad-about-yourself/

Sigala, M. (2010). eCRM 2.0 applications and trends: The use and perceptions of Greek tourism firms of social networks and intelligence. *Computers in Human Behavior*, *27*(2), 655–661. doi:10.1016/j.chb.2010.03.007

Silva, M. (2010). Educar na cibercultura: Desafios à formação de professores para docência em cursos online. *Revista Digital de Tecnologias Cognitivas*, (3), 36-51.

Silva, M. (2001). *Sala de Aula Interativa*. Editora Quartet.

Silveri, M. (2012). Adolescent brain development and underage drinking in the United States: Identifying risks of alcohol use in college populations. *Harvard Review of Psychiatry*, *20*(4), 189–200. doi:10.3109/10673229.2012.714642 PMID:22894728

Silverman, R. (2012). *Justice and development in the marketplace: Business and politics in AKP-era Turkey*. (Unpublished master's thesis). University of Washington.

Silverman, R. E. (2011). Is psychology a science? *Skeptic*, *17*(1), 36–39.

Simoncic, T. E. (2012). *Facebook depression revisited: The absence of an association between Facebook use and depressive symptoms*. Unpublished thesis. Retrieved from http://deepblue.lib.umich.edu/bitstream/handle/2027.42/91787/teagues.pdf?sequence=1

Sitkin, S. B., & Pablo, A. L. (1992). Reconceptualising the determinants of risk behaviour. *Academy of Management Review*, *17*, 9–38.

Skiba, D. J. (2013). Bloom's digital taxonomy and word clouds. *Nursing Education Perspectives*, *34*(4), 277–280. doi:10.5480/1536-5026-34.4.277 PMID:24187736

Skues, J. L., Williams, B., & Wise, L. (2012). The effects of personality traits, self-esteem, loneliness, and narcissism on Facebook use among university students. *Computers in Human Behavior*, *28*(6), 2414–2419. doi:10.1016/j.chb.2012.07.012

Slaoti, D., Motteram, G., & Onat-Stelma, Z. (2013). *Innovations in learning technology for English language teaching* (G. Motteram, Ed.). London: The British Council.

Smith, D. J. (2006). Cell phones, social inequality, and contemporary culture in Nigeria. *Canadian Journal of African Studies*, *40*(3), 496–523.

Smith, E. (2013). User education in social media applications @ your library. *The Australian Library Journal*, *62*(4), 305–313. doi:10.1080/00049670.2013.845075

Smith, S., Winchester, D., Bunker, D., & Jamieson, R. (2010). Circuits of power: A study of mandated compliance to an information systems security de jure standard in a government organization. *Management Information Systems Quarterly*, *34*(3), 463–486.

Snow, C. (2012). *Orientations towards using social media, digital and mobile technologies to improve literacy skills among diverse students in urban schools*. Harvard University Press.

Social Media Marketing, Statistics, and Monitoring Tools . (n.d.). Accessed June 23rd, 2013, from www.socialbakers.com

Social Media. (n.d.). In *Oxford dictionaries online*. Retrieved from http://www.oxforddictionaries.com/

Some Teens are Exhibiting Signs of 'Digital Dementia'. (2013). *UPI.com*. Retrieved November 8, 2013, from http://www.upi.com/Science_News/Technology/2013/06/26/Some-teens-in-South-Korea-exhibiting-digital-dementia/UPI-69441372251061/

Sönmez, M. (2010). *Türkiye'de iş dünyasının örgütleri ve yönelimleri*. Istanbul: Friedrich Ebert Stiftung. Retrieved March 6, 2014, from http://www.tuskon.org/?p=content&cl=kurumsal&i=3

SOPHOS Security Trends Report. (2013). *Social networking security threats*. Retrieved March 20, 2013, from http://www.sophos.com/en-us/security-news-trends/security-trends/social-networking-security-threats/twitter-linkedin-and-google-plus.aspx

Sparkes, A. C. (1996). The fatal flaw: A narrative of the fragile body-self. *Qualitative Enquiry*, *2*(4), 463–494. doi:10.1177/107780049600200405

Special, W. P., & Li-Barber, K. T. (2012). Self-disclosure and student satisfaction with Facebook. *Computers in Human Behavior*, *28*(2), 624–630. doi:10.1016/j.chb.2011.11.008

Spires, H., Wiebe, E., Young, C., Hollebrands, K., & Lee, J. (2012). Towards a new learning ecology: Professional development for teachers in 1:1 learning environments. *Contemporary Issues in Technology & Teacher Education*, *12*(2), 232–254.

Spitzer, M. (2012). Digitale Demenz. Droemer Verlag.

SS8. (n.d.). Retrieved October 1, 2012, from http://www.ss8.com/products-overview.php, http://www.ss8.com/industries/law-enforcement-agencies-0

Stack, S. (2003). Media coverage as a risk factor in suicide. *Journal of Epidemiology and Community Health*, *57*(4), 238–240. doi:10.1136/jech.57.4.238 PMID:12646535

Stafford, K. (2011). University keeps quiet on recent data heist. *The Eastern Echo*. Retrieved August 25, 2014, from http://www.easternecho.com/index.php/article/2011/03/university_keeps_quiet_on_recent_data_heist

Stead, L. A. (2012). How do consumer reviews on TripAdvisor affect consumer decision making when booking an international hotel. *Hospitality Management Review Student Journal at Sheffield Hallam University*, *2*. Retrieved March 27, 2014, from http://research.shu.ac.uk/domino/index.php/HMJ/article/view/21/36

Stefanone, M. A., Lackaff, D., & Rosen, D. (2011). Contingencies of self-worth and social-networking-site behavior. *Cyberpsychology, Behavior, and Social Networking*, *14*(1-2), 41–49. doi:10.1089/cyber.2010.0049 PMID:21329442

Steinfield, C., Ellison, N. B., & Lampe, C. (2008). Social capital, self-esteem, and use of online social network sites: A longitudinal analysis. *Journal of Applied Developmental Psychology*, *29*(6), 434–445. doi:10.1016/j.appdev.2008.07.002

Stepanikova, I., Nie, N. H., & He, X. (2010). Time on the internet at home, loneliness, and life satisfaction: Evidence from panel time-diary data. *Computers in Human Behavior*, *26*(3), 329–338. doi:10.1016/j.chb.2009.11.002

Stewart, D. W., & Pavlov, P. A. (2002). From consumer response to active consumer: Measuring the effectiveness of interactive media. *Journal of the Academy of Marketing Science*, *4*(30), 376–396. doi:10.1177/009207002236912

Stoddard, S., Bauermeister, J., Gordon-Messer, D., Johns, M., & Zimmerman, M. (2012). Permissive norms and young adults' alcohol and marijuana use: The role of online communities. *Journal of Studies on Alcohol and Drugs*, *73*(6), 968–975. PMID:23036215

Stompka, P. (1999). *Trust*. Cambridge, UK: Cambridge University Press.

Strasburger, V., Jordan, A., & Donnerstein, E. (2010). Health effects of media on children and adolescents. *Pediatrics*, *125*(4), 756–767. doi:10.1542/peds.2009-2563 PMID:20194281

Subrahmanyam, K., Reich, S., Waechter, N., & Espinoza, G. (2008). Online and offline social networks: Use of social networking sites by emerging adults. *Journal of Applied Developmental Psychology*, *29*(6), 420–433. doi:10.1016/j.appdev.2008.07.003

Summerfield, B. (2005). United Technologies Corp.: Learning partnerships & mobile learning. *Chief Learning Officer*, *4*(2), 42.

Sussman, S., Pokhrel, P., Ashmore, R., & Brown, B. (2007). Adolescent peer group identification and characteristics: A review of the literature. *Addictive Behaviors*, *32*(8), 1602–1627. doi:10.1016/j.addbeh.2006.11.018 PMID:17188815

Sutherland, E. (1939). *Principles of criminology* (3rd ed.). Philadelphia, PA: J.B. Lippincott.

Swartz, J. (2008). Social-networking sites work to turn users into profits. *USA Today*. Retrieved from http://www.usatoday.com/tech/techinvestor/industry/2008-05-11-socialnetworking_N.htm

Symantec Enterprise Security. (2009). *Internet security threat report* (vol. 14). Symantec Press.

Sysomos, Inc. (2010, February). *Inside YouTube videos: Exploring YouTube videos and their use in blogosphere - Michael Jackson and health care dominate*. Retrieved August 20, 2013, from http://www.sysomos.com/reports/youtube

Taiwo, R. (2010). *"The thumb tribe" and innovative English usage: Creativity and social change in the context of SMS messages in Nigeria*. Paper presented at the 3rd European Conference on African Studies, Leipzig, Germany.

Taiwo, R. (2007). Tenor in electronic media Christian discourse in South Western Nigeria. *Nordic Journal of African Studies*, *16*(1), 75–89.

Taiwo, R. (2008). Linguistic forms and functions of SMS text messages. In S. Kelsey & K. St Armant (Eds.), *The handbook of research in computer mediated communication* (pp. 969–982). IGI Global. doi:10.4018/978-1-59904-863-5.ch068

Taiwo, R. (2009). The use of socio-cultural elements for creativity in Nigeria SMS texts. *Journal of Linguistic Association of Nigeria*, *12*, 99–108.

Tapscott, D. (1999). Educating the net generation. *Educational Leadership*, *56*(5), 6–11.

Tavani, H. T. (2000). *Privacy and the internet*. Retrieved March 24, 2011, from http://www.bc.edu/bc_org/avp/law/st_org/iptf/commentary/content/2000041901.html

Taylor, B., & Kroth, M. (2009). Andragogy's transition into the future: Meta-analysis of andragogy and its search for a measurable instrument. *Journal of Adult Education*, *38*, 1–11.

Teenager's Death Sparks Cyber-Blackmailing Probe. (2013, August 13). *BBC News Scotland*. Retrieved August 16, 2013, from http://www.bbc.co.uk/news/uk-scotland-23723169

Tenopir, C., Volentine, R., & King, D. W. (2013). Social media and scholarly reading. *Online Information Review*, *37*(2), 193–216. doi:10.1108/OIR-04-2012-0062

Teo, T. S., & Choo, W. Y. (2001). Assessing the impact of using the Internet for competitive intelligence. *Information & Management*, *39*(1), 67–83. doi:10.1016/S0378-7206(01)00080-5

Teo, T. S., & Liu, J. (2007). Consumer trust in e-commerce in the United States, Singapore and China. *Omega*, *35*(1), 22–38. doi:10.1016/j.omega.2005.02.001

Testa, M., Kearns-Bodkin, J., & Livingston, J. (2009). Effect of precollege drinking intentions on women's college drinking as mediated via peer social influences. *Journal of Studies on Alcohol and Drugs*, *70*(4), 575–582. PMID:19515298

Thus, H., Chatti, M. A., Yalcin, E., Pallasch, C., Kyryliuk, B., Mageramov, T., & Schroeder, U. (2012). Mobile learning in context. *International Journal of Technology Enhanced Learning*, *4*(5), 332–344. doi:10.1504/IJTEL.2012.051818

Tickle, J. J., Hull, J. G., Sargent, J. D., Dalton, M. A., & Heatherton, T. F. (2006). A structural equation model of social influences and exposure to media smoking on adolescent smoking. *Basic and Applied Social Psychology*, *28*(2), 117–129. doi:10.1207/s15324834basp2802_2

Tokunaga, R. (2010). Following you home from school: A critical review and synthesis of research on cyber bullying victimization. *Computers in Human Behavior*, *26*(3), 277–287. doi:10.1016/j.chb.2009.11.014

Toro-Araneda, G. (2010). Usos de Twitter en la educación superior. *Serie Bibliotecología y Gestión de Información*, *53*, 1–30.

Traynor, M. (2003). Anonymity and the internet. In *Patents, copyright, trademarks, and literary property course handbook series*, (pp. 993-998). Academic Press.

Trepte, S. (2011). Preface. In S. Trepte & L. Reinecke (Eds.), *Privacy online: Perspectives on privacy and self-disclosure in the social web*. Berlin: Springer.

Trilling, B., & Fadel, C. (2009). *21st century skills: Learning for life in our times*. John Wiley & Sons.

Tsikriktsis, N. (2002). Does culture influence web site quality expectations? An empirical study. *Journal of Service Research*, *5*(2), 101–112. doi:10.1177/109467002237490

Turnbull, P. W., & Valla, J. P. (1986). Strategic planning in industrial marketing: An interaction approach. *European Journal of Marketing*, *20*(7), 5–20. doi:10.1108/EUM0000000004652

Tuten, T., & Marks, M. (2012). The adoption of social media as educational technology among marketing educators. *Marketing Education Review*, *22*(3), 201–214. doi:10.2753/MER1052-8008220301

Twumasi, A., & Adu-Gyami, K. (2013). The impact of social networking sites on the purchasing behaviours of online travel community members. *Information and Knowledge Management*, *3*(11), 105–111.

Um, S., & Crompton, J. L. (1997). Development of pleasure travel attitude dimensions. *Annals of Tourism Research*, *18*, 374–378.

University of Texas. (2012). *Texas A&M mobile strategy*. Retrieved from http://gomobile.tamu.edu/texas-am-mobile-strategy

University of Washington. (2012). *Mobile device use and allowance policy*. Retrieved from http://www.washington.edu/admin/rules/policies/APS/55.01.html

Urban, G. L., & Sultan, F. (2000). Placing trust at the center of your Internet strategy. *Sloan Management Review, 42*(1), 39–48.

Urista, M., Dong, Q., & Day, K. (2009). Explaining why young adults use MySpace and Facebook through uses and gratification theory. *Human Communication, 12*(2), 215–229.

Valente, J. A. (1999). *O computador na sociedade do conhecimento: Cadernos informática para a mudança em educação.* Brasília, DF: MEC/SEED.

Valente, J. A. (2005). *A espiral da espiral de aprendizagem: O processo de compreensão do papel das tecnologias de informação e comunicação na educação. Tese (Livre Docência) – Instituto de Artes.* Campinas: UNICAMP.

Valkenburg, P. M., & Peter, J. (2009). Social consequences of the internet for adolescents: A decade of research. *Current Directions in Psychological Science, 18*(1), 1–5. doi:10.1111/j.1467-8721.2009.01595.x

Valkenburg, P. M., Peter, J., & Schouten, A. P. (2006). Friend networking sites and their relationship to adolescents' well-being and social self-esteem. *Cyberpsychology & Behavior, 9*(5), 584–590. doi:10.1089/cpb.2006.9.584 PMID:17034326

Van der Aa, N., Overbeck, G., Engels, R. C. M. E., Scholte, R. H. J., Meerkerk, G. J., & Van den Eijnden, R. J. J. M. (2009). Daily and compulsive Internet use and well-being in adolescence: A diathesis-stress model based on big five personality traits. *Journal of Youth and Adolescence, 38*(6), 765–776. doi:10.1007/s10964-008-9298-3 PMID:19636779

van Dijck, J. (2009). Users like you? Theorizing agency in user-generated content. *Media Culture & Society, 31*(1), 41–58. doi:10.1177/0163443708098245

Van Wyck, K. (2009). How to use Facebook safely. In *IT manager's guide to social networking.* WebMediaBrands.

Vargo, S. L., & Lusch, R. F. (2004). Evolving to a new dominant logic for marketing. *Journal of Marketing, 68*(1), 1–17. doi:10.1509/jmkg.68.1.1.24036

Vargo, S. L., & Lusch, R. F. (2008). Service-dominant logic: Continuing the evolution. *Journal of the Academy of Marketing Science, 36*(1), 1–10. doi:10.1007/s11747-007-0069-6

Vargo, S. L., & Lusch, R. F. (2011). It's all B2B... and beyond: Toward a systems perspective of the market. *Industrial Marketing Management, 40*(2), 181–187. doi:10.1016/j.indmarman.2010.06.026

Vasalou, A., Joinson, A. N., & Courvoisier, D. (2010). Cultural differences, experience with social network, and the nature of "true commitment" in Facebook. *International Journal of Human-Computer Studies, 68*(10), 719–728. doi:10.1016/j.ijhcs.2010.06.002

Velliaris, D. M., & Willis, C. R. (2014). Getting personal: An autoethnographic study of the professional identit(ies) of lecturers in an Australian pathway institution. In P. Breen (Ed.), *Cases on teacher identity, diversity, and cognition in higher education* (pp. 87–110). IGI Global. doi:10.4018/978-1-4666-5990-2.ch004

Vincos. (2012). *World map of social networks.* Retrieved from http://vincos.it/world-map-of-social-networks/

Visser, L., de Winter, A., Veenstra, R., Verhulst, F., & Reijneveld, S. (2013). Alcohol use and abuse in young adulthood: Do self-control and parents' perceptions of friends during adolescence modify peer influence? The TRAILS study. *Addictive Behaviors, 38*(12), 2841–2846. doi:10.1016/j.addbeh.2013.08.013 PMID:24018228

Vogel, T. (2011) Cyber attacks launched on EU computer systems. *European Voice.* Retrieved August 25, 2014 from http://www.europeanvoice.com/article/cyber-attacks-launched-on-eu-computer-systems/

Vygotsky, L. S. A. (1989). *A formação social da mente.* São Paulo: Martins Fontes.

Walczuch, R., Van Braven, G., & Lundgren, H. (2000). Internet adoption barriers for small firms in The Netherlands. *European Management Journal, 18*(5), 561–572. doi:10.1016/S0263-2373(00)00045-1

Walker, R. (2006). *The English law of privacy - An evolving human right.* Retrieved March 27, 2013, from http://www.supremecourt.gov.uk/docs/speech_100825.pdf

Walther, J. (2011). Introduction to privacy online. In S. Trepte & L. Reinecke (Eds.), *Privacy online: Perspectives on privacy and self-disclosure in the social web.* Berlin: Springer.

Wang, W., & Benbasat, I. (2005). Trust and adoption of online recommendation agents. *Journal of the AIS*, *6*(3), 72–101.

Wang, Y. D., & Emurian, H. (2005). An overview of online trust: Concepts, elements, and implications. *Computers in Human Behavior*, *21*(1), 105–125. doi:10.1016/j.chb.2003.11.008

Wang, Y., & Fesenmaier, D. R. (2002). Defining the virtual tourist community: Implications for tourism marketing. *Tourism Management*, *23*(4), 407–417. doi:10.1016/S0261-5177(01)00093-0

Ward, M. (2006). *Tips to help you stay safe online*. Retrieved March 25, 2011, from http://news.bbc.co.uk/1/hi/technology/5414992.stm

Warren, L., & Quigley, R. (2013). Police confirm 12 year old girls suicide note said she was being cyber-bullied as her sister reveals she knew about abuse but was sworn to secrecy. *Daily Mail*. Retrieved August 20, 2013, from http://www.dailymail.co.uk/news/article-2331670/Gabrielle-Molina-Police-confirm-12-year-old-girls-suicide-note-said-cyber-bullied-sister-reveals-knew-abuse-sworn-secrecy.html

Warr, M., & Stafford, M. (1991). The Influence of delinquent peers: What they think or what they do? *Criminology*, *29*(4), 851–866. doi:10.1111/j.1745-9125.1991.tb01090.x

Warschauer, M. (2003). Demystifying the digital divide. *Scientific American*, *289*(2), 42–47. doi:10.1038/scientificamerican0803-42 PMID:12884537

Warschauer, M. (2007). The paradoxical future of digital learning. *Learning Inquiry*, *1*(1), 41–49. doi:10.1007/s11519-007-0001-5

Watkins, T. (2010). New light on Neolithic revolution in south-west Asia. *Antiquity*, *84*(325), 621–634.

Watts, D. J. (2004). *Six degrees: The science of a connected age*. New York: WW Norton & Company.

Weinberg, B. D., de Ruyter, K., Dellarocas, C., Buck, M., & Keeling, D. I. (2013). Destination social business: Exploring an organization's journey with social media, collaborative community and expressive individuality. *Journal of Interactive Marketing*, *27*(4), 299–310. doi:10.1016/j.intmar.2013.09.006

Weinberg, B., & Pehlivan, E. (2011). Social spending: Managing the social media mix. *Business Horizons*, *54*(3), 275–282. doi:10.1016/j.bushor.2011.01.008

Weir, G. R., Toolan, F., & Smeed, D. (2011). The threats of social networking: Old wine in new bottles? *Information Security Technical Report*, *16*(2), 38–43. doi:10.1016/j.istr.2011.09.008

Weisbuch, M., Ivcevic, Z., & Ambady, N. (2009). On being liked on the web and in the "real world": Consistency in first impressions across personal webpages and spontaneous behavior. *Journal of Experimental Social Psychology*, *45*(3), 573–576. doi:10.1016/j.jesp.2008.12.009 PMID:20161314

Weisgerber, C. (2009). Teaching PR 2.0 through the use of blogs and wikis. *Communication Teacher*, *23*(3), 105–109. doi:10.1080/17404620902974782

Weiten, W., Hammer, E.Y., & Dunn, D.S. (2012). *Psychotherapy and contemporary life, human adjustment*. Wasdsworth, MA: Cengage Learning.

Welch, C. (2000). The archaeology of business networks: The use of archival records in case study research. *Journal of Strategic Marketing*, *8*(2), 197–208. doi:10.1080/0965254X.2000.10815560

Wellman, B., & Berkowitz, S. D. (Eds.). (1988). *Social structures: A network approach*. Cambridge, UK: Cambridge University Press.

Wells, R. (2011). Reopening the door to tourism post Arab Spring. *Middle East*, 51.

Wenger, A. (2008). Analysis of travel bloggers' characteristics and their communication about Austria as tourism destination. *Journal of Vacation Marketing*, *14*(2), 169–176. doi:10.1177/1356766707087525

Westgate, E. C., Neighbors, C., Heppner, H., Jahn, S., & Lindgren, K. P. (2014). I will take a shot for every' like' I get on this status": Posting alcohol-related Facebook content is linked to drinking outcomes. *Journal of Studies on Alcohol and Drugs*, *75*(3), 390–398. PMID:24766750

Westin, A. F. (1966). Science, privacy, and freedom: Issues and proposals for the 1970's: Part I--The current impact of surveillance on privacy. *Columbia Law Review*, *66*(6), 1003–1050. doi:10.2307/1120997

Westin, A. F. (1967). *Privacy and freedom*. New York: Atheneum.

Westin, A. F. (2003). Social and political dimensions of privacy. *The Journal of Social Issues*, *59*(2), 431–453. doi:10.1111/1540-4560.00072

White, L. (2010). Facebook, friends and photos: A snapshot into social networking for generating travel ideas. In N. Sharda (Ed.), *Tourism informatics: Visual travel recommender systems, social communities, and user interface design*. Hershey, PA: IGI Global. doi:10.4018/978-1-60566-818-5.ch007

Whitman, M., & Mattord, H. (2010). *Principles of information security*. Cengage Learning.

Willard, N. E. (2007). *Cyberbullying and cyberthreats: Responding to the challenge of online social aggression, threats, and distress*. Research Press.

Wilson, K., Fornasier, S., & White, K. M. (2010). Psychological predictors of young adults' use of social networking sites. *Cyberpsychology, Behavior, and Social Networking*, *13*(2), 173–177. doi:10.1089/cyber.2009.0094 PMID:20528274

Wilson, R. E., Gosling, S. D., & Graham, L. T. (2012). A review of Facebook research in the social sciences. *Perspectives on Psychological Science*, *7*(3), 203–220. doi:10.1177/1745691612442904

Wistreich, N. (2009). Have some popcorn with your documentary. *Scottish Documentary Institute*. Retrieved August 21, 2013, from http://blog.scottishdocinstitute.com/popcorn_with_your_documentary_2

Wong, A. (2011). *Attacking a growing cyber terrorism threat*. Retrieved March 24, 2011, from http://www.theaustralian.com.au/australian-it/attacking-a-growing-cyber-terrorism-threat/story-e6frgakx-1226025058588

Woodhouse, P. (2012). Global social networking version 2.0. *Cambridge Marketing Review*, (4).

Woollett, K., & Maguire, E. (2011). Acquiring the knowledge of London's layout drives structural brain changes. *Current Biology, 21*(24-2), 2109-2114. Retrieved October 1, 2013, from http://www.ncbi.nlm.nih.gov/pmc/articles/PMC3268356/

World Health Organisation. (1992). *The ICD-10 classification of mental and behavioural disorders*. Retrieved July 9, 2013, from http://www.who.int/classifications/icd/en/GRNBOOK.pdf

WTTC. (2011). *Travel & tourism 2011*. World Travel & Tourism Council. Retrieved March 27, 2014, from http://www.wttc.org/site_media/uploads/downloads/traveltourism2011.pdf

Xiang, Z., & Gretzel, U. (2010). Role of social media in online travel information search. *Tourism Management*, *31*(2), 179–188. doi:10.1016/j.tourman.2009.02.016

Xu, H., Teo, H.-H., & Tan, B. C. Y. (2005). Predicting the adoption of location-based services: The role of trust and perceived privacy risk. In *Proceedings of the 26th International Conference on Information Systems* (ICIS 2005). Las Vegas, NV: ICIS.

Yacci, M. (2000). Interactivity demystified: A structural definition for distance education and intelligent CBT. *Educational Technology*, *40*(4), 5–16.

Yamagishi, T., & Yamagishi, M. (1994). Trust and commitment in the United States and Japan. *Motivation and Emotion*, *18*(2), 129–166. doi:10.1007/BF02249397

Yang, C., & Brown, B. (2013). Motives for using Facebook, patterns of Facebook activities, and late adolescents' social adjustment to college. *Journal of Youth and Adolescence*, *42*(3), 403–416. doi:10.1007/s10964-012-9836-x PMID:23076768

Yang, S. (2012). Exploring college students' attitudes and self-efficacy of mobile learning. *Turkish Online Journal of Educational Technology*, *11*(4), 148–154.

Yankaya, D. (2009). The Europeanization of MÜSIAD: Political opportunism, economic Europeanization, Islamic Euroscepticism. *European Journal of Turkish Studies*, *9*, 1–18.

Yar, M. (2005). The novelty of 'cyberthreat': An assessment in light if routine activity theory. *European Journal of Criminology*, *2*(4), 407–427. doi:10.1177/147737080556056

Yau-Hau Tse, A. (2011). *Social and psychological impacts of SMS texting on Malaysian university students*. Solls: INTECT.

Yoo, K. H., Gretzel, U., & Zach, F. (2011). Travel opinion leaders and seekers. In R. Law, M. Fuchs, & F. Ricci (Eds.), *Information and communication technologies in tourism* (pp. 525–535). Vienna: SpringerVerlag.

Yousaf, Z., & Ahmed, M. (2013). Effects of SMS on writing skills of the university students in Pakistan: A case study of University of Gujrat. *Asian Economic and Financial Review, 3*(3), 389–397.

Yousafzai, S., Pallister, J., & Foxall, G. (2005). E-banking-A matter of trust: Trust-building strategies for electronic banking. *Psychology and Marketing, 22*(2), 181–201. doi:10.1002/mar.20054

Yu, A. Y., Tian, A. W., Vogel, D., & Kwok, R. C.-W. (2010). Can learning be virtually boosted? An investigation of online social networking impacts. *Computers & Education, 55*(4), 1494–1503. doi:10.1016/j.compedu.2010.06.015

Zakaria, N., Stanton, J. M., & Sarkar-Barney, S. T. (2003). Designing and implementing culturally-sensitive IT applications: The interaction of culture values and privacy issues in the Middle East. *Information Technology & People, 16*(1), 49–75. doi:10.1108/09593840310463023

Zhao, S., Grasmuck, S., & Martin, J. (2008). Identity construction on Facebook: Digital empowerment in anchored relationships. *Computers in Human Behavior, 24*(5), 1816–1836. doi:10.1016/j.chb.2008.02.012

Zhou, Y., Lin, F.-, Du, Y.-, Qin, L.-, Zhao, Z.-, Xu, J.-, & Lei, H. (2011, July). Gray matter abnormalities in Internet addiction: A voxel-based morphometry study. *European Journal of Radiology, 79*(1), 92–95. doi:10.1016/j.ejrad.2009.10.025 PMID:19926237

Ziegler, C., & Golbeck, J. (2006). Investigating correlations of trust and interest similarity. *Decision Support Systems, 43*(2).

Zimmer, M. (2008). Preface: Critical perspectives on web 2.0. *First Monday, 13*(3). doi:10.5210/fm.v13i3.2137

Zitkoski, J. J. (2003). Educação popular e emancipação social: Convergências nas propostas de freire e habermas. ANPED 26. Reunião, GT 6, Caxambu.

Zur, O., & Zur, A. (2011). *On digital immigrants and digital natives: How the digital divide affects families, educational institutions, and the workplace*. Retrieved 11 March 2014, from Zur Institute: http://www.zurinstitute.com/digital_divide.html

Zwier, S., Araujo, T., Boukes, M., & Willemsen, L. (2011). Boundaries to the articulation of possible selves through social networking sites: The case of Facebook profilers' social connectedness. *Cyberpsychology, Behavior, and Social Networking, 14*(10), 571–576. doi:10.1089/cyber.2010.0612 PMID:21476838

About the Contributors

Vladlena Benson is an Associate Professor and a Course Director of the MA Management programme at Kingston Business School, Kingston University, London. She teaches Information Management Strategy to MBA students in the UK and Russia, and is a visiting lecturer on the IMBA programme at IAE Lyon, France. Vladlena's research interests are in the area of information security, information strategy and social networking. She publishes widely and her research is recognised by the British Computing Society (BCS) and the British Academy of Management (BAM). Vladlena publishes extensively in such journals as *British Journal of Educational Technology*, *International Journal of e-Business*, *Computers in Human Behaviour,* and others.

Stephanie Morgan is an Associate Dean, Education, for the Faculty of Business & Law, Kingston University, responsible for all aspects of learning and teaching, QA/QE, accreditations, and the student experience. She is a registered Occupational Psychologist. Her research interests include the use of technology in education and employee responses to technology change, particularly IT outsourcing. She publishes widely in both business and educational journals.

* * *

T. O. Abioye received her Master's and Doctor of Philosophy Degrees in English from Ahmadu Bello University, Zaria, Nigeria. Her academic and professional career started from Ahmadu Bello University in 1988 as a Graduate Assistant, and she rose through the ranks to become a Senior Lecturer in the same University in 2004. Professor Abioye joined Covenant University in 2005 and has previously served as the Acting Head, Department of English & Literary Studies (now Department of Languages) for four years in this university before her appointment as the Deputy Vice Chancellor (Administration) in November 2012, a position she is presently occupying. Professor Abioye has many publications in scholarly journals, books, and chapters in books. Her research orientation and interests include Discourse Stylistics, Applied Linguistics, Media Language, and English Literacy. Her hobbies, among other things, include reading, singing, and gardening.

Amos A. Alao received his Master's of Arts and the Doctor of Philosophy Degrees in Guidance Counseling from the Department of Psychological Services, Atlanta University, USA, in 1975 and 1979, respectively. He is at present a Professor of Counseling Psychology in the Department of Psychology. Prior to his appointment at Covenant University, he has taught counseling and psychology courses at the University of Botswana, where he also served as the Director of the University Careers and Counseling Centre for about 19 years. Before his move to Botswana, he worked at the University of Ibadan for about 12 years, where he rose to the post of Associate Professor in 1990. His research interests include suicide studies, interpersonal relationships, and adjustments. Professor Alao enjoys watching soccer, lawn tennis, and travelling.

Moya L. Alfonso, PhD, MSPH, is an Assistant Professor in the Department of Community Health Behavior and Education at the Jiann-Ping Hsu College of Public Health, Georgia Southern University. She received her PhD (Educational Measurement and Research) and MSPH (Social and Behavioral Sciences in Public Health) from the University of South Florida, Tampa, FL. Prior to coming to Georgia Southern, Dr. Alfonso served as Research Assistant Professor the Florida Mental Health Institute, Co-Director of the Methods and Evaluation Unit at the Florida Prevention Research Center, and Research Director for the Center for Social Marketing. Her current work focuses on translating evidence-based interventions to rural communities in the southeast, the translation of chronic disease self-management programs for use in the area of addiction and recovery, social media and substance use risk, and young adults with disabilities in rural areas. Dr. Alfonso provides research direction for the Center for Addiction Recovery.

Laura Aymerich-Franch is a Marie Curie postdoctoral fellow at the CNRS-AIST JRL (Joint Robotics Laboratory), National Institute of Advanced Industrial Science and Technology (AIST), Japan, and member of GRISS, Image, Sound and Synthesis Research Group, Universitat Autònoma de Barcelona (UAB). She holds a PhD (cum laude) in Audiovisual Communication and Advertising (UAB, 2010). Dr. Aymerich was a Fulbright/ME postdoctoral scholar at Virtual Human Interaction Lab, Stanford University (2012-2014). Before that, she was a lecturer at the Dpt. of Audiovisual Communication and Advertising, UAB (2008-2012). In addition, she was a visiting scholar at iCinema, Centre for Interactive Cinema Research, University of New South Wales, Sydney (2009). Dr. Aymerich's main areas of interest are Media Psychology and Interactive Media.

Dustin Bessette currently serves with the Oregon Parks & Recreation Department as a Park Ranger. Currently, his duties include working as the primary contact for many specific focuses such as marine mammal standing on the Oregon shore, a contact for HazMat materials found at sea, emergency enforcement personnel, as well as beach clean-up and major debris removals with approval of NOAA. Before this, Dustin worked with New York State Office of Parks & Recreation Historic Preservation as the Regional Water Safety Coordinator for the Taconic Region. His duties included various and rigorous training of lifeguard and parks staff through American Red Cross standards, conducted field visit reports, hiring and human resource duties, as well as coordination for lifeguard staff in five major outdoor swimming facilities in upstate New York. Academically, Bessette is currently a Doctoral student with the National Graduate School of Quality Systems Management earning a Doctorate degree in Business Administration (DBA). He has earned two undergraduate degrees, one Associate of Sciences in Biology and Chemistry, and a Bachelor of Science in Real Estate Studies. Further, he will earn a Master of Business Administration (MBA) degree in Marketing and Advertise Management in May of 2015, has earned 30 credit hours towards a Sustainable MBA degree and is enrolled and in process of another graduate MBA degree. Bessette presented at several conferences including, Intellectbase International Consortium (Nashville 2011, Atlanta 2011, and Las Vegas 2012), Eco Summit 2012 (Cleveland, OH),

Association for Advancement Computing Information (AACE) (Montreal, QC), virtually presented at the 5th Annual International Conference on Education, Research, and Innovation (ICERI) (Madrid, Spain), Society for Applied Learning Technologies (SALT) Conference (Orlando, FL) in March 2013, Florida Academy of Sciences (Miami, FL) in March 2013, and virtually at the 7th International Technology, Education, and Development (INTED) (Valencia, Spain) in March 2013. He has published in peer-reviewed journals for the Intellectbase International Consortium as well as reviewed graduate work for the Academy of Management.

Tuba Bircan is a statistician with PhD in Social and Political Sciences and works at the Faculty of Art and Science at Bahçeşehir University, Istanbul. Her research interests are mainly social capital, social cohesion, diversity, perceptions, inequality, crime, and quantitative methods. She is particularly specialized in role of diversity and (social) networks in communities and organisations. Dr. Bircan is currently working on legal sociology and sociology of crime in concern with the economic factors and outcomes from a quantitative approach. She has published mainly on diversity, crime, and economic disadvantages. Her work is published in international journals including *European Journal of Criminology* and *British Journal of Criminology*.

Paul Breen is a Senior Lecturer and scholar at Greenwich School of Management, more recently known as GSM London, and a Doctoral candidate with the University of Manchester. He has previously completed a Post-Graduate Certificate of Education and a Masters in Education, specialising in English language teaching and educational technology. Born in Ireland, he has worked in a number of contexts both in the British Isles and overseas, including language schools in Japan and Australia, as well as the National University of Technology in South Korea. He has articles and chapters published in a number of academic works, alongside a body of publications in other areas of interest. His research is primarily focused on identity (personal, cultural, and professional), teacher development, educational technology, and studies conducted in researchers' own workplaces.

Kim L. Brown-Jackson, ABD, MBS, CQIA, DTM, CTC, has over 18 years of leadership expertise in quality, training, program, project, and curriculum management. Currently she is a senior consultant in organizational development, quality management, leadership and talent development, and operation management. Previously, she was the director for product development in a financial management division for a training company. She has also been a learning and human capital strategist and project manager. Brown-Jackson holds certifications in Kirkpatrick Four Levels Evaluation, quality improvement (CQIA) and greenbelt experience, advanced instructional design/development, leadership, performance management, and diversity. Academically, Brown-Jackson is a Doctoral student and adjunct faculty for The National Graduate School – Quality Management. She holds a MSc in Biomedical Sciences with additional coursework towards a PhD and a MBA certificate. She holds a BA in Biological Sciences from Clemson University, cluster minor in Business Administration and language emphasis Japanese. Brown-Jackson received a National Science Foundation Fellowship. She holds an AS in Biotechnology and Forensic Science from Massachusetts Bay Community College (joint ventures at Boston University and University of Massachusetts). Brown-Jackson has prior experience as a scientist, corporate trainer, business/financial analyst, information consultant, human/financial resources. Kim L. Brown-Jackson was featured in the April 2013 edition of American Society of Quality, Quality Progress Journal as the Who's Who in Q. Brown-Jackson has presented at numerous management and leadership conferences. She co-authored and/or virtually presented over 18 conference proceedings (domestic and international peer-reviewed), contributed to academic book chapters, and written journal articles. Professor Brown-Jackson has served as peer reviewer for Academy of Management, Academic Business World, and the International Conference on Learning and Administration in Higher Education, Informing Science + IT Education Conferences, Informing Science + International Journal of Doctoral Studies Reviewer, American Telemedicine Association Conference Poster Reviewer, Journal of Educational Research and Reviews for Scienceweb Publishing Reviewer, and Association for the Advancement of Computing in Education, E-Learn Program Committee.

Maysa Bueno, PhD in Education with research in digital culture, social networks, and teacher training, Dom Bosco Catholic University (UCDB), Master's in Education with research in distance education, Federal University of Mato Grosso do Sul (2004), and holds a degree in Education with focus on translator and interpreter, is Professor of Educational Technologies of the post-graduation courses at Dom Bosco Catholic University (UCDB), works with distance learning since 2000, and currently offers courses and lectures for the insertion of technology in the school environment, teacher training for the use of digital technologies, and social networking in education. She is a Member of GETED – Group of Study and Research in Educational Technologies and the Working Group on Distance Education linked to the Permanent Forum on Education of Mato Grosso do Sul.

Darrell Norman Burrell is an alum of the prestigious Presidential Management Fellows Program, www.pmf.gov. He was selected competitively as a Presidential Management Fellow through a rigorous application process from a pool of over 7,000 applicants. Educational accolades include receiving a Doctoral degree in Health Education with majors in Environmental Public Health and Executive Leadership Coaching from A.T. Still University. He holds an EdS (Education Specialist Post Master's Terminal Degree) in Higher Education Administration from The George Washington University in Washington, DC. His graduate degrees (2) include Human Resources Management/Development and Organizational Management from National Louis University and a graduate degree in Sales and Marketing Management from Prescott College. Dr. Burrell delivers over 18 years of management experience in academia, government, and private industry. He has over 12 years of college teaching experience. Dr. Burrell has over 60 publications and 30 plus peer reviewed conference presentations. He served as an academic reviewer for the following publications: *Ethnic and Racial Studies, The Journal of Negro Education, Journal of Contemporary Issues in Criminology and the Social Sciences, The International Journal of Environmental, Cultural, Economic and Social Sustainability, The Journal of Sustainable Development in Africa, The International Journal of Social Health Information Management, Journal of Health Care for the Poor and Underserved, State and Local Government Review, The International Journal of Knowledge, Culture and Change Management, The Journal of Knowledge & Human Resource Management, Review of Management and Creativity, International Journal of Project Management and Organizations, The International Journal of Sustainability Education*, and *The Academy of Management Annual Conference*.

Sharon L. Burton received her Doctorate in Business Administration (DBA) degree in Quality Management from the National Graduate School of Quality in the Quality Systems Management department. She serves as the Director of Publishing Initiatives at American Meridian University. Serving as a consultant, she is a human capital learning & development strategist and instructor leading business process improvement through curriculum development, learning management system education, and human capital initiatives. Efforts include leading gap, task, job, audience, and system analyses to determine competencies and employ learning strategies. Burton holds the following certifications: Human Capital Strategist, and Kirkpatrick Four Levels Evaluation. She teaches quality management and business courses. Professor Burton has written over 25 conference proceedings, contributed to academic book chapters, written journal articles, and published 2 books. Burton's writings are in the areas of Andragogy, Quality Systems Management, Diversity and Inclusion, Quality Customer Service, Training and Development, Cyber Security, and more. View publications on scholar.google.com, researchgate.net, and academia. edu. She serves as an academic reviewer and has reviewed for the following publications: *The Academy of Management Annual Meeting, The Journal of Negro Education, Informing Science + Information Technology (IISIT) International Board of Reviewers, Academic Business World International Conference, International Conference on Learning and Administration in Higher Education, Interdisciplinary Journal of E-Learning and Learning Objects (IJELLO) Journal; Academic Business World International Conference*, and *The United States Association for Small Business and Entrepreneurship Journal*. She is an advocate for the rights of the people, a mentor, and coach.

Nuria Pons Vilardell Camas, Adjunct Professor at the Federal University of Paraná, PhD in Education: Curriculum, Technology, and Education in (2008) PUCSP, Master of Education in Higher Education shaft on Distance Education and Teacher Education axis (2002) PUCCamp, holds a degree in Letters from Mackenzie University (1985), specialist in Critical Reading (UNESP - 2000), has experience in the area of education, with an emphasis on distance learning, interactive learning, methods and practices in distance education, blended education in higher education, and education online distance and use of digital technologies in education. She is the coordinator of the Laboratory of Digital Culture UFPR/MINC.

Daniela Ramona Crisan currently is a Research Master student in Methodology & Statistics at Tilburg School of Social and Behavioral Sciences, Tilburg, The Netherlands. She was born and raised in Oradea, Romania, where she obtained a BSc in Psychology from University of Oradea, Faculty of Social-Humanistic Sciences (class of 2013). Her current interests are in psychometrics and educational testing.

Idowu Kikelomo Evbuoma obtained the degree of Doctor of Philosophy (Personnel Psychology) from University of Ibadan. She had her background in Education and Guidance and Counseling at the First Degree, and subsequently in Guidance and Counseling, at the Master's Degree from the same institution of higher learning. She is presently a University Lecturer in Psychology at Covenant University, Ota, Nigeria; she equally offers professional counseling consultancy services, for the University Counseling Centre. Among researches undertaken by her are studies on Employee Motivation, Work Motivation, Organizational, and Work Performance Women Studies, Gender Studies, Adolescence, and Child Parenting. Dr. Evbuoma is passionate about employee motivation, organizational excellence, and youth (and children) fulfillment. Having been trained as English and French teacher and school counselor, prior to her postgraduate and doctoral exposures, she has had a wealth of experience teaching and counseling in schools around the country.

Charalampos (Babis) Giousmpasoglou has dual background as a practitioner in luxury hospitality industry and as an academic in higher education. His research interests focus in Managerial work, Hospitality Management, Culture, Human Resources Management, and Mobile Learning. Dr. Charalampos is a holder of two first Degrees in Hospitality and Tourism from Greece (ASTER & TEI), an MSc in Hospitality Management from BCFTCS, an MA in Personnel Management (CIPD) from Leeds Metropolitan University, a PgD in Research Methodology, and a PhD in Hospitality and HRM from the University of Strathclyde.

Esra Çeviker Gürakar is an Assistant Professor at the Faculty of Economics and Administrative Sciences at Okan University, Istanbul. Dr. Gürakar's research interests are institutional transformation and political economy of institutions in Turkey and Iran. Her main focus is on formation of different political settlements and the mechanisms of transition from one to another political settlement, formalization of rent-creation and rent-distribution mechanisms, judicialisation of politics versus politicization of judiciary, and the limits of 3rd party enforcement from an open access order based organization in the process of institutional transformation. Dr Gürakar's current research is on the political economy of public procurement in Turkey, where she studies the role of public procurement processes on elite circulation, the political economy implications of legal amendments made to the Public Procurement Law, and the limits to EU-required reform in the public procurement system.

Hamil R. Harris is an award-winning journalist serving at *The Washington Post* since 1992. He has written hundreds of stories about the people, government, faith, and the communities in metropolitan Washington, DC. Harris chronicled the campaign of President Barack Obama, the Clinton White House, District government, the Million Man March, the Sept. 11 attack, the Sniper Attacks, Hurricane Katrina, and numerous other people and events. Currently, Harris is a multi-platform reporter on the Local Desk of *The Washington Post*, where he writes a range of stories, shoots photos, and produces videos for the print and online editions of the post. In addition, he is part of the Breaking News that is frequently called upon to report on crime, natural disasters, and a number of concerns. Prior to *The Washington Post*, Harris was the Senior Staff Writer for the Afro American Newspapers, Capitol Hill Correspondent for American Urban Radio Network, and a freelance correspondent for CBS News Radio and Pacifica Network News. He was a contributing writer for *Black Enterprise Magazine*. In 2006, Harris served on the team of reporters that published the series "Being a Black Man." He, also, was the reporter on the video project that accompanied the series winning two Emmy Awards, the Casey Medal, and the Peabody Award. As professor, Harris has lectured at Georgetown, George Washington University, Howard University, the American University, the University of Maryland, and the University of the District of Columbia. Additionally, he lectures several times a year to interns who are a part of the Washington semester at the Consortium of Christian Colleges and Universities.

Nina Jolani is a program analyst for the public health informatics project at the National Association of County and City Health Officials. In her position, she collaborates with internal and external stakeholders to comment on proposed legislations that impact Local Health Departments (LHDs), provides technical assistance for informatics capacity building to LHDs, and monitors policy and implementation activities related to the Health Information Technology for Economic and Clinical Health Act and its intended outcomes for public health. Her research area includes mobile health and social media methodologies that can be utilized to change public health and health care activities. Ms. Jolani received her Bachelor of Arts in political science and international studies from the University of Dayton, Dayton, Ohio.

Fritz Kohle studied at the Surrey Institute of Art and Design and as a postgraduate at the Northern Media School, Sheffield Hallam University. He currently studies for a PhD at the University of Edinburgh investigating the impact of social media on documentary production. In 2009, he obtained tenure at NHTV, University of Applied Sciences, Breda, Netherlands, as a senior lecturer teaching Film & TV production, while continuing his professional production practice. In collaboration with the Ludwigsburg Film Academy in Germany, he published the media handbook *Medienmacher Heute*. Kohle's projects include post-production management for Studio Babelsberg features in Berlin, such as Wim Wender's Soul of a Man, and Jackie Chan's 80 Days around the World. Kohle was Bigfoot Entertainment's Head of Post Production until 2007. In June 2007, he joined New York University's Tisch School of the Arts as Assistant Director for the Production and Post-production Centre, significantly contributing to the establishment of the NYU Singapore Campus.

Michelle Kowalsky is a Learning Design Librarian at Rowan University who assists undergraduates, graduate students, and their faculty in learning the art and science of research. She has been a teacher and librarian for 20 years, also at the K-12 level, and is a National Board Certified Teacher of Library Media who is renewed through 2022. She has worked in college libraries, school libraries, corporate libraries, and public libraries throughout her career, and contributes to the profession as an Education and LIS professor. Her interests focus on the intersections between libraries and technologies, and also between learning and technologies. The communication of librarians and teachers, their work in information literacy and lesson design, and the results these efforts have on student learning are her current areas of investigation.

Shanel W. Lu is an operational support professional for a financial banking institution. She executes organizational goals that sustain operational excellence through change management and workforce strategy. Lu's latest project is spearheading the research and development of custom-built in-house workforce staffing endeavors. This effort includes analyzing workforce balancing and allocation, and then consulting with senior operational leaders to strategize their workforce. Academically, Lu is a Doctoral student earning a Doctorate of Business Administration (DBA) in Quality Management from National Graduate School in Falmouth, MA. She plans to use her academic and practical experiences to support public service efforts through community outreach programs. She recognizes that quality is vital in all industries and desires to center her career on quality initiatives that will optimize more efficient processes operations. Lu believes strongly in community outreach. She is an active member of the American Asian Government Executive Network, AAGEN. Lu supports the vision and mission to uplift the community through academic and professional excellence. As a facilitator and secretary of AAGEN's Annual Leadership Workshop and Banquet, she manages weekly stakeholder meetings that ensure quality execution and delivery of service. Lu's most passionate service is mentorship and coaching. She believes that villages are created to uplift and provide pathways for future generations of emerging scholars and leaders.

Monica Mandaji, PhD in Education: Curriculum Pontifical Catholic University of São Paulo (2011), Master of Science in Communications from the University of São Paulo (2003), Degree in Social Communication at the Catholic University of Santos (1990), Full Degree at State Center for Education Technological Paula Souza (1998), Pedagogy Universidade Paulista UNIP, has Postgraduate degree in Interactive Media applied to Education PUC/SP (2003), Postgraduate Diploma in Communication from the Catholic University of Santos (1994), and Postgraduate Teacher Training for Distance Education (2010) from Universidade Paulista. She participated in the Training Course for tutoring taught by OAS (2011), is a researcher of the PUC of São Paulo, in the Graduate Program in Education: Curriculum. She is a professor at UAB, Federal University of São Carlos, in the course of Pedagogy.

Evangelia (Lia) Marinakou has an extensive teaching and dissertation supervision experience in HE at undergraduate and postgraduate level. She is a Fellow member of the Higher Education Academy (UK). She is active in research with papers presented at international conferences and published at academic journals. Her main research interests are gender issues in management, leadership, hospitality management, and education. She has also acted as project leader to European funded programmes on vocational education and training in tourism studies. She has extensive experience on curriculum design, academic quality assurance, and training the trainers. Additionally, she has worked in the hospitality and tourism industry for many years.

Rondalynne McClintock is an education and learning professional in Organizational Development Technology. She thrives at the intersection of technology, education, and information owing to the following: information helps people make informed decisions, creates opportunities, and leads to action. Using technology can transform communities and aid in addressing social injustices. Educated people communicate ideas clearly and implement plans that drive transformation and change. McClintock leverages organizational learning development, education, technical training, and coaching to serve as a higher education faculty member. She offers 19 years of experience in organizational education and learning and development as part of conducting employee training, coaching, and internal consulting. McClintock provides a well-rounded approach to teaching and training adults at all levels. She is the Founding Member and Executive Director of The Scholarship Club FPC. Academically, McClintock is a PhD student at Claremont Graduate University – Information Systems and Technology and expects to graduate in 2015. She holds a MSc in Information Systems and Technology and a MA in Education from Claremont Graduate University. She received a BS in Industrial Engineering from California State Polytechnic University-Pomona. McClintock has several conferences proceedings including, AMCIS (August 10, 2010); Transportation Research Board 89th Annual Meeting (January 10, 2010); Proceedings of the 7th International ISCRAM Conference (May, 2010); and Proceedings of the Eighteenth Americas Conference on Information Systems, (August 9-12, 2012).

Neli Mengalli, Master (2006) by the Graduate Program in Education: Curriculum, Pontifical Catholic University of São Paulo PUC-SP, Degree in Portuguese (1996), and Pedagogy (2000), works at the Education Department of the State of São Paulo-SP SEE (2009), Teaching Assistant at Technical Coordinator of Education of the Interior (2011), Technical Teaching Assistant at Virtual School Educational Programs of the State of São Paulo Coordination Management of Basic Education (2012). She was a participant at the Group Training Educators to Support Research in Digital Mode, PUC-SP (2006), worked in Project Management School and Technologies (2009), partnership Catholic University of São Paulo PUC-SP, Department of Education of the State of São Paulo, Department of Education of the State of Goiás, Centro Paula Souza of Brazil, and Microsoft.

Vasileios Paliktzoglou has several years of experience in universities such as the University of Pisa, the Aegean University, Robert Gordon University, Mediterranean University College, and the University of Wales, having an active role as: Researcher, Tutor, Supervisor, Lecturer, and Programme Manager. His research interests are in the fields of social media, Web 2.0, communities of practices, e-learning, in which he is actively involved in several international research projects. He is currently a doctoral researcher at the University of Eastern Finland and faculty member at Bahrain Polytechnic.

Sony Jalarajan Raj is Assistant Professor at the Faculty of Fine Arts and Communications, MacEwan University, Edmonton, Canada. Dr. Raj is a professional journalist turned academic who has worked as reporter, special correspondent, and producer in news media channels like BBC, NDTV, Doordarshan, AIR, and Asianet News. Dr Raj served as the Graduate Coordinator and Assistant Professor of Communication Arts at the Institute for Communication, Entertainment and Media at St. Thomas University Florida, USA. He was full-time faculty member in Journalism, Mass Communication, and Media Studies at Monash University, Australia, Curtin University, Mahatma Gandhi University, and University of Kerala. Dr Raj was the recipient of Reuters Fellowship and is a Thomson Foundation (UK) Fellow in Television Studies with the Commonwealth Broadcasting Association Scholarship.

Adam Raman is a Senior Lecturer at Kingston University in South West London in the UK. He currently lectures marketing and strategy modules on a range of undergraduate and postgraduate courses. His current research interests lie in the area of applying network theory to sustainability innovation as well as social media strategy development within organisations. Prior to joining academia, Adam spent a considerable time in industry working on numerous national, regional, and international marketing and strategy assignments.

Renata Aquino Ribeiro is a Researcher in Technological and Industrial Development at the National Council of Quality in Research - CNPQ Brazil/Federal University of Ceará, Doctor in Education: Curriculum in education and technology in Catholic University of Sao Paulo (2012) and Bachelor in Communication in the same university in 1999, Master in Arts in Hypermedia at University of Westminster recognized in Brazil at University of São Paulo. Her career included positions as a university professor at PUC/SP, Euro-Pan American Colleges, and UNIP, experience in the area of Communication and Education, with a focus on Technology and Education acting on the following topics: technology, education, cyberculture, Internet, and activism.

Gulzar H. Shah, PhD, MStat, MS, is the Associate Dean for Research and an Associate Professor of Health Policy and Management at the Jiann-Ping Hsu College of Public Health (JPHCOPH), Georgia Southern University. His interdisciplinary training and multisector work experience spans over 19 years, with appointments in both academia and public health practice agencies, nationally and internationally. Prior to joining JPHCOPH, he was the Lead Research Scientist at the National Association of County and City Health Departments (NACCHO), and the Director of Research at the National Association of Health Data Organizations (NAHDO) prior to that. He also served at the Utah State Department of Health for six years, contributing significantly to patient safety project, maternal and child health research, informatics projects (such as IBIS-PH, MatCHIIM), and health services and systems research. Dr. Shah's research interests include data improvement; practice-based PHSSR, eHealth and public health informatics, and public health finances.

Hemamali Tennakoon is a Doctoral candidate at the Faculty of Business and Law, Kingston University, London. Her research specialties are in the areas of Online Information Security, Social Media, Cyber-Crimes, and Online User Behaviour. More specifically, her Doctoral research is focused on information security issues in social media business models and its impact on behavioural intention. She has presented her work at the British Academy of Management Conference and at Kingston Business and Law Annual Research Conference. She has a BA in Business Administration from Staffordshire University, a Master's degree in Information Systems Management from University of Colombo, Sri Lanka, and an MSc in Management and Business Studies Research from Kingston University. She is also a member of the British Computer Society and an Associate Member of the Australian Computer Society.

Donna Velliaris is Academic Advisor at the Eynesbury Institute of Business and Technology (EIBT). EIBT is a specialist pre-university institution where international students work towards the goal of Australian tertiary entrance. Donna holds two Graduate Diplomas in (1) Secondary Education and (2) Language and Literacy Education, as well as three Masters' degrees in (1) Educational Sociology, (2) Studies of Asia Education, and (3) Special Education. In 2010, she graduated with a PhD in Education. Her research interests and expertise include academic literacies, transnational students/Third Culture Kids (TCKs), and schools as cultural systems. Donna is first-author of more than 10 book chapters to be published in 2014-2015.

Yoshino W. White is an alum of the prestigious GEM Fellows Program, https://www.gemfellowship.org/. She was selected competitively as a National GEM Consortium Fellow through a rigorous application process. Yoshino W. White, Product Lifecycle Professional, is an experienced leader within the consulting arena who delivers success on small and large teams and projects. She has strong implementation, communication, and leadership skills with a sound technical background. White's skills have been applied in many industries ranging from automotive, service providers, healthcare, and aerospace/defense. Academically, White is a graduate of the Florida A&M, and the Florida State University College of Engineering in Tallahassee, FL. She holds an earned Master of Science in Industrial Engineering. Her minor is mechanical engineering. She received a BS degree from Florida State University in Industrial

Engineering. White's specialties are Process Improvement and Assessments, Requirements Definition and Design, Training Delivery, Integration Implementation, and Impact Assessment. White has shared her expertise in the non-profit arena where she provided her skills in strategic planning, program management and fundraising. She provides thought leadership via company newsletter articles, peer-reviewed conference proceedings, and published journal articles.

Bruce Whitham is currently a librarian in the Research and Instruction Department of Rowan University's Glassboro, NJ campus. He has over 25 years experience, having held various senior administrative positions in college and university libraries including the positions of Head of Instruction and Research Services, Library Director, and Dean of Libraries. Recent career directions include the promotion of information literacy, digitization and online integration of library collections and resources, the development of open access, the advancement of digital resources to enhance library service delivery, and the development and repurposing of library spaces to meet changing needs and to support online learning communities. Current areas of interest include the integration of online library resources with social media applications to enhance self-directed and blended learning.

Craig Willis is Academic Coordinator at the Eynesbury Institute of Business and Technology (EIBT), as well as Senior Lecturer in the School of Civil, Environmental and Mining Engineering at The University of Adelaide. Teaching large classes of up to 550 students, Craig has developed innovative ways of providing continuous formative feedback using interactive teaching techniques, peer instruction, and professional engineering processes. In the space of two years, he was recognised with a total of seven awards for excellence in teaching and learning at faculty, university, and national levels. His research expertise extends to diverse themes, including the first-year experience, international students, active learning strategies, e-learning, engagement with large classes, peer feedback, multiple-choice assessment, and quality management processes.

Index